BELIZE
HANDBOOK

BELIZE
HANDBOOK

THIRD EDITION

CHICKI MALLAN
PHOTOS BY OZ MALLAN

MOON
PUBLICATIONS INC.

BELIZE HANDBOOK
THIRD EDITION

Published by
Moon Publications, Inc.
P.O. Box 3040
Chico, California 95927-3040, USA

Printed by
Colorcraft Ltd., Hong Kong

ISBN: 1-56691-030-7

ISSN: 1082-4863

Editor: Karen Gaynor Bleske
Assistant Editor: Michael Ray Greer
Copy Editors: Sandi K. Drewitz, Sharon Brown
Production & Design: Jim Miller, David Hurst, Carey Wilson
Cartographers: Bob Race, Brian Bardwell
Index: Deana Corbitt Shields

Front cover photo: Ambergris Caye by Oz Mallan
All photos by Oz Mallan unless otherwise noted.

Distributed in the U.S.A. by Publishers Group West
Printed in Hong Kong

Please send all comments,
corrections, additions,
amendments, and critiques to:

**BELIZE HANDBOOK
MOON PUBLICATIONS, INC.
P.O. BOX 3040
CHICO, CA 95927-3040, USA
e-mail: travel@moon.com**

Printing History
1st edition—January 1991
Reprinted June 1991
2nd edition—August 1993
Reprinted May 1994
Reprinted February 1995
3rd edition—November 1995

To my husband, Oz

CONTENTS

MAPS

MAP SYMBOLS

——— HIGHWAY	○ LARGER TOWN OR CITY
——— ROAD	○ VILLAGE OR TOWN
– – – ROAD SURFACE UNDETERMINED	▲ MOUNTAIN
▬ ▬ INTERNATIONAL BORDER	■ POINT OF INTEREST
⋯⋯⋯ DISTRICT BORDER	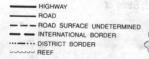 WATER
⌣⌣⌣⌣ REEF	● HOTEL/ACCOMMODATION

 GAS

AIRPORT

 ARCHAELOGICAL SITE OR RUIN

 BRIDGE

CHURCH

CATHEDRAL

CHARTS

SPECIAL TOPICS

ABBREVIATIONS

a/c—air conditioned, air conditioning
BZE$—Belize dollars
C—centigrade
d—double occupancy
f—quintuple occupancy
F—fahrenheit
FAP—full American plan (3 meals/day)
4WD—four-wheel drive
h/c—hot/cold
MAP—modified American plan (breakfast/
   dinner)
NAUI—National Association of Underwater
   Instructors

OW—one way
PADI—Professional Association of Dive
   Instructors
q—quadruple occupancy
RT—round trip
RV—recreational vehicle
s—single occupancy
t—triple occupancy
tel.—telephone number
US$—United States dollars
YH—youth hostel

ACKNOWLEDGMENTS

It's almost impossible to remember everyone who helps with the making of a guidebook! First, the people of Belize are sensational. Everyone was willing to take a few minutes to answer questions and give generously of their personal knowledge. Thanks to Phil Lanier, intrepid explorer, who trekked the jungles and cities of Belize finding new sights, new attractions, and new hotels, giving the visitor to Belize a number of options for a never-to-be-forgotten vacation. Thanks to the Fort George Hotel, and to Paul Hunt, Steve Cox at International Expeditions in Helena, Alabama, and Budget Rent a Car's Alan Auil in Belize City for their considerations. Thanks also to the many people who share our enthusiasm for Belize. The entire Moon staff pulled it off again. Thanks to my editor, Karen Bleske. It's been a pleasure working with her. Moon took my words, Oz Mallan's pictures, Kathy Sanders's and Bob Race's outstanding drawings, and Bob Race's and Brian Bardwell's maps, to make another beautiful book. Special thanks to my wonderful readers who write and let me know about new discoveries.

IS THIS BOOK OUT OF DATE?

We strive to keep our books as up to date as possible and would appreciate your help. If you find that a resort is not as we described, or discover a new restaurant or other information that should be included in our book, please let us know. Our mapmakers make extraordinary effort to be accurate, but if you find an error, let us know that as well.

We're especially interested in hearing from female travelers, RVers, outdoor enthusiasts, expatriates, and local residents. We are always interested in hearing from the tourist industry, which specializes in accommodating visitors to Belize. Happy traveling! Please address your letters to:

Belize Handbook
c/o Moon Publications, Inc.
P.O. Box 3040
Chico CA 95927-3040 USA

ABOUT THE PRICES IN THIS BOOK

As numbers go, relatively few people have shared the wonderful secret of Belize over the years. But as it happens, the secret is out—more and more adventurers, divers, sun-worshippers, and curiosity-seekers are discovering Belize. All of this attention is bringing about rapid changes to the country. Please use the prices given only as a guideline; they too are apt to change. We've tried to furnish accurate addresses as well as fax and telephone numbers where you can verify these facts. If you find the numbers have changed, we would appreciate knowing about that as well. All prices are in U.S. dollars, except where noted.

KATHY ESCOVEDO SANDERS

INTRODUCTION

Say the word "Belize" and many people think of unbelievably clear blue water and diving along a protected reef rich with brilliant sea life. Amen! Others think of twisting jungle trails overhung with exotic vines, orchids, and bromeliads, the air alive with the calls of toucans and parrots. Still others envision mysterious Maya ruins whose deserted temples and ball courts whisper the names of rulers long past. Belize is all this and much more. Home to a polyglot of people who have maintained a variety of traditions and cultures for hundreds of years, this isolated country has not paved over nature's wonders. Generally speaking, Belize is ecotourism in action.

Early recorded comments, following Columbus's fourth voyage to the New World, led the Spaniards to hastily conclude that the swampy shoreline was unfit for human habitation. Today this little-known destination is stepping quietly into the world of tourism. The government has recognized priorities and is establishing clear guidelines as the country welcomes more and more visitors. "Our tourism is based on our wildlife, the forests, the flora and fauna," proclaimed Victor Gonzalez, then-permanent secretary of Belize's Ministry of Tourism and the Environment. The country, on the cutting edge of the ecotourism phenomenon, actively protects its natural resources: wildlife, tracts of rainforest and unsullied swamplands, innumerable Maya archaeological sites, varied cultural heritages, and the largest barrier reef in the Western Hemisphere.

Belize is part of Central America's Yucatán Peninsula and of the region called **Mundo Maya,** home to the Maya for 3,000 years. An English-speaking country, Belize was called British Honduras from 1862 until 1973, when it once again became Belize in anticipation of its independence from England.

Belize was the favored hideout for pirates until pirating went out of style. Then those hard-drinking, high-seas robbers discovered an even more lucrative profession: stripping the forests of trees to fill the holds of their ships and later fetch high prices at home in England. Fortunately, they were selective and removed only a couple of species of trees.

Today Belize has one of the most peaceful, stable governments in all of Central America.

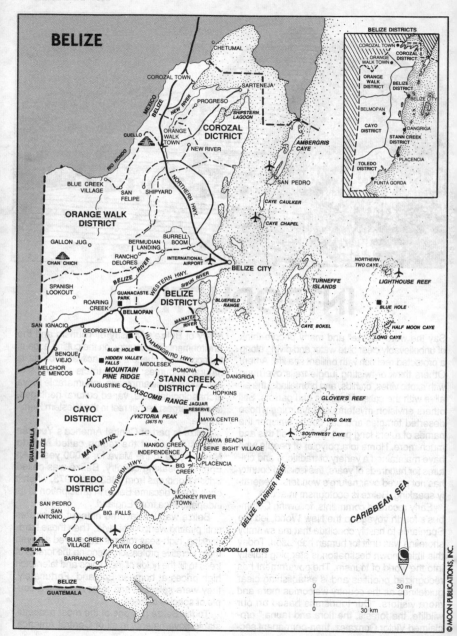

BELIZE

CHETUMAL

COROZAL TOWN

MEXICO

BELIZE

NEW RIVER

PROGRESO

SARTENEJA

SHIPSTERN LAGOON

CUELLO

RIO HONDO

ORANGE WALK TOWN

NEW RIVER

COROZAL DISTRICT

AMBERGRIS CAYE

BLUE CREEK VILLAGE

SAN FELIPE

SHIPYARD

NORTHERN HWY.

SAN PEDRO

ORANGE WALK DISTRICT

GALLON JUG

CHAN CHICH

BERMUDIAN LANDING

BURRELL BOOM

CAYE CAULKER

CAYE CHAPEL

RANCHO DELORES

INTERNATIONAL AIRPORT

BELIZE RIVER

BELIZE CITY

SPANISH LOOKOUT

WESTERN HWY.

SIBUN RIVER

BELIZE DISTRICT

NORTHERN TWO CAYE

LIGHTHOUSE REEF

ROARING CREEK

GUANACASTE PARK

BELIZE RIVER

BLUEFIELD RANGE

TURNEFFE ISLANDS

BLUE HOLE

SAN IGNACIO

BELMOPAN

MANATEE RIVER

CAYE BOKEL

HALF MOON CAYE

LONG CAYE

GEORGEVILLE

BENQUE VIEJO

BLUE HOLE

HUMMINGBIRD HWY.

HIDDEN VALLEY FALLS

MIDDLESEX

POMONA

MELCHOR DE MENCOS

MOUNTAIN PINE RIDGE

AUGUSTINE

COCKSCOMB RANGE

STANN CREEK DISTRICT

DANGRIGA

HOPKINS

GLOVER'S REEF

CAYO DISTRICT

VICTORIA PEAK (3675 ft)

JAGUAR RESERVE

LONG CAYE

MAYA CENTER

SOUTHWEST CAYE

MAYA MTNS.

MANGO CREEK INDEPENDENCE

MAYA BEACH

SEINE BIGHT VILLAGE

MAYA BEACH

BIG CREEK

PLACENCIA

SOUTHERN HWY.

TOLEDO DISTRICT

MONKEY RIVER TOWN

BELIZE BARRIER REEF

CARIBBEAN SEA

SAN PEDRO SAN ANTONIO

BIG FALLS

BLUE CREEK VILLAGE

PUNTA GORDA

PUSIL HA

BARRANCO

SAPODILLA CAYES

BELIZE

GUATEMALA

GUATEMALA

BELIZE

30 mi

30 km

© MOON PUBLICATIONS, INC.

BELIZE DISTRICTS

COROZAL TOWN

COROZAL DISTRICT

ORANGE WALK TOWN

ORANGE WALK DISTRICT

BELIZE DISTRICT

BELIZE CITY

BELMOPAN

CAYO DISTRICT

STANN CREEK DISTRICT

DANGRIGA

TOLEDO DISTRICT

PLACENCIA

PUNTA GORDA

Its growing population numbers about 200,000 (22.6 people per square mile), a quarter of whom live in Belize City. Edging the unspoiled Western Caribbean, it only recently realized its enormous potential for tourism. Divers, among the first tourists to visit this tropical country, have quietly enjoyed the Belize Reef for decades—thanks, Jacques Cousteau! Independent travelers and special interest groups (birdwatchers, archaeologists, and nature buffs) have discovered the country's beautiful cayes (meaning "islands," pronounced KEES) lying off the Caribbean coast, as well as inland rainforests and a vast number of archaeological centers. More and more middle-aged and senior travelers from the U.S. are looking into Belize as a viable, warm-weather, budget location to spend their retirement years. And at the same time, foreign industries are finding the Belizean government cooperative and willing to make tax concessions to attract outside investments. This in turn provides jobs for the locals, which the emerging country desperately needs.

The people of Belize are very aware of the importance of the pristine natural treasures in their own backyard. They realize these natural resources must be protected, and they have opted for a long-term investment in a tourism that attracts people curious about natural history. Today thousands of rainforest acres have been declared reserves, hunting certain animals (which in other parts of the world are already extinct) is illegal, and the lavish coast with miles of reef is strictly regulated. The beautiful atolls and surrounding underwater marine world that is considered second to none in the world have their reserves, as well. And ordinary farmers and landowners are banding together to form parts of their land into private reserves.

THE BELIZE NATIONAL ANTHEM

LAND OF THE FREE

O, Land of the Free by the Carib Sea,
Our manhood we pledge to thy liberty!
No tyrants here linger, despots must flee
This tranquil haven of democracy.
The blood of our sires which hallows the soil,
Brought freedom from slavery oppression's rod,
By the might of truth and the grace of God.
No longer shall we be hewers of wood.

Arise! ye sons of the Baymen's clan,
Put on your armours, clear the land!
Drive back the tyrants, let despots flee
Land of the Free by the Carib Sea!

Nature has blessed thee with wealth untold,
O er mountains and valleys where prairies roll;
Our fathers, the Baymen, valiant and bold
Drove back the invader; this heritage bold
From proud Rio Hondo to old Sarstoon,
Through coral isle, over blue lagoon;
Keep watch with the angels, the stars and moon;
For freedom comes to-morrow's noon.

THE LAND

Belize lies on the eastern coastline of Central America. Its 8,866 square miles of territory are bordered on the north by Mexico, on the west and south by Guatemala, and on the east by the Caribbean Sea. From the Rio Hondo border with Mexico to the southern border of Guatemala, Belize's mainland measures 180 miles long, and it's 68 miles at its widest point. It's roughly the same size as the state of Massachusetts. Offshore, Belize has more than 200 cayes. Both the coastal region and the northern half of the mainland are flat, but the land rises in the south and west (in the Maya Mountains) to over 3,000 feet above sea level. Mangrove swamps cover much of the humid coastal plain.

The Maya Mountains and the Cockscombs form the country's backbone, rising 3,675 feet to **Victoria Peak,** Belize's highest point.

In the west, the Cayo District contains the **Mountain Pine Ridge Preserve.** At one time a magnificent pine forest, it was destroyed in the lower plains over the decades by fires and lumber removal, and only a few straggler pine trees remain in the arid foothills. However, the upper regions of Mountain Pine Ridge provide spectacular scenery, and thick forest encompasses the **Macal River** as it tumbles over huge granite boulders. **Hidden Valley Falls** plunges 1,000 feet to the valley below. The **Rio Frio** cave system offers massive stalactites and stalagmites

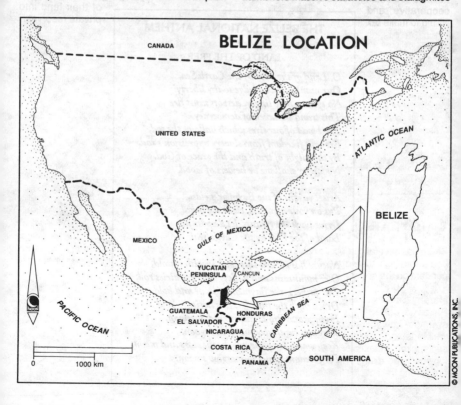

BELIZE LOCATION

CANADA

UNITED STATES

ATLANTIC OCEAN

MEXICO

GULF OF MEXICO

YUCATAN PENINSULA   CANCUN

BELIZE

GUATEMALA   HONDURAS
EL SALVADOR
NICARAGUA
COSTA RICA
PANAMA

CARIBBEAN SEA

SOUTH AMERICA

PACIFIC OCEAN

0   1000 km

© MOON PUBLICATIONS, INC.

to the avid spelunker. The diverse landscape includes limestone-fringed granite boulders.

Over thousands of years, what was once a sea in the northern half of Belize has become a combination of scrub vegetation and rich tropical hardwood forest. Near the Mexican border much of the land has been cleared, and it's here that the majority of sugar crops are raised, along with family plots of corn and beans. Most of the northern coast is swampy with a variety of grasses and mangroves that attract hundreds of species of waterfowl. Rainfall in the north averages 60 inches annually and it's generally dry Nov.-May.

Significant rainfall in the mountains washes silt and nutrients into the lower valleys to the south and west, forming rich agricultural areas. In southern Belize it rains most of the year, averaging 150 inches or more. The coastal belt attracts large farms that raise an ever-expanding variety of crops. A dense rainforest thrives in this wet, humid condition with thick ferns, lianas, tropical cedars, and palms.

WATERWAYS OF BELIZE

Heavy rains, deluging the mountains strung across the center of Belize, feed the rivers and waterways that flow from the mountains to the sea. For decades the rivers were the highways of the country; a few are deep enough to be navigable and are still used for hauling logs. These rivers are: **Blue Creek, Rio Hondo, New River, Belize River, Sibun River, Macal River, Rio Grande, Moho River, Tumex River,** and **Sarstoon River.**

HABITATS OF INLAND BELIZE

Belize has several productive habitats that support a startling variety of life. Each habitat is dependent on the soil and available water.

Marshy Havens
Belize is dotted with rivers, lagoons, and swamps. Low forests grow up around these wetlands and provide an environment for insects, birds, mammals, and reptiles. Bamboo, logwood, red mangrove, and white mangrove are among the species that find footholds in the soggy soil and grow into thickets. Numerous in-

buttress root

secto, agouti, basilisk lizards, iguanas, paca, and waterfowl are among the many creatures that inhabit these fringe forests. The wetlands themselves play host to many creatures: crocodiles, fish, turtles, and hundreds of bird species. A boat ride into one of them will give you an opportunity to see a great variety of waterfowl. The lakes of Belize (such as those at Crooked Tree) are wintering spots for many flocks of North American duck species. Among others, you might see the blue-winged teal, northern shoveler, and lesser scaup, along with a variety of wading birds feeding in the shallow waters, including numerous types of heron, snowy egret, and (in the summer) white ibis.

We once watched a peregrine falcon hunt at Crooked Tree. First it slowly circled high above the lake watching its prey and then plunged to attack a flock of American coots. Seconds before the falcon reached the ducks, the flock spotted it and began squawking loudly—warning the whole family—and diving into the water (where the falcon will not follow). After watching the falcon dive for the ducks over and over again, we moved on in our boat, feeling more secure about the destiny of these American coots.

Broadleaf Jungle and Cohune Forests

By certain scientific definitions there is no true rainforest in Belize; the quantity of rainfall is insufficient and is not evenly spread throughout the year. Instead, the magnificent broadleaf jungle of Belize is considered "moist tropical forest." Depending on its maturity this forest may have a single, double, or even triple canopy, triple being the oldest and rarest. Definitions aside, the broadleaf jungles of the Maya Mountains and parts of northern and western Belize create beneath their crowns relatively cool, damp environments that yield an explosion of life. Towering mahogany, ceiba, figs, and guanacaste live here. Bromeliads, orchids, and other epiphytes cover the limbs of these jungle giants. Lianas and vines drip from the branches to the ground. Mushrooms of many varieties and other fungi digest the remains of fallen trees. Leaf cutter ants, termites, butterflies, and spiders abound. Hummingbirds, parrots, toucans, and woodpeckers flit between trees. Anteaters, howler and spider monkeys, squirrels, and margays move among the branches. Jaguars and pumas are plentiful. Boa constrictors, fer-de-lance, and other snakes are common, as are many species of lizards.

Broadleaf forests thrive in clay soils enriched by alluvial runoff from streams and rivers. In places, cohune palms, which are typically sprinkled throughout the forest, grow in dense concentrations. This cohune forest forms a dense cover or canopy. Even so, many of the jungle giants will penetrate it as they reach upward into the sunlight. Many of the same epiphytes, vines, and animals frequent these areas.

Pine Forests and Savanna

Pine forests grow up around areas of low moisture and sandy soil. These conditions exist in certain lowland areas and the low mountains of western Belize. With its typically open canopy, the pine forest allows much more light to reach the ground. Plant and animal life is less diverse here. Palmetto palms, scrub oak, and various grasses grow in close association with pine forests. In fact, standing pines are frequently surrounded by savanna or grassland. Foxes and jaguarundis, deer, mice, squirrels and other rodents, armadillos, hawks and owls, rat snakes, and fer-de-lance frequent these areas.

THE WEATHER

The climate in Belize is subtropical with a mean annual temperature of 79° F, so you can expect a variance between 50-95° F. Belize has definite wet

*exploring the caves
along the Macal River*

WEATHER INFORMATION

	JAN.	FEB.	MARCH	APRIL	MAY	JUNE
AVERAGE INCHES OF RAINFALL (BELIZE CITY)	2.98	1.45	1.68	0.04	5.41	14.01
	JULY	**AUG.**	**SEPT.**	**OCT.**	**NOV.**	**DEC.**
	4.59	8.18	10.41	8.40	4.58	7.0
	JAN.	**FEB.**	**MARCH**	**APRIL**	**MAY**	**JUNE**
AVERAGE INCHES OF RAINFALL (PUNTA GORDA)	10.32	2.51	0.09	0.28	3.74	13.13
	JULY	**AUG.**	**SEPT.**	**OCT.**	**NOV.**	**DEC.**
	28.67	25.38	27.32	14.50	2.60	9.10
	JAN.	**FEB.**	**MARCH**	**APRIL**	**MAY**	**JUNE**
MEAN HIGHS AND LOWS IN DEGREES FAHRENHEIT	82/66	83/66	85/68	87/71	87/72	85/72
	JULY	**AUG.**	**SEPT.**	**OCT.**	**NOV.**	**DEC.**
	85/72	87/73	85/72	84/70	82/68	81/66
	JAN.	**FEB.**	**MARCH**	**APRIL**	**MAY**	**JUNE**
HUMIDITY	73%	68%	67%	74%	75%	85%
	JULY	**AUG.**	**SEPT.**	**OCT.**	**NOV.**	**DEC.**
	82%	82%	82%	67%	75%	89%

(Hurricanes may occur during the period June-Nov.,
but are most likely to occur in Aug. and September.)

and dry seasons. The dry season generally lasts Nov.-May and the wet season June-November. **Note:** In the tropics it's not unusual to have rain in the dry season; it just falls in shorter spurts. The amount of rainfall varies widely from north to south. Corozal in the north receives 40-60 inches while Punta Gorda in the south averages 160-190 inches with an average humidity of 85%. Occasionally during the winter, "northers" sweep down from North America across the Gulf of Mexico, bringing rainfall, strong winds, and cooling temperatures. Usually lasting only a couple of days, they often interrupt fishing and influence the activity of lobster and other fish. Fishermen invariably report increases in their catch several days before a norther.

The "mauger" season generally comes in August, when the air is still and the sea is calm; it can last for a week or more. All activity halts while locals stay indoors as much as possible to avoid the onslaught of ferocious mosquitoes and other insects.

Hurricanes

Belize lies in a hurricane belt. Though this powerful phenomenon seldom occurs, Belize has had firsthand experience with three in recent history (over a period of 50 years); since 1787, 21 hurricanes have hit the small country in varying degrees of intensity. In 1931, 2,000 people were killed and almost all of Belize City was destroyed. The water rose nine feet in some areas, even onto Belize City's Swing Bridge. Though forewarned by Pan American Airlines that the hurricane was heading their way, most of the townsfolk were unconcerned, believing that their protective reef would keep massive waves away from their shores. They were wrong! The next weather devastation came with Hurricane Hattie in 1961. Winds reached a velocity of 150 mph, with gusts of 200 mph; 262 people drowned. It was after Hurricane Hattie that the capital of the country was moved from Belize City (just 18 inches above sea level) to Belmopan. Then in 1978, Hurricane Greta took a heavy toll in dollar damage, though no lives were lost.

FLORA

Belize is a Garden of Eden. Four thousand species of native flowering plants include 250 species of orchids and approximately 700 species of trees. It is one of the few countries where thousands of acres of forest are still in a semi-pristine condition. The country is divided into several ecological life zones: subtropical moist, subtropical lower Montane moist, subtropical lower Montane wet, subtropical wet, tropical moist-transition to subtropical, and tropical wet-transition to subtropical. A botanist can recognize the life zones by the type of natural vegetation that occurs. The determining factor of these zones is the amount of rain that falls. Even the common mangrove grows differently depending on which life zone it is in. The trees in the subtropical moist forest along the northern coast are shorter than those growing in the wetter zones in the south. The tallest mangroves occur in the tropical wet-transition to subtropical in the southern Toledo District.

Forests of Belize

Most of the country's forests have been logged off and on for more than 300 years. The areas closest to the rivers and coast were the hardest hit because boats could be docked and logs loaded and taken farther out to sea to the large ships used to haul the precious timber. For years small patches were burned for use as *milpas* (cornfields) by the Maya. Today, the government is trying to educate the people about the advantages of using other farming methods. However, it will take a long time to break a tradition that goes back millennia.

Flying over the countryside gives you a view of the patchwork landscape of cleared areas and secondary growth. Belize consists of four distinct forest communities: pine-oak, mixed broadleaf, cohune palm, and riverine forests. Pine ridge forests are found in sandy, dry soils. Also in these soils large numbers of mango, cashew, and coconut palm are grown near

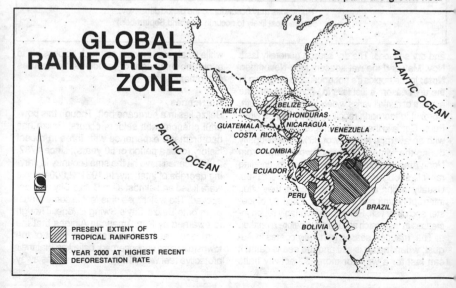

GLOBAL RAINFOREST ZONE

PRESENT EXTENT OF TROPICAL RAINFORESTS

YEAR 2000 AT HIGHEST RECENT DEFORESTATION RATE

homes and villages. The mixed broadleaf forest is a transition area between the sandy pine soils and the clay soils found along the river. Often the mixed broadleaf forest is broken up here and there and doesn't reach great height; it's species-rich but not as diverse as the cohune forest. The cohune forest area is characterized by the cohune palm, which is found in fertile clay soil where a moderate amount of rain falls throughout the year. The cohune nut was an important part of the Maya diet. Archaeologists have a saying: when they see a cohune forest they know they'll find evidence of the Maya.

The cohune forest gives way to the riverine forest along river shorelines, where vast amounts of water are found year-round from excessive rain and from the flooding rivers. About 50-60 tree varieties and hundreds of species of vines, epiphytes, and shrubs grow here. Logwood, mahogany, cedar, and pine are difficult to find along the easily accessible rivers, because of the extensive logging. The forest is in different stages of growth and age. To find virgin forest, it's necessary to go high into the mountains that divide Belize. Because of the rugged terrain, lack of roads, and distance from the rivers, these areas were left almost untouched. Even in the 1990s few roads exist. If left

undisturbed for many, many years, the forest will eventually regenerate itself.

Among the plantlife of Belize look for mangroves, bamboo, and swamp cypresses, as well as ferns, vines, and flowers creeping from tree to tree, creating a dense growth. On topmost limbs, orchids and air ferns reach for the sun. As you go farther south you'll find the classic tropical rainforest, including tall mahoganies, *campeche*, *sapote*, and ceiba, thick with vines.

Bull Horn Acacia

The bull horn acacia, or cockspur, is named after the large paired thorns that occur along its stems and branches. Depending on your point of view, these thorns may remind you of the armament of a bull or rooster. What is certain is that this tree has developed an amazing symbiotic (or cooperative) relationship with ants. The acacia provides food and shelter for the ants and they in turn protect the tree. Tunneling into the thorns near the tips, the ants hollow out areas for their colony. They find various forms of food along the branches of the acacia. In turn, foraging animals and insects, as well as passing humans who brush against the plant, are viciously attacked. The ants' painful stings are enough to drive away even large animals. Each acacia may be colonized by several groups of

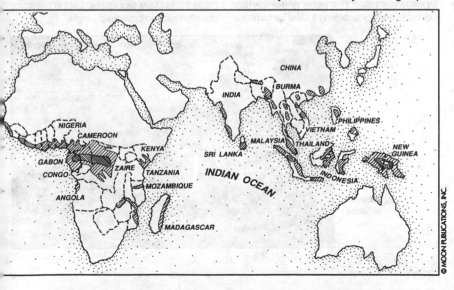

ants. But as the colonies grow larger, they attack each other, with one colony eventually prevailing.

Ceiba

The ceiba with its towering gray trunk is one of the tallest trees in the jungle. Specimens nearly 100 feet are not uncommon and some grow to twice that. Found in tropical zones around the world, the ceiba has many names. It is called the cotton tree in Belize for the fluff surrounding its seeds. This same material, commercially referred to as "kapok," has been used to stuff furniture and pillows. Young ceiba have large somewhat blunt thorns on their trunks. The number of these thorns seems to diminish as the tree matures. Ceiba are commonly found in mature broadleaf jungle.

Guanacaste Tree

The guanacaste, a member of the mimosa family, occurs from Mexico to Venezuela. Sacred to the Maya, it was called *pich*. A mature guanacaste, or tubroos, is an impressive sight with its huge gray trunk, spreading branches, and wide canopy. Total height can reach 130 feet with a six-foot-diameter trunk. The fruits, favorites of monkeys and other animals, have an ear-like shape, giving rise to the name "monkey ear tree." The wood of the tubroos is durable and light, making it ideal for furniture

and dugout canoes or *pitpans*. Guanacaste trees inhabit mature broadleaf forests as well as secondary forests. You can see a giant specimen at Lamanai Ruins and an even larger one in Guanacaste Park just north of the Western Highway at the Belmopan turnoff.

Gumbo-Limbo

With its outer layer shedding in thin papery strands, the reddish inner bark of the gumbo-limbo stands out in the jungle. This half-clothed appearance has given rise to the name "naked Indian." The Maya have for centuries used gumbo-limbo bark in preparations to treat skin rashes, especially those caused by the poisonwood tree. Fortunately, gumbo-limbos grow in close proximity to these troublemakers. Of little use for lumber, saplings are cut for use as fence posts. Amazingly, they soon become living fences as they sprout leaves and begin life anew. Tolerant of shade, the gumbo-limbo is often found in mature broadleaf jungle.

Locust

Also called *pac* by the Maya, the locust emits an aromatic resin. For centuries the Maya have used this sap for incense. Called *copal*, traces of this burnt resin have been found in some of the many caverns that dot the Cayo District and Maya Mountains. Locust trees are usually found in broadleaf jungle.

high forests
of Belize

P-L LANIER

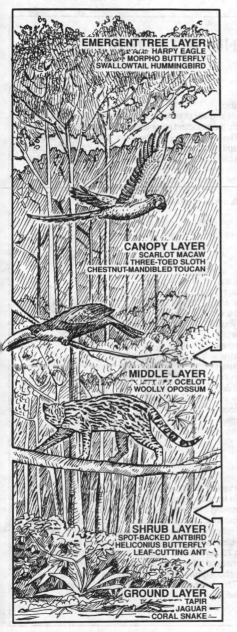

EMERGENT TREE LAYER
HARPY EAGLE
MORPHO BUTTERFLY
SWALLOWTAIL HUMMINGBIRD

CANOPY LAYER
SCARLOT MACAW
THREE-TOED SLOTH
CHESTNUT-MANDIBLED TOUCAN

MIDDLE LAYER
OCELOT
WOOLLY OPOSSUM

SHRUB LAYER
SPOT-BACKED ANTBIRD
HELICONIUS BUTTERFLY
LEAF-CUTTING ANT

GROUND LAYER
TAPIR
JAGUAR
CORAL SNAKE

Palms

A wide variety of palm trees and their relatives grow in Belize: short, fruited, even oil producers. Though similar, various palms have distinct characteristics. Royal palms are tall with smooth trunks. Queen palms are often used for landscaping and bear a sweet fruit. Thatch palms are called *chit* by the Maya; the frond of this tree is used extensively for roof thatch. Coconut palms serve the Belizeans well. One of the 10 most useful trees in the world, the coconut palm produces oil, food, drink, and shelter. The tree matures in six to seven years and then, for five to seven years, bears coconuts, a nutritious food also used for copra (dried coconut meat that yields coconut oil) and valued as a money crop by the locals.

Pines

Pine forests are less productive and diversified than broadleaf jungle but work well on the poor sandy soils of the Mountain Pine Ridge (Belizeans use "ridge" to mean forest) and lowland areas. Lowland areas support pines and savanna. The Caribbean and ocarpo are the two species most prevalent. The Caribbean has thick, rough bark and is more resistant to fire, an asset in the Mountain Pine Ridge where lightning strikes are common. It is one of the dominant trees in Belizean pine forests. With smoother bark and less hardy, the ocarpo does not fare as well in the face of fire. Pine lumber and sap have been important products in Belize since the turn of the century.

Poisonwood

The poisonwood is so-called for its toxic sap, which causes extreme skin reactions similar to those from poison ivy. The skin blisters, itches, and swells. Some locals have a resistance to the sap's harmful effects. Called "chechem" by the Maya, poisonwood is often present in mixed hardwood forests. Avoid contact with leaves, stems, or bark. If you do run afoul of a poisonwood tree, your Belizean guide will know what do to. While he or she looks for a gumbolimbo, an oral antihistamine or cortisone lotion may offer some relief.

EXOTIC FRUITS AND NUTS OF BELIZE

Tamarind

An edible pod about an inch in width and three to eight inches in length, the tamarind is reminiscent of a dark-colored string bean. The pulp around and between the two to six seeds is brown and can be 11% acidic, though as much as 20% sugar. Used in cold drinks, preserves, and chutneys, it is 3.3% protein, high in minerals, and an excellent source of vitamin B. You see stacks of them in public markets, and children enjoy them straight from the tree, a healthy snack said to be as high in food value as maize or wheat.

Cacao

Considered a stimulant plant along with coffee, the cacao bean is used to make chocolate products, including the world's favorite candy. The pods are yellow to greenish in color and look like a type of squash hanging from the tree. If you split the pod you'll find a series of 10-20 seeds surrounded by a white

creamy flesh that makes a tasty drink. Children enjoy the seeds fresh from the tree though the seeds must be dried and roasted before they acquire the familiar chocolate flavor that Americans know and love.

Bananas

Bananas come in a variety of shapes and sizes, from the tiny lady finger variety that grows in hands of about 75 fruits to the giant Cavendish, a plantain used for cooking that produces hands with about 15 fruits. The lady finger grows four to six inches long and weighs about two ounces; it has a wonderful, refreshing flavor. Most of the production in Belize is of the large market-size variety. The time from blossom to ripe fruit stage may be as short as 75 days. When a stalk of bananas is harvested, the top of the tree is whacked off and the leaves are dispersed around the base, where a new shoot grows; within eight months it will bear another stem of bananas. The continuous cycle repeats itself for seven years before the entire tree must be replaced.

Pineapple

Tropical fruits have some peculiar family traits. The pineapple, for example, is one of the bromeliad family, which is usually an epiphyte (meaning that it lives on trees and gets its nutrients from what floats around in the breeze). However, a few distant relatives of the bromeliad grow on the ground; the pineapple is one of the most famous. Each stem flowers only once and dies after fruiting. But nature in its constant battle to keep going sends up another side shoot that takes over. The plant grows to about three feet tall and the size of the fruit ranges from small (about six to seven inches tall) to the large hybrids (as tall as 12-15 inches). A sweet fruit that personifies the tropics, the pineapple is a favorite all over the world.

The *Sapote*

Also known as the mammee fruit, it grows on a tall tree that for hundreds of years has been a sacred tree to the Maya. Historians say this was the fruit that kept Cortés and his army alive on their march from Mexico City to Honduras. The oval fruit is three to six inches long and covered with a brown fibrous skin. The flesh is a beautiful salmon pink and surrounds an avocado-like seed. The "taste" of the fruit must be "acquired" by most outsiders. The texture is somewhat like a sweet potato, and the flavor reminds me of a chestnut, but taste is in the tongue of the taster. It is used in a thick jam called *crema de mamey colorado,* while the seed's commercial value becomes greater when roasted and mixed with cacao in making chocolate.

The Cashew Nut

The amazing diversity among tropical botanical relatives continues to confuse many people. For instance, did you know that the mango is a relative of the cashew nut? Actually, the family comprises some 400 species in about 60 genera around the world, but mostly in the warm-weather countries. It is said that the cashew tree furnishes food and remedies to the poor, provides a refreshing beverage to the sick, a sweetmeat for tables of the affluent, and good timber and resin for industrial use. The cashew tree is a large, spreading evergreen that grows up to 40 feet in height, often with crooked trunk and branches. The fruit is bizarre: The fleshy fruit part is called the cashew apple; the nut (the true fruit) is a kidney-shaped bean that hangs from the bottom of the "apple." It is about an inch long and covered with a thick shell. The shell contains acid substances that severely burn the skin at the touch. The cashew is roasted and then peeled to reveal a white kernel of delicate flavor. The cashew apple is a soft fleshy fruit that gives a zesty juice. It is made into jam and a wonderfully flavorful wine.

The Sapodilla Fruit

The sapodilla tree at one time was highly prized for its milky latex, which was used for many years in the production of chewing gum. It bears a fruit prized by the locals from southern Mexico, Central America, and northern South America. Fruits grow two to three inches in diameter, the skin is rough and brown, and the flesh is yellowish brown, granular, and very sweet. Unless it is well-ripened, granules stick to the teeth and feel like chewing gum. This is another "taste" that must "grow" on you.

The Passion Fruit

The name and the flower of the passion fruit may be more familiar to people than the actual fruit. Again, this beautiful purple-flowered fruit has several unlikely relatives: papaya, pumpkin, and melon. Actually there are both purple and yellow passion fruit. Both have high acidic content and are generally used for juice. Many people grow the tree strictly as an ornament because of its colorful, unusual flowers.

Quamwood

The quamwood is known for its glowing yellow flowers, which festoon the tree and carpet the ground under it in spring. The tree takes its name from the local name for the curassow or quam, a large bird that favors its seeds. Quamwood trees are usually found in broadleaf jungle and dense forests.

Strangler Fig

Imagine a creepy, leafy parasite that starts its cycle as a seed deposited by a monkey or bird somewhere in the high jungle canopy. As the fig gets down to business it sends a tendril to the ground to take root. Leaves and branches begin to grow from the budding plant. As they do, off-shoots of the original tendril begin a long process of surrounding the hapless victim's trunk. Over time the fig sends its branches above the crown of the host tree. Overshadowed above and enveloped below, the host dies. Victorious, the strangler fig is left to tower alone, a tree with a hollow heart where once the trunk of its victim stood.

From Fruit to Flowers

Central America grows delicious sweet and sour oranges, limes, and grapefruit. Avocado is abundant, and the papaya tree is practically a weed. The *sapote* (mammee) tree grows tall (50-65 feet) and full, providing not only welcome shade but also an avocado-shaped fruit with brown fiber on the outside and a vivid salmon-pink flesh that makes a sweet snack (the flavor is similar to a sweet yam's). It also produces chicle, the sap formerly used for chewing gum. Another unusual fruit tree is the *guaya* (part of the litchi nut family). This rangy evergreen thrives on sea air and is commonly seen along the coast and throughout Belize. Its small, green, leathery pods grow in clumps like grapes and contain a sweet, yellowish, jellylike flesh—tasty! The calabash tree, a friend to the indigenous people for many years, provides a gourd used for containers.

The tall ceiba is a very special tree to the Maya religion. Considered the tree of life, even today it remains undisturbed whether it has sprouted in the middle of a fertile Maya *milpa* (cornfield) or anywhere else. When visiting in the summer, you'll see *flamboyanes* (royal poinciana) everywhere. As its name implies, when in bloom it is the most flamboyant tree around, with wide-spreading branches covered in clusters of brilliant orange-red flowers. These trees line sidewalks and plazas and when clustered together present a dazzling show.

Orchids

In remote areas of Belize one of the more exotic blooms, the orchid, is often found on the highest limbs of tall trees. Of the 71 species reported in Belize, 20% are terrestrial (growing in the ground) and 80% are epiphytic (attached to a host plant—in this case trees—and deriving its moisture and nutrients from the air and rain). Both types grow in many sizes and shapes: tiny buttons, spanning the length of a long branch;

large-petaled blossoms with ruffled edges; or intense, tiger-striped miniatures. The lovely flowers come in a wide variety of colors, some subtle, some brilliant. The black orchid is Belize's national flower. All orchids are protected by strict laws, so look but don't pick.

Nature's Hothouse

In spring, flowering trees are a beautiful sight—and sound—attracting hundreds of singing birds throughout the mating season. While wandering through the jungle landscapes you'll see, thriving in the wild, a gamut of plants we so carefully nurture and coax to survive in a pot on a windowsill at home. Here in its natural environment, the croton exhibits wild colors, the pothos grows one-foot-long leaves, and the philodendron splits every leaf in gargantuan glory.

White and red ginger are among the more exotic herbs that grow in Belize. Plumeria (called *frangipani* in the South Pacific) has a wonderful fragrance and many colors. Hibiscus and bougainvillea bloom in an array of bright hues. A walk through the jungle will introduce you to many delicate strangers in the world of tropical flowers. But you'll find old friends, too, such as the common morning glory, creeping and climbing for miles over bushes and trees. Viny coils thicken daily. Keeping jungle growth away from the roads, utility poles, and wires is a constant job because warm, humid air and ample rainfall encourage a lush green wonderland.

FAUNA

Nature lovers will find a fantasyland in Belize. A walk through the jungle brings you close to myriad animal and bird species, many of which are almost extinct in other Central American countries—and the world. Tread softly—more than likely you won't see many of the beasties mentioned here since they're experts at hiding in trees, behind thick vines, in old logs, in hidden burrows, or just blending in with their background. But with concerted effort, a light step, and sharp eyes, you might get lucky.

BIRDS OF BELIZE

Since a major part of Belize is still undeveloped and covered with trees and brush, it isn't surprising to find exotic, rarely seen birds across the landscape. The Belizeans are beginning to realize the great value in this (almost) undiscovered treasure trove of nature, which attracts both scientists and laymen, and are making rapid progress in protecting natural habitats. The birds in Belize have until recent years been free of pest sprays, smog, and encroaching human beings. If you're a serious birdwatcher, you know all about Belize. Change is coming as more people intrude into the rangeland of the birds, exploring these still-undeveloped tracts in the wilderness areas of Belize. Still, there are more birds to watch here than in almost any other location in Central America.

Belize, with its marsh-rimmed shores and lakes, nearby cornfields, and tall, humid forest, is worth a couple of days to the ornithologist. One of the more impressive birds to look for is the spectacularly hued keel-billed toucan. This is the national bird of Belize and is often seen perched high on a bare limb in the early morning.

Others include chachalacas (held in reverence by the Maya), screeching parrots, and occasionally, the ocellated turkey. A good book that zeros in on the birds and animals of Belize is *Jungle Walk, Birds and Beasts of Belize,* by Katie Stephens. No color, but along with sketches of the creatures, she gives good down-to-earth descriptions of their habits. The book is available through International Expeditions, US$4.95 plus tax, postage, and handling; to order call (800) 633-4734. At the Audubon Society Office in Belize City at 12 Fort St., pick up a copy of the *Checklist of the Birds of Belize,* by Wood, Leberman, and Weyer, published by the Carnegie Museum of Natural History, Pittsburgh, Pennsylvania. Another excellent bird book that deals with the *entire* Yucatán Peninsula is *Common Birds of the Yucatán Peninsula,* with full-color photos, written by Barbara MacKinnon. It's available through Amigos de Sian Ka'an, Apto Postal 770, Cancún, Quintana Roo 77500, Mexico.

Acorn Woodpecker

This bright little creature lives an ingenious lifestyle. It's most well known for storing its supper in individual holes burrowed into tree trunks, allowing the nut to dry out without fermenting. As part of a "commune," the male birds share the breeding females, who then lay their eggs in a communal nest. The young hang around the nest for several years "helping out at home" before leaving to raise their own families. The woodpecker has black and white feathers with a red patch on the top of its head.

Jabiru Stork

The largest flying bird in the Americas is the jabiru stork, which grows four to five feet tall and has a wing span of 9-12 feet. Though the birds are scarce in the rest of the Western Hemisphere, Belize boasts a healthy community of breeding storks. Building the nest is a major construction job. The brooding nest is generally built on a high tree in an open area above the rainforest; a favorite spot is in the Crooked Tree Wildlife Sanctuary. The cumbersome birds weave a platform from large branches measur-

BIRDS OF BELIZE

Marsh Birds
roseate spoonbill
white ibis

Wading Birds
American flamingo

Water Birds
black-bellied tree-duck
fulvous tree-duck
white-fronted goose

Lowland Birds
barred antshrike
black-headed saltator
blue tanager
blue-crowned motmot
boat-billed flycatcher
clay-colored robin
crimson-collared tanager
golden-olive woodpecker
keel-billed toucan
kisadee flycatcher
masked tityra
olivaceous flycatcher
rufous-tailed hummingbird
singing blackbird
social flycatcher
spotted-breasted wren
violaceous trogon
white-tipped brown jay
yellow-throated euphonia

Birds in the Dense Forest
acorn woodpecker
black-faced grosbeak
brown woodpecker
collared trogon
flint-billed woodpecker
golden-crowned warbler
golden-olive woodpecker
gray-headed vireo
green jay
jabiru stork
keel-billed toucan
lineated woodpecker
little tinamou
lowland wood-wren
olivaceous creeper

red-crowned tanager
ruddy quail dove
short-billed pigeon
spotted wood-quail
spotted-breasted wren
sulphur-bellied flycatcher
violaceous trogon
white-bellied emerald
white-fronted dove
white-throated robin

Birds at Beaches, Bays, and Adjacent Ocean
black tern
black vulture
brown pelican
laughing gull
least tern
magnificent frigate bird
royal tern
sooty tern
spotted sandpiper

Birds Seen at Partially Cleared Archaeological Sites, Woodland Edge, or Scrubby, Deciduous Woodland
altamira oriole
Aztec parakeet
black-headed saltator
blue-black grassquit
blue-gray gnatcatcher
boat-billed flycatcher
cave swallow
common ground-dove
ferruginous pygmy owl
golden-fronted woodpecker
gray saltator
groove-billed ani
hooded oriole
laughing creeper
lesser nighthawk
mangrove vireo
masked tityra
olivaceous flycatcher
pauraque
peppershrike
plain chachalaca
red-eyed cowbird

rose-throated coptinga
ruddy ground-dove
social flycatcher
spotted-breasted wren
tropical kingbird
white-bellied wren
white-browed wren
white-fronted dove
white-lored gnatcatcher
white-winged dove
yellow-billed elaenia
Yucatán jay

Birds Seen at Lagoons, Tidal Flats, Shallow Estuaries, and Mangrove Swamps
American coot
American widgeon
black vulture
common egret
great blue heron
great-tailed grackle
jacana
killdeer
laughing gull
little blue heron
Louisiana heron
magnificent frigate bird
mangrove swallow
mangrove warbler
olivaceous cormorant
reddish egret
royal tern
snowy egret
spotted sandpiper
yellow-crowned night heron

Birds Seen in Villages and Overgrown Fields
black vulture
clay-colored robin
common ground-dove
gray saltator
groove-billed ani
ruddy ground-dove
singing blackbird
tropical house wren
tropical mockingbird
Vaux's swift

ing as much as 10 feet across. The hatchlings (two to four) are an indiscriminate gray that eventually changes into the adult coloration of black beak, white body, and black head, with a bright red band below the neck. Occasionally seen in a farmer's field, the stork from a distance looks like a bent old man wearing a red tie. The birds feed in and around swamps and ponds, preferring snails, frogs, small mammals, fish, and especially reptiles.

LOUISE FOOTE

Keel-Billed Toucan
The national bird of Belize, the keel-billed toucan is instantly recognizable by its large colorful bill, yellow front, black body, and splash of red beneath the tail. Inhabitants of the forest, toucans follow each other in small ragged flocks as they forage for fruit and small prey in the trees. Not known for their singing, toucans make short, hoarse squawks. Like that of the woodpeckers and hornbills to whom they are related, their flight has an undulating motion to it. These birds are especially numerous in sections of the Cayo, Orange Walk, and Toledo districts.

King Vulture
Certainly the king vulture or King John crow is one of the more brilliantly colored large birds of Central America. The body is white with black flight feathers on the wings, but the visual fireworks start from the shoulders up. A bright orange neck and beak, purplish head, grayish folds at the cheeks, white eyes surrounded by red, and an orange-yellow warty growth above the beak make the King John crow a real showstopper. But, like its lesser brethren the turkey and black vultures, the king must content itself

with carrion, the leftovers of the animal world. The king vulture is the only vulture in Belize to prefer forested areas, locating its food by sight alone. Rare throughout its range, the king vulture is a remarkable sight as it soars over forested valleys, hills, and mountainsides. For most visitors, though, the surest opportunity to observe this royalty is at the Belize Zoo.

Magnificent Frigate Bird
Daring showoffs, frigate birds swoop and soar in breathtaking abandon, often along the shore in San Pedro and Belize City. Easily identified by their black overall color, scissor tails and swept-back wing tips, female frigate birds have white heads and short bills while males have long black bills. The magnificent frigate bird got its name from the male's inflatable red pouch below the neck. Males inflate this twin-lobed sac only during mating displays. Frigate birds are pirates at heart, bullying other birds into releasing catches of fish in mid-air. Thus, these airborne buccaneers gain a dishonest meal without so much as getting their feet wet. The man-o'-war bird, as it is sometimes called, can be a tolerant neighbor at home, though. At Half Moon Caye they peacefully share nesting areas with rare red-footed boobies and other birds. At mealtime, of course, they revert to their pirate ways. You can easily observe all this from a treetop platform erected by the Belize Audubon Society.

Ocellated Turkey
The "peacock" of Belize, the ocellated turkey is so named because of the eyelike rings on its tail. The blue warty head sports a reddish beak. The body and legs also have a red cast. Turkeys especially like open woodland and forest edge where they hunt and peck for seeds, grasses, and fruit. They congregate in flocks of about a dozen birds most of the year. Feeding in early morning and late afternoon, turkeys select nesting sites in low horizontal branches. Considerable droppings mark these sites in white. In spring to early summer they begin their mating ritual. Like their North American counterparts, ocellated males put on elaborate displays and come equipped with spurs for jousting with rivals. They and their northern cousins are the only wild turkeys in the world. Ocellated turkeys are readily observed in Orange Walk District at the

THE QUETZAL—WORTH A TRIP

Though the ancient Maya made abundant use of the dazzling quetzal feathers for ceremonial costume and headdress, they hunted other fowl in much larger quantities for food; nonetheless, the quetzal is one of the few birds mentioned in the pre-Columbian era and it is almost extinct. Though the colorful bird is not found in Belize, we mention it because birdwatchers continuing into Guatemala or Costa Rica will want to visit its habitats. The Guatemala government has established a quetzal sanctuary not too far from the city of Coban. The beautifully designed reserve is open to hikers, with several miles of good trails leading up into the cloud forest. For the birder this could be a worthwhile detour to search out the gorgeous

quetzal. The Coban tourist office, INGUAT, hands out an informative leaflet with a map and description of the quetzal sanctuary. If in Costa Rica, take a trip into the Monteverde Cloud Forest Reserve for a possible glimpse of these shy, beautiful birds.

BOB RACE

Rio Bravo Conservation Area run by Programme for Belize.

Sooty Tern

The sooty tern is not the only seabird that lacks waterproof feathers, but it is the only one that will not land and rest on passing ships or drifting debris. The bird feeds on tiny fish and squid that swim close to the surface of the sea. While hovering close to the water they snatch their unsuspecting prey. The birds nest April-Sept., and if left undisturbed, a colony can raise 150-200 chicks in a summer. Man is the sooty tern's only predator. If frightened, the parent birds panic, leaving the eggs exposed to the hot tropical sun or knocking the young out of the nest where they cannot fend for themselves.

CATS

Jaguar

Seven species of cats are found in North America; five are distributed tropically. The jaguar is heavy-chested with sturdy, muscled forelegs, a relatively short tail, and small, rounded ears. Its tawny coat is uniformly spotted; the spots form rosettes: large circles with smaller spots in the center. The jaguar's belly is white with black spots. The male can weigh 145-255 pounds,

females 125-165 pounds. Largest of the cats in Central America and third-largest cat in the world, the jaguar is about the same size as a leopard. It is nocturnal, spending most daylight hours snoozing in the sun. The male marks an area of about 65 square miles and spends its nights stalking deer, peccaries, agoutis, tapirs, monkeys, and birds. If hunting is poor and times are tough, the jaguar will go into rivers and scoop fish with its large paws. The river is also a favorite spot for the jaguar to hunt the large tapir when it comes to drink. Females begin breeding at about three years and generally produce twin cubs.

For years the rich came to Belize on safari to hunt the jaguar for its beautiful skin. Likewise, hunting margay, puma, ocelots, and jaguarundis was a popular destructive sport in the rainforest. All of that has changed. Hunting any endangered species in Belize is not allowed. To preserve the cats, as well as other unusual animals including the tapir, paca, and dozens of bird species, Belize has designated approximately 155 square miles as **Cockscomb Basin Jaguar Preserve** (see "Cockscomb Basin Wildlife Sanctuary" under "Cockscomb Basin").

While much of the wildlife in the preserve is nocturnal, traces of animals are found by those who trek along the old logging tracks or climb up into the Cockscomb Range, including the

JAGUARS 1, HUNTERS 0

Jaguars, the biggest predators in the New World, need lots of space to roam. So it's ironic that Belize, a country so small it would fit into the hip pocket of Texas, claims to have the greatest concentration of jaguars on earth.

Apparently the cats are hanging in there and even growing in numbers. After international hunting groups brought the possibility of hunting the big cats once again before the Belize government, Alan Rabinowitz, a leading authority on jaguars with Wildlife Conservation International (the foreign service arm of the New York Zoological Society), helped it to decide that the numbers of jaguars were not enough to justify hunting. Rabinowitz did a premier study more than a decade ago on the big cat and at that time encouraged the government to protect the animals. Since 1981, hunting jaguars has been banned and thousands of acres of forest have been set aside for the big cat; 102,000 in the Cockscomb Basin Wildlife Sanctuary. Jaguars, which once ranged from the Grand Canyon to Argentina, are now extinct in the U.S. and rare or endangered elsewhere.

Changes in the countryside, such as a decline in cattle ranching, have made the jaguar more popular. Pastures have been replaced by citrus orchards, and fruit is now the country's number two export, after sugar. For jaguars at least, citrus farmers make better neighbors than ranchers, who have a deep prejudice against the prowling meat-eaters.

The new appreciation, pride, and concern expressed by Belizeans about their wildlife and their environment is the most striking change that has occurred in Belize. The image of the jaguar has changed from that of a night-stalking, dangerous, livestock killer to a source of pride and awe. Jaguars are now featured on Belizean currency, postage stamps, and nearly every tourist brochure. The most vocal advocates of jaguar protection in Belize are people involved in the country's escalating tourism business. Rabinowitz strongly advises the government to maintain its moratorium on jaguar hunting. His report is reassuring and sees the increasing public support for jaguars as an important ally in ensuring the majestic cat's survival.

highest peak in Belize, Victoria Peak (3,675 feet). South Stann Creek and the Swasey branch of the Monkey River both flow through the preserve and are good stop-offs for a cooling swim while hiking the basin. When planning a visit, go to Maya Center (a small town) first and ask about a guide, who might also take you to a minor Maya ceremonial center within the preserve. You can reach the Cockscomb Basin Jaguar Preserve from the Southern Highway, which parallels the coast between Dangriga and Placencia. Sadly, the jaguar is still illegally hunted for its skin. The animal's greatest predator is man. By establishing Cockscomb Preserve and preserves like it, Belize hopes to keep the big cat around for many centuries to come.

Margay
The smallest of the Belizean cats is the margay, usually weighing in at about 11 pounds and marked by a velvety coat with exotic designs, beautifully patterned eyes, and a bushy tail. A shy animal, it is seldom seen in open country, preferring the protection of the forest. It hunts mainly in the trees, satisfied with birds, monkeys, and insects as well as lizards and figs.

Jaguarundi
Larger and not nearly as catlike as the margay, this black or brown feline has a small flattened head, rounded ears, short legs, and a long tail. It hunts by day for birds and small mammals in the rainforests of Central America.

Ocelot

The ocelot is another of nature's great works of art, with a beautiful striped and spotted coat. Average weight is about 35 pounds. A good climber, the cat hunts in trees as well as on the ground. Its prey includes birds, monkeys, snakes, rabbits, young deer, and fish. Ocelots usually have litters of two but can have as many as four.

Puma

The puma is also known as the cougar or mountain lion. The adult male measures about 6.5 feet in length and weighs up to 198 pounds. It thrives in any environment that supports deer, porcupine, or rabbit. The puma hunts day or night.

MONKEYS

Howler Monkey

In Creole the howler monkey is referred to as "baboon" and in Spanish its called *saraguate,* though it has no close connection to its African relatives. Because the howler prefers low-lying tropical rainforests under 1,000 feet elevation, Belize is a perfect habitat, boasting a healthy family of 1,300 howlers. They are more commonly found near the riverine forests, especially on the Belize River and its major branches. The howler monkey, along with its small cousin the spider monkey, also enjoys the foothills of the Maya Mountains. To protect the howler monkey, the **Bermudian Landing Community Baboon Sanctuary** was organized to help conserve the lands where it lives. Thanks to an all-out effort involving local property owners, the Belize Ministry of Natural Resources, the U.S. World Wildlife Fund, the Belize Audubon Society, and the Peace Corps, the land that provides for the howler will be saved. The monkey lives only in Belize, southern Mexico, and parts of Guatemala. In many areas it's in danger of disappearing altogether. The sanctuary is an ideal place for researchers to study its habits and perhaps discover the key to its survival among encroaching humans. Concentrations of the howler are reasonably accessible to visitors in Belize.

The adult howler monkey is entirely black and weighs 15-25 pounds. Its most distinct trait is a roar that can be heard up to a mile distant. A bone in the throat acts as an amplifier; the cry sounds much like that of a jaguar. The howler's unforgettable bark is said by some to be used to warn other troops away from its territory. Locals, on the other hand, say the howlers roar when it's about to rain, to greet the sun, to say goodnight, or when they're feeding.

The howlers live in troops that number four to eight and no more than 10, consisting of one adult male and the rest females and young. Infants nurse for about 18 months, making the space between pregnancies about 24 months. Initially, "mom" carries her young clutched to her chest; once they're a little older, they ride piggyback. The troop sleeps, eats, and travels together. The howlers primarily eat leaves, but include flowers and fruit in their diet (when available). Highly selective, they require particular segments of certain trees and blossoms: sapodilla, hog-plum, bay cedar, fig, and buket trees.

After ecologists spent much time studying the Belizean "baboon," it became obvious that with the destruction of the riverine sections of the forest the howlers in Belize would go the way of their cousins in southern Mexico and northern Guatemala (nearly extinct). As a result, the people who live in an 18-square-mile area have joined together, voluntarily, and agreed to do or not to do certain things to encourage the lifestyle of the howler monkey. Thanks to the forward-thinking Bermudian Landing villagers, the **Community Baboon Sanctuary** has evolved. The villagers in this area maintain strips of forest between fields and along rivers and preserve the food trees of the baboon. The locals even put up with the monkey's occasional invasion of cashew trees. Although the baboon has a couple of natural predators—the jaguar and the harpy eagle—its worst foe is deforestation by man. An unexpected boon to the area has been the reappearance of other small animals and bird species that are also taking advantage of the protected area.

If you wish to visit the Community Baboon Sanctuary, contact the manager at the small interpretive museum in the village. Be aware

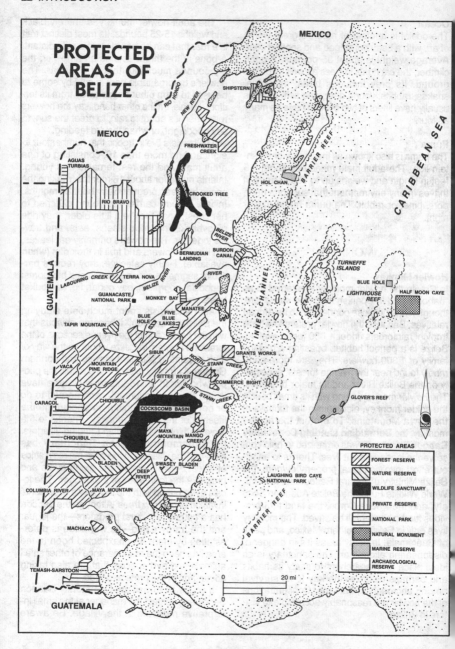

PROTECTED AREAS OF BELIZE

MEXICO

MEXICO

SHIPSTERN

RIO HONDO

NEW RIVER

FRESHWATER CREEK

AGUAS TURBIAS

RIO BRAVO

CROOKED TREE

HOL CHAN

BARRIER REEF

CARIBBEAN SEA

BELIZE RIVER

BERMUDIAN LANDING

BURDON CANAL

TURNEFFE ISLANDS

GUATEMALA

LABOURING CREEK

TERRA NOVA

RIVER

SIBUN

BLUE HOLE

LIGHTHOUSE REEF

HALF MOON CAYE

GUANACASTE NATIONAL PARK

MONKEY BAY

TAPIR MOUNTAIN

BLUE HOLE

FIVE BLUE LAKES

MANATEE

INNER CHANNEL

VACA

MOUNTAIN PINE RIDGE

SIBUN

GRANTS WORKS

NORTH STANN CREEK

SITTEE RIVER

SOUTH STANN CREEK

COMMERCE BIGHT

GLOVER'S REEF

CARACOL

CHIQUIBUL

COCKSCOMB BASIN

CHIQUIBUL

MAYA MOUNTAIN

MANGO CREEK

BLADEN

SWASEY BLADEN

DEEP RIVER

LAUGHING BIRD CAYE NATIONAL PARK

COLUMBIA RIVER

MAYA MOUNTAIN

PAYNES CREEK

MACHACA

RIO GRANDE

BARRIER REEF

TEMASH-SARSTOON

PROTECTED AREAS

FOREST RESERVE
NATURE RESERVE
WILDLIFE SANCTUARY
PRIVATE RESERVE
NATIONAL PARK
NATURAL MONUMENT
MARINE RESERVE
ARCHAEOLOGICAL RESERVE

0   20 mi

0   20 km

GUATEMALA

that the trails are on private land and visitors should not infringe on private property. A trail is maintained and it's advised that all who visit have a guide for orientation. The sanctuary employs two full-time guides. The trails are marked with numbered signs that correspond with information provided in a (good) book, *Community Baboon Sanctuary,* available in most gift shops or through the sanctuary. It's always a thrill to watch the bright-eyed black monkey as it sits within five feet of you on a wild-lime tree branch, happily munching the leaves. They seem to know they're protected here. Group trips and/or guides from local hotels are available. Ask at Bermudian Landing about locals who provide home-cooked meals and informal accommodations; in Belize City ask at the Audubon Society Office, 12 Fort St., tel. (2) 34985/35004.

Spider Monkey

Smaller than howlers, spider monkeys live in troops of a dozen or more, feeding on leaves, fruits, and flowers high in the jungle canopy. Slender limbs and elongated prehensile tails assist them as they climb and swing from tree to tree. With a border of white around their faces, adults look like little old people. Baby spider monkeys are winsome in appearance, too, and often are captured for pets. So curious and mischievous are they, however, that frustrated owners frequently cage or even release them back into the wild. Without the skills to survive or the support of a troop, such freed orphans are doomed to perish. Unlike howler monkeys, which may allow human proximity during their midday siesta, spider monkeys rarely approve. They usually dissolve into the forest canopy. On occasion, they have been known to aim small sticks, urine, and worse at intruders. Though not as numerous in Belize as howler monkeys because of disease and habitat loss, they remain an important part of the country's natural legacy.

RODENTS

Agouti

A small rodent relative of the rabbit and paca, the agouti or "Indian rabbit" has coarse gray-brown fur and a hopping gait. It is most often encountered scampering along a forest trail or clearing. Not the brightest of creatures, it makes up for this lack of wit with typical rodent libido and fecundity. Inhabiting the same areas as the paca, these two seldom meet, as the agouti minds its business during the day and the paca prefers nighttime pursuits. The agouti is less delectable than the paca. Nonetheless, it is taken by animal and human hunters and is a staple food of jaguars.

Paca

The paca or gibnut is a quick brownish rodent about the size of a large rabbit with white spots along its back. Nocturnal by habit and highly prized as a food item by many Belizeans, the gibnut is more apt to be seen by the visitor on an occasional restaurant menu than in the wild. Similar in flavor to its rabbit cousin, in Belize the gibnut is frequently fried or stewed—and it's not bad. In fact, when it comes to cuisine, the paca has been dubbed by the British press "the royal rat" after the Queen took a taste on a recent visit.

OTHER INTERESTING MAMMALS

Anteater

Without a tooth in its head the tamandua—or anteater—makes a fine living by tearing into termite and ant nests with sharp curved claws and slurping up the inhabitants. The anteater's tapered snout and long, sticky, saliva-coated tongue are perfectly adapted to this business. Ants and termites, of course, are a hard lot to stomach, but the anteater makes the most of it by employing equally tough innards. The tamandua wears a dark saddle over a lighter brown coat and its wiry hair and thick skin offer some protection against the attacks of enraged ants. Living both on the forest floor and in the treetops, the anteater uses its prehensile tail for balance or as an extra hand upstairs. Solitary by nature, anteater mothers do allow youngsters to ride along on their backs.

Coati

A member of the raccoon family, the coati—or quash—has a long, ringed tail, masked face, and lengthy snout. Sharp claws aid the coati in climbing trees and digging up insects and other small prey. Omnivorous, the quash also relishes jungle fruits. A sensitive, agile nose helps it sniff out trees bearing these favored goodies. Usually seen in small troops of females and young, coatis have an amusing, jaunty appearance as they cross a jungle path, tails at attention. The occasional solitary male is referred to as a coati-mundi or solitary coati.

Honduran White Bat

A sight that most people will never see is the two-inch Honduran white bat. It lives only in the jungles of Central America. Cuddly-looking little creatures, they have white fur with pink ears and nose. Like most bats, they feed at night on the local fruit trees found in the jungle or in a farmer's backyard. During the day, they sleep in groups of 2-15 in a "tent" they fashion by biting through the veins of a *heliconia* leaf (much like a large banana leaf) near the midrib until the sides droop. The result is a tent where they cluster under the midrib while hanging upside down by their feet. The drooping leaf protects them from the sun and rain as they sleep. The leaf also creates a perfect camouflage against predators. During the day the bright sunlight filters through the leaf, bathing the bats' fur in green hues. The green tone makes it hard for enemies, such as monkeys and snakes, to spot the bats.

Peccary

Next to deer, peccaries are the most widely hunted game in Central America. Other names for this piglike creature are musk hog and javelina. Some compare these nocturnal mammals to the wild pigs found in Europe, though, in fact, they are native to America.

Two species found in Belize are the collared and the white-lipped peccary. The feisty collared peccary stands one foot at the shoulder and can be three feet long, weighing as much as 65 pounds. It is black and white with a narrow semicircular collar of white hair on the shoulders. In Spanish *jabalina* means "spear," descriptive of the two spearlike tusks that protrude from its mouth. This more familiar peccary lives in deserts, woodlands, and rainforests, and travels in groups of 5-15.

Also with tusks, the white-lipped peccary or warrie is reddish-brown to black and has an area of white around the mouth. This larger animal, which can grow to four feet long, dwells deep in tropical rainforests and at one time lived in herds of 100 or more. They are more dangerous than their smaller cousins and should be given a wide berth.

Tapir

The national animal of Belize, the South American tapir is found from the southern part of Mexico to southern Brazil. It is stout-bodied, with short legs, a short tail, small eyes, and rounded ears. Its nose and upper lip extend into a short but very mobile proboscis. Totally herbivorous, tapirs usually live near streams or rivers in the forest. They bathe daily and also use the water as an escape when hunted either by man or by their prime predator, the jaguar. Shy, unaggressive animals, they are nocturnal with a definite home range, wearing a path between the jungle and their feeding area. The tapir is said to have bad eyesight and if attacked, it lowers its head and blindly crashes off through the forest; it's been known to collide with a tree and knock itself out in its chaotic attempt to flee! "April the Tapir" is a star attraction at the Belize Zoo. A birthday celebration is held for her each year to the delight of hundreds of Belizean schoolchildren. April gets her vegetarian "cake," and the children get the real thing as well as a good visit with the national animal. Many people attend the party that doubles as a popular fundraiser to help support the zoo. (See the special topic "The Belize Zoo" in the Belize District chapter.)

LIZARDS

Belize is inhabited by a great variety of lizards, from a skinny two-inch miniature gecko to a chameleon-like black anole that changes colors to match the environment, either when danger is imminent or as subterfuge to fool the insects it preys upon. At mating time, the male anole puffs out its bright red throat fan to make sure all female lizards will see it. Some lizards are brightly striped in various shades of green and yellow; others are marked with earthy colors that blend with the gray and beige limestone dotting the landscape. Skinny as wisps of thread running on hind legs or chunky and waddling with armorlike skin, the variety is endless—and fascinating! And don't forget the entertaining basilisk, or Jesus Christ lizard, which runs along the surface of water.

Basilisk Lizard
The basilisk lizard looks like a tiny Godzilla with its crested head and back. It's a basic brown with dark stripes on the sides. When disturbed, the basilisk proves to be equally entertaining as it tears around at breakneck speed. All you are likely to see is a flash of legs and elbows as it streaks off into the brush. In fact, its nickname, Jesus Christ lizard, comes from its ability to run across swampy areas and creeks with its webbed hind feet. Don't believe it? Just watch!

Iguana
Found all over Central America, lizards of the family Iguanidae include various large plant-eaters, in many sizes and typically dark in color with slight variations. The young iguana is bright emerald green. The common lizard grows to three feet long, has a blunt head and long flat tail. Bands of black and gray circle its body, and a serrated column reaches down the middle of its back, almost to its tail. During mating season, it's common to see brilliant orange males on a sunny branch hoping to attract a girlfriend.

Very large and shy, the lizard uses its fore-limbs to hold the front half of its body up off the ground while the two back limbs remain relaxed and splayed alongside its hindquarters. However, when the iguana is frightened, its hind legs do everything they're supposed to, and the iguana crashes quickly (though clumsily) into the brush searching for its burrow and safety. This reptile is not aggressive, but if cornered it will bite and use its tail in self-defense. The iguana mostly enjoys basking in the bright sunshine along the Caribbean. Though they are mainly herbivores, the young also eat insects and larvae. Certain varieties in some areas of southern Mexico and Central America are almost hunted out—for example, the spiny-tailed iguana in the central valley of Chiapas, Mexico. A moderate number are still found in the rocky foothill slopes and thorn-scrub woodlands. It is not unusual to see locals along dirt paths carrying sturdy specimens by the tail to put in the cook pot.

From centuries past, recorded references attest to the medicinal value of this lizard, partly explaining the active trade of live iguanas in the marketplaces of some parts of Belize. Iguana stew is believed to cure or relieve various human ailments, such as impotence. The unlaid eggs of iguanas caught before the nesting season are considered a delicacy. Another reason for their popularity at the market is their delicate white flesh, which tastes much like chicken. If people say they're having "bamboo chicken"

Iguanas love the sun.

for dinner, they are dining on iguana.

Several other species of iguana live in Belize, from the small to a gargantuan six feet long. Their habits are much the same, however. They all enjoy basking in the sun, sleeping in old hollow trees at night, and eating certain tender plants. The female can lay up to a hundred eggs, and when the pale green or tan hatchlings emerge from the rubbery egg skins, they scoot about quickly. One of the iguana's serious predators is the hawk. If an iguana sights a winged shadow while sunbathing on a high tree limb, it flings itself from the tree into the river or brush below, swimming or skittering quickly into hiding. However, man remains its most dangerous predator.

SNAKES

Snakes roam the Belize jungles and plains. The much-maligned animal is shunned by most humans, and in some cases that's a wise move. Belize has more than 20 kinds of poisonous snakes; nine are deadly. Most of these you will likely never see. Many others are harmless, and anyone who will be wandering in the bush should try to learn the difference. Pick up the Audubon Society's booklet, *Snakes Of Belize.* It's full of good information from herpetologist Dora Weyer and detailed drawings by Ellen McRae, who lives in Caye Caulker.

Boa Constrictor
The boa or wowla is one of the most handsome reptiles in the forest and its dark and light brown leafy pattern serves as good camouflage. Boas hunt for birds, lizards, and small mammals in trees and on the ground. Holing up during the day, boas prefer to hunt at night. They are able to sense the presence of prey through very sensitive heat receptors and their senses of smell and sight. As their name implies, they kill their prey by constriction, primarily suffocating their victims. Only about six feet fully grown, wowlas pose little threat to humans, but may bite if provoked. They freeze or retreat when approached. Some uninformed people kill boas as well as other snakes on sight. This is unfortunate, not only because people are rarely injured by snakes, but also because snakes help reduce the number of rodents, which keenly compete with many other creatures for food.

Coral Snake
Coral snakes are found only in the New World, mostly Central and South America, with a few in the southern U.S. In all there are about 50 species. The coral snakes in Belize average about 31 inches long. The true coral is highly poisonous and a bite is usually fatal unless treated. The harmless false coral is also found here. Its body is slender, with no pronounced distinction between head and neck. In Belize, the true coral snake is banded in a red-yellow-black-yellow-red sequence (this is not the case in other countries). If you don't know for sure, don't approach a banded snake with those colors. Remember, red means stop! One jingle says: "Red and yellow kill a fellow; red and black, a friendly Jack." Usually nocturnal, coral snakes spend the day in mossy clumps under rocks or logs.

Corals do not look for trouble and seldom strike, but will bite if stepped on; their short fangs, however, can be stopped by shoes or clothing. Even though the locals call this the "20-minute snake" (meaning if you are bitten and don't get antivenin within 20 minutes, you'll die), it's actually more like 24 hours. Reportedly, most snakebite victims are children.

The chances of the average tourist's being bitten by a coral (or any other snake) are slim. However, if you plan on extensive jungle exploration, check with your doctor before you leave home. Antivenin is available, doesn't require refrigeration, and keeps indefinitely. It's wise to be prepared for an allergic reaction to the antivenin—bring an antihistamine and Adrenalin (epinephrine). The most important thing to remember if bitten: *don't panic and don't run.* Physical exertion and panic cause the venom to travel through your body much faster. Lie down and stay calm; have someone carry you to a doctor (see the special topic "Simple First-Aid Guide" in the Health and Safety section).

Fer-de-lance
This fellow is bad news. Often aggressive, the fer-de-lance, or yellow-jawed tommygoff, is a nocturnal pit viper that comes from the same family as the cascabel (tropical rattler), water moccasin, and the jumping viper. The fer-de-lance can be found anyplace: in thick jungle,

savanna grass, or out in the open chasing prey. This nasty specimen can grow 8.5 feet long. It comes from litters of up to 75, and until it reaches adolescence it sports a prehensile tail and can and will swing and jump from any tree. As it matures it comes to the ground and pretty well stays there. It attacks with two fangs from either a coiled or extended position and will attack more than once if given the opportunity. The adult has an arrow-shaped head, is thick-set, and its dorsal coloring ranges from dark brown to olive to gray to red. It has 30 paired triangles along its sides, lighter in color and edged in black, which form a row of dark diamonds the length of the snake's back. The underside is cream or yellow beneath the jaw to the throat. The mouth is large and contains two hollow, retractable fangs, larger in proportion to its size than any other snake's. Its venom is highly poisonous and should be treated immediately. Carrying a **Cutter's Snake Bite Kit** is a possible last-ditch effort when there's nothing else, but be advised that most doctors discourage cutting the wound. Do not use a tourniquet and do not ingest alcoholic beverages. If you ask advice from a rural local about where to go if bitten, he/she might suggest a snake doctor who is little more than a healer. However, some Belizeans say, "Do not *ever* go to a snake doctor! In a desperate situation you must make a choice.

For more information, *Poisonous Snakes of the World* is available from the Superintendent of Documents, U.S. Government Printing Office, Washington, D.C.

OTHER REPTILES

Central American River Turtle
Woe the poor hicatee, too tasty for its own good! A well-armored herbivore, the hicatee or Central American river turtle has been over-hunted by man in the rivers and lagoons where it lives. Food consists of fruits, grasses, and other vegetarian fare found along the waterways. Hicatees sleep on the bottom during the day and feed at night. They mate in late spring and early summer and lay eggs in the fall to mid-December. Capable of growing to nearly 50 pounds, they rarely get the chance to do so today. As in neighboring countries, their numbers continue to decline and the Belize government has yet to declare any protection for these hard-pressed reptiles.

Crocodile
Though often referred to as alligators, Belize has only crocodiles, the American (up to 20 feet) and Morelet's (to eight feet). Crocodiles have a well-earned bad reputation in Africa, Australia, and New Guinea as man-eaters, especially the larger saltwater varieties. Their American cousins are fussier about their cuisine, preferring fish, dogs, and other small mammals to people. The territories of both

hicatee turtles

species overlap in estuaries and brackish coastal waters. Able to filter excess salt from its system, only the American crocodile ventures to the more distant cayes. Endangered throughout their ranges, both crocs are protected by international law and should be left undisturbed. Often seen floating near the edge of lagoons or canals during mid-day, they are best observed at night with the help of a powerful flashlight. When caught in the beam, their eyes glow an eerie red. Crocodiles are most abundant in the rivers, swamps, and lagoons of the Belize City, Orange Walk, and Toledo districts as well as areas around the Turneffe Islands.

INSECTS AND ARACHNIDS

Any tropical jungle has literally tens of thousands of what most people call bugs—insects and arachnids. Some are annoying (mosquitoes and gnats), some are dangerous (black widows, bird spiders, and scorpions), and others can cause discomfort (botflies) or painful bites (red ants). Many, however, are beautiful (butterflies and moths), and *all* are fascinating studies in evolved socialization and specialization.

Botfly
Ah, the lowly botfly! It looks like the common household variety but this one has developed an unpleasant trick. By depositing eggs on mosquitoes, the botfly allows its young to be transported to a unsuspecting host. As the mosquito feeds, a botfly larva is roused by the body heat of the warm-blooded host and drops onto the un-suspecting human or animal. Burrowing quickly under the skin, the maggot sets up housekeeping. To breathe it sticks a tiny tube through the skin (I'm not making this up) and there it stays until one of two things happen: you kill it, or it graduates and leaves home. Though uncomfortable and distasteful, it's not a serious health problem. To rid yourself of this pesky boarder, Sharon Matola of the Belize Zoo suggests dabbing a glob of Vaseline petroleum jelly over the air hole. This strategy draws out the varmint, intent on home repair but hopelessly mired. It is easy enough, then, to squash the squishy free-loader. Another suggested method she credits to Mr. Gregorio Sho is especially effective for the head area: take a tiny piece of tobacco (I'm not

---

DIFFERENCES BETWEEN MOTHS AND BUTTERFLIES

1. Butterflies fly during the day; moths fly at dusk and during the night as well.

2. Butterflies rest with their wings folded straight up over their bodies; most moths rest with their wings spread flat open.

3. All butterflies have bare knobs at the ends of both antennae (feelers); moths' antennae are either plumy or hairlike and end in a point.

4. Butterflies have slender bodies; moths are plump. Both insects are of the order Lepidoptera—lepidopterists, bring your nets!

---

making this up either) and stick it in the air hole. Overnight, nicotine destroys the teenage maggot. The next day you can squeeze out the un-grateful boarder at your leisure.

Butterflies and Moths
Belize has an abundance of beautiful moths and butterflies. Of the 90,000 types of butterflies in the world, a large percentage are seen here (see "Shipstern Wildlife Reserve and Butterfly Breeding Centre" under "East of Corozal Town"). You can see, among others, the magnificent Blue Morpho, orange-barred sulphur, copperhead, cloudless sulphur, malachite, admiral, calico, ruddy dagger-wing, tropical buckeye, and emperor. The famous monarch is also a visitor during its annual migration from the Florida peninsula to the Central American mountains and Mexican highlands where it spends the winter. Trying to photograph a (live) butterfly is a testy business. Just when you have it in your crosshairs, the comely critter flutters off to another spot!

Firefly
The poor firefly is really a misnomer. It's not a fly and it surely has no fire. Quite the contrary; it's a beetle that turns on a glow on the underside of its abdomen when nature's cycle brings together certain chemicals. When you see a tree in the forest literally *aglow* with tiny flashing lights, you know that it's mating season.

Both males and females locate each other by flashing an on/off pattern special to their genus. However, sometimes in a hunger frenzy, a female will fool the male of another species by imitating his flashing pattern—when the poor love-struck male approaches, she eats him! Even in the larval stage, the young can glow, perhaps to scare away predators. Occasionally fireflies eat each other, but most other jungle predators, such as birds, toads, and others searching for supper, stay away from them because the chemicals in their body taste sooooo bad.

Leaf Cutter Ant

A visitor's first glimpse of these industrious insects is likely to be a column of ants carrying green leaf cuttings across a jungle path. A quick look around may uncover an intersection where two ant "highways" cross, ants from both directions managing to get through with their leafy burdens. On first glance one would think the leaves themselves must be the object of all this effort and organization. The reality is more surprising; the ants are farmers! In a special section of their nest the insects use the cuttings as a growth medium for a preferred fungus. This cultivated fungus is what the ants harvest for food. The nest may be dozens of feet across and 10 or more feet deep, sheltering millions of ants. Like all ants, leaf cutters are highly organized, with different size members doing different tasks. Oddly, the tiny worker ants are the laborers.

Soldiers and breeding males are larger. The queen is largest and longest-lived, with a life span of more than a dozen years.

Termite

A rival to the ant's reputation for industry is that of the termite. These critters are big on building roundish nests resembling a hornet's in appearance and constructed of wood and saliva. Such termite towns are found in almost any convenient place: a hollow tree, a limb, under a porch, in a hole in the ground. The only stipulation seems to be that they must be near their favorite meal: wood is the appetizer, main course, and dessert. Unassuming, termites like to live their lives avoiding the limelight—or any light for that matter. Their nests provide them a safe dark place, ventilation, and protection from the elements. They also provide anteaters with a handy larder.

Scorpion

One of the arachnids (according to Mr. Webster: any of a class of arthropods comprising mostly air-breathing invertebrates, spiders and scorpions, mites and ticks), these pesky little creatures are believed by some scientists to be the first land animals. They can grow up to about five inches long and are equipped with robust claws. But it's the curled-up tail that you want to really avoid. When cornered, stepped on, or trapped, the scorpi-

*a giant
ant hill*

PHIL LANIER

on uses its tail and deposits what can be a fatal sting to humans. Everyone has heard that when in a jungle, never put on your shoes without checking the insides—good advice—and always give your clothes a good visual going over and a vigorous shake before putting them on. For another precaution, carry a sleeping net if you're sleeping under a *palapa* roof. We have seen scorpions drop from *palapa* roof/ceilings many times.

Tarantula
This is an ugly, furry guy, but fortunately not fatal to humans. Its bite can cause a lot of pain, but will not kill. It can grow to about six inches in diameter and some species migrate in large groups. Once while driving on a highway, about a block ahead I saw a lane-wide black spot moving across to the other side of the road; it was dozens and dozens of tarantulas. Some folks feed and train these arachnids as pets. Others in the jungle report stepping on them at night, so do wear shoes when you're out wandering, even on village sidewalks. The tarantula is able to live for long periods without food or water.

THE SEA

The Belize coast is blessed with a rich abundance of sealife, if not the sandy beaches one finds at many resorts in the Caribbean. The sandy bottom that many beachgoers worship is actually a desert supporting a limited amount of undersea life. Belize's underwater bounty, on the other hand, is due to many complex interactions among river estuaries, mangroves, sea grass beds, and reefs.

ESTUARIES

The marshy areas and bays at the mouths of rivers where salt and fresh water mix are called estuaries. Here, nutrients from inland are carried out to sea by currents and tides to nourish reefs, sea grass beds, and the open ocean. Many plants and animals feed, live, or mate in these waters. Conch, crabs, shrimp, and other shellfish thrive here. Several types of jellyfish and other invertebrates call this home. Seabirds, shore birds, and waterfowl of all types frequent estuaries to feed, nest, and mate. Crocodiles, dolphins, and manatees are frequent visitors. Rays, sharks, and tarpon hunt and mate here. During the wet season the estuaries of Belize pump a tremendous amount of nutrients into the sea.

MANGROVES

Mangroves live on the edge between land and sea, forming dense thickets that act as a protective border against the forces of wind and waves. Four species grow along many low-lying coastal areas on the mainland and along island lagoons and fringes. Of these, the red mangrove and the black mangrove are most prolific. Red mangrove in excess of 30 feet is found in tidal areas, inland lagoons, and river mouths, but always close to the sea. Its signature is its arching prop roots. Black mangrove grows almost double that height. Its roots are slender, upright projectiles that grow to about 12 inches, protruding all around the mother tree. Both types of roots provide air to the tree. Another species, white mangrove, grows inland along riverbanks. The buttonwood mangrove thrives in drier areas of the cayes and mainland.

Mangrove thickets are nurseries without equal, harboring immature fish and a variety of shellfish. Barnacles, crabs, immature gray snappers, jellyfish, snails, and sponges hide among or cling to the latticework of roots. Bonefish nose about the shallows and tarpon lie in wait. Birds of many species use the mangrove branches for roosting and nesting sites, including blackbirds,

LONGEST REEFS IN THE WORLD

Great Barrier Reef, Australia: 1,600 km
S.W. Barrier Reef, New Caledonia: 600 km
N.E. Barrier Reef, New Caledonia: 540 km
Great Sea Reef, Fiji Islands: 260 km
Belize Reef: 250 km
S. Louisade Archipelago Reef, PNG: 200 km

herons, kingfishers, pelicans, and roseate spoonbills.

Less happily for humans, even mosquitoes and biting flies find homes among the tangle. The mud beneath mangrove thickets is often malodorous with decaying plant matter. For these reasons many developers would like nothing better than to eliminate mangroves. Fortunately, the government is enforcing laws that make it difficult to disturb these natural wonders.

SEA GRASS BEDS

Standing on Ambergris Caye and looking seaward, many tourists are surprised to see something dark in the shallow water just offshore. They expect a sandy bottom typical of many Caribbean islands. However, it is this "dark stuff" that eventually will make their day's snorkeling, fishing, or dining experience more enjoyable. What they are noticing is sea grass, another of the ocean's great nurseries.

Sea grasses are plants with elongated, ribbonlike leaves. Just like the land plants they evolved from, sea grasses flower and have extensive root systems. They live in sandy areas around estuaries, mangroves, reefs, and open coastal waters. Turtle grass has broader tapelike leaves and is common down to about 60 feet. Manatee grass, found to depths of around 40 feet, has thinner, more cylindrical, leaves. Both cover large areas of seafloor and intermix in some areas, harboring an amazing variety of marine plants and animals. Barnacles, conch, crabs, and many other shellfish proliferate in the fields of sea grass. Anemones, seahorses, sponges, and starfish live here. Grunts, filefish, flounder, jacks, rays, and wrasses feed here. Sea turtles and manatees often graze in these lush marine pastures.

THE REEF

Running parallel to the coast is the Belize Reef, the longest in the Western Hemisphere and fifth-longest in the world. Scattered offshore and protected by the reef are more than 200 cayes; just outside of it lie three of the Caribbean's four atolls: **Glover's Reef, Turneffe Islands,** and

Lighthouse Reef. An atoll is a ring-shaped coral island surrounding a lagoon, always beautiful, and almost exclusively found in the South Pacific. The three types of cayes are **wet cayes,** which are submerged part of the time and can support only mangrove swamps; **bare coral outcroppings** that are equally uninhabitable; and **sandy islands** with palm trees, jungle shrubbery, and their own set of animals. The inhabited cayes lie in the northern part of the reef and include Caye Caulker, Ambergris Caye, St. George's Caye, and Caye Chapel.

The sea is a magical world. Humanity is just beginning to learn of the wonders within its depths. Some dreamers predict that a time is coming when the world's oceans will provide humans with all needed nutrients, and that people will live comfortably side by side with the fish of the sea. For now, men and women are content just to look at what's there, often through a small, round window on a diving mask.

Coral

The Belize Reef has such extraordinarily clear water that looking through a diving mask brings you into a world of color. The myriad hues of coral are rainbowlike: pale pinks, flashy reds, deep purples, flamboyant greens, and a multitude of colors in between.

Coral is a unique limestone formation that grows in innumerable shapes, such as delicate lace, trees with reaching branches, pleated mushrooms, stovepipes, petaled flowers, fans, domes, heads of cabbage, and stalks of broccoli. Corals are formed by millions of tiny carnivorous polyps that feed on minute organisms and live in large colonies of flamboyantly colored individual species. These small creatures can be less than half an inch long or as large as six inches in diameter. Related to the jellyfish and sea anemone, polyps need sunlight and clear salt water not colder than 70° F to survive. Coral polyps have cylinder-shaped bodies. One end is attached to a hard surface (the bottom of the ocean, the rim of a submerged volcano, or the reef itself), and the mouth end is encircled with tiny tentacles that capture its minute prey with a deadly sting.

Coral reefs are formed when polyps attach themselves to each other. Stony coral polyps, for example, connect with a flat sheet of tissue between their middles. They develop their limestone

CORAL MEDICAL REPAIR

Medical researchers have recently discovered that sections of coral can be placed in the human body where a piece of bone is missing, and the body's bones readily graft themselves onto the strong coral.

skeletons by extracting calcium from the seawater and depositing calcium carbonate around the lower half of the body. They reproduce from buds or eggs. Occasionally small buds appear on the adult polyp; when the buds mature, they separate from the adult and add to the growth of existing colonies. Eggs, on the other hand, grow into tiny forms that swim away and settle on the ocean floor. When developed, these begin a new colony.

How a Reef Grows

As these small creatures continue to reproduce and die, their sturdy skeletons accumulate. Over aeons, broken bits of coral, animal waste, and granules of soil contribute to the strong foundation for a reef that will slowly rise toward the surface. To grow, a reef must have a base no more than 82 feet below the water's surface. In a healthy environment it can grow one to two inches a year. One small piece of coral represents millions of polyps and many years of construction.

Reefs are divided into three types: atoll, fringing, and barrier. An **atoll** can be formed around the crater of a submerged volcano. The polyps begin building their colonies on the round edge of the crater, forming a circular coral island with a lagoon in the center. Thousands of atolls occupy the world's tropical waters. A **fringing reef** is coral living on a shallow shelf that extends outward from shore into the sea. A **barrier reef** runs parallel to the coast, with water separating it from the land. Sometimes it's actually a series of reefs with channels of water in between. This is the case with some of the larger barrier reefs in the Pacific and Indian oceans.

The Belize Reef extends from the tip of Mexico's Isla Mujeres to Sapodilla Caye in the Bay of Honduras. This 180-mile-long reef is known by various names (Belize Reef is the most common). The beauty of the reef attracts divers and snorkelers from distant parts of the world to investigate the unspoiled marinelife.

The Meaning of Color

Most people interested in reefs already know they're in for a brilliant display of colored fish. In the fish world, color isn't only for exterior decoration. Fish change hues for a number of reasons, including anger, protection, and sexual attraction. This is still a little-known science. For example, because of groupers' many colors, marine biologists are uncertain how many species of groupers exist—different species or different moods? A male damselfish clearly imparts his aggression and his desire for love by turning vivid blue. Some fish can transform into as many as 12 recognizable color patterns within seconds. These color changes, along with other body signals, combine to make communication simple between members of a species. Scientists have discovered that a layer of color-bearing cells lies just beneath a fish's transparent scales. These cells contain orange, yellow, or red pigments; some contain black, others combine to make green or other hues. A crystalline tissue adds white, silver, or iridescence. Color changes when the pigmented cells are revealed, combined, or masked, creating the final result. Fish communicate in many other surprising ways, including electrical impulses and flashing bioluminescence (body light). If fish communication intrigues you, read Robert Burgess's book *Secret Languages of the Sea* (Dodd, Mead and Company).

Conservation

The Belizean government has strict laws governing the reef, with which most divers are more than willing to comply to preserve this natural phenomenon and its inhabitants. However, there are always a few who care only for their own desires. Recently, an American bought Hatchett Caye; he has remodeled it and the local newspaper reported that he dynamited part of a nearby reef to better fit his idea of a tropical hideaway for tourists.

It takes hundreds of years to form large colonies of coral, so please *don't* break off pieces of coral for souvenirs. After a very short time out of water, the polyps lose their color and only a piece of chalky white coral remains—just like the pieces you can pick up while beachcombing. Strict fines await those who remove *anything* from the reef (spearfishing is also against the law).

SEALIFE

FISH

Angelfish

Few fish display more heavenly beauty than these disc-shaped denizens with their rounded heads, flat vertical bodies, and swept-back fins. The adult queen angelfish glistens with a burst of neon blues and yellows. It can be distinguished from the similar blue angelfish by the dark crown with light blue border on its forehead. The adult French angelfish is black overall with tasteful flecks of yellow on the sides. All live in and around the reef, pecking out a living of small shellfish and marine growth. Shy by nature, they may be approached if the diver does not pay them too much direct attention. They are found both inside and outside the barrier reef and often travel in mated pairs.

Barracuda

With its six-foot maximum length, jaws of ragged teeth, and habit of swimming directly up to divers, a large barracuda can be an unnerving sight to the novice. As with groupers, the 'cuda is territorial and investigates intruders. Yet barracuda can make good company, following a diver around like a dog. Like their freshwater cousins (pickerel and muskellunge), however, barracuda may strike at bright objects that look like injured fish. For that reason it is best not to dive near them wearing shiny watches and jewelry. Move slowly and deliberately. As with many creatures, if you like their company, avoid staring. On the other hand, a direct look or swimming toward them usually will cause barracuda to maintain more distance.

Bluestriped Grunt

These common reef fish school in large numbers in shady areas during the day. Coloration includes thin irregular blue stripes edged in black that run from nose to tail over a yellow background. The tail fin is black with a trailing edge of yellow. The bluestriped grunt is often confused with the white grunt. The latter has stripes only on the head with the rest of the body a checkerboard of yellow and blue. At night these fish

PROTECT THE MARINE HERITAGE

To ensure that the waters of Belize, particularly the reefs, remain healthy for everyone's enjoyment, please respect the following protective regulations:

1. No person shall buy, sell, export, or attempt to export black coral in any form, except under a license obtained from the Fisheries Administrator.

2. No person shall have in his possession any turtle from 1 June to 31 Aug., take any turtle found on the shores of Belize, export any turtle or articles made from turtle other than under a license granted by the Minister.

3. No person shall take fish (mollusk, scale, crustacea) using scuba equipment, except under a special permit from the Fisheries Administrator.

4. No person shall take, buy, sell or have in possession crawfish, 15 March-14 July, or conch, 1 July-30 September.

5. No person shall take, buy, or sell any coral at any time.

move out from the reef in search of shellfish in grassy or sandy areas. When grunts grind their strong molars they produce a croaking sound that is amplified by an air bladder. It is this distinct sound that gives rise to their name.

Grouper

Groupers are saltwater members of the bass family, exhibiting the heavy muscular body and large head, lips, and fins characteristic of their kind. Most members grow to about three to four feet in length. The jewfish, however, may reach eight feet and weigh hundreds of pounds. Solitary hunters, they lie in wait for smaller fish near caves, piers, reefs, and wrecks. When a likely candidate swims within range, they dart forward and open their cavernous jaws, sucking in their next meal. Rows of needle-sharp teeth ensure there is no escape. The Nassau grouper is easily identified by chocolate stripes that run more or less vertically along the length of its lighter body. It is curious and quick to approach divers. The black grouper has dark irregular horizontal patches against a pale background. Not as outgoing, it will linger near divers if ignored. Groupers of these and other species are especially numerous at Hol Chan Marine Reserve and the atolls.

Green Moray Eel

The leathery skin of this moray is an even shade of green or olive from head to tail. The long undulating fins, top and bottom, assist it in swimming. The largest of several species of eel in Belizean waters, the green moray reaches lengths of up to six feet. It hides in reef crevices during the day, venturing out at night to feed. Like all moray eels, the green moray must open and close its mouth to breathe, revealing a flash of bristling sharp teeth. Morays are easygoing but will inflict nasty bites when molested or when groping hands are thrust into their dens.

Nurse Shark

Divers often see the sluggish nurse shark resting on sand bottoms or swimming lazily about the reef. The skin varies from a shimmering copper to a slate gray. The eyes are small and light, and two barbels appear under the snout. The shape of the head, somewhat like a vacuum cleaner, may aid the nurse shark as it feeds along the bottom on crustaceans. When it comes to behavior, there is not much to report. More interesting is the shark's effect on humans. People often back away or become pests, pulling at fin or tail. Such rudeness can earn a bite. It's best to show some decorum and restraint.

Parrot Fish

The beaky mouth that gives the parrot fish its name is actually a set of fused upper and lower front teeth—the better to eat coral polyps. The result is a sandy cloud excreted by parrot fish at regular intervals as they flap about the reef with their pectoral fins. Parrot fish come spruced up in an amazing palette of bright colors. Since these colors and patterns change with age, identification is often tricky. But most divers can learn to spot several colorful characters. The largest of the group, the blue parrot fish is evenly colored a light to dark blue. Young and old midnight parrot fish appear alike in dark blue with bright blue markings on the face and head. The rainbow parrot fish is easily identified by a copper head and tail separated by a wide band of greenish blue. Adult stoplight parrot fish usually sport a calico brown and white body with a cranberry belly, tail, and dorsal fin. The queen parrot fish has a green to bluish cast but appears to have applied make-up of blue stripes bordered by yellow around the mouth and eyes.

Ray

Almost alien in appearance, rays fly through the water with the greatest of ease. The species in Belizean waters include stingrays, eagle rays, and manta rays. As defense they have camouflage, speed, and, in the case of stingrays and eagle rays, poisonous spines. Stingrays spend most of their time on the ocean bottom, often covered to the eyes with sand. The rest of the time they search for shellfish by shoveling the bottom with their pointed snouts. Stingrays are easy to get along with. When walking in shallows, a shuffling gait will give rays ample warning of your approach. They will simply flutter out of the way. Divers need only treat stingrays with a modicum of respect and the rays will return the favor. Never pull or poke at them. Freewheeling eagle rays are a graceful sight as they wing past the edge of a reef or pier. But don't even think about hitching a ride; they have several poisonous spines at the base of their tails. A bad scrape with one of these will spoil your whole day! Manta rays have no such spines, but just as you wouldn't appreciate some lout grabbing you by the shoulders, show the peaceful manta the same courtesy.

Yellowtail Snapper

This handsome fish often swims singly or in schools. Easily identified, the yellowtail snapper has a streamlined shape with a bright yellow line running from the eye down the center of the body and covering both lobes of the deeply V-shaped tail. The background of the body is a light shimmering blue above and white beneath. Yellow spots punctuate the upper sides. Curious and fast, these fish haven't a shy bone in their bodies and will readily approach divers.

SHELLFISH

Conch

A large seagoing member of the snail family, the conch spends its time dragging itself around sea grass beds where it feeds. It uses a leathery foot for locomotion and even has eyes to detect motion. The top of the shell is a yellowish brown. Underside, the shell is bright pink and white around the shell opening. The horny brown foot blocks entrance. As tasty as they are numerous, conch are caught by free-diving fishermen who sell their catches in Belize City, San Pedro, and elsewhere. Conch meat is served raw in ceviche, fried, stewed, and added to soups. Conch season lasts from October through June. After that, the conch are allowed to reproduce in peace.

Spiny Lobster

Spiny lobsters lack the large claws of their Maine relatives. Instead, they have hard spiky shells and antennae. These antennae are quite long and are useful in detecting and fencing with enemies. In fact, the protruding antennae usually are an alert diver's first indication that a lobster is at home. Bottom dwellers, spiny lobsters hide out in the reef by day, emerging by night to feed. When caught out in the open, the lobster uses its powerful tail to propel itself away from would-be gourmands, human or otherwise. Near the reef, it retreats into the first handy cranny. A favorite of seafood lovers everywhere, lobsters are legally taken in Belize by trap or free diving. Size limits are enforced; scuba divers are not allowed to take lobster. The season begins 15 June and ends 15 February. It is illegal to have lobsters in one's possession out of season, and hefty fines result from infractions. Only close management will prevent these crustaceans from being overexploited. You can do your part by refusing lobster out of season.

Feather Duster Worm

Appearing like a small flower or feather duster, this worm lives in a tube buried in the reef or sand. Its head protrudes with a flowery spiral of fronds that serve as gills and a means of collecting food. This parasol may be solid yellow, gray, or white, or it may have bands of white and red. These fronds are extremely sensitive to disturbances in the water near the worm. Get too close or move too suddenly and the feather duster disappears in a flash into the tube.

SEA MAMMALS

Bottlenosed Dolphin

Bottlenosed dolphins, called *pampas* locally, are marine mammals that breathe through a blowhole on top of their heads and are not to be confused with the dolphinfish or dorado. Bottlenosed dolphins are frequently sighted near mainland beaches as well as offshore cayes and atolls. Intelligent and playful, they will catch a free ride at the bow of passing boats. During these displays their speed, strength, and intelligence are most evident. It is not unheard of for divers to encounter dolphins singly or in pods; females tend to interact more freely than males. Single dolphins may swim very close and even allow you to touch them. Remember that these are big, powerful animals. Do not hang onto the dorsal fin or impede the animal; dolphins have been known to play roughly with those who do the same. Mothers with young may make a couple or more close passes—a wonderful experience. Or one dolphin may gain your attention while the rest move off in another direction.

Manatee

The manatee is an elephantine creature of immense proportions with gentle manners and the curiosity of a kitten. Though scarce today, this enormous animal, often called the sea cow, at one time roamed the shallow inlets, bays, and estuaries of the Caribbean in large numbers. The manatee is said to be the basis of myths and old seamen's references to mermaids. In South America certain indigenous tribes revere this particular mammal. The Maya hunted the manatee for its flesh, and its image frequently appears in ancient Maya art. In modern times, the population has been reduced by the encroachment of large numbers of people in the manatees' habitats along the riverways and shorelines. Ever-growing numbers of motorboats inflict often-deadly gashes on the nosy creatures.

At birth the manatee weighs 60-70 pounds; it can grow up to 13 feet long and weigh more than a ton. Gray with a pinkish cast and shaped like an Idaho potato, it has a spatulate tail, two

MANATEE BREEDING PROGRAM

The state of Florida, under the auspices of the Miami Seaquarium and Dr. Jesse White, has begun a captive-breeding program hoping to learn more about the habits of the manatee and to try to increase the declining numbers. Several manatees have been born in captivity; they along with others that have recuperated from injury or illness will be or have been released into Florida's Crystal River, where boat traffic is restricted. They are tagged and closely observed. Florida maintains a 24-hour hotline for people to report manatees in need of help for any reason. Rescues can include removing an adult male from a cramped storm drain or rushing to the seaquarium newborns that somehow managed to get separated from their mothers and have washed ashore. These newborns are readily accepted by surrogate-mother manatees and are offered nourishment (by way of a thumb-sized teat under the front flipper) and lots of TLC. Medical aid is given to mammals that have been slashed by boat propellers as a result of cruising boats. The manatee has a playful curiosity and investigates anything found in its underwater environment, many times sustaining grave damage.

forelimbs with toenails, pebbled coarse skin, tiny sunken eyes, numerous fine-bristled hairs scattered sparsely over its body, and a permanent Mona Lisa smile. The head of the mammal seems small for its gargantuan body, and its preproboscidean lineage includes dugongs (in Australia), hydrax, and elephants. The manatee's truncated snout and prehensile lips help to push food into its mouth. As the only aquatic mammal that exists solely on vegetation, the manatee grazes on bottom-growing grasses and other aquatic plantlife. It ingests as much as 495 pounds per day, cleaning rivers of oxygen-choking growth. It is unique among mammals in that it constantly grows new teeth—worn teeth fall out and are replaced. Posing no threat to any other living thing, it has been hunted for its oil, skin, and flesh, which is said to be tasty.

The mammal thrives in shallow warm water and has been reported (infrequently, however) in shallow Belize bays. One spring evening in the bay in front of the Adventure Inn at Consejo Shores in Belize, a curious manatee spent about an hour lazily swimming the cove, lifting its truncated snout, and often its entire head, out of the water about every four minutes. The few people (this author included) who were standing on a small dock in the bay were thrilled to see the shy animal. They are around, just keep looking. Belize reportedly has the largest population of manatees in the world, except perhaps for the Florida Sanctuary in the United States.

In neighboring Guatemala, the government is sponsoring a manatee reserve in Lago de Izabal. In the U.S. the mammal is found mostly at inshore and estuarine areas of Florida. It is protected under the Federal U.S. Marine Mammal Protection Act of 1972, the Endangered Species Act of 1973, and the Florida Manatee Sanctuary Act of 1978. It is estimated that their total population numbers about 2,000.

SEA TURTLES

In Belize sea turtles come in three varieties: green, hawksbill, and loggerhead. All have paddlelike flippers instead of feet and use the front set like wings and the rear ones to steer. Yet, as well-adapted to the ocean as they are, they all have to surface to breathe. For that reason many die in the nets of fishermen throughout the world. The largest of the three, the green turtle is so named for the green fat that encircles its body. In centuries past, mariners relied on these turtles and their eggs for sustenance. Smallest of the sea turtles, the hawksbill has been heavily hunted for its shell, which is marketed as tortoise shell. The plates of this attractive shell overlap like the shingles of a house. The loggerhead or larga is distinguished by its large head, heavy neck, and heart-shaped shell.

a sea turtle

Sea turtles are still eaten in Belize and elsewhere. Green and loggerhead turtles are legally hunted between 1 November and 1 April. Hawksbill turtles are now fully protected in Belizean waters. As the number of sea turtles continues to dwindle worldwide, responsible travelers avoid consuming any kind of sea turtle products.

People create other hazards for turtles, too. Habitat destruction, nesting disruption, and floating plastic debris threaten all three species. When people dredge turtle grass beds they destroy a primary food source for turtles. When they erect hotels, condominiums, and other buildings on turtle beaches or when they steal eggs, they disrupt key nesting sites. When they leave plastic bags and other debris floating about in the water, turtles mistake them for a favorite food, jellyfish, and suffocate upon swallowing them. On northern Ambergris Caye, Greg Smith and a group of enlightened landowners have created a sea turtle sanctuary along a six-mile stretch of beach. Their aim is to ensure nesting areas for turtles of all three species.

HISTORY

THE ANCIENTS

Earliest Man

During the Pleistocene epoch, when the level of the sea fell (about 50,000 B.C.), people and animals from Asia crossed the Bering land bridge into the American continent. For nearly 50,000 years man continued his epic trek southward. It is believed that the first people reached Tierra del Fuego, at the tip of South America, in approximately 1000 B.C.

As early as 10,000 B.C., Ice Age man hunted woolly mammoth and other large animals roaming the cool, moist landscape of Central America. Between 7000 and 2000 B.C., society

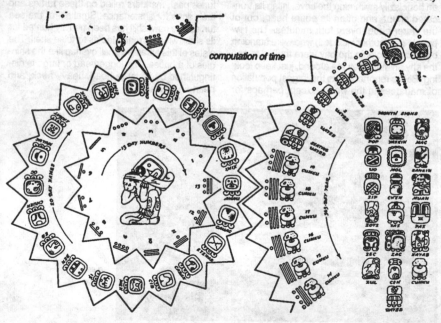

computation of time

evolved from hunters and gatherers to farmers. Such crops as corn, squash, and beans were independently domesticated in widely separated areas of Mesoamerica after about 6000 B.C. The remains of clay figurines from the pre-Classic period, presumed to be fertility symbols, marked the rise of religion in Mesoamerica, beginning about 2000 B.C.

About 1000 B.C. the Olmec culture, believed to be the earliest, began to spread throughout Mesoamerica. Large-scale ceremonial centers grew along Gulf Coast lands, and much of Mesoamerica was influenced by the Olmecs' often sinister religion of worshipping strange jaguarlike gods. They also developed the New World's first calendar and an early system of writing.

Classic Period

The Classic period, beginning about A.D. 300, is now hailed as the peak of cultural development among the Maya. Until A.D. 900, they made phenomenal progress in the development of artistic, architectural, and astronomical skills. They constructed impressive buildings during this period, and wrote codices (folded bark books) filled with hieroglyphic symbols that detailed complicated mathematical calculations of days, months, and years. Only the priests and the privileged held this knowledge and continued to learn and develop it until, for some unexplained reason, the growth suddenly halted. A new militaristic society was born, built around a blend of ceremonialism, civic and social organization, and conquest.

The Maya Mystery

For hundreds of years, modern scholars of the world have asked, "What happened to the Maya people?" We know that many Maya descendants survive today, but not the intelligentsia. However, their magnificent structures, built with such advanced skill, still stand. Many carvings, statues, and even a few colored frescoes remain. All of this art depicts a world of intelligent human beings living in a well-organized, complex society. It's apparent that their trade and agricultural methods supported the population for many centuries. They used intensive systems of farming by terracing foothill slopes and constructing raised beds in valley bottoms where soil fertility could be enriched by trapping alluvial deposits and adding organic supplements. Scholars agree the Maya were the most advanced of all ancient Mesoamerican cultures. Yet all signs point to an abrupt work stoppage. After about A.D. 900, no buildings were constructed and no stelae, which carefully detailed names and dates to inform future generations of their roots, were erected. So what happened?

Anthropologists and historians do know that perhaps as many as 500,000 Maya were killed by such diseases as smallpox after the arrival of the Spaniards into the New World. But no one really knows for sure what halted the progress of the Maya culture.

A Society Collapses

Priests and noblemen, the guardians of religion, science, and the arts, conducted their ritual ceremonies and studies in the large stone pyramids and platforms found today in ruins throughout the jungle. Consequently, more specific questions arise: What happened to the priests and noblemen? Why were the centers abandoned? What happened to the knowledge of the intelligentsia? They studied the skies, wrote the books, and designed the pyramids. Theories abound. Some speculate about a revolution of the people or decentralization with the arrival of outside influences. Others suggest the people tired of subservience and were no longer willing to farm the land to provide food, clothing, and support for the priests and nobles. Whatever happened, it's clear that the special knowledge concerning astronomy, hieroglyphics, and architecture was not passed on to Maya descendants. Sociologists who have lived with the indigenous people in isolated villages are convinced that this privileged information is not known by today's Maya. Why did the masses disperse, leaving once-sacred stone cities unused and ignored? It's possible that lengthy periods of drought, famine, and epidemic caused the people to leave their once-glorious sacred centers. No longer important in day-to-day life, these structures were ignored for a thousand years and faced the whimsy of nature and its corroding elements.

The Maya question may never be answered with authority. One nonconforming theory suggests that these stone cities were built by people from outer space. Another considers the possibility that today's Maya are no relation to the people who built the structures, made near-perfect astronomical observations, and discovered infinity a thousand years ago.

Secrets of the Ruins

With today's technology, astronauts have seen many wonders from outer space, spotting overgrown structures within the thick uninhabited jungle of La Ruta Maya. These large treasures of knowledge are just waiting to be reopened. But until the funds and plans are in hand, these mounds are left unsung and untouched in hopes that looters will not find them before archaeologists are able to open them up. Looters generally are not interested in the knowledge gained from an artifact; they're primarily interested in the dollars. Not only has much been lost in these criminal actions, but also their heavy-handed methods have destroyed countless artifacts. As new finds are made, the history of the Maya develops new depth and breadth. Archaeologists, ethnologists, art historians, and linguists continue to unravel the ongoing mystery with constant new discoveries of temples and artifacts, each with a story to tell.

COLONIAL HISTORY

The pre-Columbian history of Belize is closely associated with all of its nearby neighbors: Mexico, Guatemala, and Honduras. The Maya were the first people to inhabit the land referred to as **La Ruta Maya.** They planted corn *milpas,* built ceremonial centers, and established villages with large numbers of people throughout the region. Hernán Cortés passed through the southern part of the country on his trek northward searching for treasure. In 1530 the conquistador Montejo attacked the Nachankan and Belize Maya, but his attempt to conquer them failed. This introduction of Spanish influence did not make the impact on Belize that it did in the northern part of the Caribbean coast until the Caste War.

Hernán Cortés and Other Explorers

After Columbus's arrival in the New World, other adventurers traveling the same seas soon found the Yucatán Peninsula. In 1519, 34-year-old Cortés sailed from Cuba against the will of the Spanish governor. With 11 ships, 120 sailors, and 550 soldiers, he set out to search for slaves, a lucrative business with or without the blessings of the government. His search began on the Yucatán coast and eventually encompassed most of Mexico. However, he hadn't counted on the ferocious resistance and cunning of the Maya. The fighting was destined to continue for many years—a time of bloodshed and death for many of his men. This "war" didn't *really* end on the peninsula until the Chan Santa Cruz people finally made peace with the Mexican federal government in 1935, more than 400 years later.

Although the Maya in Mérida, in Yucatán, Mexico, were a long distance from Belize and not directly bothered by the intrusion of the Spanish, the actions of the Spanish Franciscan priests toward the Mérida Maya would have a great influence on Belize in the years that followed. The Catholic priests were wiping out ceremonies and all other traces of the Maya, further setting the stage for the bloodshed to come. The ripple effect that followed eventually ex-

Hernán Cortés

ploded into the Caste War that, in turn, brought both Maya and mestizos across the borders of Belize.

Diego de Landa was the Franciscan priest who, while trying to gather the Maya into the fold of Christianity, leaned on them and their beliefs with a heavy hand, destroying thousands of Maya idols, many of their temples, and all but four of their books. Because his methods were often cruel, in 1563 he was called back to Spain after colonial civil and religious leaders accused him of "despotic mismanagement." He spent a year in prison, and while his fate was being decided, he wrote a book, *Relaciones de las Cosas de Yucatán,* in defense of the charges. This book gave extensive information about the Maya, their beliefs, the growth and preparation of their food, the structure of their society, the priesthood, and the sciences—essentially a broad insight into the culture that otherwise would have been lost forever. Fortunately, he included in his book a one-line formula that, when used as a mathematical and chronological key, opened up the science of Maya calculations and their great knowledge of astronomy. De Landa returned to the Yucatán Peninsula and lived out his remaining years, continuing his previous methods of proselytizing until his death in 1579.

Catholicism

Over the years, the majority of Maya were indeed baptized into the Catholic faith. Most priests did their best to educate the people, teach them to read and write, and protect them from the growing number of Spanish settlers who used them as slaves. The Maya practiced Catholicism in their own manner, combining their ancient beliefs, handed down throughout the centuries, with Christian doctrine. These mystic yet Christian ceremonies are still performed in baptism, courtship, marriage, illness, farming, house building, and fiestas.

Pirates and Subjugation

While all of Mesoamerica dealt with the problems of economic colonialism, the Yucatán Peninsula had an additional problem: harassment by vicious pirates who made life in the coastal areas unstable. In other parts of the Yucatán Peninsula the passive people were ground down, their lands taken away, and their numbers greatly reduced by the European settler's epidemics and mistreatment.

British buccaneers sailed the coast, attacking the Spanish fleet at every opportunity. These ships were known to carry unimaginable riches of gold and silver from the New World back to the king of Spain. The Belizean coast became a convenient place for pirates to hole up during bad weather or for a good drinking bout. And, though no one planned it as a permanent layover, by 1650 the coast had the beginnings of a British pirate lair/settlement. As pirating slacked off on the high seas, British buccaneers discovered they could use their ships to carry logwood back to a ready market in England. These early settlers were nicknamed the Baymen.

In the meantime, the Spanish desperately tried to maintain control of this vast New World they had grasped from across the ocean. But it was a difficult task and brutal conflicts continually flared between the Spanish and either the British inhabitants or the Maya. The British Baymen were continually run out but always returned. Treaties were signed and then rescinded. However, the British relentlessly made inroads into the country, importing slaves from Africa beginning in the 1720s to laboriously thrash through the jungles and cut the timber—work that the fiercely independent Maya resisted with their lives.

In 1763 Spain "officially" agreed to let the British cut logwood. The decree allowed roads (along the then-designated frontiers) to be built in the future though definite boundaries were to be agreed upon later. For nearly 150 years the only "roads" built were narrow tracks to the rivers; the rivers became Belize's major highways. Boats were common transport along the coast and somehow road building was postponed, leaving boundaries vaguely defined and countrymen on both sides of the border unsure. This was the important bit of history that later encouraged the Spanish-influenced Guatemalans to believe strongly that Belize, failing to carry out the 1763 agreement, was their turf. Even after Spain vacated Guatemala, Guatemalans tried for generations to assume ownership across the existing Belize borders. Since 1988, however, the boundary disagreement *appears* to have blown over with the Guatemalan threat of a takeover stopping on their side of the frontier. But because no official agreements have been made, most believe this conflict is still unresolved.

Treaty of Paris

Politically, Belize (or, more to the point, its timber) was up for grabs, and a series of treaties did little to calm the ping-pong effect between the British and the Spanish over the years. One such agreement, the Treaty of Paris, did little to control the Baymen—or the Spanish. With license, British plantation owners continued to divest the forests of logs, leaving Belize with nothing more than a legacy of brutality and tyrannical control over the slaves (who worked under cruel conditions while making rich men of their masters). The Spanish continued to claim sovereignty over the land but never settled in Belize. They continued their efforts to take over by sporadically harassing and attacking the Baymen—only to fail each time when the British returned and held on to their settlement.

The Baymen held on with only limited rights to the area until the final skirmish in 1798 on a small caye just offshore of Belize City. The Baymen, with the help of an armed sloop and three companies of a West Indian regiment, won the battle of St. George's Caye on 10 September, ending the Spanish claim to Belize once and for all. After that battle Belize was ruled by the British Crown until gaining its independence in 1981.

During the first 400 years after Europeans arrived, nothing much was done to develop the country, not even roads or railroads, and you can count on one hand how many historic buildings are standing (few were ever built). Maya structures don't count—they were here before the British and will be here for many years to come.

Land Rights

In 1807, slavery was *officially* abolished in Belize by England. This was not agreeable to the powerful British landowners, though, and in many quarters it continued to flourish. Changes were then made to accommodate the will of the powerful. The local government no longer *gave* land to settlers as it had for years (the British law now permitted former slaves and other

"coloureds" to hold title). The easiest way to keep them from possessing the land was to charge for it—essentially barring the majority in the country from landownership.

Caste War

It was inevitable that the Maya would eventually erupt in a furious attack. This bloody uprising in the 1840s was called the Caste War. Though the Maya were farmers and for the most part not soldiers, in this savage war they took revenge on every white man, woman, and child by rape and murder. When the winds of war reversed themselves and the Maya were on the losing side, vengeance on them was merciless. Some settlers would immediately kill any Maya, regardless of his beliefs. Some Maya were taken prisoner and sold to Cuba as slaves; others left their villages and hid in the jungles, in some cases for decades. Between 1846-50 the population of the Yucatán Peninsula was reduced from 500,000 to 300,000. Guerrilla warfare ensued, with the escaped Maya making repeated sneak attacks upon the white settlers. Quintana Roo, adjacent to Belize along the Caribbean coast, was considered a dangerous noman's land for more than a hundred years until in 1974 when, with the promise of tourism, the territory was admitted to the Federation of States of Mexico.

Growing Maya Power

Many of the Maya who escaped slaughter during the Caste War fled to the isolated jungles of Quintana Roo and Belize. The Maya revived the religion of the "talking cross," a pre-Columbian oracle representing gods of the four cardinal directions. This was a religious/political marriage. Three determined survivors of the Caste War—a priest, a master spy, and a ventriloquist—all wise leaders, knew their people's desperate need for divine leadership. As a result of their leadership and advice from the talking cross, the shattered people came together in large numbers and began to organize. The community guarded the location of the cross, and its advice made the Maya strong once again.

They called themselves Chan Santa Cruz ("People of the Little Holy Cross"). As their confidence developed so did the growth and power

BELIZE HISTORY IN A NUTSHELL

The peaceful country of Belize is a sovereign democratic state of Central America located on the Caribbean. The government is patterned on the system of parliamentary democracy and experiences no more political turmoil than any other governments such as Great Britain or the United States.

Important Dates

1862: Became a British colony
1954: Attained universal adult suffrage
1964: Began self-government
1981: Attained full independence

of their communities. Living very close to the Belize (then British Honduras) border, they found they had something their neighbors wanted. The Chan Santa Cruz Maya began selling timber to the British and in return received arms, giving the Maya even more power. Between 1847 and 1850, in the years of strife during the Caste War in neighboring Yucatán, thousands of Maya, mestizo, and Mexican refugees who were fleeing the Spaniards entered Belize. The Yucatecans introduced the Latin culture, the Catholic religion, and agriculture. This was the beginning of the Mexican tradition in Belize, locally referred to as "Spanish tradition." The food is typically Mexican with tortillas, black beans, tamales, squash, and plantain (a type of banana that can be cooked). For many years these mestizos kept to themselves and were independent of Belize City. The colonial administration kept its distance, and a community-appointed headman made and kept the laws. Both Hispanic and non-Hispanic Belizeans who live in the northern area speak Spanish. Today, all the towns and cities of Belize come under the jurisdiction of the central Belizean government.

The Sugar Industry

Though most of the refugees ultimately returned to their homes in Mexico, the ones who stayed and began farming the land were making the first real attempt at much-needed agriculture. Large

tracts that had been cleared of trees were empty, and rich landowners were willing to rent acreage (cheaply) to the refugees for farming. Until then almost all foodstuffs had been imported from other countries (and to this day it's not unusual to see many tinned foods from Australia, England, and the United States on market shelves).

The mestizos settled mostly in the northern sections of the country, which is apparent by the names of the cities: Corozal, San Estevan, San Pedro, and Punta Consejo. By 1857, the immigrants were growing enough sugar to supply Belize, with enough left over to export the surplus (along with rum) to Britain. After their success proved to the tree barons that sugarcane could be lucrative, the big landowners became involved. Even in today's world of low-priced sugar, the industry is still important to Belize's economy.

Timber

For 300 years Belize was plundered and neglected—and not just by swashbuckling pirates and hard-living buccaneers. Its forests were denuded of valuable logwood (the heart of which provided rich dyes for Europe's growing textile industry until manmade dyes were developed). When the demand for logwood ceased, plantation owners found a viable substitute for their logging interests—removing mahogany trees from thick virgin forests. For three centuries the local economy depended on exported logs and imported food.

In a 1984 Audubon Society report, it was noted that despite the widespread use of slash-and-burn farming by the Maya a millennium ago, and the more recent selective logging of logwood and mahogany since the 16th century, Belize still has extensive forests. The large-scale abandonment of farms with the decline of the Maya civilization about A.D. 900 permitted forest regeneration that has attained what plant ecologists consider to be "climax" status. The removal of logwood only had little effect on the forest structure. It's in today's economy that logging can cause serious damage to the forest with the indiscriminate removal of large tracts of trees, no matter the variety, because of modern methods and high-tech equipment.

INDEPENDENCE

In 1862 Belize received the official title of Colony of British Honduras, though it had been ruled by the British crown since 1798. The average Belizean had few rights and a very low living standard. Political unrest grew in a stifled atmosphere. Even when a contingent of Belizean soldiers traveled to Europe to fight for the British in WW I, the black men were scorned. But when these men returned from abroad, the pot of change began to boil. Over the next 50 years, the country struggled through power plays, another world war, and economic crises. But always the seed was there—a growing desire to be independent. The colonial system had been falling apart around the world, and when India gained its freedom in 1947 the pattern was set. Many small undeveloped countries soon began to gain their independence and started to rely on their own ingenuity to build an economy that would benefit the people.

WHAT'S IN A NAME?

No one knows for sure where the name of Belize originated or what it means. The country was called Belize long before the British took the country over and renamed it British Honduras. In 1973, the locals changed it back to the original Belize as a first step on the road to independence. There are several well-known theories for its meaning. Some say it's a corruption of the name Wallis (pronounced wahl-EEZ), from the pirate (Peter Wallace) who roamed the high seas centuries ago and visited Belize. Others suggest that it's a distortion of the Maya word *belix*, which means muddy river. Still others say it could be a further distortion of the Maya word *belikin* (which is also the name of the local beer). And of course it could be another of those mysterious Maya secrets we may never learn.

Belize was dominated by outside influences until September 1981, when it gained its independence from the British Crown. But change comes slowly. This third-world country is learning through hard knocks how to be self-sustaining, self-motivated, self-governing—noncolonial. In the process of finding methods to become financially independent and raise the standard of living, Belizean leaders are discovering that the country's natural assets may indeed hold the key to bringing in dollars in the form of tourism, an industry they never before dreamed of. The government is proceeding slowly to design the proper tourist growth to fit into its scheme to preserve the ethnic cultures, the animals, the reef, and the forests. Belize is becoming a role model for other developing countries that need tourism dollars but are not willing to sacrifice their culture and natural resources. In September 1981 the Belizean flag was raised—the birth of a new era! Belize joined the United Nations, the Commonwealth, and the Non-Aligned Movement. Its work is cut out for it.

GOVERNMENT

Beginning in the mid-19th century, Belize was a British Crown colony. In 1964 the country became self-governing and in 1981, Belize achieved independence within the commonwealth. The infant country's first parliamentary elections were held in 1984. The government is directed by a prime minister; a bicameral legislature, the National Assembly, comprises an appointed Senate and an elected House of Representatives. Belize has two active political parties, PUP (People's United Party) and UDP (United Democratic Party). George Price and Manuel Esquivel have been elected prime minister back and forth. As in most democracies, the rhetoric can get very animated, but Belize is a peaceful, law-abiding country, and its citizens are proud to rule themselves.

ECONOMY

Though the country has grown on all fronts, including economically, it is still a poor country and needs money. One of the newest "events" on the money-raising agenda is the sale of citizenship for hard currency. It isn't easy to obtain, and applicants must go through rigorous scrutiny. Even that doesn't please everyone; many citizens in the country object to selling their **patrimony**. The cost to obtain citizenship is between US$75,000 and US$85,000 per family. The number of families accepted is limited to 500 per year. Anyone interested should contact the nearest Belize Consulate; in the U.S., write or call 2535 Massachusetts Dr. NW, Washington, D.C. 20008, tel. (202) 332-9636, fax (202) 332-6741.

One of the exciting aspects of a developing country is watching how the people's creative genius can turn them into entrepreneurs. The U.S. is a great example of this and a good role model for countries just putting their toes into the sea of world commerce. Belize has been independent since 1981, and after a few false starts is beginning to see the *start* of a glowing future. The *Belize Investment Code* states, "Foreign investment is welcome as long as it creates jobs and expands Belizean talent and skills; infuses foreign financial resources and good managerial skills into Belize; produces for export markets; utilizes indigenous raw materials; and engages in environmentally sound projects which make technological advances and increase the capital stock of the nation." Developing and improving the country's infrastructure promises big changes. For example, the government has brought electricity to 98% of outlying villages.

However, some critics in the country say Belize should take a hard look at what's happening. These locals are questioning how much of the country they are willing to give away to enter mainstream economics. An editorial in the local paper, *Amandala,* put it succinctly:

What we poor Belizeans have to consider is just exactly what all are we prepared to sell in order to achieve so-called "development." We've been poor for centuries in this country, and while none of us are prepared to sell our mother, we have been selling our motherland. We may not be prepared to sell our children, but we have no problem selling our children's future. We may not think we are selling our souls, but some of us are certainly selling our bodies.

We argue, when we sell our assets, that we have to get into this development race now, but when a nation sells resources which are nonrenewable, then it is giving up some of its sovereignty for money—speculative money.

Certainly these are words to ponder for any developing country.

Tourism and Ecotourism

Tourism is gradually heading to the top of the list of money-makers in the country, especially a version of it called "ecotourism." What exactly is ecotourism? Well, it depends on whom you ask. It can be anything from a walk around the Belize Zoo, to tenting in the jungle, to participation in hard-core scientific fieldwork. The general concept is easy enough to understand. Fundamentally, ecotourism means to visit a place making as little environmental impact as possible and meanwhile helping sustain the indigenous populace, thereby encouraging the preservation of scarce wildlife and habitat.

One promising step in that direction has been the rise of ecology-minded organizations such as the the Belize Eco-Tourism Association and its code of ethics and the Toledo Eco-Tourism Association with its Village Guesthouse Program. Others involved with educating as well as preserving include the Belize Zoo and Tropical Education Center, Community Baboon Sanctuary at Bermudian Landing, Programme for Belize with its Rio Bravo Conservation and Management Area, the Sea Turtle Sanctuary on Ambergris Caye, and Slate Creek Preserve in the Cayo District. Along with the government, these organizations are among those spearheading responsible tourism development and environmental protection.

AN ECOTOURISM CODE OF ETHICS

The entry-level code of ethics for the Belize Tourism Association requires members to:

- Present an invitation to all guests to be environmentally and culturally responsible.
- Eliminate plastic disposables such as cups and lunch containers.
- Avoid disturbing wildlife, flora, and coral.

Can it work? As Belize is seeing, it probably can (if the government and members of the tourist industry properly appeal to and serve those adventurous travelers who prefer real jungle to the sanitized versions of movies and amusement parks). Both local and outside investors are catching on, and the Belizean government is helping further by giving tax concessions to legitimate business, not just gold-plated Wall Street names. A few Americans who have taken the plunge into the bureaucracy describe a moderate amount of paperwork involved, such as establishing residency and obtaining work permits. Although it can take time, it isn't so difficult that it discourages potential investors.

Industry

The economy of Belize was traditionally based on logwood, mahogany, and chicle export. Today tourism along with agriculture, fisheries, and small manufactured goods give the country an important economic boost. The main exports are sugar, citrus, bananas, lobster, and timber. Thanks to tax concessions given to foreign investors, Belize has experienced a diversification of manufacturing industries, such as plywood, veneer manufacturing, matches, beer, rum, soft drinks, furniture, boat building, and battery assembly.

The **Belize Bank** offers US$ accounts for its international business corporations. This has been a big factor in attracting foreign investors.

Fishing

Belize has maintained a viable fishing industry. For years Belize fishing co-ops have been exporting rock and spiny lobster to the United States. At first it was almost a giveaway, but as the fisher-

men began working together through co-ops, prices have risen and fishermen manage to make a good living. In recent years fishing has been controlled to prevent the "fish-out" of the lobster by closing the season 15 February to 15 June and limiting the size of the lobsters. The main export markets for scale fish are the U.S., Mexico, and Jamaica. With the help of Canadian government agencies, Belizean fishermen are trained in many fields of the fishing industry. They are learning modern processing techniques, navigation, and marine engineering.

Mariculture and Aquaculture

Mariculture is a new activity in Belize. Shrimp are being harvested near the Monkey River with two species of shrimp introduced from Ecuador. Another shrimp farm is being developed near Quashie Trap Lagoon in southern Belize District. Another farm in its beginning stages will introduce the American lobster on Turneffe Islands to Caribbean waters in an at-

Belize fishing boat

tempt to stimulate faster growth. At Turneffe Islands' Northern Bogue, the spiny lobster is being raised in enclosed submerged pens. Many new "fish-growing" industries are also in the planning stages for Belize. The newest is a shrimp hatchery to be located at Mile 5 on the Western Highway. Taiwan will be providing facilities to rear post larvae (baby shrimps) so that Belize will not be so dependent on imported larvae, a system that has kept the growth of the shrimp industry in slow mode. The Taiwanese will assist in developing the process while training Belizean Fishing Department personnel.

Sugarcane

Another Belize export is sugarcane. Mestizos originally planted sugar in large tracts of land that were left empty after loggers had removed the trees. Within 10 years Belize produced enough sugar to take care of its needs, with a surplus that allowed for exporting and making rum. Sugar has continued throughout the years to be the primary money-maker for the country, despite low sugar prices in recent years. England was for years the major export/import partner for Belize. Although Belize exports to other countries, England is still an active importer for Belize, along with the United States.

Bananas

One of the attractive investments is establishing banana plantations in Belize's southern coastal

bananas

region; so far the land costs are reasonable. Limestone soil (washed down from the nearby mountains), a warm climate, and an annual rainfall of 130 inches make the area perfect for growing bananas.

BELIZE ASSOCIATION OF LOUISIANA (BAL)

BAL is a great group of people living in Lousiana who were born in Belize or whose parents are from Belize. It is a social club; everyone gets together at parties, dances, fashion shows, and other special events. But the best part is that the profits all go to Belize. The group doesn't want cash. Instead members donate toys for Christmas, books for Belizean libraries, summer clothes for adults and children, and sports equipment of all kinds; TACA airlines graciously hauls the goods to Belize. Medical supplies are always in need, even if it's just aspirin. And BAL tries to help one very special charity in

Belize, HelpAge, a home for older folks in need. For this group is always happy to get used bedding, sheets, blankets, pillows, etc.—hotels that turn over their bedding periodically are contacted in the hopes they will donate the linens to BAL.

This is one of the most sincere charities I've come across. If anyone out there wants to donate, please contact **Toucan Travel** and ask for Dulca, who is from Belize. The address is 32 Traminer Dr., Kenner, LA 70065, tel. (504) 465-0769. Remember, BAL isn't asking for cash, just goods in decent or new condition.

This cow dines on tasty water plants during the dry season.

Citrus Fruit

Stann Creek offers excellent conditions for raising citrus fruit, first introduced into the country in the early 1920s. Nine hundred grafted trees were imported from Florida and with a great deal of TLC tending them, they won blue ribbons at agricultural shows in England from 1928-1931. But as much as the Europeans were impressed with Belizean oranges, freight costs made shipping the whole fruit impossible and they had to be content with the juice.

Over the years, despite hurricanes that have flattened the trees and fluctuating prices, a combination of external events has given the Belizean citrus industry a big boost. In 1983 President Reagan removed taxes from Caribbean-grown citrus. Soon after, severe frosts damaged and limited fruit production in Florida and Texas, followed by a canker disease on Florida citrus that dealt another blow for the U.S. citrus industry. This enabled Belize to get a toehold in trading, and it has been climbing ever since.

Cattle

Not too many years ago, beef was either not available, tough and stringy (and therefore "cooked to tenderness"), or "cooked to death" for health reasons. The average Belizean family just didn't put beef on the table much. Beef-growing was a depressed business. Most Belizeans grew up eating canned meat, fried chicken, and seafood, and that was just fine. However, a new breed of cattlemen came along (mostly from the U.S.), and

showed the locals how cattle should be "wrangled." After a lot of hard work, the quality improved and the word was out—hamburgers are good! Government support of the industry has helped. And ranchers are learning the secrets of ranching in Belize. They are establishing pastures of higher-protein grasses that can support and fatten one animal per acre for one year. Next time you're in a restaurant in Belize, compliment the chef, or rather the rancher—order a tender, high-quality beefsteak raised in Belize.

The Little Guy Lives

Belize is a country where the little guy with a big idea can still make that dream come true. Marie Sharp, a native of Stann Creek District, came up with a sizzling idea one day in her kitchen—why not make and bottle a local hot sauce? **Melinda's** hot sauce, one of Belize's most successful products, was the result. It has since found its way into almost every restaurant and home in Belize, and into more than a dozen states in the U.S., including Hawaii. This is a gourmet chile pepper sauce made from the notorious habanero pepper grown only on the Yucatán Peninsula, primarily in Belize. Pepper lovers the world over agree the habanero *Capsicum chinense* is the hottest pepper known to man. Marie and Jerry Sharp grow their own on their 400-acre plantation in the Maya Mountain foothills just outside Dangriga in southern Belize.

In 1983, Marie planted five acres of peppers. After bringing along a healthy crop she was offered a ridiculous US50 cents a gallon for the peppers. She refused to give her peppers away and began experimenting with recipes to make a hot sauce. After some time she came up with the perfect recipe that includes onions and carrots, pureed raw habaneros, lime juice, vinegar, garlic, and salt. With ingredients like that, how could it miss? To get the bright red color she wanted, it was necessary to use only specially cultivated all-red peppers.

After a lot of hard work, including several packaging and marketing classes in the U.S., Marie selected the label "Melinda's. Proud Product of Belize." Because of a new arrangement with the American distributor, however, the Sharps now market the sauce as "Marie Sharp's" in Belize while retaining the original name in the States. The Sharps can barely keep up with demand in Belize. Tourists take it home by the bottle and case. Originally found only in specialty stores in the U.S. (such as Marshall Fields) and supermarket chains (such as Jewel's), Melinda's sauce is now more widely available.

Marie, meanwhile, is now buying peppers from local farmers to meet demand and has branched out to market other delicious products. Her fruit jams and spreads, all made of pure, natural ingredients, including fruits raised in the sweet earth of Belize, are already becoming equally famous. And, yes, she moved out of the family kitchen some time ago.

THE PEOPLE

THE MAYA

The indigenous people, the Maya, inhabited the area that is now Guatemala, El Salvador, southern Mexico, Honduras, and Belize. Scientists believe that at one time the Maya, the first settlers in what is now called Belize, numbered about a million. The earliest known community in the Maya world was at Cuello, in Belize's Orange Walk District, dating to 2000 B.C. Here they were pottery makers and farmers. A few of the most powerful Maya ceremonial centers have been uncovered at Altun Ha, Lubaantun, Caracol, and Xunantunich (zoo-nahn-too-NEECH).

Physical Characteristics of the Maya
Maya men average just over five feet tall, women just under five feet. Muscular-bodied, they have straight black hair, round heads, broad faces with pronounced cheekbones, aquiline noses, almond-shaped dark eyes, and eyelids with the epicanthic or Mongolian fold (a prolongation of a fold of the upper eyelid over the inner angle or both angles of the eye).

Stylized Beauty
Bishop Diego de Landa wrote in his *Relaciones* that when the Spanish arrived, the Maya still practiced the ancient method of flattening a newborn's head with a press made of boards. By pressing the infant's forehead, the fronto-

nasal portion of the face was pushed forward, as can be seen in carvings and other human depictions from the pre-Columbian period; this was considered a very important sign of beauty. Further, they dangled a bead in front of a baby's eyes to encourage crossed-eyes, another Maya beauty mark. They practiced dental mutilation by filing the teeth to give them different shapes or by making slight perforations and inlaying pyrite, jade, or turquoise. Tattooing and scarification were accomplished by lightly cutting a design into the skin and purposely infecting it, creating a scar of beauty. Adult noblemen often wore a nosepiece to give the illusion of an even longer nose sweeping back into the long flat forehead.

Modern Maya
Although the Spanish were never successful in annihilating the Maya in Latin America, they destroyed many communities. The Maya wisely left the coastal areas (where most of the outsiders were) and lived deep in the jungle interior of Belize. That, together with the influx of Maya during the Caste War, created a fairly good-sized population of Maya in the country. More-recent comers are Guatemala Maya escaping brutal treatment from the upper class. These people make up a large part of the hill areas of the Cayo, Toledo, and Stann Creek districts.

The Maya Bloodline
Isolation of the indigenous people kept the Maya bloodline pure. The resemblance of today's Maya

to the people of a thousand years ago is thus understandable, but still amazing. Three distinct Maya groups are found in Belize. Though the languages of these groups are related, they are different enough from each other that, even if you know one dialect, it's still difficult to understand another dialect. The locals call the Mopan and Yucatecs by the term Maya, and separate the Kekchi as a non-Maya group, although they, too, are Maya. Together the three groups make up about 12% of the entire population of the country. The Maya settlements are found in southwest Toledo, the upper Belize River Valley, and northwest Corozal/northern Orange Walk districts. These villages have a south-to-north pattern of Kekchi-Mopan-Yucatec. The Kekchi migrated from Guatemala to work on sugar plantations. The Yucatec, who have had the most contact with mestizos, have experienced the biggest changes in their culture. A good example is Yo Creek in the Orange Walk District. Once an all-Maya agricultural village, its first language is Spanish and more Yucatecs than ever now work for wages outside the village.

POLYGLOT

Although the first settlers, outlawed pirates, did most of their own logging, it was the second wave of settlers—the British—that changed the face of the landscape now known as Belize. Cheap labor was needed to do the grueling timber work in thick, tall jungles. The British failed to force it on the maverick Maya, so they brought slaves from Africa, indentured laborers from India, and Caribs from distant Caribbean islands, as was common in the early 16th and 17th centuries. The Caribs, much like the Maya, were a detached group and never really gave in to slaving in the sugar fields. Much later, from 1958 to 1962, a group of Mennonites (originally from 16th-century Switzerland) came looking for religious freedom and began a fine dairy and agricultural tradition. This assortment of nationalities eventually created a handsome group of people of multicolored skin and hair. Although English is the official language, a mixture of Spanish, African dialects, Carib, and English has become a patois called Creole that's pleasant to the ear, though it takes heavy-duty lis-

tening to understand. Most of the people of Belize are black-skinned Afro-Creole.

Creoles
The people who call themselves "Creoles" make up 60% of the population of Belize today. All Creoles share two distinctive traits: a degree of African ancestry and the use of the local English-Creole dialect. Skin color runs from very dark to very light, but European ancestry is usually apparent. Most Creoles believe themselves to be "true Belizeans" because their ancestors are thought to have been among the first settlers. This may not have been the case, however. Aside from the claims by resident Amerindians and European Baymen to first occupancy, many Creoles are descended from the immigrants who entered the country years after the Garifuna, Maya, East Indians, and Ladinos. Slaves were traded among the British colonials until slavery was abolished in 1833.

The center of Creole territory is Belize City, and half of the ethnic Creoles comprise more than three-fourths of the city's population. Rural Creoles live along the highway between Belmopan and San Ignacio, in isolated clusters in northern Belize District, and in a few coastal spots to the south—Gales Point, Mullins River, Mango Creek, Placencia, and Monkey River Town.

Ladinos
Spanish-speaking Belizeans, descended from Amerindians and Europeans, normally are labeled "mestizos." While the term is appropriate in a racial connotation, Ladino better describes the cultural attributes of Mexican and Central American immigrants who have given up the distinct culture of their ancient ancestors. Once the predominant population (after immigration from the Yucatecan Caste War), Ladinos are now the second-most populous ethnic group of Belize. They occupy the old "Mexican-Mestizo corridor" that runs along New River between Corozal and Orange Walk. In west central Belize—Benque Viejo and San Ignacio—indigenous people from Guatemala have recently joined the earlier Spanish-speaking immigrants from Yucatán.

Caribs and Garifuna
The Caribs came to the Caribbean islands around 1300 from South America. These warlike

*Garifuna drummers,
an important part
of any Garifuna
celebration*

tribes lived mainly in the Amazon River Valley and Guiana lowlands, and it's said the fierce warriors ate their victims. They were experts in building and navigating large plank dugouts, as well as prolific trappers, farmers, and fishermen (they fished with poison darts). Being wanderers they moved from island to island every couple of years. In the 17th century, Africans who had escaped from slavery intermarried within the Carib groups who lived on the Windward Islands in the east Caribbean. The resulting group of people is called the Garinagu or Garifuna. No pure-blooded Caribs are left in Belize.

The Garifuna (also called Garinagu) inherited the independent bloodlines of their ancestors and strongly resisted control by the Europeans. However, their arrows were no match for colonial guns, and they were ultimately defeated by the Spanish. In 1796 about 5,000 Garifuna were forced to the Bay Islands off the coast of Honduras. Over the years they migrated to the coastal areas of Honduras, Nicaragua, Guatemala, and southern Belize. A small Garifuna settlement grew in Stann Creek, where they fished and farmed. They began bringing fresh produce to Belize City, but were not welcome to stay for more than 48 hours without getting a special permit—the Baymen wanted the produce but didn't want these independent thinkers around the city, fearing they'd help slaves escape or perhaps cause a loss of the Baymen's tight control. The Baymen tried to keep the Garifuna separated from the people of Belize City by any means possible. Rumors were spread about their religious beliefs—that they were devil worshippers and baby eaters. They did have their exotic and often ritualistic ceremonies—some still do—but the dancing and singing weren't always as evil as the manipulating politicians would have one believe. (A certain amount of prejudice and fear still exists.) The Garifuna tried many times to become part of the Public Meeting (the British governing system), but were effectively refused until 19 November 1832, when they were allowed to join the community. That event, **Garifuna Settlement Day,** continues to be a major national celebration and holiday each year.

Immigrants from India

From 1844-1917, under British colonialism, 41,600 East Indians were brought to British colonies in the Caribbean as indentured workers. They agreed to work for a given length of time for one "master." Then, they could either return to India or stay on and work freely. Unfortunately, the time spent in Belize was not as lucrative as they were led to believe it would be. In some cases they owed so much money to the company store (where they received half their wages in trade and not nearly enough to live on) that they were forced to "re-enlist" for a longer period. Most of them worked on sugar plantations in the Toledo and Corozal districts, and many of the East Indian men were assigned to work as local police in Belize City. In a town aptly named Calcutta many of the population today are descendants of the original indentured East Indians. Forest Home near Punta Gorda also has a large settlement. About 47% of the ethnic group live in these two locations. The East Indians usually have large families and live on small farms with orchards adjacent to their homes. A few trade in pigs and dry goods in ma-and-pa businesses. East Indians normally speak Creole and Spanish. Apparently, descendants from the original immigrants do not speak Hindi today. A small number of Hindi-speaking East Indian merchants live in Belize City and Orange Walk Town, but they are fairly new to the country and have no cultural ties with the descendants of earlier immigrants.

Mennonites

German-speaking Mennonites are the most recent group to enter Belize on a large scale. This group of Protestant settlers from the Swiss Alps wandered over the years to northern Germany, southern Russia, Pennsylvania, and Canada in the early 1800s, and to northern Mexico after WW I. For some reason the quiet, staid Mennonites disturbed local governments in these other countries, and restrictions on their isolated agrarian lifestyle have caused a nomadic past. Most of Belize's Mennonites first migrated from Mexico from 1958-62. A few came from Peace River in Canada. They bought large blocks of land (about 148,000 acres) and began to dig in their roots. Shipyard (in Orange Walk District) was settled by a conservative wing, Spanish Lookout (in Cayo District) and Blue Creek (in Orange Walk District) were settled by more progressive members. In hopes of averting future problems with the government, Mennonites and Belize officials made agreements that guarantee freedom to practice their religion, use their language in locally controlled schools, organize their own financial institutions, and to be exempt from military service. Over the 30-plus years that Mennonites have been in Belize, they have slowly merged into Belizean activities. Although they practice complete separation of church and state (and do not vote), their innovations in agricultural production and marketing have advanced the entire country. Mennonite farmers are probably the most productive in Belize; they commonly pool their resources to make large purchases such as equipment, machinery, and supplies. Their fine dairy industry is the best in the country, and they supply the domestic market with eggs, poultry, fresh milk, cheese, and vegetables.

Rastafarians

Some Johnny-come-latelies are Jamaican Rastafarians. Primarily these people live in Belize City, but a few have made homes in Caye Caulker and other parts of the country. Rastafarians are part of a religion that believes in the eventual redemption of blacks and their return to Africa. They are easily recognizable by their dreadlocks—uncombed and uncut long mats of hair (although not all dreadlock wearers are true Rastas). Their beliefs, according to the biblical laws of the Nazarites, forbid the cutting of their hair. Rastafarians use ganja (marijuana) in their rituals (which gets them in trouble in the wrong neighborhoods) and venerate Haile Selassie I, late emperor of Ethiopia, as their god. Selassie's precoronation name was Ras Tafari Makonnen, hence the name (Ras is simply an honorific title). He allegedly descended from King Solomon and the Queen of Sheba.

LITERACY

At one time only the children of the elite were able to attend school. The Belizeans have put a top priority on education; schools are available throughout the country, and today 90% of Belizeans are literate. (There is concern that the figure may change with the heavy influx of El Salvadoran refugees.) School is mandatory for Belizean children up to age 14. High school is neither mandatory nor free—most are run by religious groups with aid from the government. As a result, not all families can afford to educate their children beyond grammar school.

(previous page) Maya site at Copan, Honduras;
(this page, top) Copan, Honduras;
(bottom left) Caracol, Belize; (bottom right) Lamanai guide (photos by Oz Mallan)

ON THE ROAD
HIGHLIGHTS

SIGHTSEEING

Belize is peppered with ruins of known Maya settlements and cities. More are being discovered all the time. **Altun Ha, Cahal Pech, Lamanai, Lubaantun,** and **Xunantunich** are among the most interesting developed sites. Others, such as **Caracol, Chan Chich, El Pilar,** and **La Milpa** are less fully excavated, but captivating, nonetheless. (See "Maya Archaeological Sites" in the Mundo Maya chapter.)

Day-trips from Ambergris Caye, Belize City, Corozal, or San Ignacio to the ruins of Altun Ha, Lamanai, Xunantunich, and others can be arranged before or after arrival in Belize. For those who would like to stay at or within sight of Maya ruins **Chan Chich Lodge, Chau Hix Lodge, Lamanai Outpost Lodge,** and **Nabitunich** (see Accommodations Index in the back of the book) all offer that experience. Lamanai Outpost Lodge also offers guests the opportunity to participate in a small archaeological dig.

RECREATION

For years the most well-known and publicized activities for visitors to Belize were diving and snorkeling. Without a doubt the Belize Reef (fifth longest in the world and longest in the Western Hemisphere) offers the diver a fulfilling experience observing the colors and variety of tropical fish and coral. Now, however, many inland attractions and activities are getting equal time. Belize is a country with a host of adventure travel and learning opportunities for all ages and abilities. The hard part is in deciding which ones to choose on your next vacation. To make the best of your decisionmaking it's helpful to keep in mind the style of traveling you like, physical abilities, and whether you will be bringing your children. A little thought given early on will help ensure your time in Belize is well spent and enjoyable.

A Matter of Style

Some folks enjoy getting dirty and being tested to the limits of their physical abilities. Others like to stay reasonably clean and experience the outdoors in a softer fashion. Some travelers like to trek through miles of muddy jungle in hopes of seeing a tapir. Others prefer to sight one in comfortable surroundings at the Belize Zoo. And while some travelers thrill to participate in a jungle research project, others are fascinated by a short visit to some excavated ruins and a guided tour. All of the above are available in Belize and can be arranged through travel agents, guides, hotels, or lodges. When making arrangements ask lots of questions to ensure that a given activity is neither too tame nor too wild for your personal style of adventure.

A Matter of Age

Today, senior travelers and and those traveling with children have many options. Active seniors enjoy Belize. Some like the tranquility of the palm-studded cayes. Many come to learn about the jungle and its creatures or about the ancient Maya ruins. ElderHostel offers fascinating tours for those who love the adventure of learning. Some resorts are planned to better accommodate the needs of active senior travelers.

Though lodges and hotels may offer discounts on accommodations for small children, Belize is best suited for families with kids old enough to enjoy outdoor activities and learning about nature. Many small children may do well at resorts, however, that offer safe beaches, games, and of course a visit to the zoo. Any of the tranquil beaches is a great place to give them their first look through the dive mask at the unique underwater world.

Photography

For the photographer, a world of beauty awaits: the sea, the people, and the natural landscape of the jungle, waterfalls, rivers, and archaeological sites. For those who want to film *everything*, small planes are available for charter in Belize City. (See "Cameras and Picture Taking" later in this chapter)

WATER SPORTS

SCUBA AND SNORKELING

Snorkeling Around

Not everyone who travels to Belize is a diver or even a snorkeler—at first. But one peek through the "looking glass"—a diving mask— will change that. The Caribbean is one of the most notoriously seductive bodies of water in the world. Turquoise blue and crystal clear with perfect tepid temperature, the protected Belizean coast (thanks to offshore reefs) is ideal for a languid float during hot humid days.

Even if you've never considered underwater sports in the past, you'll be willing—no, eager!— to learn. It's easy for the neophyte to learn how to snorkel. Once you master breathing through a tube, it's simply a matter of relaxing and floating. Time disappears once you are introduced, through a four-inch glass window, to a world of fish in rainbow colors of garish yellow, electric blue, crimson, and probably a hundred shades of purple. The longer you look, the more you'll discover: underwater caverns, tall coral pillars, giant tubular sponges, shy fish hiding on the sandy bottom, and delicate wisps of fine grass.

Diving Wonderland

For the diver, there's even more adventure. Reefs, caves, and rugged coastline harbor the unknown. Ships wrecked hundreds of years ago hide secrets as yet undiscovered. Swimming among the curious and brazen fish puts you literally into another world. This is raw excitement.

Expect to see an astounding variety of fish, crustaceans, and corals. Even close to shore, these amazing little animals create exotic displays of shape and form, dense or delicate depending on species, depth, light, and current. Most need light to survive; in deeper, low-light areas, some species of coral take the form of a large plate, thereby performing the duties of a solar collector. Sponge is another curious underwater creature and it comes in all sizes, shapes, and colors, from common brown to vivid red.

Be Selective
Diving lessons are offered at nearly all the dive shops in the country. Before you make a commitment, ask about the instructor and check his/her accident record; then talk to the locals or, if you're in a small village, ask at the local bar. Most of these divers are conscientious, but a few are not, and the locals know whom to trust.

Bringing your own equipment to Belize might save you a little money, depending on the length of your trip and means of transportation. But if you plan to stay just a couple of weeks and want to join a group aboard a dive boat by the day, it's generally not much more for tank rental, which will save you the hassle of carrying your own.

Choose your boat carefully. Look it over first. Some aren't much more than fishing boats with little to make the diver comfortable. Ask questions! Does it have a platform to get in and out of the water? How many tanks of air may be used per trip? How many dives? Exactly where are you going? How fast does the boat go and how long will it take to get there? Remember, some of the best dive spots might be farther out at sea. A more modern boat (though it'll cost a little more) might get you extra diving time.

Detailed information is available for divers and snorkelers who wish to know about the dive sites they plan to visit. *Skin Diver* magazine puts out a very informative issue on Belize at least once a year, usually in June. Many pamphlets and books are available, especially for U.S.-based dive tours. Some have been in business for many years; check them out. You also can call (800) 237-DIVE for information on dive sites. Wherever diving is good, you'll almost always find a dive shop. On both Ambergris Caye and Caye Caulker, and in Belize City, dive shops offer day-trips.

A few high-adventure dives require an experienced guide—not only recommended but also a necessity.

Underwater Hazards
A word here about some of the less-inviting aspects of marine society. Anemones and sea urchins live in Belize waters. Some can be dangerous if touched or stepped on. The long-spined black sea urchin can inflict great pain, and its poison can cause an uncomfortable infection. Don't think that you're safe in a wetsuit, booties, and gloves. The

PORTUGUESE MAN-OF-WAR

NEEDLE FISH

ELKHORN CORAL

SPONGES

TABLE CORAL

STAGHORN CORAL

ANGEL FISH

CLOWN FISH IN SEA ANEMONE

LOBED STAR CORAL

BRAIN CORAL

Laughing Bird Caye

spines easily slip through the rubber and the urchin is encountered at all depths. They are more abundant in some areas than in others; keep your eyes open. If you should run into one of the spines, remove it quickly and carefully, disinfect the wound, and apply antibiotic cream. If you have difficulty removing the spine, or if it breaks, see a doctor—pronto! Note: Environmentalists discourage divers from wearing gloves to deter their touching the fragile coral. For some varieties, just one touch is the touch of death.

First Aid
Cuts from coral, even if just a scratch, will often become infected. Antibiotic cream or powder will usually take care of it. If you should get a deep cut, or if minute bits of coral are left in the wound, a serious and long-lived infection can ensue. See a doctor.

If you should get scraped on red or fire coral you may feel a burning sensation for just a few minutes or up to five days. In some, it causes an allergic reaction and will raise large red welts. Cortisone cream will reduce inflammation and discomfort. While it wouldn't be fair to condemn all red things, you'll notice in the next few paragraphs that many of the creatures to avoid are red!

Fire worms (also known as bristle worms) if touched will deposit tiny cactus-like bristles in your skin. They can cause the same reaction as fire coral. *Carefully* scraping the skin with the edge of a sharp knife (as you would to remove a bee stinger) *might* remove the bristles. Any leftover bristles will ultimately work their way out, but you might be very uncomfortable in the meantime. Cortisone cream helps to relieve this inflammation, too.

Several species of sponges have fine sharp spicules (hard, minute, pointed calcareous or siliceous bodies that support the tissue) that should not be touched with the bare hand. The attractive red fire sponge can cause great pain; a mild solution of vinegar or ammonia (or urine if there's nothing else) will help. The burning lasts a couple of days, and cortisone cream soothes. Don't be fooled by dull-colored sponges. Many have the same sharp spicules.

Hands Off!
Some divers feel the need to touch the fish or coral they swim with. Touching coral injures it. Touching the wrong fish might injure you. Coral takes scores of years to grow a single inch. Grabbing onto a coral head damages it for years to come. Leave the reef in the same condition you found it so that others may enjoy it after you. Thoughtful divers *don't touch.*

Barracuda, moray eels, and sharks do not appreciate groping hands and all have ample means to protect themselves. Enough said.

Even sea turtles occasionally try to bite when tampered with by those wishing to prove how macho they are. Look, don't touch. In addition,

EMERGENCY NUMBERS FOR ACCIDENT EVACUATION

Divers Alert Network (DAN):   (919) 684-8111
dial this number for info about
decompression chambers

Air-Evac International
San Diego, California: (619) 278-3822
Florida: (305) 772-0003
Houston, Texas: (713) 880-9767

Life Flight (air ambulance):   (713) 704-4357
Houston, Texas: (800) 231-4357

To get the proper help to you much sooner it's important to have as much
of the following information as possible ready to give the emergency
service you call:
    name and age of the patient
    the problem
    when it happened
    name and telephone number of the doctor and medical facility
    treating the patient

sharks are attracted to blood, certain low frequency sounds (like those caused by an injured fish), electromagnetic disturbances, and certain shapes and color patterns. Avoid swimming with bleeding wounds. And while barracudas, like other predatory fish, can be excited by fish blood and jerky vibrations, they seem to be more visual hunters. They are likely to snap at something flashy, such as watches and bracelets, so leave your flashy jewelry at home.

A few sea-going critters resent being stepped on and can retaliate with a dangerous wound. The scorpion fish, hardly recognizable with its natural camouflage, lies hidden most of the time on a reef shelf or on the bottom of the sea. If you should step on or touch it you can expect a painful, dangerous sting. If this happens, see a doctor immediately.

The ray is another sinister fellow. Several varieties live in the Caribbean, including the yellow and southern sting rays. If you leave them alone they're generally peaceful, but if stepped on they will zap you with a tail that carries a poisonous sting capable of causing anaphylactic shock. Symptoms include respiratory difficulties, fainting, and severe itching. Go quickly to the doctor and describe what

caused the sting. One diver suggests a shuffling, dragging-of-the-feet gait when walking on the bottom of the ocean. If bumped, the ray will quickly escape, but if stepped on it feels trapped and uses its tail for protection.

Jellyfish can also inflict a miserable sting. Avoid particularly the long streamers of the Portuguese man-of-war, though some of the smaller jellyfish are just as hazardous.

Don't let these what-ifs discourage you from an underwater adventure, though. Thousands of people dive in Belize's Caribbean every day of the year and only a small percentage have accidents.

Safety References
Check with your dive master about emergency procedures before your boat heads out to sea. Ask about the decompression chamber in San Pedro; he or she should also know that there's a decompression chamber in Houston, Texas, and another in Isla Cozumel, Mexico, tel. 2-0140.

FISHING

Wetting a hook in Belize will probably net you a fine dinner and a bagful of pleasant memories. Inside the reef, anglers have a choice of several game and food fish. The flats are good hunting grounds for tarpon, bonefish, permit, and occasionally barracuda. In the mangroves anglers are likely to snag a snook, tarpon, mangrove snapper, or mutton snapper. Outside the reef it's deep-sea fishing for red snapper and the big trophies such as marlin, sailfish, giant groupers, and tuna.

Increasingly, Belize boat operators and resorts are turning to "catch and release" policies for many fish. The fisherman is photographed or videotaped with the catch. Then, the fish is released. Often a few food fish are kept to provide a meal and the rest turned loose. A wise choice, these policies will help ensure that Belize remains an angler's dream for generations to come.

Boats and guides are plentiful in Belize City, Ambergris Caye, Caye Caulker, Corozal, Dangriga, Placencia, and Punta Gorda. Resorts that offer fishing packages include El Pescador, Journey's End Caribbean Club, and Victoria House on Ambergris Caye; Manta Resort on Southwest Caye in Glover's Reef; Lighthouse Reef Resort on Northern Caye; and Turneffe Flats and Turneffe Island Lodge in the Turneffe Islands. It's easy to make arrangements through your hotel or tour operators in Belize and in the U.S. (see "Tour Operators" in the "Tours Organized in the U.S." section).

BOATING

Charters

Visitors have several options for chartering a boat with a captain and crew in Belize. Ambergris Caye, Belize City, Caye Caulker, and Moho Caye (just off-shore Belize City) have boats available. Motor boats and sailboats are available. Bare boats (without captain and crew) are almost impossible to find, and the companies that once specialized in them are out of business. The reason is said to be damage done to the boats by encounters with submerged coral heads, shoals, and the like.

Private Cruising

If you plan to cruise to Belize in your own boat, you must contact the Belize consulate about a permit for your vessel. Sailors will find numerous anchorages among the cayes and coastal villages of Belize. Motor boaters have limited opportunities to refuel, but marinas or dock facilities with gasoline do exist at Ambergris Caye, Belize City, Caye Caulker, Caye Chapel, Moho Caye, Placencia, and Punta Gorda.

The barrier reef provides calm inshore waters with none of the crashing surf or large swells of the open ocean. It is also pretty to observe as you approach. However, stay well clear of the reef as there are numerous coral heads that dot the water on the inland side of the reef.

Bottom conditions that affect anchoring include mud around Belize City and river mouths, sand around the many cayes farther offshore, and grass beds near the inshore cayes. Avoid anchoring in coral or, if at all possible, grass beds. If there is no choice but

LIVE-ABOARD DIVE BOATS

Stingray (45')
Fanta-Sea Charters
tel./fax (303) 226-1193,
in Belize tel./fax (2) 32712

Belize Wave Dancer (120')
Peter Hughes Diving
tel. (800) 932-6237,
(305) 669-9391

Manta IV (54')
out of Belize Yacht Club
tel. (800) 938-0860,
in Belize (26) 2797

**Belize Aggressor II (110')
and III (120')**
Aggressor Fleet, Ltd.
P.O. Drawer K,
Morgan City, LA 70381
tel. (800) 348-2628,
(504) 385-2628,
fax (504) 384-0817

Offshore Express (50')
Coral Beach Dive Shop
San Pedro, Ambergris Caye
tel. (26) 2013

**Reef Roamer I (38')
and III (34')**
Out Island Divers
San Pedro, Ambergris Caye,
Belize, C.A.,
or Box 3455
Estes Park, CO 80517
tel. (800) 258-3465,
(970) 586-6020,
fax (970) 586-6134,
in Belize tel. (26) 2151,
fax (26) 2810

M/V Hot Dive (60')
tel. (800) 468-3483,
in Belize tel./fax (2) 34058

Live-aboard dive boats cruise the cayes and atolls.

to drop anchor in sea grass, make very certain the anchor has dug in properly and that you've allowed sufficient rope for tide, wind, and wave conditions before leaving the vessel.

Those interested in cruising these waters, especially the atolls, should talk to the locals to ascertain any local undersea hazards and the best approaches.

CANOEING AND KAYAKING

Canoeing

A paddle along one of Belize's rivers, lagoons, marshes, or reefs is a great way to get some exercise and enjoy the outdoors. One of the best ways to observe wildlife in Belize is by canoe. Dawn and dusk find many creatures at the water's edge for a drink. Nights are also productive as agoutis, crocodiles, and other wildlife can be spotted within the beam of a flashlight. Rent canoes at resorts and from independent operators. Bermudian Landing Baboon Sanctuary, Chan Chich, Gales Point, and San Ignacio are prime locations.

Kayaking

Kayaking is one of those off-the-wall activities that's growing all over the world and often in unlikely places. It is fast becoming a favorite in Belize. Kayakers have a choice of river trips, sea kayaking, or a combination. The rivers are gentle enough for even beginning kayakers. An ideal way to explore the coast is paddling the calm water within the reef and touching on isolated cayes. Ambergris Caye, Dangriga, Glover's Reef, Placencia, and Punta Gorda all offer opportunities. For more information about kayaking and camping in Belize contact Monkey River Expeditions, tel. (206) 660-7777, fax (206) 938-0978, or Slickrock Adventures, tel./fax (801) 259-6996 (see "Tour Operators" under "Tours Organized in the U.S." later in this chapter).

OTHER WATER SPORTS

Depending on where you are, additional water sports may be available. Because so many of these beaches are protected by the reef that runs parallel to Belize's eastern coast, calm **swimming beaches,** though shallow, are easy to find; finding a *sandy* beach is limited to certain areas. Many hotels have pools. You can also enjoy swimming inland in various rivers and lagoons. **Glass-bottom boats** are well worth the time for the nonswimmer or nonsnorkeler and are available at Ambergris Caye and Caye Caulker. While staying high and dry, it's possible to enjoy the beauties of the underwater gardens. **Jet Skis** or **Waveriders** are available at the Ramada Royal Reef in Belize City, several resorts on Ambergris Caye, and at Tony's Inn and Beach Resort in Corozal. **Tubing** is becoming a popular Cayo activity in the dry season on the Macal and Mopan rivers.

ADVENTURES ON LAND

CAVING OR SPELUNKING

Belize offers the avid caver several opportunities for exploration. About 25 miles south of Belize City (near Gales Point) two caves, **Ben Lomond** and **Manatee,** are open to the curious. It's necessary to hire a boat to take you across the bar bordering Southern Lagoon and then to continue hiking for several miles. In Belize City or Dangriga you can find boatmen along the waterfront who know the area and will take you.

The hills outside Punta Gorda are also riddled with caves. Guides from Punta Gorda or Mayan villagers associated with the T.E.A. (Toledo Eco-Tourism Association) Village Guesthouse Program will guide you (be sure to bring a light).

entrance to a mountain cave

Farther inland, the Maya Mountains hold one of the largest series cave systems in Latin America, the **Chiquibul Cave System.** Many have never been explored. Of those that have, a large number hold evidence of use by ancient Maya. Some contain ceremonial sites, pottery, crystal-covered skulls, skeletons, or footprints. Stalactites drip from overhead, stalagmites erupt from the floor. Some caves have rivers running through them with fish and huge freshwater prawn.

In the Cayo District near Belmopan the **Caves Branch Estate** has more than 20 caves, both wet and dry, on its property. Most passageways are quite large. Some require a modicum of athletic ability and you can float through others on inner tubes. Nearby are **St. Herman's Cave** in Blue Hole National Park and **Mountain Cow Cave** at Tapir Mountain Nature Reserve. In the Mountain Pine Ridge you'll find **Rio Frio Cave,** a two-ended cavern with a stream running through it. On the Vacca Plateau, **Chechem Ha** cave contains Mayan pottery, some of which still holds kernels of grain.

Safety First

You should visit most caves only with a trained guide. Dangerous flash floods are a possibility in the rainy season. Getting lost in branching passageways can be equally hazardous. Bring an extra flashlight and batteries. Step only where your guide instructs you. When negotiating ledges always have a handhold in case you slip. Never wander away from your group.

Seeing caves in a natural state (without walkways, wired lighting, and sound system) is a rare privilege. Enjoy it and show your appreciation by never disturbing pottery or other relics in the caves. Check with your hotel or travel agent for the names of qualified guides.

ON THE TRAIL

Backpacking and Hiking

The whole country is a backpacker's delight. Catch a bus to Corozal, Dangriga, Placencia,

Punta Gorda, or San Ignacio and use any of these as a base for venturing out into the countryside. All have numerous options for budget accommodations or camping. Hang out with the locals. Pick up some Spanish, Creole, or Mayan words and phrases. Eat the local food. It's fun and you can do it on a shoestring. And if you really want to get close to nature on a tight budget, try a visit to the Cockscomb Basin Wildlife Sanctuary, Crooked Tree Lagoon, or the Programme for Belize research station in Rio Bravo Conservation Area.

Birdwatching

Birding is spectacular throughout Belize and serious birdwatchers come from all over the world. From north to south the variety of birds is broad and changes with the geography and the weather (see "Fauna"). Some of the more productive areas for waterfowl and shorebirds are the lagoons of Ambergris Caye and inland around Crooked Tree Lagoon, Gales Point, New River Lagoon, Northern Lagoon (below Belize City), and Shipstern Lagoon. Half Moon Caye has a bird sanctuary that contains the nesting sites of boobies, frigate birds, and more. The Maya Mountains and lowland jungles of southern Belize harbor Aztec parakeets, hummingbirds, scarlet macaws, and king vultures, among many others. The escarpment of the Mountain Pine Ridge shelters parrots, orange-breasted hawks, and a variety of songbirds. Northwestern Belize is rich in ocellated turkeys, toucans, and curassow to name a few. There's a lot more to see in plant and animal life while birding (see "Nature Walks" and "Nature Study," below).

Bring binoculars and wear boots and lightweight trousers if you plan to birdwatch in jungle areas. Don't forget the bug repellent and be prepared for an occasional rain shower, even in the dry season.

The **Belize Audubon Society** is very active; write if you have questions, 12 Fort St., Belize City, Belize, C.A., tel. (2) 35004 or 34985.

Nature Walks

Wherever you go in Belize you're never far from a chance to see unusual plants and wildlife. Minutes out of the heart of Belize City you may encounter anything from a boa or fox crossing the road to manatees in the Belize River. And you're not even in the jungle yet! Many hotels and resorts throughout the country have their own nature trails, some with signs identifying trees, termite nests, and other interesting flora and fauna.

Nature Study

When it comes to enjoying wildlife and the outdoors, some people want more than just fun. They want serious fun, the fun of learning about nature in more depth. This is becoming increasingly popular in Belize and is taking several forms. On Caye Caulker **Seeing Is Belizing** offers slide shows and talks on nature subjects. Maya Mountain Lodge in the Cayo District offers talks covering similar subjects as well as Maya ceramics. Chaa Creek Cottages has a Nature Study Center that houses exhibits, a library, and presentation room. On Blackbird Caye guests can participate in a dolphin research project. Lamanai Outpost Lodge offers guests the opportunity to involve themselves in a study of howler monkeys. And the list is growing all the time.

Cycling

Though once you *never* saw cyclists in Belize, you will find a growing number of comrades in Belize who are avid practitioners. However, consider a few things before you pack your bike and head for the nearest airport. If you haven't encountered tropical humidity, you may first want to rent a bike in Belize for a short trial run before you plan a long trip. The humidity can be debilitating for some; for others it might take a day or two of easy riding and your body will acclimate. Another consideration is the roads of Belize. First of all, only a few roads are paved, and those are getting busier all the time. Traffic is getting heavy on the Western Highway, which is probably the best road in the country. Most of the other roads in Belize are narrow, filled with potholes, or are dirt, which can get pretty mushy in the rain. Relinquish the roadway to motor vehicles approaching from the rear. Anyone trying to cycle around Belize City's narrow, crowded streets is looking for an accident to happen. Also, watch your bike like a hawk—take it to bed with you at night, or at least into your room. After all that, if you still want to bike the roads of Belize, have at it!

For bicycling or mountain biking you have three practical options; rent on Ambergris Caye, in Belize City, or the Cayo District. Serious cyclists can rent bikes in Belize City and ride as far as Belmopan, Corozal, Orange Walk, or San Ignacio in a day. Once in the San Ignacio area, you can arrange bike rentals at several of the lodges or through B & M Bike rentals. Mountain bikes are preferable and a patch kit is a wise precaution.

Belize now has a cycling event that's drawing an international following. It's called the **Hike & Bike for the Rainforest** and it benefits **Accion Selva** (Jungle Action), an outfit dedicated to protecting the environment. The first Hike & Bike was held in 1994 and it is slated to become an annual event the last weekend of October. For more information contact Accion Selva at P.O. Box 53, San Ignacio, Belize, C.A., tel. (92) 2037, fax (92) 2501.

Horseback Riding

The horsey set will find no end of enjoyment in Belize. The Cayo alone offers numerous ranches, lodges, and independent operators who provide adventures on horseback. You can ride around a ranch and help herd cattle or explore jungle trails or archaeological sites. You can also find horses for hire near Altun Ha in Belize City District and Gallon Jug in Orange Walk District. Even Ambergris Caye has horses.

SPORTS

Golf

Golf addicts have two quick fixes. One is a driving range on Caye Chapel at Pyramid Island

horseback riding in the mountains

Resort. The other is a chipping green at River Walk Guest House just off the Western Highway near San Ignacio. Don't come to Belize for the golf.

Tennis

Tennis courts are scarce but the tennis buff will be happy to know that a few resorts do have them: Pyramid Island Resort on Caye Chapel, Villa Holiday Inn in Belize City, and Journey's End on Ambergris Caye.

ENTERTAINMENT AND EVENTS

FESTIVALS

Come to the party! Certain holidays in Belize are signals to have fun. And the variety of activity on each holiday is vast. This is the time to sample the culture and cuisine of Belize traditions. When a public holiday falls on Sunday, it is celebrated on the following Monday. If you plan to visit during holiday time, make advance hotel reservations—especially if you plan to spend time in Dangriga on 19 November (the area has limited accommodations).

Note: On a few holidays (Easter and Christmas) most businesses close for the day; on Good Friday most of the buses do not run. Check ahead of time.

Baron Bliss Day

On 9 March this holiday is celebrated with various activities, mostly water sports. In memory of English sportsman Baron Henry Edward Ernest Victor Bliss, who remembered Belize with a generous legacy when he died, a day of sailing and fishing was designated in his will. A formal ceremony is held at his tomb below the lighthouse in the Belize Harbor where he died on his boat. Fishing and sailing regattas begin after the ceremony.

NATIONAL HOLIDAYS IN BELIZE

1 January	New Year's Day
9 March	Baron Bliss Day
March or April	Good Friday
March or April	Holy Saturday
March or April	Easter Sunday
March or April	Easter Monday
1 May	Labor Day
25 May	Commonwealth Day
10 September	National Day
21 September	Independence Day
12 October	Columbus Day
19 November	Garifuna Day
25 December	Christmas Day
26 December	Boxing Day

Ambergris Caye Celebration

If you're wandering around Belize near 26-29 June, hop a boat or plane to San Pedro and join the locals in a festival they have celebrated for decades, **El Dia de San Pedro,** in honor of the town's namesake, St. Peter. This is good fun; reservations are suggested.

St. George's Caye Day

On 10 September 1798, at St. George's Caye off the coast of Belize, the British buccaneers fought and defeated the Spaniards over the territory of Belize. The tradition of celebrating this victory is still carried on each year, followed by a weeklong calendar of events from religious services to carnivals. During this week Belize City (especially) feels like a carnival with parties everywhere. On the morning of 10 September, the whole city parades through the streets and enjoys local cooking, spirits, and music with an upbeat atmosphere that continues well into the beginning of Independence Day on 21 September.

National Independence Day

On 21 September 1981, Belize gained Independence from Great Britain. Each year to celebrate, Belizeans enjoy carnivals on the main streets of downtown Belize City and district towns. Like giant county fairs, they include displays of local arts, crafts, and cultural activities, while happy Belizeans dance to a variety of exotic rhythms from *punta* rock to *soka* to reggae. Again, don't miss the chance to sample local dishes from every ethnic group in the country. With this holiday back to back with the celebration of the Battle of St. George's Caye, Belize enjoys two weeks of riotous, cacophonous celebrating.

Garifuna Settlement Day

On 19 November Belize recognizes the 1823 arrival and settlement of the first Garifuna (Black Caribs, also called Garinagu) to the southern districts of Belize. Belizeans from all over the country gather in Dangriga and Toledo to celebrate with the Garifuna. The day begins with the reenactment of the arrival of the settlers and continues with dancing to the local Garifuna drums and *punta rock*. Traditional food is available on street stands and local cafes. The language is called Garifuna and both words, Garifuna and Garinagu, are interchangeable.

DANCES OF THE MAYA

If you happen to be one of the lucky travelers in Belize on 25 September, you should make an effort to visit **San Antonio Village** in the Toledo

FEAST OF SAN LUIS

An all-night vigil begins the festival, during which traditional masks and costumes are blessed with smoke from burning incense and food offerings. According to Maya belief a great power resides in the masks and it can be directed toward good or evil.

Drums announce the procession to the home of the prioste (holy man) each of the next nine days. Twelve dancers take part. Leading the marchers is a man dressed as the "holy deer," followed by other characters of the dance, including *el tigre* ("the jaguar"), women portrayed by men, dogs, and finally, the hunters dressed in black. Four men carry a marimba, which will be used during the celebrations. Even while being carried, the marimba is played all the way into the prioste's house and intermittently during occasional respites in the ceremonial dances. Some of the men shake rattles and an ongoing chant adds an exotic tone to the music of the dance.

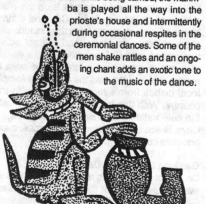

The Tiger Dance
The ancient legend of the tiger is performed in a square. The four corners and the center of the space represent the Maya's five cardinal directions north, south, east, west, and the center.

Slowly and with grace the story of *el tigre* unfolds. With active movements the tiger chases and is chased by the men in red from each of the four corners and around the center. Were they the bacabs, the Maya guardians of the directions? As a clown, the tiger impishly teases the hunters throughout the dance, stealing their hats or their rattles. At the finale the tiger is captured and killed; the hunters pantomime the killing and skinning of the tiger while the dancer steps out of his costume and runs away. Though performed with exaggerated elements of sincerity, it's a comedic performance, a warm-up of more serious things to come.

The Holy Deer Dance
The story of the holy deer, on the other hand, is performed with reverence instead of comedy, and continues for several days. The festivities include a lively procession to the San Antonio village church. The deer dances proudly, head high, acknowledges each of the other dancers, and then disappears into the forest. Enter the dogs sent by the hunters to seek out the deer. After a while the frightened deer/dancer is chased back by the dogs and with great drama the hunters kill the noble animal.

District. You have a good chance of seeing the **deer dance** performed by the Mopan and Kekchi Maya villagers. Dancing and celebrating begins around the middle of August, but the biggest celebration begins with a *novena* nine days before the feast day of San Luis.

Actually, this festival was only recently revived. The costumes were burned in an accidental fire some years back at a time when (coincidentally) the locals had begun to lose interest in the ancient traditions. Thanks to the formation of the **Toledo Maya Cultural Council,** the Maya

The Greased Pole

Preparations for the finale start two days ahead of time with an all-night vigil for the men who will cut down a tall tree the next day to be used in the pole-climbing festivities. The pillar is about 60 feet long and made from a special tree, called *sayuc* in Maya. The tree is trimmed and the dancing continues, drawing larger and larger audiences. A great procession follows as the huge pole and a statue of San Antonio (which has been in the prioste's home) are carried to San Antonio's church on the top of the hill. Occasionally the long line of people stops and lays the pole on the ground. In silence and great solemnity the pole is "blessed" by the statue of San Antonio while women manipulate censers of burning incense, sending wisps of aromatic smoke wafting around the pole. Once at the church, saints are traded. The statue of San Antonio is returned to its place, more prayers are said, and the statue of San Luis, under a protective colorful canopy and flanked by a dozen flags, is carried out on a wooden platform to "bless" the pole. The procession of people, including the statue, then makes its way to the prioste's house for another night of social dancing.

The Finale

It's 25 September, the climax day—and end of the celebration. Preparations for raising the pole begin early in the morning to the steady, low beat of a drum. Under the watchful eyes of many anxious children, bars of soap are flattened with rocks, broken into small pieces, and dissolved in buckets of water. Next, melted lard is added and thoroughly mixed. The oily compound is then generously spread on the pole. How anyone could accomplish an upward

movement on this mess is a mystery, although the first would have the most slip. Prizes that have been stored at the prioste's house—a generous hand of bananas, a bottle of rum, and a small sum of money—are placed at the top of the pole for the climber who makes it all the way. He will earn it!

After a slow procession, eating, dancing, and more blessings, the grand finale (under the watchful eye of the saint) is about to begin.

The pole-raising brings a still moment; the only sound is the low beat of the drums. The aroma of incense permeates the air. Fifty men hold ropes while others hold forked sticks and the pole slowly begins to rise, but not without a few slippery sways that bring gasps from the anticipating crowd. Finally the long pole slips neatly into the hole.

Now the fun begins—at least for the onlookers. The tiger and the hunter characters are the first to attempt to climb the pole, followed by a dozen other men; to make it more difficult each has his feet tied together. Everyone has a good laugh watching the slipping and sliding. Finally a successful challenger with great determination inches his way to the top and reaches for his prize; the crowd cheers and the church bells ring out, a happy ending to an often serious ceremony.

There is no question that this celebration is symbolic, but of what? It's doubtful that anyone really knows. So much of the ancient traditional culture has been mixed with the Christian religion that even the Maya aren't sure. The men in the village take turns as the religious caretaker for special statues of the church. This is a privilege that includes bearing the expense for most of the ceremonies for the year—a costly honor.

once again are realizing the importance of re-capturing their past. A grant from **Video Incorporated** broadcast company enabled the people to make new masks and costumes. In return the broadcasting company was granted permission to tape the festivities—a big concession for the secretive Maya. Before you decide to attend this days-long event, remember just that—it gets long. Ask the headman before you take any pictures.

MUSIC OF BELIZE

Like that of many Central American countries, the music has been heavily influenced by the rhythmic, exotic syncopations of Africa. This is toe-tapping, hip-swinging, hand-clapping music, and anyone who can just sit still and listen must be in a coma. If you manage to get to Belize in September during the festivals of the Battle of St. George's Caye and National Independence Day, you'll have an introduction to the raucous, happy music of a **jump up** (a street dance), **punta** rock (a spin-off from the original *punta,* a traditional rhythm of the Garifuna settlers in the Stann Creek District), **reggae** (everyone knows the beat of the steel drums adapted from the Trinidad cousins), **soka** (a livelier interpretation of reggae), and **brukdown** (a cadence begun in the timber camps of the 1800s, when the workers, isolated from civilization for months at a time, would let off steam with a full bottle of rum

and begin the beat on the bottle—or the jaw-bone of an ass, a coconut shell, a wooden block, anything that made a sound. Add to that a harmonica, guitar, and banjo, and you've got *brukdown*). **Creole** folk songs tell the story like it is, sad or happy, with lyrics in the Creole patois of the people.

In the southern part of Belize in Toledo District, you'll likely hear the strains of ancient Maya melodies played on homemade wooden instruments designed before memory: Kekchi harps, violins, and guitars. In the west in Cayo District listen for the resonant sounds of marimbas and wooden xylophones —from the Spanish influence across the Guatemala border. In Corozal and Orange Walk districts in the north, the infatuations of old Mexico are popularized with romantic lyrics and the strum of a guitar.

Tapes and Recordings

The music recording business is developing in Belize in its own original way—watch out Hollywood! If you want to hear Belizean music but can't get away, send for a catalog of cassette tapes available for overseas sales from **Sunrise Productions,** Box 137, Belmopan, Cayo District, Belize, C.A. Look for marimba music, Kekchi harp music, and the everloving **Waribagabaga and Children of the Most High,** combining their music of drums, turtle shells, and vocals sung in Garifuna. Also offered are typical jump up music and *punta* rock rhythms.

ACCOMMODATIONS

Picking the proper accommodations is as crucial to a good vacation as your choice of activities. That's why some folks would rather wait until they get to a destination to choose. That's not always a good idea in Belize, especially February through April. Educating yourself about the kinds of accommodations available and then matching those with your budget and preferences will reap large rewards later.

In Belize basic budget rooms are still fairly easy to find; small modern lodgings are adding more rooms to alleviate the growing shortages, and several upscale hotels have been built on Ambergris Caye and in Belize City in the last few years. Scattered about the rest of the countryside and coastal regions, small hotels and delightful intimate guesthouses range from spartan cottages with kerosene lanterns on the riverbank to luxury cabañas built of rich tropical hardwoods and surrounded by the rainforest, glorious gardens, and well-manicured grass. The rooms offer access to thousands of acres of rainforest, nature reserves, rivers, waterfalls, beautiful flowers, wild animals, colorful birds, and modern Maya villages along with ancient ceremonial sites of their ancestors. On tiny cayes just offshore, simple cabins sit in perfect locations for easy-access scuba diving and snorkeling as well as world-class permit and bonefishing. Or for other serious divers and anglers, live-aboard boats offer accommodations and the opportunity to comfortably cruise to offshore cayes. Most of the hostelries in the country are small and intimate, which, in keeping with the small country, is what the tourist majority prefers.

As you look through the listings for hotels in this book, remember that in most cases you must add 5% tax, usually 10% service charge, and in some cases an extra few percent for the use of credit cards. If you decide to stay in one of the low-key budget hotels, bring cash; most don't accept credit cards. In the more isolated areas, many of them also don't have hot water, electricity, or telephones. Adventurers won't let that stop them.

FOOD

Many of the crops now produced by U.S. farmers were introduced by the indigenous people of Mesoamerica, including corn, sweet potatoes, tomatoes, peppers, squash, pumpkin, and avocados. Many other agricultural products favored by Americans are also native to the area: papaya, cotton, tobacco, rubber, vanilla, and turkey.

PRE-COLUMBIAN AGRICULTURE

Enriching the Soil

Scientists believe Maya priests studied celestial movements. A prime function performed in the elaborate temples (built to strict astronomical guidelines) may have been charting the changing seasons and deciding when to begin the planting cycle. Farmers used the slash-and-burn method of agriculture (and the Maya still do today). When the time was propitious (before the rains began in the spring), Maya farmers cut the trees on a section of land, leaving stumps about a foot above ground. They spread downed trees evenly across the landscape to burn uniformly; residual ash was left to nourish the soil. At the proper time, they made holes with a pointed stick and dropped precious maize kernels into the earth, one by one. At each corner (the cardinal points) of the cornfield, they left offerings of *pozole* (maize stew) to encourage the gods to give forth great rains. With abundant moisture, crops were bountiful and rich enough to provide food even into the following year.

The Maya knew the value of allowing the land to lie fallow after two seasons of growth, and each family's *milpa* (cornfield) was moved from place to place around the villages scattered through the jungle. Often, squash and tomatoes were planted in the shade of towering cornstalks to make double use of the land. The coming of electricity to outlying areas brought pumps to transport water from rivers and lakes to irrigate crops. Outside of irrigation methods, today's Maya follow the same ancient pattern of farming as their ancestors. The government is suggesting more efficient management of the land with less destruction to the rainforest; this "alternate" farming method reuses a plot of ground, with the help of fertilizers, after it's been left fallow for a short time. Education, intended to teach the indigenous people alternatives to slash-and-burn, is beginning to take hold.

Maize

Corn was the heart of Maya nutrition, eaten at each meal. From it they made tortillas, stew, and both alcoholic and nonalcoholic beverages. Because growing corn was such a vital part of Maya life, it is represented in drawings and carvings along with other social and religious symbols. Corn tortillas are still a main staple of the Maya people. Grinding the corn into tortilla dough has been done by hand for centuries (and still is in isolated places). Others pay a few more cents and buy their tortillas by the kilo hot off the *tomal* (griddle). The Maya's combination of corn and beans provided a complete protein; they did not raise cattle, sheep, or pigs before Spanish times. They did include in their diets turtle, manatee, iguana, fresh seafood, and many small animals that roam the jungle.

GASTRONOMICAL ADVENTURE

Taste as many different dishes as possible! You'll be introduced to spices that add a new dimension to your diet. Naturally, you won't be wild about everything—it takes a while to become accustomed to squid served in its own black ink, for instance. A hamburger might not taste like one from your favorite "fast foodery" back home. Be prepared to come into contact with many new and different tastes—you're in *Belize,* after all, a land of myriad cultures and cuisines. You will easily find Chinese, Mexican, Creole, and European dishes. Look for such delicacies as conch, conch soup, fried lobster, iguana, armadillo, shark, black beans and rice, great fried chicken, fried plantain, papaya, and don't turn your nose up if someone invites you to a "boil up" (seafood stew). Though turtle is an endangered species, the law allows fishermen to take them at certain times of the year, so you may also see turtle offered on a menu—but perhaps if no one buys them the fishermen will quit catching them in their nets!

Seafood

You won't travel far before realizing that one of the favorite Belize specialties is fresh fish. All along the Caribbean and Gulf coasts are opportunities to indulge in piscine delicacies: lobster, shrimp, red snapper, sea bass, halibut, barracuda, conch, and lots more prepared in a variety of ways. Even the tiniest cafe will prepare sweet, fresh fish.

Try the unusual conch *(kaahnk),* which has been a staple in the diet of the Mayan and Central American along the Caribbean coast for centuries. It's often used in ceviche. Some consider this raw fish; actually, it's marinated in lime juice with onions, peppers, and a host of spices—no longer raw, and very tasty! Another favorite conch is pounded, dipped in egg and then cracker crumbs, and sautéed quickly (like

cleaning conch, still an important staple along the Caribbean coast

abalone steak in California) with a squirt of fresh lime. Caution: If it's cooked too long it becomes tough and rubbery. Conch fritters are minced pieces of conch mixed into a flour batter and fried—delicious.

If you happen to be on a boat trip the crew will probably catch a fish and prepare it for lunch, maybe cooked over an open fire, or in a "boil up," seasoned with onions, peppers, and *achiote,* a fragrant red spice grown locally since the time of the early Maya.

Garifuna Style

A very ethnic way to prepare fish is to cook it in coconut milk and local spices; it's called *seri.* In many dishes plantain or green bananas are grated into various recipes, and seaweed is used now and then. All contribute to new and unique flavors.

Wild Game

Many ethnic groups in Belize are hunters, and if you explore the jungle paths very much, you'll see men and boys on foot or on bicycles with rifles slung over their shoulders and full game bags tied behind them. Jungle game varies. Wild duck is served during certain times of the year and is prepared in several ways that *must* be tried. Iguana is common, gibnut (a rabbitlike rodent) is said to be very tasty (I haven't tried it yet, but Queen Elizabeth has!), and the Maya eat a wide variety of wild game cooked in a spicy red sauce. If you're invited for dinner by a local Maya, don't be surprised to find the likes of crested guan, tinamou, brocket deer, peccary, armadillo, agouti, paca, turtle, iguana, and iguana eggs. This is the norm for people who live in and around the forest, although I didn't say it was all legal.

Hot Stuff!

All that grand Belizean fare wouldn't be authentic without a dash or two of Marie Sharp's hot sauce. You won't have to search far; it's at nearly every restaurant in the entire country. It comes in three levels of pungency: mild, hot, and fiery hot (believe them). But be careful, the taste grows on people. Some people take it back by the case.

Brewed in Belize

When it comes to "cases," many travelers wouldn't mind taking home a case or two of the local beer, Belikin. The familiar brown bottles with the white and green label are sold all over the country. Belikin also makes a very good premium beer and a marvelous stout. All three are every bit as good as most American beers and often are favorably compared to beers from the new microbreweries in the States. The official drinking age in Belize is 18.

Restaurants

Most small cafes that cater to Belizeans are open all day until about 10 p.m. Hotels with foreign tourists offer dinner early in the evening to cater to British, Canadian, and American tastes. Most hotels and restaurants add tax and a 20% service charge to the bill. It's still gracious to leave a few coins for the waiter. If the tip isn't added to the bill, leaving 10% is customary.

Fried chicken is found on almost every menu in Belize, along with black beans and rice, which is

---

SAVE THE LOBSTER

Since the influx of tourists into the small country of Belize, a very big concern has been the safety of the lobster beds off the coast, which have provided food and support for the locals for many years. Because the price of a lobster dinner in Caye Caulker, for instance, is so much cheaper than in the U.S., the demand has increased rapidly. To keep tourists happy, a few fishermen supply the restaurants open season or closed, legal size or not! The population of lobster cannot continue to flourish with these illegal activities, and the collapse of the Belizean fishing industry will follow.

As a responsible traveler, you are urged not to order lobster during the closed season, which is 15 February-15 June. Also, if (during the open season) a restaurant is offering a lobster dinner for BZE$7-8, it is most likely a "short," which means it is under legal size. Minimum size for a lobster tail is four ounces. Ask around town for restaurants that sell legal-size tails, and then patronize them with a positive comment about saving the lobster.

All of the above advice goes for the conch as well. Closed season for conch is 1 July-30 September, and the minimum size is three ounces of meat.

considered a "typical" dinner. Some of the more local restaurants offer gibnut, a rabbitlike rodent that was served to Queen Elizabeth when she visited some years back, causing British newspapers to print half-page headlines stating the queen was served rat in Belize. Oh, well; newspapers go to any lengths to be noticed.

A ploy many seasoned adventurers use when they're tired of eating cold food from their backpacks: in a village where no cafes exist go to the local pub, grocery store, church, or city hall and ask if there's a housewife in town who, for a fee, would be willing to include you at her dinner table. Almost always you'll find someone, usually at a fair price (determine price when you make your deal). With any luck you'll find a woman renowned for her cooking. You'll gain a lot more than food in this arrangement; the cultural swap is priceless.

Food Safety
When preparing your own food in the backcountry, remember that a few possible sources of bacteria are fresh fruit and vegetables, especially those with thin, unpeeled skin, such as tomatoes or leafy vegetables, such as lettuce. When washing these foods in local water (and they should definitely be washed thoroughly before consuming), add either bleach or iodine (8-10 drops per quart) to the water, unless of course you carry your own portable filtering system. Soaking vegetables together in a container or plastic bag for about 20 minutes is easy; carrying along zipper-lock plastic bags is essential. If you're at the beach and short of water, substitute sea water (for everything but drinking). Remember not to rinse the bleached food with contaminated water; just pat dry, and if it has a distasteful lingering flavor, a squirt of lime juice tastes great and is very healthy. Some foods nature has packaged hygienically; a banana has its own protective seal so is considered safe (luckily, since they're so abundant in Belize). Foods that are cooked well are also considered safe if eaten immediately.

HEALTH AND SAFETY

TRAVELER'S DISEASE

Some travelers to foreign countries worry about getting sick the moment they leave their own country. But with a few simple precautions, it's not a foregone conclusion that you'll come down with something. The most common illness to strike visitors is traveler's disease, known by many names but, in plain Latin, it's diarrhea. No fun, it can cause uncomfortable cramping, fever, dehydration, and the need to stay close to a toilet for a few days. It's caused by, among other things, various strains of bacteria managing to find your innards, so it's important to be very careful about what goes into your mouth.

Studies show that the majority of tourists who get sick do so on the third day of their visit, and that traveler's illness is common in every country. They say that in addition to bacteria, a change in diet is equally to blame and suggest that the visitor slip slowly into the eating habits of the country, especially if the food tends to be spicy. In other words, don't blast your tummy with the habanero or jalapeño pepper right off the bat. Work into the fried food, drinks, local specialties, and new spices gradually; take your time changing over to foods you may never eat while at home, including the large quantities of wonderful tropical fruits that you'll want to eat in some countries. Also beware mixing alcohol with longer-than-usual periods of time in the tropical sun. Alchohol changes the body chemistry and it becomes very difficult to handle excessive heat.

It's the Water
While the above theories are often valid, water is probably the worst culprit. According to locals, the water from the faucet in Belize City is safe, but smaller villages and more isolated areas are still "iffy"—you'd be wise to take special precautions. A good rule of thumb: if you're not sure about the water, ask the locals or the desk clerk at your hotel; they'll let you know the status. Hotels prefer healthy guests—they'll return. If you are in an area where water is a problem, you have two options. Drink bottled water if available, or drink car-

bonated beverages without ice. The carbonation lowers the pH enough to make it inhospitable for microorganisms to grow and live.

In the backcountry, hikers may want to carry their own water and then, whether the source is out of the tap or a crystal-clear pond, boil it or purify it with chemicals. That goes for brushing your teeth as well. If you have nothing else, a bottle of beer will make a safe (though maybe not sane) mouth rinse. If using ice, ask where it was made and if it's pure. Think about the water you're swimming in; you might want to avoid some small local pools.

The easiest way to purify the water is with purification tablets; **Hidroclonozone** and **Halazone** are two, but many brands are available at drugstores in all countries. Or carry a small plastic bottle of liquid bleach (use 8-10 drops per quart of water) or iodine (use five to seven drops per quart) to purify the water. Whichever you use, let the water stand for 20 minutes to improve the flavor. Boiling the water for 20-30 minutes will purify it as well. Even though it takes a heck of a lot of fuel that you'll probably have to carry on your back, don't get lazy in this department. You can get very sick drinking contaminated water,

which you can't identify by its appearance—unless you travel with a microscope!

Giardiasis

Giardia is a parasite that can be present in streams and ponds almost anyplace in the world. You can destroy it by boiling the water. However, if fuel is a problem, you can treat the water with iodine. The amount and most efficient form of iodine (crystals or liquid?) to use are up for debate, so check with your doctor. An inexpensive water treatment kit that uses crystalline iodine is available from Recreational Equipment Incorporated. For more information, write Box 88125, Seattle, Washington 98138-0125; tel. (800) 426-4840. The company also offers the more expensive Swiss-made Katadyn PF Pocket Water Filter for those who cannot tolerate iodine for either taste or thyroid reasons. Outdoor supply shops are a good place to check for the latest in portable water purifiers.

Camping

When camping on the beach where fresh water is scarce, use sea water to wash dishes and even yourself. Before leaving home, check at a sporting goods or marine shop for **Sea Saver**

QWITCHER ITCHIN'

It's no fun to have a mosquito bite or two or a dozen. But if you're planning a trip to the tropics you say it's almost inevitable?—well not necessarily! Beware: a mosquito bite can be more than an annoyance; it can be the introduction to a particularly nasty ailment, malaria. But you can fight back against these flying, buzzing critters.

First of all, check with the Centers for Disease Control and Prevention, tel. (404) 639-1610, or with a physician who specializes in tropical diseases. They can advise you about the area you're going to visit. If it happens that you're going into a malaria-infected zone, you can take precautions. It used to be a simple matter of popping a quinine pill once a week and not to worry. But in some areas mosquitoes have developed a resistance to the common medications. Medication is still important. However, if you can avoid getting bitten in the first place, that's the way to go.

A few suggestions and a few facts to keep in mind about the mosquito:

• Wear shoes and high socks when trekking through jungle terrain. Sandals and bare feet invite trouble.

• Wear clothing with high necks and long sleeves, dark rather than light colors, and remember: the mosquito can bite right through sheer fabric.

• Leave the shiny, sparkly jewelry back at the hotel; avoid cologne, after-shave, and aromatic lotions.

• When you plan your day, remember that the worst time to be out among the beasties is at dusk and in the evening. In *most* cases, daytime trekking avoids the pests.

• Don't leave your clothes on the ground; but if you do, give them a good shake before putting them back on. Same goes for shoes.

Soap. (A rub of bar soap on the bottom of pots and pans before setting them over an open fire makes for easy cleaning after cooking.)

Other Sources of Infection

Money can be a source of germs. Wash your hands frequently, don't put your fingers in your mouth, and carry individual foil packets of disinfectant cleaners, such as Wash Up, which are handy and refreshing in the tropic heat. Hepatitis is another bug that you can contract easily if you're around it.

When in backcountry cafes, remember that fruits and vegetables, especially those with a thin edible skin (such as tomatoes), are a possible source of bacteria. If you like to eat street vendors' food (and some shouldn't be missed), use common sense. If you see the food being cooked (killing all the grubby little bacteria) before your eyes, have at it. If it's hanging there already cooked and being nibbled on by small flying creatures, pass it by. It may have been there all day, and what was once a nice sterile morsel could easily have gone bad in the heat, or been contaminated by flies. Be cautious of hotel buffets; raw shellfish, potato salad, and other cream-based salads may have been sitting out for hours—a potential bacteria source unless they are well-iced. When buying food at the marketplace to cook for yourself, use the hints given in "Food Safety" under "Food" above.

Treatment

Remember, it's not just the visitor who gets sick from bacteria. Each year locals die from the same germs, and the government is working hard to remedy the sanitation problems. Tremendous improvements ultimately will be accomplished all over Belize, but it's a slow process. In the meantime, many careful visitors come and go each year with nary a touch of the trots. If after all your precautions you still come down with traveler's illness, many medications are available for relief. You can buy most over the counter, but in the U.S. you may need a prescription from your doctor. **Lomotil** and **Imodium** anti-diarrheal medications are common and certainly turn off the faucet after a few hours of dosing; however, they have the side effect of becoming a plug. These medications do not cure the problem, only the symptoms; if you quit taking it too soon your symptoms reappear and you're back to square one. In their favor, Lomotil and Imodium work faster than **Pepto Bismol** or **Kaopectate** anti-diarrheals, and if you're about to embark on a seven-hour bus ride to Placencia you might consider either one of those "quick-stop" drugs a lifesaver. **Note:** Imodium no longer requires a prescription; Lomotil, however, does.

If you're concerned, check with your doctor before leaving home. Also ask the doctor about antibiotics to treat bacterial causes of diarrhea such as **Septra** and **Bactrim** (trimethoprim-sulfamethoxazole) or **Cipro** (ciprofloxacin), which may prove to be better against organisms with resistance to Bactrim or Septra. You should take antibiotics only if you develop diarrhea, not as prophylaxis. Something else to be aware of: Pepto Bismol can turn the tongue a dark brownish color —nothing to be alarmed about.

If you are caught unprepared and continue to have diarrhea, please be careful about dehydration, especially for infants and children. Aside from losing water, you lose cations and ions, which places a strain on the whole body system. Rehydration is key. Oral Rehydration Solution packets that you can buy where first-aid kits are sold contain glucose and various salts that aid intestinal absorption of water and critical ions. All you do is add purified water per the specific instructions.

For those who prefer natural remedies, lime juice and garlic are both considered good when taken as preventatives. They need to be taken in large quantities. Douse everything with the readily available lime juice (it's delicious on salads, fresh fruit, and in drinks). You'll have to figure your own ways of using garlic (some believers carry garlic capsules, available in most health-food stores in the U.S.). Fresh coconut juice is said to help (don't eat the oily flesh; it makes your problem worse!). Plain, boiled white rice soothes the tummy. While letting the ailment run its course, stay away from spicy and oily foods and fresh fruits. Drink plenty of pure water. Don't be surprised if you have chills, nausea, vomiting, stomach cramps, and run a fever. This could go on for about three days. But if the problem persists, or worsens (the diarrhea becomes bloody, the fever exceeds 102° F, the vomiting persists), or you still have symptoms of dehydration, *please* see a doctor.

INSECT REPELLENT

There are many insect repellents around, some better than others. Read the labels and ask questions. Some formulas were designed to spray the outdoors, some a room, others your clothes—none of these are for the skin. Some repellents are harmful to plants and animals, some can dissolve watch crystals, and others can damage plastic eyeglass lenses. This can be a particular problem if labels are written in a foreign language that you cannot read. It's best to bring your repellent from home.

Many of the most efficient repellents contain diethyl-toluamide (DEET). Test it before you leave home; the more concentrated solutions can cause an allergic reaction in some people, and for children a milder mix is recommended. Avoid use on skin with sores and abrasions.

Long Road Travel Supplies has come up with the Travel Tent. This lightweight, portable, net housing is made of ultrafine mesh netting and fits right on top of the bed. A nylon floor and lightweight poles provide you with a roomy rectangular shape and free-standing protection from flying and crawling insects that can make sleeping impossible. It's convenient with a zipper door, folding flap for extra footroom, and an inside pocket for keeping valuables close at hand. Packed in its own carrying bag, and weighing just 2.3 pounds (for single bed), it costs US$79; a double weighs 2.8 pounds and costs US$99. Ask about the budget-priced Indoor Tent II with a drawstring door; single size is US$59 and weighs 1.25 pounds. And now a new product: a **Net Canopy** that's easy to pack (comes in its own carrybag), and easy to hang over a sleeper or even

two. It comes with a simple mechanism that's simple to use on the road. The price is US$69. For more info, contact **Long Road Travel Supplies,** Box 9497, Berkeley, CA 94709, tel. (800) 359-6040 or (510) 540-4763.

When using repellents, remember:

• If redness and itching begin, wash off with soap and water.

• Apply repellent by pouring into the palms of your hands, then rubbing together and applying evenly to the skin. If you're sweating reapply every two hours. Use caution if perspiration mixed with repellent runs down your forehead and into your eyes—an absorbent headband helps.

• If you swim, reapply after coming out of the water.

• It's helpful to either dip your socks, or spray them heavily, or (as suggested by the World Health Organization) dip strips of cotton cloth two or three inches wide and wrap them around your lower legs. One strip is effective for several weeks. Mosquitoes hover close to the ground in many areas.

• Apply liberally around the edges of your sleeves, pants cuffs, or shorts cuffs.

• Sleeping in an air-conditioned room with tight-fitting windows is one good way to avoid nighttime buzzing attacks; in other situations use a mosquito net over the bed. It helps if the netting has been dipped in repellent, and make sure it's large enough to tuck well under the mattress. A rectangular shape is more efficient than the usual conical, giving you more room to sit up so you'll avoid contact with the critters that might bite through the net.

OTHER DISEASES

Many animals—cats, dogs, iguanas, birds—carry more than your average tick. A good rule of thumb: don't handle the animals.

You can acquire parasites through contact with contaminated soil, sand, water, food, or insects. Generally they enter through the skin or by being inadvertently eaten. Simple steps will help keep your exposure to them at a minimum. Wear shoes/sandals even at the beach. If you love to sunbathe on the sand, have a beach towel under you. Use insect repellent to avoid other insects such as mosquitoes, "kissing" bugs, and biting flies (see below). Symptoms of a parasite infection include but are not limited to the following: fever, rashes, swollen lymph nodes, digestive problems, eye problems, or anemia. These will not all necessarily appear while you are traveling, but may take several weeks or months to develop.

Malaria

Avoid mosquito bites: Prevention is key. This is important not only for malaria, but for dengue fever and especially for yellow fever, which has no specific therapy. No yellow fever immunization is required for travelers entering Belize except for those from countries where it is endemic, such as South America and parts of Africa. Yellow fever in Central America fortunately is rare. Dengue fever, however, occurs naturally in the region and is usually transmitted by mosquitoes that bite in the day, just the opposite of those that transmit malaria. Travelers are usually at low risk except during epidemics.

Use insect repellent that contains DEET (N,N-Diethyl metatoluamide). For adults, 30-35% DEET formulas are appropriate, for children, 6-10% DEET. Apply it to any exposed skin surfaces, including the back of the hands, feet, ankles, ears, and neck.

For those of you trekking into forest or jungle, one can also buy bednets and clothing soaked or sprayed with permethrin, another insect repellent that lasts on the order of weeks to a few months. You can buy these items at military surplus, hardware, or backpacking supply stores.

Please note that Belize does have programs for vector control and testing of the populace.

Records show that there were approximately 10,000 cases of malaria in 1994. A large share were accounted for by people from neighboring countries who moved to Belize. The regions most affected were Cayo District, Northern District, Stann Creek District, and Belize District.

As for medical prevention, consult your doctor. In Central America, prophylaxis is usually adequate with Aralen (Chloroquine). The regimen is to take it once a week beginning one week before the trip, through the trip, and then for four more weeks after returning. Side effects are rare and usually do not require discontinuing the drug. They include upset stomach, headache, dizziness, blurred vision, and itching.

Other Parasites

The "kissing bug," also known as the assassin bug, spreads Chagas' disease, or American trypanosomiasis. The insect spreads the disease when it contaminates the bite wound with its own infected feces. The one-inch bug prefers to bite its victims while they sleep; the bugs drop from their hiding places in thatch or other rural houses. The bite is followed by fever and swollen glands. Early treatment with drugs can rid the victim of the parasite, so see a doctor immediately. Untreated, it can damage the heart and other organs years later.

Although it poses almost no risk to most travelers, watch out for the flesh-eating screwworm if you have open wounds. Primarily an affliction of livestock, the female screwworm fly lays up to 300 eggs on open wounds so its larva can feed on the flesh. Without treatment, it can be fatal. Scientists have rid the U.S. and Mexico of the pest by releasing sterile male flies; they are trying to push the screwworm out of Central America as far as Panama.

The annoying botfly is much more likely to plague the traveler. It is unsightly, painful, but not dangerous and easy to treat. It burrows under the skin; you either have to draw it out or squeeze it out. (See "Insects and Arachnids" under "Fauna.")

Hepatitis A

Hepatitis A is a virus transmitted by the fecal-oral route and so occurs in areas of poor sanitation. It can be transmitted by person-to-person contact, contaminated water, raw shellfish, uncooked fruits or vegetables. Symptoms include fatigue, fever, poor appetite, nausea, vomiting, dark urine, light-colored stools, aches, pains. As with yellow fever, there is no specific therapy. Prevention generally is the same as for preventing traveler's disease and includes washing your hands before you eat. The CDC recommends a shot of gamma globulin to protect yourself before your trip.

SUNBURN

Sunburn can spoil a vacation quicker than anything else, so approach the sun cautiously. Expose yourself for short periods the first few days; wear a hat and sunglasses. Apply a good sunscreen to all exposed areas of the body (don't forget your feet, hands, nose, ears, back of knees, and top of forehead—especially if you have a receding hairline). Remember that after every time you go into the water, sunscreen lotion must be reapplied. Even after a few days of desensitizing the skin, wear a T-shirt in the water to protect your exposed back, especially if you spend the day snorkeling, and thoroughly douse the back of your neck with sunscreen lotion. PABA—para-aminobenzoic acid—solutions offer good protection and condition the skin. PABA is found in many brand names and strengths, and is much cheaper in the U.S. than in Belize. **Note:** Some people are allergic to PABA and it is said to cause cancer in isolated cases; check with your doctor before using. The higher the number on sunscreen bottles the more protection.

If, despite precautions, you still get a painful sunburn, do not return to the sun. Cover up with clothes if it's impossible to find protective deep shade (like that in the depths of a dark, thick forest). Keep in mind that even in partial shade (such as under a beach umbrella), the reflection of the sun off the sand or water will burn your skin. Reburning the skin can result in painful blisters that easily become infected. Soothing suntan lotions, coconut oil, vinegar, cool tea, and preparations such as Solarcaine sunburn relief products will help relieve the pain. Usually a couple of days out of the sun will cure it. Drink plenty of liquids (especially water) and take tepid showers (see the special topic "Simple First-Aid Guide" in this chapter).

HEALING

Most cities in Belize have a medical clinic. More than likely someone there speaks English. In the bigger cities you can usually find a doctor who will make a house call. When staying in a hotel, get a doctor quickly by asking the hotel manager; in the larger resorts, an English-speaking doctor is on call 24 hours a day. A taxi driver can be your quickest way to get to a clinic when you're a stranger in town. In small rural villages, if you have a serious problem and no doctor is around, you can usually find a *curandero*. These healers deal with the old natural methods (and maybe just a few chants thrown in for good measure). This person could be helpful in a desperate situation away from modern technology. Locals who live in the dense, jungle areas inhabited by poisonous snakes go to the local "snake doctor." Again, this might be a possibility in a remote emergency situation where you need help quickly, and yet, medical people say every time, *no matter what,* don't go to a snake doctor. A **Cutter's Snake Bite Kit** can be helpful if used immediately after a bite, though its use is controversial in medical circles because of the risk of infection. Making the cut and sucking the poison out through it could pass germs into the open wound.

Ancient Healing

A delightful lady from Chicago, Rosita Arvigo, and her husband, Greg Shropshire, have been practicing the ancient Maya art of healing for some years. Both are graduates of Chicago National College of Naprapathy; Rosita is a professor of botanical studies and has been a practicing herbalist for more than 20 years. She continues to be intrigued with the study and exploration of nature's healing herbs. For some years in Belize's Cayo District, Rosita was a student of Don Eligio Panti, a 100-year-old Maya bush doctor who has spent most of his life healing people using only the ancient Maya method plus added techniques learned from a Carib Indian during the chicle days of the 1930s. Today Rosita is his assistant. She and Don Eligio are trying very hard to keep the ancient ways alive, especially valuable because only a few Maya remember the old

Rosita Arvigo with Don Eligio Panti, a revered Belizean bush doctor who perpetuates Maya healing methods

ways. In most cases only one or two people in each group knew these ancient secrets and often they were handed down within the family. This part of the culture has dimmed over the years with the intrusion of modern medicine, which often isn't available to most of the Maya, either by choice or by circumstances.

Rosita has been recording Don Eligio's therapies, treatments, and remedies so that future generations of his people (and the world) will always have access to their effectiveness. Rosita offers her services to anyone who is willing to travel to her home, **Ix Chel Farm,** in Cayo. She is also well-known for nature walks through her forest property (for a fee), where she introduces many of the plants used in Maya treatment; strolling lectures bring the old ways into the modern world with a knowledgeable, humorous, humanitarian outlook on life. With her contagious enthusiasm, Rosita brings to life information that otherwise might be pedestrian.

While walking the **Panti Trail,** a lovely path through the woods at Ix Chel Farm, visitors

learn about the medicinal or healing value of various roots, vines, plants, and trees; each has a sign with its name. A booklet explains the use of each one. Here visitors will see the **grapevine** that provides pure water to cleanse the navel of a newborn infant; the bark of the negrito tree, also called **dysentery bark,** that treats severe dysentery (and that was sold for high prices by druggists in Europe when pirates discovered it many years past). Tea made from the **China root** is used for blood building after an attack from parasites. Another tea made from **ki bix** acts as birth control by coating the lining of the uterus.

With Rosita, her assistant, or with just the small guidebook, you will discover fruit and food sources that made it possible for the Maya of old to glean a good part of daily subsistence from the jungle. The breadnut (also known as the Ramon Tree), tasting something like a cross between a potato and a chestnut, served the Maya well for centuries when the corn crop was minimal. It can be stored up to a year, roasted over coals and eaten plain, or ground up and used to make tortillas.

This is just a tiny sampling of the information Rosita shares with her guests, plus folksy anecdotes about her experiences as a bush healer. The most recent excitement is working with scientists who come from the U.S. and other countries to Ix Chel, and with Rosita and Greg, spend weeks gathering bushels of certain barks and leaves for experimentation to find a cure for cancer and the AIDS virus. If you have a problem with mosquito or other bug bites that drive you crazy with itching, buy a vial of Rosita's **Jungle Salve;** it works! For more information about Ix Chel Farm and Rosita (see "Sights" under "San Ignacio") write to Rosita Arvigo, General Delivery, San Ignacio, Cayo District, Belize, C.A.; in Cayo, dial (92) 2267.

Self-Help

The smart traveler carries a first-aid kit of some kind. If backpacking, at least carry a minimal first-aid kit:

- ✓ adhesive tape
- ✓ insect repellent
- ✓ alcohol
- ✓ Lomotil or Immodium

- ✓ antibiotic ointment
- ✓ aspirin
- ✓ pain killer
- ✓ baking soda
- ✓ sterile, adhesive strips
- ✓ sunscreen
- ✓ cornstarch
- ✓ tweezers
- ✓ gauze
- ✓ water-purification tablets
- ✓ hydrogen peroxide
- ✓ iodine
- ✓ needle

Many first-aid products are widely available, but certain items, such as aspirin and plastic bandages, are sold individually in small shops and are much cheaper if bought in your home-town. Even if not out in the wilderness you should carry at least a few sterile strips, aspirin, and an antibiotic ointment or powder or both. Travelers should be aware that in the tropics, with its heavy humidity, a simple scrape can become infected more easily than in a dry climate. So keep cuts and scratches as clean and as dry as possible.

Another great addition to your first-aid kit is David Werner's book, *Where There Is No Doctor*. You can order it from the Hesperian Foundation, Box 1692, Palo Alto, California 94302. David Werner drew on his experience living in Mexico's backcountry to create this practical, informative book. Also useful is Dirk Schroeder's *Staying Healthy in Asia, Africa, and Latin America*, from Moon Publications.

Centers For Disease Control

Check on your tetanus shot before you leave home. If you anticipate backpacking in jungle regions, call the **International Traveler's Hotline** at the **Centers For Disease Control and Prevention,** tel. (404) 332-4559. This hotline advises callers of the conditions abroad, what areas are experiencing an outbreak of disease, and will make suggestions for immunizations. It is updated as conditions warrant. A booklet also is available, *Health Information for International Travelers,* from the U.S. Government Printing Office. To obtain a copy, send US$5 to the Superintendent of Documents, U.S. Government Printing Office, Washington, D.C. 20402.

BE SENSIBLE~STAY SAFE

Leave expensive jewelry at home. Don't flaunt cameras and video equipment or leave them in sight in cars when sightseeing, especially in some parts of Belize City. Remember, this is a poor country and petty theft is its number-one crime—don't tempt fate. (As in London, the police don't carry guns.) It is also wise not to wander around alone on foot late at night in Belize City—for the same reasons. Go out, but take a taxi. Most of the Belizeans are friendly decent people but, as in every community, a small percentage will steal anything—given the opportunity. Expect to be hustled, whether in the market, a cafe, or a bar. To the Belizeans, Americans and Canadians come off as "rich" whether they are or not. The local hustlers are quite creative when it comes to thinking of ways to con you out of some cash. Keep your wits about you, pull out of conversations that appear headed in that direction, and remember—you're in their country. Don't give out your hotel or room number freely or where they can be overheard by strangers. Don't be surprised if someone tries to sell you a controlled substance on the street; if you buy, don't be surprised if the same guy turns you in to the local authorities and earns a payoff. The police come down heavily on substance users in Belize. All of this advice is valid in Paris, downtown Los Angeles, Jakarta, and many other large cities throughout the world.

The Belize Tourist Board has issued the following list of common-sense safety tips to help visitors.

Traveler Safety Tips

It's always prudent to get the lay of the land upon arrival. Once you strike out, be reasonably sure of your destination and have a clear idea of how to get there before departing.

Always be aware of your surroundings and keep to the main streets if you have to walk. Avoid walking alone in unknown neighborhoods.

It's best not to wear expensive jewelry when traveling. And, don't carry large amounts of money, passport, or plane tickets if not necessary; if you must carry these things, wear a moneybelt under your clothes. Most hotels have safety deposit boxes.

At night, take a taxi between locations. Throughout Belize taxis can be identified by their green license plates.

In Belize City taxi prices are set. Ask your bellman, receptionist, bus driver, or other service personnel for directions and taxi prices before proceeding to your next destination.

When driving alone at night in isolated areas (which isn't too smart), use good sense, lock your doors, and keep windows up. Always keep your valuables locked in the trunk or glove compartment. And picking up strangers isn't guaranteed anywhere; only you can decide that

one. (We pick up plenty of hitchhikers in Latin America, but we are selective when we make that instant decision—usually backpackers with heavy packs get our sympathy). We try to stay off the road at night.

In the rare event that a stranger approaches you and demands your valuable items, remember that "things" can be replaced!

On any public transport, keep your belongings close by.

In emergencies, yes, you can dial 911 for police assistance; fire 90; ambulance 90.

SIMPLE FIRST-AID GUIDE

Acute Allergic Reaction
This, the most serious complication of insect bites, can be fatal. Common symptoms are hives, rash, pallor, nausea, tightness in the chest or throat, and trouble speaking or breathing. Be alert for symptoms. If they appear, get prompt medical help. Start CPR if needed and continue until medical help is available.

Animal Bites
Bites, especially on the face and neck, need immediate medical attention. If possible, catch and hold the animal for observation, taking care not to be bitten again. Wash the wound with soap and water (hold under running water for two to three minutes unless bleeding heavily). Do not use iodine or other antiseptic. Bandage. This also applies to bites by human beings. In case of human bites the danger of infection is high. (See also "Rabies" and "Snakebites.")

Bee Stings
Apply cold compresses quickly. If possible, remove the stinger by gently scraping with a clean fingernail and continue cold applications till pain is gone. Be alert for symptoms of acute allergic reaction or infection requiring medical aid.

Bleeding
For severe bleeding apply direct pressure to the wound with a bandage or the heel of the hand. Do not remove cloths when blood-soaked; just add others on top and continue pressure until bleeding stops. Elevate bleeding part above heart level. If bleeding continues, apply a pressure bandage to

arterial points. Do not put on tourniquet unless advised by a physician. Do not use iodine or other disinfectant. Get medical aid.

Blister on Heel
It is better not to open a blister if you can rest the foot. If you can't, wash the foot with soap and water, make a small hole at the base of the blister with a needle sterilized in 70% alcohol or by holding the needle in the flame of a match, drain fluid, and cover with strip bandage or moleskin. If a blister breaks on its own, wash with soap and water, bandage, and be alert for signs of infection (redness, festering) that call for medical attention.

Burns
Minor burns (redness, swelling, pain): apply cold water or immerse burned part in cold water immediately. Use burn medication if necessary. Deeper burns (blisters develop): immerse in cold water (not ice water) or apply cold compresses for one to two hours. Blot dry and protect with a sterile bandage. Do not use antiseptic, ointment, or home remedies. Consult a doctor. For deep burns (skin layers destroyed, skin may be charred): cover with sterile cloth; be alert for breathing difficulties and treat for shock if necessary. Do not remove clothing stuck to burn. Do not apply ice. Do not use burn remedies. Get medical help quickly.

Cuts
Wash small cuts with clean water and soap. Hold wound under running water. Bandage. Use hydrogen peroxide or other antiseptic. For large wounds see

"Bleeding." If a finger or toe has been cut off, treat severed end to control bleeding. Put severed part in a clean cloth for the doctor (it may be possible to reattach it by surgery). Treat for shock if necessary. Get medical help at once.

Diving Accident

There may be injury to the cervical spine (such as a broken neck). Call for medical help. (See also "Drowning.")

Drowning

Clear airway and start CPR even before trying to get water out of lungs. Continue CPR till medical help arrives. In case of vomiting, turn victim's head to one side to prevent inhaling vomitus.

Food Poisoning

Symptoms appear a varying number of hours after eating and are generally like those of the flu—headache, diarrhea, vomiting, abdominal cramps, fever, and a general sick feeling. See a doctor. A rare form, botulism, has a high fatality rate. Symptoms are double vision, inability to swallow, difficulty in speaking, and respiratory paralysis. Get to a hospital at once.

Fractures

Until medical help arrives, do not move the victim unless absolutely necessary. Suspected victims of back, neck, or hip injuries should not be moved. Suspected breaks of arms or legs should be splinted to avoid further damage before victim is moved, if moving is necessary.

Heat Exhaustion

Symptoms are cool, moist skin, profuse sweating, headache, fatigue, and drowsiness with essentially normal body temperature. Remove the victim to cool surroundings, raise the feet and legs, loosen clothing and apply cool cloths. Give sips of salt water—one teaspoon of salt to a glass of water—for rehydration. If the victim vomits, stop fluids and take the victim to a hospital as soon as possible.

Heat Stroke

Rush the victim to a hospital. Heat stroke can be fatal. The victim may be unconscious or severely confused. The skin feels hot and is red and dry with no perspiration. Body temperature is high. Pulse is rapid. Remove the victim to cool area and sponge with cool water or rubbing alcohol: use fans or a/c and wrap in wet sheets, but do not overchill. Massage arms and legs to increase circulation. Do not give large amounts of liquids. Do not give liquids if victim is unconscious.

Insect Bites

Be alert for an acute allergic reaction that requires quick medical aid. Otherwise, apply cold compresses and soothing lotions. If bites are scratched and infection starts (fever, swelling, redness), see a doctor. (See also "Spider Bites," "Bee Stings," and "Ticks.")

Jellyfish Stings

The symptom is acute pain and may include a feeling of paralysis. Immerse in ice water for 5-10 minutes or apply aromatic spirits of ammonia to remove venom from skin. Be alert for symptoms of acute allergic reaction and/or shock. If this happens, get the victim to a hospital as soon as possible.

Mosquito Bites

See "Insect Bites."

Motion Sickness

Get a prescription from your doctor if you anticipate boat traveling and this illness is a problem. Many over-the-counter remedies are sold in the United States: Bonine and Dramamine are examples. If you prefer not to take chemicals or if these make you drowsy, then something new, the Sea Band, might work for you. It's a cloth band that you place around the pressure point of the wrists. For more information write:

> Sea Band
> 1645 Palm Beach Lake Blvd.
> Ste. 220
> W. Palm Beach, Florida 33401

Medication that's administered in adhesive patches behind the ear is also available by prescription from your doctor.

Muscle Cramps

Usually a result of unaccustomed exertion, the cramp can be relieved by "working" the muscle or kneading it with the hand. If in water, head for shore (you can swim even with a muscle cramp), or knead the muscle with your hand. Call for help if needed. Do not panic.

(CONTINUED ON NEXT PAGE)

Mushroom Poisoning

Even a small ingestion may be serious. Induce vomiting immediately if there is any question of mushroom poisoning. Symptoms—vomiting, diarrhea, difficulty breathing—may begin in one to two hours or up to 24 hours. Convulsions and delirium may develop. Go to a doctor or hospital at once.

Nosebleed

Press bleeding nostril closed, pinch nostrils together, or pack with sterile cotton or gauze. Apply cold cloth or ice to nose and face. The victim should sit up, leaning forward, or lie down with head and shoulders raised. If bleeding does not stop in 10 minutes, get medical help.

Obstructed Airway

Ask if the victim can talk. If so, encourage the victim to try to cough up the obstruction. If the victim cannot speak, a trained person must apply the Heimlich maneuver. If you are alone and choking, try to forcefully cough object out. Or press your fist into your upper abdomen with a quick upward thrust, or lean forward and quickly press your upper abdomen over any firm object with a rounded edge (the back of a chair, the edge of a sink, or a porch railing). Keep trying until the object comes out.

Plant Poisoning

Many plants are poisonous if eaten or chewed. Induce vomiting immediately. Take the victim to a hospital for treatment. If the leaves of the diffenbachia (common in the Yucatán jungle) are chewed, one of the first symptoms is swelling of the throat. (See also "Mushroom Poisoning.")

Poison Ivy, Poison Oak, or Poison Sumac

After contact, wash affected area with alkali-base laundry soap, lathering well. Have a poison-ivy remedy available in case itching and blisters develop.

Puncture Wounds

Usually caused by stepping on a tack or a nail, puncture wounds often do not bleed, so try to squeeze out some blood. Wash thoroughly with soap and water and apply a sterile bandage. Check with a doctor about tetanus. If pain, heat, throbbing, or redness develops, get medical attention at once.

Rabies

Bites from bats, raccoons, rats, or other wild animals are the most common threat of rabies today. Try to capture the animal, avoiding being bitten, so it can be observed; do not kill the animal unless necessary and try not to injure the head so the brain can be examined. If the animal can't be found, see a doctor, who may decide to use antirabies immunization. In any case, flush bite with water and apply a dry dressing; keep victim quiet and see a doctor as soon as possible. See also "Animal Bites."

Scrapes

Sponge scrapes with soap and water; dry. Apply antibiotic ointment or powder and cover with a nonstick dressing (or tape on a piece of cellophane). When healing starts, stop ointment and use antiseptic powder to help scab form. Ask a doctor about tetanus.

Shock

Shock can result from any kind of injury. Get immediate medical help. Symptoms may be pallor, a clammy feeling to the skin, shallow breathing, a fast pulse, weakness, or thirst. Loosen clothing, cover the victim with a blanket but do not apply other heat, and lay the person on the back with feet raised. If necessary, start CPR. Do not give water or other fluids.

Snakebite

If the snake is not poisonous, toothmarks usually appear in an even row (the bite of a poisonous lizard, the Gila monster, shows even tooth marks). Wash the bite with soap and water and apply a sterile bandage. See a doctor. If the snake is poisonous, puncture marks (one to six) can usually be seen. Kill the snake for identification if possible, taking care not to be bitten. Keep the victim quiet, and immobilize the bitten arm or leg, keeping it on a lower level than the heart. If possible, phone ahead to be sure antivenin is available and get medical treatment as soon as possible. Do not give alcohol in any form. If treatment must be delayed and a snakebite kit is available, use as directed.

Spider Bites

The black widow bite may produce only a light reaction at the place of the bite, but severe pain, a general sick feeling, sweating, abdominal cramps, and breathing and speaking difficulty may develop. The more dangerous brown recluse spider's venom produces a severe reaction at the bite, generally in two to eight hours, plus chills, fever, joint pain, nausea, and vomiting. Apply a cold compress to the bite in either case. Get medical aid quickly.

Sprain

Treat a sprain as a fracture until the injured part has been X-rayed. Raise the sprained ankle or other joint and apply cold compresses or immerse in cold water. If swelling is pronounced, try not to use the injured part till it has been X-rayed. Get prompt medical help.

Sunburn

For skin that is moderately red and slightly swollen, apply wet dressings of gauze dipped in a solution of one tablespoon baking soda and one tablespoon cornstarch to two quarts of cool water. Or take a cool bath with a cup of baking soda to a tub of water.

Sunburn remedies are helpful in relieving pain. See a doctor if the burn is severe.

Sunstroke

This is a severe emergency. See "Heat Stroke." Skin is hot and dry; body temperature is high. The victim may be delirious or unconscious. Get medical help immediately.

Ticks

Cover ticks with mineral oil or kerosene to exclude air and they will usually drop off or can be lifted off with tweezers in 30 minutes. To avoid infection, take care to remove the whole tick. Wash area with soap and water. Check with a doctor or the health department to see if deadly ticks are in the area.

Wasp Stings

See "Bee Stings."

GETTING THERE

Many travelers are under the misguided notion that a passport is not needed to travel to Belize—wrong. You *must* have a current passport, and you may be asked at the border to show a return ticket and ample money. You do not need a visa if you are a British Commonwealth subject or a citizen of Belgium, Denmark, Finland, Greece, Iceland, Italy, Liechtenstein, Luxembourg, Mexico, Spain, Switzerland, Tunisia, Turkey, the United States, or Uraguay, provided you have valid documents. Remember to save US$11.25 for **departure tax** when going home. Mostly the officials are suspicious of people who appear scruffy and are traveling with little luggage. They're trying to discourage hippie-type "substance"-oriented squatters.

BY AIR

Charles Lindbergh
Belize is a small country that, without a national airline, is dependent on foreign airlines to bring visitors from the U.S., Mexico, and the rest of Central America. However, this may change given the history of the commuter airlines within the country and how they have grown. To Be-

lizeans, flying in and out of Belize was a farfetched idea when American hero Charles Lindbergh paid a dramatic visit to the small Caribbean nation. At the time, 1927, Lindbergh was the world's most famous pilot, having completed his flight across the Atlantic nonstop from New York to Paris. It was shortly after his famous "Lindy Hop" that he paid a visit to Latin America in his ongoing effort to promote and develop commercial aviation. On his visit to Belize, the **Barracks Green** in Belize City served as his runway, and the sound of his well-known little craft, *The Spirit of St. Louis,* overhead attracted hundreds of curious spectators. This was an exciting event for Belizeans, the beginning of an idea that would develop into the important aviation industry that has since linked the isolated parts of Belize.

AIRLINE PASSENGERS

Remember to reconfirm your airline reservations 48 hours before your arrival and departure date whether it's a national or international flight; not all airline offices have a computerized reservation service.

Philip Goldson International Airport

Most travelers planning a visit to Belize arrive at Philip Goldson International Airport nine miles from Belize City in Ladyville. (Taxi fare to and from the international airport is about US$15.) Transport to Belize is getting easier every year. The international airport extended the runway and added a modern terminal building a few years ago. Inside are several vendors selling Belizean and Central American arts and crafts and a currency exchange. Upstairs there's an observation deck and a bar/restaurant that serves decent versions of local food. Downstairs in the departure area you'll find **Jet's Bar Departure Lounge** where the drinks are tall and owner Eden Holland is known to exchange

AIRLINES SERVING BELIZE

INTERNATIONAL AIRLINES

NAME	TELEPHONE	SERVICE
American Airlines	US (800) 624-6262 Canada (800) 433-7300	from Dallas, Ft. Worth, Miami
Continental Airlines	US (800) 231-0856 Canada (800) 525-0280	nonstop from Houston
Taca Airlines	US (800) 535-8780 Canada (800) 263-4039	from Houston, New Orleans, Miami, Los Angeles, New York Kennedy, and Washington Dulles

NATIONAL AIRLINES

NAME	TELEPHONE	SERVICE
Cari-Bee Air Service	(2) 44253	charters, domestic, international, ambulance
Island Air	(2) 31140, (26) 2435 fax (26) 2192	regular service: International, Municipal, San Pedro. Charters available (including Tikal)
Javier Flying Service	(2) 45332/35360 fax: (2) 62192	charters, domestic, international
Maya Airways	US (800) 422-3435 Texas (713) 440-1867 Belize (2) 44234 fax (2) 30031	scheduled: Belize Municipal, San Pedro, Belize International, Corozal, Caye Caulker, Dangriga, Big Creek, Punta Gorda, charters, ambulance
Su-Bec Air Service	(2) 30388	charters, domestic, international
Tropic Air	US (800) 422-3435 Belize (26) 2012/(2) 45671 fax (26) 2338	scheduled: Belize Municipal, San Pedro, Belize International charters, daily flights to Tikal

excess Belizean dollars back to U.S. for good customers—that's something the currency exchange won't do!

Board direct flights from **Louisiana, Texas, Florida, Cancún,** and several points in **Latin America** daily. Airlines serving Belize include **American, Continental,** and **Taca International.** Only charter flights serve visitors from Canada, and there are no nonstop flights from Europe.

As you fly into the international airport you'll notice abandoned hangars that once housed camouflaged British Harrier jets—the ones that take off and land vertically. Today there's a single active reminder of the role Britain played in giving the young country a chance to establish its own defense—a solitary military helicopter. The British do maintain a small presence here, however, training rotating contingents of recruits in the fine art of jungle warfare somewhere inland.

After clearing customs you'll be besieged by taxi drivers offering rides into town. If you are not being picked up by a resort or tour company and Belize City sounds interesting, you may opt for one of these or you may choose to cross the parking lot to choose from several rental car firms.

If you are connecting to a domestic flight or a flight to Tikal in Guatemala you probably walked past the plane you will soon fly on your way into the terminal. Domestic flights leave from the Belize City Municipal Airport, a 15-minute cab ride away, and are generally cheaper (see "Getting Around," below).

FROM MEXICO

Traveling to Belize via Mexico's state of Quintana Roo on the Yucatán Peninsula is an efficient way to arrive. Combining a vacation in both countries is economical and a way to see a little more than usual. Shop around for budget flights from the U.S. into Cancún or even Isla Cozumel (just a short ferry ride to Playa del Carmen and its efficient bus depot, then continue by bus). From Cancún it's immensely cheap and easy to travel the 218 miles by bus to Chetumal and then across the Rio Hondo.

The Rio Hondo forms a natural border between Quintana Roo and Belize. Chetumal is the only land link between the two countries and a departure point for Batty and Venus bus lines traveling to many points in Belize.

Henry Menzies Travel and Tours, Box 210, Corozal Town, Corozal District, Belize, C.A.; tel. (4) 22725/23414, runs a taxi service and has the run between Chetumal and Corozal down to a science. Henry guides first-timers across the border with great ease. Call a day or two in advance (if in Mexico). If possible don't wait to call from Chetumal; for some reason telephoning from here can be very difficult at times. And the problem is not the phone service in Belize, which is modern. Even with short notice, Henry will usually pick you up within the hour. The trip between Chetumal and Corozal takes about 20 minutes, including the border crossing. (No matter what your travel mode, don't go at peak times such as 8 a.m. or 5 p.m.—opening and closing hours— without expecting a long wait.) He will take you any place you'd like to go in Belize. Make fare arrangements before you climb in the cab. Henry

---

SEAPORTS OF ENTRY INTO BELIZE

If you plan on traveling aboard your own vessel, these are the towns of entry:

Belize City

Punta Gorda Town

San Pedro on Ambergris Caye

In San Pedro on Ambergris Caye, you can obtain clearance, but you must pay for a custom agent to fly from the mainland.

Boats are required to have:

The vessel's official documentation.

Clearance from the last port of call.

Three copies of the crew and passenger manifesto.

Three copies of stores used or list of cargo on board; if none, an imballast manifesto.

For more information contact the Belize Embassy in Washington, D.C., 2535 Massachusetts Ave. NW, Washington, D.C. 20008; tel. (202) 332-9636, fax (202) 332-6741 or Belize Government Tourism Office, tel. (800) 624-0686.

(top left) celebrating Garifuna Day, Dangriga;
(top right) Kulcha Shack kids, Seine Bight;
(bottom) Kulcha Shack drummers (photos by Oz Mallan)

(top left) Belize City street market;
(top right) conch shells after the harvest, Laughing Bird Caye;
(bottom) Hand-cranked ferries are common in the Belize countryside. (photos by Oz Mallan)

is a good, helpful driver and an excellent guide with a comfortable a/c van.

BY CAR

If your own vehicle is a low-slung sports car, leave it home. Off the three main highways roads are rough and potholed. When it rains, you'll heave through thick mud where tires have cut deep ridges. The hot tropical sun appears and dries it into cement mounds. The higher the car the better; 4WD is best. If traveling by car you'll need Belizean insurance bought on the Belize side of the border with Belizean dollars (a couple of insurance offices are close to the border and in Corozal).

Note for the RV buff or hardy driver: the route between Brownsville, Texas, and the border of Belize is just under 1,400 miles. If you don't stop to smell the flowers along the way, you can make the drive in a few days. The all-weather roads are paved, and the shortest route is through Mexico by way of Tampico, Veracruz, Villahermosa, Escarcega, and Chetumal.

However, the Mexican government has recently changed its rules for travelers who are passing through Mexico to another destination. Travelers must buy bonds to ensure that they will not sell their cars in Mexico (often done by U.S. car thieves). You buy the bond at the border when entering Mexico—you may use a credit card only—and you must exit at the same border crossing when leaving Mexico (which sounds simple, but isn't). I suggest you call a Mexico Government Tourism Office near you for more precise information; these rules change regularly.

BY BOAT

The *Indita Maya* scheduled ferry operates Tuesday and Friday between Punta Gorda and Puerto Barrios, Guatemala (about US$10). The ferry departs Punta Gorda at 2 p.m. It's also easy to find a small boat to make the trip on the alternate days. For ferry information, call (7) 22065. (See "Cruise Ships" under "Getting Around," below.)

GETTING AROUND

BY AIR

By far the fastest and easiest way to move around Belize is by plane. The three "major" airlines are **Island Air, Maya Airways,** and **Tropic Air.** Of these Maya and Tropic have the most planes and departures. Both Island Air and Tropic are based at San Pedro on Ambergris Caye. Maya is based at the Municipal Airport along the bay. Flying on any of these is always a great adventure. If you are leaving from the Municipal Airport the runway looks about as long as two or three football fields. With the steady seabreeze, however, getting airborne is a cinch. Other airstrips look more like strips of mown grass or a short abandoned roadway, but they work just fine. Because these are such small planes, you not only watch the pilot handle the craft, but you may get to sit next to him. Coming in for a landing, you have an excellent vantage point to observe the runway looming

larger on approach. Best of all, flying low and slow in these aircraft allows you to get a panoramic view of the barrier reef, cayes, coast, and jungle.

Recently the FAA disclosed that the safety oversight by the Belize government and several other countries do not meet agency standards for airlines flying into the United States. This has caused some understandable confusion and concern among travelers to Belize. For one thing, there are no Belizean passenger airlines flying to the States. Belizean commuter airlines all have an outstanding record of safety.

A parade of regular scheduled flights leave the Municipal and International airports for airstrips offshore at Ambergris Caye, Caye Caulker, and Caye Chapel. If the scheduled flight happens to be full, another will taxi up shortly and off you go. Flight times to the cayes are 15 minutes or less. Other less frequent flights fly the coast to Big Creek, Corozal, Dangriga, Placencia, and

Punta Gorda. Corozal takes about 45 minutes with a stop at Ambergris Caye. Punta Gorda will take about an hour with a stop or two along the way. Chartered flights can be made at any time and to less frequented stops: Lighthouse Reef Resort on Northern Caye, Belmopan and Central Farms near San Ignacio, Blancaneaux Lodge airport in the Mountain Pine Ridge, and Gallon Jug airport near Chan Chich. Ask your travel agent for schedules or request them directly: Island Air, tel. (501) 23-1140; Maya Airways, tel. (501) 27-7215, fax (501) 23-0585; Tropic Air, tel. (800) 422-3435, fax (713) 521-9674.

BY BUS

Probably the cheapest way to get around the country is the bus system, which, in most cases, is surprisingly good. Most buses offer regular schedules and run frequently; for longer trips it's best to reserve your seat the day before you wish to travel. Expect lively music in fairly modern vehicles where all the passengers have seats—some even show movies on longer trips. In most cases, standing is not allowed and the driver will pack passengers three to a seat if necessary. The exceptions are the afternoon buses to Punta Gorda.

Batty and **Venus** lines serve Belize and go into Mexico and Guatemala. Get information from Batty, 15 Mosul St., Belize City, Belize, C.A., tel. (2) 72025, fax (2) 78991; in Corozal (4) 23034. Get Venus bus line information on Magazine Road in Belize City, tel. (2) 73354/77390, or on 7th Ave. in Corozal, tel. (4) 22132. Both companies offer upscale charter tours as well.

Dawson Buses leave Cinderella Plaza for Crooked Tree. **Jex & Sons Buses** pick up passengers at the Batty Bus Terminal and go to Crooked Tree. **Urbina** buses travel from Belize City to Orange Walk, departing from Cinderella Plaza. Catch the **Z-Line** to go south to Dangriga and Punta Gorda, departing from the terminal on Magazine Road, tel. (2) 73937.

James' Bus service travels to the southern part of the country, leaving Belize City from the Pound Yard Bridge. To go west to Belmopan, San Ignacio, and on to the Guatemalan border, depart from the Batty depot on E. Collet Canal or from **Novelo's** on W. Collet Canal. Novelo's buses travel to the Cayo District, tel. (2) 77372. **Carmen** buses also travel to the Cayo District, leaving from the Pound Yard Bridge.

Travel time from Belize City to Corozal or San Ignacio is about two hours, to Dangriga about four hours, and to Punta Gorda 8-10 hours (this can be a bumpy ride). Fares average about US$2-4 to most destinations, about US$7-9 for the longer routes. Remember that these are not luxury buses, but they are the cheapest way to travel. And for anyone who wants to meet the Belizean people, this is the way to go. Most of these buses make frequent stops and will pick up anyone on the side of the road anywhere—as long as space permits. The drivers will also drop you off wherever you wish if you holler when you want off.

Note: Travel aboard a newish bus line, **Caribe Express**, which operates between Mexico (Cancún, Mérida, Campeche, Chetumal) and several cities in Belize. You must get off the bus at the border and will be helped through the process when arrangements are made with **Belize Transfer Service** (BTS). The bus is modern, with a/c, movies, bathroom, an attendant, and snacks. For more information and reservations, call or write BTS, Box 1722, Palo Alto, California 94302; tel. (415) 853-1978.

CAR RENTALS

A rental car offers the independent traveler more freedom to experience Belize on a very personal level and at the driver's own pace, the itinerary changing with the urge or necessity. It also presents some challenges, not the least of which is to the pocketbook. Car rentals are expensive in Belize and there's no getting around it. Costs can be as high as several hundred dollars per week. The pool of available cars is relatively small and the wear and tear on the vehicles is unavoidably considerable.

Most of the car rental firms are in Belize City but rentals are available in Big Creek and Punta Gorda for those who arrive by air or bus and would like to tour a little on their own.

Some rental companies offer only small, midsize, and large 4WD vehicles. Vans and passenger cars are also available, some with a/c—they cost more, though prices have come down somewhat from a few years ago. Insurance is manda-

CAR RENTALS

Avis	Radisson Fort	(2) 31987
	George Hotelfax	fax (2) 30225
Crystal	Belize City	(2) 31600
		fax (2) 31900
National	Belize City	(2) 31586
		(25) 2294
Budget	Mile 3	(2) 32435/33986
	Northern Highway	fax (2) 30237
	(ask for Alan Auil)	

tory. Driving rules are U.S.-style and it's wise to obtain an international driver's license before you leave home (about US$5 at most auto clubs). Gasoline also is quite costly, about US$3 a gallon. Tour guides, package trips, and drivers are available—pricey (though maybe not compared with the cost of a car and gas)—but they offer some of the best ways to see the country.

Renting a car in Belize is usually a simple matter but is always subject to Murphy's Law. High deposits can be put on credit cards. If you know exactly when you want the car and where, it's helpful to make reservations.

Getting the Car
Check out the car *carefully* before you take it far. Drive it around the block and go over the following:

- Make sure there's a spare tire and working jack.
- Make sure all doors lock.
- Make sure the seats move forward, have no sprung backs, etc.
- All windows should lock, unlock, roll up and down properly.
- Trunk should lock and unlock.
- Check for proper legal papers for the car, with addresses and phone numbers of associate car rental agencies in towns you plan to visit in case of an unexpected car problem.
- Make sure horn, emergency brake, and foot brakes work properly.

- Make sure clutch, gear shift, and all gears work properly (don't forget reverse).
- Get directions to the nearest gas station; the gas tank may be empty. If it's full it's wise to return it full, as you'll be charged top dollar per gallon of gas.
- Ask to have any damage, even a small dent, missing door knob, etc., noted on your contract, if it hasn't been already.
- Note the hour you pick up the car and try to return it before that time: a few minutes over will get you another *full* day's rental fee.

Vehicle Condition
If you plan to motor along the Northern Highway to Crooked Tree, Orange Walk, or Corozal, you can drive the older, cheaper cars some rental companies specialize in. However, if you want to drive the rougher stretches of the Hummingbird Highway, Manatee Road, or Southern Highway you'll need a 4WD vehicle in good shape. In less-traveled areas at night or on narrow, rutted jungle trails the condition of the vehicle becomes critical. Once you've driven the teeth-rattling roads to Chiquibil Forest, Cockscomb Wildlife Reserve, Chan Chich, or Lamanai Outpost Lodge you'll understand. The local Suzuki dealership in Belize City runs the Budget Rent a Car franchise. Several recent rental experiences have indicated the cars are fairly new and well-maintained.

Insurance
Mandatory car insurance from rental car agencies runs US$10-15 per day and covers only 80% of damages (which many travelers are unaware of). In most cases in Belize, when an accident occurs the police take action first and ask questions later. With an insurance policy, most of the problems are eased over. Rental agencies also offer medical insurance for US$4-6 per day. Your private medical insurance should cover this (check).

Payoff Time
When you pick up your rental car, the company makes an imprint of your credit card on a blank bill, one copy of which is attached to the papers you give the agent when you return the car. Keep in mind that the car agency limits how much you can charge on one credit card at one time (ask the maximum when you

pick up the car). If you go over the limit be prepared to pay the balance in cash or with another credit card.

CRUISE SHIPS

For those who like traveling aboard ship, several cruise lines offer an opportunity to experience the romance of the sea along with stops at interesting cayes, ports of call, and even inland tours. Note that these ships can accommodate both active and relaxed lifestyles. And remember, airfare and port taxes are usually extra.

Caribbean Prince offers a choice of two 12-day cruises from Belize City. Stops include Ambergris Caye, numerous smaller cayes, and Punta Gorda. Both cruises call on Livingston, Guatemala, and journey up the Rio Dulce to beautiful Lake Izabal. The ship boasts a stern swim-and-snorkel deck as well as a retractable

ROAD DISTANCES FROM BELIZE CITY TO:	
Belmopan:	55 miles
Benque Viejo:	81 miles
Corozal Town:	96 miles
Dangriga:	105 miles
Orange Walk Town:	58 miles
Punta Gorda:	210 miles
San Ignacio:	72 miles

boarding ramp built into the bow. A 21-foot glass bottom boat is available for viewing reef life. Active senior travelers will find lots of company and camaraderie here. It accommodates 78 passengers. Rates are about US$1190-2525 per person double occupancy. Contact American Canadian Caribbean Line, Inc., tel. (800) 556-

DRIVING SAFETY

Unless you are accustomed to driving in Belize keep your speed a little lower than normal. This will give you an extra margin of safety while you watch for these and other road hazards:

- Soft cushions of sand or powdered clay line the sides of dirt roads. If you maneuver too quickly while passing, this mush can cause your vehicle to slalom out of control. Such hazards are especially common on the Hummingbird Highway, Manatee Road, and Southern Highway.

- Driving at night is not advised. But if you do, passing trucks and buses at night on any dirt roads can be especially tricky since these heavy vehicles tend to stay in the middle of the road. Find a long open stretch before attempting to pass and proceed carefully.

- Along parts of the Hummingbird Highway are sections with ragged paving in the center of the road and dirt on each side. It is best to avoid these center strips as their edges often harbor vicious potholes.

- Many small bridges along dirt roads have no guardrails and room only for one vehicle at a time. Approach these cautiously, especially during wet weather and when visibility of oncoming traffic is impaired.

- Approach water-filled potholes and water-covered roadways with caution; it's hard to tell the depth of the water or condition of the roadbed beneath it.

- Around the coast (especially the Hopkins area) you will occasionally come upon narrow dirt causeways with marsh on each side. If you meet an oncoming vehicle, find one of the special widened areas that allow two cars to pass. If none is present, one car must back up. Do not try to pass near the side of the causeway. The shoulders frequently give way beneath cars, causing them to slide or sink into the ooze.

- In the Cayo, people wander along the sides of the road day and night. Keep your eyes open and stay alert.

- Be aware that you may top a hill or round a curve only to come upon a stopped bus or slow-moving tractor. At night this scenario might include a vehicle with no rear lights. Be prepared to swerve, slow down, or stop quickly.

- The Chiquibul Forest Road has many spots with sharp stones in the roadbed. Drive a little more slowly than conditions would normally warrant to avoid a blown tire.

7450; or in Rhode Island, tel. (401) 237-0955, fax (401) 245-8303.

Graziya sails from Tampa, Florida, or Gulfport, Mississippi, on weekly seven-day cruises to Belize City; Port of Cortez, Honduras; and Playa del Carmen and Cozumel, Mexico. Among amenities are a pool and casino. It accommodates 400 to 500 passengers. Rates are roughly US$595-1495 per person double occupancy. Cruise Line Contact Odessa America Cruise Line, tel. (800) 221-3254.

Polaris travels between Balboa, Panama, on the Pacific coast and Belize City, originating at either port. These 13-day cruises cross the Panama Canal and their stops include the San Blas Islands, Costa Rica, and an overnight near the inland Mayan ruins of Copan. In Belize stops include Belize City, Half Moon Caye, and Lighthouse Reef. Amenities include a glass-bottom boat and zodiac boats for snorkeling and river exploration. It sails with 80 passengers. Rates are roughly US$5600-9000 per person double occupancy. Contact Special Expeditions, tel. (800) 762-0003.

Regent Spirit departs for seven-day cruises from Cozumel to Belize City, Santo Tomas in Guatemala, Roatan Bay Island and Porto Cortez in Honduras, and Cancún. Its amenities include pool, casino, gym, disco, theater, and golf driving range. It sails with up to 400 passengers. Rates

are US$899-1609 per person double occupancy. Contact Regency Cruises, tel. (800) 388-550.

Rembrandt Van Rijn spreads its sails for 4-day/8-day/15-day cruises between Belize City and Placencia. It stops at Gallows Point Caye, Glover's Reef, Half Moon Caye, Laughing Bird Caye, Lighthouse Reef, and Placencia. It sails with 36 passengers. Amenities include scuba equipment and a sightseeing dinghy, and opportunities are frequent to scuba, snorkel, or visit cayes. Rates are about four days US$575-840, eight days US$1200-1850, 15 days US$1600-2135. Contact Oceanwide Sail Expeditions, Westfalenstrasse 92, D-58636 Iserlohn, Germany; tel. (49) 2371-689333, fax (49) 2371-689335.

Triton allows a choice of three 7-day/14-day cruises departing from the Dominican Republic, Barbados, or Jamaica. Stops include many Caribbean islands such as Aruba, Cozumel, Grand Cayman, San Juan, St. Martin, and St. Thomas. Mainland ports of call include Belize, Costa Rica, Guatemala, and Panama. Amenities include pool, casino, cinema, and gym. Rates are seven days US$999-1899 per person d and 14 days US$1849-2799 per person double. Triton sails with 700 passengers. Contact Regent Holidays in Ontario, Canada, tel. (800) 263-8776.

TOURS ORGANIZED IN THE U.S.

TOURING WITH EXPERTS

Have you finally decided to do it? Is this the first time you've ever left the border of your own country? Did your curiosity about the world of Belize take hold when you watched Morley Shafer on "60 Minutes"? Are you having heart palpitations because you don't know where to start to plan this once-in-a-lifetime trip? You can stop worrying now. The first time out is a good time to read this book thoroughly, and then if you still have doubts, book a tour with an experienced group. I know, I know—you don't want to be a bus-window looky-loo! You won't be. Today's tour travelers have a world of possibilities. You can get as involved as you want in any way you wish—all with the help and encouragement of an experienced escort. The tours will include real involvement, which can be snorkeling, diving, or climbing the tall Maya ruins (there's really no way possible to see the Belizean Maya sites from a bus window). Okay, on the other hand you don't want to commit to a lot of hiking—just leave it to the expert escort. Plenty of magical places are just right for *you*. The escort can be a scuba diver, an archaeologist, a naturalist, or a zoologist. Plan your own trip with the help of one of these experienced operators.

Tours

One reason people choose a tour over independent travel is the luxury of having someone else handle all the details—especially the first time out—someone who knows about passports, visas, reservations, airline schedules, time changes, the best food, the safest water, and the most comfortable beds, plus the experience to be able to show you the best of what you wish to see.

Trip Choice

If you've chosen to visit Belize you must be someone who's interested in jungles, diving, the Caribbean, nature, wild animals, flowers, trees, history of the West Indies, the Maya, archaeology, exotic cultures, or—just Belize. Following are descriptions of some of the adventures available and a few itineraries. If any of them sound good, remember, this is just the tip of the you-know-what. In most cases telephone numbers are toll free; call them and you'll have a live human to answer all the questions you've *ever* had about Belize—and a few of its neighboring countries. The following operators have been chosen on the basis of their knowledge; all of them have a sincere feeling for the country, maybe even a love affair. All have been dealing with Belize for some time, and as in the case of Sea & Travel, they are transplanted Belizeans who maintain close ties. If you need more tour operators to choose from, call **Belize Tourist Board** in New York at (800) 624-0686 and ask for the *Belize Sales Planner*.

TOUR OPERATORS

International Expeditions, Inc.

One of the finest tour companies in the U.S. with an intimate knowledge of Belize, International Expeditions, Inc., offers planned itineraries to suit all tastes. If you are one or a dozen people interested in something out of the ordinary, call and the staff will work with you in every way possible.

Escorts/guides have been trained in their fields, and most of them are either native Belizeans or have lived in Belize for some time and know their way around the country. Expeditions run 7-14 days with two- and three-day add-ons available. Among the itineraries offered is **Naturalist Quest**, an 11-day overview of the natural wonders of Belize, including an in-depth look at the unique fauna, the rainforest, or a concentrated study of the island and reef ecology. This program is available in many combinations that include snorkeling and scuba diving—or even a workshop with the **Nature Conservancy**. The **Maya Heartland** expedition, escorted by an informed archaeologist, focuses on the ruins of the once-great ceremonial centers built by the sophisticated, ancient Maya.

One of the newest programs, **Pharmacy from the Rainforest,** has been held in the Amazon as well, and is a very popular trip. Although you don't have to be a doctor or medical person to appreciate this, people with an interest in the treasure trove of medicines that continue to come from the jungles and rainforests of the tropics are entranced. Also during the trip, field expeditions will include the Panti Trail and a reception to meet Rosita Arvigo, noted traditional healer trained by bush doctor Eligio Panti. Travelers will have an opportunity to take part in an *ethnobotanical field collection,* part of ongoing research into plant-based cancer drugs. Those interested will have a look at **Succotz Village Centre for Mayan Culture, Preservation & Women's Development; The Midwifery Centre; Smithsonian Marine Biology Institute** on Carrie Bow Caye; and lots more. Workshop leaders are prominent working scientists in their fields. Sidetrips include Tikal, Xunantunich, Belize Zoo, and a visit to the Barrier Reef, a Garifuna village, and Cockscomb Basin.

Special expeditions are planned with a variety of themes, one taking in the **Garifuna Settlement Day** celebration (see the special topic "Garifuna Settlement Day" in the Stann Creek chapter). Shorter excursions (three and four days) are planned for **Tikal** (see "Guatemala" in the Across Belize's Borders chapter), **Mountain Pine Ridge** (see Cayo District chapter), the fabulous archaeological site of **Caracol** (see "Sites in Western Belize" in the Mundo Maya chapter), and the **Cockscomb Basin Jaguar Preserve** (see the Stann Creek chapter). Hotels and restaurants are well-chosen for comfort and adaptation to the area. For more information and prices contact International Expeditions, One Environs Park, Helena, Alabama 35080, tel. (800) 633-4734, (205)428-1700, fax (205) 428-1714.

Toucan Travel

This company is run by Dulca, a transplanted Belizean living in Louisiana. She relays her intimate knowledge of the country to tourists and specializes in Placencia. For more information contact 32 Traminer Dr., Kenner, Louisiana 70065, tel. (800) 747-1381.

Great Trips

Specializing in offering Great Trips to Belize, this company provides customized travel packages to experienced travelers and sportspeople. For more information, contact 1616 W. 139th St., Burnsville, Minnesota 55337, tel. (800) 552-3419, tel./fax (218) 847-4441.

Sea & Travel

Owners Sue and Tony Castillo, native Belizeans, take pleasure and pride in sharing their country with visitors. They know every out-of-the-way destination, and go out of their way to match clients with the right areas of the country to suit their interests. Susan worked with the Belize Ministry of Tourism before coming to the United States. Whether you wish to see the cayes or the Maya sites, contact Sea & Travel, 1809 Carol Sue Ave., Gretna, Louisiana 70056, tel. (800) 345-9786, (504) 366-9985.

Roatan Charter, Inc.

This creative company specializes in **Honduras** and the **Honduras Bay Islands** (see the Across Belize's Borders chapter), one of the Caribbean's best-kept secrets. Specialties are diving, sailboating, fishing, and mountain climbing packages. Those interested in the rich history of Honduras (beginning with the Maya and then the pirates who fought over these strategically located islands), will have a chance to see and learn about it all. And if you just want to worship the sun, Roatan can arrange that also. For more information and prices, contact Roatan Charter, Inc., Box 877, San Antonio, Florida 77008, tel. (800) 282-8932, (904) 588-4131, fax (904) 588-4158.

Slickrock Adventures, Inc.

This is the outfit that will put you in an ocean kayak. Slickrock Adventures, Inc., offers a nine-day kayak adventure based on a private island at Glover's Reef. This includes charter flights from Belize City, sailboat transfers to the reef, all guides (one American, one Belizean), hotel accommodations upon arrival and departure, all meals (daily fresh seafood), all kayak and camping equipment (bring your own sleeping gear), rustic cabins on Glover's Reef, and overnight trips to neighboring cayes by kayak. Experience is recommended but not required; weather can sometimes make for strenuous days. Although the trips are made during the dry season, tropical squalls can come along at any time, delaying the ongoing passage. Conditioning before the excursion is encouraged; kayakers can expect to paddle no more than nine miles per day, often only three or four. Prices are US$1195 per person, nine days. For more information and a color brochure, contact Slickrock Adventures, Box 1400, Moab, Utah 84532, tel./fax (801) 259-6996.

Far Horizons Cultural Discovery Trips

Mary Dell Lucas is known throughout the Maya world for her excellent archaeological knowledge and insight. Her company provides trips into the most fascinating Maya sites, regardless of location. Although Mary Dell Lucas is an archaeologist herself, she often brings specialists along with her groups. For more

information call (800) 552-4575.

Best of Belize

This growing company has been bringing visitors from the U.S. to Belize for some years. For information about all parts of the country, in the U.S. call (800) 735-9520.

Belize Specialists

These folks can provide information and transport between Cancún and Belize, whether by air or by bus. A charter flight between Cancún and Belize (at press time) will cost US$99. For those interested in the orchids of Belize, Belize Specialists will set you up with a Belizean who will take you on an orchid tour and will also do all the necessary paperwork for you to return to the States with orchids from the Central American jungle. Also ask about caving trips and bicycle tours. For more information, contact (800) 4-YUCATAN.

INFORMATION

TOURIST INFORMATION

At the **Belize Tourist Board,** 83 N. Front St., Belize City, tel. (2) 77213/73255, fax (2) 77490, you'll find brochures on a number of reserves and national parks and information on various sections of the country. You'll usually find someone who's willing to talk to you and answer your questions. Or in the U.S. call Belize Tourist Office, tel. (800) 624-0686.

Belize Tourism Industry Associates, 99 Albert St., Box 62, Belize City, tel. (2) 75717, fax (2) 78710, almost always has someone on the premises to answer questions.

The consul general of the **Belize Consulate** in California is Mrs. Pearl Warren, 5825 Sunset Blvd., Suite 206, Hollywood, California 90028, tel. (213) 469-7343, fax (213) 469-7346. Her office will send you any information it has on hand.

The **Embassy of Belize,** 2535 Massachusetts Dr. NW, Washington, DC 20008, tel. (202) 332-9636, fax (202) 332-6741, and the **Caribbean Tourism Association,** 20 E. 46th St., New York, New York 10017, tel. (212) 682-0435, are both good sources of information.

Belize Online

Travelers cruising the Internet before their visit to Belize can check out the **web site** called Belize Online, Tourist and Investment Guide, which is endorsed by the Belize Tourism Industry Association and the Belize Tourist Board.

For more information, contact the site at http://www.belize.com/.

MONEY

The currency unit is the Belize Dollar (BZE$), which has been steady at BZE$2 to US$1 for some years. While prices are given in US$ in this book, travelers should be prepared to pay in Belizean currency on the street, boats, in cafes, and at other smaller establishments; however, carry both just in case. Of course, the larger hotels accept U.S. dollars. When you buy or sell currency at a bank, be sure to retain proof of sale. The banks may charge a few-cents conversion fee. The following places are authorized to buy or sell foreign currency; all are close together near the plaza in Belize City. Hours are Mon.-Fri. till 1 p.m., Saturday till 11 a.m.

Atlantic Bank Ltd.
Bank of Nova Scotia
Barclays Bank
Belize Bank of Commerce and Industry
Belize Global Travel Services Ltd.

At the Mexican-Belize border you'll be approached by moneychangers (and you can bet they don't represent the banks). Many travelers buy just enough Belize dollars to get them into the city and to the banks. Depending on your mode of transport and destination, these moneychangers can be helpful. Strictly speaking, though, this is illegal—so suit yourself. The exchange rate is the same but you'll have no receipt of sale. If selling a large quantity of Belize dollars back to the bank, you might be asked for that proof.

Airport departure tax is US$11.25 (including security tax) when leaving the country, except for in-transit passengers spending fewer than 24 hours in the country. When entering the country and flying to any other in-country destination, a US75 cents charge is required to clear security.

Credit Cards and Traveler's Checks
Credit cards are taken only at the larger business establishments, so bring traveler's checks and cash as well. You will find representatives of Visa, MasterCard, and American Express at the four commercial banks in Belize City.

Tipping
Most restaurants and hotels include the tip on the check; if the tip isn't added to the bill, then 10% is the norm. It is not customary to tip taxi drivers unless they help you with your luggage.

TIPS TO KNOW
BEFORE YOU GO

The electricity is 110/220 volt, 60 cycles. Removal of archaeological artifacts will get you thrown in jail. Religious services available are Protestant, Roman Catholic, and Anglican; ask for church locations at your hotel. While the water is said to be good from the tap in Belize City, experienced travelers still drink only bottled water. If you're looking for a water substitute, Coke signs are everywhere, and rum and Belikin beer are plentiful (both are made in Belize). Some travelers take advantage of the privilege and bring in one bottle of their own favorite liquor. The local time is Greenwich mean time minus six, the same as U.S. central time, year-round (no daylight saving time). Shops are generally open daily 8 a.m.-noon and 1-4 p.m., closed Sunday and public holidays. You can obtain visas for ongoing travel to Guatemala at the Guatemalan Embassy at Mile 6.5, New Northern Highway, tel. (2) 33150 in Belize City. When writing letters to Belize, abbreviate Central America as C.A. Be sure to include the periods; otherwise the U.S. Post Office will send your letters to California.

TELEPHONE SERVICE AND USE

Belize has a fine, modern telephone system that enables visitors to make contact with the rest of the world quickly and efficiently with direct dial service. Belize country code is 501 and the area codes follow.

The number of digits varies from city to city. When you dial from the States, use the area codes as shown. When calling within Belize, add a zero in front of the codes shown below.

AREA CODES

1	portable cellular phones	22	Caye Caulker	6	Placencia
2	Belize City	4	Corozal	7	Punta Gorda
8	Belmopan	5	Dangriga	92	San Ignacio
93	Benque Viejo	6	Independence	4	San Joaquin
3	Blue Creek	25	Ladyville	26	San Pedro
28	Burrell Boom	3	Orange Walk Town	8	Spanish Lookout

CONSULS AND VISAS

You'll find resident diplomatic and consular representatives from 20 countries in Belize, including:

British High Commission
Embassy Square, Belmopan
(8) 22146/22147

Canadian Consulate
83 N. Front Street, Belize City
(2) 31060, fax (2) 30060

Costa Rican Embassy
Hummingbird Hwy., Belmopan
(8) 23801, fax (8) 23805

El Salvador
2 3rd St., Picini Site, Belmopan
(8) 23404, fax (8) 23404

Guatemala Embassy
6A St. Matthew St., Belize City
(2) 33150/33314, fax (2) 35140

Honduras Embassy
91 N. Front St., Belize City
(2) 45889, fax (2) 30562

Mexican Embassy
20 N. Park St., Belize City
(2) 30193/30194, fax (2) 78742

Panama Honorary Consul
Princess Margaret Dr., Belize City
(2) 34282, fax (2) 30653

U.S. Embassy
29 Gabourel Lane, Belize City
(2) 77161, fax (2) 30802

Venezuelan Consulate
18/20 Unity Blvd., Belmopan
(8) 22384, fax (8) 22022

Visitors to Belize must be in possession of passports and certain categories will require visas as well. British subjects (Commonwealth citizens) and citizens of the U.S. who have return or ongoing tickets issued in their countries do not need visas. Check with your embassy before taking off.

Belize Consulates in the U.S.:

CALIFORNIA: 5825 Sunset Blvd., Suite 206
Hollywood, CA 90028
(213) 469-7343
fax (213) 469-7346

FLORIDA: 4343 W. Flagler St., Suite 400
Miami, FL 33134
(305) 442-2114

MICHIGAN: 27166 Selkirk
Southfield, MI 48076
(313) 559-7407

LOUISIANA: 1500 W. Esplanade Ave., #8B
Kenner, LA 70065
(504) 465-9904

TEXAS: 1415 Louisiana, Suite 3100
Houston, TX 77002
(713) 658-0207

Belize Embassy in the U.S.:

2535 Massachusetts Dr. NW
Washington, DC 20008
(202) 332-9636
fax (202) 332-6741

Belize Tourist Board in the U.S.:

(800) 624-0686

WHAT TO TAKE

Whatever time of year you travel to Belize you can expect warm to hot weather. Most airlines allow you to check two suitcases, and you can bring another carry-on bag that fits either under your seat or in the overhead rack; this is fine if you're planning a one-destination trip to a self-contained resort and want a couple of changes of clothes each day. But if you plan on moving around a lot, you'll be happy if you keep it light—one bag and one carry-on.

Experienced women travelers pack a small foldable purse into their carry-on, leaving them with only one thing to carry while en route. And be sure to include a few overnight necessities in your carry-on in case your luggage doesn't arrive when you do. Valuables are safest in your carry-on stowed under the seat in front of you rather than in the overhead rack, whether you're on a plane, boat, or bus.

Security

It's smart to keep passports, traveler's checks, money, and important papers in a hotel safe or on your person at all times. (It's always a good idea to keep a separate list of document numbers in your luggage and leave a copy with a friend back home. This expedites replacement in case of loss.) The do-it-yourselfer can sew inside pockets into clothes; buy extra-long pants, turn up the hem, and sew three-fourths of the way around, closing the last section with a piece of Velcro. Separate shoulder-holster pockets, moneybelts, and pockets around the neck inside clothing—all made of cotton—are available commercially. If you're going to be backpacking and sloshing in jungle streams, etc., put everything in zipper-lock plastic bags before placing them in pockets. Waterproof plastic tubes are available that will hold a limited number of items around your neck while swimming.

Clothing

A swimsuit is a must, and if you're not staying at one of the larger hotels, bring a beach towel. In today's Belize you'll see a wide variety of clothing. Unless you want to attract a lot of attention, do not wear bikinis, short shorts, or revealing tight clothes while strolling the streets of Belize City. Save that for the beach areas or the pool at your hotel. If traveling Nov.-Jan., bring along a light wrap since it can cool off in the evening. The rest of the year you'll probably carry the wrap in your suitcase. For women, a wraparound skirt is a useful item that can quickly cover up shorts when traveling through the villages and some cities (many small-village residents really gawk at women wearing shorts; whatever you do, don't enter a church wearing them). The wraparound skirt also makes a good shawl when it cools off. Cotton underwear is the coolest in the tropics, but nylon is less bulky and dries overnight, cutting down on the number needed. Be sure that you bring broken-in, comfortable walking shoes; blisters can wreck a vacation almost as much as a sunburn. For those planning long treks through the jungle, lightweight hiking boots give protection from scratching brush, flying biting insects that hover near the ground, and, yes, snakes.

Necessities

If you wear glasses and are planning an extended trip, it's a good idea to bring an extra pair or carry the lens prescription; the same goes for medication (make sure the prescription is written in generic terms). Bring your favorite toiletries and cosmetics as the selection here is small. American cigarettes are available but are pricey. If you smoke a pipe bring plenty of tobacco since it's almost impossible to find.

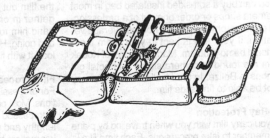

LOUISE FOOTE

Reading Material

Avid readers from the U.S. and Canada are in luck in Belize. Because the official language is English, you'll seldom have a hard time finding English-language books; however, don't expect a huge selection of best-sellers. Both small and large hotels have book-trading shelves. If they aren't obvious, ask at the desk. Most travelers are delighted to trade books. Many travelers come prepared with an "itty bitty" Book Light for rooms where there's either no electricity or dim bulbs. For books on Belize, see the Booklist.

Backpackers

If you plan to hitchhike or use public transportation, don't use a large external-frame pack; crowded buses have very little room and it won't fit in most small cars or public lockers. Smaller packs with zippered compartments that will accommodate mini-padlocks are most practical. A strong bike cable and lock secures the pack to a YH bed or a bus/train rack. None of the above will deter the real criminal but might make it difficult enough to discourage everyone else.

Experienced backpackers travel light with a pack, an additional canvas bag, a small water- and mosquito-proof tent, a hammock, and mosquito netting.

CAMERAS AND PICTURE TAKING

Bring a camera to Belize! Nature and people combine to provide unforgettable panoramas, well worth taking home with you on film to savor again at your leisure. Many people bring simple cameras such as instants that are easy to carry and uncomplicated. Others prefer 35mm cameras that offer higher-quality pictures, are easier than ever to use, and are available in a variety of price ranges. They can come equipped with built-in light meter, automatic exposure, self-focus, and self-advance—with little more to do than aim and click.

Film

Two reasons to bring film with you: it's cheaper and more readily available in the U.S. Two reasons *not* to bring quantities of film: space may be a problem and heat can affect film quality, both before and after exposure. If you're traveling for more than two weeks in a car or bus a good part of the time, carry film in an insulated case. You can buy a soft-sided insulated bag in most camera shops or order one out of a professional photography magazine. For the average vacation, if your film is kept in your room there should be no problem. Many varieties of Kodak film are found in camera shops and hotel gift shops in Belize. In the smaller towns you may not be able to find slide film.

X-Ray Protection

If you carry film with you when traveling by plane remember to take precautions. Each time film is passed through the security X-ray machine, a little damage is done. It's cumulative, and perhaps one time won't make much difference, but most photographers won't take the chance. Request hand inspection. With today's tight security at airports, some guards insist on passing your film and camera through the X-ray machine. If packed in your checked luggage, it's wise to keep film in protective lead-lined bags, available at camera shops in two sizes: the larger size holds up to 22 rolls of 35mm film, the smaller holds eight rolls. If you use fast film, ASA 400 or higher, buy the double lead-lined bag designed to protect more sensitive film. Carry an extra lead-lined bag for your film-loaded camera if you want to drop it into a piece of carry-on luggage. (These bags also protect medications from X-ray damage.)

If you decide to request hand examination (rarely, if ever, refused at the Belize airport), make it simple for the security guards. Have the film out of boxes and canisters placed together in one clear plastic bag that you can hand him for quick examination both coming and going. He'll also want to look at the camera; load it with film *after* crossing the border.

Film Processing

For processing film the traveler has several options. Most people take their film home and have it processed at a familiar lab. Again, if the trip is lengthy and you are shooting many photos, it's impractical to carry used rolls around for more than a couple of weeks. Larger cities have one-hour photo labs, but they only handle color prints; color slides must be processed at a lab out of the city, which usually takes a week or two. Kodak film mailers are another option but most photographers won't let their film out of sight until they reach their favorite lab.

Camera Protection

Take a few precautions with your camera while traveling. At the beach remember that a combination of wind and sand can really gum up the works and scratch the lens. On 35mm cameras keep a clear skylight filter on the lens instead of a lens cap so the camera can hang around your neck or in a fanny pack, always at the ready for the spectacular shot that comes when least expected. If something is going to get scratched, better a $15 filter than a $300 lens. It also helps to carry as little equipment as possible. If you want more than candids and you carry a 35mm camera, basic equipment can be simple. Padded camera cases are good and come in all sizes. A canvas bag is lighter and less conspicuous than a heavy photo bag, but doesn't have the extra protection the padding provides.

Safety Tips

Keep your camera dry; carrying a couple of big zipper-lock bags affords instant protection. Don't *store* cameras in plastic bags for any length of time because the moisture that builds up in the bag can damage a camera as much as leaving it in the rain.

It's always wise to keep cameras out of sight in a car or when camping out. Put your name and address on the camera. Chances are if it gets left behind or stolen it won't matter whether your name is there or not, and don't expect to see it again; however, miracles do happen. (You *can* put a rider on most homeowner's insurance policies for a nominal sum that will cover the cost if a camera is lost or stolen.) It's a nuisance to carry cameras every second when traveling—especially for a long period. During an evening out, we always leave our cameras and equipment (out of sight) in the hotel room; so far everything has been intact when we return. However, if this makes you crazy with worry,

some hotel safes are large enough to accommodate your equipment.

Cameras can be a help or a hindrance when trying to get to know the people. When traveling in the backcountry you'll run into folks who don't want their pictures taken. Keep your camera put away until the right moment. The main thing to remember is to ask permission first and then if someone doesn't want his/her picture taken, accept the refusal with a gracious smile and move on.

Underwater Photography

One of the newer delights for the amateur photographer is shooting the creatures of the deep in living color. If you're fortunate enough to have one of the upscale 35mm cameras put out by Nikonos or Hanimex you've got it made. Even the simple cameras, such as Weathermatic put out by Minolta, will give you a lot of pleasure and good souvenirs to take home. The simpler, inexpensive cameras are generally usable only to a depth of 15 feet. The Nikonos and Hanimex are waterproof up to 150 feet. And last but not least, check out the *disposable* cardboard underwater cameras available at most photo shops and large discount stores in the U.S. Obviously the resulting pix will not be publishable, but they're good enough to take home and put in your album to remember Bolizo and its underwater denizens.

Some hotels, resorts, and shops in Belize rent underwater cameras. Don't expect a large selection. Remember, when buying film the best for underwater is natural-, red-, or yellow-tint film; film such as Ektachrome with a bluish cast does not give the best results. A strobe or flash is a big help if shooting in deep water or into caves. Natural-light pictures are great if you're shooting in fairly shallow water. It's best to shoot on an eye-to-eye level when photographing fish. Be careful of stirring up silt from the bottom with your fins. Try to hold very still when depressing the shutter, and if you must stabilize yourself, *don't* grab onto any bright-colored coral—you will kill it. If it's colored, it's alive, so grab only the drab grayish, tannish coral; grabbing live coral can cut your hands and often cause infection. Enjoy the reef and make sure the reef enjoys you—this is a natural haven for fragile life that must be preserved and cared for.

Other Photo Information

Belize has some mighty fine local photographers. If you're not a camera carrier and decide you'd like to take home some great pictures, including underwater shots, here are a few people to check out. On Caye Caulker

stop by the photo gallery and gift shop of **James Beveridge**—look for the sign that says **Sea-ing is Belizing**. Another super place on Caye Caulker to see good photos, including underwater shots, is **Ellen MacRae's Galeria Hicaco**.

KATHY ESCOVEDO SANDERS

MUNDO MAYA

For several years five Latin American nations (Mexico, Belize, Guatemala, Honduras, and El Salvador) have discussed the need to preserve the remaining culture of the Maya, one of the greatest civilizations of all time. The Maya were dynamic engineers who created architecturally flamboyant buildings, massive reservoirs, more cities than were in ancient Egypt, and innovative farmlands. They developed a written language, tracked and recorded movements of the universe, and at its zenith the society numbered more than five million people. Present-day descendants of the Maya, along with thousands of structures hidden in thick tropical jungles, continue to tell the story of the past.

An ambitious project, tagged **Mundo Maya** ("World of the Maya"), has been designed to both exhibit and preserve, to see that the rapid growth of population—and tourism—will not destroy what has been quietly enduring nature and her elements for hundreds and in some cases as long as three thousand years. Many factors are involved in project decisions that will affect millions of people; not only the Maya who have lived in isolated pockets and out-of-the-way villages for centuries, but also the people of each country involved, plus

thousands of visitors who are discovering this culture for the first time. La Ruta Maya ("The Maya Route") will encompass the entire area that was once inhabited by the Maya, who have left their footprints in the form of amazing stone structures all over the landscape.

The project will require the cooperation of five countries, concentrating on the preservation of natural resources and rainforests, including the birds and animals that live within their boundaries (already extinct in other parts of the world). Perhaps the most important challenge the countries face is to come up with a way to encourage the development that tourism dollars can bring without infringing upon the cultural, historical, and environmental heritage of the Maya people.

A way must be found to induce the population to stop cutting the rainforest to create pastureland for raising crops and grazing cattle. Several plans are being studied. Those who have been supporting themselves in traditional ways for centuries must be taught ways to make a living without destroying the surrounding rainforest. Options include harvesting and selling such rainforest products as coffee, cacao, medicines, and fruits, and raising water buffalo (which survive nicely in the wet rainforest) rather than cattle—the meat is a viable substitute for beef. And maybe the biggest moneymaker for the people of the future is tourism—rather, ecotourism.

The five governments involved took the first step when they met in October 1988 in Guatemala City, an event hosted by then-President Vinicio Cerezo Arevalo. One of the most innovative suggestions was to build monorail-type transportation that would travel the 1,500-mile route throughout the environmentally precarious landscape to avoid bringing roads into these areas. Road development invariably brings uncontrolled settlement and destruction. There was talk of a regional Mundo Maya tourist visa and a Eurail-type pass that would allow visitors to move freely across the borders of the five countries.

No doubt it will take years of planning and agreements before these ideas come to pass, but Mexico and Guatemala have made one of the first moves by creating two adjoining biosphere reserves totaling 4.7 million acres of wildlands. In May 1989 Mexico's then-President Salinas de Gortari and Guatemala's then-President Cerezo signed an agreement to cooperate and conserve natural areas of the border zones and to protect endangered species. This is a hopeful sign for the future; in the recent past, the only things these two countries shared at the border were animosity and military patrols pointing guns at each other.

MAYA ARCHAEOLOGICAL SITES

A thousand years before modern seafarers came along, the Maya inhabited Belize. They are believed to be the first *Homo sapiens* to people the country. Archaeologists estimate that at one time, at least one million Maya lived in the area that is now called Belize. More Maya sites are discovered each year, and it's quite common for Belizean families to have ruins in their backyards without official archaeological knowledge. These are often small oratorio-style buildings or caves with artifacts that date back hundreds of years. As money becomes available, whether from the government or outside universities, more discoveries are made and it becomes apparent that Belize is a veritable treasure chest of Maya culture.

Hints for Touring the Archaeological Sites
Seven of the archaeological sites described below are open to the public. Four are visited widely and soon will be official reserves with supporting facilities. Right now visitors will find no bathrooms, snack bars, or even water in any of them. In some areas it's necessary to trek through tall grasses and jungle terrain, so dress accordingly. Wearing long pants and sturdy walking shoes with socks pulled over the cuffs (which have been previously sprayed with the type of insect repellent that can be applied to the skin) is one efficient way to approach these areas. Flying and crawling insects thrive in the jungle terrain. Of course the other usual mom-given tips apply: sun block, a loose floppy hat, and a canteen of water all help to protect the body inside and out against the hot sun and its effects.

Know the locations and distances of the sites you wish to visit. Some are lengthy treks from the closest town. Other sites are on private property and can only be visited if prior permission is obtained. For more information write or visit the **Department of Archaeology**, Belmopan, Belize, C.A., or the **Association for Belizean Archaeology** at the **Center of Environmental Studies** on Eve St. in Belize City.

SITES IN NORTHERN BELIZE

Santa Rita
Santa Rita was still a populated community of Maya when the Spanish arrived. One mile northeast of Corozal, the largest Santa Rita structure was explored at the turn of the century by Thomas Gann. Sculptured friezes and stucco murals were found along with a burial site that indicates flourishing occupation in the early Classic period (about A.D. 300), as well as during the late post-Classic period (A.D. 1350-1530). Two significant burials were found from distant periods in the history of Santa Rita: one from A.D. 300 was a fe-

male and the other was a king from a period 200 hundred years later. In 1985 archaeologists Diane and Arlen Chase discovered a tomb with a skeleton covered in jade and mica ornaments. Some believe that Santa Rita was part of a series of coastal lookouts. It has been excavated and somewhat reconstructed under the Chases' jurisdiction; only one structure is accessible to the public. Post-Classic murals, mostly destroyed over the years, combined Maya and Mexican styles that depict the ecumenical flavor of the period. Santa Rita is probably more appealing to an archaeologist than to the average tourist.

Cerros

Cerros was an important coastal trading center during the late pre-Classic period (350 B.C. to A.D. 250). It's situated on a peninsula in the Bay of Chetumal, across from the town of Corozal. Magnificent frescoes and stone heads were uncovered by archaeologist David Friedel; these signify that elite rule was firmly fixed by the end of the pre-Classic period. The tallest of its temples rises to 70 feet, and because of the rise in the sea level the one-time stone residences of the elite Maya are partially flooded. It would appear that Cerros not only provisioned the oceangoing canoes, but was in an ideal location to control ancient trade routes that traced the Rio Hondo and New River from the Yucatán to Petén and the Usumacinta basin. A plaster-lined canal for the sturdy, oversized ocean canoes was constructed

around Cerros. Archaeologists have determined that extensive fishing and farming on raised fields took place, probably to outfit the traders. But always the question remains, why did progress suddenly stop? You can reach Cerros by boat (hire it in Corozal at **Tony's Inn** or check with a travel agent in Corozal). If you travel during the dry season (Jan.-April) you can get to Cerros by car.

Nohmul

Nohmul was a major ceremonial site. It is the tallest structure in the Orange Walk/Corozal districts. Twin ceremonial groups are connected by a *sacbe* (raised causeway). The center shows it once catered to a thriving population in the late pre-Classic and late Classic periods (350 B.C.-A.D. 250 and A.D. 600-900) and controlled an area of about 12 square miles. Nohmul ("Big Hill") was named by the people living in the vicinity of the site.

The entrance to the site, in the sugarcane fields behind the village of San Pablo, is one mile down the road going west from the center of the village. Public transportation from Belize City, Orange Walk Town, and Corozal passes through the village of San Pablo several times daily. You can find simple accommodations in Orange Walk Town eight miles away.

Cuello

The ruins of Cuello were studied in the 1970s by a Cambridge University archaeology team led by

At Cuello, archaeologists have renovated the Maya ruins in the ancient manner by covering them with a white stucco coating.

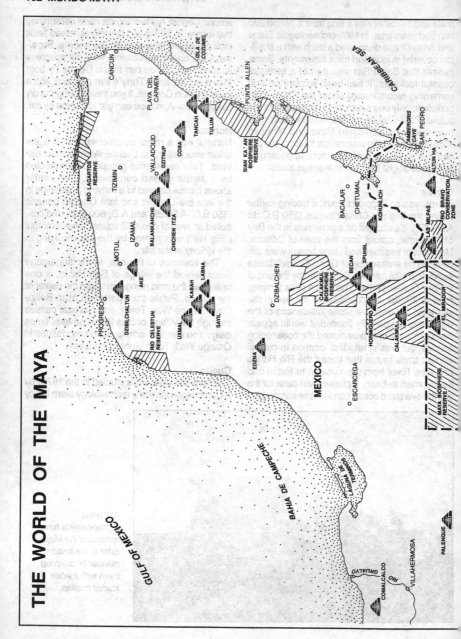

THE WORLD OF THE MAYA

GULF OF MEXICO

CANCUN

ISLA DE COZUMEL

PLAYA DEL CARMEN

TANCAH

TULUM

COBA

VALLADOLID

DZITNUP

PUNTA ALLEN

RIO LAGARTOS RESERVE

TIZIMIN

IZAMAL

BALANKANCHE

CHICHEN ITZA

SIAN KA'AN BIOSPHERE RESERVE

AMBERGRIS CAYE

SAN PEDRO

CARIBBEAN SEA

TULUM HA

MOTUL

AKE

BACALAR

CHETUMAL

KOHUNLICH

LAS MILPAS

PROGRESO

DZIBILCHALTUN

RIO CELESTUN RESERVE

UXMAL

KABAH

LABNA

SAYIL

XPUHIL

BECAN

DZIBALCHEN

RIO BRAVO CONSERVATION ZONE

CALAKMUL BIOSPHERE RESERVE

EL MIRADOR

CALAKMUL

HORMIGUERO

EDZNA

ESCARCEGA

MEXICO

MAYA BIOSPHERE RESERVE

BAHIA DE CAMPECHE

LAGUNA DE TERMINOS

COMALCALCO

RIO GRIJALVO

VILLAHERMOSA

PALENQUE

© MOON PUBLICATIONS, INC.

Dr. Norman Hammond. A small ceremonial center, a proto-Classic temple, has been excavated. Lying directly in front is a large excavation trench, partially backfilled, where the archaeologists gathered the historical information that revolutionized previous concepts of the antiquity of the ancient Maya. Artifacts indicate the Maya traded with people hundreds of miles away. Among the archaeologists' out-of-the-ordinary findings were bits of wood that proved, after carbon testing, that Cuello had been occupied as early as 2600 B.C., much earlier than ever believed; however, archaeologists now find that these tests may have been incorrect, and the age is now in dispute. Also found was an unusual style of pottery—apparently in some burials clay urns were placed over the heads of the deceased. It's also speculated that it was here that the primitive strain of corn seen in early years was refined and developed over a long period into the higher-producing plant of the Classic period. Continuous occupation for approximately 4,000 years was surmised with repeated layers of structures all the way into the Classic period. However, archaeologists are still debating the accuracy of this back dating.

These structures (as in Cahal Pech) have a different look than most Maya sites. They are covered with a layer of white stucco, as they were in the days of the Maya.

The ruins of Cuello are on the same property as the rum distillery of the same name. It's about four miles west of Orange Walk Town on Yo Creek; taxis are available. This site isn't developed, cleared, restored, or ready for the average tourist, but if you're interested in more information, contact the **Department of Archaeology** at Belmopan—if you're in the area ask at the distillery for permission to enter.

Lamanai

Set on the edge of a forested broad lagoon are the temples of Lamanai. One of the largest ceremonial centers in Belize, it was described as an imperial port city encompassing ball courts, pyramids, and the more exotic Maya features. Hundreds of buildings have been identified in the two-square-mile area. A few sites to look for:

The Mask Temple N9-56: Here two significant tombs were found, as well as two early Classic stone masks.

The High Temple N10-43: At 33-meters tall, this is the tallest securely dated pre-Classic structure in the Maya area. Among many findings were a dish containing the skeleton of a bird and pre-Classic vessels dating to 100 B.C.

Temple N10-9: Dated to the 6th century A.D., this temple had structural modifications in the 8th and 13th centuries. Jade jewelry and a jade mask were discovered here as was an animal-motif dish.

The Ball Court: The game played in this area held great ritual significance for the Maya.

Lamanai site

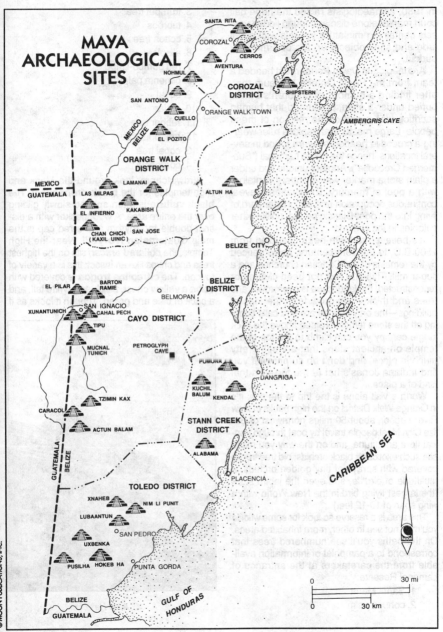

MAYA ARCHAEOLOGICAL SITES

SANTA RITA
COROZAL
CERROS
AVENTURA
NOHMUL
COROZAL DISTRICT
SHIPSTERN
SAN ANTONIO
ORANGE WALK TOWN
CUELLO
AMBERGRIS CAYE
MEXICO
BELIZE
EL POZITO
ORANGE WALK DISTRICT
MEXICO
GUATEMALA
LAMANAI
LAS MILPAS
ALTUN HA
EL INFIERNO
KAKABISH
CHAN CHICH
(KAXIL UINIC)
SAN JOSE
BELIZE CITY
EL PILAR
BARTON RAMIE
BELIZE DISTRICT
XUNANTUNICH
SAN IGNACIO
CAHAL PECH
BELMOPAN
TIPU
CAYO DISTRICT
MUCNAL TUNICH
PETROGLYPH CAVE
PUMONA
DANGRIGA
KUCHIL BALUM
KENDAL
TZIMIN KAX
CARACOL
ACTUN BALAM
STANN CREEK DISTRICT
CARIBBEAN SEA
ALABAMA
PLACENCIA
TOLEDO DISTRICT
XNAHEB
NIM LI PUNIT
LUBAANTUN
SAN PEDRO
UXBENKA
PUSILHA
HOKEB HA
PUNTA GORDA
GUATEMALA
BELIZE
BELIZE
GUATEMALA
GULF OF HONDURAS

0   30 mi
0   30 km

N

In 1980, archaeologists raised the huge ball court marker stone disc and found lidded vessels containing miniature vessels with small jade and shell objects on top of a mercury puddle.

Archaeologist David Pendergast headed a team from the Royal Ontario Museum that, after finding a number of children's bones buried under a stela, presumed that human sacrifice was a part of the religion of these people. Large masks that depict a ruler wearing a crocodile headdress were found in several locations, hence the name Lamanai ("Submerged Crocodile"). Another unique find under a plain stone marker was a pottery container with a pool of mercury. Excavations reveal continuous occupation and a high standard of living into the post-Classic period, unlike other colonies in the region.

It's believed to have been occupied from 1500 B.C. to the 19th century, as evidenced by the remains of two Christian churches and a sugar mill. This site has not been cleared or reconstructed; the landscape is overgrown, and trees and thick vines grow from the tops of buildings—the only sounds are bird calls echoing off the stone temple. To see above the thick jungle canopy you can climb to the top of the temple on ancient steps that are still pretty much in place, and don't be surprised if you find Indiana Jones's hat at the top—it's that kind of a place.

Worth a visit alone is the trip to the site; it's in Orange Walk District on the high banks of New River Lagoon about 50 miles northwest of Belize City. Most people travel by boat through tropical flora and fauna, and on the way you might see such exotics as black orchids, old tree trunks covered with sprays of tiny golden orchids, a multitude of birdlife, and even the jabiru stork (the largest flying bird in the New World with a wing span of 10-12 feet).

This area is a reserve so look for some wildlife you may not see in other, more inhabited areas. On the paths you'll see numbered trees that correspond to a pamphlet of information available from the caretakers at the entrance of Lamanai Reserve:

1. Santa Maria
2. cohune palm
3. trumpet tree
4. tubroos
5. cotton tree
6. allspice
7. red gumbo-limbo
8. pimenta palm
9. bucut
10. cedar
11. rubber tree
12. breadnut tree
13. copal tree
14. cordoncia

Birdwatchers, look around the Mask and High temples for the **black *oropendola.*** The **black vulture** is often spotted slowly gliding over the entire area. A woodpecker with a distinct double tap rhythm and a red cap is the male **Guatemalan ivorybill.** Near the High Temple, the **collared *aracari*** sits on the highest trees and chirps like an insect; this is a variety of toucan. The **citreoline trogon** is covered with color: a yellow chest, black-and-white tail, and a back of blue and green. Though it looks as if

Altun Ha

the **northern jacana** is walking on water, it's the delicate floating vegetation that holds the long-toed bird above the water as it searches along the water's edge for edible delicacies.

Other fauna spotted by those who live there are jaguarundi, agouti, armadillo, hicatee turtle, and the roaring howler monkey.

Chan Chich

In the northwestern corner of Belize in Orange Walk District, near the Guatemala border, an old overgrown logging road blazed originally by the Belize Estate and Produce Co. (logging operators) was reopened. Here, the Maya site of Chan Chich (Kaxil Uinich) was rediscovered. As recently as 1986 the only way in (for rare adventurers, pot farmers, or grave robbers) was with machete in hand and a canoe to cross the swiftly flowing river. After sweating and cutting into dense jungle to the end of the barely visible track, the adventurer's sudden reward was a 100-foot-tall rock-strewn hill—an introduction to another Maya ceremonial site! This complex has two levels of plazas, each with its own temples, all surrounded by unexcavated mounds.

When found, three of the temples showed obvious signs of looting with vertical slit trenches—open—just as the looters had left them. No one will ever know what valuable artifacts were removed and easily sold to private collectors all over the world. The large main temple on the upper plaza had been violated to the heart of what appears to be one or more burial chambers. A painted frieze runs around the low ceiling. Today the only temple inhabitants greeting outsiders are small bats.

Chan Chich has a new guard: Belizean-born Barry Bowen, owner of the property, who has built a group of simple thatch cabañas in one of the plazas of the Maya site. Though deplored by some archaeology buffs, these cabañas are very popular with birdwatchers and Mayaphiles who agree with Bowen that they will serve as a deterrent to temple looters who think nothing of defiling the ancient stone cities, and marijuana growers who find these isolated spots a perfect hiding place for their illegal crops. For more information about Chan Chich Lodge, see "West of Orange Walk Town" in the Orange Walk District chapter.

Altun Ha

Travel north 28 miles on the New Northern Highway from Belize City until it intersects with the Old Northern Highway. Take Old Northern Highway about 12 miles; a sign marks the Altun Ha access road. It's about one and a half miles to the archaeological site from here. It wasn't until the archaeologists came in 1964 that the name Rockstone Pond was translated into the Maya words Altun Ha. The site covers an area of about 25 square miles, most of which is covered by trees, vines, and jungle. Altun Ha, a trading center as well as a religious ceremonial center, is believed to have accommodated about 10,000 people. Archaeologists, working in the midst of a community of Maya families that have been living here for several centuries, have dated construction to about 1,500-2,000 years ago.

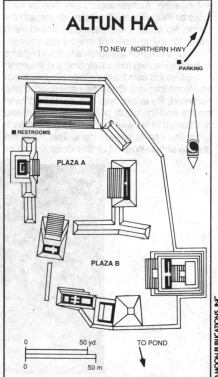

A team led by Dr. David Pendergast from the Royal Ontario Museum began work in 1965 on the central part of the ancient city, where upward of 250 structures have been found in an area of about 1,000 square yards. So far, this is the most extensively excavated of all the Maya sites in Belize. For a trading center, Altun Ha was strategically located—a few miles from **Little Rocky Point** on the Caribbean and a few miles from **Moho Caye** at the mouth of the Belize River, both believed to have been major centers for the large trading canoes that worked up and down the coasts of Guatemala, Honduras, Belize, the Yucatán, and all the way to Panama.

Near Plaza B, the **Reservoir,** also known as **Rockstone Pond,** is fed by springs and rain runoff. It demonstrates the advanced knowledge of the Maya in just one of their many fields: engineering. Archaeologists say that for centuries an insignificant little stream ran through the jungle. No doubt it had been a source of fresh water for the Maya—but maybe not enough. The Maya diverted the creek and then began a major engineering project, digging and enlarging a deep, round hole that was then plastered with limestone cement. Once the cement dried and hardened, the stream was rerouted to its original course and the newly built reservoir filled and overflowed at the east end, allowing the stream to continue on its age-old track. This made the area liveable. Was all of this done before or after the temple structures were built? Is the completion of this reservoir what made the Maya elite choose to locate in this area? We may never know for sure. Today Rockstone Pond is surrounded by thick brush and the pond is alive with jungle creatures, including tarpon, small fish, and turtles and other reptiles.

The concentration of structures includes palaces and temples surrounding two main plazas. The tallest building (the Sun God Temple) is 59 feet above the plaza floor. At Altun Ha the structure bases are oval and terraced. The small temples on top have typical small rooms built with the Maya trademark—the corbel arch.

Pendergast's team uncovered many valuable finds, such as unusual green obsidian blades, pearls, and more than 300 jade pieces —beads, earrings, and rings. Seven funeral chambers were discovered, including the **Temple of the Green Tomb,** rich with human remains and traditional funerary treasures. Maya scholars believe the first man buried was someone of great importance. He was draped with jade beads, pearls, and shells. And it was next to his right hand that the most exciting find was located—a solid jade head now referred to as **Kinich Ahau** ("The Sun God"). Kinich Ahau is, to date, the largest jade carving found in any Maya country. The head weighs nine pounds and measures nearly six inches from base to crown. It is cared for by the Department of Archaeology in Belmopan.

Cahal Pech

Altun Ha was rebuilt several times during the pre-Classic, Classic, and post-Classic periods. Scientists believe that the site was violently abandoned as evidenced by the obvious desecration of the structures. This Maya ceremonial site is open to the public 9 a.m.-5 p.m.; the small entrance fee is less than US$2.

SITES IN WESTERN BELIZE

Cahal Pech
Cahal Pech ("Place of the Ticks") is in San Ignacio in the Cayo District near **Tipu**. This medium-sized Maya site was discovered in the early 1950s, but scientific research did not begin until 1988, when a team from the University of San Diego began excavation. Thirty-four structures were compacted into a two- to three-acre area. Excavation is ongoing

and visitors are welcome. Watching the archaeological team in action gives visitors an opportunity to see how ruins look before restoration and how painstaking the work can be. You'll pay a small fee at Cahal Pech, and you can visit a new, small museum where you will see artifacts found at the site. This site is within walking distance of San Ignacio.

Xunantunich
The word Xunantunich (zoo-nahn-too-NEECH, "Stone Lady") is derived from local legend. A thousand years ago, Xunantunich was already a ruin. It's believed to have been built sometime during A.D. 150-900, the golden age of the Maya. Though certainly not the biggest of Maya structures, at 135 feet high **El Castillo** is one of the taller structures (Maya or otherwise) in Belize. El Castillo has been partially excavated and explored. The eastern side of the structure

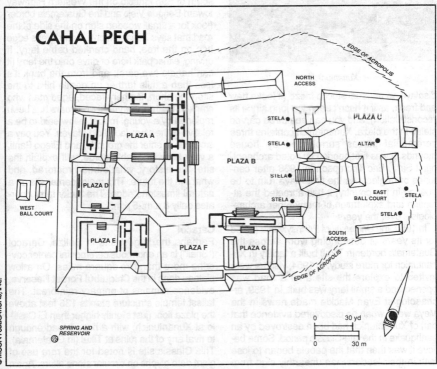

Xunantunich

displays an unusual stucco frieze (it looks new and fresh, as if it hasn't been too long since its reconstruction), and you can see three carved stelae in the plaza. Xunantunich contains three ceremonial plazas surrounded by house mounds. It was first opened by noted archaeologist Sir J. Eric Thompson in 1938 after centuries of neglect. As the first Maya ruin to be opened in the country, it has attracted the attention and exploration of many other archaeologists over the years.

In 1950, the University of Pennsylvania (noted for its years of outstanding work across the Guatemala border in Tikal) built a facility in Xunantunich for more study. In 1954, visitors were invited to explore the site after a road was opened and a small ferry was built. In 1959, archaeologist Evan Mackie made news in the Maya world when he discovered evidence that part of Xunantunich had been destroyed by an earthquake in the late-Classic period. Some believe it was then that the people began to lose faith in their leaders—an unearthly sign from

the gods. But for whatever reason, Xunantunich ceased to be a religious center long before the end of the Classic period.

This impressive Maya ceremonial site is well worth a visit and a climb—from the top the panorama encompasses the thick green Guatemalan Peten District, the Maya Mountains, and a grand view of the entire Cayo District and Belize jungle stretching for miles to the horizon. To get to the top, follow a path that meanders across the front and side of the structure. At the top is a typical small Maya temple; watch out for the large step over a hole in the cement. On one of our last visits, the site was empty except for one lone believer meditating on the very top of the temple in a perfect lotus position. He appeared to be in complete harmony with the blue sky and puffy white clouds above, the jungle below—and perhaps with the Maya gods of Xunantunich within.

To find Xunantunich, travel about eight miles south of San Ignacio on the Western Highway toward Benque Viejo and the Guatemala border (look for a small wooden sign on the side of the road that says Xunantunich). At the river's edge hop on the free, hand-cranked cable ferry. If driving, either park here or drive onto the ferry (it can handle two cars), and from the bank it's less than a mile farther up gentle hills to the site. The short, leathery-faced, aged man who cranked the ferry for years and years has been replaced by a young, robust fellow said to be a relative of the stern-faced old Mayan. You pay a small fee to enter the grounds, and Elfego Panti, a very knowledgeable guide, will explain the site: the history, what's been restored, and what's in the future. This major center sits on a natural limestone ridge. The funky ferry operates daily 8 a.m.-5 p.m.

Caracol

Perhaps the largest site in Belize, Caracol ("Snail") is an enormous ceremonial center covering more than five square miles. On a low plateau deep in the **Chiquibul Forest Reserve,** evidence remains of primary rainforest. The tallest temple structure stands 136 feet above the plaza floor (just slightly higher than El Castillo at Xunantunich) with a base broad enough to rival any of the ruins at Tikal (in Guatemala). This Classic site is noted for the rare use of giant date glyphs on circular stone altars. Again

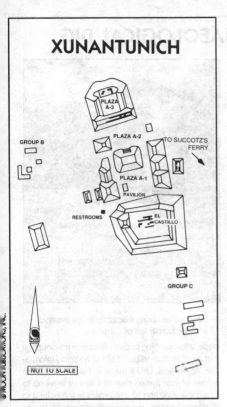

XUNANTUNICH

PLAZA A-3

GROUP B

PLAZA A-2

TO SUCCOTZ'S FERRY

PLAZA A-1

PAVILION

RESTROOMS

EL CASTILLO

GROUP C

NOT TO SCALE

the Maya exhibited their engineering skills, building extensive reservoirs and agricultural terraces. More of Caracol continues to be discovered by archaeologists Diane and Arlen Chase and their energetic assistants—student interns from Tulane University and University of Central Florida. According to John Morris, archaeological commissioner of Belize, a lifetime of exploration remains to be done within six to nine miles in every direction from today's discoveries. It's proving to have been a powerful site that controlled a very large area.

Many carvings are dated A.D. 300-600, indicating Caracol was settled about A.D. 300 and continued to flourish when other Maya sites were in decline. Carvings on the site also indicate that Caracol and Tikal engaged in ongoing conflicts, each defeating the other on

various occasions. After a war in A.D. 562, however, Caracol dominated the area for more than a century. A former archaeological commissioner named the site Caracol because of the numerous snail shells found there.

You can reach Caracol by forestry road through Douglas DeSilva (formerly called Augustine) in the Mountain Pine Ridge. However, although the site is only 30 miles farther on, visitors are advised to travel with 4WD vehicles as the road is extremely rough. **Note:** The new road should be completed by now, making the trip easier, but until I travel over it, I won't suggest you drive your sports car! The closest accommodations are near the Douglas DeSilva Forestry Station and in and around the Cayo District. Gas is not available along this road, so it behooves visitors to make all arrangements necessary to carry ample fuel. Camping is not allowed in the area without permission from the Forestry Department in Belmopan. The **Department of Archaeology** and/or the **Forestry Department, Western Division** must be informed before any visits, for permission and advice on accessibility. Once the road is complete, groups of visitors will be brought into the area by tour bus.

SITES IN SOUTHERN BELIZE

Lubaantun

Northwest of Punta Gorda, north of the Columbia River and one mile beyond San Pedro is the Maya ruin of Lubaantun ("Place of the Fallen Stones"). It was built and occupied during the late-Classic period (A.D. 730-890) and first noticed in 1875 by refugees from the southern U.S. who left the States during and after the Civil War. Its ridge location gives it a commanding view of the entire countryside. Eleven major structures are grouped around five main plazas, in addition to smaller plazas, for a total of 18 plazas and three ball courts. Most of the structures are terraced, and the tallest structure rises 50 feet above the plaza, from which you can see the Caribbean Sea, 20 miles distant. Notice that some corners of structures are rounded. Lubaantun's distinct style of architecture sets it apart from Maya construction in some parts of Latin America. This large late-Classic

LIFE ON AN ARCHAEOLOGICAL DIG

On 17 March 1992, a new tomb at Caracol was opened and the remains of at least two people were found (one a woman) along with 17 unbroken vessels. We were delighted to be invited to the archaeological site. What a time to visit! Everyone was on a natural "high," and deservedly so: day-by-day work on an archaeological dig can be tedious, and these marvelous finds don't happen on a daily basis. Archaeologists Diane and Arlen Chase and the tomb were the stars, surrounded by *National Geographic* cameras and crew, Belizean Archaeological Commissioner John Morris, American Consul Eugene Scassa and his wife, "Voice of America" broadcasters, and several Belize City reporters. Three young British hikers were also present.

Archaeologists come with an insatiable curiosity and an auto-wind wellspring of energy, motivation, and love for their work. And these scientists always manage to attract student workers of the same ilk.

Students generally spend the digging season (the dry season) carefully prodding the soil, brushing away thousand-year-old dirt, washing and scrubbing shards, and climbing up and down the multitudes of

Solar panels bring electricity to the isolated archaeological site of Caracol.

steps, often carrying buckets filled with precious soil that might contain valuable bits of historical information. At Caracol, unlike many archaeological sites, a crew of four armed men remains year-round to guard the site, and all equipment is left behind to discourage looters who regularly damage structures and steal valuable artifacts.

Everyday life here adapts to the environment. Housing is simple *palapa* huts and separate latrines; the shower house is a small mazelike affair with tiny roofless cubicles separated with walls of palm fronds. The "shower" is nothing more than buckets of water hauled up from the river and left to warm in the sun. But a solar panel does provide limited electricity for such necessities as a refrigerator and freezer.

Food, as usual, is an important part of daily life. Supplies, including frozen chicken and beef, are brought in on the weekend. Meats are served about three times a week; the rest of the time the menu is supplemented with canned foods and beans. At each meal the *fogon* (stone grill) is fired up and covered with handmade tortillas; birthdays are always celebrated with a homemade cake.

A student archaeologist washes shards dug up around Caracol.

One very young archaeologist enjoys Mickey Mouse in the middle of the jungle, with the help of solar panels.

Work on the new road into Caracol had just begun at the time of our visit. We barely made it to the site by bouncing, slipping, and sliding on the muddy mire of a road; we hit only one tree and afterward had to tie the right passenger door shut with a rope. But it was all worth it.

Our first surprise at Caracol occurred soon after we climbed out of the mud-covered Land Rover and wandered over to a group of thatched, pole houses clustered just beyond the entrance. We discovered a kitchen, a dining room, and experienced mild shock when we walked into another room to find Mickey Mouse on the small screen in living and talking color! And what's more, a tiny three-year-old boy sat on his trike mesmerized by the TV. At first I thought this was just a weird dream. After I looked around, it was obvious that this was a gathering place for the "community," with its bleacherlike arrangement of boards and logs and solar-powered VCR.

The average city dweller would readily admit that life is not easy here. The weather is very hot and humid. In the past it's been necessary to regrade the road each year after the damaging rains (the new all-weather road should make a big difference). The bug problem never quits; mosquitoes are the bane of the tropics. Yet many archaeologists quickly admit they have it a lot easier today than did the earliest scientists long before solar panels.

Caracol's Canaa (Sky Palace) stands 140 feet high.

Lubaantun

site has been studied and surveyed several times by familiar names, such as Thomas Gann and, more recently, by Norman Hammond in 1970. Distinctive clay whistle figurines (similar to those found in Mexico's Isla Jaina) illustrate lifestyles and occupations of the era. Other artifacts include a unique, carved glasslike skull, obsidian blades, grinding stones (much like those still used today to grind corn), beads, shells, turquoise, and shards of pottery. From all of this archaeologists have determined that the city flourished until the 8th century A.D. It was a farming community that traded with the highland areas of today's Guatemala, and the people worked the sea and maybe the nearby cayes just offshore. To get to Lubaantun from Punta Gorda, go 1.5 miles west past the gas station to the Southern Highway, then take a right. Two miles farther you'll come to the village of San Pedro. From here go left around the church to the concrete bridge; cross and go almost a mile—the road is passable during the dry season. Park before you reach the aged wooden bridge. This site has not been made into a park, so it's largely overgrown with brush and jungle; wear your hiking boots and long pants.

Nim Li Punit

Right off the Southern Highway before the San Antonio turnoff, 25 miles north of Punta Gorda town, you'll find Nim Li Punit (a 15-minute walk from the highway along a trail marked by a small sign). The site has enjoyed only preliminary ex-

cavations (1970), and is believed to have held a close relationship with nearby Lubaantun. One of the memorable finds was a 30-foot-tall carved stela, the tallest ever found in Belize—and in most of the rest of the Maya world. About 25 stelae have been found on the site dated A.D. 700-800. Rediscovered in 1974, the site was looted almost immediately. However, the looters missed a tomb later uncovered by archaeologist Richard Leventhal in 1986. If you're not driving a car, it's best to make arrangements to see these ruins and the villages with a guide before your arrival in Punta Gorda.

Uxbenka

Found only recently (1984), Uxbenka has revealed more than 20 stelae, seven of which are carved. One dates from the early Classic period, an otherwise nonexistent period in southern Belize and a rare date for stelae in the entire Maya area. The site is perched on a ridge overlooking the traditional Maya village of Santa Cruz and provides a grand view of the foothills and valley of the Maya Mountains. Here you'll see hillsides lined with cut stones resembling massive structures. This method is unique to the Toledo District. Uxbenka ("Old Place") was named by the people of nearby Santa Cruz. It's located just outside Santa Cruz, about three miles west of San Antonio Village. The most convenient way to see the site is with a rental car. However, if you're staying in San Antonio or Punta Gorda ask around town; a local may be willing to take you and act as a guide. Arrange your price in advance.

OTHER SITES

Hundreds of unexcavated and probably undiscovered Maya sites lie hidden in the shadows of Belize's forests. Because of the attraction of big bucks on the black market attached to Maya art, a partially excavated site is an open invitation to looters. The government is willing to leave these unknown sites undisturbed hoping that looters will not find them first. A few other sites that have been documented are in various stages of excavation:

Actun Balam, near Caracol in the Cayo District.

Tzimin Kax ("Mountain Cow"), in the Cayo District.

Pusilha, on the Moho River near Lubaantun.

This is far from a complete list. As growth in the country continues and money becomes available, the mysterious Mundo Maya will continue to reveal itself.

Rio Azul

Beyond Blue Creek and across the border into Guatemala, one of the newest and most exciting archaeological sites, Rio Azul, was rediscovered a couple of years ago. Without roads, it is not yet accessible from the Belizean side, but has already produced new and exciting artifacts, such as a screw-on-lid pottery jar—a few more pieces to fit into the puzzle of the advanced Maya civilization.

BELIZE DISTRICT

Of all the districts, probably the Belize District most clearly defines the country. Here on the banks of Haulover Creek the country was founded, its hopes were kindled, its present success was forged, and many of its greatest problems have arisen. It is a district of much ethnic diversity. It is also a district that encompasses swamps, mangroves, thickets, marshes, broadleaf forest, and a couple of hundred cayes. It juxtaposes Maya ruins with the commercial capital of the country, Belize City, where the population is also the most heavily concentrated. Within the Belize District to the east are island playgrounds, the largest of them Ambergris Caye; to the west are the Baboon Sanctuary and the Belize Zoo; to the north rises the pyramid of Altun Ha; and to the south lie the lagoons of the Gales Point area.

BELIZE CITY

Belize City straddles the estuaries of Haulover Creek, part of the Belize River that empties into the Caribbean Sea. In this bustling harbor-city of about 50,000 (mostly Afro-Creoles), small businesses abound. With independence, Belize is implementing slow but sure changes. However, if you want to get a taste of what colonial life was like "back when," don't wait. Come before the town is spiffed up, painted, and highrises line the coast. Visit before the old Swing Bridge is replaced—nothing is quite like watching the traffic jams at 5:30 a.m. and 5:30 p.m. each day, when the low-lying bridge across Haulover Creek closes to cars while it pivots to allow tall-masted boats to pass through. (If you happen to drive across the Swing Bridge after dark, be sure to turn your headlights down as there's a hump in the bridge—car headlights blind oncoming traffic.) Haulover Creek is a name left over from the time when cattle were attached to each other by a rope wrapped around their horns and "hauled" across the river.

(top) Kayaking with the Slickrock group is always an adventure. (Norm Shrewsbury);
(bottom) Fallen Stones Lodge feeding butterflies (Phil Lanier)

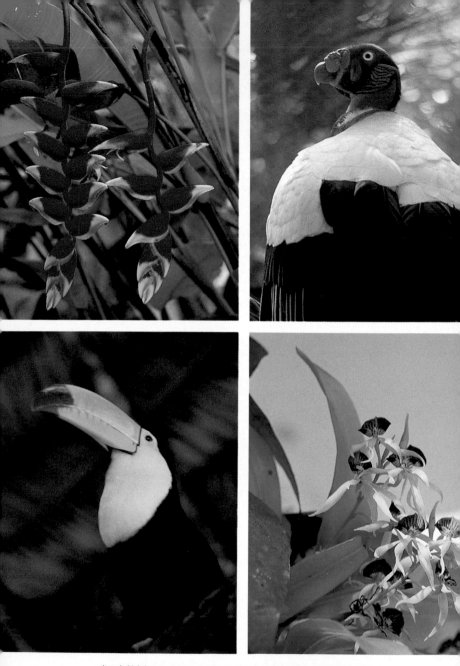

(top left) lobster claws growing at Chaa Creek; (top right) king vulture;
(bottom left) Rambo the Toucan is the free-wheeling pet at the Belize Zoo.
(bottom right) Black orchids are the national flower of Belize. (photos by Oz Mallan)

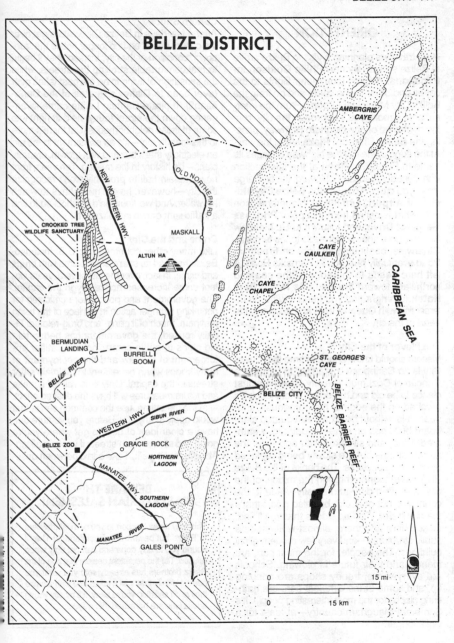

ORIENTATION

Most travelers planning a visit to Belize arrive at Belize's relatively new **Philip Goldson International Airport** (commuter flights to the cayes and other towns come and go from the Belize City Municipal Airport). From the international airport, you'll approach the city from the northwest on the Northern Highway, passing the **Belize Biltmore Plaza** along the way. At the edge of the city the highway changes its name to **Freetown Road** at the intersection with Central American Boulevard, the first large street you cross. To reach the **Belize City Municipal Airport,** turn left at this intersection onto what is called from this point **Princess Margaret Drive,** and follow it to St. Matthew Street, where another left leads to the terminal. Otherwise, continuing straight on Freetown Road eventually puts you at Barracks Road. A left here heads to the edge of the sea and northward toward the **Ramada Royal Reef Hotel;** turn right and you head toward an intersection with **Queen Street** and access to the heart of the city.

The Flavor of the City

Visitors should know ahead of time that Belize City is no Caribbean "paradise" in terms of a Cancún or Cozumel. The city appears at first glance to be old and run-down, and, though it's perched on the edge of the gorgeous Caribbean, it is without beaches. Antiquated clapboard buildings on stilts—unpainted, weathered, tilted, and streaked with age—line the narrow streets but are slowly being replaced by concrete structures. The banks of the Belize River, meandering through the middle of the city, are often dirty and smelly—face it, the country is not only old, but also poor; that's the *down* side. The *up* side is that you'll find, tucked here and there, almost-white sedate public structures—and very few modern glitzy buildings. The people, for the most part, are friendly and their future is glowing. Schools are everywhere, trendy shops are popping up, and some of the simplest bars are gathering places for the most interesting people. It's Somerset Maugham country—at least for a while longer.

Culture Shock

After a few days in Belize City visitors get over the culture shock and no longer notice the "rundown" condition of the city. Instead, they'll begin to feel comfortable strolling the streets, while the sensation of living in an era past takes over (ever been to Disney's Pirates of the Caribbean?). If pirate-Captain Lafitte came swaggering down the street today, he'd fit right into some of these neighborhoods. But there's more to this friendly city—it's an excitement in the air, an electricity that's buzzing with growth, dreams, plans—it's history in the making. Ten years from now Captain Lafitte probably won't recognize the city—however, he still might have to watch his wallet. And we *know* he'd be shocked to find a traffic light or two in Belize City.

Crime and the City

Like many other countries, the U.S. included, Belize has had its share of problems with drugs and crime. In fact, over the last several years violent crime increased noticeably in the capital. The government and police were criticized for not taking stronger action in the face of the rising mayhem, much of it gang- and drug-related. Finally roused, the government has begun taking steps to battle crime, including stiffer enforcement of the law and the deployment of army troops when necessary to maintain safer streets in the capital. Only time will tell if these and future measures will have the desired effect.

In the meantime, use the common sense that would apply in any city. Before you venture out, have a clear idea of how to get where you're going and stick to main streets if you're walking. At night, don't walk. Take a taxi between desti-

---

BEWARE THE RASTAFARIAN SALESMEN!

This may never happen to you or most travelers to Belize but beware the Rastafarians! They'll hound you to buy dope and can get ugly when refused. Tell the persistent dealers that one of the Rasta brothers has already sold you what you need. Usually that's all it takes and with a smile they're off satisfied you're okay. It's mostly young adults who are harassed this way.

nations, or if you're driving, keep your windows rolled up and your doors locked. Don't flash money, jewelry, and other temptations, but if you're threatened, hand them over. And in emergencies, call 911 for the police, 90 for fire or ambulance.

Hub of the Nation

Belize City is not for everyone. However, there are many practical reasons travelers include Belize City in their explorations. At certain times of the year it becomes difficult to find comfortable accommodations within one's budget in the smaller towns and caye resorts. In fact, sometimes it's impossible to find any accommodations without reservations. Because of the number and variety of accommodations in Belize City, it's a good base for forays into other parts of the country on day-trips.

Belize City has access to rivers, ocean, and three of the five major roads in the country: the Northern Highway, Western Highway, and Manatee Highway. The city is ideally located for reaching any part of the country within a day's time. Because of this access, Belize City is also where you'll find the headquarters of the bus lines, rental car agencies, and airlines, as well as the Texaco Station where you catch most water taxis to offshore cayes and coastal towns.

Stocking Up

Whether you're heading off by bus to Punta Gorda, driving to the Rio Bravo Research Center in Orange Walk District, cycling out to the Cayo District, or catching the boat to the Turneffe Islands, there is nowhere in the country better suited for stocking up on necessary provisions. Supermarkets, pharmacies, hardware stores, and bike shops have a greater selection than you will find elsewhere.

SIGHTS

North of the Swing Bridge

An early morning stroll through the weathered, old clapboard buildings of Belize City gives you a genuine feeling of the city. This is when people are rushing off to work, kids are all spiffed up on their way to school, and housewives are out and about doing their daily shopping.

For most travelers, Belize City revolves around the **Swing Bridge** at Haulover Creek. You reach it from either airport from the northwest side of town. This is where you catch boats to the cayes, do your banking, check in with the Belize Tourist Board, post a letter, buy local handicrafts, and much more. The streets are crammed with small shops (many operated by East Indian and Chinese merchants), a stream of pedestrians on the sidewalks, and lots of traffic.

On this side of the creek, Queen and Front streets are the crucial thoroughfares. As you face the Swing Bridge a look to the right will reveal the **Texaco Station,** where you catch boats to Ambergris Caye, Caye Caulker, and elsewhere (another boat, the *Andrea,* is available at the dock in front of the Bellevue Hotel across the creek). On the corner to the left, in the multistory wooden building, is the **post office.**

Moving down Front Street you'll find the **Belize Tourist Board,** 83 North Front St., tel. (2) 77213, on your right.

Continuing to the point, you'll see the **Bliss Memorial** and the **Fort George Lighthouse.** The seabreeze can be very pleasant here as you glimpse numerous cayes as well as ships at anchor offshore.

Once you round the point, the road becomes Marine Parade and runs past the modern-**Radisson Fort George Hotel, Chateau Caribbean Hotel,** and **Memorial Park,** a grassy salute to the 40 Belizeans who lost their lives in WW I, and ends at Hutson Street. The **U.S. Embassy** sits at the end of the block on the right. The old colonial house was built in New England, dismantled, and transported to Belize as ship's ballast. It was reconstructed 120 years ago and houses the entire U.S. Embassy, which has been in Belize since 1840.

From the **Radisson Fort George** dock you'll get a good view of the harbor. Originally this was Fort George Island; until the 1850s it was the location of the army barracks. The strait separating the island from the mainland was filled in during the early 1920s and dedicated as a memorial park for the dead of WW I. Today it is the site of the **Baron Bliss Memorial** and the Fort George Hotel. After WW II, visiting dignitaries from England surveyed the country with plans for various agricultural projects; they also could find no place to stay. Accommodations went to the top of their

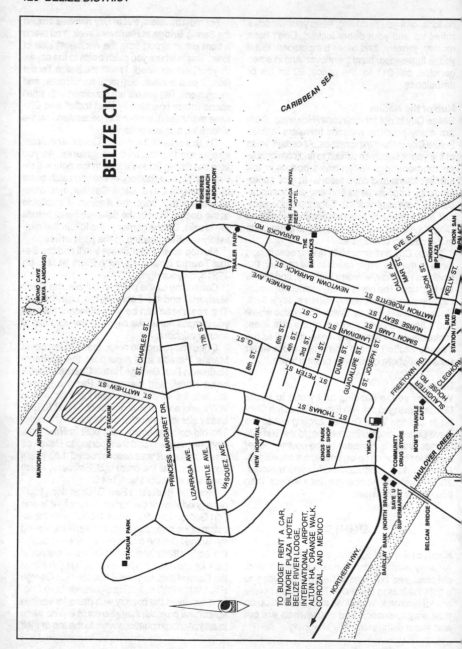

BELIZE CITY

CARIBBEAN SEA

MOHO CAYE
(MAYA LANDINGS)

MUNICIPAL AIRSTRIP

NATIONAL STADIUM

ST. MATTHEW ST.

ST. CHARLES ST.

17th.

PRINCESS MARGARET DR.

LIZARRAGA AVE.

GENTLE AVE.

VASQUEZ AVE.

STADIUM PARK

TRAILER PARK

BAYMEN AVE

NEWTOWN BARRACK ST.

CALLE AL

BARRACKS RD.

THE RAMADA ROYAL
REEF HOTEL

THE BARRACKS

EVE ST.

MAR ST.

WILSON ST.

CINDERELLA
PLAZA

CHON SAN
PALACE

KELLY ST.

FISHERIES
RESEARCH
LABORATORY

6th ST.

4th ST.

3rd ST.

1st ST.

C ST.

G ST.

8th ST.

ST. PETER ST.

DUNN ST.

GUADALUPE ST.

ST. JOSEPH ST.

MATRON ROBERTS ST.

NURSE SEAY ST.

SIMON LAMB ST.

LANDIVAR ST.

NEW HOSPITAL

ST. THOMAS ST.

KINGS PARK
BIKE SHOP

YMCA

FREETOWN RD.

CLEGHORN

SLAUGHTER
HOUSE RD.

BUS
STATION / TAXI

MOM'S TRIANGLE
CAFE

COMMUNITY
DRUG STORE

SAVE U
SUPERMARKET

BARCLAY BANK (NORTH BRANCH)

BELCAN BRIDGE

HAULOVER CREEK

NORTHERN HWY.

TO BUDGET RENT A CAR,
BILTMORE PLAZA HOTEL,
BELIZE RIVER LODGE,
INTERNATIONAL AIRPORT,
ALTUN HA, ORANGE WALK,
COROZAL, AND MEXICO

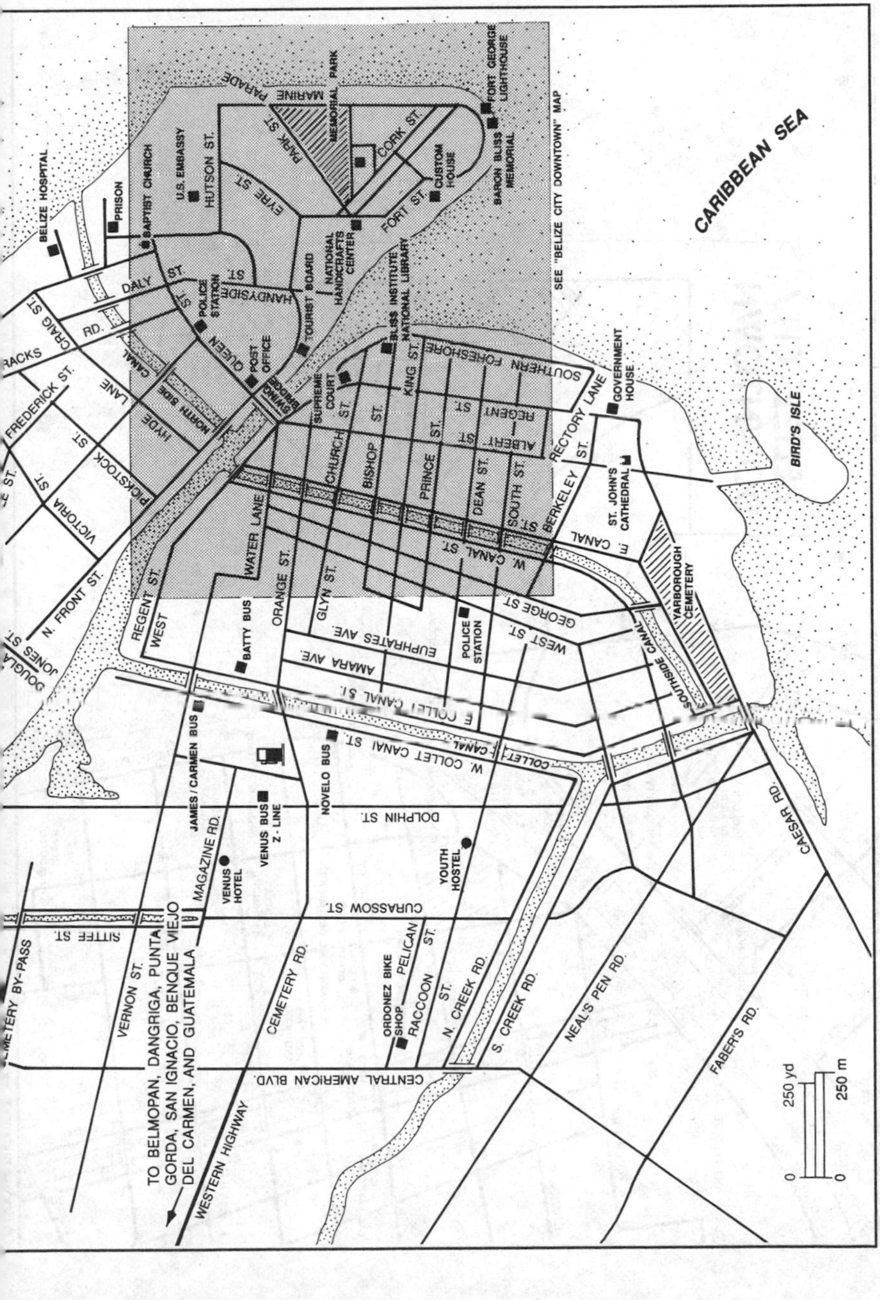

CARIBBEAN SEA

BELIZE HOSPITAL
PRISON
BAPTIST CHURCH
U.S. EMBASSY
HUTSON ST.
EYRE ST.
PARK ST.
MARINE PARADE
MEMORIAL PARK
CORK ST.
FORT ST.
FORT GEORGE LIGHTHOUSE
BARON BLISS MEMORIAL
CUSTOM HOUSE
NATIONAL HANDICRAFTS CENTER
SEE "BELIZE CITY DOWNTOWN" MAP

DALY ST.
CRAIG ST.
BARRACKS RD.
POLICE STATION
QUEEN ST.
CANAL
NORTH SIDE CANAL
HYDE LANE
HANDYSIDE ST.
TOURIST BOARD
POST OFFICE
SWING BRIDGE
BLISS INSTITUTE
NATIONAL LIBRARY
SOUTHERN FORESHORE
GOVERNMENT HOUSE

FREDERICK ST.
VICTORIA ST.
PICKSTOCK ST.
N. FRONT ST.
WATER LANE
REGENT ST.
WEST ST.
CHURCH ST.
SUPREME COURT
KING ST.
BISHOP ST.
PRINCE ST.
DEAN ST.
SOUTH ST.
ALBERT ST.
REGENT ST.
BERKELEY ST.
RECTORY LANE
ST. JOHN'S CATHEDRAL
BIRD'S ISLE

DOUGLAS JONES ST.
ORANGE ST.
GLYN ST.
W. CANAL ST.
GEORGE ST.
E. CANAL
YARBOROUGH CEMETERY
BATTY BUS
EUPHRATES AVE.
AMARA AVE.
POLICE STATION
WEST ST.
SOUTHSIDE CANAL

E. COLLET CANAL ST.
W. COLLET CANAL ST.
COLLET CANAL
CAESAR RD.

JAMES / CARMEN BUS
NOVELO BUS
DOLPHIN ST.
VENUS BUS Z - LINE
VENUS HOTEL
MAGAZINE RD.
YOUTH HOSTEL
CURASSOW ST.
SITTEE ST.
CEMETERY BY-PASS
VERNON ST.
ORDONEZ BIKE SHOP
RACCOON ST.
PELICAN ST.
N. CREEK RD.
S. CREEK RD.
NEAL'S PEN RD.
FABERS RD.
CEMETERY RD.
CENTRAL AMERICAN BLVD.

TO BELMOPAN, DANGRIGA, PUNTA
GORDA, SAN IGNACIO, BENQUE VIEJO
DEL CARMEN, AND GUATEMALA
WESTERN HIGHWAY

250 yd
250 m
0

© MOON PUBLICATIONS, INC.

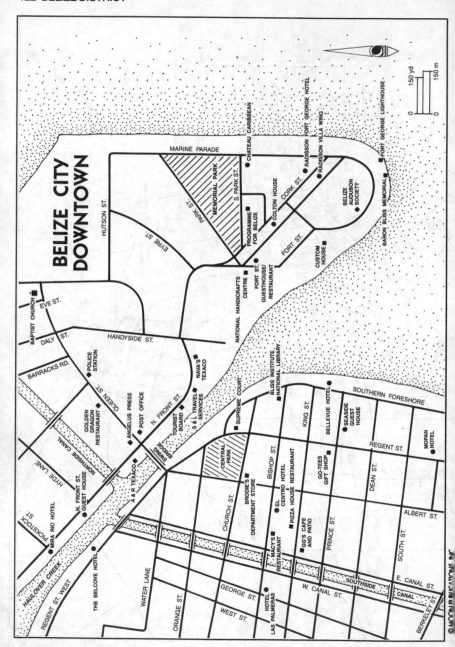

BELIZE CITY DOWNTOWN

MARINE PARADE

MEMORIAL PARK

S. PARK ST.

PARK ST.

HUTSON ST.

EYRE ST.

CHATEAU CARIBBEAN

COLTON HOUSE

CORK ST.

RADISSON FORT GEORGE HOTEL

RADISSON VILLA WING

FORT GEORGE LIGHTHOUSE

BARON BLISS MEMORIAL

BELIZE AUDUBON SOCIETY

FORT ST.

PROGRAMME FOR BELIZE

CUSTOM HOUSE

FORT ST.

GUESTHOUSE/ RESTAURANT

NATIONAL HANDICRAFTS CENTRE

BAPTIST CHURCH

EVE ST.

DALY ST.

HANDYSIDE ST.

BARRACKS RD.

POLICE STATION

QUEEN ST.

NAVA'S TEXACO

SUPREME COURT

BLISS INSTITUTE

NATIONAL LIBRARY

SOUTHERN FORESHORE

GOLDEN DRAGON RESTAURANT

ANGELUS PRESS

POST OFFICE

N. FRONT ST.

TOURIST BOARD

S & L TRAVEL SERVICES

SWING BRIDGE

KING ST.

BELLEVUE HOTEL

SEASIDE GUEST HOUSE

MOPAN HOTEL

REGENT ST.

NORTHSIDE CANAL

HYDE LANE

N. FRONT ST.

GUEST HOUSE

A & R TEXACO

CENTRAL PARK

CHURCH ST.

BRODIE'S DEPARTMENT STORE

BISHOP ST.

EL CENTRO HOTEL

PIZZA HOUSE RESTAURANT

GO-TEES GIFT SHOP

DEAN ST.

ALBERT ST.

PICKSTOCK ST.

MIRA RIO HOTEL

HAULOVER CREEK

REGENT ST. WEST

THE BELCOVE HOTEL

WATER LANE

ORANGE ST.

GEORGE ST.

WEST ST.

HOTEL LAS PALMERAS

MACY'S RESTAURANT

GG'S CAFE AND PATIO

PRINCE ST.

SOUTH ST.

W. CANAL ST.

SOUTHSIDE

CANAL

E. CANAL ST.

BERKELEY ST.

150 yd

150 m

priority list and became one of the first postwar projects in the colony. An easygoing, low-key charmer with excellent service and tasty meals, Fort George was the best hotel in town. Today, the hotel is part of the Radisson chain and has taken over the Villa hotel across the street, one block off the waterfront. The Radisson Fort George is the most noticeable structure in the area, especially since the addition of the modern, six-story-tall glass wing.

In general, the Fort George area is one of the most pleasant in Belize City. Meander through the neighborhood and you'll pass some lovely homes and a few charming old guesthouses as you head back toward town.

Turning right onto South Park Street will take you past **Programme for Belize** on the right. This worthy organization is striving to combine education, ecotourism, and sustainable jungle agriculture along with administration of the **Rio Bravo Conservation and Management Area.**

South of the Swing Bridge

As you cross the bridge, fishing boats at anchor bob in the current downstream. You're in for quite a spectacle if you are lucky enough to be there as the bridge is opened to allow boat traffic upstream.

On the south side of the bridge, you'll encounter even more traffic and more local color. Vendors sell fruits and cold drinks along the southeast side of the bridge. Bliss Promenade skirts the waterfront and eventually brings you to the **Bliss Institute;** social functions and seminars are held here. It is also the location of a theater, museum, and library, as well as the National Arts Council. Take a look at the display of Maya stelae and altars retrieved from the Cayo District.

In the main business section of Regent and Albert streets (originally called Front and Back streets—the only streets in 18th-century Belize City) you'll see old brick slave houses, with timber-and-shingle second floors. Slaves were kept in chains in the brick basements when they were not working in the fields.

The Market

Saturday-morning market in Belize City will never be the same. The seedy, old colonial

---

BARON BLISS

Henry Edward Ernest Victor Bliss, also known as the "Fourth Baron Bliss of the former Kingdom of Portugal," was born in the County of Buckingham, England. He first sailed into the harbor of Belize in 1926, though he was too ill to go ashore because of food poisoning he had contracted while visiting Trinidad. Bliss spent several months aboard his yacht, the *Sea King,* in the harbor, fishing in Belizean waters. Although he never became well enough to go ashore, Bliss learned to love the country from the sea and its habitués—the fishermen and officials in the harbor all treated him with great respect and friendliness. On the days that he was able only to languish on deck, he made every effort to learn about the small country. He was apparently so impressed with what he learned and the people he met that before his death he drew up a will that established a trust of nearly two million dollars for projects to benefit the people of Belize.

So far, more than a million dollars in interest from the trust has been used, for the erection of the Bliss Institute, Bliss School of Nursing, Bliss Promenade, and In-transit Lounge at the Belize International Airport, plus contributions to the Belize City water supply, the Corozal Town Board and Health Clinic, and for land for the building of Belmopan.

An avid yachtsman, Bliss stipulated that money be set aside for a regatta to be held in Belize waters, a focal point of the gala Baron Bliss Day celebrations each year. The baron's white granite tomb is at the point of Fort George in Belize City, guarded by the Bliss Lighthouse.

---

marketplace on the southern side of the Swing Bridge has been replaced by a modern three-story concrete structure. It's not quite as crowded as the old, tin-roofed, open-sided building, but friendly people still sell vegetables, skinned iguanas, fish, meats, and exotic fruits, as well as Belizean handicrafts. When you're strolling through the market and a lovely black lady with a bright-colored kerchief wrapped around her head says, "Try a tamarind, darlin'," go ahead (peel it and enjoy the flesh around the seeds). A tamarind is tasty and looks like a dark reddish brown string bean; it has the texture of dried fruit. Man doesn't live by apples alone—the tropics have many exotic fruits to try. All those who said that the historical Belize market was the seediest, darkest, most run-down market in the country will be in for a big surprise when next they visit.

Albert Street, just before you reach Belize City's **Central Park,** is the banking center of the city.

The market square offers frequent flea-market activity with a mishmash of gewgaws set out on small blankets, park benches, or the ground. This is a colorful scene with owners huddling close together under brilliant-hued umbrellas to screen out the hot sun. On close examination, it looks as though everyone is selling the same "attic treasures." This is the location of the original courthouse built in 1818. It has since been twice rebuilt (once after a demolition in 1878, and again after a fatal fire in 1918 that took the life of then-governor William Hart Bennett). Today, there is no courthouse, just a bit of green in the middle of the city.

The **Supreme Court building** sits between the Central Park and Haulover Creek. The antiquated town clock atop the white clapboard building shows a different time from all four sides—each wrong since the clock stopped running a while back (like most clock towers in Belize), but who's keeping time anyway? (Actually a visitor wrote to say that one side of the clock was showing the correct time. So noted!) The structure is decorated with a graceful white-metal filigree stairway that leads to the long veranda overlooking the square.

Church and State

Belize has the oldest Protestant church in Central America, **St. John's Anglican Cathedral.** This lovely old building, the only typically British structure in the city, is surrounded by well-kept green lawns. The slaves in Belize in 1812 helped to erect this graceful piece of architecture using bricks brought as ballast on sailing ships from Europe. Several Mosquito Coast kings from the Waiki tribe were crowned in this cathedral with ultimate pomp and grandeur; the last was crowned in 1815.

Behind the cathedral, at the southern end of Regent Street and also on Southern Foreshore,

clock tower

is **Government House,** which before Hurricane Hattie and the ensuing construction of Belmopan was the home and office of the governor general, the official Belizean representative of the Queen of England. The Prime Minister of Belize still keeps an office here. (Today the governor general can be found in Belmopan at **Belize House.**) Mostly, the lovely old structure now serves as a guesthouse for visiting VIPs and a place for social functions. Queen Elizabeth and Prince Philip were houseguests here on their visit in 1994. The old wooden buildings (built 1812-14) are said to have been designed by acclaimed British architect Christopher Wren, and until recently were described "as elegant as it gets." It's surrounded by sprawling lawns and wind-brushed palms facing the sea along Southern Foreshore.

RECREATION

Bike Shops and Tours

Who would dream of taking a bike tour of Belize City? Obviously some! Lindy Gillett at **Karakta,** 16 St. Thomas St., tel. (2) 33458, and his cast of top Belizean cyclists conduct city tours on very comfortable 18-speed bicycles. He detours you through streets *away* from the heavy traffic often encountered in Belize City. These are local cyclists, so they know their way around. *Karakta* is Creole for "character" and Lindy must be one to come up with such an audacious idea. He is planning to expand with tours of Altun Ha, the Baboon Sanctuary, and other nearby locations, maybe by the time you get there. Lindy also owns and operates **Kings Park Bike Shop.** He carries a good selection of touring and mountain bike parts and accessories.

Ordonez Bike Shop, 14 Pelican St., tel. (2) 78751, (just off Central American Blvd. near the Western Highway turnoff) is a popular supplier, biker, and booster of the "Hike & Bike to Save the Rainforest." Owned by Andrew Ordonez, it's a quality shop that carries parts and accessories for serious cyclists.

Boat Charters for Diving and Fishing

About the time this book goes to press, the *Belize Aggressor III,* tel. (800) 348-2628, will be taking up residence at the Ramada Royal Reef Marina. It's 120 feet long with nine cabins, a wet bar on the sundeck, and a jacuzzi. It makes trips of five and a half days to Lighthouse Reef and the Turneffe Islands with five dives per day. Rates are about US$1500 for the package.

Four other boats are chartered out of the Ramada Royal Reef Marina with captain, crew, and fuel: *Barracuda,* a 38-foot motor yacht, sleeps 20 people and costs US$330/day; *Royal Roamer,* a 36-foot dive boat, can accommodate up to 16 divers and goes for US$385/day; *Fish N' Diver* is a 30-foot boat outfitted to accommodate fishing or diving enthusiasts and costs US$440/day; and *Santa Katarina,* a 38-foot luxury cruiser, is especially well-suited for parties and rents for US$600/day.

Mike and Donna Hill of **Fanta-Sea Charters,** tel./fax in the U.S., (303) 226-1193, in Belize, tel./fax (2) 32712, charter the 45-foot catamaran, *Stingray,* out of Maya Landings on Moho Caye. They suggest an itinerary based on the customer's budget and time, anything from a day sail to the cayes to a trip up the Rio Dulce in Guatemala. Cost per day

for groups of up to three people is US$180 per person; for groups of four to six, US$150 per person, including food and beverages (except liquor).

Also based out of Moho Caye, the 60-foot ocean yacht *M/V Hot Dive,* in the U.S. tel. (800) 468-3483, in Belize, tel./fax (2) 34058, is available for day tours, packages, or customized itineraries. One package goes to the Rio Dulce in Guatemala. Depending on clients' interests, the boat can be rigged for deep-sea fishing, diving, or a combination. Chris Berg is the captain. Trips are priced according to package desired.

The dive shop at **Black Line Marina,** Mile 2.5 on the Northern Highway, offers NAUI openwater scuba certification courses for US$300 per person and dive packages. Full-day fishing trips with experienced guides can be exciting light-tackle excursions on the rivers, shallow saltwater flats, or the barrier reef. Overnight charter trips are available. For more information, call (2) 33187 or write Box 332, Belize City, C.A.

Marinas

Boat owners note: Vessels traveling to the area must have permission before entering Belize. Contact the Belize Embassy in Washington, D.C., tel. (202) 332-9636.

At Rogue's Point, **Radisson Fort George Hotel,** Marine Parade, tel. (2) 77400, fax (2) 30276, is a picturesque place to tie up, especially morning and evening. Rates are US$1/foot for boats 50 feet in length and longer, US50 cents/foot for under 50 feet.

Not only do the *Belize Aggressor, Wave Dancer,* and other charters dock at **Ramada Royal Reef,** Kings Park, Barracks Road, tel. (2) 32670, fax (2) 32660, but numerous boats belonging to the island resorts tie up on their trips into town. You can, too. Rates for docking run about US50 cents per foot per day.

Another marina boaters will want to check out is **Maya Landings,** tel. (2) 35350, fax (2) 35466, on Moho Caye. Ice, diesel, gas, and basic supplies are available. It should be fine for boats up to about 75 feet. Rates are US$1/foot. Credit cards are accepted.

You can also tie up at the **Black Line Marina,** Mile 2.5 on the Northern Highway, tel. (2) 33187. For radio contact from boats use VHF Channel

70 (143.500 MHz). It offers full marina facilities, marine ways, hookups, and supplies including fuel, water, and ice.

ACCOMMODATIONS

Most hotels all over the country add about 20% to listed prices for service charge and tax. And if the business accepts a credit card (many don't), be prepared to pay three to five percent more. One of the publications put out by the Belize Tourist Board says you can find rooms from US$12 and up. Well, the "and up" rooms are easy to find, but you'll have to look a little harder to find the cheapies. And then you should study them carefully. Expect community bathrooms and only cold water in some. Ample economy-types are around for those willing to search for them. Upscale hotels are growing in size (literally)—many have added rooms in response to the keen interest in Belize. Two newer hotels are the **Ramada Reef** and the **Biltmore Plaza.**

Budget

The small, simple **North Front Street Guest House,** 124 N. Front St., Belize City, Belize, C.A., tel. (2) 77595, offers eight rooms with shared bath; breakfast and laundry service are available. Near the center of town, it's just one block from where the water taxis tie up for trips to Ambergris Caye and Caye Caulker. Room rates are US$15 s, US$25 d. A group room with four beds goes for US$5 per person. Write or call for more information.

The **Mira Rio Hotel,** 59 N. Front St., Belize City, Belize, C.A., tel. (2) 44970, is ultrasimplicity downtown. With communal bathrooms and clean small rooms, rates are US$16 s, US$25 d; check out the new penthouse. This is the pickup spot for travelers going to **Ricardo's Beach Huts and Lobster Camp.** The restaurant on the premises, **Bistro Caribe,** serves a great barbecue and an unusual seaweed drink. A liquor store is also on-site. The owner, Dimas Villas, lives on the premises.

Owned by Hugh Weir and Adelma Broaster, the **Belcove Hotel,** 9 Regent St., Belize City, Belize, C.A., tel. (2) 78339, fax (2) 74007, features six simple rooms with ceiling fans and either private or shared bath with h/c water. Rates are

US$15 s/d with shared bath, US$20 with private bath. These folks also run a resort on **Gallows Point Caye** and operate **Native Guide Systems,** their own tour and travel agency. A restaurant is in the works.

More than a few blocks off the beaten path, the small **Hotel Las Palmeras,** 39 George St., Belize City, Belize, C.A., tel. (2) 73345, fax (2) 76815, sits on the corner of George and Bishop streets. It offers small economical rooms, some with private bathroom; a boutique and a cafeteria are on the premises. Rates with private bathroom are US$20 d, with community bathroom US$15 d, no credit cards. Write for more information.

Seaside Guest House, 3 Prince St., Belize City, Belize, C.A., tel. (2) 71689, is a little gem with rooms that are clean, though small. It has only cold water and a community bathroom, but it has a sea view, and it's kept cool by the trade winds. It's quiet, only six blocks from the bus station, and three blocks from the central square. Breakfast and dinner are available (fresh fish, rice, salad—about US$7). It's undergone lots of renovation. Owners Leonard Williams and John Self live on the premises and are willing to help with ongoing hotel, sightseeing, and transportation arrangements. Rates are about US$14 s and US$20 d; a dorm room is available with four beds for US$8 per person; there are five rooms in all. The water system has been improved. Write for more information.

For those traveling by bus, it doesn't come more convenient than the **Venus Hotel,** 2371 Magazine Rd., Belize City, Belize, C.A., tel. (2) 73354/73390. Immediately beside the Venus Bus Station you'll find nine basic rooms with restaurant and night security. Rooms have cold-water private baths and ceiling fans. Rates are about US$13 s, US$19 d.

Moderate

Colton House, 9 Cork St., Belize City, Belize, C.A., tel. (2) 44666, is an old charmer owned and operated by Alan and Ondina Colton. It's obvious from the sparkling hardwood floors that a lot of love (and labor) went into renovating the house, which is more than 60 years old. Some of its appeal lies in the white wooden hanging swings on the front porch, the green plants scattered about, and the sheer white curtains on

Ramada
Royal Reef
Hotel

the windows. Bedrooms are fan cooled. Both of the Coltons are usually on hand to give good information about Belize; they live downstairs. The Coltons offer four rooms, two with private bathrooms; the other two share a bathroom. The Colton House, down the street from the Radisson Hotel, doesn't offer food, but it's near quite a few cafes, a Chinese spot, and (just around the corner) the **Fort Street Restaurant.** Rates with shared bath are about US$33 s, US$40 d; with private bathroom, US$38 s, and US$45 d, US$52 t.

Just off Albert Street on Bishop, **El Centro,** 4 Bishop St., Belize City, Belize, C.A., tel. (2) 72413, fax (2) 74553, is an old standard of Belize City that offers a central location, a good restaurant downstairs, and upstairs, small, carpeted rooms with private bath, a/c, phone, and TV. The owner, Alfred Sikaffy, lives on the premises. Rates for all 13 rooms are about US$38 s or d.

Costing a little more money but very delightful is a small guesthouse in a charming old Victorian building simply called **Fort Street Guest House.** Hugh and Teresa Parkey are the owners and they enjoy making guests feel at home and sharing information about the city and sightseeing on the cayes and in the countryside. Conveniently located, the guest house is within easy walking distance of the entire Fort George area as well as the action around the Swing Bridge area. The cooking here remains outstanding and a favorite with local Belizeans

when they want a special evening out. By night the simple, tropical Victorian decor takes on a crystal, linen, and candlelight sparkle. Lime garlic shrimp has its followers as does the longtime signature dessert, Death by Chocolate Cake, with chocolate ice cream and topping.

The relaxing Casablanca-style decor of the rooms with wooden shutters, wicker furniture, slow-moving ceiling fans, and clean community bathrooms is special! Put your order in the night before and fresh coffee is delivered to your room at 7 a.m. Room rates are US$45 s, US$60 d, US$75 t, US$85 q including breakfast. For more information and reservations, write or call Theresa Parkey, Box 3, Belize City, Belize, C.A., tel. (2) 30116, fax (2) 78808. In the U.S. contact **Magnum Belize,** tel. (800) 447-2931.

The **Bakadeer Inn,** 74 Cleghorn St., Belize City, Belize, C.A., tel. (2) 31286/31400, fax (2) 31963, owned by Belizean Kent McField, gets rave reviews from guests for its good food, friendly staff, and comfy rooms. It's near the intersection of Cleghorn and Mapp streets, with a lush tropical patio and parking for cars and trailers. Do you want to know where you'll see great undersea scenery in the cayes or do you need a discussion on the difference between a dolphin and a dolphin fish? Ask Kent's wife, Melanie Dotherow; she's a marine biologist as well as the inn's manager. Rooms come with extra nice mattresses, h/c water, private bath, a/c, carpeting, and phone. A full American breakfast is included in the price, US$45 s, US$50 d. Write for more information.

In the same area of town as the Bakadeer Inn you'll find the **Royal Orchid,** Box 279, Belize City, Belize, C.A., tel. (2) 32783, fax (2) 32789, a four-story yellow and red building that serves as a store and hotel on the corner of Douglas Jones St. and New Road. Upstairs on the top floor is a bar/restaurant with panoramic views of the city, said to be especially nice at night. Owner Willie Chang offers 22 rooms with h/c water, private baths, a/c, TV, and phones. Rates are US$45 s, US$55 d, US$60 t.

The **Mopan Hotel,** 55 Regent St., Belize City, Belize, C.A., tel. (2) 77351/73356, fax (2) 75383, is another simple but friendly hotel with reasonable rates. The bar is known far and wide as a meeting place for regular Belizean travelers, interesting people, or just those who want to watch a Super Bowl game (hijacked from the U.S. via satellite) while sipping Belikin beer and enjoying friendly kibitzing. The roomy, old house has eight rooms, with a/c in some, and private bathrooms. Rates for fan-cooled rooms are US$21 s, US$32 d; for a/c US$32 s, US$37 d. Write or call for more information and reservations.

More Expensive

One of the most upscale hotels in Belize City is the **Radisson Fort George Hotel,** 2 Marine Parade on the waterfront. Rooms are nicely appointed, with private bath, a/c, TV, and a minibar; some have ocean views. The hotel has a swimming pool and its own marina. Rates start at US$114 s/d, US$134 t in the executive and colonial wings. The rates are US$139 d for the tower, and a superior room in the new section with a water view is US$159 d. The hotel dining room serves a full buffet breakfast daily and offers a different special each day; on Thanksgiving count on a turkey dinner. You'll also find the **Seventh Heaven Guest Deck,** a bookstand, and gift shop. And if you see a big bowl of bananas in the lobby, help yourself!

Inside the compound is **Rachel's Art Gallery,** which carries prints and original art by various artists, including those by Rachel herself. **Emory King Real Estate** also has a small office here (the main office is at 9 Regent St., tel. 2-77453). This establishment is owned by cigar-chomping author, raconteur, humorist, scriptwriter, sometimes actor, and man about town/country Emory King, a U.S. transplant. How did he get to

Belize? According to Emory, by "accident." As Emory tells it, while he was on a world cruise aboard the *Vagabond,* the vessel crashed into a reef of staghorn coral at English Caye one moonlit night. Though the boat was repaired, he never left—that was in 1953. In the early years he lifted his pen to agitate for Belize's independence (accomplished in 1981) as well as to write several popular books and a couple of videos on Belize. King's *Driver's Guide to Beautiful Belize* would have to be considered a Belize best-seller. Today he describes his adopted country as "a little bit south of Paradise, a little bit north of frustration."

Across the street is the **Radisson Villa Wing,** now a part of the Radisson Fort George Hotel. The Villa, 13 Cork St., also overlooks the sea. All rooms have a/c and TV. The Villa has a bar and a restaurant. The 30 new rooms are really quite nice. The service charge is *not* added to your bill; rates are US$110 s, US$120 d, US$130 t; credit cards are okay. For more information and reservations, write or call Radisson Fort George, Box 321, Belize City, Belize, C.A., tel. in Belize (2) 77400/77242, fax (2) 73820. In the U.S. or Canada call (800) 333-3333 or fax to (402) 498-9166.

The **Chateau Caribbean,** on the waterfront at 6 Marine Parade, Box 947, Belize City, Belize, C.A., tel. (2) 30800, fax (2) 30900, has all the amenities of a fine hotel, including a restaurant and bar. Rates are US$69 s, US$ 79 d, US$89 t, US$95 d deluxe. Write or call for reservations and more information.

The **Bellevue Hotel,** 5 S. Foreshore, Box 428, Belize City, Belize, C.A., tel. (2) 77051/ 77052, fax (2) 73253, is a charming old hotel that was built as a private home in the early 1900s. The family that built this hotel still owns and operates it. Most of the rooms are spacious with private bathrooms, a/c, and telephones. The hotel features a pool, restaurant, bar, and a lively disco that makes music into the wee hours of the morning. The **Bellevue Bar** is a good meeting place for the locals. The restaurant has a very tranquil atmosphere and serves excellent food with a great wine list, personally chosen by owner Roger Dinger, from the vineyards of Europe. Rates are US$79 s, US$83 d. The in-house tour company, **Maya Circuit Tours,** offers a variety of trips to the Maya ruins, as well as fishing, diving, birdwatching, and nature tours. Write or call for more information and reservations.

One of the newer Belize City hotels, the **Biltmore Plaza,** Mile 3, New Northern Highway, Belize, C.A., in the U.S., tel. (800) 528-1234, in Belize, tel. (2) 32302, fax (2) 32301, is comfortable and attractive. Seven miles from the airport in the Bella Vista area near town and across the highway from Budget Rent a Car, the Biltmore is a convenient stop for those intending to stay overnight before renting a vehicle.

You'll find nothing rustic about these 92 rooms; they're midsize, with good beds, TV, direct-dial phones, tile bathrooms and showers, and the upper story opens onto cool verandas. All the rooms surround a green garden with a pool in the middle that has a swim-up bar. The **Victorian Room** is an upscale dining room open daily 7 a.m.-11 p.m. The **Squires Lounge** is adjacent to the restaurant and opens at 4:30 p.m. for pre-dinner drinks or a handy game of darts. This really gives the feeling of an English pub; were they still around, you might find a group of British soldiers having an ale and tossing darts! Prices are US$70 s or d.

The **Ramada Royal Reef Hotel,** Box 1248, Newtown Barracks, Belize City, Belize, C.A., tel. (800) 228-9898, (2) 32670, fax (2) 32660, is another newish hotel along the waterfront in Belize City on Barracks Road, 20 minutes from the international airport and just a few minutes from downtown. It continues to grow in importance as a source of upscale lodging, water-related activities and nighttime entertainment. A beautiful mural by Belizean artist Carolyn Carr brightens the lobby. The resort offers a gift shop, travel agency, landscaped grounds, outdoor pool, sunning beach, marina, charter boats, Jet Skis, and small sailboats. The 114 rooms have a/c, ceiling fans, direct-dial phones, tile bathrooms and showers, and room service—rooms facing the sea have a fine view. Nonsmoking rooms are available. Rates are US$115 s/d. Suites are available for US$198. A huge, double-level presidential suite for US$440 has amenities fit for a king. **The Reef** offers oceanfront dining, and the **Toucan** is a casual, poolside dining area for light meals and drinks. The **Blue Hole** is a lobby bar with terrace seating and live entertainment. The **Calypso Bar & Grill** at the hotel marina is a breezy, popular spot for drinks,

lunch, and dinner. At night there's live entertainment. At the marina you'll find the dive boats *Belize Aggressor* and *Wave Dancer* dock and the charter boats offered by the hotel.

Trailers

North of Haulover Creek toward the airport on Barracks Road is a trailer park that's little more than a parking lot with full hookups for trailers. Across the street from the sea, its rates are about US$10 depending on how much electricity you use.

Outlying Accommodations
In Belize District

On the New Northern Highway near the international airport you'll find the **Belize River Lodge,** Box 459, Belize City, Belize, C.A., tel. (25) 2002, fax (25) 2298, a laid-back guesthouse run by Margarite Miles. When you reach the sign, ring the bell on the tree, and someone will come across the river and pick you up. This is supposed to be especially good for serious fishermen. Write or call for more information; call for package prices.

On Moho Caye just a short water taxi ride from the city, **Maya Landings,** Box 86, Belize City, Belize, C.A., tel. (2) 35350, fax (2) 35466, offers comfortable rooms, a restaurant, marina, and condominiums. The **Quarterdeck Bar/ Restaurant** serves good versions of local cuisine on an airy covered patio. Rooms come with h/c water, full private bath, ceiling fans, and windows looking out on the cayes. Rates are US$50 s/d and US$10 per person additional. Credit cards okay. Also docked here are the charter boats *M/V Hot Dive* and *Stingray.* Extra slips are available for visitors. A courtesy water taxi takes guests and restaurant patrons to and from Moho Caye and the mainland. Call or write for more information and directions to the water taxi landing.

Owners Beth McBride and Ray Packer run the unusual little **River Haven Cabins and Houseboats,** Box 78, Belize City, Belize, C.A., tel. (2) 70530, fax (2) 70529, about 18 miles from Belize City on the Sibun River. Not only do they have a couple of rooms and a cabin, but a couple of houseboats, too. After a short training session, modern-day Huck Finns can pilot themselves down the Sibun River and through the canal into the Northern Lagoon. This seems a good bet for birders (sun-grebes, boat-billed herons, bat falcons and many more are regularly observed) and those who like trying something a little different. The boats feature basic accommodations for four, with a bath, kitchen (fully equipped), linens, and two private sleeping areas. Rates are US$790/week, US$525/midweek (Mon.-Fri. a.m.), US$395/weekend (Fri.-Sun.).

Rooms ashore are $40 s/d. The cabin sleeps four for US$65. All come with private bath, fan, and 24-hour electricity. Children's activities are a plus here; the resort offers a summer camp. River Haven attracts a following of travelers from North America and Europe, and accepts Visa/MC.

FOOD

For years it was the custom for international travelers to Belize to eat in their hotels, where simple food was prepared. Few restaurants were available, and even those were really nothing to speak of. However, more and more travelers are opting to try the cuisine of the country. As a result a few more restaurants are opening each year.

Local Cuisine
While in Belize take the opportunity to try the country favorites: Creole-style beans, rice, and stewed chicken. Favorite side dishes are coleslaw and fried plantain (large cooking bananas). Fried chicken and potato salad are Sunday-best dinners. And fresh fish is beginning to come in fancy wrappings. If staying at a guesthouse, ask if the cook makes "fried bread" for breakfast. One of the staples of the Caribbean for years has been conch: conch fritters, stewed conch, even conch ceviche.

Fragile Foods from the Sea
Don't order seafood out of season. The ocean is being exploited, and even some fishermen somehow don't realize that if you keep eating the babies of any species, they don't grow up to produce. The once-prolific lobster is getting more scarce in Belizean waters. And conch (really the staple of the Caribbean people) is not nearly as easy to find as it once was. Most reputable restaurateurs go along with the "rules" and don't buy these fragile seafoods undersized or out of season; however, a few have no scruples. Closed season for lobster is 15 Feb.-15 June, and conch season is closed 1 July-30 September. Lobster season has been shifted to help the crawly red critters get ahead of the hunt.

Wild Game
For the adventurous, at least one restaurant in Belize City Macy's serves wild game. The old favorites, such as venison, are seldom seen on menus because of their position on the about-to-become-extinct list. I've heard that even "bamboo chicken" (iguana) is getting harder to find.

Belize street

But you will see some dishes that you probably won't see anyplace else. For the most part, armadillo and gibnut are fixed in a stew.

Hotel Food

Belize City is not a "gourmet delight" *yet,* but things are looking up. Hotels are beginning to discover good chefs, and a few outstanding restaurants (such as **Fort Street** and **The Grill**) are becoming known outside the country. All of the more luxury-oriented hotels offer continental cuisine in lovely surroundings, though the food is apt to be a little pricey. And don't forget the small hotels. Some of the guesthouses have some of the tastiest meals around.

The **Bellevue Hotel** is known for good food and surroundings and a bar upstairs that offers a panoramic view of the harbor. The **Radisson Fort George Hotel** serves a beautiful buffet with a multitude of delicious seafood delicacies. The **Ramada Royal Reef** has a whole selection of dining experiences on the premises.

International Food

Among the better small restaurants is the **Fort Street Restaurant,** 4 Fort St., (2) 30116. Fort Street is a popular spot with an excellent menu for a special candlelight dinner, but don't give short shrift to breakfast and lunch. (We had one of the all-time great Thanksgiving dinners at Fort Street.) **The Grill,** 164 Newtown Barrack St., (2) 34201, a short walk from the Ramada Royal Reef Hotel, is popular with upscale travelers and if you like that sort of thing, you can rub shoulders with the ministers of Belize while enjoying a glass of wine and a good steak or tasty pasta.

Belizean Specialties

The **El Centro Hotel** restaurant, 4 Bishop St., and **Macy's Restaurant,** 18 Bishop St., are good bets for excellent Creole food for reasonable prices. If you see conch fritters on the menu at Macy's, give them a try. Adventurous eaters who revel in wild game can try armadillo, gibnut, and other exotic dishes. Try **GG's Cafe & Patio,** 2-B King St., where you can choose from Belizean specialties or great burgers in an alfresco tropical setting.

Simple and Good

Mom's Triangle Cafe (at its new location on Slaughterhouse Road, about a block from

Belize lobster boat

Bakadeer Inn) is known for good American-style and Belizean homo cooking—it has a good gift shop, too. **Goofy's,** 6 Douglas Jones St. serves a tasty hamburger. A pleasant place for lunch with American and Belizean food is **Kadel's,** second floor of the market, (2) 70103. From here you can watch the activities on the river and the bridge.

Chinese Cooking

You'll find a lot of Chinese food in Belize City, some really not so good. But everyone raves about the Chinese food at **The Royal Orchid Hotel,** 153 New Rd., (2) 32789, and at **Chateau Caribbean Hotel,** 6 Marine Parade, (2) 30800. A few others worth trying are the **Golden Dragon,** just off Queen St., and **Chon San Palace,** 1 Kelly St., just off Freetown Road. For Indian dishes, check out **Natraj, Gateway of India,** 5 Amara Ave., (2) 74723, where you'll find a menu that includes chicken tika, mutton egg fry, and fish baryani. If you're longing for Mexican food, we hear there's a place that

DRINKING WATER IN BELIZE CITY

Use your common sense as far as food and water are concerned. The water in Belize is commonly runoff from rooftops that is then stored in cisterns or tanks. In some cases it's perfectly safe; in others it's *iffy!* If you're concerned, ask for bottled water. In case it's not available, carry a small bottle of laundry bleach as a backup. Add a couple of drops per quart of water, shake, and let stand 30 minutes before drinking. Another option is to travel with a small, portable water purifier. (See "Health and Safety.")

might soothe the cravings called **The Mexican Corner,** King St. Let us know how it is.

Snacks and Sweets

Feel like having a snack? For a pizza fix, try the **Pizza House,** 11 King St., west of Albert Street. Ice cream lovers go to **Scoops,** Gaol Ln. at Eve St., for ice-cream cones and sundaes. Or for a tropical fruit drink and more ice cream, stop in at **Bluebird Ice Cream Parlour,** Albert Street. You can always check out the deli case at **Brodie's Dept. Store** with luscious-looking cold cuts and sandwiches to go.

NIGHTLIFE

Travelers looking for nightlife in Belize City will find the best at hotels such as the **Bellevue,** where the views of the harbor are great at sunset and the music goes on often until the wee hours of the morning. The breezy **Calypso Bar & Grill** at the Ramada Royal Reef Hotel has entertainment in the evenings, even on Sundays. The restaurant/bar at the top of the **Royal Orchid Hotel** offers panoramic views. **The Big Apple Disco,** 67 N. Front St., tel. (2) 44758, can get lively on a Friday night. And for more live music, check out the **Red Roof Lounge,** 3580 Sittee St., tel. (2) 33508. Call (2) 33507 and the Red Roof will send a car to pick you up at your hotel. It has both a restaurant and a bar, open 5 p.m.-3 a.m. on Friday and Saturday.

Look around, ask at your hotel, take a taxi; something's always going on at night in Belize.

SHOPPING

Gifts and Souvenirs

At 3 Fort Street across from the Fort Street Guest House sits an old warehouse. But don't be fooled: the **National Handicrafts Centre,** tel. (2) 33636, is one of the best sources of Belizean arts and crafts in the country. Inside, you'll find carved wooden plaques and bowls, jewelry, bags, ceramics, slate carvings, baskets, maps, music, and more. (**Note:** Bringing black coral jewelry or any other form of the coral into the U.S. is illegal.)

Rachel's Art Gallery, in the courtyard of the Radisson Fort George Hotel, 2 Marine Parade, is a small shop big on the quality of Belizean paintings and prints displayed. A talented artist herself, Rachel also has a few of her own for sale.

For those traveling by car, **El Papagayo Gift Shop** at Mile 3 on the Northern Highway, tel. (2) 33374, has a wide selection of handicrafts, towels, T-shirts, and postcards.

At the corner of Regent and Prince streets, **Go-Tees,** tel. (2) 74082, is a great spot to drop in for all sorts of gifts, postcards, and books, but especially T-shirts and other clothing.

If you're looking for souvenirs and gifts, go to the second floor of **Brodie's Department Store,** Albert and Regent streets, tel. (2) 77070, and you'll find a modern boutique where you can collect lots of goodies to take home.

Groceries and Sundries

Brodie's Department Store, Albert and Regent streets, tel. (2) 77070, is an institution in Belize. It's a modern emporium that sells a wide variety of foodstuffs and personal hygiene products, shampoos, soaps, aspirin, toilet tissue, razors, shoe polish, and much, much more.

Stock up on your way into or out of the north edge of town at **Sav U Supermarket.** This modern, air-conditioned market sells everything any supermarket in the U.S. would carry, and it's reasonably priced.

Film and Photo Processing

Photo processing in Belize has come a long way in the last several years. Now, you can get fast, professional processing of slides or prints at **Belize Photo Lab,** corner of Bishop and Canal streets, tel. (2) 74991; **Spooner's 1-Hour Mini-**

Ziricote carving with carver

Hotel room tax 6%
Service charge (a tip placed on a bill) 10%
Airport departure tax US$10

Airport security fee from international airport to domestic airport in Belize is US75 cents, international airport to foreign international airport US$1.25.

If you use your credit card it will cost you a little more at most businesses. Ask first if that's a problem. You will be approached by street vendors selling Belize dollars for less than the official rate. You might be lucky and hook up with an honest peddler (and many are), but on the other hand you might find the guy who has already cheated a lot of tourists in the exchange business. The official rate of exchange is two Belize dollars for one U.S. dollar.

Post Office
To post a letter or pick up stamps, stop by the **Paslow Building,** at the corner of Queen and Front streets. Lots of folks buy the beautiful Belize stamps for framing and for gifts. They really are lovely. If you just want to post a letter, expect a letter to the U.S. to travel for US30 cents, a postcard US15 cents; to Europe a letter will cost BZE75 cents, and a postcard BZE40 cents. If you visit in the outlying cities or cayes, bring your mail to Belize City to post It's more apt to get quickly to its destination.

Emergency Numbers
For the **police,** call 911. For **fire** and **ambulance,** call 90.

Medical Services
If you should need a doctor, the U.S. Embassy recommends **Dr. Manuel Lizama,** 13 Handyside St., Belize City, Belize, C.A., tel. (2) 45138. **Belize City Hospital** is a public government facility, tel. (2) 32723/32724/77251/77252.

Downtown pharmacies are **Community Drug Store,** Albert St., tel. (2) 73842; **Brodie's Department Store,** Albert and Regent streets, tel. (2) 77070; and **Central Drug Store,** 1 Market Square, downtown and Farmers Market, tel. (2) 45587.

lab, 89 Front St., tel. (2) 31058. And both chrome and print film is available. Film and other supplies are available at **Belicolor Photo Service,** 4 Gabourel Ln., tel. (2) 30818.

SERVICES

Money Matters
Go south over the bridge on Albert Street and you run into a string of banks including: **Atlantic Bank,** 6 Albert St., tel. (2) 77124; **Bank of Nova Scotia,** Albert St., tel. (2) 77027; **Barclay's Bank,** 21 Albert St., tel. (2) 77211; **Belize Bank,** 1 Market Square, tel. (2) 77132. All the banks keep the same hours and days: Mon.-Thurs. 8 a.m.-1 p.m.; Fri. 8 a.m.-1 p.m. and 3-6 p.m.

Be prepared for some additions on your bills for taxes and service charges:

INFORMATION

Tourist Information

For general information sources and a list of consulates, see "Information" in the On The Road chapter. While in Belize City, visit or call the **Belize Tourist Board**, 83 N. Front St., tel. (2) 77213, fax (2) 77490, for information on reserves, national parks, and various sections of the country.

You'll usually find someone in at **Belize Tourism Industry Associates**, 99 Albert St, Box 62, tel. (2) 75717, (2) 72464, fax (2) 78710, to answer questions.

Travel Agents

Want to book transportation, tours, or accommodations? **S & L Travel Services**, 91 N. Front St., Box 700, tel. (2) 75145, (2) 77593, fax (2) 77594, is just down the street from the Belize Tourist Board. Owners Sarita and Lascelle Tillet run a first-class and very personable operation. They've been in business for 25 years; we have worked with them for eight years. They can get as creative as you like, whether you want a custom vacation, a photo safari, a birding adventure, or anything else you can imagine. You also can get all the usual things—airline tickets, car rentals, hotel reservations.

To the east and on the left is another agency, **Belize Travel Adventures**, 168 N. Front St., tel. (2) 32618. Using local agencies to make arrangements is often better than trying to wing it completely on your own. These agencies can get you all the information you need and when rooms are tight (a not too infrequent situation February-April), they are more likely to be able to get you accommodated.

Conservation Organizations

The **Belize Audubon Society** has offices and representatives all over the country. They are a splendid source of information for travelers who wish to investigate any of the wildlife reserves in Belize. In each case they are involved in managing the reserves. They have the most up-to-date information about current seasonal conditions, and can tell you when and if you can use each reserve. Ask about the **Community Ba-**

boon Sanctuary at Bermudian Landing, **Cockscomb Basin Wildlife Sanctuary, Crooked Tree Sanctuary,** and **Half Moon Caye Natural Sanctuary.** Roughing it at these locations (and that's pretty much the way it is at all of them) is not for everyone, but for those willing to stay in very basic accommodations or camp, each of these offers unique experiences. Although you'll see offices scattered about the city, the one at 12 Fort St., tel. (2) 34985/35004, is probably the best equipped to answer tourists' questions. Stop by to buy books on natural history and to pick up free pamphlets on parks. Birdwatchers, ask about the *Belize Bird Guide*. This office is also where you can arrange overnight accommodations in Cockscomb Basin Wildlife Sanctuary.

Located in an unassuming building on Park Street just about a block from the Radisson and on the edge of Memorial Park, the **Programme for Belize**, 2 S. Park, Belize City, Belize, C.A., in the U.S. tel. (617) 259-9500, in Belize tel. (2) 75616, fax (2) 75635, is the group that manages the **Rio Bravo Conservation Area** with the support of the Belize Audubon Society, The Nature Conservancy, and the World Wildlife Fund. Stop in here to arrange for accommodations or tours at Rio Bravo in Orange Walk District.

Publications

In most of the large hotels you'll find a shop with English language novels and popular history and picture books put out by Belize's own **Cubola Productions.** It publishes a selection of history books, an atlas of the country, and several collections of short stories and poems written by locals. They aren't necessarily all Pulitzer quality, but they give a great insight into the country from the early days to today. Several bookstores in town are worth investigating. The **Book Centre**, 144 N. Front St., tel. (2) 77457, and **Belize Book Shop**, corner of Regent St. and Rectory Ln., tel. (2) 72054, both have a good selection and variety. If you still aren't satisfied, check out the **Spear** library, North Front Street.

Though the **Angelus Press**, 10 Queen St., tel. (2) 35777, north of the Swing Bridge, is a large stationery shop, it offers a good selection of books about Belize, maps, a variety of paper supplies, pens, and stamps, plus all kinds of equipment for architects, etc.

For complete, accurate survey maps of the entire country, check out the **Survey Department**, above the post office on Queen St., tel. (2) 73221. The **Belize Tourist Board** also has maps available; they re not of Survey Department caliber, but they'll get you around. And of course, Emory King's *Road Guide* (pick up from his real estate office at 9 Regent St., tel. 2-77453) for the country is charming, though not necessarily perfectly accurate. It will also serve the purpose.

If you're looking for **local newspapers,** you'll find several in the city; we subscribe to *Amandala*. Reading the local news is just one more way to keep abreast of current affairs in the city and country.

For American news, **Mom's Triangle Cafe** on Slaughterhouse Road generally carries the *Miami Herald, Newsweek,* and *Time* magazines.

GETTING AROUND

Getting around the city by foot is fairly easy since most of it is clumped close together. However, if you wish to see Belize's outlying areas you can go by taxi, bus, boat, or plane.

Rental Cars

Belize City has various rental car agencies. They are all expensive. However, at **Budget Rent a Car,** Mile 3, Northern Highway, tel. (2) 32435/33986, fax (2) 30237, owner Alan Auil breaks in the 4WD cars himself and offers new cars that are well-maintained. On several trips we have driven his cars into the dirt (and mud); they've taken the bumpy roads and deep water and kept going. When you're out in the wilderness, that's what counts. **Safari Car Rental,** 73 Eve St., tel. (2) 35395, fax (2) 30268, in the U.S. tel. (800) 447-2931, offers all four-door 4WD vehicles and a small pickup for driving around town. Other companies have offices in town; these just happen to be our favorites. Price them all—you never know when you can make a good deal. And of course, always check out your car thoroughly.

Using Your Odometer

If you're driving the **Western Highway,** start your trip odometer at the cemetery; if you're driving the **Northern Highway,** start the odometer at the northern edge of town just north of the intersection of the Northern Highway with Central American Blvd./Princess Margaret Drive.

Gas Stations

Two stations that are easy to find downtown are **A & R Texaco** on North Front St., just upriver from the Swing Bridge where the water taxis park, and **Nava's Texaco** on North Front St., down the street from the post office about a block and on the right. You'll find **Shell** and **Esso** stations around town, as well as on the way out of town on the Northern and Western highways.

By Taxi

Taxi fares are controlled by the government. Even so, they should be determined before getting in the cab. From the international airport to Belize City the fare is usually US$15, from the municipal airstrip, US$4. The fare for one passenger carried between any two points within Belize City (or any other district town) is US$1.50. For two or more passengers it is US$1 per person. If you plan to make several stops, tell the cabbie in advance and ask what the total will be; this eliminates lots of misunderstandings. Generally speaking, most of the city is accessible on foot, even the bus stations. Taxis can be hired by the hour (US$12.50) or for long trips out of town.

By Bus

You'll find a choice of buses available going off in all directions. Since the schedules change regularly, contact the companies when you're ready to travel. Fares are reasonable. The bus lines are:

Batty Brothers Buses, 15 Mosul Street, tel. (2) 72025, fax (2) 78991.

Novelos' Bus Service, 54 E. Collet Canal, tel. (2) 77372.

Venus Bus Lines, Magazine Road, (2) 73354.

Z-Line Bus Service, Magazine Road, tel. (2) 73937, in Dangriga tel. (5) 22211.

Other small lines, which don't have phone numbers, are **Jex Brothers Buses,** Magazine Road, which go to Crooked Tree; the **Dawson Buses,** Cinderella Plaza on Barracks Road; and **Chan Buses,** Vernon Street at the bridge, which go to the Altun Ha area.

This is one way to cross a river.

PHIL LANIER

By Sea

If you want to take a trip to the cayes or any of the other coastal communities along the Caribbean Coast, go to the Texaco station near the Swing Bridge on North Front Street. This is where the boats come to fill up. It's a great way to meet the locals and to get a glimpse of out-of-the-way canals, rivers, and coastal towns; of course, establish the cost before you climb aboard.

Most of the "water taxis" will stop at Caye Chapel or Caye Caulker on their way to Ambergris Caye, if you alert the captain as you board. On calm, sunny days it's a very pleasant trip. In windy or rainy weather a light wrap comes in handy. Or take the *Andrea,* which is enclosed, from the dock at the Bellevue Hotel. Transit to Caye Caulker takes about 45 minutes; the trip between Belize City and Ambergris takes about 75 minutes. The trips cost about US$10 one-way, less than US$20 roundtrip. The **Caye Caulker Water Taxi Association** is working to standardize rates; if the boat captain you talk to wants more, talk to a member of the association.

For Ambergris Caye, the *Andrea II,* tel. (2) 74988, makes the run from Belize City daily at 3 p.m. (from the Bellevue Hotel dock) to San Pedro (it departs San Pedro at 7 a.m.). Pay on board or buy your tickets at **Universal Travel Services,** 8 Handyside St., tel. (2) 30963, in Belize City just off Queen St. or at its San Pedro office on Barrier Reef Drive.

Zippy Zappy Boating Services, tel. (2) 32844, fax (2) 34480, has three boats that operate from the Texaco station—*Can't Touch This, Our Boat,* and *Zappy.* All three are available for water taxi service and trips for birdwatching, fishing (deep-sea, flats, and river), snorkeling, and swimming.

Miss Belize leaves from the dock behind the Supreme Court building. The *Hustler* leaves San Pedro daily at 7 a.m. and returns from Belize City at 4 p.m. from the new dock near the courthouse and new market; rates are US$10 one-way, US$17.50 roundtrip. The *Thunderbolt* docks at the Swing Bridge in Belize City and has the same schedule as the *Hustler.* Also check with the chamber of commerce regarding who might direct you to one of the freight boats that make occasional trips to the island, or ask around the dock near the Swing Bridge. A few regularly scheduled trips run between the cayes.

By Air

The Belizean commuter planes provide a great service in and out of Belize City to the outlying airports all over the country. In many cases taking the plane really beats the bumpy, rough (often muddy) roads for long distances (like to Punta Gorda). Call for current schedules and prices. Airlines and charters are:

Caribee Air, Muni. tel. (2) 44253.

Island Air, Intl. tel. (2) 52219, Muni. tel. (2) 31140.

Javier's Flying Service, Muni. tel. (2) 45332/ 35360.

Maya Airways, Intl. tel. (2) 52336, Muni. tel. (2) 44234.

Su-Bec Air, Muni. tel. (2) 34906/30388.

Tropic Air, Intl. tel. (2) 62338, Muni. tel. (2) 45671.

Tour Operators

Savvy travelers know Belize offers much for the visitor to see and many ways to do it: travel independently with a rental car or by bus, hire a taxi, or travel with a tour operator who provides transportation as well as guidance. For those interested in letting someone else do the driving, various tour operators are reliable. In Belize City, for example, Sarita and Lascelle Tillet of **S & L Guided Tours,** Box 700, 91 N. Front St., Belize City, Belize, C.A., tel. (2) 75145, (2) 77593, fax (2) 77594, operate as a husband/wife team. They drive late-model a/c sedans or vans and travel throughout the country with airport pickup available. The Tillets have designed several great **special interest vacations** and will custom design to your interests, whether they be the Maya archaeological zones (including Guatemala's Tikal), the cayes, or the caves and the countryside. Lascelle is a great birdwatcher; he always seems to spot the unique before anyone else and knows the names and living habits of each winged creature—it was he who pointed out our first jabiru stork in Belize.

Formerly Belize Mesoamerica, **Adventure Expeditions Belize,** 4 S. Park St., Box 1217, Belize City, Belize, C.A., tel. (2) 30748, fax (2) 30750, is another excellent Belizean tour agency. Tell the agents what you want and they will make it easy for you. They have an office at the Belize International Airport and offer tours to all the attractions in the country, whether natural history, archaeology, or adventure.

Other reputable agencies include **Belize Travel Adventures,** 168 N. Front St., tel. (2) 33064, fax (2) 33196, and **Belize Tours & Expeditions,** tel./fax (2) 35721.

VICINITY OF BELIZE CITY

SOUTH~GALES POINT

To get to Gales Point by car choose either the Manatee Road or the Hummingbird Highway; and make sure it's not raining! Going by way of the Hummingbird is about 25 miles longer. In dry weather the Manatee Highway is preferable. Also, it's a drive best done in daylight because: first, it's safer; and second, there's such a lot to see—beautiful jungle views, Maya villages, and the Maya Mountains in the distance.

A small village originally established by logwood cutters sits on a two-mile-long peninsula that juts into the Southern Lagoon; both are called Gales Point. Gales Point is about 15 miles north of Dangriga in Stann Creek District and 25 miles south of Belize City.

Southern Lagoon

The lagoon is part of an extensive estuary surrounded by thick mangroves. Their tangled roots provide the perfect breeding grounds for sport fish, crabs, shrimp, lobster, and a host of other marinelife. Rich beds of sea grass line the bottom of the lagoon and support a population of manatees. These gentle mammals are often seen basking on the surface of the water or coming up for air (which they must do about every four minutes). This concentration of manatees is a popular spot for boaters to bring visitors to swim with the manatees or just to observe.

Access from Belize City by boat is a pleasant way to Gales Point. The boat winds through mangrove-lined canals and across the Sibun River before going through the Northern and Southern lagoons.

Accommodations

The only accommodations available in the area are at **Manatee Lodge,** Box 170, Belmopan, Belize, C.A., in the U.S. tel. (800) 334-7942, (904) 222-2333, fax (904) 222-1992; in Belize tel. (8) 23320, fax (8) 23334. On the northern end of Gales Point, this property is a companion to Hidden Valley Inn in the Cayo District. In fact, some travelers stay a few days here before or after visiting the Mountain Pine Ridge. What they have access to here is a completely different habitat and wildlife that exist in the broad expanses of shallow brackish water and mangroves called the Southern Lagoon. The number of shore and waterfowl is impressive, and to aid guests in seeing local wildlife, the lodge provides each room with a canoe. Binoculars are a must, as is bug repellent. A motor boat and guide are US$125/half-day for a group of up to four people. Expeditions to other area nature reserves can be arranged as can roundtrip ground/water transport between Belize International Airport and Gales Point. The lodge caters to birders and independent travelers who enjoy the outdoors. You can fish for a little diversion (a limited number of rods are available at the lodge). The kids especially seem to enjoy baiting a hook and seeing what comes up on the other end of the line. Snook and snappers are likely and tasty catches. The lodge will prepare them for lunch or dinner. Fly fishing for the small tarpon of the lagoon can be fun. The lodge also has a couple of Sunfish sailboats for the enjoyment of guests.

The eight rooms of the lodge are spacious, have private bathrooms, and are connected to the main buildings by elevated walkways. Children under six are free, 6-12 half-price. Room rates are US$77.50 s, US$105 d; lunch costs US$7.50, dinner US$17.50.

WEST~THE BELIZE ZOO

On Freetown Road headed out of Belize City, turn left onto Central American Boulevard and cross the Belcan Bridge. At the first big intersection you come to—it has a turnaround in the center of the intersection—take a right and you are now on Cemetery Road, which becomes the Western Highway. Set the trip odometer at 1. Follow the Western Highway to about Mile 28 and look for the turnoff on the right.

BERMUDIAN LANDING BABOON SANCTUARY

Driving the Northern Highway

If you are driving to Bermudian Landing from downtown Belize City, leave town on Freetown Road. You'll pass through the intersection with Central American Boulevard (to the left) and Princess Margaret Drive (to the right). Continue straight out of town. As you cross this major intersection, the road becomes the Northern Highway; set your trip odometer just a couple of hun-

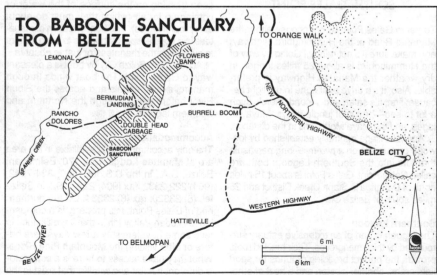

TO BABOON SANCTUARY FROM BELIZE CITY

TO ORANGE WALK

LEMONAL

FLOWERS BANK

BERMUDIAN LANDING

RANCHO DOLORES

DOUBLE HEAD CABBAGE

BURRELL BOOM

NEW NORTHERN HIGHWAY

BABOON SANCTUARY

SPANISH CREEK

BELIZE CITY

WESTERN HIGHWAY

HATTIEVILLE

TO BELMOPAN

BELIZE RIVER

0   6 mi

0   6 km

© MOON PUBLICATIONS INC

THE BELIZE ZOO

The Belize Zoo, established in 1983, has brought together some of the country's fascinating animals. For now they live in thatched-roof cages, and the environment is fairly simple and small. However, money is being raised with pledges, contributions, and fundraisers sponsored by the private sector to build modern housing for the animals. The financial goal has not yet been reached and the galas continue. One yearly event is April's birthday party, vegetarian birthday cake and all. April is a Baird's tapir (the national animal)—also known as a mountain cow—and spends much of her time happily submerged in her own pond. She's the hands-on favorite attraction. Besides April, another animal of special interest is the jaguar. The zoo, at Mile 30 on the Western Highway, is open 10 a.m.-5 p.m. The admission is US$5.

Note: The local buses will drop you off only on the highway at the entrance road (you must ask the driver to stop at the zoo road). From there it's about a mile walk to the zoo. You can also take taxis from Belmopan for under US$10, depending on how many people are going.

Sharon Matola, the founding director of the Belize Zoo, tells the story of the zoo with affection and love: "Some people call it funky; others say that it's the best zoo they have ever seen, and everyone tells us that the animals who live at the Belize Zoo seem . . . well, they seem so happy. Welcome to the Belize Zoo!" As the founding director, she thrives on the unique opportunity to work among rare species of tropical animals, and to work with a local staff of employees who proudly share their natural heritage—the dramatic wildlife of Belize—with visitors to the zoo.

April

One of the Belizean zookeepers gives everyone who comes through the gates a tour of the zoo, including a visit with April. An old superstition says that the tapir can skin a person alive with its nose, but of course, as a guide explains, this is not true. And as April, the five-hundred-pound tapir, trundles over to get a closer look at the curious visitor, you can see that the personal touches of animal care and wildlife education have intermingled to produce a unique zoo experience.

Education

Hand-painted, homespun signs provide simple educational messages that cause visitors to laugh as well as learn. A glance at the sign in front of the peccary enclosure tells visitors, "We are warries, and we like the way we smell." Warries are members of the piglike peccary family. Peccaries do smell funny, but a sign explains the purpose of this odd scent in a way that helps observers to appreciate this animal's unusual natural history.

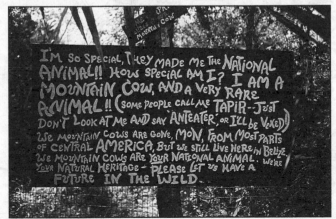

The "backyard" feeling is promoted by these clever signs at each exhibit.

BELIZE ZOO

SPIDER MONKEY

DEER

TRAIL (PINE SAVANNAH)

TAPIR

BARRIER

OCELOT

WHITE-LIPPED PECCARY

KINKAJOU

WHITE-COLLARED PECCARY

SPECIAL EXHIBITS

VULTURE

PUMA

LAGOON

TAYRA

RESTROOMS

GIFT SHOP

MACAW

OFFICES

TOUCAN

HOWLER MONKEY

CURASSOW

GUAN

AGOUTI / PACA

GREAT HORNED OWL

PARROTS

JAGUAR

HAWK

COATI

SERVICE AREA

SPECTACLED OWL

MARGAY

FOX

TAMANDUA

JAGUARUNDI

REPTILES

CROCODILES

WADING BIRDS

BCB

NOT TO SCALE

TO BELIZE CITY

© MOON PUBLICATIONS, INC

April, the national animal, loves the attention and TLC she gets at the Belize Zoo.

Beginnings

Sharon Matola started the Belize Zoo in January 1983. Coming to Belize to begin a zoo and build a wildlife education program was not what she considered part of her destiny at that time. She had arrived in Belize to manage a small collection of local animals for a natural film company. However, after she had worked only five months on the project, its funds were severely reduced, and it became evident that the group of animal film stars would have to be disbanded.

Get Rid of the Animals?

Sharon says that besides the fact that these wild cats, birds, anteaters, and snakes had become her friends and companions, other reasons made getting rid of them difficult. Once a wild animal has become semi-tamed and dependent on people for care, returning to a life in the wild is impossible.

So, as an alternative, she told herself, "This country has never had a zoo. Perhaps if I offered the chance for Belizeans to see these unique animals, their existence here could be permanently established."

And so a zoo was born. From the very beginning the amount of local interest shown in the zoo was incredible. The majority of the people in Belize live in urban areas, and their knowledge of the local fauna is minimal. The Belize Zoo offered many Belizeans the opportunity to see the animals that share their country. It was touching to see the looks on the faces of small children who were experiencing for the first time the animals of their homeland. The modest beginnings of the zoo were based upon the simple idea that children deserved the chance to grow up knowing animals, especially those living in the thick forests and jungles not too many miles from their city homes.

School Programs

This initial interest was exciting and prompted Sharon to begin a country wide education program. She took colorful slides of the animals to schools along with invitations for the teachers to bring their children—free of charge—to the new zoo. Those modest beginnings have evolved into a major wildlife awareness program that has touched the hearts of thousands of children and adults throughout Belize. The zoo now has a collection of Belizean fauna that numbers well over one hundred species. The zoo staff is a dedicated crew of Belizean zookeepers who not only provide excellent care for the animals but also travel around the nation with wildlife education programs.

Special events at the zoo further enhance wildlife awareness efforts. Every child in the nation is invited to come to the zoo and join in the celebration. Besides singing "Happy Birthday" to a tapir, eating cake, and being entertained by Rose Tattoo (the famous clown of Belize), the children learn more about their special natural heritage.

Learning about their country's animals is important. Today, throughout Central America, much of the wildlife is standing on the brink of extinction. To lose, forever, the roaring call of the howler monkey, the dramatic flashes of red that belong to the scarlet macaw, or the discreet presence of the mighty jaguar, would be a tragedy.

One of the zoo's important messages is to let visitors know where they can view the animals of Belize in the wild. When watching the howler monkeys playing in the trees at the zoo, a nearby sign informs zoo guests that they can see these monkeys at the Bermudian Landing Community Baboon Sanctuary. A walk by the jaguar exhibit not only provides an impressive look at these beautiful big cats but also encourages visitors to visit the Jaguar Preserve in the Cockscomb Basin Wildlife Sanctuary—"the only place in the world where the big cats can roam protected and forever free."

A Success Story

This type of progressive wildlife education has helped to bring about a growing pride among the people of Belize for the animals of their country. This sense of pride will lead to a feeling of propriety that will ultimately help to ensure the animals future in the Belizean wild. The zoo's success story will develop further, and the future is an exciting one. The little zoo will be moving to an underdeveloped piece of land where both animals and zoo visitors will have more room to roam about. Using a master plan for development that was donated by zoo architects from Seattle, Washington, the goal is to display each Belizean animal in a natural, wild setting.

Raising money to implement this master plan has been a local as well as an international effort. It has not been easy, but slow and steady progress is being made. A visit to the Belize Zoo is fun, inspiring, and educational for the local as well as foreign visitors. The funky, "down home" approach puts people from all walks of life in touch with the magic of the animals of Belize—animals that are the natural heritage of this unspoiled, tropical country, and are also the natural treasures of the entire world.

Role Model

The Belize Zoo is becoming increasingly well known throughout the world. The unique educational programs and the conservation efforts of the zoo have consistently made international environmental news. The publishers of the *Belize Handbook* believe that the efforts of the Belize Zoo should be encouraged and supported by all. If you wish to help, it s easy! All you have to do is make the appropriate donation to become a member of the Belize Zoo. Join today by sending your name and mailing address to:

The Belize Zoo
P.O. Box 474
Belize City, Belize, C.A.

Membership categories are (in U.S. dollars):
Individual, $25
Family, $35
Patron, $65
Participating, $130
Sustaining, $250
Supporting, $500
Benefactor, $1,000

Every single dollar helps! Whatever your contribution, you will receive the zoo's informative newsletter and other benefits, depending on your level of participation. Plus, you'll have the personal satisfaction of knowing you're helping to educate the world around you and protect the unique wildlife of Belize.

---

dred yards farther, where the road begins a gentle bend to the right.

Expect a good deal of traffic in the mornings and afternoons on the stretch past the Bella Vista suburb and the Belize Biltmore Hotel. You'll encounter lots of school buses, vehicles pulling over to pick up riders, and speed bumps. The **Belize River** is off to the left. At about Mile 5.5 you'll come to **Haulover Bridge** (one way traffic at a time) and continue skirting the river northward on Northern Highway.

At a little less than Mile 9 you'll see the turnoff to **Philip Goldson International Airport** to the left. Continue to mile 14, where the road forks. Take the left fork toward Burrell Boom and Bermudian Landing. Readers are telling us about an excellent eatery in this town called **El Chiclero Restaurant,** tel. (28) 2005, which purportedly has great barbecue. Stop and ask for directions, though how hard can it be in a small village?

About seven miles past Burrell Boom you'll be in Bermudian Landing. Check in with the sanctuary manager for up-to-date information on directions, room and board, and guide fees.

Accommodations and Food

Situated on a lush hillside is the relatively new **Jungle Drift Lodge,** Box 1442, Belize City, Belize, C.A., tel. (2) 78160, fax (2) 32842. Owned and run by John Estephan and Madeleine Lamont (yes, of the same Lamont family who own Glover's Reef Resort in Stann Creek District), it provides simple accommodations in an exciting area. The lodge is only 300 yards from the natural history museum sponsored by the World Wildlife Fund. On 20 acres they've fashioned their little piece of paradise with basic cabins with cold water, private baths, electric lamps, and fans. Rates are about US$15 s, US$20 d, US$30 t. Camping is also available (bring your own tent) at US$5 per person per day. Meals are local dishes prepared by villagers. The lodge

offers canoes and kayaks for rent for US$5/hour. Fully guided canoe trips through the sanctuary cost US$20 per person.

The two available rooms at **Little Eden Guest House,** Box 1317, Belize City, Belize, C.A., tel./fax (2) 82129, cost a little more and you must share a bath. The rooms have electric fans, and there's a small gift shop. Rates start at US$26.

Getting There

By Bike: If the traffic doesn't bother you, it's an easy trip (do wear a helmet), and don't let the speed bumps surprise you.

By Bus: Catch the **Orange Bus** operated by the Russells; it leaves Orange Street and Euphrates Avenue Mon.-Fri. at 12:30 p.m., Saturday at noon. Rates are about US$1.75 each way.

By Car: It's an easy drive and well-signed once you're on the Northern Highway.

By Taxi or Tour: This is close enough to the city or either airport that you can consider a taxi or an escorted tour for a day-trip. Negotiate taxi prices ahead of time. Check with your hotel or travel agent for a tour.

BELIZE CITY
TO ALTUN HA
AND CROOKED TREE

NORTH~THE ROAD TO ALTUN HA

Back on the Northern Highway, continue past the Burrell Boom turnoff and continue to about **Mile 19** where the road forks; the right fork leads to Altun Ha and Maskall Village.

Ten and a half miles from the intersection you reach the Altun Ha entrance. The ruins of Altun Ha have become one of the more popular day-trips to Maya archaeological sites for groups and individuals venturing from Belize City, Ambergris Caye, and Caye Caulker. It was from a tomb at Altun Ha that archaeologists unearthed the largest Maya jade carving ever found (see "Maya Archaeological Sites" in the Mundo Maya chapter).

Nearby Accommodations

Just two miles north on the Old Northern Highway, Albert and Marilyn Gill have created **Genesis in the Jungle,** an unusual experience for guests who wish to experience Belizean living. Albert is a musician who, with his band, plays reggae and *punta* rock. Marilyn runs a tropical winery that makes sweet wines of cashews,

THE DEVELOPMENT OF A LIVING ANIMAL SANCTUARY

THE BERMUDIAN LANDING HOWLER MONKEY SANCTUARY

When zoologist Robert Horwich from the University of Wisconsin at Milwaukee began a population survey thoughout the range of the **howler monkey,** it was the beginning of what would become the first viable animal sanctuary. The scientist spent time in the howler's range, which covered southern Mexico, northeast Guatemala, and Belize. Until then, no one had formally studied the primate and its rainforest habitat.

The results were disturbing. In Mexico the monkeys were hunted by the locals for food and their living habitat was fast being eliminated with the destruction of the rainforest. Conditions in Guatemala were only slightly better. Here, too, the monkeys were hunted by locals in the forests around Tikal, and as the forest habitat shrank in the country, so too did the numbers of howler monkeys.

It was the last survey that was surprising. In Belize, at Bermudian Landing, the communities of monkeys were strong and healthy, the forest was intact, and the locals seemed genuinely fond of the noisy creatures. This was definitely a place to start talking *wildlife reserve.*

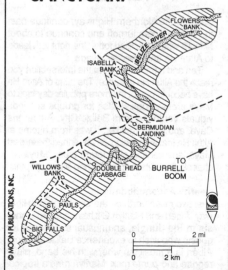

Horwich, with the help of Jon Lyon, a botanist from the State University of New York, began a survey of the village. After many meetings with the town fathers, excitement grew about the idea of saving the "baboon" (the local name for the monkey). Homeowners agreed to leave the monkey's food trees, hogplums and sapodillas, and small strips of forest between cleared fields as aerial pathways for the primates, as well as 60 feet of forest along both sides of waterways.

The landowners signed voluntary pledges promising to follow the management plans set forth by Horwich and Lyon—a sanctuary was born. At last count more than 70 landowners (in seven villages covering 18 square miles along a stretch of the Belize River that measures 20 miles) were taking part. Villages include Double Head Cabbage and Flowers Bank.

The monkeys are happy and the population has grown to a whopping 1,000. By now sanctuary management may have acted on the plan to move some of the troops south into the Cockscomb Basin Wildlife Sanctuary. One of only six species of howler monkeys in the world, the black howlers are the largest monkeys in the Americas.

BERMUDIAN LANDING COMMUNITY BABOON SANCTUARY

BELIZE RIVER

FLOWERS BANK

ISABELLA BANK

BERMUDIAN LANDING

WILLOWS BANK

DOUBLE HEAD CABBAGE

TO BURRELL BOOM

ST. PAULS

BIG FALLS

0   2 mi

0   2 km

© MOON PUBLICATIONS, INC.

BOB RACE

One of the outgrowths of this innovative plan in Belize is the knowledge that educating the people about conservation and arousing in them a basic fondness for all of nature has been much more successful than enacting a stringent hunting law. The managers of the sanctuary are local villagers who understand their neighbors; much of their time is spent at with children at schools and adults in interested villages. Part of their education includes basic farming techniques and sustained land use that eliminates the constant need to cut forest for new corn *milpas;* this might be the most important feature of learning for the forest inhabitants.

A museum at Bermudian Landing gives visitors an overview of rainforest ecology along with specific information and lore about the black howler monkey and other animals living within the sanctuary. From the museum, visitors can explore three miles of forest trails that surround Bermudian Landing. The tourist brings in a few extra dollars for the subsistence economy of the area. Plans include building guest cabañas, selling wood carvings created by locals, and offering visitors a trip down the river into monkey country.

If it all sounds perfect, it isn't! Some people from the more urban areas come to the sanctuary to kidnap baby monkeys to sell for pets. The only way anyone can kidnap a baby howler is by killing the mother, since she will never relinquish her young without a fight. A lively debate continues among traditional conservationists about allowing the people to live within a wildlife preserve. However, Belize's grass-roots conservation is proving that it can succeed. Other countries such as Australia and Sierra Leone are watching carefully to see how this same concept can be adapted to the needs of their own endangered species without kicking out the people who have lived on the land in some cases for many generations.

mangos, soursop, ginger, or pineapple. A screened, thatched-roof restaurant on the grounds serves traditional Belizean dishes, jerk chicken, and homemade tofu. Camping on raised covered platforms is available for about US$2.50. Hammocks are available for rent. Write the Gills at Mile 2 Northern Highway, Maskall Village, Belize, C.A., or leave a message at Maskall Village Community Phone, tel. (3) 22041.

Named by a Maskall Village first-grader in a contest held by the owners (how's that for local involvement?), the **Pretty See Ranch,** Maskall Village, Belize, C.A., tel. (1) 49672, is eight miles north of Altun Ha. It offers 1,360 rolling green acres for horseback riding and river and fishing trips. A thatched-roof restaurant with a wood oven turns out barbecue and local dishes. All vegetables are grown on the premises. Cabins are spaced apart for privacy.

About a mile out of Maskall Village lies **Maruba Lodge,** a small retreat that could be described as an oasis of charm and grace—or a jungle spa. Visitors to the resort, in the heart of the forest, will find an emphasis on health and rejuvenation of the body and mind. Guests are pampered with exotic drinks, a Japanese tub, swimming pool, excellent food, jungle expeditions, river rides, caving, and—for those interested—a weight-control program, body massage, tropical herbal wrap, seaweed body wrap, mineral baths, African honeybee pat, and exercise classes. Each thatch room is decorated in a different flamboyant style; the jungle suite has its own jacuzzi and balcony. Prices begin at US$133 s, US$116 d, US$280 suite; they're less in the summer, and all prices include breakfast and dinner. Contact Maruba Resort, Box 300703, Houston, TX 77230, tel. (713) 799-2031, (800) 552-3419; in Belize (3) 22199.

Getting There

Catch the **Dawson Bus** at Cinderella Plaza on Barracks Road leaving at about 1 p.m., or the **Chan Bus** at Vernon Street, leaving the bridge at about 2 p.m.; each makes the return trip in the morning about 6 a.m. and 6:30 a.m., so unless you're spending the night in the area, find another way to get back. Altun Ha is close enough to the city, or either airport, that you can arrange for a taxi or a day tour that shouldn't be extraordinarily expensive.

CROOKED TREE

Crooked Tree is 33 miles northwest of Belize City and two miles off the Northern Highway. After you take the turnoff to Crooked Tree, it's another two miles down the dirt road and over a one-mile-long narrow causeway (be prepared to give way to allow another vehicle coming from the opposite direction to pass). Hunting and fishing are not permitted.

History

Crooked Tree is made up of a network of inland lagoons, swamps, and waterways. **Crooked Tree Lagoon** is up to a mile wide and more than 20 miles long. Along its banks lies the town of **Crooked Tree**. It was settled during the early days of the logwood era, an island surrounded by fresh water, accessible only by boats traveling up the Belize River and Black Creek. The waterways were used to float the logs out to the sea.

CROOKED TREE WILDLIFE SANCTUARY

In 1984 **Crooked Tree Wildlife Sanctuary** was established on the island for the protection of resident and migratory birds of the area as well

as for the varied jungle creatures that make Crooked Tree their home. The wildlife sanctuary is divided into two sections. The largest is a series of six connected lagoons open to visitors and accessible by boat and road. A smaller water area, Mexico/Jones Lagoon, is not open to tourists.

Audubon Society

Although several organizations had a hand in founding the park with financial aid, ongoing credit for supervision goes to the Belize Audubon Society. The Society, with the continued help of devoted volunteers, maintains a small business center/museum in a small building on the right just after you cross the causeway. Do sign in; this validates the sanctuary and gives the Society a reason to sponsor it. For now there is no admission fee, but that will be changing. You will always find a knowledgeable curator willing to answer questions about the birds and flora encountered at the sanctuary. By the way, you'll find an outhouse-type toilet in the back yard.

Flora and Fauna

Multitudes of birds find the sanctuary a safe resting spot during the dry season, with enor-

Local canoes are carved from one large log.

mous food resources along the shorelines and in the trees. After a rain, thousands of miniscule frogs (no more than an inch long) seem to drop from the sky. They're fair game for the **snowy egret** and **great egret**—quick hunters with their long beaks. A fairly large bird, the **snail kite** picks up the **apple snail** all around the lake, then returns to its nesting tree and gorges—a dead giveaway with piles of empty snail shells underneath. Two varieties of ducks, the **black-bellied whistling duck** and the **Muscovy**, nest in trees along the swamp. All five species of **kingfishers** live in the sanctuary, and you can see **ospreys** and **black-collared hawks** diving for their morning catch. On one trip, we watched from our dory as a **peregrine falcon** repeatedly tried but failed to nab one of a flock of floating **American coots**. Black Creek, with its forests of large trees, provides homes to **black howler monkeys, Morelet's crocodiles, coatimundis, turtles,** and **iguanas**.

THE VILLAGE

The village is divided into three neighborhoods: **Crooked Tree, Pine Ridge,** and **Stain,** with a total population of 800. Villagers operate farms, raise livestock, and have a small fishery. Visitors will find the village spread out on the island; it consists of a cricket field, two churches, and neat wooden houses (many on stilts) in the middle of large, well-kept plots of land, each with its own tank to catch rainwater—a tranquil community.

Crooked Tree mainly attracts nature lovers. But visitors will find barefoot boys going home for lunch with fishing poles over their shoulders and, maybe, a string of healthy-looking fish. Ladies with floppy hats gabbing over back fences always flash a friendly smile with a gracious hello. And if you indulge in conversation you'll have a chance to hear the lovely soft Creole patois that is common throughout the country. While strolling through the village you might see the local boys having a hard workout on the cricket field.

The Cashew Seed/Nut

The village is also known for its thick stand of cashew trees. In the past the trees yielded a mild infusion into the budgets of the local women. Once a year they picked, processed, and sold about 400-500 quarts of bulk cashew nuts to a distributor in Belize City, who then packaged and sold them to the consumer. A new business is growing in Crooked Tree. The townspeople will be doing what they did before, only now they will go on to package the nuts for visitors and local consumers in shops and hotels around the country.

The cashew is very unusual—it's the only plant that grows its seed on the outside of the fruit (see the Special Topic, "Exotic Fruits and Nuts of Belize"). One bean-shaped pod hangs from the bottom of each fruit—one fruit, one

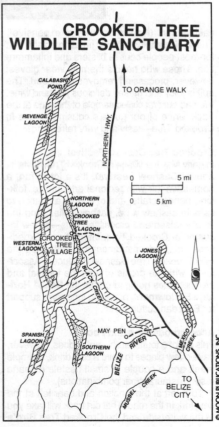

CROOKED TREE
WILDLIFE SANCTUARY

CALABASH POND

REVENGE LAGOON

TO ORANGE WALK

NORTHERN HWY.

0   5 mi

0   5 km

NORTHERN LAGOON

CROOKED TREE LAGOON

WESTERN LAGOON

CROOKED TREE VILLAGE

BLACK CREEK

JONES LAGOON

SPANISH LAGOON

MAY PEN

SOUTHERN LAGOON

BELIZE RIVER

MEXICO CREEK

MUSSEL CREEK

TO BELIZE CITY

© MOON PUBLICATIONS, INC.

Crooked Tree
Audubon Society
Visitors' Center

cashew nut. (No wonder they're expensive!) The shell contains a highly irritating poison that for most people causes blisters and inflammation. Those who handle the nuts wear gloves; however, processing removes all poison. The fruit is juicy and makes delicious jelly and wine. We had our first chilled sample of the wine at the back fence of our guide's cousin's house in Crooked Tree—tasty and very refreshing!

Crooked Tree Cashew Festival
In early May the village of Crooked Tree hosts its annual **Cashew Festival.** It's a lot of fun, a hometown fair with regional arts, music, folklore, dance, crafts, and of course a chance to sample cashew wine, cashew jellies, and the locally raised and processed nuts—a new industry for Crooked Tree. International Expeditions, Inc., was instrumental in setting up the new Crooked Tree Cashew Producers Association, with the profits of both the festival and product sales going to create the **Belize Heritage Endowment,** providing long-term support for Belizean cultural arts.

Accommodations and Food
This is not a tourist area—yet. It does, however, have a few places to have a cold drink, a simple meal, and a couple of small hostels (cabaña resort/restaurant/bar combinations).

Turn left at the junction and bear left at the next fork in the road. That dirt track will take you to the waterside and the **Crooked Tree Bird's**

Eye View Resort, formerly Crooked Tree Lodge. All rooms are spacious and have h/c water and private baths. Campers, ask about an area set aside for tents. Rates for room only are US$50 s/d; a dorm room that sleeps eight is US$10 per person. Meals are available: US$3.50-7 dinner. The resort has five boats for taking guests birdwatching. For more information, write or call Box 1976, Belize City, Belize, C.A., tel. (2) 44101, or fax (2) 77594.

Molly and Steve Tillett run **Molly's Rooms,** Crooked Tree, Belize District, Belize, C.A., no phone—five simple rooms in a clapboard building. Bathing is by bucket and they have a latrine for a toilet. Rates are US$10 s, US$15 d. Meals of local cooking are US$3 each. They also offer boat rentals, horseback riding, and overnight jungle tours.

Take a right at the junction and eventually you'll find **Paradise Inn Resort,** Crooked Tree, Belize District, Belize, C.A., tel. (2) 44333, in the U.S. tel./fax (718) 498-1122, CompuServe 75512,2552 (from other Internet providers: 75512.2552@compuserve.com)—a restaurant and five thatched-roof cabañas constructed of native hardwoods and operated by Rudy Crawford and his family. Each features private bathroom, h/c water, and is simple but comfortable. The evening breeze is intoxicating after a hot day on the water. Rates are about US$37 s, US$48 d. Meals are separate; US$3 breakfast US$4-6 lunch, US$7-20 dinner; package rates are available. The Crawfords also provide horse-

(top left) The Blue Hole is a favorite dive site off the Belize coast. (Belize Tourism Office);
(top right) Caribbean sunset (Phil Lanier); (bottom left) blue waters off Belize (Oz Mallan);
(bottom right) Clouds of fish swarm the reefs off the Belize shore. (James Beveridge)

Warrie Head Creek waterfall (Oz Mallan)

back rides, carriage rides, and a variety of tours.

Sam Tillett's Hotel, tel. (2) 44333, is another tiny (three rooms) hostel that's clean, has private baths, and is budget priced. Meals are available. Room rates are about US$26 d. Call for more information.

Take a right at the junction and it won't be long till you see **A & B Restaurant** on the left. It offers three meals a day, seven days a week, usually Belizean fare. T-bone steak is US$3.25, gibnut is US$3, deer US$3; it also serves pies and puddings.

Getting There

Independent travelers catch the **Jex Bus** to Crooked Tree in Belize City at 34 Regent St. at 10:55 a.m., 4:30 p.m., and 5:15 p.m.—from Crooked Tree to Belize City at 5:15 a.m., 6:30 a.m., and 7 a.m. This is fine for those who plan to spend the night. If not, check with the Audubon Society for further transport info, rates, and updated schedule. Other options are to go

cashew fruit with nut hanging below

by taxi, with a local tour operator, or by bike (a medium-long ride).

GUIDES AND TOURS

Local Guides

One recommended way to visit Crooked Tree is to hire a local guide who really knows his digs. Locals take you in boats to really experience the lagoon. Sam Tillett (now owner of a small hotel) was a local guide. Ask him if he's available to paddle you around the lagoon in his dugout canoe (a dory); this silent transport enables you to get very close to the shoreline without a motor that might tangle with thick plants, such as water lilies (called "tum tum") that grow on the surface of the lagoon. This is Sam's country, and after years of practice he knows what he's doing; he silently glides across the water to the birds without a swish. Sam, like most Belizeans, speaks a wonderful Creole (as well as good English) and will tell you, in English and Spanish, the names of unusual birds, plants, and animals. A profusion of wild ocher pokes up from the water covered with millions of pale pink snail eggs. Grazing cows wade into the shallows of the lagoon to munch on the tum tum, a delicacy that keeps them fat and fit when the grasses turn brown in the dry season.

From Belize City, if you want to be sure you'll have a guide and transportation once in Crooked Tree, check with the people at the Belize Audubon Society office in Belize City and they will be happy to have a guide and boat waiting for you when you arrive.

Naturalist Quest Tour

If you're really a nature lover, and want to squeeze every moment you can into the outdoors, including a trip to Crooked Tree Sanctuary, then take the **Naturalist Quest Tour** with International Expeditions, Inc., One Environs Park, Helena, Alabama 35080, tel. (800) 633-4734, (205) 428-1700. The Naturalist Quest gives Belize visitors a look into the heart of the country accompanied by a knowledgeable guide who will explain birds, animals, plants, growth patterns, seasonal curiosities, the weather, and a lot more. You arrive at Crooked Tree by way of one of the many waterways that crisscross the country. You'll pass by banks lined with jungle vines, plants, thick trees, and exotic birds. I can't think of a better way to "discover" Crooked Tree the first time. (Okay, I still like to pretend I'm Katharine Hepburn on the *African Queen*.)

This tour originates in the United States. Travelers board the boat from just outside Belize City, and Crooked Tree is just one of the stops. From here you'll travel a short distance up the wide Belize River over gentle rapids to a narrow, winding jungle stream. Keep your eyes open and you'll see (and undoubtedly hear) black howler monkeys, giant iguanas sunning on tall tree limbs, as well as myriad birds, including squawking species of parrots and maybe even the elusive and almost-extinct jabiru stork. The photographer will have several miles of jungle stream to capture exotic shots on film before reaching Crooked Tree Lagoon and *its* concentration of trees, plants, and birds. The boat makes a stop at **Crooked Tree Village,** where travelers are given a chance to explore the scenic settlement.

SOUTH OF CROOKED TREE

Chau Hiix Ruins
A new archaeological site, Chau Hiix, is being studied nearby. Under the auspices of the University of Indiana at Indianapolis, Dr. Kay Anne Pyburn is leading the dig. They have already made some startling discoveries that include a ball court and ball-court marker, along with small artifacts. Preliminary studies indicate the site was occupied from 1200 B.C. to A.D. 1500. **Sapodilla Lagoon** is south of Crooked Tree on Spanish Creek. A small guesthouse, aptly named Chau Hiix Lodge, is available near the site.

Chau Hiix Lodge
For now it has four rooms, each with private bathroom, hot showers, good spring water, screened windows, fans, rich mahogany wood interiors, and a wraparound screened-in porch

Crooked Tree cruise canoe

where meals are served. A nature trail winds its way through the trees to the archaeological site and is a wonderful place for birders. You might also see the hicatee turtle, which is on the endangered-species list. Guests at Chau Hiix Lodge have access to canoes and day-trips to the Community Baboon Sanctuary, or they might choose to just wander the trails on the 4,000-acre grounds of the lodge. Although drop-ins are welcome, most stays are packaged, including airport pickup, arrival by boat through beautiful lagoons, all meals, guided trips, and other lodge activities. Rates are listed for per person double occupancy: three-night packages are US$525, four nights US$635, seven nights US$935. In the U.S. call (800) 654-4424, fax (407) 322-6389; in Belize City call (2) 73787.

THE CAYES

INTRODUCTION

Along the coast of Belize, more than 200 cayes (pronounced "KEES" and derived from the Spanish word *cayo*) lie off the mainland. They range in size from no more than a half-block-long patch of mangrove forest to the largest, Ambergris Caye, which is 25 miles long and nearly 4.5 miles at its widest point. Some of these islands are inhabited by people, others only by wildlife.

THE LAND AND SEA

If you're out boating off the coast of Placencia, you might pass what in the distance looks like a tiny house rising straight from the sea. The small wood structure sits on a caye that just barely provides enough ground around the building to keep it dry. A caye starts as a tiny dot of mangrove, which in turn attracts birds, guano, and bits of sand in the breeze; it continues to grow until it's a true little island. And so the size of

this caye will also grow. In Belize the locals say it is rising. Perhaps this funny little house was a form of "homesteading" the sea.

Most of the cayes lie within the protection of the Belize Reef (almost 200 miles long), which parallels the mainland. Without the protection of the reef—in essence a breakwater—the islands would be washed away by the constantly pounding surf. Within the reef the sea is calm, shallow, and inviting; in some areas with a white sandy bottom, the color of the water is a rich aqua—even more inviting. Mangroves provide wonderful breeding grounds for the magnificent sealife that attracts divers worldwide.

FAUNA

The uninhabited islands are alive with all manner of exotic wildlife, though fewer animals and birds are seen on the larger cayes as

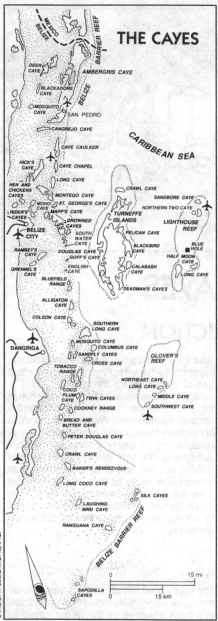

THE CAYES

MEXICO
BELIZE

BARRIER REEF

DEER CAYE
AMBERGRIS CAYE

BLACKADORE CAYE

MOSQUITO CAYE
SAN PEDRO

CANGREJO CAYE

CARIBBEAN SEA

CAYE CAULKER

HICK'S CAYE
CAYE CHAPEL

HEN AND CHICKENS CAYES
LONG CAYE

CRAWL CAYE

MONTEGO CAYE

MOHO CAYE
ST. GEORGE'S CAYE
SANDBORE CAYE

MAPPS CAYE
TURNEFFE ISLANDS
NORTHERN TWO CAYE

RIDER'S CAYES
DROWNED CAYES
LIGHTHOUSE REEF

BELIZE CITY
SOUTH WATER CAYE
PELICAN CAYE

BLACKBIRD CAYE
BLUE HOLE

RAMSEY'S CAYE
DOUGLAS CAYE
GOFF'S CAYE
HALF MOON CAYE

GRENNEL'S CAYE
ENGLISH CAYE
CALABASH CAYE
LONG CAYE

BLUEFIELD RANGE
DEADMAN'S CAYES

ALLIGATOR CAYE

COLSON CAYE

SOUTHERN LONG CAYE

DANGRIGA
MOSQUITO CAYE
COLUMBUS CAYE
SANDFLY CAYES
CROSS CAYE
GLOVER'S REEF

TOBACCO RANGE
NORTHEAST CAYE
LONG CAYE
MIDDLE CAYE

COCO PLUM CAYE
TWIN CAYES
SOUTHWEST CAYE

COCKNEY RANGE

BREAD AND BUTTER CAYE

PETER DOUGLAS CAYE

CRAWL CAYE

BAKER'S RENDEZVOUS

LONG COCO CAYE

SILK CAYES

LAUGHING BIRD CAYE

RANGUANA CAYE

BELIZE BARRIER REEF

0   15 mi
0   15 km

SAPODILLA CAYES

© MOON PUBLICATIONS, INC.

more people visit them. However, you will see the common **iguana,** which can grow to more than six feet (a local food source), along with its smaller cousin, the **wishwilly** or **spiny-tailed iguana** (note the lethal-looking jagged spines that run down its back); both avowed vegetarians and usually harmless, they can devastate a garden in no time. Also lurking in the underbrush are **opossum, armadillo, raccoon, peccary, deer, paca (gibnut),** and maybe even **ocelot.** The **giant blue land crab** is an unusual critter, as is the **hermit crab,** which graduates from one abandoned mollusk shell to the next, leaving its outgrown one behind—sometimes in the crook of a tall tree. Two snakes make their home on the islands: the **boa constrictor** and the **black-tailed indigo.** Both are good rat catchers and supposedly harmless to adults (who are too big to be crushed). These snakes will bite if cornered; do guard small pets and children. The many frogs and lizards are fun to search out, especially the **Central American basilisk.** This small lizard often streaks past, upright on its hind legs—even along the surface of the water. It's often referred to by the locals as the **Jesus Christ lizard.** The black **anole** has a colorful habit of spreading a bright, salmon-pink throat pouch when claiming territory or looking for a female.

Birds

The most impressive members of this wild kingdom, however, are the birds that thrive on the multitude of cayes, whether they're tiny mangrove patches or busy tourist destinations. Colorful land birds number in the hundreds, including 27 varieties of migrant warblers. Birdwatchers will also find the **magnificent frigate bird, brown pelican, cormorant, royal tern, laughing gull,** and **brown-** and **red-footed boobies.** The best time to be a watcher on the cayes is September and October, when thousands of birds are migrating south. Many go no farther and spend the winter right here. Wading birds have found the islands the perfect place to live year-round. Look for the **snowy egret, green heron, great egret, cattle egret, little blue heron,** and **great blue heron,** along with many, many others.

HISTORY

The Maya
The first "islanders" on the cayes were the Maya. Little is known about the culture of the cayes in that era except on Ambergris Caye, where shards of pottery still litter the ground at **Marco Gonzalez, Chac Balam,** and **Santa Cruz.** Remnants indicate that Ambergris Caye was an important hub for trading. It is possible to visit these sites, and it's best to go with a guide. Contact the **Belize Tourist Board** in Belize City, tel. (2) 77213, fax (2) 77490; and in San Pedro on Ambergris Caye, contact the **San Pedro Town Board** at (26) 2198/2402, fax (26) 2492. They will put you in touch with someone who knows the ins and outs of Maya territory on the island.

Spanish Speakers
In the mid-1800s, Spanish-speaking refugees from Mexico's Caste War came for relief from the killing and bloodletting between the Maya and the Mexicans. Many of these people stayed in Belize, starting dynasties that continue to grow several generations later.

Buccaneers
By the 17th century, pirates found the cayes around the Belizean mainland perfect for lying low, riding out a storm, resting, drinking rum, refurbishing their ships, and replenishing water and food supplies. Small treasures of gold coins and antiquated bottles dating from the era indicate the pirates used these islands regularly. In the past, locals "strenuously" discouraged outsiders from using metal detectors for fear they'd find one of the legendary "gold treasures" buried on the island by pirates.

Tourists
The cayes first opened the doors to tourism with a boat that made the trip from Belize City in the 1920s. But it really began in earnest when the cayes started to attract a large influx of divers in the 1960s. One of these islands, Ambergris, is one of the most popular diving hubs in Belize.

PRACTICALITIES

Accommodations and Food
At one time the only island with a hotel was Ambergris, and that came surprisingly early in its history. But it was many years before any of the other cayes had the same amenities. Caye Caulker was next with friendly folks who would rent out an extra room or hammock space with guests/tourists welcome to join the family for meals. That has all changed. About 25 cayes now offer simple to elaborate accommodations. Some cayes offer an entire island with an exclusive hotel. It doesn't always mean the hotel falls into the luxury category; in fact, many of these are "diving" islands with simple cabinlike accommodations. However, guests have a selection of prime vacation options if they want to dive or fish. These resorts are generally noted for excellent food.

Almost everything must be brought over by boat, including food, furniture, fuels, everyday living essentials, and building materials. Expect the prices to be a little higher than on the mainland for similar lodging and meals.

Getting There
Each caye has its own method of transport. Caulker and Ambergris have regular public transport daily. For some you must make arrangements with private boat owners. The resorts can give you details. Private yachts and seaplanes may land at a few of the cayes. Check with the Belize Embassy in Washington, D.C., for rules concerning paperwork when bringing in a foreign-registered vessel. A few cayes have small air strips for charter planes (available in Belize City). Remember that when you leave the protection of the barrier reef to get to the atolls, you will be in open sea and it can get quite choppy. Those who tend toward seasickness should come prepared with their favorite preventatives.

THE MANGROVES AND TURTLE GRASS

Developers and certain segments of the tourism industry frown upon two Belizean eco-systems: mangroves and the accompanying grass flats.

Many people see mangroves as an eyesore, a breeding place of mosquitoes and sandflies. As beachfront property becomes more desirable, developers are apt to remove mangroves and turtle grass to make way for a white beach, clear swimming areas, and hotels for visitors.

Fortunately, biologists and lovers of nature are informing the public that without the mangroves and the turtle grass, the cayes will erode and lose many feet of land mass.

Caye Caulker shows a good example of erosion at the Split, which originally was a shallow ditch dug across the island for easy dory transport. But in 1961 Hurricane Hattie blasted through the small ditch, making a much larger cut. It was made worse in the early 1980s when a small resort cut down the protecting mangroves to make a beach. Since then, the erosion has continued and the buttonwood mangrove trees along the edge have fallen one by one into the swiftly flowing waters of the channel.

As the mangroves and grasses are uprooted, cayes lose their "anchors." And what makes turtle grass important? Lobster, conch, and stone crab proliferate in the protection of the wispy grass. And it's an important food source for Belize's manatees and sea turtles. These marine creatures, globally endangered, are just two who have managed to survive in Belize's waters. Turtle grass, along with a variety of mangroves, is a natural hatchery for many fish species, which in turn provide the fry to feed larger fish, pelicans, cormorants, and other sea birds.

Mangroves are salt-resistant, growing where most other plantlife find it impossible. In Belize, two species of the four known in the country—the red mangrove and the black mangrove—shield large areas of the Belizean coastline and hundreds of cayes. Red mangrove in excess of 30 feet grows in tidal areas, inland lagoons, and river mouths, but always close to the sea. Its signature is its arching prop roots. Black mangrove grows almost double that height. Its roots are slender, upright projectiles that grow to about 12 inches, protuding all around the mother tree. Both types of roots provide air to the tree. Another species, white mangrove, grows inland along riverbanks. The buttonwood mangrove thrives in drier areas of the cayes and mainland.

Mangroves are amazingly resilient, second only to the barrier reef in providing hurricane protection. When wiped out, they immediately begin to regrow. They propogate by their prop roots and by seeds that germinate on the tree. As soon as the seeds hit the mud, they begin their growth cycle. If the seeds fall into the water, they can survive for six months floating and bobbing until they happen upon the right conditions in which to set down roots. Mangrove cayes nurture invertebrates and reptiles, including boa constrictors, iguanas, and saltwater crocodiles. Sea turtles, including loggerhead and hawksbill, thrive on encrusted sponges and crustaceans clustered at the roots. Wading birds, spoonbill, ibis, and heron feed around the roots; frigates, pelicans, and cormorants roost and nest in the rich, green foliage.

Mangroves and turtle grass are Belize's most important eco-systems. Again, Belizeans are becoming role models to other developing countries with their choice of priorities. And though the tourist dollar is very important to the economy, the people are making decisions now that will protect their natural assets; they are choosing now the type of tourist who will visit the country in the future.

AMBERGRIS CAYE

Ambergris is the largest caye along the Belizean coast, and if it weren't for a very small canal separating the island from the Yucatán mainland, Ambergris could easily have been part of Mexico. In fact, Mexico has occasionally staked its claim over the years. As for its name, ambergris is a waxy substance occasionally found floating in or on the shores of tropical seas. Believed to originate in the intestines of the sperm whale, it is rare and valuable, used in the manufacture of perfume.

San Pedro is the only town on Ambergris and for years has been the main tourist attraction of Belize. This may change with the development of hotels and guesthouses all over the country. But despite its many new hotels and golf carts, this small island still offers the "feeling" of old Belize and I hope it will never change. Activities are pretty low key, but if you're looking you will find a couple of discos and bars with a lively nightlife.

Enjoy a Belikin beer at one of the waterfront hangouts and watch the sometimes-hectic but mostly quiet traffic in the harbor. It's not unusual to see a small sailboat balancing a car on wooden planks across its bow (the official way to get a car to the island) and locals

say only one or two have been lost over the side! At one time cars were really a rarity, but more are showing up on the sandy roads. The government eliminated the duty on electric golf carts, which should bring more of the quiet vehicles instead of cars to the island. In harbor traffic you might also see a small boat hanging heavy in the sea, loaded to the waterline with a tall mound of sand brought from the mainland or another caye for construction; watch as the men shovel it out onto the shore (San Pedro sand has too much salt).

Don't be surprised if a local Creole comes into the bar or cafe where you're having a Belikin and offers to sell you an old beer bottle filled with a potion made in his kitchen from seaweed; it is said to ease hangovers, cure ulcers, and soothe colicky babies. No hard sell here; he's just offering a needed service. The waitress or potion-peddlers will be happy to talk to you, tell you about their families, their island, their lives. For a special holiday celebration, visit San Pedro during the Dia de San Pedro holiday, 26-29 June. Many of these friendly, sociable people can trace their family roots to the beginnings of Ambergris, even before James Blake bought the island (see "History," below). Enjoy Belize for

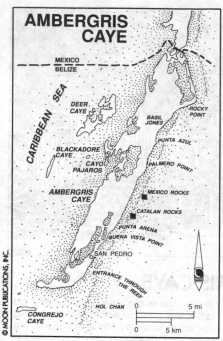

AMBERGRIS CAYE

CARIBBEAN SEA

MEXICO
BELIZE

DEER CAYE

BASIL JONES

ROCKY POINT

PUNTA AZUL

BLACKADORE CAYE

CAYO PAJAROS

PALMERO POINT

AMBERGRIS CAYE

MEXICO ROCKS

CATALAN ROCKS

PUNTA ARENA

BUENA VISTA POINT

SAN PEDRO

ENTRANCE THROUGH THE REEF

HOL CHAN

CONGREJO CAYE

0   5 mi
0   5 km

© MOON PUBLICATIONS, INC.

what it is and don't expect something it isn't: a luxury resort—à la Cancún.

THE LAND

Twenty-five-mile-long Ambergris is three-quarters of a mile off the Belize Reef and 35 miles from Belize City. Its beach runs parallel to the reef except at Rocky Point, where they briefly come together. Four and a half miles north of Rocky Point, at Boca Bacalar Chico, a narrow channel separates Belize and Mexico. Legend says the ancient Maya dug the scant strait by hand so that they could bring their canoes through rather than going all the way around the peninsula. In dry years when the water receded it was impossible to get a boat through, so in 1899 the Mexican government dug the channel deeper and wider to allow its warships easy access to the other side of the peninsula.

Ambergris Caye was formed by an accumulation of coral fragments. That, along with the silt

emptied nearby from the Rio Hondo, has created a lovely bit of terra firma where people have been making a living since pre-Hispanic times as fishermen. The caye is made up of mangrove swamps, 12 lagoons, a plateau, and sand ridges. The largest lagoon, fed by 15 creeks, is 2.5-mile-long **Laguna de San Pedro** on the western side of the village. San Pedro sits on a sand ridge at the southern end of the island. Over the years the constant wind, rain, and tide have reduced the shoreline and beachfront of the village by 30 feet. The water surrounding the caye offers rich fishing grounds and has supported fishermen for more than 300 years. At the southern end of Ambergris, navigable channels (often only big enough for a skiff) meander in and out of mangrove swamps and small and large lagoons. The backside is a haven for myriad varieties of birds, including the rare spoonbill.

HISTORY

The Maya
As with the rest of Belize, the first people on the caye were the Maya. They managed to rout the invading Spaniards as early as 1508. Very little is known about these Maya. However, a small post-Classic site in the Basil Jones area and a few jade and carved ornaments have been found along with obsidian flakes and fragments of pottery. At the southern end of the caye the ruins of Marco Gonzalez are also considered of strategic importance. It is presumed that because of the location of Ambergris Caye (in the center of the sea-lane) it was a stopover for Maya traders traveling up and down the coast. And because of its close proximity to Mexico, no doubt it had great military value as well.

The Blakes
Between 1848-49, during the Caste War on the Yucatán Peninsula, Yucatecan mestizos migrated to Belize, and four families were the first permanent residents of what has developed into present-day San Pedro on Ambergris Caye. Before long there was a population of 50 self-sufficient fishermen—also growing corn and vegetables. Life was idyllic for these people—until 1874 and the coming of the Blake family.

fishing industries, though in the end (after almost 100 years) the good guys won out—or so it seems today. After many years of complaints, the tyrannical rule of the Blake family came to a close when the Belizean government stepped in and made a "forced purchase" of San Pedro. It redistributed the land, selling lots and parcels to the same islanders who had been living on the land for generations.

The Fishing Industry

The caye saw industry change according to the political climate: from logwood to chicle to coconuts, and then to lobsters. Before 1920, the spiny lobster was thrown away and considered a nuisance, constantly getting caught in fishing nets. That all changed in 1921 when the lobster became a valuable export item. Though the fishermen were getting only a penny a pound, the business became lucrative when freezer vessels and freezer-equipped seaplanes began flying between the cayes and Florida. After struggling long and hard, the islanders established fishing cooperatives. Once the fishermen shook off the human "sharks," the fishing industry on the cayes became successful, with the benefits finally going to the fishermen.

Today's Ambergris

The island is rich in lore, some of which still reaches out and taps the modern islander on the shoulder. The establishment of the fishermen's co-op enabled the population of Ambergris to develop a good middle-class economy over the years. The financial upswing has allowed the town to improve the infrastructure of the island, which in turn has created a good atmosphere for tourists. Lots of stores, cafes, and hotels are waiting to be enjoyed, and the streets are becoming crowded with golf carts as the island develops.

The earliest tourists came to Ambergris Caye aboard the boat *Pamelayne* in the 1920s. By 1965 the first real hotel was established, and the industry has been growing ever since. The caye is considered the most developed and successful tourism area of Belize. It boasts 24-hour-a-day electricity, modern telephone communication to anywhere in the world, and medical service. You can buy the beautiful Belizean stamps and mail letters from the caye. On the downside, who knows how this influx of out-

James Blake paid the Belize government BZE$650 for Ambergris Caye (taking over every parcel of land except one parcel set aside for the Catholic Church) and began collecting rent from people who had been there for many years. After this, the history of the island was tied up with the fortunes of the Blakes and their in-laws, the Parhams and Alamillas. Their story reads like a script from a soap opera—including illicit love affairs, illegitimate children, unlikely marriages, and (some say) oppression of the poor. The Blakes controlled everybody and everything on the island, including the coconut and

siders will affect the culture, values, and traditions of the tiny island? The ecology is threatened, but scientists in the country are on the alert and taking precautions to preserve the flora and fauna. Ambergris Caye is a laid-back combination of tropical paradise (with accommodations from simple to upscale, but not glitzy) and old-flavor fishing village: the best of both worlds, which must be seen and experienced.

WATER SPORTS

Diving and Tourism

A circus of underwater color and shapes is the main reason people first started traveling to Belize in large numbers to explore its pristine dive areas. Today, get together with a group of serious divers anywhere in the world and at least one will rave about an underwater adventure in Belizean waters. Since dive stories can be even more remarkable than fish stories, neophytes normally should take it all with a grain of sand—except in Belize. Divers tell of swimming with wild dolphins, swarms of horse-eye jacks, and more than two dozen eagle rays at one time. Some divers go strictly to photograph the eerie underwater beauty and color. Others enjoy the excitement of coming head to head with pelagic creatures that are carrying on with life as though the two-legged outsider were invisible, such as during the January full moon when hundreds of groupers gather at their primeval mating grounds on the reef. These stories tell of so many groupers (hundreds!) that the reef face is covered with these thick-lipped, ugly fish releasing sperm and eggs in such a fury and quantity that you cannot see two feet in front of you.

Coral and Sponges

Belizean waters are universally clear except where, during heavy rains, the river outlets gush silt-clouded water into the sea. Particularly pristine areas are around the atolls, the reef, and certain cayes. In some cases visibility is extraordinary: more than 200 feet. Coral heads are magical with unique shapes reaching, floating, and quivering, interspersed with minute-to-immense fish all with personalities of their own. Garish-colored sponges decorate steep vertical walls that drop into black nothing. Bright red and yellow tube sponges grow tall, providing habitat for similarly colored fish.

Ships and Treasure

Some divers prefer searching for sunken ships. All have heard the stories of magnificent sunken treasure never found—but then who would tell if they did find it? For more than 300 years the Belize Reef has served as a watery grave for ships thrown into the destructive limestone wall during forceful unexpected storms, including hurricanes. According to some divers, the bottom of the sea along the Belize Reef between Mexico's Isla Mujeres and Honduras Bay is littered with wrecks both ancient and modern.

Diving the Cuts and Atolls

When flying over the reef and as you approach Ambergris Caye, study the seascape around the island. The Belize Reef is clearly visible about a half mile in front of the island. If the plane is low enough you can see marinelife suspended in the sea, coral heads, large fish, and, of course, the inviting multicolors of blue that lure even the nonscuba diver to learn how to snorkel. You can also see the layout of the

REEF FISH

Atlantic spadefish	green moray	Spanish grunt
banded butterfly fish	honey damselfish	spotfin butterfly fish
bar jack	nurse shark	spotted drum
blue tang	queen triggerfish	trunkfish
bluestriped grunt	schoolmaster	white grunt
dog snapper	sergeant major	yellow jack
four-eyed butterfly fish	smallmouth grunt	yellowtail damselfish
French grunt	southern stingray	yellowtail snapper

*snorkeling off
Ambergris Caye*

reef, how shallow the water is, and how close to the surface the corals rise, making it impossible for even the most shallow-draft craft to cross over.

The cuts (or channels) are also clearly visible; these seven channels are the areas where most day boats bring their divers to explore, both on the seaward side and at the cut itself. This part of the Caribbean attracts divers for many reasons, one of which is the location of three of the only four atolls in the entire Caribbean Sea: **Turneffe Islands Atoll, Lighthouse Reef Atoll,** and **Glover's Reef Atoll.**

Almost every hotel on Ambergris employs the services of local divers and some have on-site dive shops and dive masters. Local guides for the most part have lived on the island most of their lives and operate island-built skiffs 20-30 feet long that are generally powered by two outboards. Other options for the visiting diver are live-aboard dive boats that travel farther and stay out at sea longer, from overnight excursions to seven-day cruises that originate from a variety of ports in the U.S., Belize City, or San Pedro. This is a world meant for divers.

Other Dive Locations around Ambergris

Probably no "secret" dive spot is left along the Belizean mainland or island coasts. But if you talk to divers who continue the search, some go away with curious smiles on their faces—do you suppose they know something they aren't sharing? **Hol Chan Marine Reserve** is probably the most popular dive destination of the cuts or channels. The words *hol chan* mean "little channel" in the Maya language. The reserve covers about five square miles and is located four miles southeast of San Pedro in the northern section of the Belize Reef. The channel is about 30 feet deep, and since no fishing is permitted in the reserve, it is rich with sealife of every description. Divers can expect to see abundant angelfish, blue-striped grunts, schoolmaster snapper, and hundreds of other varieties. It's also well-known for the green moray eels living in tiny caves along the wall. The areas for recreation are marked with buoys. The usual rule: take only photos! It is clearly spelled out; do not collect coral or fish whether with spear or handlines. Mooring buoys are in place to help protect against anchor damage.

Note: The current at Hol Chan is very strong. Snorkelers should take note. At least one person has drowned because of the current.

Palmetto Reef is another dramatic dive site for the experienced. Divers will see flamboyant blue vase and purple tube sponges along with

---

DIVE EMERGENCIES

A decompression chamber, manned by volunteers, is now available in San Pedro on Ambergris Caye. Divers are urged to donate US$1 per tank to help support this important system.

other reaching and twisting corals. Coral shelves plunge 50-150 feet into dark chasms. **Mexico Rocks** offers a variety of coral heads and clouds of tiny fish. **Caverns** offers swim-through caves filled with colorful fish and sponge-covered walls. At **Sandy Point Reef** myriad caverns and deep canyons provide dramatic diving.

Diving Instruction

Most dive shops on Ambergris give diving lessons, with a choice of either a brief resort course or full NAUI and/or PADI certification. **Reef Divers, Ltd.,** tel. (2) 2965/3134, based at Royal Palm Inn, and **Amigos del Mar,** tel. (800) 938-0860, are known to be among the best. Other reputable shops to check out are **Belize Dive Center,** tel. (26) 2797, **Hustler Tours Pro Dive Shop,** tel. (26) 2693/2538, fax (26) 2719, **Out Island Divers,** tel. (800) 258-3465, in Belize (26) 2151, **Paradise Dive Club,** tel. (26) 2149, and **Tortuga Dive Centre,** tel. (26) 2804, based at the Holiday Hotel, tel. (26) 2014.

Boating and Snorkeling

Take a boat ride. Explore the Caribbean Sea in and around the many cayes of the area. Some vessels are **glass-bottom boats,** such as the *Reef Seeker,* tel. (26) 2804, at the Holiday Hotel, so the nonswimmer can enjoy the beauty of the sea, too. Snorkeling is also part of the activity on many boats, and gear is readily available. Ask at your hotel about trips to Hol Chan Marine Reserve or Caye Caulker.

A day-boat with a long history of success is the *Rum Punch II,* run by brothers Tony and George. A snorkeling stop at the **Coral Garden,** lunch at Caye Caulker, and captivating stories make a pleasant day. True to the boat's name, rum punch is served throughout the trip.

The *Winnie Estelle,* tel. (26) 2394, is a converted freight boat offering comfortable daytrips to the reef and Caye Caulker for snorkeling. This classic wooden 66-foot island trader docks at the Paradise Hotel.

But man does not boat by day alone. *The Dolphin,* tel. (26) 2870, makes sunset and dinner cruises from the dock of the Playador Hotel.

Many guides who lead snorkeling trips also do fishing trips. Among the many who offer both are **Fred Alamilla,** tel. (26) 2006; **John Alamilla,** tel. (26) 2009; **Alfonso Graniel,** tel. (26) 2584; **Abel Guerrero, Jr.,** tel. (26) 2517; and **Andy Nunez** with his boat, *Flashdancer,* tel. (26) 2442.

Live-Aboard Dive Boats

For some real excitement, take a dive trip on the *Manta IV* with **Belize Dive Center.** Eye to eye, fish to human, you can be the director of your own video, take still photos, or just watch the activity of the classic denizens of the deep. The *Manta IV* also provides dive trips leaving from the shores of Ambergris Caye (operating out of **Belize Yacht Club** in San Pedro) to magnificent locations that all divers yearn to visit: **Blue Hole, Half Moon Caye, Long Caye,** and **Turneffe Islands.** You have your choice of daytrips or overnight excursions. The *Manta IV* is a 54-foot diesel, fiberglass V-hull, with freshwater showers. It was used in the film *Cocoon II.* For more information about prices and reservations in the U.S., call (800) 938-0860; in Belize call (26) 2797.

The owners of *Reef Roamer I* and *III* are the people who put Blue Hole trips on the tourist map. **Out Island Divers** has run dive tours to Lighthouse Reef and the Blue Hole for more than a decade. The captains and crews are experienced at making neophytes feel comfortable in open water. They explain to the uninitiated that Belize got its great reputation for diving from the atolls, not the barrier reef. The famous Blue Hole is only part of the excitement, because the vertical walls surrounding the atolls and the myriad forms of sealife are fantastic. *Reef Roamer I,* 38 feet with a wide beam, is used for day-trips, and *Reef Roamer III,* 34 feet, has the flexibility for day runs or overnighters. The three-day trip to Lighthouse Reef is hard to beat for value, variety of undersea life, and excitement. You get nine dives in all and eight meals for around US$350. For more information, write or call Box 3455, Estes Park, Colorado 80517, tel. (800) 258-3465, (970) 586-6020, fax (970) 586-6134, in Belize tel. (26) 2151, fax (26) 2810.

Other boats to check out include *Offshore Express,* tel. (26) 2013, fax (26) 2864, managed by the Coral Beach Dive Shop, tel. (26) 2817.

Fishing

The area within the reef is a favorite for such fish as tarpon and bonefish. Outside the reef the choice of big game is endless. Most hotels and dive shops will make arrangements for fishing, including boat and guide. One resort, **El Pescador,** (26) 2975, specializes in fishing packages that include all types of angling.

Good local fishing guides include **Freddie Waight** through the Belize Yacht Club, tel. (26) 2777; **Jose Gonzales,** tel. (26) 2344; **Nestor Gomez,** tel. (26) 2063; **Luz Guerrero,** tel. (26) 2705; and **Luis Perez** through Amigos del Mar, tel. (26) 2706.

For a trip on one of the best-equipped large sportsfishing boats on the island, contact Captain Tom Thomas of *Sea Boots,* tel. (26) 2911, a 52-foot cruiser docked at **Journey's End.** Captain Tom offers reef and deep-sea fishing, as well as flats fishing for tarpon and bonefish.

At the Marina

The **Belize Yacht Club** offers up to 33 slips to visiting boaters. Rates are US$25/night plus gas and water. For the boater, supplies including Shell petroleum products, ice, and snacks are available, tel. (26) 2777, fax (26) 2768.

Water Toys and Where to Find Them

Ambergris has joined the high-tech tourist community, and most of the upscale hotels have fun toys for rent. Along with the latest in diving equipment and dive boats, fun-seekers will find **Windsurfers, Jet Skis, catamarans,** and **water skis.** If you've never done any of these things, schools and instructors are available.

Catamarans are available for guests at **Ramon's Village** and **Journey's End. Innovative Water Sports,** tel. (26) 3337, at The Palms (next to Ramon's Village) rents **Wave Runners** for US$50-60/hour.

Kayaks and **canoes** are available from **Island Adventures,** tel. (26) 2697, on the beach in front of Fido's Courtyard.

Windsurfers are available in town through **Rock's Inn** and **Ramon's Village. Victoria House** south of town also offers them for rent. Instruction is additional. North of town, **Journey's End Caribbean Club** offers free use of boards to guests. For more options check at your hotel or at one of the larger hotels on the island.

OTHER RECREATION

Beachcombing

Ambergris doesn't have miles of beachfront to walk. Along much of the main part of town the beach is narrow and the water comes almost to business doorways. And because the reef breaks up the wave action along the shore,

San Pedro docks

windsurfing along the caye

there are not the numbers and kinds of shells one might like, but the views and the salt air are just fine for early morning walks—you never know when you'll find a small treasure lying on the sand. Shelling trips are available; ask your hotel.

Birdwatching
The birdlife in Belize is renowned. On Ambergris the frigate birds glide and dive just off the beachfront. You need only travel a short distance out of town to see an enormous variety, including the **white egret, white heron,** and **roseate spoonbill.** The best places on Ambergris to watch for these birds is in the mangrove bays. Of course, you can arrange boating trips to the back side of the island where birdlife is abundant. Check with your hotel or one of the local travel agencies.

Biking
It's possible to bike from south of Victoria House all the way to the Parrot's Nest up north with only a break for the ferry at the cut. For those who want to see the island by bike, hotels and resorts including **Caribbean Villas, Journey's End,** and **Ramon's Village** provide or rent bikes to guests. Independent operators, such as **Oscar's Rentals,** (26) 2008, rent bikes by the hour, day, or week.

Horseback Riding
Those who would love to see San Pedro from horseback will find horses at the north end of town at the stables of **Isla Equestrian** just off Pescador Drive, behind Paradise Resort, (26) 2895.

Inland and Island Tours
If you're a newcomer to this sort of vacation, but want to see it *all,* including the land and the sea, don't worry. Most hotels and local travel agencies will arrange for day-trips to the mainland to see Maya ruins at Altun Ha, Lamanai, and Xunantunich; the bird sanctuary at Crooked Tree; Belize Zoo; and more. One to check out is **Abel's Tours,** tel. (26) 3402. **Aero Belize,** tel. (26) 3200, has packages to **Mayan Katut Resort** on its own tiny island. And, **Island Air,** tel. (26) 2435, has packages available to the Maya ruins of Tikal in Guatemala.

Seaplane Tours
Adding a bit of adventure to your sightseeing excitement by using a bush-pilot classic, the de Havilland Beaver seaplane, two of the many Leslie brothers of **Hustler Tours** take visitors on trips to Lamanai or Crooked Tree Lagoon; US$175 per person with four to five people. As an example, the Lamanai trip includes the flight to and from, lunch, and a swim at the Lamanai Outpost Lodge. You depart at 8:30 a.m., arrive at 9 a.m., and return at 3 p.m.

Tennis
Journey's End Caribbean Club and **Royal Palm Inn** offer tennis among other amenities to their guests. Bring your own gear.

Weightlifting and Aerobics
In case you haven't had enough exercise already, if you're staying at the **Belize Yacht Club,** tel. (26) 2777, you can bench press, use the squat machine and the Nautilus machines,

Belizean Reef Suites

curl a dumbbell or two, and ride the cycle machines to your heart's content. Step- and pool-aerobics classes also are available. The cost is US$5/day and hours are 6:30 a.m. till 9 p.m., Mon.-Saturday.

ACCOMMODATIONS

For such a tiny island you'll find a wide variety of accommodations. Don't expect a lot of luxury; most rooms downtown are very simple, with several upscale exceptions. A few have a/c; most have fans. The majority of the hotels are downtown, in some cases in a cluster separated by narrow walkways in between and along San Pedro's narrow beachfront. In the center of town most of the "beach" is little more than a narrow strip of sand on which to pull up boats, and a pedestrian walkway. Many of the hotels on Front Street (on the eastern side of the island and running north and south) provide porches that look out over the sea and reef just offshore. The

downtown hotels are right in the middle of things, close to the restaurants, bars, gift shops, dive shops, and all other commerce. For something a little more deluxe, check out the hotels on the edges of town, where you'll find more traditional beach resorts—and where you'll pay considerably more as well.

Note: Most hotels offer special rates during the summer and early fall. Also, a 5% government tax is added to your room rate, and in many hotels a 10-15% service charge is also tacked on. In some cases an extra 4-5% is charged for the use of a credit card. This raises the quoted rate considerably! Prices also change frequently; traveler's checks usually are accepted.

Make reservations as soon as you decide to travel to the cayes—especially if you are planning your trip Dec.-March. In most cases accommodations are limited, and even on the largest island, Ambergris, reserve well in advance.

Budget

Not a whole lot of budget lodgings are left in San Pedro, with the exception of the following gems that will remind longtime travelers of "old" San Pedro.

Take a look at **Rubie's,** San Pedro, Ambergris Caye, Belize, C.A., tel. (26) 2063, fax (26) 2434, on Barrier Reef Drive at the south end of town. It's still one of the least expensive hotels on the caye, offering clean rooms with ocean views. Rooms come with shared or private baths. With shared baths, they cost about US$14 s/d; with private baths US$27-38 s/d. You can arrange a wide array of activities through the hotel, including snorkeling and dive trips. Fishing is a specialty; tailored trips feature light spin casting or fly fishing for bonefish and tarpon or trolling for reef fish with live bait. Rubie's also has a cafe serving breakfast, lunch, and dinner, 6 a.m.-6 p.m. Credit cards are okay.

No, **Martha's Hotel and Cafe,** is not on the beach but this great little budget hotel, Box 27, San Pedro, Ambergris Caye, Belize, C.A., tel. in the U.S. (800) 365-6232, in Belize (26) 2053, fax (26) 2589, is two blocks from the waterfront, close to everything, and across the street from **Elvi's Kitchen.** Upstairs are the rooms, downstairs a general store where you can pick up

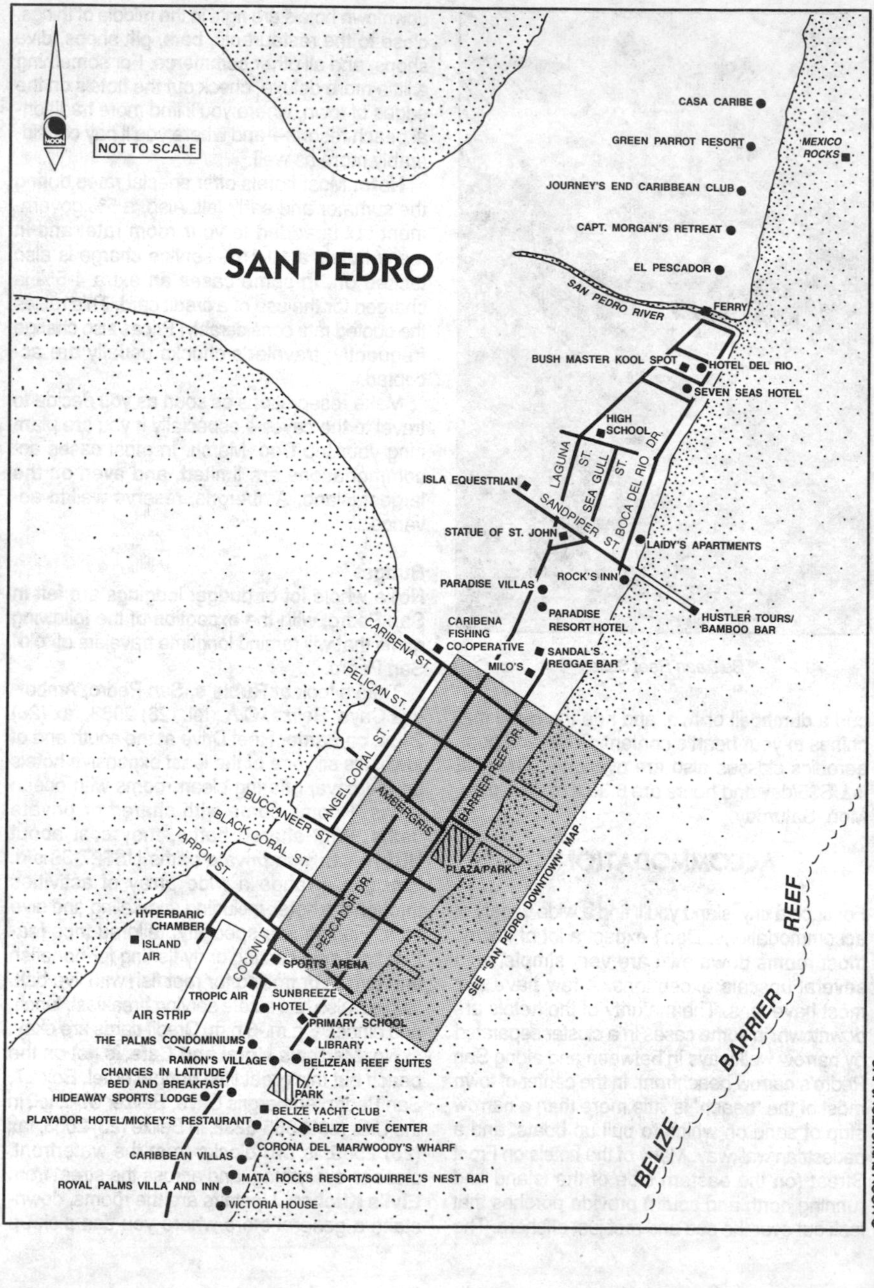

NOT TO SCALE

SAN PEDRO

CASA CARIBE

GREEN PARROT RESORT

MEXICO ROCKS

JOURNEY'S END CARIBBEAN CLUB

CAPT. MORGAN'S RETREAT

EL PESCADOR

SAN PEDRO RIVER

FERRY

BUSH MASTER KOOL SPOT

HOTEL DEL RIO

SEVEN SEAS HOTEL

HIGH SCHOOL

LAGUNA ST.

SEA GULL ST.

BOCA DEL RIO DR.

ISLA EQUESTRIAN

SANDPIPER ST.

STATUE OF ST. JOHN

LAIDY'S APARTMENTS

PARADISE VILLAS

ROCK'S INN

PARADISE RESORT HOTEL

HUSTLER TOURS/ BAMBOO BAR

CARIBENA ST.

CARIBENA FISHING CO-OPERATIVE

SANDAL'S REGGAE BAR

MILO'S

PELICAN ST.

ANGEL CORAL ST.

AMBERGRIS

BARRIER REEF DR.

BUCCANEER ST.

PESCADOR DR.

BLACK CORAL ST.

PLAZA/PARK

TARPON ST.

SEE "SAN PEDRO DOWNTOWN MAP"

HYPERBARIC CHAMBER

ISLAND AIR

COCONUT

SPORTS ARENA

AIR STRIP

TROPIC AIR

SUNBREEZE HOTEL

THE PALMS CONDOMINIUMS

PRIMARY SCHOOL

LIBRARY

RAMON'S VILLAGE

BELIZEAN REEF SUITES

CHANGES IN LATITUDE BED AND BREAKFAST

HIDEAWAY SPORTS LODGE

PARK

PLAYADOR HOTEL/MICKEY'S RESTAURANT

BELIZE YACHT CLUB

BELIZE DIVE CENTER

CARIBBEAN VILLAS

CORONA DEL MAR/WOODY'S WHARF

MATA ROCKS RESORT/SQUIRREL'S NEST BAR

ROYAL PALMS VILLA AND INN

VICTORIA HOUSE

REEF

BELIZE BARRIER REEF

© MOON PUBLICATIONS, INC.

almost anything from a cooler of ice to a pair of sandals. Originally someone's home, the rooms are clean and unpretentious with private baths, ceiling fans, linoleum floors—and about the least expensive in town at about US$23 s, US$35 d. Ask for a corner room. Credit cards are okay. You can arrange a variety of tours for diving, fishing, caving, and other land tours. Bicycle and golf cart rentals are available.

The old classic **Hotel San Pedrano,** Barrier Reef Drive, Ambergris Caye, Belize, C.A., tel. (26) 2054, fax (26) 2093, is just a block from the ocean on the corner of Barrier Reef Drive. From the breezy upstairs veranda it's easy to eat a bite, read a book, or watch the streetlife below. It's a favorite of both European and American travelers, who offer nothing but favorable comments. It offers good value for your dollar. Each room has h/c water, private bath, ceiling fan, or a/c. Some have full kitchens. Rates with fan are US$25 s, US$30 d, US$43 q; with a/c US$35 s, US$40 d, US$58 q. Credit cards are okay. You can buy toiletries, soft drinks, dishwashing liquid, and suntan lotion in the store downstairs. The hotel can arrange a variety of excursions including diving, fishing, shelling, and beach picnics.

Right on the beach and around the corner from Hotel San Pedrano, **The Conch Shell Hotel,** San Pedro, Ambergris Caye, Belize, C.A., tel. (26) 2062, is inexpensive and has simple rooms with private baths, ceiling fans, linoleum floors, wood panel walls, and simple furnishings. Some have kitchenettes; ask for Room 5. Rates are about US$20 s, US$53 d. Credit cards are okay. Across the side street is a bar called **Cholo's,** where a lot of the fishing guides hang out after work, have a drink, and play pool. You may see this as adding to the local color of the area or as a detraction.

Moderate

If there's one thing in San Pedro's favor—besides its village charm, sandy streets, friendly people, and easy pace—it is that this town offers travelers a wide choice of lodging at reasonable prices.

In the center of town and across from the park, the **Barrier Reef Hotel,** Barrier Reef Drive, Ambergris Caye, Belize, C.A., tel. (26) 2075/ 2049, fax (26) 2719, has 11 rooms, a restaurant, sports bar with big-screen TV, beauty parlor (with Nexus products), and second-floor pool. It seems especially popular with the diving crowd. The pool is especially nice on a hot day and the restaurant is known for its seafood pizza. Rooms have h/c water, private baths, and ceiling fans or a/c. Rates are US$48 s, US$65 d, US$75 t; credit cards are okay. If you like being near the pool, ask for Room 9. The owners, John and Jeanne Bremekamp, live on the premises.

Allan and Helen Forman offer guests at the **Coral Beach Hotel and Dive Shop** a welcome

*Victoria House
Resort*

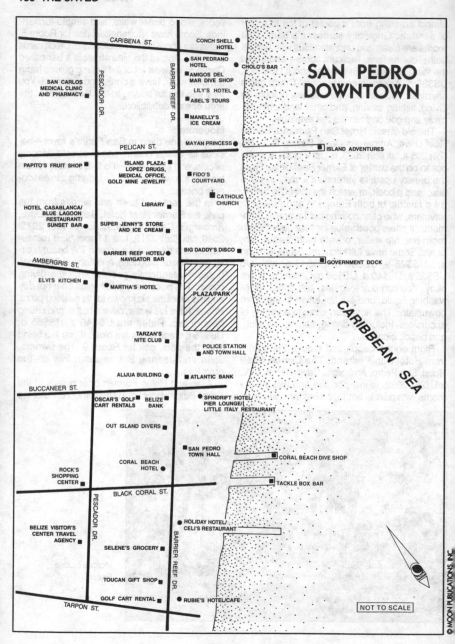

SAN PEDRO DOWNTOWN

CARIBENA ST.

CONCH SHELL HOTEL ●

● SAN PEDRANO HOTEL
■ CHOLO'S BAR

■ AMIGOS DEL MAR DIVE SHOP

● LILY'S HOTEL

■ ABEL'S TOURS

■ MANELLY'S ICE CREAM

SAN CARLOS MEDICAL CLINIC AND PHARMACY ■

PESCADOR DR.

BARRIER REEF DR.

PELICAN ST.

MAYAN PRINCESS ●

■ ISLAND ADVENTURES

PAPITO'S FRUIT SHOP ■

ISLAND PLAZA: LOPEZ DRUGS, MEDICAL OFFICE, GOLD MINE JEWELRY ■

■ FIDO'S COURTYARD

CATHOLIC CHURCH

LIBRARY ■

HOTEL CASABLANCA/ BLUE LAGOON RESTAURANT/ SUNSET BAR ●

SUPER JENNY'S STORE AND ICE CREAM ■

BARRIER REEF HOTEL/ NAVIGATOR BAR ●

BIG DADDY'S DISCO ■

AMBERGRIS ST.

ELVI'S KITCHEN ■

● MARTHA'S HOTEL

PLAZA/PARK

■ GOVERNMENT DOCK

CARIBBEAN SEA

TARZAN'S NITE CLUB ■

POLICE STATION AND TOWN HALL ■

ALIJUA BUILDING ●

■ ATLANTIC BANK

BUCCANEER ST.

OSCAR'S GOLF CART RENTALS ■   BELIZE BANK ■

● SPINDRIFT HOTEL/ PIER LOUNGE[/ LITTLE ITALY RESTAURANT

OUT ISLAND DIVERS ■

■ SAN PEDRO TOWN HALL

CORAL BEACH HOTEL ●

■ CORAL BEACH DIVE SHOP

ROCK'S SHOPPING CENTER ■

■ TACKLE BOX BAR

BLACK CORAL ST.

PESCADOR DR.

BARRIER REEF DR.

BELIZE VISITOR'S CENTER TRAVEL AGENCY ■

● HOLIDAY HOTEL/ CELI'S RESTAURANT

SELENE'S GROCERY ■

TOUCAN GIFT SHOP ■

GOLF CART RENTAL ■   ● RUBIE'S HOTEL/CAFE

TARPON ST.

NOT TO SCALE

© MOON PUBLICATIONS, INC.

piña colada and 19 clean rooms, each with private bathroom, h/c water, and a/c or fan. The building is across the road from the sea. Rates without meals are US$45 s, US$65 d, and with meals US$74 s, US$122 d. The Coral Beach offers several package prices as well. A diving tour, four days/three nights based on double occupancy, is US$350 per person; seven days/six nights is US$550 per person. A fishing tour, four days/three nights based on double occupancy, is US$400 per person. Dive and fishing packages include a boat, guide, equipment, room, meals, transportation to and from Belize International Airport, tackle, etc. All packages include tax. The hotel bar, **The Tackle Box**, is out at the end of the dock. For info contact Coral Beach Hotel, Box 16, San Pedro, Ambergris Caye, Belize, C.A., tel. (26) 2013/2001, or Coral Beach Travel, 172 N. Front St., Box 614, Belize City, Belize, C.A., tel. (2) 7036.

Owners Norman and Deon Gosney say they'd rather their cleverly decorated **Hotel Casablanca**, Pescador Drive, Ambergris Caye, Belize, C.A., tel. (26) 2327/2992, fax (26) 2992, was written up in design magazines than those on travel. And attention to design is certainly evident here, from the classic white and blue exterior to the attractive rooms, no two of which are exactly alike (ask about the Elvis Room). Eccentric little decorating touches have to make you smile: an unusual table top here, blue lights in a ceiling-fan fixture there. Rooms come with h/c water, large private baths, a/c, mirrors; rates are US$85 s/d. The restaurant, **Blue Lagoon**, is one of the best in town, serving an eclectic menu (where else will you find tasty coq au vin?). Norman, a savvy transplanted New Yorker, has turned the roof of the building into **The Sunset Bar** and the view of the rooftops, surrounding lagoons, and ocean is fantastic at the appointed hour.

On the north end of town near the San Pedro River, in a more remote location by the mangroves and the sea, are a couple of cabañas known as the **Hotel del Rio**, Ambergris Caye, Belize, C.A., tel./fax (26) 2286. Here, surrounded by sea grapes, palms, lilies, banana trees, and hibiscus you'll find a pleasant family atmosphere. Linda and Fido Badillo offer **Cabana Chica** and **Cabana Grande**, with thatched roofs and a pleasing mixture of rustic simplicity and modern convenience. The smaller unit has sides of palm saplings and a small veranda. Inside, you'll find a ceiling fan, coffee maker, fridge; it sleeps up to three for US$40. The Grande features wood paneling, ceiling fan, gray tile floor, kitchen with fridge and stainless steel sink, and can sleep up to five for US$60. Anglers, take note—husband, Fido, is a well-known fishing guide with his own 28-foot boat.

Just around the corner from the Del Rio is a little store/bar called **Bush Master Kool Spot,** where you can stock your fridge and buy toiletries and such. You don't have much of a beach here, but then most of San Pedro doesn't; there is a dock for Fido's boat and you can go off the end of it for a swim or walk to any likely spot nearby.

It's hard to miss **Laidy's Apartments,** Ambergris Caye, Belize, C.A., tel (26) 2682, just north of Rock's Inn about a hundred paces or so. The building is painted a bright blue and white. You'll find four simple, clean apartments with king-size beds, h/c water, private baths, and ceiling fans (two also have a/c). Rates are US$50 s/d with fan only, US$65 with a/c. No meals here but you are near enough to quickly walk to any of San Pedro's restaurants. You can, however, make arrangements for laundry, diving, fishing, and water taxis to Caye Caulker and Belize City.

The old standard of budget travelers, **Lily's Hotel,** San Pedro, Ambergris Caye, Belize, C.A., tel. (26) 2059, has moved up a notch with air conditioning. The simple hotel is run by the Felipe Paz family—friendly, long-time residents of San Pedro. Lily's has been known for years for offering excellent local food in plentiful family-style servings—let Felipe know in the morning if you plan to eat dinner that evening. In addition, Lily's offers 10 basic clean rooms with a/c, h/c water, and private bathrooms. Ask for one of the six rooms with an ocean view. Rates in winter are about US$60 s/d. Lily's accepts Visa/MC.

At the north end of Barrier Reef Drive you'll find the entrance to the compound, **Paradise Resort Hotel,** Box 888, Belize City, Belize, C.A., in the U.S. tel. (800) 451-8017, in Belize tel. (26) 2021, fax (26) 2232. This casual resort has a pleasing range of amenities and a good location on a sandy beach with its own dock and beachside bar, conveying a relaxed "barefoot" feeling. The hotel's **Palm Restaurant** has a good reputation for tasty food; try the chicken picata, sautéed lobster, or fish with lime or caper butter. You'll find a deli, gift and dive shops, and you can make all fishing arrangements on the premises. You'll have your choice of a room, a thatch cabaña, villa, or a minisuite with a/c. Room rates vary according to season, location, and type: Cabañas start at US$70 s, US$90 d; rooms start at US$50 s, US$70 d; villas are available starting at US$80 s, US$100 d. Those are minimum rates (they go up from there), and expect a US$10 surcharge for a/c; meal plans are available. Paradise Hotel charges five percent service charge.

At first glance the **Spindrift Hotel,** Barrier Reef Drive, Ambergris Caye, Belize, C.A., tel. (26) 2174, fax (26) 2251, reminds one of the great old Florida hotels with the soft, art deco corners and the center courtyard. Within its complex are a romantic little Italian restaurant, a lively bar, a small second-floor sundeck, 21 rooms, and three suites. It's one of the few hotels in the country with economy rooms and suites under one roof. All rooms have h/c water, private baths, and ceiling fans. Suites have a/c and so do some of the more expensive rooms. Rates begin at US$47.50 s/d and go to US$82.50 s/d. Suites go for US$110-165 s/d. For economy rooms, ask for a patio room with the inner balcony. In the higher-priced brackets check out Rooms 1, 2, or 20, if available. Up to

two children under 12 are free with adults. Credit cards are okay.

For More Money

More and more "resort" types are taking hold on the island. Prices are relatively high, but considering the isolated location, they offer pretty good value for those looking for a little more luxury compared with the prices of many other Caribbean resorts.

In a bright modern building on the corner of Barrier Reef Drive and Buccaneer Street are a travel agency, arts and crafts store, juice bar, post office, and **Alijua Hotel Suites,** Barrier Reef Drive, Ambergris Caye, Belize, C.A., tel. (26) 2113/2791, fax (26) 2362. It's worth checking out if you're in the mood for a suite. The seven rooms are priced at US$88 s, US$104 d, US$125 t, US$140 q. The management will allow more than four guests per room for a fee of US$10 per person additional.

This delightful full-service resort, **Ramon's Village,** in the U.S., P.O. Drawer 4407, Laurel, Mississippi 39441, tel. (800) 624-4215, (601) 649-1990, fax (601) 425-2411; in Belize tel. (26) 2071, has the best beach (all 500 feet of it) on the island. Just south of San Pedro, its attractive surroundings, great restaurant and bar, a myriad of activities, and a long pier with a palapa at the end make it a favorite among divers and nondivers alike. The recreational pier features a dive, photo, and video shop; boats, guides, and

Green Parrot Resort

PHIL LANIER

all diving equipment are available for reef trips. The saltwater pool is steps away from the cabañas. Airport pickup is just one of the courtesies provided guests.

If you stayed at Ramon's years back you'll notice it has expanded and added a lot more cabañas so the space on the beach is more crowded. Lovers of thatched-hut cabañas will fall in love with the castaways look of the place. Sixty well-appointed palm-thatched beachfront cabañas are cooled by fans, five have a/c. Simple and charming, each has private bathroom, hot water, and daily maid service, with laundry service and child care on request. Room rates are US$125 s/d, US$135 t, US$145 q, higher during some peak holidays; suites are US$290/ night and sleep up to four (ask for Suites 27, 28, 31, 32—they're right on the beach). Credit cards are okay. Meal packages are available. Dinner is about US$20. Recreational rentals include sailboards, aqua cycles, speed boats, bicycles, and motor scooters. Scuba instruction is available, too.

Ah, the suite life! Kenneth Krohn has created a wonderful getaway, **Belizean Reef Suites,** San Pedro, Ambergris Caye, Belize, C.A., tel./fax (26) 2582, where you can have gleaming white suites with a/c and many of the amenities you'd expect in fancier Caribbean locations. Everything looks spotless, the large one or three bedrooms, the big bathrooms, and the spacious kitchens and living rooms. The shady verandas are especially pleasant on a hot sunny day with beautiful views of the ocean. Guests can use the facilities at Ramon's with the understanding that a little patronage of bar, etc., would be appreciated. Fair enough; Ramon's has the nicest slice of sand on the island. Rates are US$125 d, US$250 up to six; US$10 per person additional. Laundry service, bikes, water toys, tours on land or sea, and transportation can all be arranged.

Another charming suite hotel, **Mayan Princess,** Box 1, San Pedro, Ambergris Caye, Belize, C.A., in the U.S. tel. (800) 345-9786, in Belize tel. (26) 2778, fax (26) 2784, sits near the center of town. All 23 units face the ocean and have wicker furniture, a bed, a small kitchen with a microwave oven and eating counter, a/c, a hide-a-bed, and a tropical ambience. Spacious verandas overlook the sea and provide

shady views of the beach and ocean. Nonsmoking and luxury honeymoon suites are also available. Ask for the corner suite Room 17. Rates are about US$115 s, US$125 d. Credit cards are okay.

Take a look at **Paradise Villas Condominiums,** Ambergris Caye, Belize, C.A., in the U.S., tel. (800) 626-3483, tel. (510) 792-2639, fax (510) 791-5602, in Belize, tel. (26) 3077, fax (26) 2831 or e-mail Susan Garcia at susangg @aimnet.com. These deluxe resort suites next door to the Paradise Hotel have all the amenities of a hotel plus a fully equipped kitchen and a spacious living room. The one-bedroom units feature h/c water, private baths, a/c, full kitchen, and daily maid service. Each unit accommodates up to four adults (two on a sofa sleeper). High-season rates are US$150/ day. As with all resorts on the island, prices fall during the off-season.

Inside an elegant three-story building of tropical colonial design, on the corner of Sandpiper Street and the ocean, are the 14 suites of **Rock's Inn,** Ambergris Caye, Belize, C.A., tel. (26) 2326, fax (26) 2358. All suites have fully decorated bedrooms, living rooms, and kitchens with h/c water, private baths, ceiling fans, and a/c, and can accommodate up to six adults. Rates are US$95-115 s, US$105-125 d, US$115-135 t; children under 12, free with parents. Credit cards are okay. Shady verandas provide a pleasant perch from which to take in the ocean and beach scene. Hammocks and easy chairs under the palms make for lazy afternoons. For those not so inclined to siestas, fishing, diving or seaplane trips, Jet Skis, and Windsurfers can be arranged. The inn picks up guests at the airport and offers a free bottle of champagne for honeymooners. Immediately in front is the dock for **Hustler Tours** and the **Bamboo Bar.** Water taxis to Journey's End dock here, too.

From the palm-studded beach outside, the weathered clapboard exterior of **Seven Seas Hotel,** Ambergris Caye, Belize, C.A., tel. (26) 2382, fax (26) 2472, conjures visions of an aging tropical inn. Once inside, however, the illusion evaporates with gracious suites that include two bedrooms, h/c water, private baths, kitchenettes, ceiling fans (one room has a/c, but you probably won't need it, add US$15), Belizean furniture, and tile floors. Credit cards are okay. Rates are US$85 s, US$95 d, US$105 t, US$115 q. Maid service even takes care of dishes. Views from the upper floor are especially nice. Ask for Rooms 9 and 12, if available. **Note: Children under 12 are not allowed.** The hotel can arrange tours and trips of all kinds.

The pleasant **San Pedro Holiday Hotel,** Box 1140, Belize City, Belize, C.A., in San Pedro tel. (26) 2014, in the U.S. (800) 633-4734, just keeps getting better. It offers a charming ambience—the pink and white wooden structure faces the sea with wide verandas open to the cooling trade winds of the tropics. On the waterfront, a fenced-in piece of the Caribbean is the Holiday's "open saltwater pool." Other services include a full-service dive shop, **Tortuga Dive Center,** and the glass-bottom boat, *Reef Seeker.* On the premises are a small but pleasant lobby bar known for its ceviche and bartender (Chico), an economical deli, and popular **Celi's Restaurant.** Celi's serves delicious food, and dinner is by reservation only. Try the fish dishes.

Rooms come with h/c water, private baths, and fans or a/c. Some have refrigerators. Rates with fans are US$74 s/d, US$94 t; with a/c US$84-94 s/d, US$104-114 t. The Holiday Hotel also has larger apartments for families and groups. Apartments include a/c in the bedroom, tabletop stove, and fridge. Sofa sleepers allow them to sleep up to four. Rates are US$120 s/d, US$140 t, US$160 q. Credit cards are okay. Write or call for more information and reservations.

At the southern end of San Pedro—on the beach amidst pleasant palmy surroundings sits the **SunBreeze Hotel,** San Pedro, Ambergris Caye, Belize, C.A., tel. (26) 2191, fax (26) 2346. They don't come more convenient for arriving air passengers than this; it's across the street from San Pedro's small air strip. Because of the U-shape of the building, with the open end toward the ocean, and the small size of the planes, the proximity to revving aircraft engines is not the problem you might expect. Also on the site are a good bar and restaurant, a gift shop, beauty salon, and dive shop. Barrier Reef Drive starts next door, so it's an easy walk to almost any point in town. Rooms come with a/c, h/c water, private baths, ceiling fans, TVs, telephones, and balconies to enjoy the sea view. Rates are US$90-125 s, US$100-135 d, US$110-145 t. Credit cards are okay.

South of San Pedro

San Pedro is so comfortable and centrally located there's often no urge to look farther afield. However, some great accommodations lie within two miles of town and are included here in order of their proximity.

How about a little bed and breakfast near the beach and next to the yacht club? **Changes In Latitude B&B,** San Pedro, Ambergris Caye, Belize, C.A., tel./fax (26) 2986, has strong appeal for divers looking to spend their days in the water and then have comfortable rooms and beds for the evening. It's a quiet little place run by Canadian transplants Lori Reed and Susan Vesala. Their cleverly painted sign says it all with an igloo perched on a tropic isle. In fact, cleverness has everything to do with how they run their B&B and the way they've furnished the six rooms. They live upstairs while catering to the needs of guests in the six downstairs rooms. At one end of the lower level is a common room that serves as a kitchen/eating area and library. Inside the small but comfortable rooms you'll find fans or a/c, h/c water, private baths, good mattresses, phones, lots of wood furnishings, and Maya design bedspreads. They do great breakfasts, especially Susan's Apple Pancakes with coffee and fresh fruit. Rates with fans are US$65 s/d, with a/c US$75 s/d. Credit cards are okay. After a pickup at the airport, Lori and Susan provide their guests a packet that contains tips on the best places for food, fun, and diving. They also point out that **Jade Garden** Chinese restaurant is just down the road a hundred steps or so. Dive boats pick you up at the end of the pier. The pool and workout facilities at the Belize Yacht Club are available next door for US$5/day.

Even from the air it's easy to spot the **Belize Yacht Club,** Ambergris Caye, Belize, C.A., tel. in the U.S. (800) 396-1153, in Belize (26) 2777, fax (26) 2768. Its red tile roofs and white walls surround a swatch of green and turquoise. About a 10-minute walk south of town, the complex boasts a friendly staff, pier/marina, dive shop, workout room, gift shop, pool, manicured lawns, 44 units, and on-site security.

These are among the plushest suites on the island and they are priced accordingly. All units come with h/c water, private baths, a/c, full kitchens, huge closets, and large verandas. Rates for one-bedroom suites are US$150 s/d, US$165 t. Two-bedroom suites go for US$300 d, US$315 t, US$330 q. Children under 12 are free with parent. Credit cards accepted.

The workout room includes cycles, free weights, exercise machines, bench press, and showers. Five days a week there is circuit training using steps and weights. Pool and step aerobics are also available several times weekly.

The **Hideaway Sports Lodge,** Box 43, Ambergris Caye, Belize, C.A., tel. (26) 2141, fax (26) 2269, is another spot that's a short distance from the beach and a favorite of divers and active vacationers. The Hideaway has 15 rooms at reasonable rates, a bar/restaurant, and a nicely tended pool. It also has a close relationship with **Belize Dive Center** at the pier of the Belize Yacht Club across the road. Once guests return from their daily adventures they can lounge by the pool or have a drink at **Hernado's Restaurant and Bar,** where they'll find tables, a couch, game area, and dart board. Come lunch- or dinner-time, guests can opt for full vegetarian fare if they please. A separate dining area serves large groups. Breakfast is free

Rooms vary in size and number of beds, accommodating from two to four people. Some rooms can be joined to house up to six. Rooms come with h/c water, private baths, and fans or a/c. Rates range US$40-90 per night per room, some of which hold six people comfortably. More than the established number of people per room costs US$15 per person additional. Credit cards accepted.

Past the yacht club you'll pass some private property and then about half a mile from town you come upon the **Playador,** Ambergris Caye, Belize, C.A., tel. (26) 2870, fax (26) 2871, and **Mickey's Place Bar/Restaurant.** The welcome beachside bar serves drinks and coolers while the restaurant upstairs offers a good view and tasty, reasonably priced food; meal packages are available. This is also the dock for the *Dolphin,* which runs sunset and dinner cruises. During the day it does snorkel trips.

All accommodations have an ocean view. Rooms in the main building feature h/c water,

private baths, a/c, and large verandas for US$105 s/d. Ten thatched-roof cabañas have h/c water, private baths, fans, and small verandas for US$95 s/d. One cabaña has a/c for US$125 s/d. The cost for additional people is US$10. Children under 12 with adult are free.

A little farther down the beach you'll find good value in **Corona del Mar,** Box 37, Ambergris Caye, Belize, C.A., tel. (26) 62055, fax (26) 62461, an all-suites hotel known to many locals as **Woody's** after **Woody's Wharf.** Longtime residents Woody and Helen Canaday own the four one-bedroom suites, each with h/c water, private bath, a/c, full kitchen, and veranda. The wooden doors with the carved Maya motif are a nice touch. Rates are US$110 s/d, US$10 per person additional. The hotel accepts Visa/MC. Laundry service, diving, fishing, glass-bottom boat tours, and windsurfing can be arranged. Bikes are US$10/day.

Will and Susan Lala have one of the finest suites-type accommodations on the island in **Caribbean Villas,** Box 71, Ambergris Caye, Belize, C.A., in the U.S. tel. (800) 345-9786 or (913) 468-3608, in Belize tel. (26) 2715, fax (26) 2885. In a lovely two-story building with white-washed walls and red tile roof, it's close enough to town to bike in and out at your leisure (bikes are compliments of the hotel). Relax in a hot tub, go horseback riding, fishing, diving, snorkeling, or just take in the view. Climb up to the "people perch" and watch the birds at treetop height, or at night, gaze at the stars.

Spacious, attractively furnished lodgings come in all sizes from a double room to a deluxe suite with a loft. Rooms have h/c water, private baths, ceiling fans and cost US$85-95. More-luxurious suites include a/c, full kitchens, and more living and sleeping area. They range in price US$150-245 and can accommodate up to six people. Double couples will prefer Unit 4 with its wrap-around loft, large balcony, and dual bathrooms.

Just a bit farther down the beach is **Mata Rocks Resort,** Box 47, Ambergris Caye, Belize, C.A., tel. (26) 2336, fax (26) 2349, a hangout for locals and travelers alike. Why so popular so far from town? Partially because of the friendly beach bar atmosphere of the **Squirrel's Nest Bar,** the palm-covered beach, and the "Famous Bar-b-cue" for Sunday lunch. When they say you get a healthy portion of ribs, fish, and chicken, they're not exaggerating. Only the heartiest of appetites can eat it all.

Rooms are comfortable wood-sided suites with stucco exteriors and tile roofs. Inside, they have h/c water, private baths, ceiling fans, a/c, kitchens, and maid service. The resort can arrange a full range of island activities. It accepts Visa/MC.

The **Royal Palm Inn,** Box 18, Ambergris Caye, Belize, C.A., tel. (26) 2148, fax (26) 2329, boasts a beautiful pool, tennis court, workout room, dive shop, and a white sandy beach shaded by swaying palms and edged by the clear blue Caribbean—perfect for snorkeling, scuba diving, fishing, with the reef just off shore. The condo resort also happens to be strategically located next door to the Squirrel's Nest at Mata Rocks for drinks and lunch, and it's within walking distance of Victoria House Resort for fancier dining. The pool is well-maintained with a small waterfall, and **Reef Divers Dive Shop** is one of the best operations on Ambergris. The villas are comfortable, large one-bedroom apartments with a/c, h/c water, private baths, and fully equipped kitchens. The staff is conscientious and cheerful.

The handsome **Victoria House,** with lush tropical gardens two miles south of town, offers delightful (though pricey) oceanfront casitas or deluxe rooms. The resort includes stucco and thatch casitas with tile floors; rooms have ocean views, private bathrooms, and ceiling fans or a/c. Excellent meals are included, and diving and fishing equipment is available; a bar and a gift shop are on the premises. Rates for casitas are US$170 d, for rooms US$110 s, US$130 d. Rates for rooms without meals are available. Packages are the best deals if you're content to sit tight on the premises for all meals; seven-night packages for rooms are US$989 per person double occupancy, for casitas US$1079 per person, including roundtrip airfare from Houston, New Orleans, or Miami to Belize, roundtrip airfare from Belize to San Pedro, transfer to hotel, three meals a day, four days of diving or four half days of fishing, plus one night dive, boat, guide, and equipment. For more information and reservations, write or call Box 20785, Houston, Texas 77225, tel. in Texas (713) 662-8000, outside Texas (800) 247-5159, fax (713) 661-4025; in Belize, tel. (26) 2067.

North of San Pedro

True to its name, **El Pescador Lodge,** Box 793, Belize City, Belize, C.A., tel. (800) 245-1950, in Belize tel. (26) 2398, three miles north of San Pedro, is focused on fishing, though some come just to get away from it all. Anglers will find one of the best selections of quality gear in the country: line, lures, rods and reels. Boats and guides specialize in tarpon fishing and cast the lagoons for ladyfish or snook, much of which is catch-and-release. Others take guests outside the reef for sailfish or wahoo. Or they troll the reef for kingfish and barracuda and jig the bottoms with bait for snapper and grouper—something for every fisherman. Fishing package rates include transfers from Belize City, all meals, boat and guide; guide tips, bar tab, and gear are extra. Packages are structured for couples of avid anglers and for those where only one likes to wet a hook. Packages begin at US$1450 per person.

The resort has 10 rooms and one suite, all with private baths in a large colonial building.

Ambergris coast

A long veranda faces the sea within sight of the reef just 200 yards offshore. For snorkelers, beach bums, and less-active types, the lodge offers less-expensive packages at about US$925 per person. Rooms only, on a daily basis, are also available at US$120 s, US$196 d.

What would it be like to be a castaway on a luxurious tropical paradise, where the palms really sway, and the staff is to love? Guests at **Captain Morgan's Retreat** will find out with 21 clean, attractive beachfront casitas with a freshwater pool and excellent food. Fishing, diving, snorkeling, and sailing trips are available. As at most of the resorts, its prices per cabaña rise and fall with the season. High season rates—1 Nov.-30 April—are US$130 s, US$170 d, US$190 t, a little more during holidays, considerably less in summer. A meal plan is available for US$35 per day (three meals) and US$25 (two meals). Ask about a couple of great package plans (including airfare from the U.S.). Captain Morgan's is a couple miles north of San Pedro and it's almost impossible to walk to. Boat transport is available; call in the U.S. (800) 447-2931, in Belize (26) 2567, fax (26) 2616.

Four miles north of San Pedro on a broad beachfront with seawall, **Journey's End Caribbean Club**, Box 13, Ambergris Caye, Belize, C.A., in the U.S. tel. (800) 541-6796/447-0474, in Belize tel. (26) 2173, fax (26) 2028, offers a wide range of activities and accommodations, three bars, and a good restaurant. This is the resort to visit for isolation and an all-in-one kind of vacation. Here, you will find a swimming pool with waterfall, volleyball, a fine dive shop (operated by Reef Divers) snorkeling trips, mountain bikes, tennis, sailboats, Hobie cats, Windsurfers, canoes, paddle boats, and a well-equipped deep-sea fishing boat, *Sea Boots.* While additional charges are associated with some of these activities, they are all conveniently available. Less-active types have ample opportunity for beachcombing, sun worshipping, or reading a book by the pool.

Transportation back and forth between the resort and San Pedro is by water taxi. It takes about 10 minutes one way and the resort has a schedule of three trips daily with two additional trips Wednesday and Saturday. Otherwise, you can arrange to pay for trips on your own schedule.

Guests have a choice of rooms overlooking the back lagoon (great sunsets), pool cabañas toward the center, or thatched cabañas off to one side. The rooms by the lagoons offer the most isolation and views of wildlife. The poolside cabañas are the most charming and convenient to the sundeck and poolside bar/grill. The thatch cabañas are nearer the restaurant and beachside activities. Weekly packages cost about US$1700 and up.

The small, intimate **Green Parrot Resort,** Box 36, San Pedro, Ambergris Caye, Belize, C.A., tel. (26) 2175, fax (26) 2270, six miles north of San Pedro but just a quarter mile from famous Mexico Rocks, offers spectacular snorkeling. The Green Parrot has four double cabañas and two triple cabañas set on the beach, and a dining room and bar are available for guests and locals. Full American Plan (FAP, three meals) and Modified American Plan (MAP, two meals) are available. All cabañas have ceiling fans and hot showers. Snorkeling and fishing are provided by the resort at a minimum fee. Diving, deep-sea fishing, and numerous tours are also available. Rates are MAP US$90 s, US$65 d per person; FAP US$95 s, US$70 d per person. Write or call for more information.

FOOD

Those who like to eat are in for trouble in San Pedro and not for lack of good food. Instead, there are almost too many tempting chances to sample the culinary arts. This is a change from years past. At one time, the only place to have a good meal was at your hotel. Most of the hotels still serve good food—in fact some are outstanding—but today the visitor also has a choice of other cafes springing up around town. The selection grows each year.

Inexpensive
Rubie's has good pastries and coffee in the morning. Several good spots to try for sandwiches and quick fare are **Celi's Deli** at the Holiday Hotel, **Elvi's Kitchen,** and **H & L Burger,** a block down Buccaneer from the Alijua Hotel (try the jerk burger). **The Hut** is another little spot that serves good food.

At **Tarzan's Nite Club** the conch fritters and ceviche are worth a try; and **Ambergris Delight,** just down from the Hotel Casablanca, does a decent job on seafood for a small price.

For inexpensive Mexican food, **Luigi's** will work. Better yet, **Tropical Takeout,** across the street from the airport and next to the Sun-Breeze, has great homemade salsa *(muy picante!),* the better to douse tasty tacos of chicken, pork, or beef. A good value, a plate of them will put you back about US$2.50. And they're good! So are the *boletos,* Tropical Takeouts version of a sandwich, but actually a taco by still-another name. And you can get eggs and trimmings any time of day. No wonder the cabbies hang out here.

An attraction of Fido's Courtyard on Barrier Reef Drive, the **Pizza Place** makes good on the namesake dish "by-the-slice," or a deluxe large combination pizza costs about US$20. It's enough to feed you and your whole diving crowd (well, *almost*). It also serves deli-style sandwiches, seafood, and local cuisine. Eat it there or carry it away.

When Mike Perez of **Sandals Reggae Bar,** north end of Barrier Reef Drive by the entrance to Paradise Resort, fires up his barbecue at lunchtime or dinner, it takes more willpower than ours to resist the aroma of fish, chicken, and pork chops sizzling over the flames. The addition of coconut husks to the coals yields especially tasty results. His own spicy sauce accompanies the meal with all the fixings for US$4-6. It's said he makes a good ceviche as well. The bar accepts Visa/MC.

Nothing could be better on a hot day than a tall drink of fresh juice at **Vitamins,** in the back of the Alijua Building on the corner of Barrier Reef Drive and Buccaneer Street. You have your choice of assorted tropical fruit or vegetable juices. Shakes and smoothies, ice cream, and sandwiches also are available.

Moderate
La Parilla in Fido's Courtyard is a good choice for breakfast or lunch with American and Mexican selections. Salads are good here, too. Next door, **Big Daddy's** has great barbecue, especially the lobster. At **Duke's Place,** try the T-bone in lemon garlic butter. Or better yet, the mixed kabob (fish, chicken, shrimp, and steak)

is a good bet. The sautéed conch steak wins good reviews. Creole shrimp swimming in garlic and wine is tasty, too.

A relative newcomer, **Le Classique,** next to Rock's Shopping Center on Pescador Drive, is a cool refuge from the afternoon heat and the place to get Steak Classique, a T-bone covered in onion gravy; specialties are Caribbean food. **Mata Rocks Resort** serves a Sunday barbecue of fish, ribs, and chicken that satisfies the heartiest appetites.

More Upscale
How about chicken satay, pasta fagioli, and coq au vin on the same menu? You'll find these and more tasty dishes at **Blue Lagoon,** the restaurant at the Casablanca Hotel. The coq au vin, tender pieces of chicken cooked in red wine with mushrooms, onions, and bacon, is a very decent rendition and a value at US$9.

Customers enjoy a thatched-roof, fan-cooled tropical cafe at **Elvi's Kitchen,** Pescador Drive and Ambergris Street. The seafood specials are especially good (quality and quantity) even though they may cost a bit more. Burgers are good, too.

Would an icy piña colada and some of the best conch ceviche on the island put you in the proper mood? **Celi's Restaurant** at Holiday Hotel, Barrier Reef Drive between Black Coral and Tarpon streets, delivers the goods. Barbecue lovers: the Wednesday night barbecue is not to be missed.

The **Jade Garden,** a short walk south of Ramon's Village, serves fairly good Chinese food in very pleasant surroundings. Try the broiled fish or the pepper steak. The service is great.

Located in the Spindrift Hotel, **Little Italy,** corner of Barrier Reef Drive and Buccaneer Street, is an intimate place for couples, especially on the little veranda. The lobster alfredo is terrific. Chicken and pork dishes in wine sauces are good. The tomato sauces are just okay but the homemade icebox key lime pie is to die for.

The restaurant at **Ramon's Village** is a dining spot overlooking the beach. The chef whips up great seafood, Asian meals, and surprisingly good Cajun dishes. It's said that chef Rommie Kie, a transplant from Hong Kong, learned the Cajun touch from Paul

*Journey's End
Caribbean Club
on Ambergris Caye*

Prudomme of Louisiana fame. The fresh seafood is great, along with Kie's Hong Kong specialties.

At **Victoria House**, if you happen to hit the right night, the chef here can turn out sumptuous meals. Other times we hear it just doesn't measure up. Fresh seafood and Asian, Italian, Mexican, American, and typical Belizean fare are on the menu.

ENTERTAINMENT

If you collect statistics of this sort, in the small town of San Pedro you can count 22 bars. We'd love to hear from readers with a rating list. Here's ours.

At the north end of town, **Bamboo Bar** is perched on the end of the pier by Rock's Inn. It's a great place to shoot pool and watch music videos while downing a fresh fruit drink or piña colada. It's also the favorite hangout for both local guides and visitors.

Barefoot Bar & Grill at the SunBreeze Hotel has a great location on a breezy stretch of palm-dotted beachfront. A little music is always playing and tables are at several levels so you can pick your view. At the south end of town past the end of Barrier Reef Drive and across from the airport, it might be a good spot to drown your sorrows before heading back to the real world.

Something is always going on at **Big Daddy's Disco,** on the edge of the park and the ocean at Ambergris Street, especially Thurs-

day (Macho Night) and Friday (Ladies' Night) when it offers special drink promotions. Saturday night the place rocks to live music. Big Daddy's sells good barbecue, too.

The **Holiday Hotel** is another popular local hangout on long hot afternoons, especially if Chico is running the bar. He makes some of the best piña coladas in town and the conch ceviche is right up there.

For some really funky entertainment, drop into the **Pier Lounge** (in the Spindrift Hotel at Buccaneer Street and Barrier Reef Drive), a favorite haunt of divemasters and other locals. On Monday evenings the hotly contested crab races take place. And on Wednesday evenings is the observance of the "World Famous" **Chicken Drop.**

Located in Fido's courtyard, **Purple Parrot Bar,** at Barrier Reef Drive between Ambergris and Pelican streets, is one of the livelier spots in town. Several nights a week it offers live entertainment and with two restaurants, an art gallery, and a camera shop in the courtyard, there are always lots of new faces around.

With a sand floor and lots of funky sandals hanging from the ceiling, **Sandals Reggae Bar,** north end of Barrier Reef Drive by the entrance to Paradise Resort, is a great spot to shoot pool, shoot the bull, and listen to one of the best collections of reggae music on the island. It has lots of friendly locals to get to know. Owner Mike Perez makes a tasty Coco Loco. He also sells his homemade Bitters, an aged herbal and bark concoction that's steeped in high octane rum and is said to be good for upsets of almost any kind. A couple of these and you'll forget what it was that was ailing you.

Sunset Bar, atop the Hotel Casablanca, between Ambergris and Pelican streets, is the place to be for the perfect end of the day. A rum punch puts a rosy glow on things before the sun has even begun to disappear. As the sun calls it a day, the colors keep changing and getting prettier by the moment. Often the best visual fireworks, though, happen **after** the sun has set for 15-30 minutes. Things begin to get dark and then suddenly the sky glows the most gorgeous pink and orange. Budding astronomers as well as meteor lovers will have a good time up here, too. It's a great place to pop the question. The bar takes cash only.

The caged sea creatures in the ocean corral of the dockside **Tackle Box Bar,** end of Black Coral Street, at the end of the pier, may strike you as interesting or tacky at best. That aside, this waterfront establishment is a daytime favorite of locals and travelers who have some time and a thirst. You never know whom you'll run into—a boat captain, a government minister, or an eye surgeon from the States.

Tarzan's Nite Club, Barrier Reef Drive and Ambergris Street, across from the park, is another jumping joint on Thursday through Saturday nights. And with tasty and inexpensive edibles next door at **Tarzan's Huts,** you have the option of eating before or between dance sessions.

SHOPPING

Arts and Crafts

Gift shops abound in San Pedro, especially on Barrier Reef and Pescador drives. If you want postcards, shells, colorful swim and beach apparel, towels, hats, T-shirts, or any of the other usual knickknacks, they're easy to come by, either in the hotels or independent stores. Some are more than just souvenir shops and have displays of fascinating crafts—Belize has several artists who create world-class art with excellent portrayals of life and nature in Belize on canvas and at least one artist who works in clay. Browse them all.

In Fido's Courtyard is the ambitious little **Belizean Arts,** tel. (26) 2638, fax (26) 63347. Owned by Belizean artist Walter Castillo, it carries a nice selection of his originals in oils and acrylics as well as numbered prints and some craft items. You can see Castillo's work around the country and it is beginning to draw a larger audience outside of Belize with exhibitions in England, Japan, and the United States. Originally an immigrant from Nicaragua, Castillo has lived in Belize, primarily the Punta Gorda area, since the '60s and is now a Belizean citizen. Today, much of his work portrays in vivid color and energetic forms the simplicity and joys of coastal Belizean life.

Artist John Westerhold has made himself right at home near Rubie's in **Iguana Jack's,** Ambergris Caye, Belize, C.A., tel. (26) 2767. Here, he has a shop and kiln where he creates and sells his paintings (and those of others), along with his ceramic sculptures, masks, and signature pots with the whimsical iguanas. Pass by on the beach and watch John at work through the back of his shop while pots dry on the little veranda before glazing. An amiable type, John enjoys talking to visitors. Stop by for a look and a brief word at the south end of Barrier Reef Drive.

The spacious **Best of Belize** on Pescador Drive at the south end of town has a wonderful selection of Belizean wood furniture (tables, clam chairs, and calypso chairs), cutting boards, other wood items, and ceramics.

Just around the corner from Best of Belize, on Tarpon Street, is the little **Arts and Crafts of Central America,** tel. (26) 2623, with a wide array of items both Belizean and Guatemalan. The prices may not be the absolute cheapest but the quality is high. The shop carries cloth rubbings of Maya wall carvings, hammocks, leather bags, ceramic flutes, masks, vases, and textiles. Credit cards accepted.

In the Alijua Building, at the corner of Barrier Reef and Buccaneer streets, you'll find that the **National Handicraft Centre** has a small but noteworthy collection of Belizean crafts, including wooden bowls, slate carvings, postcards, and ceramics.

Shop 1001 across the street from Holiday Hotel has an especially large selection of T-shirts among other gifts.

Groceries, Sundries, and Other Basics

You can buy groceries and basic supplies at a number of stores. **Rocks Shopping Center** on the south side of town, at the corner of Pescador Drive and Buccaneer Street, has cereal, bread, meat, vegetables, cleaning solutions, wines, and just about anything else you'd expect to find in a grocery store in the States.

Patty's Fresh Fruit & Vegetables, tel. (26) 2388, has a wonderful array of whatever's in season: star fruit, papayas, pineapples, grapefruit, watermelon, grapes, limes, bananas, squash, chayote, okra, lettuce, ginger, bell peppers, and potatoes. Patty's, just south of Elvi's Kitchen, delivers free to condos and docks. More centrally located, **Martha's Store** at the corner of Pescador Drive and Ambergris Street sells everything from food items to clothing, shoes, pots and pans, even ice—and it delivers. The **San Pedrano Hotel** has a small convenience store that carries a lot of basics.

On the south side of town, **Super Jenny's** on Barrier Reef Drive carries dry goods to frozen food, bottled beverages (alcoholic and not), medicines, and cleaning compounds. Within the same building check out **World Fantasy,** an ice-cream parlor and tiny movie theater in one.

Those on the north end of town also will find **Bush Master Kool Spot,** near Hotel del Rio. It carries a limited but useful selection of canned goods, cereal, eggs, bread, meats, garlic, dried beans, paper products, and cleaning supplies. Remember: This is an island and everything must cross the sea, so the choice is limited and pricey. But you should find just about everything you need on the shelves, along with Belikin beer and Belizean rum.

SERVICES AND INFORMATION

The **Atlantic Bank** is across the street from the **Spindrift Hotel.** The **Belize Bank** is across the street and south of Buccaneer Street. The **Post Office** is in the **Alijua Building** on the corner of Barrier Reef Drive and Buccaneer Street, open Mon.-Fri., 8 a.m.-5 p.m. It's always fun to look at Belize's beautiful, artistic, and often very large postage stamps; they make great gifts for the folks back home and are perfect for framing or for the traditional stamp collector.

Visitors will find answers to all of their travel questions at several local **travel agencies** in San Pedro; a few hotels have their own agencies. Three independents (all on Barrier Reef Drive) are **Amigo Travel** in the Alijua Building, tel. (26) 2180; **Travel & Tour Belize,** the oldest in San Pedro, tel. (26) 2137; and **Universal Travel,** tel. (26) 2562. They can handle all of your travel needs, whether airline tickets or a tour into the countryside of Belize.

Have a **real estate** question? Many people fall in love with the easygoing, water-oriented lifestyle of Ambergris Caye. For all those who just can't tear themselves away, condos and property are for sale on Ambergris Caye and elsewhere in the country. The **Belize Yacht Club, Belizean Reef Suites, Mayan Princess,** and **Royal Palm Inn** are just a few examples of the condominiums around San Pedro. More are on the way. For more information, contact John Edwards of **Southwind Properties,** Box 1, San Pedro, Ambergris Caye, Belize, C.A., tel. (26) 2005/2060, fax (26) 2331.

Camera enthusiasts who want to have their film processed or need film should look in Fido's Courtyard for **Joe Miller Photography,** which will process normal and underwater slide film (E-6 film). The shop also rents underwater cameras and videos. **Belicolor Quality Photo Finishing,** at the corner of Pescador Drive and Buccaneer Street, offers one-hour processing and more costly commercial-quality work.

Medical Services are available at **San Carlos Medical Clinic,** Pescador Drive, tel. (26) 2918. You'll find prescription and over-the-counter drugs, ear medication, remedies for stomach distress, antihistamines, and salves; and Dr. Giovani Solorzano is in. **San Pedro Massage Clinic,** tel. (26) 3428/3301, offers relaxing massages by Rosario Uejbe, a licensed masseuse who specializes in Swedish massage and facials. She takes appointments at the office or she will come to your hotel; rates are about US$15/half-hour, US$30/hour.

GETTING AROUND

Even on an island this small the occasional need for a **taxi** arises. Some hotels offer a steady stream of them. Otherwise, you can have one called or take matters into your own hands and call **Chi's Friendly Taxi Service,** tel. (26) 2635/2850, or **Tun's Taxis,** tel. (26) 2038.

The most frequently seen modes of transport are **golf carts and mopeds.** Anyone can get in on that action at **Ramon's Wheel Rentals,** at the south end of town near Ramon's Hotel. Very few cars exist on the island and it really is fun to explore San Pedro and the rest of the island with one of the ever-present golf carts. Ramon's rents two-wheel or four-wheel golf carts by the hour, half-day, day, or week. Prices start at US$10/hour, US$25/half day, US$60/ day, US$225/week.

Polo's Golf Cart Rental, (26) 62080, is another golf cart operation at the opposite end of town by Paradise Resort, and **Oscar's Rental Center,** tel. (26) 2008, rents golf carts and mopeds, as well. And, yes, San Pedro *does* have a **gas station** a short distance south of town.

GETTING THERE

By Air

A 2,600-foot-long runway accommodates both private and commercial small planes on Ambergris, and from the strip it's just a few minutes' walk to downtown San Pedro (although there's been talk of moving this strip to a 550-acre spot south of town for years). Three airlines (Island Air, Maya Airways, and Tropic Air)

run regular and frequent flights to San Pedro and Caye Caulker. From Belize City it's 15 minutes to the caye; flights to Ambergris are available from other towns in Belize as well. For schedules and prices contact U.S. travel agents, or **Island Air,** San Pedro, Ambergris Caye, Belize, C.A., tel. (26) 2435/(2) 31140; or **Maya Airways,** 6 Fort St., Box 458, Belize City, Belize, C.A., tel. (2) 77215/72312. **Tropic Air,** Box 20, San Pedro, Ambergris Caye, Belize, C.A., tel. (800) 422-3435 in the U.S., except in Texas (713) 440-1867, in Belize (26) 2012, offers the same service. Tickets are available at the **Universal Travel Agency** next to Mom's in Belize City. Several charter planes make custom flights: **Cari-Bee Air Service,** Municipal Airstrip/San Pedro, Belize City, C.A., tel. (2) 44253, for local and international charters; and **Su-Bec Air Service,** Box 182, Belize City/San Pedro, Belize City, C.A. tel., (2) 30388.

The flight from Belize City to San Pedro takes about 15 minutes and fare is about US$66 roundtrip.

By Boat

The trip by boat between Belize City and Ambergris takes about 75 minutes. It's possible to arrange boat travel to and from San Pedro at any time of day but, unless you take one of the regularly scheduled water taxis, you may pay more than necessary (it depends on your negotiating skills).

downtown Ambergris

Among the boats making regular runs, *Andrea II* leaves San Pedro for Belize City at 7 a.m. daily from the Texaco dock by the Conch Shell Hotel. On a windy or rainy day, you stay dry on this vessel because it's enclosed. In Belize City, the *Andrea II* departs for San Pedro from the Bellevue Hotel pier (south of the Swing Bridge) at 3 p.m.

The *Hustler* leaves San Pedro daily at 7 a.m. and returns from Belize City about 4 p.m. The *Thunderbolt* docks at the Swing Bridge in Belize City and has the same schedule as above. Rates for all these boats should be around US$8 one-way, US$16 roundtrip. If in doubt check with a travel agency or any member of the **Caye Caulker Water Taxi Association**, to which many of the boat operators in Belize City belong. This organization is trying hard to standardize prices to the benefit of tourist and boat operator alike. Do *not* pay in advance; wait until you're safely on your way or at your destination. No regularly scheduled trips are available between cayes other than Ambergris and Caye Caulker; ask around the docks at Caulker and San Pedro and you'll probably find a private boat owner willing to take you for a fee.

Rough Weather Ahead

The sea is usually calm on trips to the cayes thanks to the offshore reef. However, there's always the exception. (If it's extraordinarily rough, the boats will not run to the cayes.) But, if you happen to be traveling by boat when there're lots of whitecaps, sitting toward the stern of these boats usually nets you a smoother ride. In the case of an enclosed boat, such as the *Andrea II,* you may also smell more fumes back there. So, you have to weigh which will affect you more. And some sailors say that keeping your eyes on the horizon in rough weather helps to avoid seasickness. If you're always prone to seasickness, whether calm or rough, there are always seasick pills or seasick wrist bands. Both of these are best brought from home just in case you can't find them here in a pinch.

CAYE CAULKER

This tiny island offers its own special brand of laid-back tourism. Though the major industry traditionally has been fishing, tourism is beginning to edge up as a close second, maybe even number one by now. Traditionally, only a few cars mar the tropical scenery and disrupt the two main sandy roads running north to south, cut by a number of cross roads. However, even that is changing "a little" with more cars than ever before. Caulker is a place to recover from "burnout"—no traffic, no smog, no high-tech "anything," no business meetings (for anyone), no lawn mowers (no lawns), no Burger Kings, no cake mixes (yet?), and no frozen orange juice. To rejuvenate the psyche, Caulker does have swimming, snorkeling, diving, and a chance to study the sea and sky and all of God's creatures above and below. There's little else to do besides "experiencing" the small "desert island." And the best part? It's *cheap!*, though not quite as cheap as in the past.

THE LAND

Caulker lies 21 miles northeast of Belize City, 11 miles south of Ambergris Caye, and one mile west of the Belize Reef. The island is four miles long; however, the inhabited part is an area less than a mile long, measuring south from the Split at the northern end. The land north of the Split is uninhabitable, consisting mostly of mangrove swamps with a narrow strip of land along the east coast. The dry season is Dec.-February. Because the island sits on a limestone escarpment, most houses have wells. The water, though drinkable, is used mostly for utility purposes because of its slight saline flavor. Drinking water is collected in rain gutters from the aluminum roofs and then channeled into tanks kept by the side of most houses. In the dry season drinking water becomes scarce.

New Development

At least eight houses have been built recently on the south end of Caulker, causing a little friction between pro-development and no-devel-

opment. Some in the area do not want to bring in electricity, others do, and so the discussion continues. All agree that there will be no signs in this neighborhood.

No doubt the ecology of the island will be an ongoing debate as long as there are those who *want* and those who *don't want* to further develop the small island. The most recent issues of disagreement are the sewage treatment plant and the recently built airport. Seventeen acres of crocodile and bird nesting lands were destroyed with the construction; 120 species of birds nest on the southern end of Caye Caulker. As is, the island can ill afford much more development.

FLORA AND FAUNA

Flora

Caulker is a sandy island that does not support general agricultural production, although coconut, papaya, lime, breadfruit, banana, plantain, and cacao flourish. Colorful flowering trees and plants such as hibiscus, ginger, *flamboyanes*, crotons, succulents, spider lilies, bougainvillea, and periwinkle add an exotic touch to the otherwise stark white (sandy) landscape. The ziricote tree does nicely and locals candy the fruit, or use it in salads. Jungle weeds and vines thrive in the sandy soil, and no matter how often they are cut back (by hand with machetes), they soon reappear.

Fauna

Pelicans and frigate birds decorate the sky as they soar along the coast hunting for fish. Birdwatchers can see ospreys dropping on fish in the shallows or perched occasionally on the post of a pier. One has even built a nest by the air strip.

A few creatures are endemic to the island, such as a variety of lizards, a few snakes (including the boa constrictor), and two types of crabs. During the rainy season, May-Sept., sand flies and mosquitoes are on the attack and drive all human life indoors. On rare occasions malaria and dengue fever have shown up on the island, but not in recent history.

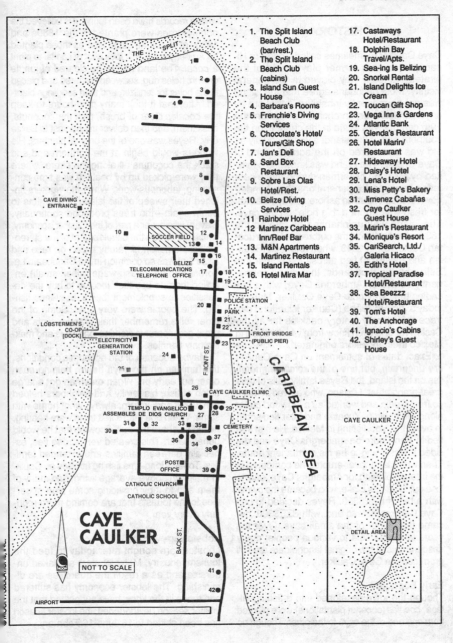

1. The Split Island Beach Club (bar/rest.)
2. The Split Island Beach Club (cabins)
3. Island Sun Guest House
4. Barbara's Rooms
5. Frenchie's Diving Services
6. Chocolate's Hotel/Tours/Gift Shop
7. Jan's Deli
8. Sand Box Restaurant
9. Sobre Las Olas Hotel/Rest.
10. Belize Diving Services
11. Rainbow Hotel
12. Martinez Caribbean Inn/Reef Bar
13. M&N Apartments
14. Martinez Restaurant
15. Island Rentals
16. Hotel Mira Mar
17. Castaways Hotel/Restaurant
18. Dolphin Bay Travel/Apts.
19. Sea-ing Is Belizing
20. Snorkel Rental
21. Island Delights Ice Cream
22. Toucan Gift Shop
23. Vega Inn & Gardens
24. Atlantic Bank
25. Glenda's Restaurant
26. Hotel Marin/Restaurant
27. Hideaway Hotel
28. Daisy's Hotel
29. Lena's Hotel
30. Miss Petty's Bakery
31. Jimenez Cabañas
32. Caye Caulker Guest House
33. Marin's Restaurant
34. Monique's Resort
35. CariSearch, Ltd./Galeria Hicaco
36. Edith's Hotel
37. Tropical Paradise Hotel/Restaurant
38. Sea Beezzz Hotel/Restaurant
39. Tom's Hotel
40. The Anchorage
41. Ignacio's Cabins
42. Shirley's Guest House

THE SPLIT

CAVE DIVING ENTRANCE

SOCCER FIELD

BELIZE TELECOMMUNICATIONS TELEPHONE OFFICE

LOBSTERMEN'S CO-OP [DOCK]

ELECTRICITY GENERATION STATION

POLICE STATION

PARK

FRONT BRIDGE (PUBLIC PIER)

FRONT ST.

CARIBBEAN SEA

CAYE CAULKER CLINIC

TEMPLO EVANGELICO ASSEMBLES DE DIOS CHURCH

CEMETERY

POST OFFICE

CATHOLIC CHURCH

CATHOLIC SCHOOL

BACK ST.

CAYE CAULKER

NOT TO SCALE

AIRPORT

CAYE CAULKER

DETAIL AREA

HISTORY

Caye Caulker (sometimes called Corker or Hicaco) is another former playground of the pirates—at least they played in the general vicinity. Most historians agree that the island was not permanently inhabited in that era by anyone. However, an anchor dating from the 19th century was found in the channel on the southern end of the island; a wreck equally as old was discovered off the southern end of Caye Chapel. The island was known to be visited by Mexican fishermen during those centuries because for generations they handed down stories of putting ashore at Caye Caulker for fresh water from a "big hole" on the caye. The island was uninhabited as late as the 1830s. It wasn't until the outbreak of the Yucatán Caste War in 1848, when refugees (Spanish and mestizos) fled across the border into Belize by the thousands, that many permanently settled on Ambergris Caye, with a few finding their way onto Caye Caulker. Many of today's **Jicaqueños** (Caulker Islanders) can trace their family history back as far as the Caste War and even know from which region in Mexico their ancestors originated.

Exact dates of settlement on Caye Caulker are uncertain, but one of the remaining families on the island, the Reyes family, tells of their great-grandfather, Luciano, who arrived in Mexico from Spain and worked as a logwood cutter along the coast of Yucatán and later fled south to avoid the bloodletting in Mexico. He first settled in San Pedro on Ambergris Caye and decided it was going to be his permanent home. Then when land fever erupted he competed in the intense bidding for Ambergris Caye, only to lose out to James Blake, who became the owner with a bid of BZE$650. Reyes decided to buy Caye Caulker instead and, with BZE$300, became the owner of the small caye. Over the years land was sold to various people; many descendants of the original landholders are still prominent on Caye Caulker.

Early Economy

Though the town developed into a fishing village, *cocales* (coconut plantations) were planted from one end of the caye to the other. Though no written records have been found, it is believed the original trees were planted in the 1880s and 1890s at about the same time as those planted on Ambergris Caye. It took a lot of capital to plant a *cocal*. The land had to be cleared of jungle growth, holes dug, seaweed gathered and placed in the holes for fertilizer, and then seedlings planted. After that it took many man-hours to keep the *cocales* clear of brush, pick the coconuts, husk them, and then deliver the harvest to Belize City. Reyes was one of the original planters. His workers would begin at the northern end and stack the coconuts all along the shore, where they were picked up by boats. It was time-consuming, laborious work. When the workers finished their sweep of the island, it was time to begin again—the trees produced continually. Slavery was never a part of the Caulker economy, which prevented the development of the stereotypical plantation hierarchy based on race and class that was so common in the Caribbean. Laborers earned a cash wage (albeit small) enabling them to use their income to buy the necessities to supplement their subsistence fishing. The people were very poor. Some of the older folks remember their grandparents and great-grandparents working long days and making only pennies.

Maybe because of the economic conditions, the families on the caye began helping each other out early on. When one man got a large catch of fish, his family and neighbors helped him with it and, in turn, always went home with some. When one man's fruit trees were bearing, he would share the fruit, knowing that he would benefit later. This created very strong ties, especially between families and extended families. Today's long-time fishing families on Caulker make an above-average living, and many of them add to it by providing some type of service to the tourists that are coming more regularly every year.

Lobstering

Lobsters are sought after today to feed the tourism industry. Many lobsters are taken undersize and as a result the quantities are diminishing. The lobster economy has suffered and those in the know have suggested that the lobster season be shortened; the lobster season has been shifted to 16 June-16 February.

Caulker docks

THE PEOPLE

In the early days fish brought in very little cash. However, fishing was still preferred to working on the *cocal*. It was less strenuous and less time-consuming, and the fishermen enjoyed greater independence. Eventually fishing began to pay off for the people and co-ops were established. Lobster was an important part of their success as it was on Ambergris. Fishermen liked being their own bosses and, as a result, to this day Jicauqueños (in Spanish the island name is Cayo Jicaco, which has degenerated into Caye Caulker) are independent thinkers with a lot of self-assurance. They take pride in their early roots on the island, and while color-class social thinking is seen in other parts of Belize, the distinction between peoples in Caulker is not based on color, rather on whether they are *islanders* or *nonislanders!* Along with the title "Jicauqueños" you usually know an islander from such comments as, "I belong to Caye Caulker." Most of the original island families were mestizo (commonly referred to in Belize as Spanish). But today the mixture also includes Creoles and a few immigrant Anglos. The Caulker community has been fairly successful in keeping the ownership of land among the locals. Every once in a while someone talks of bigger and better tourist accommodations, but face it: The locals are happy with their small island, small guesthouses, small home-style cafes and want to keep it just the way it is. It appears they don't really *want* more outsiders!

TOURISM

Early Tourism
Until the 1960s few visitors reached the shores of Caye Caulker. But once the hippie backpackers discovered the small relaxed island, more and more travelers began arriving. This was becoming the hushed secret among adventurers making their way south along the Central American trail. Although most people had never heard of Belize in the 1970s, they did recognize the name of British Honduras with a rough idea of location. The usual description was that Belize was the next country past Mexico. Such people as Jacques Cousteau and *National Geographic* writers began spreading the word that Caulker was the place for the young or the young at heart. It soon became apparent to islanders that incoming visitors *needed* food and lodging, and this was a new way for the women to earn extra money. The men's lives changed little with the influx as they continued their fishing. Houses on Caulker were generally wooden structures built on stilts with a separate cooking shack. The first accommodations, such as **Edith's Hotel,** were simple cubicles created by enclosing the space under the house. Others followed and soon is-

landers built simple hotels next to their homes. Most offered only the barest of necessities with shared toilet, no hot water, and were often dormitory style, but they served the purpose and were satisfactory for the young adventurers who came. The first cafes were women selling food out of their windows on the sandy lanes. Some women would place chalkboards in front of their houses announcing that they were cooking boilup, or fish, or *whatever,* that evening and the price. If you wanted to come for dinner, all you had to do was knock on the door early in the day and tell her. It was wonderfully casual, unbelievably cheap, and a marvelous opportunity to get to know the warm, friendly people of Caulker. Probably the only black mark during this era was the substance users who became obnoxious and insulting. The people didn't approve of having "stoned" or drunken folks wandering around the small comunity. In the Caulker of the 1990s, a close watch is kept on anyone who looks the part—that's not to say that the islanders themselves have never indulged in growing a little pot.

Tourism Today

Today's Caulker is changing—a little. The population has grown from 500 to 1,000 in the last decade. The islanders don't want to "lose" their island as they believe the San Pedranos have lost San Pedro on Ambergris Caye. The islanders have adamantly kept out foreign investors, and they keep the prime pieces of land for their homes. Newer hotel cabañas now provide private bathrooms and some even have hot water and dining rooms, but they still maintain the wonderful, low-key Caribbean ambience. Many are just simple thatch huts.

Visitors are not just backpackers anymore. Though the island still attracts many young adults, it also finds whole families visiting who thrive on the low-key, unhurried, uncrowded atmosphere. Visitors can expect nice people, productive fishing, exotic snorkeling and diving, a laid-back atmosphere—and reasonable prices! More small hotels are springing up around the island each year. In February and March you'll run into the largest number of tourists from the States. In August the island is filled with the European contingent. The slowest months are the fall months and January. According to some

readers, at any particular time "hustlers" from Belize City can pester visitors to the point of wanting to leave. Hope the city fathers do something about that in a hurry!

The caye has sandy streets and very few are marked with street signs; just ask anyone for directions. You can walk from one end of the island to the other, and backside to frontside on a lazy morning, including a stop at **Tropical Paradise Restaurant** for a cold fresh glass of orange juice or a tasty ice cream. Or follow the aroma of baking pastries into the spotless big kitchen at **Daisy's Hotel** (watch your step— don't walk on the family's pet spider monkey). Try a powder bun or coconut crust and sweet fresh orange juice (served all day), and then continue your tour of the island. Look around and you'll find plenty of these Caulker "fastfood" outlets with some of the best home-cooked snacks, whether they're fruit yogurt, lobster pies, pastries, or fresh-squeezed orange juice.

If you want to take a little rest first, flake out on one of many wooden docks (locals call them

This wooden cistern catches precious water.

"bridges") that jut out over the clear turquoise sea along the waterfront. In case you didn't know, that's what Caye Caulker is all about—being lazy, lying on your back, and studying the sky and all the winged creatures that prefer flying just *above* Caulker. You might see the graceful and magnificent frigate (fish bandit extraordinaire that never gets its feathers wet), always on the lookout for a handout from any *real* fishing bird flapping away with its loaded beak—whammo! The frigate steals the fishing bird's catch and it doesn't know what hit it. In spring you might see the black male frigate's brilliant red gular pouch (under its beak) inflated like a bright red balloon —that means it's courting. When you get tired of that view, flip onto your stomach and look over the side of the dock—you can spend the rest of the day studying the constantly changing underwater scene through crystal-clear water, no glass needed.

OFFICIALDOM

The pace here is very slow and the cost is low. The townsfolk do not happily entertain bums or hippie-types, and they're doing their best to keep the small village from being overrun by substance and alcohol users. (Apparently, Caulker has enough over-imbibing locals that it doesn't need to import any more.) The mayor says they love the low-budget travelers—as long as they don't sleep on the docks or wander around nude (both against the law). However, the town has two problems: too few police to do the enforcing and a frequently "broken" jail—prisoners come and go at will. Fortunately, the crimes on Caye Caulker are small transgressions. Also, keep in mind the law does not allow camping on public or private property without permission. The only "official" camping now is at Vega Inn and Gardens (see "Accommodations," below) and as at many places in Belize, the price is almost as much as a cheap room.

ORIENTATION

Caye Caulker is cut into two pieces. **The Split** or **the Cut** separates the southern inhabited part of the island from the northern mangrove swamps. This feature earned its name after a hurricane widened a channel causing a "cut" or "split" in the island. This is where travelers and locals alike come to enjoy the sandy beach around the Cut.

Moving south past the Cut toward town on **Front Street,** the street that skirts the eastern shore (there are two more streets, inland), the traveler soon encounters the first of seven sandy roads that cut across the island. The **public pier** is at the fourth and main road, which also has a pier at the western side of the island. Between the two you'll pass **Chan's Mini Mart** and the noisy **B.E.L. Power House.**

The western pier is where water taxis between Belize City, Caye Caulker, and Ambergris Caye pickup and deliver. A fuel pump is here as well. Sailors exploring the nearby cayes anchor in the shallow protected waters offshore.

Back on Front Street, the **cemetery** lies at the sixth road inland. This is also where Front Street dead-ends. By turning right and then cutting to the left one street over, you'll come upon the seventh and final street. Follow this street west one block, take a left, and you can follow this dusty track called **Back Street** (even though there's one farther west then this), all the way to the air strip. Of course, you could have kept to the beach on the eastern side and reached here just as well.

The island continues past this point some distance south, but there's nothing for visitors in that area yet.

WATER SPORTS

Diving Services

Three very reputable diving services on the island offer trips as well as certification courses. You'll find **Frenchie's Diving Services,** tel. (22) 2234, at the first major dirt cross street from the Split and just about 25 yards off Front Street. These folks always get good reviews from divers—the night dive at Hol Chan (US$35), especially.

Belize Diving Services, tel. (22) 2143, fax (22) 2217, offers NAUI/PADI certification. To find it, turn west at the Martinez Caribbean Inn and proceed across the width of the island past the soccer field. Belize Diving will be on the right.

Caye Caulker School of Scuba, tel. (22) 2292, owned by local guide Abel Novelo, offers certification as well as dive trips, boating, and snorkeling. Ask around for directions.

Cave Diving
The Caye Caulker Blue Hole (not *the* Blue Hole at Lighthouse Reef) is now off limits to divers; a few unfortunates have lost their lives over the years in these caves. This is the opening to a cave system that is immense and also very dangerous. Local guides know safer cavelike passageways in the reef face that are more appropriate for sport divers. Ask the dive shops for more information.

Snorkeling Guides
The people of Caye Caulker are perfect examples of democracy at work. Not only have they formed a water taxi association to standardize rates and services for the good of local boatmen and visitors, but they've now created **Caye Caulker Tour Guide Association** for the same purpose. This should mean a lot less guesswork for the tourist and higher standards for guides.

Touring with Chocolate
Probably the best known of all the guides is Captain Chocolate, owner of **Chocolate's Tours,** Caye Caulker, Belize, C.A., tel. (22) 2151. Chocolate and his boat *Soledad* are near-legends in the trade. Whenever you talk with groups of travelers who've been to Caulker, the name Chocolate is bound to come up. For years he has run a water taxi service. During this time, he became the first to begin taking people on trips to a nearby caye to see manatees. Today, he also gives river tours, tours of Gales Point and surrounding lagoons, and a tour to Goff's Caye that includes two stops to observe the manatees (US$27.50). The first stop is in an open area where it is possible for snorkelers to leave the boat and approach manatees in their element. The effect is exhilarating as you near a creature weighing hundreds of pounds, yet who, with the flick of a tail, can leave you far behind.

The second stop is an area that Chocolate describes as the manatees' home. He approaches this area slowly and quietly with his engines off to ensure no harm comes to the sluggish beasts

Captain Chocolate provides dependable transport aboard his SS Soledad to and from Caye Caulker.

(they are rarely swift of thought or action). Instead, he uses a stout stick to pole in close. A couple of minutes' wait and the curious manatees begin to surface around the boat to breathe and continue feeding.

Other guides are often not so careful; some manatees show recent scars from boat propellers. Captain Chocolate is very protective of local manatees, and when guides from other islands come to visit the area with engines running, he sees to it that they learn the ground rules in a hurry.

Goff's Caye is Chocolate's next stop. This tiny spit of sand has great beaches, a cluster of palm trees, a pier, and good snorkeling on the east side of the island. Chocolate can also arrange overnight tenting trips here (about US$70 including tent).

More Good Guides and Boats
A former mate on Chocolate's boat, **Harrison,** tel. (22) 2263, is also a safe, reliable boatman for day-trips to Hol Chan Marine Reserve and San Pedro, Ambergris Caye, and Goff's Caye.

Like Chocolate, Harrison stops for snorkeling with manatees in open areas where they graze and poles his boat into the areas where the marine mammals congregate and doze. He docks his boat at the same dock as Chocolate.

Captain Jim Novello, Caye Caulker, Belize, C.A., tel. (22) 2195/2239, takes snorkeling trips to the reef, San Pedro, Turneffe Islands, Lighthouse Reef, and several smaller islands south of Caye Caulker. From Caye Caulker to the reef, divers have three snorkeling/diving stops, US$8 or US$13, including snorkeling gear. Captain Novello heads a popular snorkeling trip with stops at the Turneffe Islands, the Blue Hole, and Half Moon Caye. You also have an opportunity to see the endangered red-footed booby. It's an all-day adventure that costs about US$68.

Even the nonswimmer can enjoy spectacular underwater sights with **Belizario** and son Denis Martinez on trips to the reef, Hol Chan, and San Pedro in their **glass-bottom boat;** cost is about US$10 to the reef, US$15 to Hol Chan. Inquire at **Martinez Restaurant.**

Note: It only makes sense that divers and passengers check out the boat they're boarding. Ask questions—does it have two motors? extra gas? how far will you be going? what's the weather outlook both inside the reef and outside? In short, take steps to ensure your own safety. Ask a local about the diving reputation of your divemaster.

Fishing

This is good fishing country; inquire at your hotel about making arrangements with a fisherman (tackle provided) to take you on a hunt for the sweetest seafood in the Caribbean. Or take a walk to the backside of the island, where you'll find fishermen cleaning their fish, working on lobster traps, or mending their nets in the morning. Many will be willing to take you fishing. Main trophies are groupers, barracuda, snapper, and amberjack, all good eating. Small boats are available for rent by the hour; if you want a more organized trip contact **Porfilio Guzman,** tel. (22) 2152, is a well-known fishing guide for reef or flats fishing. Guide **Roque (Rocky) Badillo,** tel. (22) 2214, owns **Roque's Fishing and River Tours** and is another good choice.

Fishing and Diving Charters

Rolando "Roly" Rosado offers fishing and diving charters. He'll take you to the reef to dive, or on day-long fishing expeditions. Talk to Roly or his brother Ramon at Box 743, Belize City, Belize, C.A., tel. (22) 2058/2073. **Raul Young,** tel. (22) 2133, takes travelers snorkeling or fishing on the reefs and is known for flats fishing. **Tom Young, Sr.,** tel. (22) 2134, is known for his trips to Turneffe Islands.

Swimming the Split

While meandering around the island you'll notice the Split, a channel that was widened by Hattie's big blow in 1961. The violent force of the wind and water rammed through the land, blowing away a piece of the mangrove forests —and suddenly the island was cut in two by a wider swath of water. One of the few sandy Caulker beaches is on this end of the island, but be aware that swimming in the "new" channel can be dangerous; this is a shallow and heavily trafficked area. The pull of the swift

---

FISHING TIPS

BEST FISHING TIMES FOR LOCAL FISH

Barracuda, Bonefish, Bonito, Jack, Mackerel, Permit, Snapper, Tuna, Wahoo	Year-round
Grouper	December
Marlin	March-May
Sailfish	March-June
Snook	January-May, November, December
Tarpon	March-July, November

current is enough to overpower children or weak swimmers. Another and even more dangerous threat is the passage of fast skiffs through the Split. Fatal accidents have occurred. Around the bend only a few meters out of the channel, the water is calm and safe. Swimming off the "back bridge" on the western side of the caye is even safer.

ACCOMMODATIONS

None of the hotels on the island is luxurious (one room at **Chocolate's** is an exceptiom); some just offer more than others. Most of the budget hotels on Caulker have shared bathrooms and are very basic. The newer ones offer electricity, private baths, and ceiling fans—a taste of tropical island life without the frills. The following is not a complete list of hotels; more accommodations are available. Remember, prices are negotiable depending on the time of the year, the number of tourists on the island, and how persuasive you are. You're never too far from the sea on Caulker, but few places are right on the water's edge. **Note:** Don't expect long white beaches in Caulker; for the most part the shore is lined with sea grass. One of the best sandy beaches is at the Split. During the high season, most rooms are taken as soon as the tourists from Belize City arrive. Make reservations if possible.

Simple Rooms

A spot that might interest backpackers, **Barbara's Rooms,** Caye Caulker, Belize, C.A., tel. (22) 2215, is on a dirt track between the Split and the first cross street. Just turn at **Island Sun Guest House** (both are reached by the same phone) and it's on the left. It has six basic rooms on the first floor of a two-story building. All rooms have cold water, shared baths, and wooden floors. The cost is about US$10 s/d.

Castaways Hotel, Caye Caulker, Belize, C.A., tel. (22) 2294, is next door to the Hotel Mira Mar and a couple of blocks north of the public pier. Castaways has eight rooms that are clean and reasonably priced. All rooms have cold water, shared baths, and fans. Guests receive free coffee in the mornings. Rates are US$7 s, US$11 d. Castaways also has a restaurant/bar and the menu is one of the largest on the island.

If you follow Front Street south to the dead end and turn right, **Caye Caulker Guest House,** Caye Caulker, Belize, C.A., tel. (22) 2249, will be two blocks inland and on the right. Here Soloman Nicholas rents out rooms with h/c water and shared baths for US$17 s/d.

Lena's Hotel, Caye Caulker, Belize, C.A., tel. (22) 2106, is right on the water and therefore a popular choice. It has 16 rooms in an old building. Half have shared baths; the other eight have private baths. Rooms come with fans. Rates with shared bath are about US$16

Vega Inn and Gardens

s/d, with private bath US$27-32 s/d. Manager Conchita Marin can help arrange diving and fishing trips.

Daisy's Hotel, Caye Caulker, Belize, C.A., tel. (22) 2123, is another great oldie. Run by a great family of many daughters, Daisy's is on the east side of the island, on the main street and south of the public pier, just inland from Lena's Hotel. Daisy's has 11 simple rooms with fans in several buildings. Those with private bath are US$18; rooms with shared bath go for US$11 s/d.

Check at Ellen MacRae's gift shop, Galeria Hicaco, Caye Caulker, Belize, C.A., tel. (22) 2178 (near the Tropical Paradise), to see **Ellen's Rooms.** Each of the two rooms has a private baths with cold water and solar-heated black-barrel showers. One room has a double and 3/4 bed and the other has one double bed. Call or write for new rates.

Edith's Hotel, Caye Caulker, Belize, C.A., tel. (22) 2161, with smallish, tidy rooms is a hallmark on the center street of the island. Four rooms come with h/c water, private baths, ceiling fans; another four have shared baths. Rates are US$25 with private bath, with shared bath US$20. Two cabañas have h/c water, private baths, and fans for US$22.50.

Hideaway Hotel, Caye Caulker, Belize, C.A., tel. (22) 2103, is across the street from the Hotel Marin and next door to the Assembly of God church. Actually the Hideaway has no place to hide when the church breaks into song, and no place to hide from the sun. These bare, sultry lodgings are aimed at longterm stays but the owners may be willing to negotiate shorter engagements if you're really desperate. Rates are negotiable but hover around US$12.

Hotel Marin, Caye Caulker, Belize, C.A., tel. (22) 2110, is farther inland from Daisy's and across the street from the church. Sarah Marin has 15 rooms on a fairly shady lot. Rates with shared bath are US$12.50 s/d, with private bath US$25.

Formerly The Reef Hotel, the **Martinez Caribbean Inn,** Caye Caulker, Belize, C.A., tel. (22) 2196, with its friendly staff has been around for a long time under various names. The 17 rooms are basic with h/c water, private baths, fans, and ocean views that afford a glimpse of breakers crashing against the Belize Reef. We hope new owners have raised the standards here. Rates are US$17.50 s/d, US$22.50 t, US$25 q. This is a noisy area. The hotel has a restaurant/bar nearby (also noisy).

Hotel Mira Mar, Caye Caulker, Belize, C.A., tel. (22) 2157, is a two-story hotel a couple of blocks north of the public pier on Front Street. Its 19 rooms face the ocean across the street and each has cold water, shared or private bath, and fan. Rates for shared bath are US$6 s, US$9 d, US$12.50 t; for private bath US$22 s/d.

M & N Apartments, Caye Caulker, Belize, C.A., tel. (22) 2111, fax (22) 2257, are on the corner of the second cross street south of the Split. Rooms come with h/c water and are simply furnished. Rates are US$12.50 s/d. These are the same folks who rent the golf carts.

Monique's Resort, Caye Caulker, Belize, C.A., tel. (22) 2140, is across the street from the post office. You'll find two cabañas owned by Edward Reyes. Both include two beds, h/c water, private bath, and ceiling fan. Rates are US$25 s/d, US$5 per person each additional.

Tom's Hotel, Caye Caulker, Belize, C.A., tel. (22) 2102, is popular with the young crowd and backpackers: simple bungalows (36 rooms), clean, with h/c water, shared or private baths, fans, louvered windows, tile floors, and a sea view. Rooms with shared bath are US$10.50-17.50 d, depending on the "newness" and simple amenities provided. Five separate cabins with private baths and hot water go for US$26.75.

Vega Inn and Gardens, Box 701, Belize City, Belize, C.A., tel. (22) 2142, fax (22) 2269, is one of the originals, and still a favorite. Vega Inn offers simple rooms in an old two-story building on the sand. Owned by the Vega family, longtime island residents, the hotel has a warm and friendly atmosphere. This is a family affair and they're a font of information about the island —past and present. The family will talk for hours about establishing the fishing cooperatives, struggling against the big money-and-power folks who controlled the cayes—and winning out. Lydia rents the rooms and with only 10, reservations are a must, especially during the holiday seasons (Christmas and Easter). Rates for a room with a private bath are US$53 s/d, US$59 t; with shared bath US$22.50 s/d, US$27.50 t. The inn accepts Visa/MC.

You can rent campsites on Vega Inn and Gardens property, but the management doesn't put up with loud or drunken parties! Camping fees are US$7 per person per night. For more information about rooms and camping contact Maria Vega. Ask about arrangements for snorkeling and fishing.

Mary Jo Wilson's **Anchorage,** Caye Caulker, Belize, C.A., tel. (22) 2002, is three clean, thatched-roof cabañas on a white sandy beach with scores of swaying palms, just a bit south of Tom's Hotel. Each cabaña has cold water only, private bath, Robinson Crusoe simplicity, and appropriate tropical ambience. Rates are US$15 s/d, US$8.50 per person additional for up to five people. Beer and soft drinks are also available.

A Cut above the Others
Local guide Chocolate runs a well-known guide service. With the help of his wife, Annie Seashore, he also runs a giftshop, and above it they have opened **Chocolate's Hotel,** Box 332, Belize City, Belize, C.A., tel. (22) 2151. It's a stretch to call this a hotel with just one room, but what a beautifully furnished room it is—many say the best on the island! If you're lucky enough to snag this one, you'll have h/c water, private bath, fan, cross ventilation, coffee maker, bedpost lights, tile floors—even terry cloth robes. Rates are US$60 s/d. And staying here makes it a good bet you'll get a spot on one of Choco-

late's trips to Goff's Caye and a swim among manatees along the way, an experience you'll not soon forget.

In a concrete building by the water Ilna Auxillou runs **Dolphin Bay Apartments.** The two fully furnished apartments are rented to those wishing to stay for a week or longer. Both feature cold water (soon to be upgraded to h/c), private bath, full kitchen with stove and fridge, and fans. The upstairs apartment is larger, catches a bit more of the sea breeze and rents for US$175/week s/d. The lower apartment rents for US$125/week s/d. Contact Dolphin Bay Travel, Caye Caulker, Belize, C.A., tel. (22) 2214.

Ignacio's Cabins, Caye Caulker, Belize, C.A., tel. (22) 2212, are north of Shirley's and you'll find 13 colorful, small clapboard wooden huts along the beach with a scattering of palms, sea grapes, and cassarina trees. Each room comes with a private, cold-water bath, and costs about US$15 s/d. These are very small and may not be everyone's cup of tea but they have lots of island character.

Island Sun Guest House is just south of the Split and its cabañas. Island Sun sits on the corner of a dirt track that goes a short way inland. It has two downstairs guest rooms with hand-painted floral patterns on the walls. The effect is charming. The rooms have h/c water and fans and cost about US$30 s/d. You can make arrangements by calling Barbara's Rooms, Caye Caulker, Belize, C.A., tel. (22) 2215.

Sea Beezzz Hotel

Formerly known as Jimenez Huts, the six **Jimenez Cabañas,** Caye Caulker, Belize, C.A., tel. (22) 2175, are owned and operated by George Jimenez. Like many folks, Mr. Jimenez thought it was time to boost the image of his lodgings rather than promote a traditional image of backwater simplicity. The cabañas have h/c water, private baths, ceiling fans, and night lights. Rates are US$24 s/d.

Two stories high, the **Rainbow Hotel,** Caye Caulker, Belize, C.A., tel. (22) 2123/2172, sits on the edge of the lane going north of the public pier toward the Split. Here are 17 clean, motel-style stucco rooms with h/c water, private baths, electricity, fans, TVs, and tile floors. Rates are about US$24-30 s, US$30-34.50 d. For more information contact Ernesto Marin. The hotel accepts Visa/MC.

For a real touch of Belize hospitality, check out the **Sea Beezzz** Hotel, Box 812, Belize City, Belize, C.A., in the U.S. tel. (602) 451-0040, in Belize tel./fax (22) 2176. It's open five months a year, late November through Easter. The hotel has its own dock and will make arrangements for diving or other water activities. Out front there's a little garden with flower beds edged with conch shells. The family restaurant (below the rooms) serves American breakfasts for about US$4.50, a great shrimp scampi dinner, "freshly cut sandwiches," cinnamon rolls, coconut crusts, pineapple upside-down cakes, and lots of other homemade goodies. You'll find six very clean double units, each with h/c water, private bath, fresh linoleum, electricity, and fans, run by a family who can tell you all about the island. The room rate is US$40 s/d.

Clean and comfortable, **Shirley's Guest House,** Caye Caulker, Belize, C.A., tel. (22) 2145, fax (22) 2264, has nine rooms built with beautiful tropical woods—great wooden floors and walls. The outside is neatly painted white with a green trim. It has private bathrooms; all are on the beach. This is the lodging closest to the airstrip on the eastern side. Shirley charges US$45 for rooms with shared bath, s/d; about US$125 for double rooms with private bath and fridge. She's been on Caye Caulker for 22 years—a pleasant no-nonsense lady.

Sobre Las Olas Hotel, Caye Caulker, Belize, C.A., tel. (22) 2243, is just south of the Sand Box. This hotel has a restaurant on the water and across the street are the rooms. They range in size, price, and amenities. Rooms have h/c water, private baths, and fans or a/c, and some have TVs. Rates are US$20-38 s/d.

The Out Island Beach Club and Tiki Bar, Caye Caulker, Belize, C.A., tel (22) 2054/2053, in the U.S. (800) 771-1133, is where you'll find the nicest sandy beach on the island. It gets very busy during the high season, and tourists come from the rest of the island to soak up the rays and swim in the comparatively grass-free water. Recent construction has provided more sandy beach frontage and a safe swimming area. A snack stand/bar a few steps away is open for drinks till midnight. Managed by O.J., it makes for an "in" location for travelers who want to absorb the most activity the island offers. Formerly called the Split Island Beach Club, the hotel is a group of nine small wooden cabins on short stilts in the sand. Each has a/c, h/c water, private bath, fans, and all are clean and tidy. The hotel has a desalination plant that provides lots of fresh water. Rates are US$50 d per cabin in season, US$35 in low season (Sept.-Nov.).

Ramon Reyes has one of the more popular spots on Caye Caulker and with good reason: **Tropical Paradise Hotel,** Caye Caulker, Belize, C.A., tel. (22) 2124, represents good value and has an equally good restaurant. It is separated from the colorful village cemetery by a neat white picket fence—both look out to sea. The wooden cabañas have private ceiling fans, baths, h/c water, and a small, clean cafe/ice-cream parlor with a friendly staff. Rates for cabañas are US$32.50 s, US$35-40 d; rooms are US$25 s, US$25-30 d. The suites offer a/c, color TV, and a refrigerator, US$60-65 per night, breakfast included. From the Tropical Paradise you can make arrangements for snorkeling, fishing, or lobster trapping with guides. You can also hire a guide and boat to take you to neighboring cayes.

FOOD

For such a tiny island, Caye Caulker boasts a number of small cafes and other eateries; just don't expect lace and linen service. For the most part, meals are simple, with fresh seafood and chicken as the featured menu items.

Probably the two best restaurants on the island are **Sand Box** and the **Tropical Paradise Restaurant**. At the **Sand Box**, north on Front Street, you'll find a sand floor inside and a line waiting for a table, especially for one outside. This is an evening spot to see and be seen. Fish fillet with curry rice is US$5, conch ceviche is US$2.25, lobster salad is US$4, seafood jambalaya is US$8, and jerk chicken is US$4.50. Beer, liquor, soft drinks, and fresh juices (watermelon, orange, and pineapple) round out the menu.

Tropical Paradise Restaurant, at the south end of Front Street, has a pleasant interior. Among other selections, it serves pancakes and bacon for US$2, scrambled eggs and lobster with toast for US$4, and fresh orange juice for US$1.50. For lunch or dinner, lobster ceviche costs US$4, burgers cost US$1.50-3.25, fried fish US$6, curried lobster US$9, and pork chops US$7.50. The outdoor area, called the **Cascade Lounge,** is perfect for drinks or alfresco dining.

Sobre Las Olas, a beachfront bar and grill near the Sand Box, serves lobster, shrimp, crab claws, pork chops, and burgers. **Sea Beezzz Restaurant** serves great breakfasts of eggs and bacon/ham/sausage for US$3.25, pancakes with bacon/ham/sausage for US$4.75, coffee for US50 cents, and freshly squeezed orange juice for US$1. **Castaways** is known for breakfast and burgers (US$2.50-3.50), steak in mushroom sauce (US$7), vegetarian chow mein (US$4.50), lobster in fresh garlic sauce (US$8.50), and Thai chicken (US$6).

Marin's, down the street from the Tropical Paradise, has a good menu and always-fresh fish; **Glenda's,** on the west side of the island, serves inexpensive Mexican food and delicious lobster burritos. In the morning try her homemade cinnamon rolls, delicious cheese rolls, and fresh squeezed orange juice. **Syd's,** east of Glenda's, designs good burritos and has a great Saturday night barbecue. **Daisy's Hotel** serves tasty capuccino. **Mad Annie's** (formerly Fisherman's Wharf), a block north of the public pier, serves a variety of fresh seafood at reasonable prices. **Martinez Restaurant** offers three meals a day year-round with burgers, tacos, and lobster heading the menu. **Chan's Garden,** on Back Street across from the Hotel Marin, serves

Chinese food and decent T-bone steaks. **I & I Restaurant**, across the street from Monique's Resort and west of the Front Street dead-end, has an outdoor deck and constant reggae in the background.

Groceries
A little different, **Jan's Deli** is actually a grocery store with all the makings for tasty sandwiches, cold drinks, champagne, pastries, fresh vegetables, ice cream, ready-to-go lunches, sundries, and snacks.

If you're lucky, you may run into some cute kids strolling the sandy lanes balancing pans of homemade sweet crusts and wheat bread on their heads—for sale, of course! The banana bread is heavenly.

Look around and you'll find **Chan's Mini Mart** (across from the Atlantic Bank), and a few other small grocery stores. And if you want fresh fish or lobster, ask at the Lobstermen's Co-op Dock on the backside of the island what time the fishermen come in with their catch. This is always a good place to buy fresh fish.

ISLAND ART AND GIFT SHOPS

You'll find a sprinkling of small shops in and around Front Street. Several sell T-shirts, island art, photos, books, shells, suntan lotion, maps and typical Belizean souvenirs.

Chocolate's Gift Shop, Box 332, Belize City, Belize, C.A., tel. (22) 2151, is operated by Captain Chocolate's wife, Annie Seashore. On the waterfront road going toward the Split in a beautiful natural-wood building, Chocolate's shop offers T-shirts (hand silk-screened and painted by Annie), a good selection of Guatemalan/Mexican handcrafted items, Indonesian sarongs, plus hammocks, jewelry, postcards, stamps, and other memorabilia to help you remember the caye.

Just ask anyone—he or she will point you to Ellen MacRae's **Galeria Hicaco,** a small gift shop at the south end of Front street near the Tropical Paradise. It's in the same building as **CariSearch, Ltd.,** Ellen's guiding/chartering/consulting business. Here, she sells art, crafts, and clothing made by the Kekchi and Mopan Maya, Garifuna, mestizos, and Creoles. Ellen is a marine biologist/artist who takes outstanding

local girls selling powder buns, lemon crusts, and other homemade pastries

underwater photos of the reef. Ask her about guided trips to the reef or her suggestions for nature lovers. For more information about rooms available at Ellen's contact CariSearch, Ltd., tel. (22) 2178.

One-time local artist **Philip Lewis** lived on Caulker for many years and produced flamboyantly decorated T-shirts. An earthy primitive artist, he was co-designer of the national currency. Though he now lives in Switzerland, some prints of his excellent drawings are still on display at the Galeria Hicaco, along with his popular (though now aging) map of Caye Caulker.

James Beveridge, an excellent photographer of underwater marinelife, terrestrial wildlife, and people pictures, owns another shop featuring island art, **Sea-ing Is Belizing**, Box 374, Belize City, Belize, C.A., tel. (22) 2189. Browse around the shop/gallery (near the soccer field and Belize Diving Services) and you'll find a book exchange, gift items, and invitations to

special slide shows on weeknights at 8 p.m., with subjects such as the scenics of Belize, underwater reef shots, and flora and fauna, including the jaguar preserve. You can get photo processing done here.

Don't stop looking; there are more. Wander through **Coco's Gift Shop,** near the police station, **Salty Dog** and **Sea Shell Gift Shop,** both near Atlantic Bank, and **Toucan Gift Shop.** In addition, **Mayan Secrets** (just west of Tropical Paradise Hotel) and **Tracy's Island Wear** (between The Reef Bar and Martinez) offer T-shirts, sarongs, towels, postcards **with stamps,** and bug repellent. Both accept Visa/MC/AmEx. Ask about **Wendy,** who makes and designs her own T-shirts across the street from Dolphin Bay.

SERVICES AND INFORMATION

Because of the size of the island and limited number of visitors to Caulker, most of the businesspeople who make a living from tourism do so through multiple services. For the most part the local men carry on with their fishing; their wives are the backbone of the food businesses and hotels. You'll find that the shops are generally owned by multitalented people who are artists, photographers, guides, or divers. They all have one thing in common; they're dedicated to saving their natural resources—especially the reef and its rich sealife.

Among other services that you will find helpful: **Atlantic Bank,** open 9 a.m.-1 p.m., is on Back Street, half a block south of Chan's Mini Mart and the cross street with the public piers at each end.

The **Post Office** is also on Back Street at the last crossroad as you go south and across from the primary school and church. It's open 9 a.m.-noon, 2-5 p.m. Mon.-Fri.; 9 a.m.-noon only Saturday.

If you should have a medical problem, a small clinic on Front Street just north of Lena's Hotel offers limited services.

Guide Services
Marine biologist Ellen MacRae is a vital advocate in Caye Caulker's ecological climate. Through her **CariSearch, Ltd.** (southern end

of Front Street), Box 47, Caye Caulker, Belize, C.A., tel. (22) 2178, she offers an **ecology tour,** in which clients are oriented with a one-hour lecture in the morning and then spend an afternoon of guided snorkeling with Ellen. She also offers bird/caye ecology hikes, guided lecture tours to mangrove lagoons, and she takes camping charters to atolls and southern cayes. All tours must be scheduled at least one day in advance, longer for camping charters. Ellen is very involved with the local **Siwa-Ban Preserve.**

James Beveridge is a recommended guide as well as a representative of the **Belize Audubon Society** and very involved with preserving the country's natural resources. Ask about his underwater photo safaris and sailing trips at his shop **Sea-ing Is Belizing,** Box 374, Belize City, Belize, C.A., tel. (22) 2189, where he can also arrange diving lessons. James sponsors underwater photo safaris as well as sailing trips. Write or call for more information.

Travel Agencies
Need a local travel agent to arrange dive trips, plane reservations, inland trips, or accommodations? **Dolphin Bay Travel,** tel. (22) 2214, is near the pier and next door to Sea-ing Is Belizing.

Now there's a choice in local travel agencies on Caye Caulker with **Hicaco Tours and Travel,** tel. (22) 2073, fax (2) 74007. Besides being a

member of the Caye Caulker Water Taxi Association, Ramon Rosado can make arrangements for tours in the cayes or inland.

TRANSPORTATION

Getting Around
Caye Caulker is so walkable and the pace so languid most people hoof it wherever they go. However, taking a spin around town in a **golf cart** is a pleasant way to get one's bearings upon first arriving. At **Island Rentals,** tel. (22) 2111, carts are rented by the hour or day. Credit cards are accepted.

Getting There
Island Air, Maya Airways, and **Tropic Air** now make regular flights to Caye Caulker, flying to both the Belize Municipal and the International airports. The airstrip on Caulker is pretty simple —you wait under a tree or on the veranda of the small building that serves all flights. Fares are US$16.50 one-way and US$30 roundtrip to the municipal airport (about 10 minutes); or US$35 one-way and US$70 roundtrip to International (about 15 minutes).

If you prefer getting there by boat, outboard skiffs/launches go to and from Caye Caulker every day. The **Caye Caulker Water Taxi Association** is working hard to standardize

Galeria Hicaco
Gift Shop

the controversial Caulker airstrip and one of the commuter planes that make daily stops at Caye Caulker

prices (US$7.50 one-way, US$15 roundtrip) and service. Among some of the better known boats are *Blue Wave, Elsy, Good Grief, Libra, Pegasus, Sea Train,* and *Soledad.* These boats haul travelers, groceries, dive equipment, and other small freight to the island daily, leaving Caye Caulker 6:30-7 a.m. and returning from Belize City about 9 a.m. on their first round trip. It takes about 45 minutes between Belize City and Caye Caulker and is usually an enjoyable ride, allowing passengers to get in the island mood a bit before they touch shore at Caye Caulker. Boats will stop at Caye Chapel if requested. A light wrap is handy for windy trips. A poncho is a godsend on rainy voyages.

OTHER POPULAR CAYES

CAYE CHAPEL

Just one by three miles long, this privately owned caye is about 25 minutes by boat from Belize City (15 miles)—and has its own 3,600-foot-long landing strip. Caye Chapel, with its waving palms, beautiful wide beach, and coral heads at the reef a mile offshore, pampers visitors at its only hotel, **Pyramid Island Resort and Marina,** Box 192, Belize City, Belize, C.A., in the U.S. tel. (800) 458-8281, in Belize tel. (2) 44409, fax (2) 32405. Run by the owners of the caye, the hotel offers 32 large, a/c, comfortable rooms, good food, a golf driving range, tennis and basketball courts, a dive shop, fishing and diving boats, sailboards, and a marina for those who wish to cruise in on their own boats. The caye is set up to provide excellent diving services for the most experienced divers. Prices (depending on the season) include use of the tennis and volleyball courts and Sunfish sailboats. Rooms are US$40-60 s, US$60-96 d; the beach house costs US$150-175. For a complete meal plan, add US$30 per person per day (the resort raises all of its own vegetables, will cook your catch, and provides barbecues if you choose to grill it yourself). Ask about good-value, all-inclusive dive packages.

ST. GEORGE'S CAYE

This small caye, nine miles from Belize City, is shaped something like a boomerang with its open ends facing the mainland. The caye is steeped in history and was the first capital of the British settlement (1650-1784). It is also the

TURTLE PENS TURNED SWIMMING POOLS

In the days when pirates roamed the high seas for months at a time, they had regular stopping places; islands with abundant supplies of water were probably the most important. St. George's Caye was a favorite spot to pick up giant sea turtles. The seamen built large square pens (called kraals) at the end of wooden docks and would keep the captured turtles here until they left for the bounding main. Several turtles were taken on board and fed, kept mostly on their backs and out of the way (they would live that way for a month or two), until they were slaughtered for their meat. Often, turtle was the only fresh meat the crews would eat for many months. No doubt animal-rights groups would have plenty to say about that today!

Over the years the pirates dwindled and St. George's Caye became the unofficial capital of Belize. Many more homes were built along the waterfront, and kraals became "crawls," swimming pens for people. Today many of the bright-white wooden houses still have the small "pools" at the end of their docks.

scene of the great sea battle between Spaniards and British settlers. Today the small cemetery gives evidence of St. George's heroic past.

St. George's Caye is far from commercialized—on the contrary, it's very quiet with mostly residential homes and their docks. However, two small resorts, **Cottage Colony** and **St. George's Lodge,** attract divers and people searching for total peace and relaxation near the sea. Both have great diving and snorkeling facilities.

Bela Carib is another commercial endeavor on the island. Karl, originally from Austria, has a workshop on the beach where he builds glass aquariums, collects tropical fish (which he breeds and exports), and now makes personalized St. George's T-shirts for the few tourists who stop by. Ask around and you'll find him; his sales room is about the size of a closet, with a few gift items for sale. Another small gift shop along the waterfront between Cottage Colony and St. George's Lodge has a small col-

lection of Belizean artwork and souvenirs. Hours are pretty sporadic, probably any time a client climbs up the stairs to the front door.

Accommodations
Cottage Colony is a marvelous little resort of small colonial-like white- and pastel-painted wooden cottages surrounding a large sandy courtyard with hammocks slung between shady palms (for a leisurely nap or a good read). The attractive second-floor dining room/bar overlooks the sea, has classy marine decor, and serves tasty food. The collection of individual cottages accommodates as many as 25 people. The suites have a sitting room, a kitchen, and a/c. The rooms are fan-cooled, simply but comfortably furnished, and have private bathrooms. The resort is 20 minutes from the **Bellevue Hotel** dock in Belize City. Both the Bellevue Hotel and the Cottage Colony are owned by the Dinger family, so it's easy to make a smooth trip/connection to Belize City and St. George's Caye. Cottage Colony has a good diving program with several boats capable of handling large dive groups. PADI certification classes are available. Room rates are about US$100 s/d. Ask about dive packages for about US$1000; fishing packages are about US$1400. You can make reservations at either the Bellevue Hotel, 5 S. Foreshore, Box 428, Belize City, Belize, C.A., tel. (2) 77051, fax (2) 73253, or at Cottage Colony, tel. (2) 12020.

At the southern end of the caye and less than a mile from the reef, visitors are invited to stay at the delightful **St. George's Lodge,** Box 625, Belize City, Belize, C.A., in the U.S. tel. (800) 678-6871/(813) 488-3953, in Belize tel. (2) 44190, fax (2) 31460. Divers are regulars here, but it's a quiet and relaxing spot for anyone who takes pleasure in the beauty of the sea, sky, and lovely surroundings. Don't expect a nightlife other than the good fellowship of other travelers, either in the comfortable bar/lounge or outdoors under the palms watching the stars over the sea. The main building consists of a lovely dining room, secluded sun deck, and bar—all made of beautiful Belizean hardwoods—and 10 lodge rooms with h/c water, private baths, fans, and 24-hour electricity. Six thatch cottages with the same amenities sit on a dock over the water. Electricity is provided by the lodge's own wind-

Cottage Colony is a relaxing spot between diving or snorkeling trips.

mills, and a solar-heated hot tub is always available for the guests. Good home cooking is provided—lots of fresh fish, fresh breads, and great lobster pizza.

Rooms are priced at daily package rates with meals and airport transfers, tanks, weights, and full diving privileges with boats and guides (two boat dives daily) included, varying by whether or not the guest is a diver. Lodge rooms cost about US$247-285 per person for divers, US$183-212 per person for nondivers; cottages cost about US$265-303 per person for divers, US$195-228 for nondivers. A 20% tax and service charge is additional.

SOUTH WATER CAYE

South Water Caye is another scenic, postcard-pretty, privately owned island 35 miles south/southeast of Belize City and 14 miles offshore from Dangriga. Carrie Bow Caye, where the Smithsonian Institution has a research station, is just a mile southeast.

Onshore are several lodging choices and a research operation. A British organization called **Coral Caye Conservation** has a group of volunteers with headquarters at South Water Caye studying how tourism affects the cayes and their environment. The volunteers (fewer than 30) are all divers and study the fish, sea grasses, algae, currents, and tides, and test seawater samples regularly looking for changes. Volun-

teers also investigate the culture of the people, lifestyle changes, and their boating activities.

Accommodations
Blue Marlin Lodge, Box 942, Belize City, Belize, C.A., in the U.S. tel. (800) 563-2354/

THE GRAY LADY

As in all good myths and legends, details are sketchy, but facts are usually delicious. It is said that Henry Morgan often roamed the waters of the Caribbean, frequently off the coast of Belize City. In his wanderings, Henry brought his lady-fair with him, a very independent miss. It's easy to imagine that lovers occasionally got testy living in such close quarters aboard a caravel. And though Henry and his lady-fair usually kissed and made up, one lightning-slashed night, just off the coast of St. George's Caye, they were unable to settle a nasty argument—something to do with the seaman standing watch the night before? He was the captain after all; his word was law! The lady ended up walking the plank into the stormy sea, gray gossamer gown whipping around her legs in the angry wind. Since that fateful night the lady in gray has been roaming the small caye of St. George trying to find her blackguard lover—they say. Don't scoff; some islanders will speak no ill of the Gray Lady, and on stormy nights they stay safely behind closed doors.

798-1558, in Belize tel. (5) 22243, fax (5) 22296, offers 15 double rooms and six cabañas just steps away from the sea. The domed cabañas have a/c, beautiful furniture, and immense bathrooms, phone service at the office, and well-kept grounds. All rooms come with h/c water, private bath, and electric fans; the bar/dining room over the sea serves meals, snacks (included), and drinks. Diving equipment, divemaster, fishing boats, and guides are available—and best of all South Water Caye is only 120 feet from the reef. Day-trips are available to Glover's Reef, the Blue Hole, and other wonderful nearby dive spots. Diving classes for certification are available.

Lodging prices are based on five-day or eight-day packages, all transfers and meals included. For diving, rates are about US$1095 s for five days, US$1400 s for eight days. This includes two day dives and one night dive from the boat and unlimited shore dives. For anglers a five-day vacation package is US$1350 s, and for eight days US$1950 s. A five-day vacation package is US$825 s and an eight-day package is US$1100 s. Rates are somewhat less per person for doubles and triples.

In addition to their mainland Pelican Beach Resort in Dangriga, Stann Creek District, the Raths family owns Belizean-style vacation homes on stilts on South Water Caye. Called **Osprey's Nest** and **Frangipani House,** they have great views of the ocean, each sleep six, and are fully furnished. You have no refrigeration here; cooling is by block ice in coolers. All lighting is solar. Cooking can be your own or you can hire a cook for an additional charge. Cost of the cottages is US$95/day. Call or write Pelican Beach Resort, Box 14, Dangriga, Stann Creek District, Belize, C.A., tel. (5) 22044, fax (5) 22570.

Nearby, you'll find **Leslie Cottages** (elevation three feet) right on the beach. Inland is an octagon-shaped marine lodge that can house groups of up to 15 and has bath and dining facilities. Each of the three cottages (one on the east side, two on the west side of the island) has a kitchen and private bathroom. There are two cabañas as well, which have no bathrooms; guests use the lodge. Kayaks, Sunfish sailboat, and Windsurfer are free for guests to use.

Accommodations are rented by the week and include meals and transfers from Dangriga Airstrip on the mainland to South Water Caye. Rates for lodge and cottages are US$725 per person per week for fewer than four people, US$675 per person for four or more. Rates for cabañas are US$575 per person per week. For more information contact International Zoological Expeditions, 210 Washington St., Sherborn, Massachusetts 01770, tel. (508) 655-1461, fax (508) 655-4445.

LESSER KNOWN CAYES

Scattered along the coast are a constellation of small (and not so small) cayes. You can make arrangements to visit well in advance or wing it, if you feel like taking a chance. Accommodations are limited.

BLUEFIELD RANGE

Accommodations

The Bluefield Range is a group of cayes a short distance south of Belize City. On one of the islands, 21 miles south of the city, is **Ricardo's Beach Huts and Lobster Camp,** the ultimate of funky. Originally two shacks on stilts built over a sand spit of shallow water leading out from a mangrove island, Ricardo's now is four very basic huts built on cleared land. A path has been built up and leads to the swimming and snorkeling beach on the west side of the island. Units face east, overlooking a lagoon surrounded by more mangrove islands. Some manatees live in the lagoon and you might see them at sunrise and sunset. Ricardo's father cooks fresh seafood and local dishes. Fish and snorkel the nearby reefs and cayes. That's where dinner comes from.

Ricardo and his father appreciate the conservation value of mangroves and have underbrushed just enough so guests can watch the birdlife of the area. It's one of the best anchorages for any weather (even a recent tropical wave with 30- to 40-knot winds caused nary a problem).

Expect camp-out conditions: outhouse, bucket shower, bugs. Bring mosquito coils, repellent, and a mosquito-net bed/tent. On the up side, this is one of the few chances to experience outer-island living just as it has been for the people who spend their lives fishing these waters. Ricardo's is "bloody ethnic with some really genuine people running it," observed a recent visitor.

A trip here is a package deal, a fish and lobster camp. Because the island has no bar, feel free to bring your favorite bottle; soft drinks and ice are provided. Bring your own fishing and snorkeling gear. For two people the rate is about US$150 per person; for five or more it drops to US$100. The price includes two nights and three days at Ricardo's, including accommodations, meals, and roundtrip boat transfers to and from Belize City. Visitors are picked up at the **Mira Rio Hotel,** 59 N. Front St., Belize City. For more information, contact Ricardo Castillo or Anna Lara, Box 55, Belize City, Belize, C.A., tel. (2) 44970.

CARRIE BOW CAYE

Just one mile from **South Water Caye** and two miles from **Twin Cayes** (where manatees play in the sea), **Smithsonian Marine Biology Institute Laboratory** welcomes visitors. Accommodations are simple. Trips to both nearby islands and other destinations can be arranged at the main building. Write or call for more information, Box 21, Dangriga, Belize, C.A., tel. (5) 22243, fax (5) 22296.

ENGLISH CAYE

Though this is just a small collection of palm trees, sand, and coral, an important lighthouse sits here at the entrance to the Belize City harbor from the Caribbean Sea. Large ships stop at English Caye to pick up one of the two pilots who navigate the 10 miles in and out of the busy harbor. Overnights are not allowed here but it's a pleasant day-trip location.

GOFF'S CAYE

Near English Caye, Goff's Caye is a favorite little island-stop for picnics and day-trips out of Caye Caulker and Belize City, thanks to a beautiful sandy beach and promising snorkeling areas. Sailboats often stop overnight; camping can be arranged from Caye Caulker by talking with any reputable guide. Bring your own tent and supplies. Goff's is a protected caye, so note the rules posted by the pier.

GALLOWS POINT CAYE

Accommodations
On its own island at the doorstep of the Belize Reef, **Gallows Point Resort** is only seven miles from Belize City. Here vacationers enjoy snorkeling, scuba diving, fishing, and glass-bottom boat trips. At the **Wave Hotel,** rates include three meals, room, reception at the airport, and transport to the island; they are US$87 s, US$120 d. Ask about **ElderHostel,** designed with people 50 and older in mind. Contact your travel agent for rates. For more information, write or call Gallows Point Resort, 9 Regent St. West, Belize City, Belize, C.A., tel. (2) 73054. **Note:** Boaters will find on the island **Weir Dow Marina,** a landlocked yacht anchorage with chandler and a shuttle service to Belize City.

LAUGHING BIRD CAYE

Another protected area, **Laughing Bird Caye National Park** is a popular day trip from Placencia. It's easy to see why. Swaying palms, small but beautiful beaches, an absence of biting bugs, shallow sandy swimming areas on the leeward side of the island, and interesting diving on the ocean side add up to a lot of pleasure in a relatively small package.

This particular kind of caye is referred to as a *faro* island, and the arms on each end make a kind of enclosure around a lagoon area on the leeward side. In this way the island acts much like a mini-atoll. That's good news for those wishing to dive the eastern side of the island. You'll find a lot of elkhorn coral and fish life.

Grunts, damselfish, parrot fish, houndfish, bonefish, and even rays and nurse sharks are to be found here.

MONTEGO CAYE

Not much is on this small caye 10 miles from Belize City besides the **lobster camp** of Luis Rosado, in the U.S. tel. (415) 584-9384, in Belize (2) 33029, and **Mangrove Manor,** a rustic educational center operated by his wife, Wendy Berkelman, a U.C. Berkeley graduate. She provides small children's groups a different kind of educational experience. Activities revolve around observing marine life or participating in the lobster fishery. Campouts can be arranged at nearby **Hicks Caye.** For those who would like to come and hang out that's okay, too.

Accommodations are in small clapboard buildings or tents. Your food is prepared over an open fire, and you eat in the main house. It's heavy on local flavor as well as local seafood—especially lobster, in season. You pay a small maintenance fee if you use equipment to catch your own dinner. Rates are US$25 per person. But bring your own food and the rate drops to US$10 per person.

SPANISH LOOKOUT CAYE

Accommodations

When you approach the **Spanish Bay Resort** from the sea on a sunny day, the simple white cabañas built over the blue-green water are quite spectacular. It's on Spanish Lookout Caye, 10 miles east-southeast of Belize City, about a 30-minute boat ride. Five cabañas with 10 rooms, hot showers, and private baths are connected to the island by a dock. The rooms are furnished with two double beds, and a circular bar/dining room overlooks the sea. Power is solar, with backup generators. Diving is one of the favorite activities here with a PADI divemaster and instructor on-staff. A number of boats, including the 57-foot live-aboard *Reef Maiden,* are available for divers and snorkelers to get to and from the nearby reefs. The resort is only one mile west of the main barrier reef and about eight miles west of central Turneffe Island. Most dives are done in front of Shag Caye to Rendezvous Caye. The resort offers weeklong packages that include seven nights, all meals, airport transfers, two day-trips with lunch on neighboring cayes, hotel tax, and 12 dives for dive-package guests. Nightlife is good conversation, though in late afternoon guests enjoy climbing up to the **Crow's Nest** to watch the sinking sun—if you stay long enough you'll see nature's sparkling light show in the sky. A three-night package for nondivers is US$341 per person d, US$479 for divers, US$395 for snorkelers, with many other options. For more information, write or call Box 35, Belize City, Belize, C.A., in the U.S. tel. (800) 359-0747, in Belize (2) 77288/72725, fax (2) 72797. The departure point for Spanish Bay Resort is from N. Front St., Belize City.

AND MANY MORE CAYES

A myriad of other little-known cayes have names such as **Baker's Rendezvous, Deer, Drowned, Frenchman's, Hunting, Little Peter, Long, Middle Long, Negro, Pajaros, Paunch, Ramsey's, Rider's, Romero, Rosario, Sapodilla, Simmonds, Spanish, Swallo,** and **Tostado.**

While some of the tinier cayes, which were around in days long gone, have been washed or blown away by hurricanes and other natural forces over the years, new mangrove-bits and sandy cayes are forming all the time. And there are still plenty of others that are hundreds of years old. If some of this latter group could only speak, they'd probably have exciting stories to tell—tales of ancient Maya ceremonies, of battles won, treasure lost, and the shenanigans of rip-roaring pirates.

THE ATOLLS
INTRODUCTION

The atolls are startlingly beautiful when approached by sea or air. Like necklaces of coral, the islands and reefs surrounding the lagoons create large areas of protected waters. Boating, diving, fishing, sailing, and windsurfing in these areas is exhilarating. The islands vary from palm-covered spits of sand to lush mangrove cayes. Most of the islands have mangroves; it is best to come prepared with plenty of bug repellent containing at least 30% DEET. Citronella seems to work well, too. The mosquitoes are sometimes fierce.

Dolphin sightings are common in the atolls as well as around the cayes of Belize. Often dolphins in a playful mood will catch a ride on the bow wave of boats. The power and grace of the animals are remarkable. Other times, divers may see them underwater. Usually, dolphins make a pass or two and go about their business. Sometimes they pay no attention at all; other times they approach closely. It all depends on the time of day, their mood, and the presence of young. It's okay to touch them if the animals approach closely; dolphins enjoy the stroke of a hand. Do not, however, grab the dorsal fin or impede the animal in the water. These creatures are immensely strong and occasionally respond aggressively to rough treatment or what they perceive to be threats.

DIVING AROUND THE ATOLLS

Live-Aboard Dive Boats
Several excellent live-aboard vessels based in Belize City take their guests to Lighthouse Reef and Turneffe Islands atolls. These boats are designed for scuba divers, but can also accommodate an avid diver's companion if he or she is a sea lover and/or a casual angler. Nondivers pay less, too. Your hotel and chef travel with you to some of the most scenic spots in the tropical world. Tariff includes all meals, diving, fishing, cruising, guides, and equipment. Alcohol

DIVERS, MIND YOUR MANNERS

Unfortunately, many divers **and some dive-masters** do not show proper etiquette when dealing with undersea life. Instead, they want to grab hold and ride any creature large enough. While many divers take great pride in such macho/macha behavior, it should be noted that swimmers have been injured by dolphins in Belizean waters, at least one seriously (the diver sustained a concussion, broken ribs, and internal injuries). After the incident in question, a marine biologist observed what was possibly the same dolphin interacting with people and exhibiting occasional rough play. Divers were also observed trying to grab or ride it. It has been conjectured that this boorish pulling and tugging on the dolphin has led to correspondingly rougher behavior by the dolphin. Who can blame it?

and tips are extra. (See the chart "Live-Aboard Dive Boats.")

In the luxury category and accommodating 14-18 people, the **Aggressor II** (soon to be replaced by **Aggressor III**) offers carpeted, a/c staterooms with single and double berths, hot water, a desalination water maker, self-service bar, stereo, and VCR, as well as a spacious dining room for buffets and barbecues on the sundeck, and plenty of good food.

Divers enjoy unlimited diving (twin compressors for an unlimited air supply, tank, backpack, weightbelt, and weights are provided). A personal dive locker is available right on the dive deck with a wide dive platform plus two ladders. Camera buffs will find a complete video and photo center with daily E-6 processing (camera rentals available). You'll also find certification courses, photo and wildlife seminars, and lots of TLC, including airport transfers. Live the good life from Saturday to Saturday. For more information, contact Aggressor Fleet Limited, P.O. Drawer K, Morgan City, Louisiana 70381, tel. (800) 348-2628, fax (504) 384-0817. Rates for a one-week diving vacation are US$1395 per person based on double occupancy.

Equally famous as the Agressor Fleet, **Peter Hughes Diving,** tel. (800) 932-6237, (305) 669-9391, has a fleet of top-end dive boats. The **Belize Wave Dancer,** which goes to Turneffe Islands, Lighthouse, and Glover's Reef, is no exception. The boat accommodates 20 guests on a dive adventure they will not soon forget. Guests have a choice of five dives per day on two separate sites; one of these is a night dive. Dive instruction is available including advanced certifications. The 120-foot *Wave Dancer* has E-6 processing and video center onboard. In addition, it has a sun deck, outside bar, and freshwater showers on the stern to rinse off body and soul when boarding the boat. All cabins have a private head and shower.

Dive trips are available from a few other live-aboards that cruise these waters, including **M/V Hot Dive,** tel. (800) 468-3483; the 60-foot boat has an onboard compressor.

TURNEFFE ISLANDS ATOLL

The islands are mostly small dots of sand, mangrove clusters, and swampy land, though **Blackbird Caye** and **Douglas Caye** are quite large. With the preponderance of mangroves and coconut palms, many cayes are home only to sea and wading birds, ospreys, manatees, and crocodiles; a few support small colonies of fishermen and divers.

This atoll is a great fishing destination, just 25 miles east of Belize City. If you're into bonefish and permit, miles of crystal "flats" are alive with the hard-fighting fish. Tarpon are abundant late March-June within the protected creeks and channels throughout the islands. Those who seek larger trophies will find a grand choice of marlin, sailfish, wahoo, groupers, blackfin tuna, and many more. Check with fishing guides in Belize City or Ambergris Caye, or the resorts listed below under "Accommodations."

DIVING

Divers will find different dive spots every day and any type of diving they want—wall dives, shallows for photography, fish life, creek dives, coral heads, or drift dives. At the northern end of the atoll, divers especially enjoy the walls

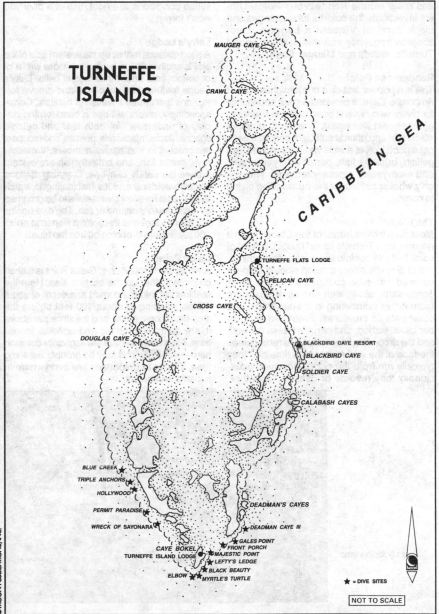

TURNEFFE ISLANDS

MAUGER CAYE

CRAWL CAYE

CARIBBEAN SEA

• TURNEFFE FLATS LODGE

PELICAN CAYE

CROSS CAYE

DOUGLAS CAYE

• BLACKBIRD CAYE RESORT

BLACKBIRD CAYE

SOLDIER CAYE

CALABASH CAYES

BLUE CREEK ★
TRIPLE ANCHORS ★
HOLLYWOOD ★
PERMIT PARADISE ★
WRECK OF SAYONARA ★

DEADMAN'S CAYES

★ DEADMAN CAYE III

★ GALES POINT
★ FRONT PORCH
CAYE BOKEL ● ★ MAJESTIC POINT
TURNEFFE ISLAND LODGE ★ LEFTY'S LEDGE
★ BLACK BEAUTY
ELBOW ★ ★ MYRTLE'S TURTLE

★ = DIVE SITES

NOT TO SCALE

© MOON PUBLICATIONS, INC.

and reefs around **Rendezvous Point.** Others investigate the colorful tube sponges and black coral at **Vincent's Lagoon.** Liveaboards frequently visit this northern end of Turneffe Islands and **Mauger Caye.**

Rendezvous Point

This is a popular first-dive of overnighters out of Ambergris Caye. It provides a great opportunity for divers who haven't been under in a while to get their feet wet again. The depth is about 40-50 feet and affords sufficient bottom time to get a good look at a wide variety of reef life. Angelfish, butterfly fish, parrot fish, yellowtails, and morays are represented well. This will only whet appetites for the outstanding diving to come.

The Elbow

Most divers have heard of the Elbow (just 10 minutes from Turneffe Island Lodge), a point of coral that juts out into the ocean. This now-famous dive site offers a steep sloping drop-off covered with tube sponges and deep-water gorgonians, along with shoals of snappers (sometimes numbering in the hundreds) and other pelagic creatures. Predators such as bar jacks, wahoo, and permits cruise the reef, and the drop-off is impressive. Currents sweep the face of the wall most of the time and they typically run from the north. However, occasionally they reverse or cease all together.

When conditions are right, this is a dive you won't forget.

Lefty's Ledge

A short distance farther up the eastern side of the atoll is another dive to excite even those with a lot of bottom time under their weight belts. Lefty's Ledge features dramatic spur-and-groove formations that create a wealth of habitats. Correspondingly, divers will see a head-turning display of undersea life, both reef and pelagic species. Jacks, mackerels, permits, and groupers are present in impressive numbers. Wrasses, rays, parrot fish, and butterfly fish are evident around the sandy canyons. Cleaning stations are also evident, and it's fascinating to watch large predators allow themselves to be groomed by small cleaner shrimp or fish. The dive begins at about 50 feet and the bottom slopes to about 100 feet before dropping off into the blue.

Gales Point

Another "don't-miss" dive, Gales Point is a short distance farther up the eastern side. Here the reef juts out into the current at a depth of about 45 feet, sloping to about 100 feet before the drop-off. Along the wall, and the slope just above it, are numerous ledges and cavelike formations. Rays and groupers are especially common here—some say this may be grouper breeding area. Corals and sponges are everywhere in numerous varieties.

ready for lounging

Sayonara

On the leeward or eastern side of the atoll the wreck of the *Sayonara,* a tender sunk by Dave Bennett of Turneffe Islands Lodge, lies in about 30 feet of water. Close by is a sloping ledge with interesting tunnels and spur-and-groove formations. Healthy numbers of reef fish play among the coral, and some barracudas tag along. Large schools of permits are often drawn down by divers' bubbles. They give a marvelous three-dimensional quality to the dive as you see them spiraling down from the surface like a squadron of fighter planes.

Hollywood

A bit farther up the atoll, Hollywood offers divers a relatively shallow dive (30-40 feet) with moderate visibility unless the currents have reversed. Here you'll find lots of basket and tube sponges and lush coral growth. Many angelfish, parrot fish, grunts, and snappers swim here. So, although not as dramatic as an eastern side dive, Hollywood has plenty to see.

ACCOMMODATIONS

While limited in number, accommodations fall neatly into three categories: one that appeals primarily to divers but can easily accommodate anglers or beach bums, another for those who would like to participate in an ongoing research project, and a third for avid fishermen.

The motto of guests at the friendly **Turneffe Island Lodge** could well be captured in the words written on the first sign a new arrival sees, "We're not here for a long time, just a good time!" How true. And that's what's in store for up to 16 guests on Little Caye Bokel, 12 acres of beautiful palm-lined beachfront and mangroves. It's a popular location for divers, anglers, and those who just want to swing in a hammock under the palms.

At the southern tip of the atoll, the resort is a short distance north of its larger relative, Big Caye Bokel. This strategic location offers enthusiasts a wide range of underwater experiences within minutes of nearly 200 dive sites. Shallow areas are perfect for photography or snorkeling; you can see nurse sharks, rays, reef fish, and dolphins in the flats a few hundred yards from the dock. All the dives mentioned earlier and many more lie within 15 minutes by boat. The dive operation run by Kevin is first rate, and advanced instruction and equipment rentals are available. This would be an excellent place to get that underwater photography certification.

One diver we met had been on a 14-day visit, had dived three different sites each day (never repeating one of them), and had half an hour of underwater video of dolphins. He yawned at every diving tale he heard. Rather ostentatious, actually!

Anglers have a choice of fishing for snappers, permit, jacks, mackerel, and billfish off the drop-offs. They can stalk the near-record numbers of snook, bonefish, and tarpon in the flats and mangroves. George, the fishing guide, has an uncanny way of knowing where the fish will be.

The lodge is fish-camp comfortable. The friendly ease about the place, fostered by owners Dave and Jill Bennett, makes even shy guests feel at home. Rooms are next to the sea, have h/c water, private baths, and 24-hour electricity. The main lodge boasts a small bar with wood deck overlooking the grounds, a spacious pine-paneled dining room that serves tasty meals in ample quantities, and a comfy lounge with TV, VCR, and ample reading material. The lodge also has a gift shop and evening activities so the guests won't get bored on their desert island. A one-week package includes meals, sports facilities, and transfers from Belize International Airport, with emphasis on either diving or fishing. The dive package is about US$1300 per person per week; the fishing package is about US$1600 per person per week. For more information and reservations, write or call Box 480, Belize City, Belize, C.A., in Belize fax (2) 30276, in the U.S. contact 11904 Hidden Hills Dr., Jacksonville, Florida 32225, tel. (800) 338-8149, (904) 641-4468.

On the eastern side of Turneffe Islands lies **Blackbird Caye Resort,** 4,000 acres of a planned, environmentally responsible resort. At present, it offers 10 thatch cabañas, with coldwater showers, private baths, and single and double beds. **Note:** For several months of the year, Blackbird Resort exclusively caters **Oceanic Society Expeditions** to the fondly nicknamed **Dol-**

phin Embassy on Blackbird Caye. A favorite of the Oceanic Society, the Dolphin Embassy is a modern research center created to study communications between humans and dolphins. A resident researcher takes groups out to spot and count dolphins, and sometimes to swim with them. Plan on a 1.5-hour boat ride from Belize City. The reef is a stone's throw from the resort beach; prepare to snorkel in an untouched area. Seven-day packages start at US$1100 per person and go up to US$1350 per person (diving); US$1550 per person (fishing); US$1450 per person (combination). Packages (land only) begin with your pickup at the Belize International Airport and include all meals; no alcoholic drinks are available on the island—feel free to bring your own. For information and reservations, write or call 1415 Louisiana St., Suite 3100, Houston, Texas 77002, tel. (713) 658-1142. For prices and information about the Oceanic Society Expeditions to Blackbird Caye, call (800) 326-7491.

For vacationing folks who want to concentrate on just a few things—fishing, fishing, or fishing—**Turneffe Flats Lodge,** Box 36, Deadwood, South Dakota 57732, tel. (800) 815-1304/(605) 578-7540, fax (605) 578-7540, is the place to go. Flats fishing for bonefish, tarpon, snook, and permit have put the resort on the map with fly fishermen. A fleet of boats and guides is available or anglers can wade. Larger boats venture out for reef fish, including snappers, wahoo, and groupers. Blue-water fishing for tuna and billfish is also available. Fishing packages, including all transfers, shared guide and boat, meals, and lodging, are US$1795.

Guests who want to dive or mix diving with fishing will have ample opportunity to indulge. Seven-day dive packages, including three dives per day and a trip to Lighthouse Reef, go for US$1295. Mixed fishing and diving costs US$1795.

The resort features tidy raised wooden structures along the beach with h/c water and private bath. Meals are served on a pleasant breezy deck just off the lodge building.

LIGHTHOUSE REEF ATOLL

ORIENTATION

The most easterly of Belize's three atolls, Lighthouse Reef lies 50 miles southeast of Belize City. The 30-mile-long, eight-mile-wide lagoon is the location of the **Blue Hole,** a favorite destination for divers that was made famous by Jacques Cousteau, and a favorite destination of dive boats from Belize City, Ambergris Caye, and Caye Caulker. The best dive spots, however, are along the walls of **Half Moon Caye** and **Long Caye,** where the diving rivals that of any in the world.

Think of the atoll as a large spatula with a short handle and a long blade. At the northern tip of the spatula blade, **Sandbore Caye** is home to a rusty lighthouse and a few fishing shacks. It is also the favorite anchorage of several of the dive boats doing overnight stops, including *Reef Roamer II.*

Big Northern Caye, across a narrow strait, is the location of **Lighthouse Reef Resort.** A landing strip just behind the resort is a con-

venient means of entry for resort guests and divers who wish to make only a day-trip without the long water crossing going and coming, which eats up most of the day. Here are long stretches of beach to walk, beautiful vistas, and large areas of mangroves and lagoons, home to snowy egrets and crocodiles.

Halfway down the spatula-shaped atoll, about where the blade meets the handle, lies the magnificent Blue Hole, a formation best appreciated from the air, but impressive from the bridge of a boat.

At the elbow of the handle, and looking like some kind of Gilligan's Island, is Half Moon Caye with its lighthouse, bird sanctuary, shipwrecks, and incredible diving offshore.

Finally, on the imaginary handle we come upon Long Caye, a lonely outpost with a small dock, large palms, and glassy water.

Some anglers and beach bums do come to Lighthouse, but the lure of diving attracts most visitors. And at Lighthouse Reef, they are not disappointed.

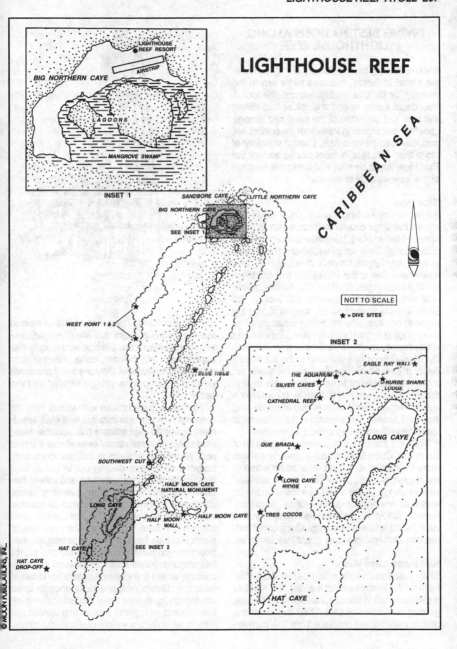

LIGHTHOUSE REEF

INSET 1

LIGHTHOUSE REEF RESORT

BIG NORTHERN CAYE

AIRSTRIP

LAGOONS

MANGROVE SWAMP

CARIBBEAN SEA

SANDBORE CAYE
LITTLE NORTHERN CAYE
BIG NORTHERN CAYE
SEE INSET 1

NOT TO SCALE
★ = DIVE SITES

WEST POINT 1 & 2

BLUE HOLE

INSET 2

SOUTHWEST CUT

HALF MOON CAYE
NATURAL MONUMENT

LONG CAYE

HALF MOON
WALL
HALF MOON CAYE

HAT CAYE

SEE INSET 2

HAT CAYE
DROP-OFF ★

EAGLE RAY WALL ★

THE AQUARIUM ★
SILVER CAVES ★
CATHEDRAL REEF ★

NURSE SHARK
LODGE

QUE BRADA ★

LONG CAYE

LONG CAYE
RIDGE ★

TRES COCOS ★

HAT CAYE

© MOON PUBLICATIONS, INC.

DIVING DESTINATIONS ALONG LIGHTHOUSE REEF

If you're looking for spectacular diving, Belize is the place. In Belize, this area rivals any in the country, or for that matter, around the world. You could easily spend a week or two diving this atoll and never tire of the coral and sponge growths, the amazing variety of invertebrates, and reef and pelagic fish. Expect visibility of more than 100 feet in most places except the Blue Hole (it can be silty) and the upper reaches of the leeward side of the atoll.

Blue Hole

If flying over the offshore coast, you'll easily recognize this large circular formation with its magnificent blue-to-black hues surrounded by neon blue. Though there are other, smaller, blue holes around Ambergris Caye, Caye Caulker, and elsewhere, this is the Blue Hole to beat them all. The submerged shaft is a karst-eroded sinkhole with depths that exceed 400 feet. In the early '70s Cousteau and his crew explored the tunnels, caverns, and the listing stalactites that were angled by past earthquakes. This twilight world has suspended sediment and little fish life. Most dive groups descend to the caves at a depth of about 135 feet. Technically, this is not a dive for novices or even intermediate divers, though thousands have done it. It requires a rapid descent, a very short period at depth, and a careful ascent. For a group of 10 or more, at least three divemasters should be present.

From the standpoint of undersea life, the lip of the crater, down to about 60-80 feet, is a much more interesting dive. Be prepared for some of the largest midnight parrot fish you will see anywhere. Stingrays are also to be found in sandy areas, as are feather duster worms. Angelfish, butterfly fish, and small reef fish cluster around coral heads and outcroppings. Occasional barracudas and small groupers guard their territories.

Half Moon Caye Wall

They just don't come much better than this. Here on the eastern side of the atoll, the reef has a shallow shelf in about 15 feet of water where garden eels are plentiful. Their heads and a part of their bodies protrude from the burrows

lighthouse

that protect them. They look to the untrained eye like blades of grass, but when you get closer to get a better look, the shy eels quickly disappear back into their tiny holes. Interesting to watch from a distance, they are but a precursor to what is in store as you go deeper into the water.

The sandy area broken with corals extends downward till you run into the reef wall, which rises some 20 feet toward the surface. Most boats anchor in the sandy area above the reef wall. Numerous fissures in the reef crest form canyons or tunnels leading out to the vertical face. In this area sandy shelves and valleys frequently harbor nurse sharks and gigantic stingrays. Feather duster worms of various types, sea anemones, shrimps, crabs, and starfish live here. All the reef fish you like to photograph are here: angelfish, damselfish, surgeonfish, triggerfish, butterfly fish, and parrot fish abound. You'll also see several cleaning stations, where tiny wrasses or shrimp rid fish of parasites. Divers who are lucky enough to be staying at Lighthouse Reef Resort or diving off live-aboards with photo processing aboard are sure to return with a wealth of wonderful slides.

Cruise through one of the canyons and experience the sight of the reef falling vertically out of sight on a drop of a thousand feet and more. The wall here is simply spectacular with overhangs, caves, a riot of sponges, and coral growths of every kind. Gorgonians and sea fans grow everywhere. The eye hardly knows where to settle. Schools of the tiniest fish hover like gnats in protected crevices. Sea turtles, barracuda, lobsters, and morays are evident, along with the larger pelagics—jacks, wahoos, and groupers of various species. Occasionally, you'll see eagle rays and mantas. This is a site you could dive many times without boredom, if there weren't so many other good areas to see.

Tres Cocos

On the western wall, "Three Coconuts" refers to trees on nearby Long Caye. But you'll hardly notice land. Your eyes will be focused on the neon shades of blue beneath your boat—lighter shades signifying shallower water with sand bottom, darker indicating coral growth, indigo signifying the deep. The sandy bottom slopes from about 30 feet to about 40 feet deep before it plunges downward. Overhangs here are common features, and sponges and soft corals adorn the walls. Another fish lover's paradise, Tres Cocos does not have the outstanding coral formations you'll see at several other dives in the area, but who cares; there's a rainbow of marine life all about. Turtles, morays, jacks, coral, shrimp, cowfish, rays, and angelfish are among the actors on this colorful stage.

Silver Caves

The shoals of silversides (small gleaming minnows) that gave this western atoll site its name are gone. But Silver Caves is still impressive and enjoyable. The coral formations are riddled with large crevices and caves that cut clear through the reef.

As you enter the water above the sandy slope where most boats anchor, you'll be in about 30 feet of water and surrounded by friendly yellowtail snappers. Once again you'll see the downwardly sloping bottom, the rising reef crest, and the stomach-flipping drop into the blue.

The crevices and sandy canyons provide ample habitat for a panoply of undersea life.

Expect to see nurse sharks, gigantic stingrays, file fish, angelfish, morays, parrot fish, wrasses, and a multitude of small reef fish hovering around the reef crest, above, and slightly below. Cleaning stations are evident here, too. You'll find feather dusters, sea fans, sea cucumbers, and starfish (including occasional basket stars).

Off the face of the reef, you'll see mackerel, jacks, barracuda, sea turtles, eagle rays, and large groupers. Barrel, tube, and vase sponges abound.

West Point

Farther north and about even with the Blue Hole, West Point is well worth a dive. Visibility may be a bit more limited (60-80 feet) than down south, but it's still very acceptable. The reef face here is stepped. The first drop plunges from about 30 feet to well over 100 feet deep. Another coral and sand slope at that depth extends a short distance before dropping vertically into very deep water. The first and shallow wall has pronounced overhangs and lush coral and sponge growth. Divers are likely to encounter triggerfish, morays, parrot fish, file fish, wrasses, and angelfish in abundance. Garden eels and rays inhabit the shallow sandy slope.

HALF MOON CAYE

As you approach Half Moon Caye you'll believe you have arrived at some South Sea paradise. Offshore, boaters use the rusted hull of a wreck, once known as the *Elksund*, as a landmark in these waters. Its dark hulk looms over the surreal blue and black of the reef world. The caye, eight feet above sea level, was formed by the accretion of coral bits, shells, and calcareous algae. It's divided into two ecosystems. The section on the western side has dense vegetation with rich fertile soil. The eastern section primarily supports coconut palms and little other vegetation.

Besides boasting offshore waters that are among the clearest in Belize, the caye's beaches are also Robinson Crusoe wonderful. You must climb the eight-foot-high central ridge that divides the island and gaze south before you see the striking half-moon beach with its unrelenting surf erupting against limestone rocks.

Half Moon Caye's first lighthouse, built in 1820, sits on the eastern side of the caye. Another was built in 1848 and modernized and enlarged in 1931; today the lighthouse has entered the age of high technology with solar power.

Half Moon Caye Natural Monument

Dedicated as a monument in 1982, the crescent-shaped island was the first reserve created within the new climate of protecting Belize's natural beauty. The caye, at the southeast corner of Lighthouse Reef, measures 45 square acres.

Flora and Fauna

The variety of vegetation is not large, but you will see the **ziricote** forest, the **red-barked gumbo-limbo, ficus fig, coconut palms,** and the **spider-lily plant.**

The endangered **red-footed boobies** are the principal inhabitant of Half Moon Caye and the main reason for its status as a monument. Ninety-eight percent of the 4,000 adult breeding birds on the caye are a very rare white. Naturalists must travel to an island near Tobago in the West Indies to find a similar booby colony; most adult red-footed boobies are dull brown. Along with the boobies, 98 other species of birds have been recorded on the caye and include the **magnificent frigate, white-crowned pigeons, mangrove warblers,** and **ospreys.** A couple of varieties of iguana skitter through the underbrush, and in the summer **hawksbill** and **loggerhead turtles** return by instinct to lay their eggs on the beaches.

The Tower

Everyone should go to the observation tower provided by the Audubon Society in the ziricote forest and climb above the forest canopy for an unbelievable view. Every tree is covered with perched booby birds in some stage of growth. In the right season you'll have a close-up view of nests while feathered parents tend their hatchlings. The air is filled with boobies coming and going, attempting to make their usually clumsy landings (those webbed feet weren't designed for landing in trees). Visitors have a wonderful opportunity to see the myriad inhabitants of the caye. Thieving magnificent frigates swoop by while iguanas crawl around in the branches, both always mindful of an opportunity to swipe a few eggs left unguarded.

Camping

Guests must register at the park warden's office near the lighthouse. You'll be directed to maps, camping and sanitation facilities, and given other general information about the caye. The biggest concern is the preservation of Half Moon Caye and its plants and animals. Please observe the rules of the house: bring your own water (island water is very scarce); no pets allowed; when camping use only designated sites and firepits; stay on trails to avoid damage to fragile plantlife and to avoid disturbing nesting birds; no hunting or fishing; carry everything out with you; don't litter; and, finally, do not collect *anything*—eggs, coral, shells, fish, plants—even sand!

Getting There

If you go by boat, expect to spend a couple of hours or more getting to Half Moon Caye from Belize City, depending on the sea conditions. On occasion, the sea can be rough, and not all small-boat captains will leave the protected waters inside the barrier reef. Besides, on rough days divers will find poor underwater visibility at the atoll anyway. These conditions, especially the ones fed by strong northerlies in winter, seldom last more than a few days at a time.

Only chartered or privately owned boats and seaplanes travel to Half Moon Caye Monument; so far no regular public transportation is available. An option would be to take an inexpensive water taxi from Belize City to Ambergris or Caye Caulker and take one of the Reef Roamers out to Half Moon Caye (US$40 one-way, US$80 roundtrip) the next day. You could catch a ride back with the same outfit the following week. All of this would have to be worked out in advance. Check with **Out Island Divers,** tel. (26) 2151, on Ambergris Caye. Or you could check with **Belize Audubon Society,** (2) 34987, in Belize City for other suggestions.

Bringing in Your Own Vessel or Plane

Note: People traveling to Belize on their own vessels must clear with the authorities before entering Belizean waters. Check with the Belize Embassy in Washington, D.C., tel. (202) 332-9636, fax (202) 332-6741.

On the leeward side of Half Moon Caye, sailors will find a dock with a pierhead depth of about six feet. Large ships must anchor in designated

boating along
the atolls

areas *only*. This will help to protect the reef from further (irreversible) damage such as that caused by large anchors in the past. Amphibious planes are welcome to land here.

NORTHERN TWO CAYE

When people talk about the fantastic sunrises and sunsets out here, believe them. Long walks on the shore, swims in the shallow waters offshore, and fantastic diving/snorkeling are hallmarks of Northern Two Caye and the **Lighthouse Reef Resort,** tel. (800) 423-3114. The island covers 1,200 acres, though almost half is mangrove lagoon with resident bonefish, crocodiles, and birdlife. Sandbore Caye lies a short distance away.

On shore, the resort offers 16 acres of tropical beauty, and nature has provided wonderful, long alluring beaches, swaying palms, and a variety of bird and reptilian life. Accommodations are in villas or duplex cabaña-like rooms. The three villas (one two-bedroom with kitchen, and two with one bedroom for two people) are colonial-style architecture with solid wooden roofs, facing the sea and the northeasterly trade winds. They have wallpapered walls, Persian rugs, "antique-type" furnishings, baths and showers, h/c water, a/c, space for diving equipment, an immeasurable supply of fresh water from four wells, and a dining room/bar where family-style meals can be served. The cabaña rooms have mahogany interior ac-

cents, Mexican-tile floors, h/c water, private baths, a/c, and modern interior decoration.

Diving, snorkeling, and fishing (bonefishing and deep-sea game fishing) are unsurpassed. Divers must have certification cards with them and should bring their own gear as rental equipment is limited. Slide processing is available. You're likely to spot dolphins nearby. It's possible to come into close contact with them. Remember: treat them with respect—if in doubt, ask the dive guide what to keep in mind. Anglers usually bring their own gear, too. Consult with the resort for further information.

The one-week package price is US$1200 per person, double occupancy; the nondive package is US$900 per person; the fishing package is US$1600 per person. Special fishing/diving packages cost US$1400. Rates include three meals, snacks, three dives daily, guide, and boat.

Getting There

You can arrange air transportation from Belize International Airport to Northern Two Caye by way of **Tropic Air** or charter. For more information and reservations, write or call Box 1435, Dundee, Florida 33838, tel. (800) 423-3114, (813) 439-6660, in Belize tel. (2) 31205.

If you want to go by boat, hitch a ride with one of the *Reef Roamers* (US$40 one-way, US$80 roundtrip) owned by **Out Island Divers,** tel. (26) 2151, on Ambergris Caye. You could catch a ride back with the same outfit the following week. Just remember, it all depends on the weather.

GLOVER'S REEF ATOLL

Seventy miles (a five-hour boat trip) southeast of Belize City brings you to **Glover's Reef,** a dream-come-true of island fantasy—white sand, blue sea, and coconut palms with a fringe of white water breaking over the nearby reef. It was named for pirate John Glover, who, in his own swashbuckling manner, also loved this offshore reef. The atoll is a circular necklace of almost continuous coral reef around an 80-square-mile lagoon with depths to 50 feet; the various colors of blue in the water are so intense they seem phony. Within the lagoon divers will find 700 shallow coral patches. And for the adventurer looking for sunken ships, the sea on the north and northeastern sides of the reef embraces the bones of at least four ships. This is a favorite destination for boaters large and small, including live-aboard dive boats that come from the U.S. and Belize City.

Anglers will have a chance at bonefish and permit, as well as the big trophies, including sailfish, marlin, wahoo, snapper, and grouper.

Diving
Glover's Reef is rightly known for the abundance of its marine life, especially turtles, manta rays, and whale sharks. Corals and sponges of many types crowd the walls and reeftops. The names of dive sites such as **Shark Point, Grouper Flats, Emerald Forest Reef, Octopus Alley, Manta Reef, Dolphin Dance,** and **Turtle Tavern** conjure visions of what lies in store. Because of the Caribbean swells, most of the frequently dived locations lie in the southern parts of the atoll.

Northeast Caye Base Camp
Slickrock Adventures leads sea-kayaking trips to Glover's Reef December through April. This is a nine-day adventure for those interested in doing some serious or casual ocean kayaking, windsurfing, beach bumming, snorkeling, fishing, and scuba. Extensions inland as far away as the Cayo District and Tikal in Guatemala are also offered. One look at the brochure and video and even those who didn't previously have the slightest interest are often sold. The cabins here are simple but comfortable, meals include lots of fresh fish (how

does poached grouper in horseradish sauce sound?), and kayakers can easily explore other cayes. The trips are run by seasoned outfitters and the rate for a nine-day package is US$1350 per person. For information, write or call Box 1400, Moab, Utah 84532, tel./fax (801) 259-6996.

Accommodations
Manta Resort, tel. (2) 31895, in the U.S. tel. (800) 342-0053, fax (813) 594-5613, which lies on Southwest Caye on the southern tip of Glover's Reef, is a 13-acre speck of sand that is pure, simple pleasure. Available arrangements for fishing and diving include equipment and scuba instruction. Each of the cabañas has a private bath, warm-water showers, and daily maid service. Each mahogany cabaña has a private porch, a hammock close by, and is cooled by the trade winds. The rooms are simple but comfortable. A spacious restaurant/bar is built on a pier that extends over the water under a thatch roof. Fortunately, the owner *loves* good food; the guests have it good here. Homemade chocolate-chip cookies are favorites! Expect great salsas and sauces, maybe even the "five-alarm garlic hot sauce"—a remarkable potion. When you're sitting around in the late evening, ask the staff about the ghosts that still wander the cayes off the Belize coast—tingling stories for late at night. Only eight-day, seven-night packages are available; the diving package (high season) is US$1600 s, US$1195 per person double occupancy, US$1150 per person triple occupancy; the seven-night fishing package is US$1595 per person double occupancy. Ask about prices for nondivers and nonfishermen. These prices are all-inclusive from the moment you land in Belize City (airfare to Belize City not included). Actually, you are welcome to spend as much time at Manta Resort as you wish, but unless you travel on a Saturday, you must take a marine charter (ask at the resort). It is a 57-mile, two-and-a-half-hour ride to Manta Resort. For more information contact the resort.

Glover's Reef now has a few more options for accommodations. One of these, **Glover's Atoll Resort,** Box 563, Glover's Reef, Belize

City, Belize, C.A., tel. (5) 23048, is right on top of Long Caye, a striking reef surrounded by crystalline water. It's especially popular with the independent backpacker, adventurer, and anyone who's looking for a budget paradise and enjoys camping. The members of the Lamont family are born hosts and invite all to come and experience their lifestyle of 24 years. They also have one of the most eccentric, in-depth, and interesting newsletters around—get on the mailing list.

Guests have a choice of camping or of a simple but delightful beach cabin on stilts that overlooks the reef. The cabin has two beds, a cooking corner equipped with everything (except food), shower, private outhouse, candlelight, and rainwater for drinking. Basic groceries and simple meals are available, or you are welcome to carry all of your own groceries and beverages with you from the mainland. Prices for cabins or tents are US$95/week per person, US$150/two weeks per per-

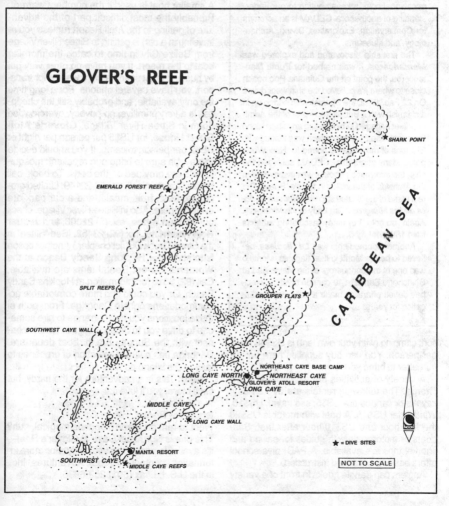

GLOVER'S REEF

★ SHARK POINT

★ EMERALD FOREST REEF

CARIBBEAN SEA

★ SPLIT REEFS

★ GROUPER FLATS

★ SOUTHWEST CAYE WALL

NORTHEAST CAYE BASE CAMP
LONG CAYE NORTH ● ● NORTHEAST CAYE
● GLOVER'S ATOLL RESORT
LONG CAYE

MIDDLE CAYE

★ LONG CAYE WALL

★ = DIVE SITES

● MANTA RESORT
SOUTHWEST CAYE ★ MIDDLE CAYE REEFS

NOT TO SCALE

SEARCHING FOR SUNKEN TREASURE

CEDAM, a group of Mexican divers from nearby Quintana Roo, allied in the early 1950s and has salvaged several old vessels along the reef. The booty from these old ships wasn't gold treasure but other practical items such as equipment, kitchen implements, tools, arms, beads, and an occasional coin, all contributing to our understanding of another era. CEDAM is an acronym for Conservation, Exploration, Diving, Archaeology, and Museums.

The first ship discovered and explored was *Mantanceros.* It was named for Punta Mantanceros, the point off the Quintana Roo beach close to where it's believed the ship went down. On 22 Feb. 1742, the Spanish ship ended up in a skirmish with a British ship—part of the Admiral's fleet engaged in blockading any ships along the coast. The Spanish galleon was loaded with 270 tons of mixed cargo bound for New World ports. Many years after CEDAM salvaged the ship, the information about it was discovered in the Archives of the Indies in Seville, Spain. The real name of the ill-fated ship was *Nuestra Señora de los Milagros* ("Our Lady of the Miracles"). Again, no gold, but many fascinating artifacts from 18th-century Spain.

Another doomed ship was *La Nicolasa,* believed to be the Montejo fleet flagship. Montejo was one of the conquerors of the Maya. And at Chinchorro Banks, a 40-cannon mystery wreck has defied efforts to make a definitive identification for years.

son; camping (with your own tent) is US$70/week per person. You can buy supplies here but it's far better to bring your own.

A variety of activities are available at extra charge. The following rentals are by half day: kayaks or canoes are US$5; sea kayak US$10, Windsurfer US$15. A boat with motor is US$20 the first hour and US$10/hour after that. Sailboats or motorboats with guides for sailing and snorkel trips are available. A PADI dive school offers basic to advanced instruction.

Anglers can dangle hooks in front of a variety of fish. Bonefish are at the top of the chart and resident fishing guide Breeze Cabral is known to be an expert fly fisherman. Expect to see barracuda, tarpon, kingfish, grouper, and wahoo.

Getting There

Transportation to the atoll is provided from **Sittee River Village** (also called Middle Bank) in Stann Creek District aboard a 50-foot diesel sailer; it departs once weekly at 8 a.m. Sunday. A smaller boat is used if the numbers warrant. Probably the most difficult part of the adventure of getting to the Atoll Resort (unless you're traveling in a car) is getting to Sittee River Village from Belize City in time to catch the morning boat to the resort. If you have no other way but by bus and must spend a night waiting for transport, you have several options. For a long time the only available, and probably still the cheapest, is a *very* primitive, no-privacy, overcrowded dorm in Sittee River Village, **Glover's Atoll Guest House,** for US$5 per person per night or US$2 per person to camp. If you should decide to stay, be sure to bring bug repellent; mosquito nets are provided on the beds. To book, call Belize Communications, (8) 22149. Limited groceries, fresh fruit, meals, and a car park are available here. Also in Sittee River Village, check out **Toucan Sittee,** tel. (5) 22006, and **Jaguar Reef Resort,** tel./fax (92) 23452. (See "Sittee" in the Stann Creek District chapter.) Another option is to stay near **Hopkins Sandy Beach** at the **Women's Co-op.** Rental tents are available. Call (92) 3310 for information at Hopkins Sandy Beach. Or you could find more comfortable accommodations right in Dangriga. From both of these locations you must arrange to hire someone to drive you to Sittee Village in time to connect with the Sunday 8 a.m. boat departure. Dangriga has a larger selection of groceries to take to the island as well.

Note: This is an adventure for the hardy; but once there, you'll love it.

Island for Rent

Want to rent an island? Sounds magical, huh? This one is Northeast Caye at Glover's Reef—it's available part of the year only. For more information, contact Slickrock Adventures, Inc., in the U.S. tel./fax (801) 259-6996.

COROZAL DISTRICT

Corozal is the northernmost district in Belize. The ambience is "Spanish," but with a Belizean flavor. If arriving from Mexico, you'll immediately notice the difference between the two countries. The people of Corozal are a happy bunch, and you'll discover dozens of American expats enjoying the slow pace of Belizean living.

Fauna
Nature lovers will not be disappointed by the Corozal District. Crocodiles, tapirs, jaguars, manatees, peccaries, tree frogs, and more live in the forests and creeks. Birdwatching is especially good around the bays, lagoons, marshes, and mangroves of the coastal areas. Wading birds and waterfowl of all types frequent these areas. In drier places parrots, toucans, hawks, and songbirds are plentiful. **Shipstern Wildlife Reserve and Butterfly Breeding Center** offers excellent opportunities to see all of the above and a treasure-trove of wild butterflies as well. More than 200 species may be observed fluttering about on sunny days.

COROZAL TOWN

Just nine miles (15 minutes) from the Rio Hondo (the border separating Belize and Mexico) and 96 miles north of Belize City is the small town of Corozal. The population is about 9,000. While English is the official language, Spanish is just as common since many are descendants of early-day Maya and mestizo refugees from neighboring Quintana Roo. Historically, Corozal was the scene of many attacks by the Maya Indi-ans during the Caste War. What remains of the old fort can be found in the center of town (west of Central Park). Today, it's a quiet little village that lies near the tranquil shores of the Caribbean and close to the Bay of Chetumal.

The town was almost entirely wiped out during Hurricane Janet in 1955 and has since been rebuilt. Strolling through the quiet streets you'll find a library, town hall, government adminis-

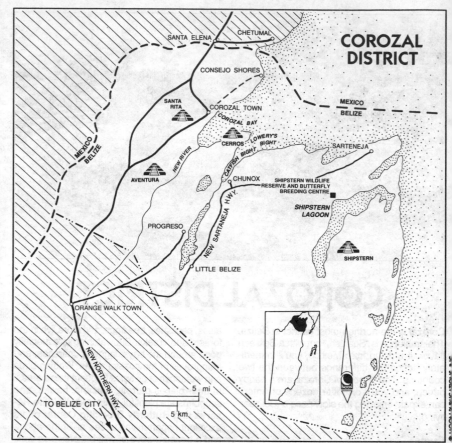

trative offices, a Catholic church, two secondary schools, five elementary schools, three gas stations, a government hospital, a clinic, a cinema, a couple of small hotels, a couple of funky bars and discos, and several restaurants. Not a whole lot of activity goes on here, unless you happen to be in town during special holidays. The biggest excitement is during the Mexican-style "Spanish" fiestas of Christmas, Carnaval ("Carnival"), and Columbus Day.

Many houses are clapboard, raised on wooden stilts to avoid possible floods and to catch the wind, creating a cool spot for the family to gather. More of the newer houses are built out of cement blocks—almost all display TV anten-

nas. Be sure to go into the town hall and take a look at the dramatic historical mural painted by **Manuel Villamour.** The flamboyantly colored mural depicts the history of Corozal, including the drama of the downtrodden Maya, their explosive revolt called the Caste War, and the inequities of colonial rule.

The Corozal District economy has for years depended on the sugar industry with its local processing factory. One of the oldest (no longer in operation), the **Aventura Sugar Mill** began operating in the 1800s. Little is left today, but you can still see the antiquated chimney when driving past the village of Aventura on the New Northern Highway, seven miles from Corozal Town.

Orientation

Enter Corozal either from the north (many drivers cross the Mexican border here) or from the south on the Northern Highway. Getting oriented to Corozal is easy since it's laid out on a grid system with **avenues** running north and south and **streets** running east and west. Corozal's two primary avenues, 4th and 5th, run completely through town. The majority of restaurants or stores of interest to travelers lie on, or adjacent to, these. The town square is in the center of town, with streets numbered outward from there in each direction (1st St. North, 1st St. South).

SIGHTS AND RECREATION

Corozal Town is a great base camp for fishing, nature watching, and water sports. Lots of folks just *hang out* for a couple of days, wander over to the town square, have a drink or two somewhere, and strike up a conversation with the locals and a few of the expats who've come to love the laidback lifestyle.

Maya Archaeological Sites

Though not of the scope or interest to the casual traveler as Lamanai in Orange Walk District or Caracol and Xunantunich in the Cayo District, the nearby ruins of **Cerros** and **Santa Rita** are easy to visit. Both are mostly unexcavated. Cerros is especially intriguing as it looms over the jungle across the bay from Corozal Town. On a peninsula in Corozal Bay you'll find Cerros, an important coastal trading center during the late pre-Classic period (350 B.C.-A.D. 250).

You can reach Cerros by boat (hire it either in downtown Corozal or **Tony's Inn**.) The trip is pleasant if a bit pricey (US$75-100). If there's no one else to split the cost of the trip and it's dry season (Jan.-April), you can get to Cerros by car.

Today's Corozal Town is built on the site of what was once the ancient Maya province of Chetumal. The bay was an important trading port. The remaining ruins are called Santa Rita. To explore this site either strike out on your own, or go with a guided group from your hotel. It's on the edge of town. Women traveling alone should team up with others or hire a guide.

River Trips

A favorite excursion from Corozal is a boat ride up the New River to Lamanai in Orange Walk District. Travel 30 miles past mestizo, Maya, and Mennonite settlements on a sun-dappled, jungle-lined river until you come to a broad lagoon and then to the temples of Lamanai. The trip is through tropical flora and fauna and you might see such exotics as black orchids and jabiru storks, the largest flying birds in the New World, with a wing span of 10-12 feet. This is an all-day trip. The price for one to four people to Lamanai runs about US$250 (check with Henry Menzies, tel. 4 22726). During the dry season (Jan.-April), you can reach Lamanai by road from San Felipe, preferably in a 4WD. See "Maya Archaeological Sites" for more detailed information about all the Maya sites.

*Corozal Town Hall
historical mural*

Across the Border

Tours to Chetumal for shopping or to Bacalar with its Spanish fort and blue hole are popular activities. Henry Menzies, tel. (4) 22725, specializes in such tours. In fact, Henry takes visitors back and forth to Tulum, Akumal, and Cancún in quality a/c vehicles.

Other Activities

If you're a biker and want to rent a bike, check with **Leslie's Travel,** tel. (4) 22377, which has a few mountain bikes in good repair for rent. **Fishing** is good in Corozal. With its numerous creeks, bays, inlets, and the ocean, Corozal offers the angler a choice of fishing for saltwater or freshwater species. Tarpon fishing is especially popular.

ACCOMMODATIONS

Look for the sign for **Tony's Inn and Resort,** Box 12, Corozal Town, Corozal District, Belize, C.A., tel. (4) 22055, fax (4) 22829; from the U.S. call **International Expeditions,** tel. (800) 633-

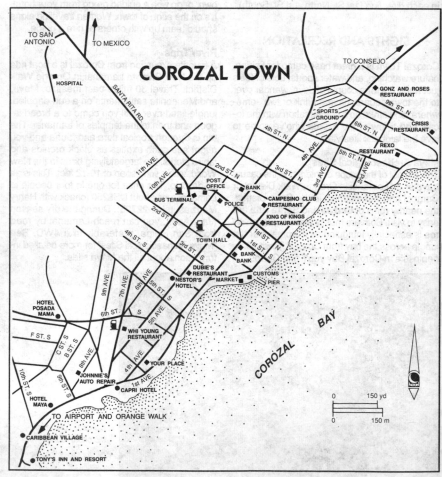

4734. On the sea facing the Maya site of Cerros across the bay, it is one of Corozal's nicer hotels. This two-story sparkling-white stucco building is a clean modern hotel with large rooms that have a/c, private baths, electricity, and h/c water. It has a good restaurant, well-cared-for grounds, and a manmade sandy beach and beach bar (a good evening hangout) where you can enjoy the tradewinds off the Caribbean, swimming and other water sports, and pleasant companionship with fellow travelers. Tony's has 21 double rooms. Winter rates for standard rooms are US$35 s, US$45 d; for moderate rooms, US$40 s, US$50 d, US$55 t; for deluxe rooms, US$60 s, US$70 d, US$75 t, US$80 q. They cost less in the summer; credit cards okay. The restaurant serves a tasty selection, including such dazzlers as curried lobster or a plain filet mignon (à la carte). Tony's is 80 miles from the Philip Goldson International Airport in Belize City, 18 miles from Chetumal, Mexico, and 150 miles from Cancún, Mexico. Owners/managers Dahlia and Tony Castillo are friendly and always ready to assist their guests. Write or call for more information and reservations.

About a hundred yards north of Tony's and on the left is **Caribbean Village,** South End, Corozal Town, Belize, C.A., tel. (4) 22725. Formerly known as the Caribbean Motel and Trailer Park, this pleasant shady resort was once an old standard for RVers, campers, and those looking for the simplest of cabins. Today, the five cabins, renovated by owners Henry and Joan Menzies, appeal to travelers who want simple but clean accommodations and good food at reasonable prices. Across the street from the bay, under palms that catch the breeze, the onsite restaurant is a pleasant place to grab a bite to eat or to hang out. It serves great local food, hamburgers, fish, and pies made from scratch. If you're lucky you may even get the occasional taste of gibnut, armadillo, or peccary. It serves breakfast, lunch, and dinner. Campsites with 24-hour security are about US$5, and cabins with electricity, private baths, and fans rent for about US$15 s, US$20 d, US$10 per person additional. The Menzies accept Visa/MC. An added plus: Henry is a travel agent and knowledgeable guide who specializes in tours of northern Belize and Mexico.

Across from the bus stop at the south end of 7th Ave. is **Hotel Maya,** Box 112, Corozal Town, Belize, C.A., tel. (4) 22082/22874, a small hotel and restaurant run by Rosita Menzies and Sylvia Hamil. Two buildings house the office, restaurant, and rooms. The building is fairly well maintained and the help is friendly. Mexican and regional dishes are served in the comfy little cafe. Enjoy a cold beer and ceviche at the bar; swimming is across the street. Although far from fancy, all rooms have private baths, h/c water, and fans. The furnishings are simple but comfortable. Corner rooms on the second and third floors facing the ocean are especially desirable. Rates are US$17.50 s, US$27.50 d, US$30 t. The hotel accepts Visa/MC. This is also the agency for **Island Air.**

Tony's Inn and Resort

If you want cheap, the **Capri Hotel,** Box 59, #14 4th Ave., Corozal Town, Belize, C.A., tel. (4) 22042, is a place to check out. This budget roadhouse offers a huge, rather dark bar and pool hall downstairs; it gets very noisy and the sound drifts up into the rooms. Upstairs are 28 sparely furnished rooms. Rates for rooms with shared bath are US$4.25 s, US$6.25 d, US$8.25 t; private bath US$6.25 s, US$9 d. It accepts traveler's checks.

Off the beaten track in a residential neighborhood, **Hotel Posada Mama,** 77 G St. South, Corozal, Belize, C.A., tel. (4) 22107/23245, is hard to find but the small blue hostel is worth it. Very clean, tiny rooms have a toilet and shower tightly placed in separate corners. The eight colorful cement rooms have a/c, color TV, h/c water, and telephones. Rates are US$26 s, US$35 d. There isn't a restaurant here, but the owners will direct guests to their favorite eateries.

Nestor's Hotel, 123 5th Ave., tel./fax (4) 22354, has been a budget favorite for a long time, but it sometimes has been a little loosely managed. However, the new owners are running a tighter establishment. Rooms are small, simple, and have fans and private cold bath. The hotel plans to upgrade to hot water (ask). Rates are US$10 s, US$12.50 d, US$17.50 t. Downstairs a pleasant restaurant and bar with audio and video systems attracts locals and travelers. Also, an outdoor bar at the front veranda is in the works. Try the barbecue dip steak sandwich for under US$5 or a T-bone in one of three sizes. It serves good vegetarian fare, too. A locked parking lot is available.

South of Corozal Town

Just past Libertad and the Sugar Mill owned by Petrojam, a Jamaican firm, is **Santa Cruz Lodge,** Box 84, Corozal Town, Belize, C.A., tel. (4) 22441. One of the newer resorts in the area, it used to be the living compound of the sugar executives and their families years ago. All we can say is that these folks lived pretty well. The 37-acre resort has manicured grounds, a pool, tennis/basketball courts, two bars, excellent dining facilities, 22 deluxe rooms, and plans for a golf course. Credit cards are okay. Rates are US$79 s, US$89 d, US$109 executive suite, US$119 honeymoon suite. Contact Gervis Menzies for information.

FOOD

Corozal has a good number of places to eat a decent meal. None of it is gourmet, but a variety of places serve Creole and Mexican-style food. Chinese food in Corozal is usually the quality of the inexpensive takeout variety.

The popular **Campesino Club** at 47 4th Ave. is good for a cold drink and lively conversation with the *campesinos* (countryfolk). It serves lunch and dinner and prepares takeout orders. Burgers are good at a little over US$1 and fried chicken dinners will cost you US$2-3. You'll find fresh orange and tomato juice here, too.

King of Kings Chinese Restaurant on 3rd Avenue in the center of town serves Chinese, barbecue, chicken salad, fried fish, steak (about US$6-7), and a variety of soups (lobster US$4.50)—liquor also. A separate room is provided for families. It's open 8:30 a.m.-1:30 a.m.

Crisis (pronounced CREE-sees) is a neat little place with a lot of atmosphere, good local food, and reasonable prices. On the 9th Street North, Crisis features a lounge, dancing, and live music on weekends. The rice and beans with stew beef is good for US$2.25. Check out the conch ceviche or steak for under US$4. *Chimole* or *escabeche* cost about US$2.25 each. Other features include oilcloth tables and fans. It's open Sun.-Mon. 10 a.m.-10 p.m., closed Saturday morning, but open till midnight Saturday.

Serving three meals a day, **Dubie's Bar & Restaurant,** 5th Avenue north of Nestor's Hotel, opens about 8 a.m. The fare is reasonably priced and good. The menu isn't set, but Dubie's offers soup, rice and beans, and fish. Stew chicken with rice and beans costs US$2.50. You'll find lots of locals here.

At the north end of town on the right you'll find **Gonz and Roses,** 5 4th Ave. North, tel. (4) 23137, a quaint eatery with a cool interior, tables and private booths, all brightened by tiny blinking Christmas lights. Here, from 11 a.m. till midnight, Ms. Gonzalez serves a variety of local and Mexican food. Tostadas are a bargain at US30 cents, fried chicken with potatoes and veggies costs US$2.50, and conch ceviche sells for US$4.

For local color and good Chinese food try **Rexo,** 9 6th St. North. (Okay, it also has pizza, lasagna, and hamburgers—with French fries.) You'll also find fresh orange juice and a limited selection of groceries in a glass case. It's open 11 a.m.-10 p.m.

Whi Young Restaurant, across from the Texaco station at the south end of town, is easy to find and locals recommend it. Specials include chow mein (to US$7.50), chop suey (to US$6.50), and curry (to US$5.50).

Your Place, by the edge of the bay on 1st Avenue in a grassy stretch of park, has a large *palapa* with a half dozen tables, chairs, a bar, and six stools. Outside you'll find palms and greenery; inside, shade, a little music, and your choice of beer and soft drinks. Relax, what's the hurry, anyway; this is Corozal.

SHOPPING AND SERVICES

Corozal has lots of little shops, grocery stores, book stores, and a few gift shops. You'll find locally made jewelry, pottery, a variety of wood carvings, clothing, textiles, and a host of other mementos at **White Sapphire Jewelry and Gift Shop,** 7th Ave. at the south end of town. Don't be surprised if one of the craftspeople drops by with his or her latest piece.

Money
If you need to change money, go to **Belize Bank, Nova Scotia Bank,** or **Atlantic Bank** Mon.-Thurs. 8 a.m.-1 p.m., Friday 8 a.m.-1 p.m. and 3-6 p.m.

Local Guides and Tour Companies
Two good local guides know the country well, especially the Corozal District, and have well-kept vans: **Henry Menzies Travel & Tours,** Box 210, Corozal Town, Belize, C.A., tel. (4) 22725, and Manuel Hoare of **Ma-Ian's Tours,** 13 6th St., South Corozal Town, Belize, C.A., tel. (4) 22744, fax (4) 23375.

Alvin Leslie arranges bike tours. Contact **Leslie's Travel,** 57 7th Ave., Corozal Town, Belize, C.A., tel. (4) 22377.

Garage Service
If you're driving your own car and have a mechanical problem, don't fret—**Johnnie's Auto Repair,** 23 8th Ave. South, offers 24-hour service.

GETTING THERE

By Air
The fastest way to Corozal is by air, either from Belize City or Ambergris Caye. **Island Air,** tel. (4) 22874, has two flights from Belize City Municipal Airport, with a stop at San Pedro, at 10:30

Posada Mama hotel

PHIL LANIER

fishing from the docks in Corozal

a.m. and 2:30 p.m. daily except Sunday. Flights from Corozal to San Pedro and Belize City at 8 a.m. and 3:30 p.m. are available daily except Sunday. Buy your tickets in downtown Corozal; the airstrip is about three miles south of town and taxi service is available. **Tropic Air,** tel. (4) 22725, has flights daily to Corozal from San Pedro at 10 a.m. and 3 p.m.; the flight takes 20 minutes.

By Bus
Both **Venus** and **Batty** buses travel between Chetumal and Belize City and stop in Corozal about every two hours until 6 p.m.; Sunday service is more infrequent.

By Car
In this area, driving is easy along the Northern Highway. Signs are plentiful, but watch for speed bumps outside Orange Walk and in some small hamlets.

NORTH OF COROZAL TOWN

Consejo Shores
This suburb of Corozal Town is seven miles northeast of the town center. Look for the turnoff downtown; it brings you to **Consejo Shores,** which the locals call the "Miami Beach" of Belize (a wild stretch of the imagination unless you've seen the rest of the country). The name is rather odd, too, since Corozal has no "real" beach. Mostly this is an upscale neighborhood with some lovely homes (many owned by expats). Walking along the coast it's easy to find a place to enter the lovely blue sea; you'll find good swimming, for example, at Four Mile Lagoon.

Lagoon Campground
Off the Santa Elena Highway on Four Mile Lagoon, about 1.5 miles from the Mexican border, a couple of Americans have recently opened a campground that sounds pretty nice. We haven't seen it yet, but they offer full hookups for RVs as well as primitive camp sites. Sailboat rentals, a stone dock, and a boat launch are available too. One of the owners is a registered nurse, and both are ardent travelers, knowing all of Belize and surrounding countries well enough to give good travel information for those traveling with RVs. For more detailed info and prices, write to Rosalie and William Dixon, Lagoon Campground, General Delivery, Corozal, Belize, C.A.

EAST OF COROZAL TOWN

SARTENEJA

When you arrive you'd almost think you were in Mexico; but why not? The small fishing village in northern Belize was established by Yucatán settlers from Mexico in the 19th century. The fishermen continue to use the skills handed down over the years along with the knowledge of boat building. Obviously the immigrants were not the only people who felt that Sarteneja's location on the Corozal District coast was ideal for the seafaring life; it is apparent that the ancient Maya spent many years here also. To date, only one Maya structure has been partially restored and archaeologists note that the remains of more than 350 structures have been discovered—but not excavated.

For generations, the people of nearby villages have robbed the Maya sites of building materials such as stone blocks and limestone to make plaster and cement. As the scavengers picked and dug around the structures over the years, artifacts made of gold, copper, and shells continued to turn up. Scientists believe Sarteneja was occupied by the Maya from the early Classic period into the 1700s.

Agriculture

Today Sarteneja is home not only to fishermen, but also to farmers. Pineapples grow well and for years were transported to Belize City by boat twice a week and sold at the Belize City wharf. But since the all-weather road from Sarteneja opened, the fruit can be delivered more frequently by truck. Farmers are planting other crops, and with the freedom of coming and going to Belize City more easily, this may develop into a major agricultural community—if tourism doesn't beat it out first! Already there are sport fishermen who prefer Sarteneja's mild climate (with rich catches of fish) to the southern, more humid part of the country.

Accommodations

So far, only one small hotel takes care of visitors at Sarteneja; it is pleasant, clean, budget priced, and recently expanded by owner Pedro Cruz. Ask around town for **Hotel Diani's,** tel. (4) 32084. Now that Sarteneja village has electricity, you can use the overhead fans all night. There's a nice little cafe, too. It's all family run, and dad Pedro Cruz also has a small general store in town.

SHIPSTERN WILDLIFE RESERVE AND BUTTERFLY BREEDING CENTRE

Shipstern is in the northeastern corner of the Belize coast. Thirty-two square miles of moist forest, savanna, and wetlands have been set aside to preserve as-yet unspoiled habitats of well-known insect, bird, and mammal species associated with the tropics. The reserve encompasses the shallow **Shipstern Lagoon,** which, although hardly navigable, creates a wonderful habitat for

Pineapple is a lucrative crop for Sarteneja.

a huge selection of wading and fish-eating birds. The reserve is home to about 200 species of birds, 60 species of reptiles and amphibians, and nearly 200 species of butterflies.

The **Audubon Society** and **International Tropical Conservation Foundation** have been extremely generous in their support. As at most reserves, the object is to manage and protect its habitats and wildlife, as well as to develop an education program. This entails educating the local community and introducing children to the concept of wildlife conservation in their area. Shipstern, however, goes a step further by conducting an investigation of how tropical countries such as Belize can develop self-supporting conservation areas through the controlled, intensive production of natural commodities found within such wildlife settlements. Developing facilities for the scientific study of the reserve area and its wildlife is part of this important program.

Shipstern began the production of live butterfly pupae through intensive breeding. Around the world, tourist attractions such as Disney World are providing butterfly habitats, where visitors can wander through an enclosure designed to resemble the deep jungle, with flitting tropical birds and colorful butterflies—all flying free. These butterfly habitats are gaining popularity and showing up all over the world. Great Britain has 60—10 years ago there were only two. Many of the large animal parks in the U.S., such as Marine World Africa USA in Vallejo, California; San Diego Wild Animal Park; the San Francisco Zoological Society; and many others have either opened a habitat or are designing one. They are so much more pleasant than dead collections!

The Butterfly Life Cycle
A butterfly goes through four stages in its life cycle: egg, caterpillar, pupa, and adult. Shipstern gathers breeding populations of typical Belizean species in the pupal stage. Depending on the species, butterflies live anywhere from seven days to six weeks.

In many areas of Belize, butterfly populations have been almost totally depleted for many reasons, including habitat destruction (from logging, for instance) and changing farming practices, particularly the use of pesticides. Shipstern's untouched steamy marshes, swamps, and rainforest have been a natural breeding ground for beautiful butterflies for thousands of years and maybe will continue to be so.

For a while, the pupae were gathered at Shipstern, carefully packaged in moist cotton inside a cardboard box, and then shipped. Once the pupae were unpacked they were carefully "hung" in what is called an emerging cage with a simulated "jungle" atmosphere—hot and humid. A short time later they shed their pupal skin, and a tiny bit of Belize fluttered away to the amazement and joy of children and adults who came to visit these popular habitats. However, costs were exceeding benefits, so the export business was stopped. But the butterfly breeding program continues for education and science.

Botanical Trail
Before starting your trek along the Botanical Trail, pick up a book with detailed descriptions of the trail and the trees at the center's headquarters. The lovely trail starts at the parking lot by the office and meanders through the forest. You will have the opportunity to see three types of hardwood forests and 100 species of hardwood. Many of the trees are labeled with their Latin and Yucatec Maya names.

Admission to the Visitor's Center and the Butterfly Breeding Center is free; however, it's really best to go with a guide. A guided tour of both centers and the Botanical Trail costs US$12 per person, less if you have more than four people. The guides' discerning eyes spot things that most city folk often miss right in front of them. The forest is alive with nature's critters and fascinating flora. Hours are daily 9 a.m.-12 p.m. and 1-3 p.m., except for Christmas, New Year's Day, and Easter. It takes about one hour to drive from Orange Walk to Shipstern Wildlife Reserve. Don't forget a long-sleeved shirt, pants, mosquito repellent, binoculars, and a camera. For more information, write Box 1694, Belize City, Belize, C.A.; in Switzerland, International Tropical Conservation Foundation, Box 31, CH-2074 Marin-Ne, Switzerland.

BOB RACE

ORANGE WALK DISTRICT
INTRODUCTION

Orange Walk is the second largest district of Belize and its history is inexorably linked to **Orange Walk Town,** near the northern tip of the district. This busy town is one of the largest commercial and farming centers in the country. It was settled in the last century by refugees from southern Mexico during the Caste War; you'll still hear more Spanish than English. What's left of two forts, Mundy and Cairns, reminds one that this was the scene of violent battles between Belizean settlers and war-minded Maya trying to rid the area of outsiders. The last battle took place in 1872. Today the most striking people you'll notice on the streets aren't the Maya but the Mennonites, who still maintain their simple cotton clothes, horse-drawn buggies, and a stoic countenance.

THE LAND

Orange Walk District is blessed with a wide array of habitats and wildlife. Like its neighbor, Corozal, it has a riverine lagoon, marshes, and deep tropical forest. You'll find three primo areas around Lamanai ruins on the New River Lagoon, the Rio Bravo Conservation Area, and Chan Chich Lodge. The vast New River Lagoon is Belize's largest body of fresh water (28 miles long). Its dark waters are smooth and reflective, changing with every cloud that passes over the sun. Morelet's crocodiles and hicatee turtles inhabit these waters along with numerous species of fish and waterfowl.

Logging

For more than 100 years, before settlement by farming-inclined mestizo refugees from Yucatán in 1849, this was timber country. If you travel about two miles north past Orange Walk Town, you'll find a reasonably new toll bridge over the **New River.** In years past all the timber logged from the north and middle districts was floated down the New River to Corozal Bay, and then to Belize City; from there it was shipped all over the world. Today you'll encounter large logging trucks crossing the toll bridge.

Sugarcane

At one time sugarcane was the most important Belizean crop. Now farmers grow more and more citrus, and beef producers supply not only the local market but also the export market. **Caribbean rum** (a product of sugarcane) is still big business in this area. During the cane harvest the one-lane highway is a parade of trucks stacked high with sugarcane and waiting in long lines at the side of the road to get into the sugar mill. Night drivers beware: the trucks aren't new and often have no lights.

Mennonite Country

The picturesque Mennonite farming areas of Orange Walk seem strangely out of place as you ride through the countryside. At times you could believe you were in North Dakota or even Pennsylvania as you near Blue Creek and the mountains that straddle the Mexican border behind it. Today's Mennonite farmers have created lovely green pastures and rich gardens; they specialize in the dairy and egg industries. Agriculture is blossoming in many directions in Orange Walk.

ARCHAEOLOGICAL SITES

Lamanai, one of the most impressive Maya ruins in Belize, huddles to one side of New River Lagoon and the abandoned 19th-century sugar mill built by U.S. Confederate refugees at Indian

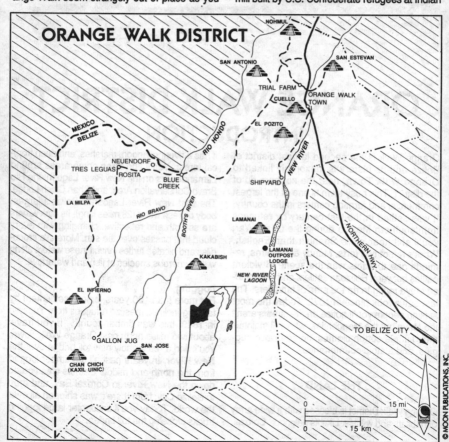

sugar mill

BOB RACE

Church, which harbors its own memories of the past. Besides Lamanai, the nearby ruins of **Cuello** beckon the visitor as does the distant site of **La Milpa** in the **Rio Bravo Conservation Area** to the far west.

Archaeological Research And Nature Study

Programme for Belize operates a Rio Bravo exploration tour offering a couple of days' involvement on the La Milpa ruins archaeological survey. Participants are allowed the time to study the flora and fauna of the area. Lamanai Outpost Lodge's ongoing archaeological program allows guests of the lodge to get involved. For more information, contact Programme for Belize, 2 S. Park St., Belize City, C.A., tel. (2) 71248/75616.

ORANGE WALK TOWN

Orange Walk Town (population about 10,000), just off the Northern Highway, is easy to get to. Roads from Orange Walk Town enable you to explore, in four directions, as many as 20 villages. Daily buses from Orange Walk link Belize City and Corozal. Lying 66 miles north of Belize City and 30 miles south of Corozal Town, Orange Walk town is one of the larger communities in Belize. Though it does not qualify as a tourist destination, it's another facet of Belize with its own history and style. If passing through, stop and look around. The town has two banks, a cinema, a few hotels, and a choice of many small, casual cafes. Close by you'll find several interesting historic sites: **Indian Church,** a 16th-century Spanish mission; the ruins of Belize's original sugar mill, built by U.S. Confederate Civil War refugees; and if you head west and then southwest you'll find **Blue Creek,** a Mennonite development where Belize's first hydro-electric plant is located.

SIGHTS AND RECREATION

Cycling

Motivated cyclists with mountain bikes should have no trouble in most of Orange Walk District. Wet conditions in the rainy season can make riding impossible in some isolated areas, but the roads to Rio Bravo Conservation Area and Chan Chich are all-weather. Allow plenty of time and avoid night travel between Blue Creek and Gallon Jug. In the hilly country around Blue Creek the road rises over a short distance and curves around a *lot*. A gas station/general store at the top, **Linda Vista Credit Union,** offers food and drinks. Other than this section of road, the less than 40 miles to Chan Chich should be a good ride for the experienced cyclist, especially from the point you bear off to the left a little before Tres Leguas till the point you reach Chan Chich. On this last bit expect fast-moving jeeps rounding the sharp turns in a hurry; there're no shoulders much of the way. It's a jungle out there!

Orchid Tours

The **Audubon Society** is very involved with the preservation of Belize's wildlife. One of Belize's most important features is 150 species of orchids growing wild throughout the country. **Godoy and Sons,** 4 Trial Farm, Orange Walk Town, Belize, C.A., tel. (3) 22969, offers a tourist guide service that, along with the usual attractions, leads orchid tours. Luis Godoy, the eldest son, has developed an exciting tour during which visitors will see a variety of tropical blossoms, including the black orchid (the Belizean national flower). Ask about orchid sales. When not involved with touring, the Godoys export orchid plants for the Audubon societies from various parts of the country. Many resorts around the country buy the plants from the Godoys to use for landscaping.

Orchid fanciers who wish to buy Belizean orchids must go through special procedures to bring the blooms into the United States. Luis Godoy is one of just a handful of people in the country who know all the legal procedures involved and he can handle all of it for you. Call or write the Godoys for information or look them up when visiting Orange Walk Town.

River Trips

Trips up and down the New River and around the New River lagoon are fun adventures for the entire family, with a chance to see Morelet's crocodiles and iguanas sunning on a bank. Night safaris are equally, if not more, exciting. It's a chance to see the habits of animals who come out to play only after the sun sets; you'll need the help of a good spotlight of course.

By day you'll see the sights of verdant jungle and wildlife along the river. Many people combine a river trip with a visit to the ruins of Lamanai. It is the most impressive way to approach the site, and a time-saver as well compared to going by land. Contact **Jungle River Tours,** tel. (3) 22293, fax (3) 23749, at Lovers Lane road and talk to Antonio or Herminio Novelo, who run river tours to Lamanai and the surrounding area.

ACCOMMODATIONS

Most of the hotels in Orange Walk Town are simple and not designed for upscale tourist comforts. However, the rooms are basic, clean, and, for the most part, inexpensive.

D Star Victoria, 40 Belize Rd., Orange Walk Town, Belize, C.A., tel. (3) 22518, fax (3) 22847, was formerly known as the Baron Hotel. This refurbished version is easily the best of the downtown hotels and is on the main road between Belize and Corozal. With 31 rooms it is also the largest. As you come into town it is hard to miss with its coral and white exterior. Even the pool appears to have had a facelift. Its disco comes to life in the wee hours. All rooms have h/c water, private baths, and ceiling fans or a/c. Rates are US$25 d, with a/c US$42.50.

Mi Amor Hotel, 19 Belize/Corozal Rd., tel. (3) 22031, is a roadside hotel on the town's main thoroughfare. It offers private bathrooms and a choice of a/c or fan; rates start at about US$21 s, US$30 d; TV is extra. It also has a restaurant and a bar.

Chula Vista Hotel, tel. (3) 23414, is a few miles beyond Orange Walk Town at **Trial Farm Village.** Take a look at this attractive motor court hotel. The Reyes family offers seven clean simple rooms with private bath for about US$18 s, US$23 d, and a restaurant and bar.

Two other budget accommodations are **Jane's Hotel,** 2 Baker St., which offers tiny rooms overlooking the New River and **Tai-San Hotel,** 30 Queen Victoria Ave., tel. (3) 22752, which has six inexpensive rooms and a small restaurant.

FOOD

There's really only one good reason to linger in Orange Walk Town—on the far side of town in a nice neighborhood near the hospital is the best restaurant around, **The Diner,** 37 Clark Street, tel. (3) 23753. Here you'll find a surprising menu: peppermint steak (US$5), smoked pork chops (US$8), filet mignon (US$12.50), lobster thermidor or grouper in bechamel sauce (US$15). Try the coconut pie or the homemade soursop ice cream! Watermelon, papaya, and orange juices are available; the staff will prepare special requests. It's open 10 a.m.-10 p.m.

It's easy to find Chinese food in Orange Walk Town, maybe because at one time it was home to so many Chinese laborers who worked the sugarcane fields. Now you can find Belizean, Mexican, and Jamaican specialties, even hamburgers, mixed in with so-so oriental offerings. Most of these eateries have little in the way of decor, many are inexpensive, some for whatever reason ask too much for what you get in return. **Lee's Chinese Restaurant,** 11 San Antonio Rd. near the fire station, serves passable versions of chicken chow mein (US$3.25), sweet and sour fish (US$7.50), black soybean lobster or shrimp (US$12), and cocktails from a colorful bar on Yo Street. A few more to check out are **Camie's Restaurant,** Queen Victoria St., tel. (3) 22174; **Jane's Chinese Food Center,** 21 Main St., tel. (3) 22389; and **Happy Valley Chinese Restaurant,** 38 Main St., tel. (3) 22554. If you're looking for Belizean food, stop by **Golden Gate Cafe,** tel. (3) 22460, or **Orange Walk Restaurant** on the Belize/Corozal Road.

Entering town on the Belize/Corozal Road you will see a **service station/convenience store** on the left. This store has light snacks, cold drinks, a few staples, medications, and cosmetics. If you are headed by car to Rio Bravo or Chan Chich this is a good place to top off the gas tank.

GETTING THERE

By Bike
Orange Walk is rideable in one day from Belize City for above-average cyclists. **Tips:** the Northern Highway is busy; the Old Northern Highway, which takes a bit longer, might offer more interesting villages and potential stopovers (best with a mountain bike). Don't travel on either of these roads at night.

By Bus
Batty Brothers and **Venus Bus Lines** travel between Chetumal and Belize City with stops in Orange Walk and Corozal about every two hours until 6 p.m.; Sunday service is more infrequent.

By Car
Traveling to Orange Walk on the New Highway is easy; just point the car and go. Watch out for speed bumps as you near the toll bridge south of Orange Walk. The Old Northern Highway is more comfortable with a 4WD vehicle because of the high clearance needed during the rainy muddy season.

AROUND THE DISTRICT

SOUTH OF ORANGE WALK TOWN

About due south of town and west of Crooked Tree is **New River Lagoon** and the ruins of the Maya ceremonial center of **Lamanai.** You can reach both by boat.

Sights
Lamanai is another exciting Maya site and one of Belize's largest Maya ceremonial centers. It was an imperial port city encompassing ball courts, pyramids, and the more exotic Maya features. Lamanai is believed to have been occupied from 1500 B.C. to the 19th century. Historical Spanish occupation is apparent with the remains of two Christian churches, and the sugar mill was built by U.S. Confederate refugees. You can reach Lamanai by boat from Shipyard or by road during the dry

season from San Felipe. A visit to this unreconstructed ceremonial center, which dates from 3500 B.C., is an Indiana Jones adventure into the deep shadowed home of the mysterious Maya. (See "Maya Archaeological Sites" in the Mundo Maya chapter for more details and descriptions of Lamanai.)

Accommodations
Right next door to Lamanai Reserve along the shore of the New River Lagoon is the comfortable **Lamanai Outpost Lodge,** tel./fax (2) 33578. Guests of the lodge, just a half mile from the reserve's dock, can either walk or take a quick water taxi ride over. The lodge boasts 16 comfortable thatched-roof cabañas made of natural wood and other mostly Belizean materials. Below the resort's lodge and dining room, the cabañas lead down to the lagoon's shore, where you'll find a dock, swimming area, canoes, boats

Lamanai pottery
artifacts

of various types, and a Windsurfer. This is a low-key, escape-to-nature kind of setting, perfect for the birdwatcher, Mayaphile, naturalist, or traveler who wants to get away from the tourist trail for a while. Overnight rates are US$70 s, US$90 d; packages, including meals and activities, run US$340-620. The area is rich in animal life, including more than 300 species of birds as well as crocodiles, margays, jaguarundis, anteaters, arboreal porcupines, and the fishing bulldog bat.

The owners are involved in several scientific research projects that also allow nature study opportunities for guests. One study concentrates on howler monkeys, another on recording birdcalls, and another on spiders. Guests through programs such as ElderHostel and Oceanic Expeditions can participate in the work. Dr. Herman Smith leads a new archaeology project that will allow guests the chance to roll up their sleeves and help with a dig. Quarters for the researchers will soon be completed. Ask about daily herbal and bird walks as well as night safaris.

WEST OF ORANGE WALK TOWN

Four miles west of Orange Walk Town are the minor ruins of **Cuello.** As the road meanders west from there, numerous small villages dot the border region. Occasionally, you'll see a soft drink sign attached to a building, but there's not much else

between Orange Walk and Blue Creek but wide open fields of crops, low forest, and dirt road.

Near **Blue Creek** the road rounds a bend to reveal a pleasant valley. The small village to the right is **La Union** on the other side of the Mexico border. Then the road angles up sharply. At the top is **La Vista Credit Union,** the gas station/general store mentioned earlier. Fill the tank if you're driving to Rio Bravo or Chan Chich Lodge, it's your last gas station until you come back this way.

Rio Bravo Research Station

Here, on 250,000 acres of prime tropical jungle in the Rio Bravo Conservation Area is a cluster of small thatched-roof buildings. The station, run by the Belizean conservation group **Programme for Belize,** 2 S. Park St., Belize City, Belize, C.A., tel. (2) 71248, fax (2) 75616, is dedicated to scientific research, agricultural experimentation, and the protection of indigenous wildlife and the area's Maya archaeological locations—all this while creating self-sufficiency through development of ecotourism and sustainable rainforest agriculture such as chicle production. A scientific study continues to determine the best management plan for the reserve and its forests.

Another focus is on environmental education. Every year the organization, which receives support from the Belize Audubon Society, the Nature Conservancy, and the World Wildlife Fund, expends a goodly effort in educating Belizeans and eco-specialists from abroad. In one program young Belizean students are recruited to become field biology trainees. This one-year program allows young people the opportunity to work alongside international researchers in gathering knowledge of the jungle and its inhabitants. Another program, sponsored through Save The Rain Forest, Inc., brings in groups of high school teachers and students to experience and learn about the forest and its ecosystems.

For visitors here, Rio Bravo provides the chance to experience the outdoors while supporting a worthy environmental effort. You'll have opportunities to experience the wilderness and see archaeological work under way at La Milpa, the ancient Maya ruins on the property. Activities include nature walks (both day and night), more in-depth study of local birds, mammals, and reptiles, and swims in the Rio Bravo. Visitors may or may not see crocodiles, deer, peccaries, fer-de-lances, coatis, boa constrictors, margays, and jaguars in the surrounding jungle. Birdlife is plentiful with waterfowl and jungle birds represented. Scientists, research volunteers, donors, and interested travelers are encouraged to contact Programme for Belize.

Chan Chich

Built in the center of an ancient Maya plaza and surrounded by miles of steaming jungle, Chan Chich has an ambience all its own. When you're flying in, it's apparent that civilization is scarce. Driving in on the miles of oft-times bumpy road confirms it. For birdwatchers, naturalists, horseback riders, canoers, or those who love being out in the middle of nowhere (125,000 acres of it here), the experience can be exhilarating. Cleared trails wind through the rainforest, with a green canopy high above. Almost daily, guests run into a flock of beautiful ocellated turkeys out for their morning feed or hear the nightly roar of the howler monkey. Deer, peccary, puma, spider monkey, tapir, and the jaguar live in this country. Parrots and toucans, great currasows, crested guans, and several hundred other species inhabit the branches overhead.

Chan Chich means "little bird." Actually the word has many translations, depending on which

Maya dialect you use. The Maya site itself is a fairly recent discovery in the northwestern corner of Belize. Because of its isolation, it was a favorite spot to raise marijuana, and looters attempted to steal the treasures buried within the tombs. But no more! Now, with **Chan Chich Lodge,** Box 37, Belize City, Belize, C.A., tel. from the U.S. (800) 343-8009, fax (508) 693-6311, or from Belize (2) 75634, fax (2) 76961, under the watchful eye of managers/builders Tom and Josie Harding and the ardent guests wandering the jungle trails, it is no longer an *easy* task for robbers to dig their trenches and tunnel unseen.

The lodge offers an adventurer's ambience with a jungle location and rustic architecture that blends surreptitiously into the surroundings of Maya and nature. Each of the 12 cabañas has a thick thatched roof (good natural insulation against the jungle heat), beautiful hardwood interior, private bathroom with hot-water shower, electricity, ceiling fan, two queen-size beds, veranda, and walkways (paved with rounds of cabbage bark logs) that lead to the river. A charming community dining room/salon offers excellent food and a handsome outdoor bar. Guides are available for birdwatching. Canoeing the New River or the adjoining lagoon is a pleasant way to spend a few hours and have a chance to see some wildlife along the way. Guests at Chan Chich Lodge can arrange to ride quarter horses from nearby Gallon Jug stables and explore numerous jungle trails, fields, and sparsely traveled dirt roads. Additional Maya ruins are hidden in the recesses of the jungle. Nearby lakes are pretty sites for picnics. You must have a guide.

Chan Chich is 130 miles from Belize City, a 3.5-hour drive on all-weather roads from the international airport, or (much easier) take a 30-minute charter flight to nearby Gallon Jug. Rates are US$85 s, US$100 d, full meal packages US$35 adults, US$25 children under 12; all-inclusive prices are US$180 s, US$125 per person, double occupancy, including most activities, meals, rooms, Belikin beer, soft drinks, and tax. Tours and guides to the surrounding areas are easily arranged through Josie. Call or write for more information.

CAYO DISTRICT
INTRODUCTION

The largest of the six districts of Belize, the Cayo is also one of the most interesting. Here you'll find not only the nation's capital but the booming tourist center of San Ignacio. Maya, Mennonites, mestizos, Anglos, Creoles, and Chinese all commingle in government, commerce, and agriculture. The **Maya Mountains, Vaca Plateau,** and **Mountain Pine Ridge** are important geological features. Several major rivers drain the highlands, including the **Branch, Macal, Mopan,** and **Sibun.** Savanna, broadleaf jungle, and pinelands form a patchwork of habitats. Protected lands and private reserves include **Blue Hole National Park, Chiquibul National Park, Guanacaste National Park, Slate Creek Reserve,** and **Tapir Mountain Reserve.** A myriad of interesting caves and ruins were once used by the Maya. Among these are **Cahal Pech, Caracol, Chechem Ha Cave, El Pilar, Rio Frio Cave,** and **Xunantunich.**

While traveling in this part of the country you'll pass through many quaint-sounding villages.

Towns with names such as **Roaring Creek, Black Man Eddy, Holdfast, Double Head Cabbage, Washing Tree, Teakettle** add their own exotic charm.

HISTORY

The Mestizo Past
The Spanish influence is much stronger in the Cayo District than in either Belize City or Stann Creek. At one time the majority of the people in the Cayo were mestizo, their families having lived in the area for generations. In those days this bustling area depended mostly on the forests to survive, especially at the river port of San Ignacio from which logs and chicle were sent down the river to the sea, loaded onto ships, and sent across the world's oceans. Access to the area around San Ignacio, bordered on two sides by rivers, was limited to river traffic. Thus arose the name, Cayo, or "island" in Spanish.

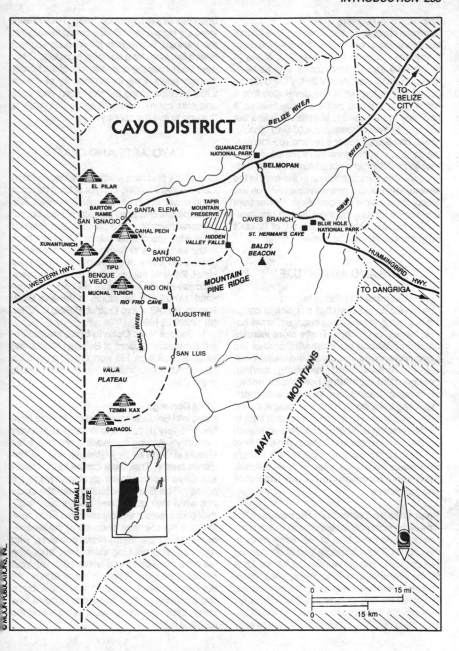

The Boom in Tourism

But times change. Today, while many residents are descendants of the original settlers, a great many are refugees from unsettled areas in Guatemala and El Salvador as well as newcomers from all over. And while the Cayo District still produces lumber, it has developed into a citrus, peanuts, and cattle area as well as a booming tourist center. Mennonite farms dot the area between Belmopan and San Ignacio. Small hotels and cottage resorts are increasing rapidly, attracting travelers worldwide who recognize Belize as a hot adventure travel destination. One recent advance in the area is the development of the hydroelectric dam on the Macal River below Benque Viejo. Power from the dam is lighting up the Cayo in unprecedented fashion, making it the envy of Belize's neighbor just across the border.

INLAND ADVENTURE

From Roughing It to Resorts

The traveler to the Cayo has a choice of camping or staying at numerous cottages, small hotels, lodges, or ranches. These more intimate accommodations are scattered across the Cayo countryside and attract the visitor interested in **birdwatching, canoeing, caving, cycling, fishing, hiking, horseback riding, swimming, tubing,** and **general adventuring.** Long treks through tropical foliage, canoe rides on a choice of rivers, horseback trips to hidden waterfalls, and quiet safaris to search out the shy animals and flamboyant birdlife of the Belizean forest are popular with visitors who return year after year to their favorite. Each accommodation has its own ambience and specialties.

River Trips on Yesterday's Highways

One of the most popular activities in Belize is canoeing along the banks of the many rivers in the country. This is a special kind of sightseeing —a chance to see the wonders of nature. Look for the ever-changing flora: plants, trees, vines, and blossoms that thrive along the river banks. Watch for the shy animals that live within their own private microcosms, including small underground burrows, sandy river beds, and leafy branches of tall hardwood trees. These rivers were the highways of Belize during the days of the Baymen. Sometimes it's so quiet you can hear a fish jump for a hovering mosquito. Other days you'll hear the dramatic roar of the howler monkey announcing its territory. By all means while traveling along the river keep your eyes and ears open—most will agree this really is the way to see the country.

CAYO ARTS AND CRAFTS

One of the premiere artists of Belize, **Carolyn Carr** creates haunting images of local Belizean life in acrylic at her studio near Belmopan. Animals, too, are cherished subjects of hers, but our personal favorite is the painting that reminds us of what the old marketplace was like back in the early days of Belize. One of her murals graces the lobby of the Ramada Royal Reef Hotel. Prints of her canvases are sold in many Belizean shops; an original will cost you thousands. You'll find her studio at **Banana Bank Ranch,** Box 48, Cayo District, Belize, C.A., tel. (8) 12020/23180.

In Benque Viejo **Octavio Sixto** creates detailed miniature replicas of Belizean shacks and landmark buildings. His work is sold around the country but, not surprisingly, more of it is available in the Cayo.

Slate Carvings

Maya and Belizean motifs set out in slate have become very popular and in some cases very expensive. Among the leading artists are the **Garcia sisters, Lesley Glaspie,** and the **Maganas family.** Their work can be found in several Cayo shops as well as elsewhere in the country. The Garcia sisters started the craze and while their quality has always been high, their prices remain equally elevated. Slate carvings are never cheap because of the time required to create them. Now, however, with more artists producing them, wise shopping will net a treasured piece without draining your personal treasury. Though many artists use the same subject matter, if you find a piece that excites you, it's a good idea to buy it now rather than later since you'll seldom find the identical piece.

Wood Furniture

Mennonite furniture is becoming increasingly popular as a take-home item. Cleverly executed chairs and small tables in mahogany and other tropical woods are the mainstays. In San Ignacio they are conveniently boxed ready for baggage check at the airport.

Arts and Crafts Shops

Of the art houses that you are apt to hear about in Belize, many are in Cayo; a couple of them are really outstanding. Most of the gift shops at various resorts around the countryside offer the same things. Check out the jewelry. We found charming little necklaces, bracelets, and earrings made from the vertebrae of a shark. The clever artist buys the carcass after the fishermen are finished butchering the fish. She then buries the bones in the ground and lets nature's tiny subterranean creatures do the rest, and shortly the bones are clean of all lingering flesh. From there the artist's methods are secret, but in the end she has created pure white, lightweight, attractive jewelry of symmetrical "fish beads."

In Belmopan look into **El Caracol Gallery & Gifts,** 32 Macaw Ave., Belmopan, Belize, C.A., tel. (8) 22394. East of San Ignacio, **Caesar's Place,** a friendly hotel/bar/restaurant/gift shop at Mile 62, Western Highway, tel. (92) 2341, fax (92) 3449, has encouraged local artists and artisans to create jewelry, slate carvings, and other works for sale. As a result, it has a huge selection,

probably the largest in the area. Ask about its locally made furniture.

In San Ignacio, **Eva's Restaurant,** 22 Burns Ave., San Ignacio, Cayo District, Belize, C.A., tel./fax (92) 2267, has a small but first-class selection of Belizean arts and crafts in the gift shop area. **Farmer's Emporium,** 24 Burns Ave., San Ignacio, Cayo District, Belize, C.A., tel. (92) 2253, carries among its array of arts and crafts a selection of Mennonite furniture that can be boxed for check-in at Belize International Airport. **Arts and Crafts Center,** 24 Burns Ave., San Ignacio, Cayo District, Belize, C.A., tel. (92) 2211, displays some fine Belizean arts and crafts. Behind it, **Arts and Crafts of Central America,** 1 Wyatt St., San Ignacio, Cayo District, Belize, C.A., tel. (92) 2253, specializes in "just what you're looking for." The **New Hope Trading Co.,** Buena Vista Rd., San Ignacio, Belize, C.A., tel. (92) 2188, offers exotic woodcrafts.

The Magana family has two shops, **Magana Zactunich Art Gallery** south of Cristo Rey Village and **Magana's Art Center** at the east edge of San Jose Succotz. Both sell Belizean and Guatemalan arts and crafts of good quality and at reasonable prices.

On the north edge of San Antonio the Garcia sisters have their **Tanah Mayan Art Museum** and store, San Antonio Village, tel. (92) 3310, fax (92) 3235. Prices and quality are high. In Benque Viejo, **Galeria del Arte de Gucumaz** has a choice of Belizean and Guatemalan crafts at reasonable prices.

ALONG THE WESTERN HIGHWAY

As you pass the Belize Zoo and head west along the Western Highway the sense of adventure begins to build. Savanna and pines border the road and the traffic is rarely heavy. The milepost markers that run between Belize City and San Ignacio will help you find your way around the countryside. If you're driving, just set your odometer to match the markers as you turn onto Cemetery Road at the western edge of Belize City. You'll pass two service stations between the Western Highway and the turnoff for Belmopan. Another lies down Constitution Drive on the way into Belmopan.

Manatee Junction

Driving west, note the junction with the **Manatee Road** on your left at about Mile 29. Look for the **Midway Resting Place,** a service station and motel of sorts on the southeast corner. Its tall Texaco sign makes it an especially good landmark at night when the sign is lit up. This improved dirt road is the shortcut to Gales Point, Dangriga, and the Southern Highway. It's always a good idea to top off your tank, stock up on cold drinks, and ask for current road condi-

tions here. Heavy rains can cause washouts on a lot of these "highways." It's a drive best done in daylight because of the picturesque views of jungle, Maya villages, and the Maya Mountains in the distance.

Monkey Bay Wildlife Sanctuary

A couple of miles farther down the road and on the left you will come to a sign at Mile 31 for Monkey Bay Wildlife Sanctuary. Take the short road up to the main building and have a look around. Matt Miller, an American transplant to Belize, runs this 1,070-acre private reserve with a board of directors and the financial assistance of Monkey Bay Wildlife Fund Tokyo. The main house has a gathering place upstairs with library, bulletin boards, and panoramic views of the pines, palmettos, and savanna. There's a casual feeling here of a college student union. That's little wonder, since the main focus is on educating the student groups Miller and staff bring in from the States.

You'll find two miles of trails, a 20-acre arboretum, and good swimming at nearby Sibun River. With the declaration by the Belize govern-

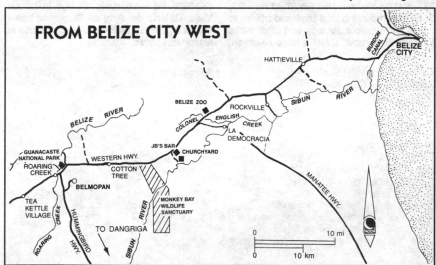

FROM BELIZE CITY WEST

ment in 1992 of the 2,250-acre **Monkey Bay Nature Reserve** across the river, there now exists a wildlands corridor between the **Manatee Forest Reserve** to the south and the sanctuary.

About a dozen raised platforms are available for camping. You can rent tents or bring your own. Meals are available at the main house as are cold showers. No, there are no monkeys and no bay, but the river does flow through and this is a good meeting place for backpackers. Rates for campers are US$5 per person per night. Vegetarian meals are available for US$3-5. For more information, write or call Box 187, Belmopan, Belize, C.A., tel. (8) 23180, fax (8) 23235.

PRACTICALITIES

J.B.'s Watering Hole

At around Mile 32, legendary J.B.'s Watering Hole, tel. (1) 49311, presents the traveler an opportunity to slake a thirst and chew the fat with locals and other travelers. This "watering hole" in the middle of nowhere has been around for years. A former favorite of British forces (now gone), it's one of the few such places worth stopping for between Belize City and San Ignacio. Locals say Harrison Ford was a regular during the filming of *Mosquito Coast.* Originally run by J.B., it's long since under new management. It's a good stop for a burger, or stewed chicken and a Belikin. Lift one to J.B.'s memory and the fair ladies who run it still; you'll be in good company.

Banana Bank Ranch

Originally one of the older working cattle ranches in the country, Banana Bank Ranch, run by artist Carolyn Carr and Montana cowboy-husband John, offers a change of pace in accommodations. Today, most of its pastures have been converted to growing corn and beans. It has electricity and a phone. Yet the place retains the ambience of the tropical ranch it was. Rooms and cabañas are fanciful and no two are alike. And the food is great, served family style! An unusual sidelight is a small menagerie that includes a resident jaguar and spider and howler monkeys, most of which were given to the Carrs as pets who had outworn their welcome.

Half of the 4,000-acre ranch is covered in jungle and within its borders guests will discover not only a wide variety of wildlife but a respectable-size Maya ruin. Its accompanying lagoon, hand-dug centuries ago, today harbors several Morlet's crocodiles. Scattered around the property are many more small "house mounds." With more than 20 saddle horses, Banana Bank Ranch features horseback riding; however, visitors can birdwatch, fish, hike, or take a boating trip down the Belize River with plenty of time left for a cooling swim. A lazy ride via horse-drawn buggy into the surrounding countryside is another treat, as is nighttime stargazing with an eight-inch telescope.

Five cabañas each sleep up to six people, and five more rooms in the main house accommodate guests, three with shared bathroom; one room is furnished with a water bed and has a private bath. In the lodge rates are US$47 s, US$65 d, US$90 t, US$104 q for shared bath; for private bath US$70 s, US$90 d; for the cabañas US$80 s, US$97.50 d, US$115 t, US$137.50 q, and US$149.50 f. Children under 12 are charged half price. Breakfast comes with the room; lunch is US$8, dinner US$12. For more information, write or call Box 48, Belmopan, Cayo District, Belize, C.A., tel. (8) 12020/22677. In the U.S. book through Great Trips, tel. (800) 552-3419, fax (218) 847-4442. Transfers are available; you'll be picked up in Belmopan for US$12.50 per person or in Belize City for US$70. Discounts for five or more people.

You'll find Banana Bank Ranch at Mile 47 on the right. Follow the signs; from the highway it's 1.25 miles on an all-weather road through fields and low jungle to the river. Park your vehicle to the right under the trees and amble down to the dock. Someone will pull a boat along the rope stretched from bank to bank to fetch you shortly. If you miss the first turnoff road, there's another past Roaring Creek Village at Mile 56, on the right. The sign says to take the road to the ferry, cross the river, and proceed to the ranch—a total of four miles.

Hector Silva Airport

Back on the Western Highway you'll pass Hector Silva Airport on the left with its monument and grassy field. So far there are no scheduled flights, but charter trips are available on **Maya Air, Island Air,** or any of the other airlines flying commuters around the countryside.

At Mile 48 on the left you'll find the **Hummingbird Highway,** which leads toward Belmopan, Dangriga, and the sea. To the right is **Guanacaste National Park.**

GUANACASTE NATIONAL PARK

A mere 56 acres, Guanacaste National Park packs a lot within its small area. This gem of a

park is sponsored by the **Belize Audubon Society, MacArthur Foundation, World Wildlife Fund,** and the government. It gets its name from the huge specimen of guanacaste or tubroos tree near the southwestern edge of the property. Ceiba, cohune palms, mammee apple, mahogany, quamwood, and other trees also populate the forest. Agouti, armadillo, coati, deer, iguana, jaguarundi, and kinkajou have all been observed in the park, along with more than 100 species of birds. Among the rarer finds are resident blue-crowned motmots. Picnic tables, benches, restrooms, and trash cans have been added slowly to the site, mostly by Peace Corps volunteers.

If you're going to Guanacaste, pack a lunch, bring a swimsuit, and take some time out at this quiet spot where the Belize River and Roaring Creek meet—you'll need very little coaxing to cool off with a swim.

The park was originally the home of the former British city planner who was commissioned after Hurricane Hattie in 1961 to relocate the capital. It's said that he chose the spot because of the proximity to the spectacular old guanacaste tree. The official decided almost immediately that the meadow should be set aside as a government reserve for future generations to enjoy. The huge tree, well over 100 years old, is more than 25 feet in diameter and host to more than 35 species of exotic flora, including orchids, bromeliads, ferns, philodendrons, and cacti, along with a large termite nest and myriad birds twittering and fluttering in the branches—a tree of life! When rivers were the main method of transport, travelers stopped here to spend the night under the protection of its wide-spreading branches. The only thing that saved the tree from loggers was its crooked trunk.

As you enter the park, walk across the grassy field; go left to get to the trail that brings you to the guanacaste. Beyond the tree there's a looter's trench—someone long ago thought there was treasure buried here—that demonstrates how a looter excavates and works a would-be treasure site (including Maya structures). Farther on, the path meets the shore of **Roaring Creek,** the westernmost boundary of the park. This is a wonderful and easy trail; you may or may not see another hiker, but you'll certainly see birds, delicate ferns, flowers, and long parades of wiwi ants—"cutters"—on the trail carrying their green mini-umbrellas (really pieces of leaves that they're carrying back to their nest).

From the entrance to the park, cross the meadow and veer to the right for the steps that lead down to the **Belize River.** Along the shore nature quietly continues its pattern of creation and subsistence. The *amate* fig grows profusely on the water's edge and provides an important part of the howler monkey's diet. In the center of this scheme is the tuba fish, which eats the figs that fall into the water, dispersing the seeds up and down the river—starting more *amate* fig trees. And so it goes—on and on. At dusk on a quiet evening, howler monkeys roar the news that they're having dinner—keep your distance, world! Park hours are 8 a.m.-4 p.m.

BELMOPAN

Opposite the entrance to Guanacaste National Park the Hummingbird Highway heads south past Constitution Drive, the turnoff to Belmopan. From there the Hummingbird continues toward the forest-covered hills beyond and Dangriga 55 miles away.

The New Capital City

About 50 miles from Belize City, Belmopan is the new capital of the country. The small, unpretentiously planned city was built far away from the coast to be safe from floods after two hurricanes in 30 years rammed their way through the coastal region with amazing destruction. After Hurricane Hattie in 1961, when the relocation was ordained, the government expected large numbers of the population of Belize City to move along with the government center; it didn't happen. Industry stayed behind and so did the jobs—the masses are still in Belize City, which remains the cultural and industrial hub of the country. Some capital employees continue to commute the 50 miles back and forth each day. However, Belmopan was designed for growth and continues to expand. You can see the tiny city very quickly, but it's a good hub for a variety of explorations.

Located in the geographical center of the country, Belmopan seems more like a quiet suburb than the capital of the country. It's worth a visit just to amble around the market, listen to the several languages being spoken, and buy a *punta* rock cassette tape or some fresh produce. As for the government buildings, they aren't particularly attractive with their all-over gray look and vaguely Maya design. Built of concrete, they should be sturdy enough to withstand the next hurricane. Government employees are friendly, though, and senior members are remarkably accessible.

Until a museum is built, the archaeological treasures of the country are stored in rooms in the government buildings. The town does have a large complex of sporting fields that includes basketball, volleyball, and tennis courts, as well as lots of space for spur-of-the-moment gatherings.

Orientation

From the Western Highway it's just a couple of miles down smooth pavement to the turnoff to Belmopan. Two roads allow the traveler to see what's useful and interesting. **Constitution Drive** curves gently to the left as it enters town, passing a handy gas station on the right and crossing **Bliss Parade** a couple of streets farther. This is one of the two most significant intersections in Belmopan. If you turn right onto Bliss Parade, the **Belmopan Hotel** will be immediately on your right, the **bus station** and **market square** on your left. If you follow Bliss Road to the right it joins **Ring Road**. As the name implies, this multilane extension describes a loop around the central town district, meeting Constitution Drive, the other important intersection, north of town. Along the way the **Bull Frog Inn** sits on the left at the back end of town. After you turn the corner and head back west toward Constitution Drive, an unnamed road to your right leads to Moho Street and the budget **El Rey Inn.** Keep following the Ring Road and you will pass various government buildings and embassies on the left before you meet up with Constitution Drive again.

Once you're on the access road that runs west through the market and toward Constitution Drive, to your left will be the bus station. Past the

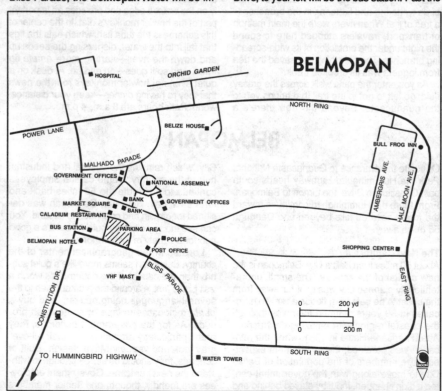

station on the left is Bliss Parade. Ahead and to the right across the access road is the **Caladium Restaurant.** Closer and across a parking lot to the right are the two **banks.**

Market Square

This is where the action is for visitors, its lines of stalls alive with the commerce and gossip of the area. Hang out here for a little while and you are sure to see a parade of local farmers, government workers, and colorful characters going about business. Try a tasty tamale for next to nothing. Bananas, oranges, mangos, tomatoes, chiles, and carrots are cheap, too, and there's even some produce you won't recognize, such as wild cilantro, which is just as tangy as the cultured herb back home.

Archaeology Department

If you're interested in antiquities, visit the vaults of the **Department of Archaeology** in the capital. Here the government is preserving finds from Belize's Maya sites. The Museum Building Fund is growing, and one day construction on the new museum must surely begin. Right now, visitors and Mayaphiles must still view these valuable traces of the last 1,000 years all crammed into a small vault. According to one archaeology commissioner, "Tourists on occasion become irate when they are denied access to the vault. This happens if they come on the wrong day, time, and/or without an appointment." So to avoid this problem, remember that the vault is open to the public Monday, Wednesday, and Friday, 1:30-4:30 p.m., and an appointment *must* be made two days in advance; tel. (8) 22106, or fax (8) 23345. Admission is free. Anyone interested in helping out financially should contact the **Association for Belizean Archaeology,** Belmopan, Belize, C.A.

ACCOMMODATIONS AND FOOD

Convenient to market square, government buildings, and the bus station, the contemporary **Belmopan Hotel** establishment encourages groups to hold meetings and conventions here. It offers meeting rooms, swimming pool and poolside bar, restaurant, group facilities, and a communications center. The 20 comfortable rooms have a/c, fans, and cable television. Some of the carpeting is a bit long in the tooth and the interior decorating is a little confused at times, but the people are friendly and eager to please. Ask for one of the rooms with a refrigerator. Grilled lobster, seafood, surf and turf, and T-bone steak head the menu here. The restaurant, tel. (8) 22130, serves three meals daily. Room rates run US$50 s, US$60 d, US$65 t; the hotel accepts traveler's checks, MasterCard, and Visa. For more information, write or call Box 237, Belmopan, Cayo District, Belize, C.A., tel. (8) 22130, fax (8) 23066, telex 146 Belcon BZ.

Long a favorite of Belmopan visitors, the **Bull Frog Inn,** 25 Halfmoon Ave., Belize, C.A., tel. (8) 22111, fax (8) 23155, sits in a quiet residential neighborhood with convenient access from Ring Road at its back. With the clean modern lines of a prosperous motel chain, the inn has 24 a/c or fan-cooled rooms with private baths, cable television, and lush tropical gardens. Rates for studio rooms are US$32.50 s, US$37.50 d; for lawn terrace rooms US$50 s, US$62 d.

The Bull Frog's indoor/outdoor restaurant and bar have a solid reputation among even the elite of Belmopan, and this is one of the most popular spots in town to dine. The fish fillet, roast beef with creamed potatoes, grilled lobster, chicken, and burgers are all good here. The inn serves fresh orange, lime, and grapefruit juice. Red and white tablecloths complement its breezy open-air design. Prices are moderate.

With economical daily specials listed on the chalkboard, the air conditioned, family-run **Caladium Restaurant** is a convenient place to sip a milkshake or a beer, or to linger over a lunch of local Belizean fare as you plan your next excursion. As a rule Belizean beef can't stand up to the quality of its pork. Here, however, the sirloin steak smothered in onions, bell peppers, and a rich gravy is excellent. The prices are right, the waitresses couldn't be friendlier, and the service is quick. Look for the Caladium, tel. (8) 22754, across the access road from the bus terminal, on Market Square.

GETTING THERE

There's really little reason to fly into Belmopan,

but if that's your choice, only charter flights are available into **Hector Silva Airport.** Most hotels in Cayo can arrange for pickup. Busses are much cheaper; take your choice of **Batty** Brothers, Novelo's, or Z-Line buses. All buses from Belize City to San Ignacio and Dangriga stop in Belmopan at Novelo's bus station in Market Square.

SOUTH OF BELMOPAN

Along Hummingbird Highway
The Hummingbird Highway is a real paradox. It boasts some of the best paved road in Belize and some of the worst. Beyond the turnoff for Belmopan are intermittent stretches of rough, partially paved road as well as quality, scenic highway. It's this good/bad quality of the road surface that presents a problem. Drivers may be lulled into complacency by smooth paved stretches, only to be rudely awakened by yet another round of dusty road and vicious potholes—not to mention the huge citrus trucks that ride down the center of the highway! All of the above create the challenge of driving the Hummingbird.

Another 10 miles down the road after passing the Belmopan turnoff, you drive by towering hills and lush jungle on each side as you cross the **Caves Branch Bridge** and enter the **Valley of Caves.** Nearby are the many caverns of **Caves Branch Estate, Blue Hole National Park,** and **St. Herman's Cave.** Put 20 more miles under your wheels and you have climbed into the **Maya Mountains,** passed the access road to **Five Blue Lakes National Park,** and experienced the high pass known as **Over the Top.** Now you're descending toward the sea.

Belize is improving the Hummingbird, but stretches between Over the Top and the Southern Highway still are in miserable shape. The junction with the Southern Highway is 20 miles farther—Dangriga is 25. (See the Stann Creek District chapter.)

SIGHTS

Maya Mountains
The high forested hills and green valleys of the northern end of the Maya Mountains provide beautiful scenery along much of the Hummingbird Highway. Sibun Valley is the most impressive of these. You'll see citrus orchards heavy with fruit, sleepy villages perched on the banks of rocky streams, craggy cliffs and gorges crusted with deep green beards of heavy jungle, and tracts of thick cohune forest. All will beckon you to stop, to explore, to linger a bit longer.

Blue Hole National Park And St. Herman's Cave
At about Mile 12.5 past Belmopan is a sign that indicates St. Herman's Cave; ignore it, and continue to the main entrance about a mile down the road. You'll find a parking area and a "cabaña" for those wishing to change for a dip in the deep blue waters of the Blue Hole. Covering 575 acres, Blue Hole National Park encompasses this water-filled sink, St. Herman's Cave, and the surrounding jungle. (Belize's other Blue Hole lies in the ocean at Lighthouse Reef.) Rich in wildlife, Blue Hole National Park harbors the jaguar, ocelot, tapir, peccary, tamandua, boa constrictor, fer-de-lance, toucan, crested guan, blue-crowned motmot, and red-legged honeycreeper.

The pool of the **Blue Hole** is an oblong collapsed karst sinkhole 300 feet across in some places and about 100 feet deep. Water destined for the nearby Sibun river surfaces briefly here only to disappear once more beneath the ground. Steps lead down to the swimming area, a pool only 25 feet deep or so.

St. Herman's Cave is not as convenient. As you face the Blue Hole the trail to St Herman's Cave lies to the right and requires a hike of a little more than a mile and a half over rugged ground that rises and falls. The trail begins by the changing cabaña. A flashlight and rugged shoes are necessities, a light windbreaker or sweater a wise choice for extended stays. The nearest of the three entrances is a huge sinkhole measuring nearly 200 feet across, funneling down to about 65 feet at the cave's lip. Concrete steps laid over the Maya originals aid explorers who wish to descend. The cave doesn't offer the advanced spelunker a real challenge, but neophytes will safely explore it to a distance of about a mile. Pottery, spears, and the remains of torches have been found in many caves in the area. The pottery was used to collect the clear water of cave drippings, called *Zuh uy Ha* by the Maya.

The entire area is a labyrinth of caves where the ancient Maya once lived and roamed; some of the chambers still show signs of rituals long past. A variety of caves lie in the hilly limestone nearby and include **Mountain Cow** and **Petroglyph Caves.** These can have cathedral-like ceilings hundreds of feet high or narrow cramped passageways. Some have crystal-coated stalactites and stalagmites; others have underground streams that seem to speak at times in murmured voices. And while you won't likely find any Maya living in the caves, you will find a number of harmless bats. Expect plenty of human company at these sites on weekends, too; during the week you'll usually have the place to yourself. Bring a flashlight, extra batteries, and sturdy walking shoes. The surrounding lush jungle is thick with tropical plants, delicate ferns, bromeliads, and orchids.

It's best to visit most of the caves with a guide, and at the least, don't visit the park unless the wardens are there. Make sure you lock your car and don't leave valuables in view.

ACCOMMODATIONS

Caves Branch Jungle River Camp

About the time you see the sign for St. Herman's Cave (Mile 12.5), you should see another sign to Caves Branch Jungle River Camp. Turn left and follow the dirt track about a mile into the jungle before you see signs of habitation to the left. Rounding a bend you'll drive directly into the camp and up to the main building. Behind and to the left are the open-sided dining area, about five cabins, and a couple of latrines, all linked by gravel paths. The camp has no electricity—all lighting is by kerosene—and no showers. Below a steep embankment, the Caves Branch River swirls over sand and gravel. It is handy for swimming—and bathing, depending on your modesty. Several spots are perfect for Tarzanlike dives into the refreshing waters below—if only there were a sturdy vine!

Each cabin has two accommodations. Three walls in each room have screened windows chest high and up. Though these are open-sided affairs, you feel a sense of coziness in the lantern's light before drifting off to sleep. Camping is also available at US$5 per person; tent US$10.

Adventure is the draw here. Owner Ian Anderson delivers with an array of choices for adventurous spirits; jungle treks both day and night offer glimpses of elusive jungle creatures. Don't be surprised to see coati, kinkajou, boa constrictors, fer-de-lance, paca, and more. You'll even find a Maya ruin nearby to explore.

This area is not called Caves Branch for nothing; on the 58,000 acres of the estate are 27 known caves, of which only about 15 have been mapped. Ian has developed a variety of trips around several of these. He offers tubing trips through river caves where at times the murmur of the water takes on the sound of human voices. Pristine dry caves glisten with crystal formations. Some caves still have pottery shards, skeletal re-

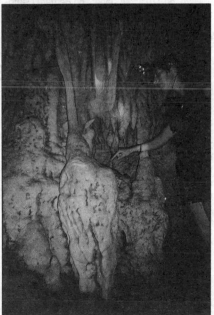

exploring caves at Cave Branch

PHIL LANIER

mains, and footprints coated with an icing of rock crystals. Caving activities range in price US$45-95. For the especially bold there are three- and six-day **Jungle Quest** survival treks in which an experienced guide teaches you tricks necessary to live off the land. Prices range from US$15 for the nature walk to US$450 for the six-day survival trek.

Room rates are: bunkhouse US$10 per person; cabaña US$20 s, US$35 d, US$45 t, US$55 q. Contact Ian Anderson's Adventure Tours, Box 356, Belmopan, Belize, C.A., tel. (8) 22800.

Tamandua Jungle Experience Cabañas
Just getting to Tamandua (named after the arboreal anteater) is an adventure. Look for the sign at **Over the Top** around Mile 32. Leaving the highway to the left, follow a dirt road out of town, cross a stream (not too deep), and go up and down a hilly dirt track (watch for peccaries). Finally you'll spot planted trees, some thatched-roof cabañas, Land Rovers, and a small gate to your left.

Here, on 170 acres, Janet and Bernard Dempsey have carved out a little paradise, surrounded by towering limestone karst hills and jungle. Fruit trees planted on the premises include custard apple, mango, passionfruit, coconut, guava, soursop, and banana; most are still quite small. The covered dining area and handful of airy cabañas sprinkled around a flowing stream seem to snuggle into the landscape. They are based on traditional Maya designs, sit on short stilts, and are made mostly of *santa maria,* a very durable hardwood. Each cabaña can sleep two to three people. Toilets are of the eco-friendly composting type. You bathe in the stream below. Lights are kerosene—there's no electricity. In a rare concession to civilization, a butane fridge in the kitchen keeps wine and beer cold. The Dempseys offer trips to many sites around the farm and surrounding area, including caves, waterfalls, and **Five Blue Lakes National Park** nearby. This is another destination for those in good physical condition. Bring a rain poncho, water, and bug repellent. Guided tours are US$20/day, minimum two people. Meal prices are: breakfast US$5; packed lunch US$7; dinner US$15. Cabaña rates are US$30 d; each additional person US$10. This is too far to come without a room waiting, so reservations are suggested. Contact the Dempseys, Box 306, Belmopan, Belize, C.A.

WEST OF BELMOPAN

Westward from Belmopan on the highway, anticipate lots of big trucks, slow-moving traffic, and pedestrians.

Tapir Mountain Nature Reserve
Covering 6,741 acres, Tapir Mountain is one of the newest jewels in the country's crown of natural treasures. The deep, steamy jungle is ripe with an abundance of plantlife. Every wild thing native to the region roams its forests, from toucans to tapirs, from coatis to kinkajous. To the southwest lie the towering cliffs of the Mountain Pine Ridge, the lush valley called the **Vega** in **Slate Creek Preserve,** and the vast forest lands of the **Chiquibul Forest Reserve.** For access to these areas contact the Belize Audubon Society, Box 1001, Belize City, Belize, C.A., tel. (2) 35004/34987, fax (2) 34985/78562.

ACCOMMODATIONS AND FOOD

Pook's Hill Lodge
At Teakettle Village (around Mile 52.5) look for the sign to the lodge, Box 14, Belmopan, Belize, C.A., tel. (8) 12017. Turn to the left onto a dirt road. More signs will lead the way. After four miles turn right and the property begins less than a mile down the road. Another three-quarters of a mile will take you to the lodge. Located in a 300-acre jungle reserve adjacent to Tapir Mountain Reserve, the lodge is owned by Ray and Vicki Snaddon. Many birds and animals use the property, and the lodge surrounds a small Maya plaza. You can go birdwatching, hiking, rafting, or tubing. Horseback riding costs $35 a half day, US$50 a full day. The bar/lounge overlooks the creek. All cabins are doubles, have palm-thatched roofs, private baths with

h/c water, and kerosene lamps. At press time three cottages were completed with four more nearly ready. Breakfast is included with the room. Lunch is US$9; dinner US$15. Rates for cabins are US$60 s, US$75 d. Children under 12 are free.

Warrie Head Creek Lodge

Another great Cayo lodge! A stroll down a grassy hillside brings you to bubbling cascades where the Belize River and Warrie Head Creek meet, a walking trail, and a spring-fed pool that's perfect for swimming. This is a bit of paradise

with orchid trails, 189 species of birds, and 40 varieties of fruit trees. Eight comfortable rooms are fan-cooled, and have h/c water, showers, and bar service; the dining room serves delicious food. Owners Bia and Johnny Searle offer river trips, trips to the popular sights in the country, and horseback riding. If you have the chance, take the time to talk to Bia. She was born and raised in Belize and can tell you about Belize past and Belize today. She has wonderful stories about growing up with a Creole nanny who became her surrogate mother and grandmother to her children for many years before

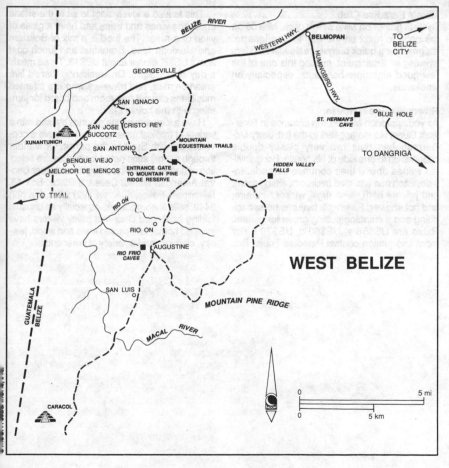

WEST BELIZE

her death. Ask her about "ground" food (giant yams and potatoes), *calalu,* and *ackee* (a Jamaican tree that produces a substitute for eggs). Bia is collecting antique Belizean colonial furniture. Eventually she will have it in all of the rooms; for now the upstairs lounge is furnished with it. Ask about a canoe trip to Iguana Creek, with or without a paddler, US$10 half day. Contact the lodge, Box 244, Belize City, Belize, C.A., tel. (2) 77257, fax (2) 75213; in the U.S. call International Expeditions, (800) 633-4734. Rates are US$60 s, US$70 d, breakfast US$6, lunch US$9, dinner US$18.

Mike's Paradise Club
Cyclists gather on Mike's high deck, Mile 58 on the right, to relax on the way to San Ignacio. It's great for a quick burger break. Mike's offers evening entertainment, making this one of the few good nighttime hangouts, especially on weekends.

Riverwalk Guest House
As you approach Mile 60, the entrance to Riverwalk Guest House appears to the left. Jerry McDermott has built two very classy double cabañas off to one side of his house. Bougainvillea twines above their common veranda. Inside, each has a/c, tiled bedroom, sitting room, and private bath, area rugs, wicker furniture, and hot shower. Riverwalk features horseback riding and a chipping/putting green for golfers. Rates are US$50 s, US$60 d, US$70 t. For more information contact Paradise Tours, Box

42809-400, Houston, Texas 77242, tel. (713) 850-1664, fax (713) 785-9528.

Caesar's Place
A hotel/gift shop/restaurant/bar of some renown sits on the right at Mile 62. Caesar Sherrard rents a number of clean garden rooms. Each has a private bath, h/c water, tile floors, and ceiling fans. Camping is available for US$5 per person; full RV hookups can be negotiated, too. Rates for rooms are US$55 s, US$65 d, US$70 t. For simple cabañas in beautiful jungle river surroundings at the same price ask about **Black Rock.**

This is also a lovely spot to sit in the shade under the vines and trees and have a glass of wine or a meal. The food is a mix of Belizean and Mexican food. Breakfast and lunch cost about US$6, dinner about US$13. Three meals a day cost US$25. On weekends there's live entertainment, and travelers who are talented musicians can get free room and board for jamming with the house band.

Have a look around the grounds planted with a variety of tropical greenery. And do have a conversation with Stanton the parrot. Or wander through the gift shop noted for its massive selection of handmade Belizean crafts and other Central American wares. Caesar's Place, Box 48, Belmopan, Belize, C.A., tel. (92) 2341, fax (92) 3449, sells fine woodwork, especially an unusual folding hardwood chair that many visitors have shipped home, and carved slate and wood, jewelry, clothing, and a variety of other crafts.

GEORGEVILLE TO MOUNTAIN PINE RIDGE

Georgeville is not much more than a bump in the road at Mile 63. For the traveler it has no real attraction, other than—it is across the road from an abundance of small lodging signs where one turns left onto the Pine Ridge Road (also known as Chiquibul Forest Road). Down this long, curving, bumpy road lie the treasures of the Mountain Pine Ridge. For some travelers to Belize this area is the highlight of the trip. The road winds through the tropical foothills past orange and cattle farms before the terrain begins to gradually change to sand, rocky soil, then red clay, and tall pine trees. Soon the road rises and you are surrounded by tall pines, rushing streams, small and large waterfalls, and patches of thick forest with the echoing calls of the *chachalaca* and *tinamou*. Creases of land within narrow river valleys are rich with stands of tall hardwood trees, many covered with orchids and bromeliads. At certain times of the year bright-colored clouds of flamboyant butterflies float from tree to bush. Here and there small clearings have been carved out of the jungle by *milperos* (slash-and-burn farmers), and picturesque clusters of thatch huts surrounded by banana and cohune trees with delicate blossoms show Belizean life in the slow lane.

This is another "wily" road; some of it is fine, the rest is rocky, uneven, and bumpy, and will shake even the sturdiest vehicle. Certain sections are impassable during the rainy season; check out conditions before you head up.

SIGHTS

While there is plenty of opportunity to relax in the piney woods, broadleaf jungle, or by rushing streams, the Mountain Pine Ridge tends to draw energetic people. This is as true of those who manage its resorts as the guests themselves. For active people of all ages the Mountain Pine Ridge offers **bird-watching, caving, Maya ruins, horseback riding, jungle treks, mountain biking, opportunities for nature study,** and **swimming.**

Slate Creek Preserve
Mountain Equestrian Trails and several other private landowners have set aside 3,000 acres as a private preserve. The purpose of the preserve is to protect the watershed, plants, and animals of a valley called the Vega. Within this limestone karst area is a myriad of life. Mahogany, santa maria, ceiba, cedar, and cohune palms tower above. Orchids, ferns, and bromeliads are common. Birds such as the aracari, emerald toucanet, keel-billed toucan, keel-billed motmot, king vulture, and various parrots and hummingbirds are to be found here. Puma, ocelot, coati, paca, and anteater roam the forests. Resident biologist Jan Meerman shares information about his work and the surrounding ecosystems with visitors. For more information contact Mountain Equestrian Trails, Mile 8, Mountain Pine Ridge Road, Central Farm Post Office, Cayo District, Belize, C.A., tel. (8) 23180; fax (8) 23235.

Hidden Valley Falls
Mountain Pine Ridge Forest Reserve covers almost 300 square miles, and only controlled logging is allowed. Follow the reserve's main road for about two miles beyond the entrance and you'll come to the turnoff for Hidden Valley Falls. From the turnoff the road keeps going down for about four miles and brings you to the falls and a picnic area. These spectacular falls plunge about 1,000 feet over the granite edge down to the jungle. It's a moderately difficult hike to climb the rocks to the falls.

Rio On Pools
Continuing south toward Augustine Village you will cross the Rio On. It's well worth the climb over an assortment of worn boulders and rocks to a delightful site with waterfalls and several warm-water pools; don't forget your camera. There's a parking area just off the road.

Rio Frio Cave
Back on the highway, turn right at **Douglas De Silva** (the western division of the Forestry Department) and continue for about five miles. Follow the signs to the parking lot. From here

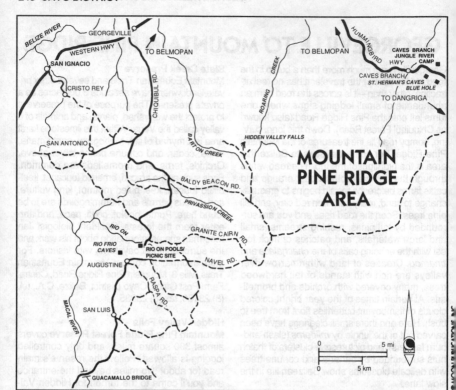

MOUNTAIN PINE RIDGE AREA

visitors have a choice of exploring nature trails (note the purple ground orchids growing along the paths) and two small caves on the road or continuing to the largest and most well-known river cave in Belize, the Rio Frio, with an enormous arched entryway into the half-mile-long cave. Filtered light highlights ferns, mosses, stalactites, and geometric patterns of striations on rocks. Each step stirs up the musty smells of the damp rocky cave. Watch where you walk; sinkholes are scattered here and there, and a narrow stream flows along the gravel riverbed.

Caracol Archaeological Site
This is the Maya city state that toppled Tikal. Located in a nationally declared archaeological preserve, within the Chiquibul Forest Reserve, this site offers a wealth of natural wonders

as well as the fabled Maya ruins. (See "Maya Archaeological Sites" in the Mundo Maya chapter.)

ACCOMMODATIONS

Travelers will find only a handful of places to stay near Mountain Pine Ridge. But, within that limited number is great variety. Visitors have a choice of a working citrus farm, a couple of ranch/equestrian resorts, or resorts with miles of hiking trails and panoramic vistas of the river gorges and their roaring waterfalls. Cabañas on piney hillsides offer caving hikes nearby. Two resorts sit on the banks of Privassion Creek: one a luxurious resort owned by Hollywood director Francis Ford Coppola and the other a more modest lodge owned by local Belizeans. You can't find much more variety than that in ambience and budget.

Those interested in camping must get permission from the forest guard at the entrance of Douglas De Silva Reserve (formerly called Augustine); camping is permitted both at the entrance to the reserve and at Augustine Village, about 10 miles south. Neither spot is particularly scenic. But traveling the circular route will take you past beautiful scenery and to the falls and the caves.

Cool Shade Farm

At about Mile 2.5 on the Pine Ridge Road a sign on the left points to **Barton Creek Farms** and a cluster of buildings on a hill in the distance. This small handsome resort sits on the breezy hilltop with panoramic views of the surrounding citrus groves and the hills beyond. The resort has six double rooms and a cabaña off to one side. Meals are available. Rates are US$65 d and US$10 each additional person. Most major credit cards are accepted. Contact Marla Holder, Box 255, Belmopan, Belize, C.A., tel. (92) 2146; fax (92) 3089.

Maya Ranch Guesthouse

This lodging, owned by John and Beth Roberson, is situated on a 5,000-acre working cattle ranch at Mile 4.5 on the right. While John rides the range, Beth runs **Guacamallo Treks Horse Excursions** and puts up guests in the comfortable house behind their home. The guest house is filled with the warm tones of tropical wood and has two bedrooms, full kitchen, living room, h/c bath, area rugs and tapestries, veranda on three sides, and easy chairs in which to take in the view. Lights are on between 5 p.m and 9 p.m. only; kerosene lamps are used at all other times. The Robersons offer tours to many sights, from nearby nature trails to Caracol Ruins. If guests prefer they can join John in "moving" cattle. Buggy rides to the Barton Creek Mennonite Village are another highlight. The horses are a quarter horse mix and the tack is American. Prices for rides start as low as US$35 for a breakfast ride (includes hearty breakfast afterward) to US$280 for a two-day Caracol/Chiquibul Forest Excursion.

Room rates are US$60 s, US$70 d, US$85 t, US$95 q. Continental breakfast is included; Beth will provide lunches for US$7. Generally, though, you're on your own; this is not for those who want to be pampered. Contact Beth Roberson, Box 198, Belmopan, Belize, C.A., tel. (1) 49117, fax (92) 3075.

Mountain Equestrian Trails

At Mile 8 turn left at the MET sign and follow the road back to the left. Jim and Marguerite Bevis offer a wonderful change of pace and an opportunity to see areas of Belize that are without roads—this is especially interesting if you're an equestrian. Before the Bevis family took over and built the lovely cabañas, only the "horse people" thought of coming here. No more. This small resort now

Rio On River cascades through the mountains.

CAYO COTTAGE COUNTRY

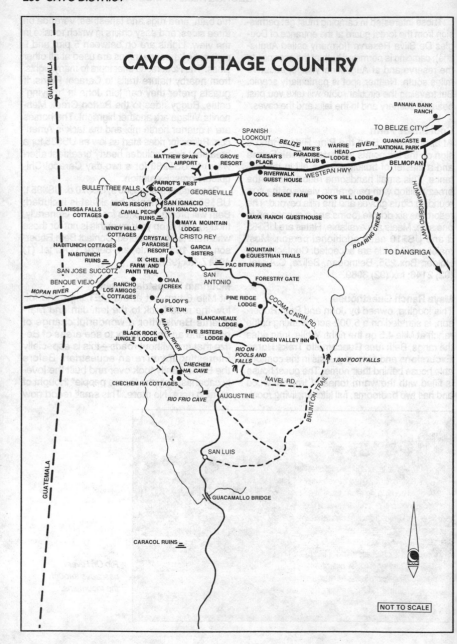

NOT TO SCALE

THE OLD AND NEW WEST OF BELIZE

Cayo District reminds many visitors of America's Old West. San Ignacio Town projects the flavor with narrow streets, old buildings with wooden store fronts and broad overhangs, a general mercantile, an abundance of Chinese restaurants, and country folk coming to town for their weekly supplies.

Just a short distance out of town, Mountain Equestrian Trails Ranch (referred to as MET) is a sample of the new "West" of Belize. Ranchers Jim and Marguerite Bevis, together with their four children, live the typical ranch life of the '90s in the tropics. They thrive on their way of life. And although living in this isolated area has its problems, it's nothing this family (and many others just like it) hasn't conquered. School lessons are learned at the dining-room table under Marguerite's supervision, though sometimes a student-teacher from the U.S. comes to live with them for a few months at a time. As the kids get tall enough to climb a horse on their own, they learn the skills to become excellent horsemen and horsewomen under the watchful eye of dad, Jim. And the whole family takes part in running the ranch, one way or another.

Jim moved to Belize with his parents in 1962 when he was 11. By the time he was 13 he had bought his first dory (dug-out canoe), which he traded for one bottle of White Horse whiskey. He speaks fluent Spanish and Creole, knows Belize's rugged bush, the local culture and folklore, and gives a lot of himself to Belize and those interested in Belize. He learned his equestrian skills while growing up and today has a reputation as one of the best expeditionary guides in the country.

Marguerite is a registered nurse from Texas. She's had to use her medical training on more than one occasion in the countryside. To deal with the infrequent emergencies around the ranch, she was taught how to suture (she practiced on a chicken's foot) by a Boston physician. The school desk/dining-room table serves as an examining table. As for children's illnesses, she tells how she

has depended on Rosita Arvigo's earthy remedies. She recalls with a shudder one frightening bout with amoebic dysentery; in the end it was Rosie's herbal *negrita* that cured her daughter.

Though spread out in the hilly district, with neighbors usually a long distance apart, this is a close-knit community alive with pioneer spirit—no telephone lines, television stations, supermarkets, or movie theaters.

They have developed communication using telephone lines in Belmopan and radio frequencies. If you call one of the out-of-the-way jungle cottage resorts in Cayo District, everyone with a radio hears the call come through and the conversation—a lot like small-town party lines in the Old West. As Marguerite puts it, "We have no secrets." And because of this open community "telephone," neighbors also know when there's an emergency. If help is needed, they give it freely.

Adventurers/guests enjoy visiting MET. Always looking for new challenges, Jim awhile back took seven people across the Maya Mountain Divide on foot. The group rode horses to Caracol and then to Las Cuevas, an old sheep campsite deep in the Chiquibul Forest. From here the group began a trek that took 14 days, "some of the most difficult hiking I've done," according to Jim. Although the group was elated by the trek, it had a dramatic ending when the Maya guide slipped on a steep rocky precipice and fractured his pelvis. Fortunately, Jim had a high-frequency radio and was able to get help

right away; a military helicopter airlifted the injured man to a hospital in no time. Will the visitors make that trek again? They can't wait, not even the guide!

MET is a working guest ranch and the whole family helps to entertain. Teen-age son Arran started a truck garden. He plants cucumbers, Chinese cabbage, and other vegetables that he then sells to his parents to use in the restaurant. Already learning to be an entrepreneur, he sells the excess at market with the other farmers. Lacy is learning the joys of being a gourmet cook in the dining room. Heather and Trevor still would rather hang around the stables and the horses, run through the grassy fields, or walk the nature trail.

Marguerite and Jim are very concerned about the preservation of their beautiful countryside, and with other landholders are creating Slate Creek Preserve, a privately owned reserve. Jim and the kids are establishing a butterfly trail on the ranch for visitors to wander. They've made a study of which plants to leave alone and which they can bring in to attract the beautiful fluttery creatures that live in the jungle throughout Belize.

If you happen along the road, you'll know MET by the beauty and tranquility of the land, healthy horses grazing in green pasture with tall and short trees (covered with brilliant blossoms in March), a lovely house perched on the side of a hill, and a bunch of happy kids who may not know much about the latest Saturday cartoons, but who can tell you which is a gumbo-limbo tree, where you can find a Baird's tapir, and who can saddle up a horse in double time (see "Accommodations" in the "Georgeville to Mountain Pine Ridge" section).

offers a relaxing alternative to a seaside vacation. To take advantage of the location—close to the Mountain Pine Ridge area, the mountains, Caracol, and the entire Cayo District—it helps to have a car to get around in. No matter that the small cantina is a 20-minute drive from San Ignacio, it still attracts visitors and locals from all around for drinks, dinner, and good conversation.

For the horseperson, this is a working farm/ranch, with 20 beautiful quarter horses in peak condition and expertly trained on the 150-acre ranch; you have your choice of a gentle or spirited horse. Trips are designed to suit every taste, from mountain trails that wander past magnificent waterfalls and pools where everyone is lured for a swim, to pine forests that take in creeks, Maya caves, Caracol, exotic butterflies, and more than 150 species of orchids. The equestrian trails are only a few miles from Rio Frio Caves and Hidden Valley Falls, where the water drops into the jungle below. Programs are designed for both beginners and experienced riders—children from age 10 with previous riding experience are welcome. Kids feel right at home with the Bevis brood; all are excellent riders, even down to the youngest, Trevor. Ask about customized tent/camping trips called Chiclero Trails.

Guests will find lovely cabañas of thatch, stucco, and exotic wood interiors with private bathrooms and h/c water (no electricity—yet); very comfortable. Meals are served in the cozy cantina/restaurant, which serves a variety of excellent food (breakfast is included with the room, lunch US$10, dinner US$15). Room rates are US$85 s, US$90 d, US$100 t, plus US$5 service charge per person per night; riding fees are extra. Riders are required to carry personal liability insurance to cover themselves while touring. For a brochure and more information write to Mountain Equestrian Trails, Central Farm Post Office, Cayo District, Belize, C.A., or Box 180, Belmopan, Belize, C.A., tel. (8) 23180, (8) 22149, fax (8) 23235. For a special look at the Bevis family, see the Special Topic, "The Old and New West of Belize."

Hidden Valley Inn

Those looking for the solitude of long hikes through pines and jungle to waterfalls and pristine pools should take a look at the lovely Hidden Valley Inn, Mountain Pine Ridge, Box 170, Belmopan, Belize, C.A., tel. (8) 23320, fax (8) 23334, in the U.S. (800) 334-7942. It's always a surprise to find this upscale resort in the midst of tall sparse pine trees in the middle of nowhere. To get there turn left at Mile 14 onto Cooma Cairn Road. Then just follow the signs. On the left, set on 18,000 acres of private reserve, this is really a "get-away" vacation. The main house is the gathering place for guests in several spacious public rooms: a comfortable lounge, card room, TV room, library filled with good reading material, and the dining room, where dinner is served in candle-lit splendor. The 12 cottages have *saltillo* tile floors, vaulted ceilings, cypress-paneled walls, fireplaces, ceiling fans, screened louvered windows, comfy beds, and private baths with h/c water. When the main electricity goes out at night, 12-volt bedside lamps and night-lights are available. For those who enjoy hiking, well-tended trails on the property lead past **Tiger Creek Pools and Falls, King Vulture Falls** (where the king vulture nests), **Dragonfly Pool, Butterfly Falls** and **Crystal Pools, Lake Lollyfolly,** and the famous **Hidden Valley Falls** (also known as **1,000 Foot Falls**). For birders, bird blinds are set up where you can glimpse such beauties as orange-breasted falcons, rose-breasted grosbeak, indigo bunting, and the ocellated turkey. Picnic lunches are provided. Bed and breakfast rates are US$77.50 s, US$105 d; lunch is US$7.50, dinner US$17.50.

Pine Ridge Lodge

Set on a hill beside the Little Vaqueros Creek, Pine Ridge Lodge, Box 2079, Belize City, Belize, C.A., tel. (92) 3310, from the U.S. (216) 781-6888, is a few miles inside the Mountain Pine Ridge Reserve (be prepared to stop at

the gate) and a bit past Mile 14. Turn right at the sign. Owners Vicki and Gary Seewald have extensively planted the grounds, and various epiphytes and orchids live on the pines. The lodge consists of eight renovated cottages, each with a colorful Maya-inspired wall painting on the exterior. All the cottages have screen porches, lanterns, private bathrooms with coldwater showers (they are being upgrading to hot water), original Maya-style art, pottery, and Guatemalan textiles. The open-air cafe serves good home cooking, fresh juices and fruits, eggplant parmigiana, and, as Gary (the owner) says, the best French toast in Belize (he makes it). A large outdoor grill awaits barbecues, and two screened palapas nearby allow parties to eat together in semi-privacy. The Sewalds advertise the **Pine Ridge Tavern** as being the "last stop for a cold beer before heading off to Caracol." Ask for a Riverview cottage; the calming sound of the stream is wonderful. Room rates are US$70 d, continental breakfast included, summer rates US$50, US$15 per person for each additional person. Dinner and lunch are $7 per person. The lodge is only seven miles from the Rio On pools. Write or call for more information.

Blancaneaux Lodge

This is the place for people who *do* want to be pampered! It's a director's fantasy on a bluff overlooking the rocks and falls of Privassion

Hidden Valley Inn

Creek. Here Francis Ford Coppola has created a little hideaway for those who want a softer, more exclusive, experience in Belize. At about Mile 14.5 turn right at the sign for Blancaneaux Lodge, Box B, Central Farm, Cayo District, Belize, C.A., tel./fax (92) 3878. The **Blancaneaux Airstrip** will appear on the right. Turn left at the splashy gate and head down to the end of the drive; don't be put off by the stockade fence to the right. You'll notice a grassy courtyard (perfect they say for croquet) and fountain to one side, the lodge and planted gardens to the other, and the cabañas and villas below. The lodge of rustic wood and stone features a restaurant, bar, deck, fireplace, and two double rooms upstairs.

Cabañas of native woods are constructed in a tropical design with panoramic screened decks in back. In fact, the deck with its flamboyant view is the focus of each cabaña; it can be screened off from the rest of the room at night. The rest is simply comfortable and fanciful. A few luxurious villas include kitchens; but who wants to cook here when the lodge has a gourmet chef? The dining room offers delicious pastas (a *lot* of pastas) and other Italian foods with a selection of wines from Coppola's vineyards—costly. If you like exotic drinks try the one they call "Jaguar Juice." The staff is friendly and hard-working and comes from a variety of ethnic backgrounds. The staff even includes a licensed massage therapist; the word from guests is that he really gets the kinks out. Got that screenplay to finish? Computer hookups, fax, and other modern communications are available. Rates for lodge rooms are US$65 s, US$90 d; for cabañas US$110 s, US$145 d; for villas US$225 s, US$275 d; US$25 per person additional. Meals are expensive by Belize standards; a continental breakfast is about US$12, dinner is US$30, a lunch/dinner package is US$40.

Five Sisters Lodge

Past Blancaneaux a couple of miles, a locally owned resort sits above a well-known attraction called Five Sisters, five small waterfalls. At press time the lodge was not quite finished, but there was a restaurant/bar with deck and a commanding view of the Privassion Creek. In addition, about half a dozen cabañas overlook the creek and the small island in its center. Steps leading down allow the hardy access to a swim and a drink at the island. This trip down involves a lot of steps (both ways) so anyone with health problems might just enjoy the view from the top. It's a good opportunity to mingle with the locals who come here on weekends. Contact Carlos Popper, (92) 3184.

GEORGEVILLE TO SAN IGNACIO

Grove Resort

Between Belmopan and San Ignacio at Mile 65.5 on the Western Highway, start looking for a sign that will direct you to the Grove Resort, Box 1, San Ignacio, Cayo District, Belize, C.A., tel./fax (92) 2421. Set on 50 wooded acres, the unexpected upscale resort includes six deluxe villas. Each contains two-room suites with a/c, fans, Italian marble, rattan furniture, refrigerator, and a veranda overlooking the tropical countryside. The concrete buildings are pink and white, with sliding glass doors that open onto private patios. For fun there's a swimming pool, volleyball court, tennis court, horseshoes, outdoor fitness center, and a nature trail. Touring is made easy with on-premises car rental or escorted day-trips to the cayes or other destinations in the country. Dining is either poolside or in the upstairs clubhouse dining room with a great view.

Daily room rates are US$100 s, US$125 d, US$10 per person additional, children under 5 free; meal plans are per person, US$35 FAP or US$27 MAP. For more information contact Bob or Peg Hufstutler, who have a fine reputation for running resorts after four successful years at Caye Chapel.

Mennonite Country

Follow the sign to **Spanish Lookout Village**. It's always a surprise in the tropics—the landscape suddenly changes from ragged forest covered with vines and creepers and shaggy ferns to neat barns and rolling green countryside. This is one of the Mennonite communities whose founders brought a small bit of Europe with them and, over the years, developed a fine agricultural industry that supplies a large part of the milk, cheese, and chicken for the country.

Santa Elena

At the moment there's not much of interest to the average visitor in Santa Elena other than its proximity to its sister city across the Macal River. That is going to change, however, and there is already a notable exception.

Run by Michael and Diane Waight, the **Snooty Fox Guest House**, 64 George Price Ave., Santa Elena, Cayo District, Belize, C.A., tel. (92) 2150, fax (92) 3556, is a sign of things to come in Santa Elena. It seems geared for the younger set. Overlooking the Macal River from a lofty perch, it boasts a large suite with kitchen, stocked refrigerator, cable TV, and h/c private bath; two cabañas with cable TV, private baths, and fans; and two budget rooms with a shared bath. A pleasant bar has a pool table and canoes for rent. Rates run from US$20 for a budget room to US$50 for a suite.

SAN IGNACIO

San Ignacio is the largest city in western Belize and the district capital. This agricultural community is a peaceful, though busy, hub nestled in rolling hills with clusters of houses scattered on hillsides and valleys along with the remains of once-elegant Maya ceremonial centers. The Maya, the country's first farmers, also appreciated these rich valleys.

At one time a busy port, now the river is a placid part of both San Ignacio and Santa Elena. Here you'll see women doing their wash, kids splashing around to keep cool (and accomplishing a bath at the same time), and car-washing in the shallows on Sunday.

ORIENTATION

Hawksworth Bridge

The impressive Hawksworth Bridge links the highway between Santa Elena and San Ignacio. As the only suspension bridge in Belize, it's a high-tech dot on the landscape of the low-key Belize countryside. It even has one of the few traffic lights in the entire country. In the past, whoever reached the center of the one-lane bridge first had the right of way, and the other vehicle had to back off the bridge; occasionally the local gendarme had to come along and measure car distances to settle the drivers' arguments. But that's a thing of the past now with a neat line of traffic waiting patiently at the red light. Old-timers say the water rose as high as this bridge during Hurricane Hattie!

The police station and post office are immediately to your left as you leave the Hawksworth Bridge. But the main action in town is to your right down Burns Avenue. This short strip about two blocks long is where the heart of the town pulses. Here you'll find Eva's Restaurant. You'll also find several hotels in a row, a bank, and stores to provide you most anything you need. It's as convenient a street as you will find in all Belize. But there's more to explore within a block or two east or west.

San Ignacio Tourist Center

Although the city doesn't have an *official* government tourist office, what sometimes appears to be the nerve center of the entire Cayo is the "surrogate" tourist office called **Eva's Restaurant and Bar**, 22 Burns Ave., San Ignacio, Cayo District, Belize, C.A., (92) 2267. The government should take a lesson; this is probably the best information center in the entire country. Some say the Cayo is its own little universe. If so, then Eva's Restaurant must be the center of that cosmos. Many experienced travelers make it their first stop in town. Eva's is a gathering spot not only for knowledgeable wanderers but also for many people who run the cottages and activities in the area. Bulletin boards on two walls keep diners up to date on all the activities offered in the area. The biggest asset is owner Bob Jones, a walking database of information for just about anything that's happening in San Ignacio and along the river.

So, if you need help finding a budget room (Eva's has pictures and rates of most of the budget resorts along the river), or a guide, or a tour operator, or information on almost anything in the area from nightlife to natural history, ask for Bob. He's never impatient though he undoubtedly answers the same questions thou-

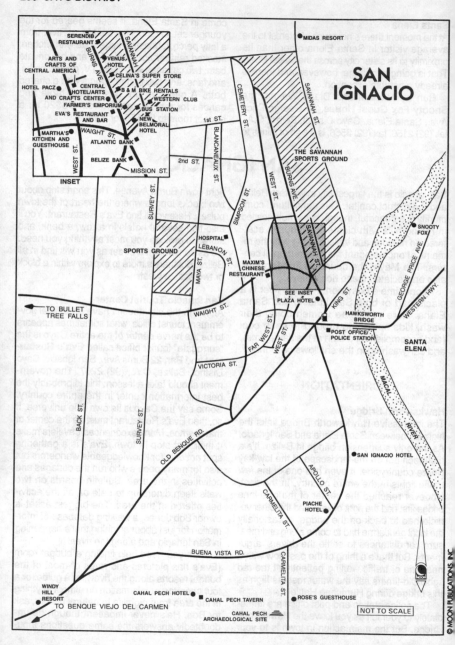

SAN
IGNACIO

SERENDIB
RESTAURANT

ARTS AND CRAFTS
OF CENTRAL AMERICA

VENUS
HOTEL

CELINA'S SUPER STORE

HOTEL PACZ

CENTRAL
HOTEL/ARTS
AND CRAFTS CENTER

B & M BIKE RENTALS

WESTERN CLUB

FARMER'S EMPORIUM

BUS
STATION

EVA'S RESTAURANT
AND BAR

NEW
BELMORAL
HOTEL

MARTHA'S
KITCHEN AND GUESTHOUSE

WAIGHT ST.

ATLANTIC BANK

BELIZE BANK

MISSION ST.

INSET

BURNS AVE.

SAVANNAH ST.

WEST ST.

1st ST.

2nd ST.

CEMETERY ST.

BLANCANEAUX ST.

SAVANNAH ST.

BURNS AVE.

MIDAS RESORT

THE SAVANNAH
SPORTS GROUND

SNOOTY
FOX

SURVEY ST.

SIMPSON ST.

HOSPITAL
LEBANON ST.

MAYA ST.

SPORTS GROUND

MAXIM'S
CHINESE
RESTAURANT

TO BULLET
TREE FALLS

WAIGHT ST.

FAR WEST ST.

WEST ST.

SEE INSET
PLAZA HOTEL

KING ST.

HAWKSWORTH
BRIDGE

POST OFFICE/
POLICE STATION

GEORGE PRICE AVE.

WESTERN HWY.

SANTA
ELENA

MACAL RIVER

VICTORIA ST.

BACK ST.

SURVEY ST.

OLD BENQUE RD.

SAN IGNACIO HOTEL

APOLLO ST.

PIACHE
HOTEL

CARMELITA ST.

BUENA VISTA RD.

CARMELITA ST.

WINDY
HILL
RESORT

TO BENQUE VIEJO DEL CARMEN

CAHAL PECH HOTEL

CAHAL PECH TAVERN

CAHAL PECH
ARCHAEOLOGICAL SITE

ROSE'S GUESTHOUSE

NOT TO SCALE

© MOON PUBLICATIONS, INC.

Hawksworth Bridge

sands of times each month. If you're happy with his help, stop and have a (good) meal, and then send him a postcard when you get home (note the collection on his wall).

SIGHTS

Cahal Pech Archaeological Site

Though they have been partially excavated and restored, the ruins of Cahal Pech ("Place of the Ticks") still have a covering of jungle around them. The site was discovered in the early 1950s, but scientific research did not begin until 1988, when a team from San Diego State University's Department of Anthropology began excavation. (For more information see "Maya Archaeological Sites" in the Mundo Maya chapter.) Info and a pamphlet about the site are available at the site and at the Piache Hotel. Nearby **Tipu** was an important Maya-Christian town during the early years of colonization. Tipu was as far as the Spanish were able to penetrate in the 16th century.

Chechem Ha Cave

Loaded with Mayan pottery, this ceremonial cave is near the farm of the same name owned by the Morales family. The government allows only guided tours and (of course) nothing can be removed from the cave. The pottery inside is estimated to be as old as 2,000 years. You can climb and explore various ledges and passageways but the highlight is a deep ceremonial chamber in the heart of the hill. In some places you need a rope to help you get around. While those of only average physical abilities can enjoy Chechem Ha Cave, you should take care when moving amidst the pottery; a clumsy patron some years ago seriously damaged one of the pots. Though rewarding, the cave is not easy to reach. Take your choice—it's either a very long drive via Benque Viejo and the hydro dam road followed by a short walk, or a short drive to a parking spot down Chaa Creek Road and a long hike down the river and up the face of the Vaca Plateau. For more information contact Eva's, tel./fax (92) 2267.

Ix Chel Farm and the Panti Trail

About Mile 4.5 out of San Ignacio a sign indicates the turnoff to the left for duPlooys and Chaa Creek. Down this road you bear left at the fork to go to Chaa Creek. Past the parking area and to the left is Ix Chel Farm and the Panti Trail. Visitors are welcome to take part in a walking tour through the forest, where they will see examples of plants and trees that can cause damage (scratches, rashes, poison) and then, close by, the antidote. Rosita Arvigo and husband, Greg Shropshire, are both graduates of Chicago National College of Naprapathy. Anyone interested in holistic medicine will be fascinated with the Panti Trail, named for the elderly Maya bush doctor, Don Eligio Panti, good friend, teacher, and

Maya vessels discovered in Vaca cave system

mentor of Rosita's. It's a fun trip that can start in San Ignacio with a canoe ride down the placid Macal River to the docks at Ix Chel, by car (next door to Chaa Creek Lodge), or with any number of tour operators. From there, after checking in with Rosita, Greg, or one of her assistants, enjoy the stroll along the shady, tree-lined trail. Expect to pay a fee, and if you want Rosita to escort you, the fee is more (*if* she is even available; there are other knowledgeable guides as well). You can just pay the fee, get a guide booklet, and do it on your own. Around the house, small garden plots produce fresh vegetables and a pineapple or two, and fruit trees are scattered about. This is a highly recommended way to spend a day; often you won't see Rosita, but if she's available, be sure to say hello. Research groups from around the world frequently come to huddle with Rosita and Don Eligio in their quest for a possible solution from the jungle-apothecary for both the AIDS virus and cancer. For more information about the herbs and roots, and details about the Panti Trail and Don Eligio Panti, the 100-year-old Maya healer, write to Rosita Arvigo, General Delivery, San Ignacio, Cayo District, Belize, C.A., tel. (92) 3870.

ACTIVITIES

San Ignacio is a great base camp for almost any activity the Cayo and nearby Guatemala have to offer. Most hotels and resorts can arrange for any of them. However, when in doubt, drop in at Eva's Restaurant and check the bulletin boards.

Animal Observation and Birdwatching
Looking for the furred and feathered inhabitants is especially productive in the Mountain Pine Ridge, the national parks and forest reserves, along the Macal and Mopan rivers, and the remote reaches of the Vaca Plateau. Lodges at Black Rock, Chaa Creek, Chechem Ha, Crystal Paradise, duPlooys, Ek Tun, Hidden Valley, Mountain Equestrian Trails (MET) all have large tracts of land where you'll likely find abundant wildlife and knowledgeable staff members. Most lodges can arrange for trips to productive areas with qualified guides who know the area well.

Nature Study
Many study groups come to Belize to learn about the rainforest, its wildlife, and ancient cultures. Workshops are held all over the countryside. If this kind of a vacation interests you, check with **Chaa Creek Cottages,** tel. (92) 2037, fax (92) 2501, where there's a local natural history museum and learning center. **Maya Mountain Lodge,** tel. (92) 2164, fax (92) 2029, gives regular classes in ecology and multiculturalism. **MET,** tel. (8) 23180/22149, fax (8) 23235, a participant in Slate Creek Reserve, has a resident biologist and organized

study in the reserve through its Chiclero Trails organization. **International Expeditions,** a stellar U.S. tour operator (see "Tours Organized in the U.S." in the On the Road chapter), organizes archaeology and rainforest workshops in the area.

Exploring Ruins

With **Cahal Pech, Caracol, El Pilar,** and **Xunantunich** within easy driving distance of the town, exploration is a very popular activity among those visiting San Ignacio. Countless other mounds and ruins are scattered throughout the surrounding jungle. Ask at your lodging. Two independent guides who specialize in such trips are **Ramon Silva** (ask at Eva's) and **Herman Velasquez,** (92) 2467.

Hiking

The areas listed above also lend themselves well to extended hikes. Even the smaller resorts can accommodate the desires of the average tourist and can arrange for more-serious hikes.

Hardcore Treks

Want to cross the Maya Mountains? Want to trek deep into the Chiquibul Forest? Want to test yourself to the limits? Jim Bevis at **MET,** tel. (92) 3310, is one of the most experienced hikers, horsemen, and trekkers in Belize.

Cycling

Getting around the Cayo under your own power can be exhausting if you're hoofing it. A mountain bike might be the answer. **B & M Bike Rentals,** 26 Burns Ave., San Ignacio, Belize, C.A., tel./fax (92) 2382, specializes in **Trek, Diamond Back, Peugeot** and other bikes. Expect to pay at least hourly US$5, daily US$30, weekend US$50, weekly US$120. This outfit delivers locally and has all the repair kits, locks, helmets, and other paraphernalia needed; it also provides emergency service. Contact Eric Barber.

Guests at **Chaa Creek** and **Hidden Valley Inn** have access to mountain bikes and trails on the lodge properties.

Hike & Bike for the Rainforest

This annual competition held in October combines an eight-kilometer footrace with a 32-

Rosita's fascinating Panti trail at Ix Chel Farm

kilometer cycling contest. The three-day event attracts serious competitors from several countries, including the United States. Various events appeal to nonparticipants who still want to support the cause and have a good time. Proceeds go to help **Accion Selva** (Jungle Action), a nonprofit organization that serves to promote sustainable land use among rainforest communities. Accion Selva has donated proceeds in the past to benefit the Belize Zoo and and Tapir Mountain Reserve. For more information contact Accion Selva, Box 53, San Ignacio, Belize, C.A., tel (92) 2037, fax (92) 2501.

Horseback Riding

The equestrian resorts offer good riding adventures. Those who like to saddle up should also check with **Guacamallo Treks,** part of Maya Ranch, tel. (1) 49117, fax (92) 3075. Another, **Easy Rider,** (92) 3310, is an independent operator who charges reasonable rates and gives good service.

Caving

Numerous caves lie in the surrounding hills along Mountain Pine Ridge and Vaca Plateau. Check with **Jim Bevis,** tel. (92) 3310; **William Morales** (ask at Eva's); **Jeronie Tut,** tel. (92) 2823; or **Gary Seewald,** (92) 3310.

Canoeing and Tubing

These are exhilarating ways to enjoy the Macal and Mopan rivers. Most hotels and cottage resorts in Cayo District have canoes and tubes; **Tony's Guided Tours** is probably the most economical, independent trip on the river at US$25 per person. **Snooty Fox,** tel. (92) 2150, fax (92) 3556, across the river in Santa Elena has a fleet of canoes. River travel is best during the wet season, May-Oct., and not good during an extremely dry season when the water gets very low. However, Fred Prost claims to run tubing trips from the **Parrot's Nest,** tel. (92) 3702, north of town to San Ignacio during the dry season with success; check it out.

Swimming

It's pretty easy to find a "swimming hole" in the San Ignacio area. Rivers, ponds, and creeks are abundant. Many hotels built along or above the river have small beaches along the water, and of course several hotels offer pools as well.

ACCOMMODATIONS AND FOOD DOWNTOWN

Accommodations

On San Ignacio's main street, the **Plaza Hotel,** 4A Burns Ave., San Ignacio, Belize, C.A., tel. (92) 3332/3375, is one of the newest hotels in town with h/c water, private tile bathrooms in each room, four rooms with a/c, five with phones, and coffee in the dining room. Rates for rooms with a/c are US$30 s, US$38 d; non-a/c US$18 s, US$25 d. The hotel has rather a strange entry from the street; it's next to Beto's Shopping Center and near the bank and fruit stands.

Since renovation, the **New Belmoral Hotel,** 17 Burns Ave., San Ignacio, Belize, C.A., tel. (92) 2024, fax (92) 3502, has jumped a level in class from its previous life. Like the Plaza, it has a lobby on the second floor and comfortable wicker furniture for guests. Centrally located, the Belmoral has Eva's across the street one way, the bank and produce stands the other, and the bus station behind. The large common balcony allows guests to check out the local scene from above. Some of the back rooms have nice views of the surrounding hills. It has 11 rooms in all, and accepts traveler's checks and Visa/MC. Rates are US$25 s, private bath US$30 d.

You can't be more centrally located than this budget favorite, the **Central Hotel.** It's next door to Eva's and above the **Arts and Crafts Center.** With eight rooms to keep his eye on, manager Tony Wells keeps the place running in an easygoing fashion. Lots of interesting folks in their 20s to 40s from Europe and the States stop by here. Cash or traveler's checks only. Rates are US$9.50 s, US$11 d, US$14. Contact 24 Burns Ave., San Ignacio, Belize, C.A., tel. (92) 2253.

Just a few steps farther down Burns is another good-value, low-cost lodging, the **Venus Hotel,** 29 Burns Ave., San Ignacio, Belize, C.A., tel. (92) 3203, fax (92) 2225. From the second-floor lobby you look over the rooftops westward and streetlife below. The hotel has a range of rooms. Some of the rooms toward the back have attractive views of the river and surrounding hills. (Ask about the cabañas at its sister hotel, Cahal Pech). It accepts traveler's checks and Visa/MC. Rates are shared bath US$10 s, private bath US$17.50 s, a/c US$22.50 s, US$2.50 per person additional.

In the center of town on Far West Street, **Hotel Pacz,** a small newer hostelry owned by Peter and Diana Zugrzycki, has five clean, simple rooms with h/c bath. Free tea or coffee is available in the morning. Rates are US$15 s, US$17.50 d, US$20 t.

Just a couple of streets behind Burns and on the corner you'll find **Martha's Kitchen and Guesthouse,** 10 West Street, San Ignacio, Belize, C.A. John and Martha August let out three rooms that offer an atmosphere of privacy and conviviality in a homey setting. The rooms go for US$13-15 s depending on the size of the bed; US$3.50 per person additional. Laundry services are available. Food is also available downstairs; breakfast is US$3.50 and a lunch or dinner T-bone steak with rice, salad, and fried plantains is US$5.

Other basic hotels include the **Hotel San Juan** and the **Hi-Et**. Some rooms may have a/c or TV, private or shared baths, but look at these budget rooms very carefully before you make your decision. These are good places if the budget is most important.

Food

Eva's Restaurant and Bar, 22 Burns Ave., tel. (92) 2267, is not only the tourist and activity center; it s also the right place for a good meal and a cold Beliken. Expect good fried chicken for about US$4.50; peas, rice, and stewed chicken for about US$3; and burgers for about US$2. And don't forget the *salbutes,* an open taco with lots o' goodies for just US50 cents.

Eva's is a clearing house for fellow travelers and the latest gossip. Bob keeps a list of names

Eva's Restaurant and tourist center

to share a ride to "anywhere," cheaper by the group.

Near the Venus Hotel you'll find the **Serendib Restaurant,** 27 Burns Ave., tel. (92) 2302, a cafe owned by Sri Lankan Hantley Pieris. Along with good hamburgers and chow mein, he serves excellent curries. Reasonably priced, a broiled lobster dinner or "San Ignacio Giant Steak" will set you back only about US$10. A coffee shop serves continental breakfasts for about US$2.25 and a full breakfast for about US$4. The Serendib accepts traveler's checks and Visa/MC.

Maxim's Chinese Restaurant, 23 Far West Street, (92) 2283, is a Chinese spot with some reputation among the locals. It has numerous ceiling fans and a freezer in the main dining area. Bing Run Liu and family serve mainly lunch and dinner. Prices are moderate; you won't pay much over US$10 for the best meal in the house and a beer.

ACCOMMODATIONS AROUND TOWN

North Edge of Town

About a quarter mile out of town at Branch Mouth Road, take a look at **Midas Resort,** a small family-run lodging. You'll find six circular cottages with thatched roofs, situated on five acres along the banks of the Macal River (a 300-yard path from the cottages). All cabins offer private bathrooms. No electricity is available yet, but oil lamps and hot water are provided. Campers are welcome; rates are US$7 per adult. Cabaña rates with bathroom are US$30 s, US$35 d. For more information and reservations call (92) 3845. Ask about day trips to the surrounding areas, including Tikal, Guatemala.

South Edge of Town

You could say the **San Ignacio Hotel,** Box 33, San Ignacio, Cayo District, Belize, C.A., tel. (92) 2034/2125, fax (92) 2134, is a hotel fit for a queen; Queen Elizabeth *did* stay here on a visit to Belize in 1994. To try it for yourself, you'll have to take the first left (Buena Vista Road) after crossing the Hawksworth Bridge into town.

Because of the one-way street just past the end of the bridge, you will have to circuit the little center triangle until you can cross over and take Buena Vista Road up the hill. The hotel is a hundred yards up on the left. The San Ignacio Hotel overlooks the Macal River and the hills of Cayo. Its 25 rooms are pleasant and roomy with private bathrooms and h/c water; the hotel also has a restaurant and bar, patio deck, swimming pool, ball court, disco, gift shop, sightseeing tours, and convention facilities. As an added touch it has 10 acres of forest along the river with marked trails and a swimming beach. Birdwatching tours are available with a guide or a birding list. The kitchen has a good reputation and reasonable prices: breakfast US$6, lunch US$10, packed lunch US$6, dinner US$15. Rates for balcony rooms are US$43 s, US$50 d, US$60 t; deluxe rooms are US$65 s, US$75 d, US$85 t. Most major credit cards are okay. Write or call for more information.

Run by local Garifuna Godsman Ellis, **Piache Hotel** offers 12 clean comfortable rooms and an outdoor bar at 18 Buena Vista St. in San Ignacio. Godsman has a wealth of info on San Ignacio and all of Belize. He offers tours to the surrounding ruins and into Tikal. Transportation to and from the airport is available; he can provide meals and transportation for large groups. The Piache (Garifuna for "doctor") is a small quiet hotel on a hill overlooking town, but close enough to walk to most everything. It's not fancy but, as Godsman says, "It's very Belizean." Peanut butter lovers: Godsman makes some of the best peanut butter anywhere. Rooms with fans are US$18 s, US$24 d, US$30 t; a/c room US$35 d. For more information, write or call Box 54, San Ignacio, Cayo District, Belize, C.A., tel. (92) 2032, (92) 3264, fax (92) 2685.

Poised high upon Cahal Pech Hill, the cozy **Rose's Guesthouse** is an undiscovered gem with panoramic views of the surrounding countryside. It's also the lodging closest to **Cahal Pech Ruins.** Rose and family rent five rooms at value prices, especially when you consider breakfast is included and Rose's has h/c bath, postal and laundry services, even a fax for workaholics. As with many of the lodgings

she can arrange pickup from Belize City, or most any other arrival point. She also offers arranged tours to reserves, caves, parks, and archaeological sites. Room rates are US$32.50 s, US$40 d, US$7.50 per person additional. Contact Rosalind Lee at 1178 Cahal Pech Hill, San Ignacio, Belize, C.A., tel. (92) 2282.

Near the the crest of Cahal Pech Hill is the **Cahal Pech Hotel,** a sprinkling of about a dozen cabañas owned by the Venus Hotel (stop by its Burns Avenue location for directions and arrangements). The views are panoramic and the breeze refreshing. The cabañas are built with an updated Maya theme using a blend of traditional and modern materials. Some cabañas have walls made of small palm trunks or bush stick. Each has a thatched roof with double beds, h/c water, private bath, louvered windows, and veranda. A main building houses a restaurant. For prices and questions contact Mark Bedran, Venus Hotel, 29 Burns Ave., San Ignacio, Belize, C.A., tel. (92) 2186; fax (92) 2225.

West Edge of Town

Once about a mile out of town on the Western Highway, **Windy Hill Resort** today sits at the edge of San Ignacio—the town has grown out to meet it. Things are changing in the Cayo. Here, on **Graceland Ranch,** you'll find rustic charm with thatched-roof cottages, green grass, private baths, h/c water, ceiling fans, 24-hour electricity, a swimming pool, and recreation hut complete with TV, hammocks, bar, table tennis, and billiards. Guests enjoy the friendly efficiency with which the place is run and the variety of activities: canoeing, caving, horseback riding, nature tours, and hiking trails. Ask about escorted tours to Guatemala and archaeological sites in the area. Cottage rates are US$50 s, US$70 d, US$85 t, US$100 q; credit cards accepted. Meals served in a casual thatched-roof dining room are: breakfast US$6, lunch US$8, dinner US$15. For more information, write or call Windy Hill Cottages, Graceland Ranch, San Ignacio, Cayo District, Belize, C.A., tel. (92) 2017; in the U.S. contact Sea & Explore, 1809 Carol Sue Ave., Suite E, Gretna, Louisiana 70056, tel. (800) 345-9786, (504) 366-9985, fax (504) 366-9986.

ENTERTAINMENT AND SERVICES

Cayo Nightlife

If you have the energy after a day on the river or hiking the jungles, you have several good choices for a quiet drink or more boisterous nightlife. You'll find a placid atmosphere and a nice view at the patio of the **San Ignacio Hotel** or the bar at **Windy Hill Resort. Eva's Restaurant** on Burns Avenue and the **Western Club** behind the New Belmoral Hotel are centrally located and have lots of conviviality. At the Western Club you can also try out your footwork on the dance floor. **Discovery 2000,** 2 Far West Street, owned by the Serendib Restaurant, offers drinks, a jukebox, pool tables, and gaming machines.

For high-visibility nightlife try the **Cahal Pech Tavern,** tel. (92) 3380, the giant longhouse on top of the hill just south of town. It probably has the largest palapa roof in the entire Cayo, if not the country. This lively tavern also has great views of the area at night and plenty of sociable goings-on, with lots of dancing space and enough seating space to accommodate a thousand. This is a fine choice to meet fellow travelers and mix with the locals. It's so popular, in fact, the local cable company broadcasts from here each Friday, including various contest nights.

If you want to go a little farther than San Ignacio you'll find nighttime activity at **Caesar's Place** (Mile 62), **Mike's Paradise Club** (Mile 58), and **Snooty Fox** in Santa Elena.

Shopping

For gifts, **Eva's Restaurant, Farmer's Emporium** (24 Burns Avenue), **Arts and Crafts Center** (41 Burns Avenue—under the Central Hotel), and **Arts and Crafts of Central America** (1 Hyatt Street) sell Belizean arts and crafts. Farmer's Emporium also offers fresh bread and orange juice. **Celina's Super Store,** 43 Burns Avenue, tel (92) 2247, sells groceries.

Services

The **post office** and **police station** are in the large government building at the foot of Hawksworth Bridge. **Atlantic Bank** and **Belize Bank** are on Burns near the Plaza Hotel. The station for all buses, **Novelo, Batty,** and **Z-Line,** is behind the New Belmoral Hotel.

GETTING THERE

By Air

Chartered flights into **Spanish Lookout** and **Blancaneaux** airports are the most expensive way to arrive. They are also the quickest. Blancaneaux is a less dependable point for a return flight because of frequent foggy conditions in the rainy season and weight limitations due to altitude and runway length. However, if conditions aren't right, a 30-minute ride to Spanish Lookout is a good fallback plan.

All the resorts can arrange for a pickup at the **International Airport** in Belize City. The cost for such a transfer is about US$120-130 but can be split. Bob Jones at Eva's can always arrange it, too, if necessary.

By Bus

Novelo and **Batty** run through here from Belize City to the Guatemala border. The first bus reaches San Ignacio from Belize City about 9 a.m. and continues to the Guatemala border; the last one leaves in the opposite direction at about 6 p.m. The buses stop at the town circle near the police station, at the bridge, or at the parking area off Burns Avenue. Expect only limited service on Sundays. For current schedules between Belize City, San Ignacio, and Benque Viejo (Guatemala border), call the **Batty Bus** in Belize City, tel. (2) 72025, or the **Novelo Bus,** tel. (2) 77372.

By Bike

Just keep pedaling! Just be careful of traffic passing from behind, and relinquish the road to vehicles. Remember, too, that dark comes quickly in the tropics. Check with locals to get a fix on when the sun will set. It's best to be in San Ignacio by dusk; road travel after that becomes much more hazardous.

By Car

Armed with the map the rental car agent will supply, the drive is simple; enjoy the scenery and follow the signs. You'll be happy to note that many of the speed bumps that peppered the roadways in years past are gone. Keep your eyes peeled for the few that remain and drive more slowly than the locals; they know what's ahead.

VICINITY OF SAN IGNACIO

NORTH OF TOWN

Sights

A few dusty miles north of town is the little village of **Bullet Tree Falls**. Not much here, just a playing field and an intersection. But continue to the far side of town to where the road splits just before the bridge. This is an important landmark. Go forward and you're going toward El Pilar Ruins, take a right and you are headed to the **Parrot's Nest**.

The fascinating **El Pilar Ruins** lie on about 50 hilly acres northwest of Bullet Tree. Here, two groupings of temple mounds, courtyards, and ball courts overlook a forested valley. Aqueducts and a causeway lead toward Guatemala, within sight 500 meters away. Unexcavated except for the handiwork of looters here and there, the ruins hold onto their air of mystery. Many trees shade the site: allspice, gumbo-limbo, ramon, cohune palm, and locust. It's a beautiful hiking area with ridge after ridge of beckoning jungle.

Accommodations

After taking the right at the above intersection, the gate to the **Parrot's Nest** is just a hundred yards or so, past the edge of town. Once you're at the gate, pastures appear under the trees ahead and to the right. The cemetery is to the left. Now move the stick/gate out of the way and enter the field (please remember to replace them—Fred hates to chase loose horses). From this point follow the tracks around the field and to the left.

Getting here takes a little effort but it's worth it. Fred makes guests feel at home in his own laidback way. And maybe you've seen him before; Fred ran the Seaside Guesthouse, a favorite among backpackers and wanderers, for years. Parrot's Nest has four simple yet comfortable clapboard cabins with thatched roofs. A couple sit just inches off the ground on short stilts. Two more are treehouses on 10-foot stilts under the spreading limbs of a gigantic guanacaste tree. Each cabin has a fluorescent light, linoleum

floor, simple single or double bed, with the breeze providing "natural" air conditioning.

A couple of *palapas* on the grounds have sinks, toilets, and cold-water showers. Rates are US$17.50 s/d. All meals are available. In the past guests have eaten at tables on Fred's back porch. However, he is in the process of adding a separate dining room. Fred offers horseback riding and can arrange for larger numbers of riders with 24 hours' notice. He organizes tubing trips (the Macal River winds around two sides of his property) from his place to San Ignacio. He also offers overnight camping trips to El Pilar. Contact Fred Prost, Bullet Tree Falls, Cayo District, Belize, C.A., tel. (92) 3702.

Getting There

Catch the bus in San Ignacio at noon or 3 p.m.; rates are about US$1. Or hire a cab for less than US$10. If you're mountain biking, it's an easy 20-minute ride.

SOUTH OF TOWN

Sights

The Magana family has opened the **Magana Zactunich Art Gallery** at about Mile 7 to compete with the nearby Tanah Museum. Like the family's other establishment in San Jose Succotz, it sells a wide variety of Belizean crafts.

Probably the most famous Maya art gallery and museum is the **Tanah Mayan Art Museum**, featuring the well-known Garcia sisters. Originally five, the Garcia sisters took their Maya heritage and began re-creating slate carvings reminiscent of their ancestors. Today they have made a nationwide name for themselves. The Tanah Museum is built in the old Maya way with limestone and clay walls; the floor is a parquet of logs and limestone, and the roof is typical thatch of bay and palm leaves, picked and placed on the nights of the full moon to give them a longer life. These sisters are charming ambassadors of the San Antonio neighborhood, as well as clever artists who make hand-drawn art cards depicting the wildlife of Belize, Belizean dolls, native jewelry, and medicinal herbs (who more qualified than the nieces of Don Eligio Panti, Belize's most renowned bush doctor? See "Ancient Healing" in the Health Care chapter). If you're traveling to **1,000 Foot Falls, Rio Frio Cave,** or the falls of the **Rio On,** stop by and visit the Garcias in San Antonio, Box 75, San Ignacio, Belize, C.A.

Accommodations

At Santa Elena a sign directs you to **Maya Mountain Lodge,** Box 46, San Ignacio, Cayo District, Belize, C.A., tel. (92) 2164, fax (92) 2029, (800) 344-MAYA. The jungle hideaway is operated by Susie and Bart Mikler. A meandering trail with signs introduces the neophyte to a variety of plants and trees. The rooms and cottages are clean and comfortable and the Miklers serve a menu that includes Belizean, international, and Mexican food, along with homemade breads and buckets of fresh-squeezed orange juice; no liquor is sold (you can, however, bring your own). Electricity, hot water, private bathrooms, and friendly people are provided. The rate for cottages is US$59 s or d, with meals served family style. Rooms with private bath are US$39; with bath down the hall US$25. Children under 12 are free. Breakfast costs US$7, lunch US$6, dinner US$15. Ask about family workshops on biodiversity and multiculturalism. Write or call for reservations and more information.

At about Mile 4 and only a quarter of a mile past Cristo Rey Village you'll find the friendly, family-owned **Crystal Paradise Resort** off to the right. The patriarch of the Tut family runs a successful thatching business; ever wonder who does all those roofs you see in the area? Mrs. Tut is in charge of the resort's kitchen and the rest of the clan run tours and entertain guests. In fact, son Jerone is a well-known birding, horseback riding, river, and cave guide with an impressive and growing library of nature guides.

Accommodations come in several styles on the property. If you're lucky you may get one of the simple thatched cabañas near the dining *palapa* that overlooks the river. These have compelling views of the valley and feature cement walls, tiled floors, h/c showers, and shaded verandas for relaxing. Others are clean and comfortable but more of a clapboard style. All offer ceiling fans and electricity. The Tuts also own other property nearby that's great for birdwatching and nature walks, and they offer a number of tours around the countryside. Traveler's checks and Visa/MC are accepted. Rates for rooms are US$55 s, US$75 d, US$100 t; thatched-roof cabañas US$75 s, US$95 d, US$115 t, breakfast and dinner included. Lunch is US$8, packed lunch US$6. Contact Jerone Tut at Cristo Rey Village, Cayo District, Belize, C.A., tel. (92) 2823.

WEST OF SAN IGNACIO

No less an authority than cigar-chomping Emory King, in his *Driver's Guide to Beautiful Belize,* suggests starting one's odometer at the San Ignacio Hotel rather than at the foot of Buena Vista Road. Why argue with success? We do the same.

ACCOMMODATIONS

Clarissa Falls Cottages

At Mile 5.5 on the Western Highway is a laid-back resort where guests camp or stay in three simple stick-and-thatch cottages, lighted by kerosene lamps, with inner paneled walls, two twin beds, and a hammock space in each,

with room to add a cot; the shared toilet and shower building is separate. Night and day watchmen are provided. Activities include horseback riding, US$10 per hour, per person (with guide), tube rentals US$1.50, boats US$10/hr., and from here it is a nice walk along the Mopan River to the Maya archaeological site of Xunantunich. You can see the ruins from Clarissa Falls Cottages. These are very basic accommodations, so check them out carefully. The dining room serves mostly Mexican food, including a few specialties such as black mole soup and great Mexican-style tacos. It also serves vegetarian fare. Overnight rates are US$2.50 per person for camping; US$7.50 per person for cottages. Food can

Chaa Creek Lodge

be as inexpensive as US40 cents for an order of tacos, to US$6 for a meal such as stuffed squash. This is a food hangout for locals. Call owner Chena Galvez for more information, tel. (92) 3916.

Chaa Creek

From simple to the sublime (well almost). On the Western Highway about Mile 4.5, look for the Chaa Creek sign and make a turn onto the dirt road to the left. Stay to the left at the fork and the road leads to a secluded hideaway on the edge of the Macal River. This is a favorite to which guests return year after year. If you arrive in the middle of the afternoon and approach from the parking lot in back of the thatched-roof kitchen, you'll see pans of unbaked homemade rolls lining the windowsill and rising in the warm afternoon shade. Check in at the bar/lounge *palapa* across from the dining *palapa,* where you'll probably meet owners Mick and Lucy Fleming. This American wife/British husband team are both world travelers who came to visit Belize in the late '70s, fell in love with it, and never left. Chaa Creek was one of the first cottage resorts in Cayo, and if you ask Mick he'll tell you its colorful history, from overgrown farm to private nature reserve of 330 acres where three small Maya plaza groups lie along the resort's Ruta Maya trail system; ask for a map or take one of the daily walks with a Chaa Creek guide.

A bright, flower-lined path brings you to the white stucco cottages with tall peaked *palapa*

roofs and wooden shutters that close over bright-colored curtains (you don't need glass—no mosquitoes here!). The 19 double cottages (two rooms in each with two double beds in each room) have private baths and h/c water, Mexican-tile floors, decor of rich Guatemalan fabrics, and oil lamps that are lit when the sun sets (no electricity). The cottages, reminiscent of Africa from the Flemings's earlier years in Kenya and Uganda, are scattered across the brow of a grassy hillside that slopes down to the edge of the Macal River. Guests can swim along the shore, go sightseeing on the trails, or paddle a dory down the river to San Ignacio (the trip takes about two hours). The river meanders through thick trees and tangled growth. Local housewives pound sudsy clothes clean on river rocks under a leafy arbor, while iguanas blink at you in the lazy afternoon sun. It's a great outing and you can relax knowing that someone will pick you up in the van or Land Rover in San Ignacio for the trip back if you wish.

Chaa Creek is an easy gateway to the Guatemala border and the fabulous **Tikal** ruins. Day-trips to the ruins of **Xunantunich** (close by) as well as to Tikal can be arranged here. Rooms are available either with breakfast, lunch, or dinner, or all three, but you must decide in advance and are charged accordingly. After dinner, enjoy the art of conversation or enjoy the starry sky; look for the magic light show in tall trees around the grounds—fireflies do their mating dance and cast a sparkling glow on the spreading branches.

Ever innovators, the Flemings have created **Chaa Creek Natural History Museum,** located in a forest setting a short hike above the resort. The museum includes exhibit areas that examine ecosystems, geology, and Maya culture in the Cayo area, a research room and archives, a lecture area, and a reading porch. Outside the contemporary wooden structure is a breeding facility for the Blue Morpho butterfly.

Room rates are US$95 s, US$115 d, $US130 t; breakfast is US$8, a packed lunch is US$7, lunch US$10, dinner US$22, plus tax and service charge. Ask about Chaa Creek's **Chiquibul Camp Site,** four hours away between Mountain Pine Ridge and the Chiquibul Reserve on the banks of the Macal River. This is great for anyone who enjoys camping and trekking in a remote setting—the habitat of tapir, Morelet's crocodile, and scarlet macaw. For canoe rental fees, inland expeditions, reservations, and prices, write or call Box 53, San Ignacio, Cayo District, Belize, C.A., tel. (92) 2037, fax (92) 2501.

DuPlooy's Cottage Resort

If you received a "challenge" in the mail offering a free weekend in an isolated jungle guesthouse in Central America's Belize to the first couple who brought a gallon of still-frozen Häagen-Dazs ice cream to said resort, what would you do? Well, several adventurers *did;* they packed up their Häagen-Dazs and hit the airport on the run. The first couple (from Davis, California) ar-

rived undaunted by jungle heat with a cooler filled with dry ice and not one, but two gallons of their favorite flavors. DuPlooy's Cottage Resort had one heck of a party all weekend. And not only did the resort guests enjoy, but also special friends from all over Belize came with a multitude of exotic fruit toppings and lots of chocolate sauce.

This is typical of the feeling you get at duPlooy's—a really fun place to stay that's a kind of nature-inspired Disneyland. This is a family-run resort (all daughters) with fun-timers Judy and Ken duPlooy at the helm. The small resort is set on what was originally 20, now 60, acres of rolling countryside wrapped on the east and north by the Macal River. The duPlooys have planted the additional 40 acres with 2,000 trees, part fruit orchard and part botanical garden, and built a pond that is already attracting lots of birds and fish (where do they come from?). You can use duPlooy's as a place to relax on a sandy beach by the river, or as a base from which to explore the caves, the nearby waterfalls, the Maya ruins, or even Guatemala and Tikal. Guests choose their mode of exploring either on horseback, ferry, canoe, or on foot. Don't miss exploring duPlooy's grounds. Ken is a great gardener, and an even greater birdwatcher/guide. Take a look at the orchids hanging on the trees, and, as Ken says, if a cutting isn't *stolen,* it won't grow well. Ken in his birding hat holds fort on the "deck" every morning, and

At duPlooy's, paths lead around green grassy hills down to the cottages along the riverbank.

one of the bird guides guarantees 75 birds before breakfast from the deck every morning—before the bird walk. **Night birding** expeditions in the back of his pickup with a powerful beam is a new world of birds that play in the dark.

Horsemen enjoy **night riding** when the moon is full. Or by day, a ride through the woods to Cahal Pech Maya ruins, followed by a ride into San Ignacio and tying up in front of a restaurant, feels remarkably like an old Western adventure. Check out the Maya medicine garden, run by an old healer, Mr. Green, and the Maya hut where Maya-style lunches will soon be served. The trail along the river is a pleasant place to walk and observe nature at its finest.

Guests have several choices. The **Jungle Lodge,** with its stucco cabañitas with red tile roofs, screened porches, private bathrooms, hot showers, and ceiling fans, has large rooms with many windows to bring in the pleasant views. **duPlooy's Bungalows** is three large rooms in single buildings, each with its own deck looking down on the bird-laden bush and beautiful Macal River. Each room has a king bed and queen-size sofa bed, refrigerator, coffee pot, bathtub, and hammocks on the deck. **Jungle Lodge Connecting Rooms** with two rooms connected by a bath, is perfect for a family and can sleep as many as seven. **The Pink House** guesthouse has six rooms with two shared bathrooms, living room, and screened-in porch around the building with comfy hammocks and seating areas, and a dining area where simple meals are served.

Meals can be included for US$30 per day. Lunch can be a voucher in a local restaurant, a packed picnic, or served in the river-view dining room. Dinner consists of four courses served in the dining room. Vegetarian meals are available, and do try some of the great exotic fruit dishes (many fruits and veggies come straight from the garden.) Rates for the bungalows are US$130 s, US$190 d, US$235 t; and for Jungle Lodge are US$100 s, US$145 d, US$190 t (please check; the prices were in the process of change). Guesthouse prices are US$30 s, US$40 d, US$50 t, and include continental breakfast. Package rates, including sightseeing trips, are available; for more information call duPlooy's, tel. (92) 3101, fax (92) 3301, or in the U.S. (803) 722-1513.

Ek Tun

Getting to this isolated resort along the Macal River offers guests an adventure before they arrive. At about Mile 4.5 turn left at the Chaa Creek sign. From there it's 10 adventurous miles to the resort; the last leg you make by boat. Once there, the adventure continues on 200 acres with jungle trails, a waterfall, and Maya mounds and ceremonial cave to explore. Tapir, deer, peccary and a variety of birdlife use the property. Jaguars and howler monkeys have been heard nearby. Other excursions include river trips that explore limestone caves in the nearby **Vaca Cave** system.

Accommodations include two luxurious stick-and-thatch huts that can house up to four people each. The cabins are charming and about 500 square feet with two double beds in the loft and another downstairs. Antiques are among the furnishings and each hut offers h/c water, flush toilets, stucco walls in the bathroom, and kerosene lamps described by former guests as *rustic elegance.* At the present only one generator is used for electricity, and it usually goes off early. Readers, just ask and you'll receive a mini book light. Food cooked by Phyllis (the wifely half of the partnership) includes such specialties as chilled papaya soup, jicama salad, Indonesian chicken, green chili, and who knows what tomorrow's surprise might be. Most of the fruits and vegetables served are grown in the Ek Tun gardens. Meals are served in the open dining room overlooking the surrounding mountains and the surging Macal River. Rates are US$110 s, US$140 d, US$170 t, US$200 q; meals are MAP US$32 per person. Children under 12 stay for half price. Packages are available. Transfers to San Ignacio are US$30 for up to 4 people. If driving, call ahead for a detailed map and directions. For more information, contact Merlin Dart in the U.S., Box 18748, Boulder, Colorado 80308-8748, tel. (303) 442-6150; or Ken and Phyllis Dart in Belize, General Delivery, Benque Viejo, Cayo District, Belize, C.A., tel. (92) 2881, fax (93) 2446.

Black Rock Belize Jungle River Lodge

General directions to reach Black Rock require turning at the road to Chaa Creek, Mile 4.5, and taking the right fork toward duPlooy's. Then there's a 20-minute walk along the Macal River, the *only* way in—hope you're traveling light. A mountain bike might make the trip easier. On your way stop by Caesar's Place, at Mile 62 on the Western Highway, for details and exact directions. Getting to the lodge may not be for everyone, but for those who thrill to the outdoors, the vistas include jungle foliage, wildlife, and the unspoiled Macal River. Guests have a choice of "tent cabañas" or cabañas with two beds, screens, and palapa roofs overhead. Excellent food is served in an open-air dining pavilion. Though in a primitive setting of 250 jungle acres, Black Rock uses modern technology to provide solar electricity, solar hot water, and solar water pumps.

From here guests strike out on their own to hike, explore on horseback or canoe, swim and lounge around the riverside beach, watch birds, or take day-trips to nearby caves and Maya archaeological sites. Caesar's Place will arrange for pickup and transfers. Rates for shared bath are US$36 s, US$42 d, US$46 t; private bath US$55 s, US$65 d, US$70 t. Meals are US$6 full breakfast, US$6 lunch, US$13 dinner. For more information, contact Caesar Sherrard, Box 48, San Ignacio, Belize, C.A., tel./fax (92) 2341.

If you aren't driving a vehicle, the easiest way to get to Black Rock is to hop the airport bus going to Belize City, get on either Novelo's or Batty's bus on the way to San Ignacio, and ask to be dropped off in front of Caesar's Place.

Chechem Ha Cottages

On the edge of the Vaca Plateau the farm of Antonio and Lea Morales looks out over the magnificent Macal River Valley. Here they offer simple accommodations to travelers who want to visit Chechem Ha cave. Though this farm is just upstream from Black Rock and Ek Tun, the easiest way to reach it is by taking the turnoff at Benque Viejo by the cemetery and heading toward the new hydroelectric dam about 10 miles (ask at Eva's in San Ignacio for directions or to share a ride). This is truly living with the locals as you witness around you family life on a small jungle farm. Bunks are simple affairs in clap-board buildings. Fireflies will light up the night and all manner of jungle birds will call from the trees. You'll eat under a thatch palapa and bathe in the nearby stream or under the waterfall below the lip of the plateau. The toilet is a latrine.

Nabitunich

Within walking distance to Xunantunich, Nabitunich is about Mile 5.5 out of San Ignacio on the Western Highway and a half-mile off to the right. Look for the entrance on the right and open a couple of gates to get in; the Juans, who own the farm and used to run the lodging, raise cattle. The grounds are located near the river, with rolling grass to the bank and a clear view of the temple top at Xunantunich—especially beautiful at sunset—a relaxing atmosphere. Just keep to the left past the farmhouse. Nabitunich is to the side and behind. Here a group of cottages with eight double units is run by the new proprietor, Theresa Graham. Ask for the "stone cottage"; though all are nice, some still have an open common ceiling. Hot and cold water are available, as well as an electric plug and good lights in the bathroom for shaving; but if you like to read in bed, bring a clip-on book light with plenty of batteries.

Wander the grounds. Admire the lushly planted vegetation and palms. Pick and enjoy a fresh orange or grapefruit from the trees of the compound. Make yourself at home in the comfortable screened lounge. Nabitunich is for the independent traveler, though guests have access to canoes and horses.

Nabitunich continues its reputation for delicious multicourse meals. Breakfasts are simple but tasty with fruit, cereal, yogurt, French toast, and huevos rancheros. Dinner is an elaborate affair with lace and linen, a tradition carried over from when the Juans ran the place. Theme nights feature French, Greek, or Italian food. Beer, wine, rum, and soft drinks are available at reasonable prices. Rates with breakfast and dinner are US$75 s, US$95 d, US$120 t. For more information call (93) 2096, fax (93) 3096. Nabitunich is closed June through September.

TO THE GUATEMALA BORDER

SAN JOSE SUCCOTZ

About Mile 6.5 you'll find the village of San Jose Succotz. Ancestors of the Mopan Maya migrated from San Jose (in Guatemala's Petén) and throughout the years have preserved the ancient Maya culture and folklore they brought with them to the isolated small village. In Succotz the first language is **Mopan,** and the people still wear the bright-hued fabrics that the women weave on their back-strap looms. The most colorful time to visit is during one of their fiestas. The two biggest celebrations are 19 March (feast day of St. Joseph) and 3 May (feast day of the Holy Cross).

Sights
If you're interested in local art, check out **Magana's Art Center** at the entrance to San Jose Succotz village, not too far from the Xunantunich ferry. David Magana has been working with the youth of the area, encouraging them to continue the art and crafts of their ancestors. You'll find the results inside in the form of local woodcarvings, baskets, jewelry, and stone (slate) carvings unique to Belize. It's open 9 a.m.-4 p.m.

The **Xunantunich Archaeological Site,** an impressive Maya ceremonial center, rests on a natural limestone ridge and provides a grand view of the entire Cayo District and Guatemala countryside. The tallest pyramid on the site, **El Castillo,** has been partially excavated and explored, and the eastern side of the structure displays a stucco frieze. The plaza of the ceremonial center houses three carved stelae. Eight miles past San Ignacio on the Western Highway going toward Benque Viejo and the Guatemala border, you'll reach the turnoff and the Succotz Ferry (look for a small wooden sign on the side of the road). After another mile you'll reach Xunantunich. You can park here, hop on the hand-cranked ferry (free) that shuttles you across the river, and you have about a mile's hike up gentle hills to the site. If you wish, drive your car on the ferry, which operates daily 8 a.m.-5 p.m., and then motor on to Xunantunich.

You'll pay a small fee to enter the grounds, and a guide will explain the site: the history, what's been restored, and what's in the future. For more details about Xunantunich, see "Maya Archaeological Sites" in the Mundo Maya chapter.

As you make your way south on the Western Highway past the Xunantunich turnoff and before you arrive at Benque Viejo, the **Mopan River** runs alongside the road—more than likely you'll see women under shady trees scrubbing the family laundry on the rocks. Close by the kids have a good time playing and splashing around in the cool water. These are Mopan Maya from San Jose Succotz.

Accommodations
Here, on 88 acres about a mile from San Jose Succotz and the **Xunantunich ferry,** is a jungle hillside camp, **Rancho Los Amigos Cottages,**

river ferry boat on the way to Xunantunich

tel. (93) 2483, that's big on value. You won't find electricity or tiled bathrooms; instead four huts (three accommodating up to five people) are built on a Maya mound. Each is made with white-washed adobe sides and thatched roofs. Their interiors are simple but clean. There is an outside shower and pit-style toilets. A spring on the property provides water for cooking and bathing, and a creek runs to one side. From the covered cooking and eating area you look out over jungle and trails at the back of the property that are handy for early morning animal watching and birdwatching.

The family that runs these budget *casitas* (Ed and Virginia Jenkins and clan) exemplifies the hospitality of Belize. Virginia is a great cook, especially with vegetarian fare; don't miss her fettuccini Alfredo and scrumptious home-baked bread. And where else can you get acupuncture and massage as relaxing and reasonably priced options? Activities include birdwatching and trips to many of the area attractions. Whether it's the vibes from the ancient history buried below or otherwise, the sky seems bluer here, the spring water purer, and the stars brighter than usual; rates are US$25 per person including room tax, breakfast, and dinner daily.

Getting There
Batty Brothers and **Novelo** buses both stop here on their way to neighboring Benque Viejo. If you're traveling by car watch for the speed bump (sleeping policeman) at the east end of town. There are several more between here and the center of Benque.

BENQUE VIEJO DEL CARMEN

Eight miles beyond San Ignacio on the Western Highway going toward the Guatemala border lies **Benque Viejo,** the last town on the Belize side (the border is about one mile farther). Like the rest of the area, the houses sit on posts, and the town is scattered across hillsides with lush mountains standing guard.

This is a quiet little town with a low-key, peaceful atmosphere. Benque Viejo has been greatly influenced by the Spanish, both from its historical past when Spain ruled Guatemala and later when Spanish-speaking *chicleros* (chicle workers) and loggers worked the forest.

The Latin influence persists with today's influx of Guatemalans. A group of foreign doctors who donate free medical assistance visit **Good Shepherd Clinic** in Benque Viejo every year. People come from all over the district for this needed service; families even come from across the Guatemalan border.

Many residents are Mopan Maya Indians, and even more of these descendants live in the nearby Maya village of **San Jose Succotz.** At one time Benque Viejo ("Old Bank"—riverside logging camps were referred to as banks) was a logging camp. This was the gathering place for chicle workers, and logs were floated down the river from here for shipment to England.

Accommodations and Food
The couple of places around Benque appeal primarily to backpackers and budget travelers. According to readers, **Maxim's Palace Hotel and Restaurant,** 41 Churchill Street, Benque Viejo, Belize, C.A., tel. (93) 2259, is the best of the bunch. Or you can try **Oki's Hotel,** George St., tel. (93) 2006.

Vista del Carmen Cafe perches at the east end of town up on a high hill overlooking Benque and the surrounding countryside. Like the Cahal Pech Tavern, this you can see from some distance away. Once there, you'll see a large *palapa* with tables and a bar. Off to one side are two simple, whitewashed cabañas.

Shopping
Galeria de Arte Gucumaz sells Belizean and Guatemalan handicrafts at some of the best prices around. Otherwise there's not much shopping. A few small general stores sell a little of everything: canned goods, sweets, sundries, and cold drinks. You'll also find a gas station, police department, fire station, and telephone service. This is a good place to fill your gas tank before entering Guatemala.

By Bus to and from Guatemala
Both **Batty** and **Novelo** buses move through town fairly often, starting with a 6:30 a.m. departure from Belize City. Some bus drivers going to the border pick you up and waive the fee since it's so close. Traveling in the other direction (from Benque Viejo to Belize City), buses begin moving through at 4 a.m. Remember when

traveling on Sundays in Belize that the schedule is much shorter, so check ahead of time.

At the Guatemala Border

The border is open 8 a.m.-noon and 2-6 p.m. Someone will let you through during off hours, but will charge an extra fee, both for you and your car. If you're trying to get to **Tikal,** take the 6:30 a.m. **Batty bus** from Belize City, which passes through Benque Viejo, crosses the border, and arrives at the first town, Melchor de Mencos, about 10 a.m. Here it meets with the bus to Flores, where you'll hope to connect with a bus to Tikal from the El Cruce junction. Occasionally you can hitch a ride, but if you're not a gambler, you may want to go directly to Flores, where buses run more frequently to Tikal. (For more detailed information about crossing the border, traveling into Guatemala and Tikal, accommodations, and Maya archaeological sites, see "Guatemala.") Those going straight to Tikal should change money at the bank in Melchor de Mencos (or even with the money-changers who hang out at the border station). The bank at Flores closes daily at 2 p.m. Tikal has no banks, and though hotels and restaurants will accept U.S. dollars and traveler's checks for payment, they will *not* change traveler's checks into Guatemalan *quetzals*.

STANN CREEK DISTRICT
INTRODUCTION

For those looking for the *real* rainforests of Belize, beautiful beaches, and fascinating local culture, a trip to the Stann Creek District in southern Belize is in order. This section of the country has not been high on the list of advertised destinations, but that is all beginning to change. Of course this means more and more resorts will come along, changing life here ever-so-slightly at first. However, as more people arrive in response to the Mundo Maya movement, many new doors of financial opportunity are opening for the locals. This southern district of the country has a lot to offer, especially those who are looking for Mundo Maya ("World of the Maya"). As well as being one of the richer rainforests in the country (with more than 120 inches of rain per year), southern Belize offers white sand and blue sea, waterfalls, jungle pools, vine-edged trails, and a plethora of hidden Maya cities of the past. Another plus—more and more divers are discovering the southern cayes and their opulent undersea life and comparing them with the best of the more touristed regions.

THE LAND

Stann Creek District begins just after Over The Top ridge on the Hummingbird Highway where the surrounding lush rainforest is thick with tropical plants, delicate ferns, bromeliads, and orchids. As you get closer to Dangriga, the rainforest gives way to vast groves of citrus. Stann Creek is not the smallest district in Belize but it's next in line.

Agriculture
Over the millennia, rivers and streams gushing from the Maya Mountains have deposited a rich layer of fertile soil, making the coastal and valley regions ideal farming areas. The banana industry, once vital in the area, was wiped out by a disease called "Panama Rot" many years back. However, with new technology, a strain of bananas has been developed that appears to be surviving and promises to grow into a profitable operation.

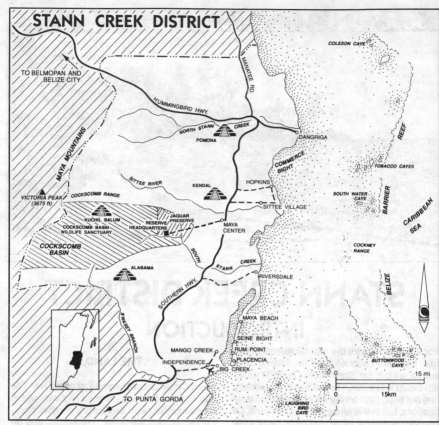

Stann Creek's citrus industry produces Valencia oranges and grapefruit, which are then processed (on-site) into juice—one of Belize's most important exports. The business center of the citrus industry, Dangriga has rebounded with vigor since being wiped out by Hurricane Hattie in 1961. The town itself bears little resemblance to its big brother, Belize City. Dangriga has a bright potential in agriculture.

ON THE ROAD

Hummingbird Highway
For those who drive into Stann Creek, the Hummingbird Highway holds pleasures and perils.

The beauty of picturesque villages, bountiful orchards, and jungle landscapes can abruptly disappear behind the dusty red cloud of a citrus truck barreling down the road in front of you. Lots of potholes lie hidden along the 20 or so miles leading up to the turnoff to the Southern Highway. Don't despair, the highway has fine stretches of dirt and pavement as well.

Manatee Road
Another route into Stann Creek District and onward to Dangriga or the Southern Highway is to take the Manatee Road (check conditions before you head out during wet weather). This, too, is a dirt road that can charm you with beauty one moment and jar your fillings loose the next.

Dangriga coastline

Many short wooden bridges with no rails are large enough for a single vehicle only. Sections of the twisting road are lined with jungle or pine forests on each side, with not a sign of human intrusion. You'll drive through washouts, where rain-swollen streams empty over their banks and carve rim-bending channels and pits into the submerged roadway. But you'll be rewarded with the sight of eclectic Maya villages, towering forests, and distant looming mountains.

HISTORY AND THE PEOPLE

Stann Creek, as all of Belize, is a rich mix of cultures, including Garifuna, East Indian, European, and Maya. Historically, African heritage is especially strong here, and for that reason both Stann Creek and Toledo districts are considered by some to be the most "Caribbean" sections of Belize. The indigenous people of southern Belize (dating back 3,600 years) are the Maya, and they, too, are still well-represented.

MAYA

Small villages of Maya, still practicing some form of their ancient culture, dot the landscape. Little is known of their early history except what has been learned from the amazing structures that are continually uncovered in thick jungle. Records show that in more recent times (soon after Columbus visited the New World), many of the Maya moved away from the coast to escape hostile Spanish and British intruders who

arrived by ship to search for slaves. The independent Maya refused to be subjugated, so traders brought boatloads of African slaves into the Caribbean. Both the Maya and the Africans had religious beliefs that were extraordinarily inconsistent with the lifestyles of Christians, who considered them subhuman. As a result, the Maya and the Garifuna for years kept to themselves.

Even now, the Mopan, Yucatec, and Kekchi continue to live much as their ancestors did. Most of them practice some form of Christian religion integrated with ancient beliefs—in southern Belize the Kekchi have their own Mennonite church. But ancient Maya ceremonies are still quietly practiced in secluded pockets of the country, many in southern Belize, by the Maya people. Curiously, today's Maya have little connection with the Maya structures that remain. Not too far from Dangriga, many of these ceremonial centers have been discovered, with indications that many more lie waiting under thick jungle growth.

local produce market

GARIFUNA

The earliest Black Caribs were farmers, fishermen, trappers—and warriors—originating on St. Vincent Island in the West Indies. Here, escaped West African slaves mixed with the aboriginal people called Red Caribs.

Though the Black Caribs were dominated by the Europeans and confined to the islands of St. Vincent and St. Dominica, they never stopped their fight for freedom. They were persistent warriors, and under the leadership of a valiant fighter, Joseph Chatoyer, they continued the battle. But with European firepower against their bows and arrows, they were no match. The Caribs were put down in 1796, and to try to contain them, the victors moved about 5,000 captives once again to the Bay Islands off the coast of Honduras.

From the time that ships flying the Spanish flag began using the ocean to export the riches of the New World to Spain, the Bay Islands (because of their location) were thrust into the middle of the fight over who would control these sea-lanes. At one time or another the fight included Dutch, English, French, and U.S. ships, either pirating or smuggling goods in and out of what Spain considered its personal territory. The Bay Islands off Honduras shifted ownership regularly as all of those countries vied for control of the sea-lanes.

After arriving in the Bay Islands, the Caribs,

still seeking peace, began wandering in their dugout canoes and over the years began to settle in coastal areas of Honduras, Guatemala, Nicaragua, and southern Belize. In 1802 the beginnings of a settlement took hold in Stann Creek with 150 Caribs. The isolated band supported itself by subsistence fishing and farming. In 1823 a civil war in Honduras forced more Caribs to leave and they headed for Belize. They landed in Belize under the leadership of Alejo Beni and began what has been a peaceful, poor community. Only recently, after more than 150 years, has Dangriga become a thriving agricultural center thanks to the efforts of the whole community, including the Maya and the Caribs.

The Black Caribs are known today by the language they speak, referred to as both Garifuna and Garinagu. According to Phylis Cayetano, who devotes much of her time and effort to preserving the Garifuna culture and language, the group is a mixture of Amerindian, African, Arawak, and Carib, but the mothers were mostly Arawak. The Garifuna developed their own language, and, according to a dictionary that dates from the 1700s, very few words are African; most are Carib.

The Garifuna continued to practice what was still familiar from their ancient African traditions—foods, dances, and especially music, which consisted of complex rhythms with a call-and-response pattern that was an important part of their social and religious celebrations. An eminent person in the village is still the drum maker

GARIFUNA SETTLEMENT DAY

The hour before dawn we made our way through the darkness along the edge of the sea heading toward the persistent beat of distant drums. Orange streaks began to widen across the horizon as we climbed over a half-fallen wooden bridge spanning a creek, cutting a muddy path to the Caribbean. We were on our way to Dangriga on Garifuna Settlement Day, one of Belize's lively national holidays celebrated each year on 19 November to commemorate the arrival of the Garifuna people to Belize.

The ancestors smiled. Rains that had been pouring down for a week subsided, and by the time we reached the center of town and the river shoreline, crowds of revelers were beginning to gather in the breaking dawn. This was a day of reflection and good times in Belize, a severe contrast to Garifuna beginnings that for decades were filled with misery and tragedy.

Settlement Day is a happy celebration. Everyone dresses in colorful new clothes, and while waiting for the "landing," family, friends, and strangers from all over Belize catch up on local gossip, make new acquaintances, and enjoy the party. Sounds of beating drums emanate from small circles of people on both sides of the river, from the backs of pickup trucks and from rooftops. In lieu of drums, young men push through the crowds shouldering giant boom-boxes that broadcast the beat. Excitement (and umbrellas) hang in the air as the assemblage waits for the canoes and the beginning of the pageant.

Garifuna history really began more than 300 years ago when two ships filled with African slaves were wrecked on the Caribbean's Windward Islands. The next century is shadowy and the only certainty is that with the passage of time they intermarried with the Carib people, creating the Garifuna. They were defeated and con-

trolled over the years by the Spanish and British, the latter deporting them to the inhospitable island of Roatan off the coast of Honduras.

But now, in the early dawn, the crowd cheers. It spots two dugout canoes paddling from the open sea into the river. Years ago, the first refugees from Roatan—men, women, and children—crowded into just such boats along with a few meager necessities to start a new life in a new land. Today's reenactment is orchestrated according to verbal history handed down through generations. Leaves and vines are wrapped around the arrivals' heads and waists. Drums, baskets that carry simple cooking utensils, young banana trees, and cassava roots are all among the precious cargo the Garifuna originally brought to start their new life in Dangriga.

The canoes paddle past cheering crowds. No matter that this pageant is repeated every year (like the U.S.A.'s Fourth of July); each November is a reminder of the past, and even this outsider is swept along in the excitement and thoughts of what this day represents to the Garifuna citizens of Belize.

Like a winning athlete passing in review, the canoes travel up the river and under the bridge and back again so that everyone lining the bank and bridge can see them. When the "actors" come ashore they're joined by hundreds of onlookers. The colorful procession then proceeds through the narrow streets with young and old dancing and singing to the drum-

beats; they proudly lead the parade to the Catholic church where a special service takes place. Dignitaries from all over Belize attend and tell of the past and, most important, of the hopes of the future.

The Catholic church plays a unique part in the life of the Garifuna. Some years back the church reached an unspoken, working agreement with the Garifuna: nothing formal, just a look-the-other-way attitude while their Garifuna parishioners mix Catholic dogma with ancient ritual. It wasn't always this way. For generations the people were forced to keep their religion alive in clandestine meetings or suffer severe punishment and persecution.

Rain, much like time, has not stopped the Garifuna celebrations nor the dancing that is an integral part of the festivities. Street dances traditionally held along village streets for many nights leading up to Celebration Day continue and are moved indoors to escape the flooded streets. Small bars and open *palapa* (thatch) structures are crowded with fun lovers and reverberate with the pounding of exotic triple drums (always three). Drums bring their magic, and parties continue with both modern *punta* rock and traditional dances into the early hours of the morning. The Garifuna are a people filled with music. The songs sung in the Garifuna language tell stories— some happy, some sad—and many melodies go hand-in-hand with daily tasks.

At an open *palapa* hut, three talented drummers begin the beat. The old Garifuna women, heavily influenced by their African beginnings, insist on marshaling the dances—the old way. The first tempo is the *paranda*, a dance just for women. A circle is created in the dirt-floored room and the elderly women begin a low-key, heavy-footed, repetitive shuffle with subtle hand movements accompanied by timeworn words that we don't understand but are told tell a tale of survival.

Every few minutes a reveler filled with too much rum pushes through the circle of people and joins the dancing women. He's quickly chased out of the ring by an umbrella-wielding elder who aims her prods at the more vulnerable spots of his body. If that doesn't work she resorts to pulling the intoxicated dancer off the floor by his ear—a little comic relief that adds to the down-home entertainment.

The *paranda* continues, and little kids energetically join in the dances on the outside of the "circle" or watch wide-eyed from the rafters near the top of the *palapa* roof, entranced by the beat, dim light, and music—the magic of the holiday. The recurring rain adds an extra beat to the exotic cadence of the drums; dance after dance continues.

The *huguhugn* dance is open to everyone, but the sexy *punta* is the popular favorite, one couple at a time in the ring. Handsome men and beautiful women slowly undulate their bodies with flamboyant grace and sexual suggestion. This is the courtship dance born in their African roots. In case you miss Settlement Day parties, stop by a bar or nightclub anywhere in Belize and you'll see locals doing a modern version called *punta* rock.

The Garifuna are a matriarchal society, and the elder women are trying hard to keep the old traditions alive. While English is the language of the country and taught in the classrooms of Belize, one of the concerns of the elders is the preservation of the ethnic language of the Garifuna.

Most of the older Garifuna women wear bright-colored dirndl skirts and kerchiefs tied low over their foreheads, symbolic of days spent in the fields. Only a few wear the traditional costumes trimmed with

shells; today's young women and girls prefer T-shirts and jeans or modern tight skirts—and none wears a kerchief. The men wear jeans and years ago they traded their straw hats for baseball caps.

Freedom and integration into Belize in the 1800s was not easy. And though the Garifuna were allowed to settle in the Stann Creek District when they first arrived, the British isolated them from the rest of the country. They allowed the Garifuna into Belize City only with 48-hour passes to let them sell their harvest. City dwellers who did no farming and for years were forced to exist on limited imported food welcomed this fresh produce.

The populace in general was frightened of the Garifuna, believing the lies that they ate babies and cast evil spells; these stories were spread by slave owners who were convinced that their own slaves would run off and live with the outsiders if they got the chance to see the relative freedom that the Garifuna enjoyed in southern Belize. Finally, on 19 November 1832, the Garifuna were accepted and given a voice in government affairs at the public meeting in Belize City.

During Settlement Day, a walk down the narrow streets takes you past small parties and family gatherings under stilted houses where dancing and singing is the rule; others enjoy holiday foods (including cassava bread), and drinks. If invited to share a cup of coffee dipped from an old blue porcelain kettle and heavily laced with rum, join in!—it could turn out to be the best part of the celebration!

who continues the old traditions, along with making other instruments used in these often night-long singing and dancing ceremonies.

Obeah

One of the most enduring customs, the practice of black magic known as obeah, was regarded with great suspicion and concern by the colonialists in Belize City. Even after laws were enacted that made it illegal for any man or woman to take money or other effects in return for fetishes or amulets, ritual formulas, or other magical mischief that could immunize slaves from the wrath of their masters, the practice continued—though in more secretive ways. (No doubt, if you have a need and have established a trust with the Garifuna, you can find an obeah man today.) The obeah works through dances, drumbeats, trances, and trancelike

contact with the dead. Small, black puchinga (cloth dolls) stuffed with black feathers can strike dread into the hearts of the Garifuna; if buried under the doorstep of an impending victim the doll can supposedly bring marital problems, failure in business, illness, or death. It's not unusual for sacrifices to involve the blood of live chickens and pigs. Small Garifuna children occasionally are seen with indigo blue crosses drawn on their foreheads to ward off evil spirits.

Exile

Shortly after the Garifuna established themselves in southern Belize they brought their produce in dugouts to sell in Belize Town, where the people were delighted to have fresh vegetables. But because of the fear generated by the slave owners of Belize Town, these southern people were ostracized when they tried to become part of the Town Public Meeting. The fear pervaded the colonial town for many years.

Now, each year on 19 November, the whole country remembers the day the Garifuna arrived in Belize, and **Settlement Day** is celebrated with a reenactment of the landing in 1823 —a happy celebration and an opportunity for the curious to witness the exotic tempos of Garifuna dancing and singing. Be adventurous and taste the typical, though unusual, Garifuna foods. If you drink too much "local dynamite" (rum and coconut milk), have a cup of the strong chicory coffee said by the Garifuna "to make we not have *goma*" (a Garifuna hangover).

Recognizing that schooling is essential, the Garifuna, along with the entire country of Belize, are staunch advocates of education—every desk in the classrooms of Dangriga is filled. In schools all across the country, Garifuna women excel as teachers.

The people are, generally, still farmers; their plots often are 5-10 miles outside of town. In the early days they walked the long distances; today they take a bus, tending their fields from early morning to late afternoon. The district's leading crop is citrus, and the people of Dangriga figure strongly in this production.

Traditions

Traditionally and continuing today, the Garifuna raise cassava to make *eriba,* a flat bread made from the meal of the cassava root. The large bulbous roots of the shrubby spurge plant are peeled and grated (today mostly by electric graters, but formerly by hand—a long, tedious job on a stone-studded board). The grated cassava is packed into a six-foot-long leaf-woven tube that is hung from a hefty tree limb, then weighted and pulled at the bottom, squeezing and forcing out the poisonous juices and starch from the pulp. The coarse meal that remains is dried and used to make the flat bread that has been an important part of the Garifuna culture for centuries.

Today's Garifuna are still aloof and seldom marry out of their group. Many are still superstitious; however, a friend is treated warmly. The women are extremely hard-working, the central influence of the family, and generally the caretakers of the family farm.

WHITE SETTLERS

The earliest white settlers were Puritans from the island of New Providence in the Bahamas. These simple-living people implemented their knowledge of raising tobacco on nearby offshore cayes (today called Tobacco Cayes), began a trading post (also known as a "stand," which over time deteriorated to "Stann"), and spread south into the Placencia area. The trading post ultimately faded away, and Dangriga continued its almost stagnant existence. During the American Civil War, arms dealers became familiar with the Belizean coast. In the 1860s British settlers in Belize encouraged Americans to come and begin new lives in Belize. Hundreds of Confederates did arrive after the Civil War and began clearing land to develop. However, it was not to last. Most of the American settlers returned to the U.S., though one group of Methodists from Mississippi stayed in Toledo District long enough to develop 12 sugar plantations. By 1910 most of the Mississippians were gone. During U.S. Prohibition, boats decked out as fishing crafts ran rum from Belize to Florida.

Despite its slow start, today's Dangriga is a community, population about 9,000, with a bright future of growth.

DANGRIGA

The town of Dangriga, a Garifuna word meaning "standing waters," was formerly called Stann Creek. The small community is on the coast, 36 miles south of Belize City as the crow (or Maya Airways) flies. However, by bike, bus, or car the trip is much longer, roughly 75 miles along the twisting Manatee Road or about 100 miles on the unpredictable Hummingbird Highway from Belmopan. By Stann Creek standards, the city of Dangriga is a bustling, though easygoing, place that is thriving because of the successful citrus industry that has finally begun a healthy growth (after more than 50 years). Tourism today attracts a moderate number of curious citizens-of-the-world, especially divers, owing to Dangriga's location near the enticing underwater world of the sea.

Dangriga Culture

Dangriga is home to the well-known **Warribaggabagga Dancers** and the **Turtle Shell Band.** It is the heart of Garifuna folk culture. The music and dancing, including syncopated African rhythms, are an enchanting mixture of the various cultures of southern Belize. Some of Belize's most ac-

complished artists live in Dangriga. **Austin Rodriquez,** 32 Tubroose St., is known for his authentic Garifuna drums. **Benjamin Nicholas** paints the local scene from his studio at 27 Oak St., and **Mercy Sabal,** 22 Magoon St., makes colorful dolls that are sold all over the country.

Arts and Crafts

Drums and other typical musical instruments are favorite souvenirs. Women make charming purses woven from reeds. Another memento is a mask, carved and painted by an artisan, used during various ceremonies in the south of Belize, both in Maya and Garifuna ceremonies. **Note:** There have been a couple of complaints from readers who have commissioned artwork with payment in advance. Some of these people did not receive exactly what was expected when it was due. Perhaps only a partial advance payment would be better.

Activities

Activities include cycling, exploring ruins, fishing, hiking, nature watching of all kinds, snorkeling, and scuba diving.

Pelican Beach Resort

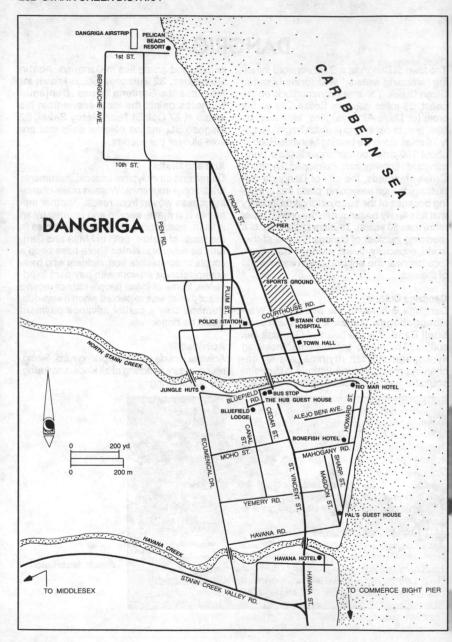

DANGRIGA AIRSTRIP

PELICAN BEACH RESORT

1st ST.

BENGUCHE AVE.

10th ST.

CARIBBEAN SEA

DANGRIGA

FRONT ST.

PEN RD.

PIER

SPORTS GROUND

PLUM ST.

COURTHOUSE RD.

POLICE STATION

STANN CREEK HOSPITAL

TOWN HALL

NORTH STANN CREEK

N
Moon

0   200 yd

0   200 m

JUNGLE HUTS

BLUEFIELD RD.

BLUEFIELD LODGE

CANAL ST.

CEDAR ST.

BUS STOP

THE HUB GUEST HOUSE

ALEJO BENI AVE.

BONEFISH HOTEL

RIO MAR HOTEL

HOWARD RD.

MOHO ST.

ECUMENICAL DR.

ST. VINCENT ST.

MAHOGANY RD.

MAGOON ST.

SHARP ST.

YEMERY RD.

HAVANA RD.

PAL'S GUEST HOUSE

HAVANA CREEK

HAVANA HOTEL

HAVANA ST.

TO MIDDLESEX

STANN CREEK VALLEY RD.

TO COMMERCE BIGHT PIER

ACCOMMODATIONS

The traveler to Stann Creek has a choice of staying on the mainland or visiting the offshore cayes, and of camping, staying at small lodges and resorts, Maya and Garifuna guesthouse programs, or in the Cockscomb Basin Wildlife Sanctuary.

You'll find the casual **Pelican Beach Resort,** Box 14, Dangriga, Stann Creek District, Belize, C.A., tel. (5) 22044, fax (5) 22570, along the beachfront just north of town. It's run by Therese and Tony Rath; she is president of the Belize Audubon Society, and he's a gifted nature photographer whose work appears all over the country. The most attractive lodging in Dangriga and the closest to the small local airstrip, Pelican Beach offers a fine waterfront location, friendly atmosphere, and good food prepared by local cooks in the restaurant/bar. Iguanas, turtles, land crabs, and butterflies inhabit the surrounding greenery. A palm-studded beachfront adds to the charm. Rooms are clean, simply but comfortably furnished, and include fans, h/c private baths, and telephones; some have balconies. The resort has its own travel agency, and sightseeing trips to the cayes or to Cockscomb Basin Wildlife Sanctuary are easily arranged. Dangriga is a 15-minute walk along the shore. Ask about their cottages and group accommodations on South Water Caye (see "Other Popular Cayes" under "The Cayes"). Rates on rooms at the resort vary according to two meal plans and several floors, US$45-100 s, US$60-150 d, US$70-195 t. Discounts for longer stays, and children under 12 are free with adult. All major credit cards are okay. Follow Ecumenical Drive past the tall transmission tower, across the bridge, and until the road dead-ends. Turn right and it's by the beach on your left. Contact the resort for reservations.

On the second street south of Central Bridge and a couple of blocks west of Havana Street in a quiet residential area on the second floor of a clapboard building is the charming little **Bluefield Lodge,** #6 Bluefield Road, Dangriga, Stann Creek District, Belize, C.A., tel (5) 22742. The owner, Miss Louise, has seven clean, attractively furnished rooms with fans, h/c water, private or shared baths, and special little touches in wallpaper, bedcovers, and curtains. Everything about the place bespeaks the pride and care she takes in her lodge. Parking is on the street. No food service but sodas are available for purchase at the front desk. Rates are with private bath US$17.50 s; with shared bath $12.50 s, US$14.50 d.

An old favorite of divers, the **Bonefish Hotel,** #15 Mahogany Rd., Box 21, Dangriga, Stann Creek District, Belize, C.A., tel. (5) 22165, fax (5) 22296, is a pleasant little place with 10 rooms and a second-floor lobby and bar. It's in downtown Dangriga a couple of blocks east of Havana Street and across the street from a grassy park at the end of Mahogany Road. It caters to active travelers who want to tour the area, fish, or dive. Across the street to the east is the ocean a short distance away. The resort is allied with Blue Marlin Lodge on South Water Caye. Rooms are clean and simple, carpeted, and include private h/c bath, TV, a/c; rates are US$35-45 s, US$60 d. It accepts Visa/MC.

The brightly painted **Havana Hotel,** 490 Havana St., Dangriga, Stann Creek District, Belize, C.A., tel. (5) 22375, sits on the south bank across Havana Creek from Pal's Guest House. Here, in his backyard, owner Gayburn Elijio has opened a two-story building with three single and three double rooms. Each comes with cold water, private bath, ceiling fan, and louvered windows. Rooms are named after animals with a corresponding painted wood plaque on the door; there is a jaguar, tapir, and toucan room, among others. The double rooms have TVs and there's a laundry room on the premises, especially handy if you've just come in from the bush. Rates are US$13 s, US$19 d.

Worth a look for backpackers, buses bound for Placencia and Belize City leave from **The Hub Guest House,** 573A 8th, Riverside, Dangriga, Stann Creek District, Belize, C.A., tel. (5) 22397. It has five (usually clean) basic rooms with private baths, two with shared bath; some rooms have picturesque river views (look at the rooms before you check in and make certain security on windows and privacy is satisfactory). The restaurant downstairs serves good versions of local food and the shaded area in front offers a fine opportunity to mingle with locals and fellow travelers. Room service is available during restaurant hours; breakfast, lunch, and dinner are served. Rates are US$25 s, US$40 d. The staff is always willing to offer tourist info. The **James** bus for Placencia leaves daily from the Hub at 3 p.m.

Along the river on the west side of town, look for an unexpected surprise just by the bridge. **Jungle Huts Hotel,** Ecumenical Drive, Box 10, Dangriga, Stann Creek District, Belize, C.A., tel. (5) 23166, is run by the local dentist, Arthur Usher, and his wife, Beverly. You'll find hot water, tiled private bathrooms, pleasant furniture, and two double beds in each of the four rooms in the main building. Some have a/c. In addition, there are four basic cabañas of a rustic Belizean design. All feature private h/c baths or showers. The hotel and its cabañas are very secure (behind the Usher home). Prices for hotel rooms with fans are about US$30 s, US$35 d, US$45 t; with a/c they are about US$43 s, US$48 d, US$53 t. The whole family is very friendly and you have more of a feeling of staying with relatives than with strangers.

If you are looking for waterfront accommodations in the center of Dangriga, **Pal's Guest House,** 868 Magoon St., Dangriga, Stann Creek District, Belize, C.A., tel. (5) 22095, is the place. You'll find nine clean, modest rooms at the corner of North Havana Road and Magoon Street. Across the road and on the beach is another building. Five rooms are available with parquet linoleum floors, ceiling fans, h/c private showers, TVs, and balconies with ocean views. Louvered windows on both ends of the rooms create good cross-ventilation. Five more rooms will soon be ready upstairs. Guests and locals alike cool off in the brackish water beyond the beach. Fishermen's boats are beached or tied nearby. Rates on seafront rooms are US$22 s, US$31 d.

Rio Mar Hotel, 977 Waight St., Box 2, Dangriga, Stann Creek District, Belize, C.A., tel. (5) 22201, is a budget guesthouse whose tiny clean rooms with paper-thin walls rent for about US$10 s, US$15 d. You may not be enthralled by the blaring music that issues from the bar downstairs or the computerized games and machines that sometimes add to the din. But there are those who say this is the place to be on Garifuna Settlement Day. And for travelers interested in exploring the offshore cayes, the manager

at Rio Mar can arrange trips to South Water Caye. Excursions to these smaller cayes are usually more expensive than those to the more well-known cayes, such as Caye Caulker. For more info write or call the hotel.

Other inexpensive basic hostelries are **Catalina's Hotel,** 35 Cedar St., tel. (5) 22390, and **Riverside Hotel,** 5 Commerce St., tel. (800) 256-7333, (5) 22168, fax (5) 22296, simple and comfortable with shared baths and fans.

FOOD

In Dangriga Town don't forget what time it is; the small cafes are open only during meal times. **The Hub** serves good traditional Creole dishes of rice and chicken for about US$2. For a change of pace try the **Burger King.** Yes, the Burger King—maybe not *the* Burger King, but it serves great burgers, fries, shakes, ice cream—oh yes, and conch soup. The **Rio Mar Hotel** also has a bar and restaurant. **Pelican Beach Resort** has delicious food prepared by Creole cooks.

GETTING THERE

By Air
The 20-minute flight from Belize City to Dangriga is by far the easiest and quickest way to arrive. Maya Airlines has up to five scheduled flights in and out of Dangriga from the two Belize City airports Monday-Saturday. It's also possible to fly back and forth between Dangriga, Placencia, Big Creek, or Punta Gorda. The strip itself is similar to the Belize Municipal, about the length of a few football fields. Check with **Maya Airways,** tel. (2) 44032, fax (2) 30585, for fares and Sunday schedules. **Tropic Air,** tel. (2) 45671, (6) 23184, fax (2) 62338, flies into Dangriga three times daily, with one flight on Sunday and holidays. Call for reservations.

By Boat
Dangriga is roughly 36 miles by boat from Belize City. Because there isn't a scheduled boat trip to Dangriga, ask around—at the Belize City docks by the Texaco station, your hotel, or the Belize Tourist Board, 83 N. Front St., in Belize City.

By Bus

From Belize City's Magazine Road terminal, the **Z-Line Bus** offers several departure times daily: 10 a.m., noon, 2 p.m., and 4 p.m. (fare US$4); departure times from Dangriga daily: 5 a.m., 5:30 a.m., 9 a.m., 10 a.m. (US$4). Call for schedule changes; in Belize City call (2) 73937, in Dangriga call (5) 22211, (5) 22160. It's about a five-hour ride.

Check out the **Promised Land Bus Line**, which makes daily trips between Dangriga and Placencia, tel. (5) 23012.

By Car

It pays not to be in a big rush when meandering the highways and byways south of Belize City. Building roads through swamps and marshes takes lots of money, so up until now it's just been easier to go around the problem areas. Remember, "highway" doesn't necessarily denote a smooth, paved road. Most of the highways in southern Belize are graded, potholed, dirt roads that can be impassable during the rainy season (June-Oct.).

Those inclined to drive, however, will do best with a 4WD vehicle (rentals available); the reward is a chance to see the lovely countryside up close.

Drivers Note: Fill up your gas tank whenever you run across a gas station; a fill-up at Belize City should get you to the next gas at Dangriga.

ALONG THE SOUTHERN HIGHWAY

HOPKINS

Hopkins is a low-key Garifuna fishing village about eight miles south of Dangriga. Wooden boats are dragged onto the beach when fishermen are finished for the day, making picturesque photos. Craftsmen carve dugout canoes out of one large tree trunk and weave their own nets—life is simple here. The small seaside village, four miles from the main road, has about 800 people with the main source of income from fishing. Until recently Hopkins has been virtually untouched by tourism, getting only the occasional visitor. This is reflected in the basic accommodations available.

Accommodations and Food

Hopkins is one of the best places to join in the festivities for Garifuna Settlement Day. You can probably drop in and find a room most of the year, *except* around Garifuna Settlement Day (19 November). Or you can make a couple of phone calls in advance. I say a *couple* because Hopkins has only a community phone. The procedure is to call (5) 22033 and tell whoever answers what time you will call back and that you want to talk to someone about finding a room. You have a couple of choices.

At Sandy Beach at the end of the village, **Hopkins Women's Cooperative/Sandy Beach Lodge** offers three buildings with nine rooms for rent. Four have private baths; others share a bathroom, outhouse-style. These accommodations are *extremely* basic, but generally clean. Meals are served. Prices start at about US$7 twin, outside bath, and the most expensive is less than US$30 d, private bath. Don't expect too much and you'll enjoy your stay in the village. Though the Co-op is right on the beach, sometimes the shoreline looks pretty trashy, although the women try to clean it. Contact tel. (5) 22033 (community phone, leave a message) or write Hopkins Village, Stann Creek District, Belize, C.A.

The name of **Swinging Armadillos' Hammock Lounge and Tourist Information Center** may sound a little crazy, but you'll find a friendly bar/restaurant specializing in seafood and traditional Garifuna dishes, with hammock rentals at laidback prices. For more information contact Michael Flores, tel. (5) 22033 (community phone, leave a message) or write Hopkins Village, Stann Creek District, Belize, C.A.

Ask around; some women in the village are happy to have a guest at the table for a small fee. The same goes for pitching a tent along the beach.

SITTEE

A couple of miles farther down the Southern Highway brings you to the turnoff to the left for Sittee. This qualifies as a village only in the loosest sense; it's just a cluster of fishing shacks, other houses, **Reynold's Store,** and amiable people scattered around the Sittee River. And that's the way it's been for a long, long time. But things change even here. In years past the accommodations were limited to a clapboard home offering the most basic of accommodations and owned by congenial locals. Today, there are a few more.

Accommodations and Food

Glover's Guest House, Box 563, Belize City, Belize, C.A., tel. (5) 23048, is a very spartan lodging primarily for guests of Glover's Atoll Resort, a palm-studded caye on the barrier reef. Backpackers may want to try here; if it's full, there's always room for camping at about US$3 per person. Meals are available. A boat arrives to take guests to Glover's Atoll Resort every Sunday at 8 a.m. (See "Glover's Reef Atoll" in the Atolls chapter.)

A short distance farther down the river, you'll find the **Toucan Sittee,** Sittee River, Stann Creek District, Belize, C.A., tel. (5) 22006, a pleasant basic lodging with very good local food. On the right as you head for the ocean you'll see the sign, two spacious raised wooden cabins, and a main house. The cabin nearest the river has two doubles, each with a kitchen, cold water, private bath, and a screened porch. The rate is US$50 d, US$5 per person additional. The other cabin is a bunkhouse with shared cold water bath. Travelers can lodge here for US$6 per person, private groups of four or more for US$8 per person. One of the owners, Neville Collins, can arrange guided river and lagoon fishing. Snook, tarpon, peacock bass, sheepshead, and barracuda are his specialties. A boat with a guide is US$125/day; boat only is US$50. He also rents canoes for about US$38/day. Delicious meals are based on local dishes, including *serre* (fish cooked in coconut milk), steak with onions and bell peppers, baked barracuda with yogurt, curries, and fresh fruit pies. Meal prices start at US$2.50-4 breakfast, US$2-3 packed lunch, US$3.50-5 dinner.

Head out the causeway to **Sittee Point,** where the river meets the sea, and you'll notice homes going up, parcels of prime beachfront marked for development, and the attractive thatch cabañas of **Jaguar Reef Resort,** Hopkins Village General Delivery, Stann Creek District, Belize, C.A., tel/fax (92) 3452. A good sign of the times is this lodge's pledge to donate profits from the resort to various conservation charities, including the Belize Audubon Society. It's all the work of two ecotourism-minded individuals, Canadian Bruce Foerster and noted adventure guide Neil Rogers. Together, they have overseen the creation of the lodge with its dozen (and growing) thatched-roofed cabañas on the beach. Made of mostly traditional materials, the cabañas have hardwood decks, screened windows, private h/c baths. Rates are US$100 s, US$120 d. Meals are available for about US$6 breakfast, US$9 lunch, US$17 dinner. Rates drop considerably in low season (1 June-31 Oct.). Ask about their great packages, including tours, meals, transfers, and snorkeling on the cayes. Mountain bikes are available at about US$20/day, tel./fax (2) 12041.

The water just off the beach can be a bit muddy at times (like most Belizean mainland beaches) because of the close proximity of rivers and streams. Clear water is only a matter of minutes out to one of the nearshore cayes. But the reason to come here is the interesting mix of tours available, including dive trips to offshore cayes and Glover's Reef Atoll or trips to the nearby Cockscomb Basin Wildlife Sanctuary. Tours are available that combine both. Ask about the mountain bike trip to the Cockscomb that allows adventurers to bike to the park (the road to the overnight area is deep within the park) and then hike several of the more impressive trails. Trips to nearby Hopkins are also very bikeable. Write or call for more information.

Drivers Note: Driving the causeway (mentioned above), which cuts through the marsh from the mainland to a kind of barrier island by the beach, is a one-way affair. A couple of places have been fashioned to allow one vehicle to pull over while another passes. Do not attempt to pass a vehicle on this causeway, especially in wet weather; the shoulders have a habit of crumbling beneath the weight of vehicles, allowing them to slide or roll into the marsh.

COCKSCOMB BASIN

The land rises gradually from the coastal plains to the **Maya Mountains;** the highest point in the Cockscomb Basin range is **Victoria Peak** (3,675 feet). Geologists believe that Victoria Peak is four million years old, the oldest geologic formation in Central America. Mountain climbers find this peak a real adventure. The first climbers (a party that included Roger T. Goldsworth, governor of then-British Honduras) reached the peak in 1888; British soldiers recorded another climb in 1986. Heavy rain along the granite peaks of the Maya range (as much as 160 inches a year) runs off into lush rainforest thick with trees, orchids, palms, ferns, abundant birds, and exotic animals, including peccaries, anteaters, armadillos, tapirs, and jaguars. Until recently, the jaguar was a prize for game hunters. Today the beautiful cat has thousands of acres to roam protected from man in the **Cockscomb Basin Jaguar Preserve.**

The archaeology buff should check out the ruins in the vicinity of Cockscomb Basin: **Pomona** on North Stann Creek, **Kendal** on the Sittee River, and **Pierce** on South Stann Creek.

COCKSCOMB BASIN WILDLIFE SANCTUARY

Maya Center Village

A few miles south of the Sittee turnoff you'll come to the entrance to the sanctuary at Maya Center Village. This small town's claim to fame is the entry into the **Sanctuary.** Check in here if you're interested in seeing the reserve (or the remains of the Maya ceremonial site called **Kuchil Balum.**) You'll find a selection of Belizean crafts for sale, including carved slate Maya images. Maya families within the sanctuary were relocated to this small village to protect the sanctuary environment. Since then the Maya have changed their lifestyles; the men work as guides

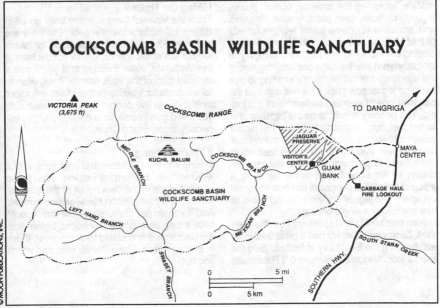

and the women concentrate more on crafts. They have organized a crafts co-op, and their art is for sale at the **Visitors' Center** about seven miles into the Sanctuary.

The Cockscomb Basin Wildlife Sanctuary is one of the wildest places in the country and easily one of the most beautiful. If you came to Belize to see luxuriant jungle, if you came to get close to the "skeeters" and all of God's creatures, and if you came to share sleeping space in a clapboard building with a bunch of strangers from all over the world who have the same interests as you, then you've come to the right place.

Most of the hotels in southern Belize provide transportation and guided tours of the wildlife sanctuary, or you can make arrangements with your hotel in other parts of the country for a side trip to southern Belize.

Sanctuary Beginnings

A large tract of approximately 155 square miles of forest was declared a forest reserve in 1984, and in 1986 the government of Belize set the region aside as a preserve for the largest cat in the Americas, the jaguar. The area is alive with wildlife, including the margay, ocelot, puma, jaguarundi, tapir, deer, paca, iguana, kinkajou, and armadillo (to name just a few), hundreds of bird species, and some unusual reptiles, including the red-eyed tree frog. And though you probably won't see the large cats roaming during the day (they hunt at night), it's exciting to see the large jaguar paw print; it's a real sign that the cat does indeed exercise ownership of this jungle. The peccary is said to be the jaguar's preferred diet, but, according to locals, the jaguar enjoys a love/hate relationship with the animal. Maya legend has it that the jaguar learned to climb trees to get away from the peccary because, as large and feared as the jaguar is, a group of the piglike peccaries can tear the great cat apart. The jaguar prefers to search from its tree branch for a single peccary.

Alan Rabinowitz and sponsors from the **New York Zoological Society** had a great deal to do with bringing the Sanctuary to fruition. (See the special topic "Jaguars 1, Hunters 0.") Rabinowitz did extensive research in this area, studying the jaguar, its habits, and its range. He lived in the jaguar's neighborhood for about 18 months and urged the government to create this protective hideaway for the large cat. He has put it all down in a book titled *Jaguar*, published by Arbor House, New York.

Visitors' Center and Accommodations

Seven miles into the Sanctuary you'll find the Visitors' Center with its small museum, picnic area, and outhouse/restroom. You'll also find an "office" of the **World Wildlife Fund,** an important sponsor of the park, along with the **Belize Audubon Society** and the government. The overnight accommodations are between these in a couple of clapboard buildings with about a dozen bunks and zinc roofs. A walled-off washing area has buckets, and a separate cooking area has a gas stove, a few pots and such; we're talking basic here. Rates are US$12 per person; or bring your own tent (US$3). No campfires. And just in case, bring a poncho, mosquito netting, and insect repellent with enough DEET to pack some punch (30% or higher).

Hiking the Trails

From the Visitors' Center, many trails go off in different directions into the park. The trails are well-cared-for and comfortable even for hikers without lots of experience. Check out the front of the Visitors' Center Building and you'll see a detailed map of the trails nearby. If you wish to take a guide for trekking farther afield, ask about availability at the center. Bring your swimsuit; you'll find good pools for a cooling plunge, especially along Stann Creek.

If You're Driving

Driving into the Cockscomb is best done with a 4WD vehicle. In the rainy season, even these can get stuck in the parking lot of the Visitors' Center—the best stretch of level ground in miles! And if you do get stuck, on a slow day it could take a long time and a few bucks before you are discovered and pulled free; however, there is a villager from Maya Center who can winch you out.

PLACENCIA PENINSULA

Continuing on the Southern Highway, take the road to Riversdale, about 10 miles. In Riversdale a right turn will put you on the road down the strip of land called the Placencia Peninsula.

Belizeans and visitors alike agree that the finest beaches in the country are along this 11-mile slender strip of land called the Placencia Peninsula. It feels like an island with the Caribbean on one side and the Placencia Lagoon on the other. It is predicted that eventually this will be the next big tourist development—*come quickly!* Placencians will tell you that the best time to vacation here is *anytime* (although more rain falls May-Nov.). The informality and relaxed atmosphere are very special and highly contagious. Nature provides white sand fringed with waving green palms and the azure sea; the reef is visible in the distance. The water is clear enough to watch fish through the glasslike surface only occasionally rippled by gentle breezes. And from the Placencia coast you can hoist anchor and within a short time find a score of idyllic offshore cayes.

MAYA BEACH

As you proceed south on the peninsula you'll come to a small cluster of houses. Its particular attraction is a nice beach and almost complete isolation from tourists.

Australians Bruce Larkin and Sally Steeds run **Singing Sands,** Maya Beach, Placencia Peninsula, Belize, C.A., tel./fax (6) 22243, in the U.S. tel. (800) 617-2637, a small resort of six thatched-roof cabañas and a bar/restaurant along a beach sprinkled with palms. It's a retreat far from much of anything—and that especially appeals to the travelers who seek it out. Each of the cabañas has paneled wood walls, screened windows, ceiling fan, private bath, h/c water, and porch out back. Rates are US$75 s, US$95 d. Credit cards are okay. Meals are available for US$2.50-8 breakfast, US$8-20 dinner. The active set will find available mountain bikes, a couple of Windsurfers, 45-foot catamaran, ski boat, and slalom skis at reasonable

rates. The resort has a dive shop, too; Sally is a certified PADI instructor. In addition, she and Bruce frequently arrange boating trips for guests to fly-fish or to observe manatees and dolphins in the lagoon.

SEINE BIGHT

Seine Bight, 2.5 miles south of Maya Beach, is a Garífuna village of simple one-room wooden houses on stilts and about 550 people. Most of the men are fishermen and the women tend the family gardens, which they depend on for their basic food needs. It takes a while for the locals to strike up a friendship. In fact, unless you make the first move, about all that happens is that people will look you over, especially the kids.

The people here are different; they have a carefree intact culture that reflects ancient tribal customs. Men and women have a major split; the women have their own language that they say the men don't understand. The men will do absolutely nothing that might be construed as women's work. According to the women, the men lounge around in hammocks and drink most of the day. However, they have been known to help a stranger with car trouble. Ask before you take pictures, and accept "no" graciously.

Entertainment/Culture/Art

If you need a little additional diversion, head on over near the hurricane shelter to a little place called **Sunshine.** It's the local bar/disco and features natural wood on the outside walls, pale blue inside, four *huge* speakers, and room to dance to *punta* rock and reggae. Take your choice of soft drinks, fresh squeezed orange juice, beer, tropical brandy, or bitters (a potion made of various roots and herbs marinated in rum). "De bitter, de better, mon!" It does taste bitter. But not bad, especially after the first one or two. Herbert also serves barbecue or fried chicken. A paper on the wall reads, "Attention: No loafers allowed. No bad words allowed. Avoid

KULCHA SHACK MENU~ A FEW GARIFUNA DISHES

Hudut: fish simmered in thick coconut milk with herbs and cooked over an open fire served with *fu-fu* (beaten plantain).

Tapow: green banana cut in wedges and simmered in coconut milk with fish, herbs, and seasonings—served with white rice or *ereba* (cassava bread).

Seafood gumbo: a combination of conch, lobster, shrimp, fish, and vegetables, cooked in coconut milk, herbs, and grated green banana or plantain—served with rice or *ereba* and Irish Moss (a seaweed shake).

unnecessary arguments. No credit until tomorrow. Please do not spit on the floor."

Take an evening to discover the one-of-a-kind **Kulcha Shack** (pronounced "shock"). By day it's just another small forlorn structure on the beach with some friendly people serving drinks and snacks. But at night it takes on magic. You'll hear the haunting drums of the Garifuna accompanied by melodies from the past. If you're lucky enough to have a translator with you, you'll learn a bit of Garifuna melodrama. The drummers know their craft well, and with reservations on the weekends, you'll see modern entertainment (such as *punta* rock) as well as the traditional fare. The lamp-lit cafe serves

authentic Garifuna food, provides good entertainment. For a great souvenir to take home, ask to see Darlene's (the owner's wife) handmade Garifuna dolls (about US$20). For the special dinner and show, minimum of four people, the price is US$25 per person; make reservations and call before 6 p.m., tel. (6) 22015. Ask about the simple cabins on the beach.

Lola's Art is in the center of town. Lola sells handmade dolls, too. But she sells a selection of other interesting artwork, including oil and acrylic paintings on canvas (US$14-150), notecards (US50 cents), and holiday cards (200 varieties in all). She also sells shellcraft of different kinds, carvings, and painted plaques and coconut shells. If you miss her sign, just ask around for Lola Delgado.

Accommodations

On a clean, shallow beach about a half mile north of Seine Bight is **Blue Crab Resort,** Seine Bight, Placencia Peninsula, Belize, C.A., tel. (800) 359-1354. American-owned, the resort offers a couple of cabañas, camping facilities, and camper hookups. Each of the cabañas has a high thatched roof, louvered windows, h/c water, private bath, and three fans. Rates are US$50 s, US$75 d, US$25 per person additional; children under 16 free in adult's room. Camping rates are US$10 s, US$18 d, and include use of beach and bathroom. Camper hookups (electricity and water) are US$25 per

tasting bitters

PHIL LANIER

PHIL LANIER

Auntie Chigi's Place

day. Meals are for guests only and include a mix of Asian and American cuisine; US$25 per person/day. The resort arranges trips for night and day fishing, diving, snorkeling, Maya ruins, and the Cockscomb.

Just north of town sits a small resort that seems transplanted from Hilton Head, South Carolina. The buildings of **Nautical Inn** have finished wood exteriors with shingled roofs. In fact, all the structures are based on an octagon and all the names and interior decoration on a maritime theme. Besides a bar/restaurant called the **Oar House,** the resort has an outside barbecue, an onsite travel agency, beauty salon, giftshop, and massage service. The 13 rooms feature Belizean-made furniture, ceiling fans, h/c water, private baths with deftly designed glass shower stalls, and "porthole" motif mirrors. Four rooms have a/c. Ask for an upper-level room, right at "coconut" height. Rainwater is used for drinking and in the showers and toilets. Rates are US$80 s, US$90 d. Children under 12 free in same room with

adults. All major credit cards are okay. Three meals are provided daily for US$30 per person. On the beach, a catamaran, canoes, and volleyball net await energetic guests. Beyond the beach stretches a 100-foot dock with a *palapa* at the end. In addition, the inn has eight motor scooters that rent for US$25/day, a 24-foot boat for snorkeling and scuba trips to the **Silk Cayes** and elsewhere, and a 22-passenger bus for touring Maya ruins and the area. Contact Ben and Janie Ruoti, Seine Bight, Placencia Peninsula, Bolizo, C.A., tel./fax (6) 22310.

In the middle of town you'll find **Auntie Chigi's Place,** the colorful green building with the yellow trim. It's of simple wood frame construction that will appeal to backpackers and those who really want local flavor. Auntie Chigi's offers five rooms with very simple but clean surroundings, shared bathrooms. Rates are US$20 per room. Meals are about US$1-2 breakfast and lunch, US$3-4 dinner and is "whatever's in the pot." Write to Edna Martinez, Seine Bight Village, Placencia Peninsula, Belize, C.A.

PLACENCIA TOWN

Sitting at the southern tip of the palm-dotted peninsula, Placencia Village is more than 100 miles south of Belize City. To get there you can travel by land, sea, or air. Placencia has been a fishing village from the time of the Maya, outside of the intrusion of a pirate settlement now and then. Even with the arrival of tourists, it is still home to many fishermen. Modern conveniences (including electricity and telephones) also have arrived!

The town itself is about a mile long. Delightful guesthouse resorts continue to develop in the area along the coast, and the people who run these isolated resorts offer a warm pioneer spirit of cordiality. Fortunately (for now at least) they all fit into the environment—Placencia hasn't been spoiled by high-rise, jet-set, hundreds-at-a-time tour groups that have filtered into and transformed many other once-placid Caribbean locations.

In lieu of a newspaper, local cafes are the places to hear all the news and daily gossip of Placencia. If something is really important, it'll be posted on a tree or a fence around the gas pump and Harald's grocery store. On a trip awhile back we saw notices on trees and bulletin boards telling of the arrival of a medical team from the Arkansas National Guard. They set up business at each village along the peninsula and gave free medical and dental examinations. With them were several veterinarians who were greeting all the local dogs and cats and vaccinating them on the spot. Made this American feel *good!*

ORIENTATION

In Placencia, there really isn't a main road through the "downtown business section," but there *is* a mile-long "main sidewalk." The road into town (Placencia Road) comes down the peninsula, skirts the airport, runs alongside the lagoon, and parallels the sidewalk on the west. More and more businesses are springing up along Placencia Road. The road passes a large soccer field and at the road's far end you'll see a turquoise building with a red roof (the Galley Restaurant); it continues to the service station, ice house, bus stop, and main dock at the end of town.

"Downtown" Placencia

This stretched-out community doesn't really have a "downtown," but if I had to pick a "central downtown" or "heart" of Placencia Town it would probably be along the shoreline near where the old post office once held fort. Placencia's post office is an open-air affair near the sea. A gas pump sits just a few feet away, and close by is a small harbor with cafe/bars—gathering places for locals and visitors alike.

Use the gas pump as a reference point; just east of it is the dock and marina, which accommodate good-sized vessels. You'll see a mixture of fishing boats and yachts in the harbor. This is a good mooring area for visitors, and for those looking for a boat to head out to the cayes, ask at the dock, the post office, or the grocery store—someone will direct you. Need a boat ride to Big Creek? This is the place to get that as well. Allow a good half hour on the water to get to Big Creek and then a short taxi ride or a 20-minute hike to the airport. You'll need to make arrangements ahead of time to have a taxi pick you up shoreside in Big Creek. The Placencia airstrip is just north of Rum Point Inn, and the bus stop is close to the gas pump.

South of the Gas Pump

South of the gas pump, you'll find a sandy path that leads southwest along the water past a few houses and businesses, including **Chili's** and **Mike's Caribbean Club.** Farther down, past a few mangroves and houses, you'll find **Brenda's Cafe,** an ongoing favorite in Placencia. Keep going and you'll pass **Paradise Vacation Resort.** Next to the resort is **Tentacles Restaurant,** and out on the dock, **Dockside Bar.** Both are relaxing places to spend the cocktail hour meeting other travelers and locals; sip a little, nibble a little, and enjoy the end of the day.

Back at the gas pump going in the opposite direction, across from the post office and the road, you'll see a warehouselike building; that's

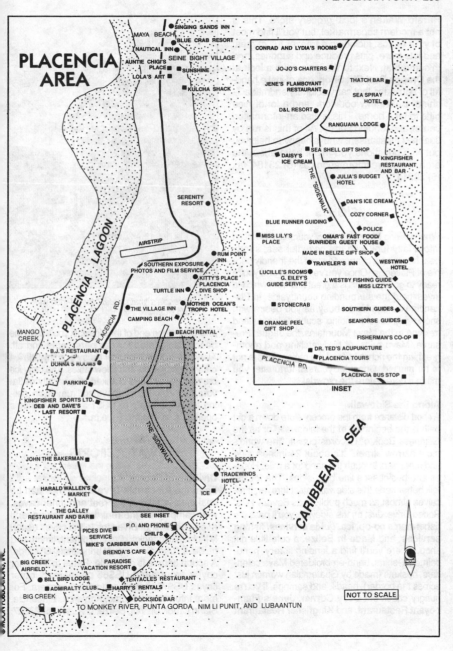

PLACENCIA AREA

SINGING SANDS INN
MAYA BEACH
BLUE CRAB RESORT
NAUTICAL INN
SEINE BIGHT VILLAGE
AUTIE CHIG'S PLACE
SUNSHINE
LOLA'S ART
KULCHA SHACK

PLACENCIA LAGOON

SERENITY RESORT

AIRSTRIP

RUM POINT INN
SOUTHERN EXPOSURE PHOTOS AND FILM SERVICE
KITTY'S PLACE PLACENCIA DIVE SHOP
TURTLE INN
MOTHER OCEAN'S TROPIC HOTEL
THE VILLAGE INN
CAMPING BEACH
BEACH RENTAL

MANGO CREEK

B.J.'S RESTAURANT
DONNA'S ROOMS

PARKING

KINGFISHER SPORTS LTD.
DEB AND DAVE'S LAST RESORT

JOHN THE BAKERMAN

THE SIDEWALK

HARALD WALLEN'S MARKET

THE GALLEY RESTAURANT AND BAR

SEE INSET

PICES DIVE SERVICE
MIKE'S CARIBBEAN CLUB
BRENDA'S CAFE
PARADISE VACATION RESORT

P.O. AND PHONE
CHILI'S

SONNY'S RESORT
TRADEWINDS HOTEL
ICE

BIG CREEK AIRFIELD

BILL BIRD LODGE
ADMIRALTY CLUB
HARRY'S RENTALS
TENTACLES RESTAURANT
DOCKSIDE BAR
BIG CREEK
ICE
TO MONKEY RIVER, PUNTA GORDA, NIM LI PUNIT, AND LUBAANTUN

CARIBBEAN SEA

NOT TO SCALE

INSET

CONRAD AND LYDIA'S ROOMS
JO-JO'S CHARTERS
JENE'S FLAMBOYANT RESTAURANT
THATCH BAR
SEA SPRAY HOTEL
D&L RESORT
RANGUANA LODGE
SEA SHELL GIFT SHOP
DAISY'S ICE CREAM
KINGFISHER RESTAURANT AND BAR
JULIA'S BUDGET HOTEL
THE "SIDEWALK"
D&N'S ICE CREAM
COZY CORNER
BLUE RUNNER GUIDING
POLICE
MISS LILY'S PLACE
OMAR'S FAST FOOD/SUNRIDER GUEST HOUSE
MADE IN BELIZE GIFT SHOP
TRAVELER'S INN
WESTWIND HOTEL
LUCILLE'S ROOMS
G. EILEY'S GUIDE SERVICE
J. WESTBY FISHING GUIDE
MISS LIZZY'S
STONECRAB
SOUTHERN GUIDES
ORANGE PEEL GIFT SHOP
SEAHORSE GUIDES
FISHERMAN'S CO-OP
DR. TED'S ACUPUNCTURE
PLACENCIA ROAD
PLACENCIA TOURS
PLACENCIA BUS STOP

© MOON PUBLICATIONS, INC.

Harald Wallen's local grocery store. This is not a modern supermarket, but you'll find most of your needs, including a freezer full of meat and lots more, plus produce and sundries, and this and that. Next to Wallen's, take a look at the **Orange Peel Gift Shop,** one of just a handful of boutiques that carry colorful handmade T-shirts, Belizean woodwork, and a lot of nice gifts to take home. This is also an information center and lending library. All of this is run by Joanne Christiansen, who is happy to help you out with questions you might have about the area. For more information call (6) 23184, fax (6) 23211.

SIGHTS

When visiting Placencia allow yourself to be lolled into a lazy funk with the beautiful sea, sandy beaches, and a chance to meet the friendly people of Placencia. Once you've relaxed and you're ready to go again, this is a great hub from which to investigate the surrounding countryside. In Placencia you can be as busy as you desire with snorkeling, beachcombing, scuba diving, or land trekking to the Maya Mountains, the Jaguar Preserve, Maya ruins, or birdwatching and photographing the rich wildlife of the region. This is not to be missed. Consider yourself fortunate; you made it here before the crowds!

Along the Sidewalk

A short distance from the grocery store down a dirt path is the beginning of the "sidewalk" or as the Guinness Book of Records puts it, "the world's most narrow street." It's about 24 inches wide and meanders through the sand for a mile. Houses and businesses line both sides. The townsfolk better keep this sidewalk intact forever; it receives almost as much publicity as Beverly Hills' Rodeo Drive. Just off the sidewalk you'll pass the **fishermen's co-op, ice, guide services, fishing services,** and **Made in Belize,** a cute little gift shop, where you'll find a lending library, hand-painted T-shirts, hand-embroidered Maya calendars, baskets (made by Guatemalan women just across the border), beads, and earrings. If you're hungry check out **Cozy Corner, Jene's Flamboyant Restaurant,** and **Kingfisher Restaurant**

Placencia's "main street," the 24-inch-wide main sidewalk

and Bar. At the end of the sidewalk you'll be at the beach designated for campers, tents and all. Along the sidewalk look for **Daisy's,** a tiny little ice cream/pastry shop with a few tables. The tasty ice cream here is hand-cranked in a variety of flavors, including local papaya and rum raisin, selling for US50 cents or US$1 a cup; the shop's open 11 a.m.-5 p.m., 7-9 p.m.

WATER SPORTS

Diving and Snorkeling

From the **Placencia Dive Shop** trips can be designed to take in the reef and inner cayes, with camping on the reef, lagoon fishing, and deep-sea fishing. Dive trips to the cayes usually include two tanks, dive equipment, lunch, and guide. Scuba divers must bring their "C" cards. A scuba course is available. Rates to the inner cayes are around US$65 per person, outer cayes US$75, based on four passengers. For more information contact Kitty Fox, Placencia, Stann Creek District, Belize, C.A., tel. (6) 23227.

Rum Point Divers is yet another good dive shop. Divers travel to the cayes and other dive destinations on the *Auriga,* a comfortable PRO 42-foot dive boat. Dive packages are offered for extended or short periods. For more information, contact Rum Point Inn at (6) 23239, fax (6) 23240; in the U.S. call the Belize specialists at Toucan Travel, 32 Traminer Dr., Kenner, Louisiana 70065, tel. (800) 747-1381, fax (504) 464-0325.

Sea Kayaking

This is a great way to explore the near shore cayes, mangroves, creeks, and rivers. Kayaks are available to guests at several resorts, including **Kitty's** and **Turtle Inn,** as well through **Kevin Madeira,** tel. (6) 23178.

Windsurfing

This is a great activity when the wind's up. The lightly choppy water presents a fairly flat surface and the long reaches possible off Placencia make for easygoing fun. Guests at **Singing Sands** and **Rum Point Inn** will find a couple of boards available for a "wind fix" most anytime since this is not a sport that's in heavy demand in Placencia.

Exploring the Cayes

Find a boat and captain through your hotel or around the dock or post office. Take a morning

to cruise around the southern sea and discover tiny little islands scattered about, including **Laughing Bird Caye.** This mini-atoll is a narrow S-shaped caye with three small harbors and easy access for snorkelers to discover, just off shore, a crystalline underwater world of fascinating corals and beautiful tropical fish. Clumps of palm trees offer a tiny bit of shade, and the sea around the caye is brilliant turquoise—no lie!

Along the way you'll see a tiny little house that from a distance looks as if it's floating on the water. On closer inspection, you'll see that it's set on a tiny sand bar that locals say gradually started rising from the sea more than 15 years ago. This prompted a Belizean entrepreneur to haul out to the bar the materials to build this tiny, unusual house. The caye is called **Lazy Caye,** and my theory is that the gentleman who built the house is squatting and hoping that the land will continue to rise large and broad from the sea, and he will have his own estate someday. Along the way you'll pass other private cayes with lovely homes and small resorts.

Fishing

Fishermen consider Placencia the "permit capital of the world." And **Kingfisher Sports, Ltd.,** is noted for a good fishing operation. Fishing guide Charlie Leslie has a reputation for being *the* best fly fisherman anywhere. He has more than 16 years' experience in these waters and some

homesteading the sea

visitors have been returning almost that long because of Charlie.

Kingfisher Sports takes you to a wide variety of fishing spots, from inshore fishing spots that include nearby flats to **Tarpon Caye,** to the remote area of **Ycacos.** Fishermen will find bonefish, tarpon, snook, snapper, and permit that weigh in at up to 30 pounds.

Offshore fishing will take you outside the reef, where the depth increases dramatically. It's common to find wahoo, sailfish, marlin, kingfish, and dolphin fish. Sightseeing trips inland, as well as diving and picnicking trips on the nearby cayes, are available. Ask about package prices, which include room, food, boat, guide, and fishing. For more information contact Robert Hardy in the U.S., 107 Lafayette Ave., San Antonio, Texas 78209, tel. (512) 826-0469, fax (512) 822-6415. In Placencia, contact Charles Leslie, tel. (6) 23104/23175, fax (6) 23204, or Joel Westby, tel./fax (6) 23138.

Another great place to catch bonefish to your heart's desire is **Big Creek,** a short skiff-ride away from Placencia. Fishermen can expect "good bones," as well as wily permit and torpedo-size tarpon. Ask about boat charters to Guatemala.

Hints for the Fisherman

Come prepared; there's little choice of equipment in Placencia. For bonefishing, experienced fishermen suggest a sturdy reel, a good nine-foot fly rod, and a No. 8-weight, floating, saltwater, tapered fly-line.

A few hints for the newcomer to tropical fishing locations: Bring good polarized glasses with side shields and a heavy-duty sunscreen (don't forget the ears, nose, and lips). Wear a long-sleeved shirt to keep out the sun, and lightweight ripstop nylon pants for wading as the sun's rays will go right through the water and burn your legs. For even more protection, wear a hat—those funky, double-billed, fore- and aft-style hats with bandannas are excellent sun shields. You will need shoes for wading knee-deep along the coral flats; sneakers or Patagonia Reef Walkers serve the purpose. Standing in the shallow water with the sun's reflection for three or four hours can burn your skin to a crisp unless you take precautions. Above all, have fun and remember, fishermen, *catch and release!*

Jungle Explorations

Placencia is a good base for exploring some beautiful jungle areas. A one-hour boat ride brings you to the mouth of the **Monkey River,** a good picnic spot with noisy howler monkeys, tall trees, toucans, oropendulas (birds that nest in hanging bags that they weave), and wading birds. By boat you'll float through a labyrinth of mangrove channels. If possible go to **Golden Stream** this side of Nim Li Punit. Go by boat across Mango Lagoon to more lush forest, small pools, and waterfalls—these can be chilly, although a higher waterfall is warmed as it flows across hot rocks into an eight-foot-deep pool, complete with tiny aquarium fish to keep you company. Nearby, stop at a small craft shop where you'll find carved slate, small baskets, embroidery, and other crafts of the area; there's an outhouse here. If you have a chance while visiting in Placencia, take a trip out of town to the banana packing plant—very interesting. Ask one of the locals for directions.

OTHER RECREATION

Cycling

Biking between outlying resorts and Seine Bight or Placencia Town is an excellent way to see everything there is to see on the lower part of the peninsula while burning off some of those Seaweed Punches. Singing Sands and Rum Point Inn have mountain bikes available for their guests. Those with their own sets of wheels can easily take a boat over to Big Creek or Mango Creek and head out into the surrounding countryside for some exploring. Or, when you're ready, take off for Punta Gorda and points south. It's only about a 20-minute trip through the mangroves and channels into Big Creek. Check with the locals at the main dock for prices. And if you do go, you might consider shipping out in the late afternoon and spending the night at the **Bill Bird Lodge.** It features a very pleasant shaded veranda out front, and stepping into the bar in the early evening is like walking onto the set of a tropical version of *Cheers,* complete with local characters.

Placencia Tour Guides

A number of guides are available in Placencia to take you to the surrounding area. Local Sam

Burgess drives a taxi in town, but his main occupation is as a guide for his company, **Jaguar Tours,** which you can reach at his **Sea Shell Giftshop,** tel. (6) 23139. He has a well-running, clean, 12-passenger van and escorts guests to Garifuna villages, nearby caves, rivers, and to the Jaguar Reserve and Maya ruin sites.

Placencia Tours, tel./fax (6) 23186, does a fine job. Owner Ellis Burgess takes visitors to Cockscomb Basin Wildlife Sanctuary for day or overnight trips, and if you really want to look for the jaguar taking a nocturnal stroll, he will lead you on a night walk through the forest (an overnight trip with a night stroll including food costs US$67 per person). Ellis tells us that howler monkeys are being moved to the Jaguar Preserve and are being sighted about every third trip. He also travels to the Maya sights of Lubaantun, Nim Li Punit, Uxbenka, and Blue Creek; day-trips are US$60. The tour includes pickup (or drop off) in Cayo or Belize City International Airport, with optional stops such as

Rum Point Inn

the zoo, Belmopan, parks, etc., along the road to Placencia. At US$60 per person, it's a good deal! Placencia Tours is in Placencia Village, across from the ball field; Ellis says, "Drop by the veranda for information." Other guide services are available through most of the hotels and guesthouses. Kurt and Earl Godfrey, who are experienced in manatee watching, camping, river tours, and fishing, operate reliable **Southern Guides,** tel. (6) 23277.

ACCOMMODATIONS

Budget Lodgings
Most of these budget lodgings lie within the central part of Placencia Town, and many are close to the "sidewalk."

Check out **Jamie's Rooms,** four rooms with fans, shared bath, cold water for US$6 per person. **Lucille's Rooms** offers five rooms; four share a bathroom for US$5.50 dorm, private bath for US$10 s, US$13 d, tel. (6) 23190. **Sunrider Guest House** has two rooms over **Omar's Fast Foods** with fans, cold water, private baths for about US$18 d, with stove US$30. **Traveler's Inn** offers several colorful rooms, cold water, shared or private bath for US$5-7.50 s, US$10-13 d. **Julia's Budget Hotel** offers prices of US$7.50 s, US$11 d, no phone. At **D&L Resort,** tel. (6) 23243, prices range from US$18 s, US$55 d, to US$75 for four. **Conrad & Lydia's Rooms,** tel. (6) 23117, are US$7.50-12.50 s, US$11-20 d. **Paradise Vacation Resort** near Tentacles Restaurant has large rooms, king beds, private baths, and ceiling fans downstairs, and smaller rooms with two twin beds, shared baths, and free-standing fans upstairs. The rate for shared bath is about US$13, for private bath about US$23. Contact owner/host Dalton Eiley, tel. (6) 23179, for more information. Also check out **Deb & Dave's Last Resort,** tel. (6) 23207, on the back road into town and **Harry's Rentals** near the tip of the peninsula past Tentacles Restaurant.

Moderate Lodgings
Conveniently located **Sonny's Resort,** tel. (6) 23103, is a slightly worn but comfortable beachfront hotel. Bar and restaurant, as well as fishing, snorkeling, diving, and beachcombing, are avail-

Kitty's Place

TODD CLARK

able. Try Sonny's version of the famous seaweed drink—not bad. Rates are about US$58 cabañas, US$33 s, US$44 d.

South of Sonny's look for the **Tradewinds Hotel,** tel. (6) 21322, on five acres near the sea. Three cabañas with spacious rooms, fans, refrigerators, coffee pots, and private yards are US$50 per night for four people.

The **Sea Spray Hotel,** tel. (6) 23148, 30 feet from the beach on the point, offers five cabañas and eight rooms with private bathrooms. Attached to the hotel you'll find the **Thatch Bar.** Rates for cabañas with refrigerators, h/c water are US$53; rooms with a community bath, about US$25-35 s, with a private bath US$50-60 d.

Westwind Hotel, tel. (6) 23255, is priced higher than most other lodgings in Placencia Town, and it is also one of the most attractive and comfortable. It offers eight rooms in all with bright modern interiors, great views, sunny decks, kitchens, h/c water, private baths, and fans. This resort provides all the amenities of some of the resorts north of town, right in the heart of the village. Rates are US$25 s, US$55 d, suites are US$90.

Accommodations North of Town

Serenity Resort, tel. (6) 23232, fax (6) 23231, in the U.S. (800) 331-3797, is an attractive family resort. The northernmost of the Placencia Village area accommodations, it must be doing something special; it has been open only since 1992 and has doubled in size with more on the way.

By this printing there should be 12 cabañas and 10 additional rooms in a new building, making this the largest accommodation on the peninsula with 21 acres of land. Cabañas have tiled roofs and floors, high ceilings, h/c water, ceiling fans, private bathrooms, and patios. Rates per cabaña are US$75 s, US$85 d, US$110 t.

The dining room, with blue tablecloths and blue-upholstered chairs, has a thatched veranda that faces the sea; meals are US$7.50 breakfast and lunch, US$15 dinner. There's no bar here and no alcoholic beverages are sold on the property, though guests can enjoy them in their rooms. Owner Ted Giblin, no prude himself, says he instituted the policy because Serenity is a family destination. The pricing structure bears him out; children under 5, free; 5-11 no room charge/half price meals; 12-18 years US$10 per person/day and full price meals.

Rum Point Inn is operated by George and Corol Bevier and is a favorite of guests and divers from around the world. There's a closer airstrip now, but in days gone by the closest one could land was the strip in Big Creek. Then, you hopped a small boat (dory). No more. Yet, the good things at Rum Point remain the same; it still offers some of the best accommodations on the peninsula and a bustling dive business. In fact, the 42-foot jetboat *Auriga* is considered the best dive boat on the peninsula. And then there's the little matter of the cabañas; do they look more like mushrooms or igloos? It's a toss-up. But no one disagrees that once you're inside, they become magical—presenting a cool, spacious, tropical atmosphere, each attractively furnished with two queen beds, brightly woven Guatemala fabrics, rich hardwood furniture, tropical plants, roomy bathrooms, tile floors, and fans. Each dome-shaped cabaña is pristine white inside and out, with artfully shaped openings of glass cut into the walls and ceilings to let in the light, moon, and stars—viewing stations from bed during a tropical lightning storm. It's probably the most modern and unusual hotel in Placencia.

The warmth and conviviality of the resort is bested only by its outstanding gourmet cooking (according to some, the best food in all of Belize). Each night the table linens are a different color and design, and in a week the daily menu never repeats itself. Foods are fresh and innovative, and a lovely dining room and veranda overlook the water for long evenings under the stars. The Beviers make you feel as though you're a guest in their lovely home, perfect hosts at candle-lit family-style dinners each evening.

George is a medical entomologist and the perfect guide to accompany visitors into special places in the Belize jungle or on boat trips to the reef to snorkel or dive. A new dive boat takes divers on special trips with qualified dive instructors. Fishing is great, but relaxing on the porch in a hammock is a must. An alluring beach and sea are just a few steps from the cabañas, perfect for beachcombing. A while back a guest

discovered a bottle—yes, with a message in it from a sailor who had thrown it overboard three months before from a ship off Grenada! Granted, it wasn't as traditional as our daydreams would conjure—the bottle was a two-liter plastic job with a screw-on lid instead of glass with a cork, but nevertheless an exciting discovery. In the main house, Corol runs a nice little gift shop, and the lounge has a wonderful library with a huge variety of books about Central America, mammals, invertebrates, the Maya, plants, mammals—you name it. The cozy bar is a great gathering place for cocktails and delicious toasted coconut chips before dinner. Town is about a 20-minute walk. Each cabaña rents for US$175 s, US$224 d, US$15 per person additional; children under 12 US$50, including meals. Summer prices are lower.

Have a little fun on the Windsurfer or take a bike to town. Tours to the cayes and reef start at US$65 per person and up. Trips for up to four people to the Maya ruins, the rainforest, and rivers start at US$150. Complete fishing and dive packages are available. Credit cards are accepted. For more information write to Rum Point Inn, Placencia, Stann Creek District, Belize, C.A., tel. (6) 23239, fax (6) 23240; in the U.S. call the Belize specialists at Toucan Travel, 32 Traminer Dr., Kenner, Louisiana 70065, tel. (800) 747-1381, fax (504) 464-0325.

Another diving favorite, **Kitty's Place,** Box 528, Belize City, Belize, C.A., tel. (6) 23227,

Nautical Inn, north of town in the Seine Bight

PHIL LANIER

fax (6) 23226, is owned and operated by Kitty Fox and Ran Villanueva. Just on the other side of the airstrip from Rum Point, this is a small but growing spot, with a nice beach and comfortable rooms and apartments. Kitty no longer offers camping but she has expanded the number of rooms and apartments. Rates for rooms are from US$33-63 s to US$43-78 d. The Colonial apartment sleeps up to six and rents for US$93 s, US$108 d, US$15 per person additional. The Belizean apartment sleeps three and goes for US$63 s, US$78 d, US$88 t. Ask for the combination weekly price for apartment and rooms. Kitty's offers **Franco's Restaurant** (three-course dinner each evening) with an authentic Italian chef who serves luscious specialties, bar service, a great gift shop, and daylong trips. Sea kayaks rent for about US$20/half day, US$35 full day. Kitty's also offers camping or a house on **French Louis Caye,** about six miles off the coast. You can rent the whole island for around US$75/day! (See "Glover's Reef Atoll" under "The Atolls.")

Down the road just a bit is the **Turtle Inn** off to the left on a palmy beach. They don't come much more comfortably casual than this lodging run by American Skip White. The place is so laid back, for the longest time there's been no sign on the road to direct you in through the low trees, and there may not be one now, either. Yet, once you do find it, Turtle Inn offers great atmosphere, diving, adventure travel, and ecotourism. Skip is a versatile camper, hunter, diver, and general adventurer. The curious will find excursions to far-off cayes, the reef, and deep into the Maya Mountain jungles, where few outsiders have gone. Skip offers 8- to 10-day jungle tours in the heart of the jungle, river trips, dive and camping trips, and trips to the Maya ruins. Sea kayaks are also available by the day and half day. The Turtle Inn offers six quaint thatched-roof cabañas on the beach with ceiling fans, cold-water baths, verandas, and hammocks for US$86 s, US$150 d, US$192 t, US$236 q, meals included; rates are a bit cheaper with breakfast only. All electricity is solar-powered. But no mention of Turtle Beach is complete without mentioning the bar/restaurant area. The wood deck that spills out onto the beach at just above sand level invites one to step up, plop down, and strike up a conversation with the nearest fellow wayfarer. It's a great spot for late afternoon drinks about the time the guests have come in from their adventures. Sharing tales of a day in the ocean or jungle whets the appetite for food as well as conversation. And the restaurant here won't disappoint with a menu heavy on seafood and local dishes. Even natives and guests from elsewhere show up. For more information contact Turtle Inn, Placencia, Stann Creek District, Belize City, Belize, C.A., tel. (6) 22069, or Dr. Lois Kruschwitz, 2190 Blue Bell, Boulder, Colorado 80302, tel. (303) 444-2555.

Just a half mile north of Placencia on what may be the widest single strip of beachfront on the island (1,000 feet) is **Mother Ocean's Tropic Hotel,** tel. (6) 23233, fax (6) 23224, in the U.S. (800) 662-3091, six waterfront cabins on a cleared lot with palms swaying in the breeze. It formerly was known as The Cove Resort. Many activities, including equipment, are available: snorkeling, scuba diving, fishing, trips to the Jaguar Reserve and the Maya Mountains, and now participation in data collection of the environmental research station operating out of the same facility. It has a tennis court and rackets on site. Each renovated cabin has two queen size beds, private bath, and large sceened porch; some have kitchenettes. Stays require a three-night minimum. Rates are US$75 s, US$77 d, US$87 t, US$97 q; with kitchenette add US$8/day.

A short distance down the way from Mother Ocean's is a spot that spans the road, **Village Inn,** Placencia, Stann Creek District, Belize, C.A., tel. (6) 23217, (6) 23267. This small establishment has a trailer on the beach side of the road and two double rooms. Across the road is a cabaña with one room upstairs and two downstairs. All these accommodations have fans. The beachside rooms are about US$33/night; the trailer holds up to four, and has kitchen, h/c bath for US$65. Across the road the upstairs cabaña with kitchen, h/c water, full bath is US$65 d; downstairs rooms with shared bath are US$20 d each. The inn offers special rates for rentals by the week or month. Meals are also available.

FOOD

You'll find some of the finest Creole cooking in Belize in Placencia. Most of the cafes are low-key and the real "stuff" includes fresh seafood cooked in coconut milk and local herbs, with liberal amounts of plantain or banana. However, if something less daring sounds good, you'll find sandwiches, tamales, hamburgers, and great Italian food.

For a quick burrito or hot dog, try **Chili's**; it's owned by Buddha Bill, formerly of Belize City. Chili's serves burritos, chili dogs, barbecue chicken, and other fast food, but has nothing to drink and nowhere to sit really. Next door, the **Caribbean Club** serves drinks of all kinds and has lots of seating but nothing to eat—a good combination.

Omar's Fast Food can fix you up with pork chops, T-bone steak, or conch steak for about US$6, lobster for US$10; breakfast specials are about US$3.

The Galley Restaurant and Bar, tel. (6) 23133, should not be missed by jazz lovers or those who enjoy good food. Owner Cleveland is a jazz and blues musician, handy with a guitar, flute, or keyboard. Some evenings he'll play his own music, other times covers of the greats. This restaurant also has the best jazz CD collection in the whole of Belize. And where Cleveland leaves off the kitchen picks up. The T-bone steak is recommended here, about US$8, as well as stuffed baked fish, US$7; Creole style lobster, US$12.50; shrimp fried rice, US$9; and vegetarian stir-fries. Prompt smiling service has been a hallmark of this establishment. Try the Galley's famous "Seaweed Drink"; it claims to have created this common Placencia concoction in its present frothy form. It's similar to egg nog with a pleasing flavor and a shot of brandy for good measure. Local men (especially husbands) chuckle sheepishly and say, "It's good for de back mon!"

Brenda's Cafe, tel. (6) 22137, is known for excellent Creole food (very ethnic) and easy hours. If you want to be certain she will be open, make a reservation and for sure she'll be there. Brenda serves tasty and economical breakfasts and terrific local specialties for lunch and dinner; lobster with all the local fixin's costs US$12.50. If you want something special, call her and make a request; you'll get a good (ample) meal.

Franco's at Kitty's Place has really tasty, authentic Italian food, served from 7 a.m.-10 p.m.

You can't miss **Jene's Flamboyant Restaurant**, tel. (6) 23174, or at least you can't miss the tree just across the sidewalk that it's named after, especially if it's in full bloom. Uncle Jay, the proprietor, prides the place in using fresh ingredients and accommodating special requests. Every day he offers Belizean specials for about US$6-8. Continental specials appear frequently in the evenings. And Sunday is the day for open-pit barbecue and Garifuna drummers. Holidays mean smoked meats.

Tentacles Restaurant, tel. (6) 23156, is a large cafe with a grand thatched roof over a rich hardwood deck where you can watch the sea. Here you can expect good seafood, hamburgers, Italian, and local food. Ask about the Reggae Salad! Try the steak for about US$8, half a chicken for US$6, or a lobster dinner for about US$15. It's open 8 a.m.-2 p.m. and 6-10 p.m.

Dockside Bar hosts a popular Saturday-afternoon happy hour, 4-6 p.m. It serves hot dogs and great ceviche (and rum drinks for half price). The owners here operate a VHF radio for the convenience of boaters. This a great gathering place for visitors and local boatmen, and the rumor is that Placencia will soon be a port for visa renewals.

Other options include **B.J.'s Restaurant**, Placencia Rd., tel. (6) 23108, which offers fresh orange juice and good fried chicken in a screened dining room with wooden tables. Serving simple fare, it's open 7 a.m-10 p.m. **Sonny's** also serves everything from seafood to burgers. And just a 20-minute walk from town or a short bike ride is **Turtle Inn**, where the seafood and Creole food are first rate. **Stonecrab** restaurant serves good seafood.

Sweet Stuff

Got a sweet tooth? The Belizeans will fix that. Downtown, ask where to find **Miss Lily's**; she's a great baker and makes delicious powder buns to sell from her house (under the stilts). Like all of the ladies (following), she works on Belizean time—when she sells out, she closes up. They all make the favorites of the villagers (and visitors): Creole bread (with shredded coconut), cinnamon rolls, Johnnie cakes (journey cakes), and other favorite snacks. Anyone will point you to these local bakers: **Miss Elsie's, Miss Lydia's, Miss Lizzy's, Miss Cuncu,** and, to these lady bakers, let's add **John the Bakerman** (great breads!).

PRACTICALITIES

Placencia Laundromat, tel. (6) 23123, is a reasonably new service with washers and dryers. It's open daily 8 a.m.-5 p.m.

At **Harald Wallen's Market,** tel. (6) 23128, often referred to as just Harald's, you can find most all of your needs, including groceries, dry goods, and sundries. If you need something special, call.

Next to Harald's, you'll find the **police** at Orange Peel Gift Shop.

Southern Exposure, tel. (6) 23239, fax (6) 23240, offers photo processing and a lot more. It's a photo lab/image bank at Rum Point Inn, with talented photographer **Wade Bevier** available. If photographers request, he will set up "blinds" in reserves for nature "shoots." He knows the area well. He sells film and batteries and offers a two-day print film service. He also takes passport pictures.

GETTING THERE

By Air
Flying is easiest, quickest, and gentlest to the body. For current schedules and fares call **Maya Airways** in Belize City, tel. (2) 44234.

By Bus
The **Promised Land Express** leaves Dangriga for Seine Bight and Placencia every day at 2 p.m., arriving in Seine Bight about 4:30 p.m. and Placencia about 5 p.m. From Placencia to Dangriga it's a 6 a.m. departure; arrival time in Dangriga is 8:30 a.m. Cost is less than US$5 each way.

Or take the **Z-Line** bus to Mango Creek for US$7.50; ask at the post office about the boat to Mango Creek or the mail boat for Big Creek. The buses also continue to Punta Gorda for US$8.50. A bus leaves from Dangriga at **The Hub** guesthouse for Punta Gorda at 3 p.m.; fare

is about US$5. This particular bus ride gets three goose eggs for discomfort. From Mango Creek you travel by dory across the lagoon to Placencia.

By Car
If driving, continue past the Dangriga turnoff (can it be possible that this strip of road to Placencia is worse than other southern roads? Yes!). Four-wheel-drive is a necessity, especially for the last five miles from the small village of **Seine Bight** to **Placencia Town** on the very tip of the peninsula.

BIG CREEK SOUTH OF PLACENCIA

This small community is growing into the banana capital of Belize. Planes land at **Big Creek Airfield,** not as often as they once did when this was the closest you could fly to Placencia, but frequently. Mango plantations are becoming more common and shrimp farming is a new, successful industry. When flying between Belize City and Placencia you'll get a bird's-eye view of **Laguna Madre,** a shrimp farm and processing plant. Note the 12 large ponds next to the sea. This could be an invaluable asset for the fisherman.

But bananas are putting Big Creek on the map. Somehow it was a surprise to see a bright yellow crop duster doing its thing in the surrounding green banana groves. It seemed so high tech! After you travel around southern Belize, the high-tech world seems far distant. But the growing banana industry of southern Belize is changing the scene. Small and large banana ranches are springing up, many run by Americans who see the entrepreneurial potential of Belize.

The Big Creek dock also shows signs of successful development with a new deep-channel port. For years small container boats and barges were loaded with bananas by cranes and hauled through the shallow harbor. The fruit then was transferred into seagoing container ships that headed across the Atlantic to England and Ireland. With the new deep harbor, bananas, as well as citrus products, arrive at their destination in Europe in 15 days rather than in 21 days.

This represents a big savings in fruit, time, and hence, money.

The deep port will also enable cruise ships to make stops along Belize's southern coast someday, in turn encouraging more locals to open tourist attractions, mainly hotels and restaurants. It's easy to understand why the government refers to the brisk banana business as "yellow gold." Thriving industry is providing jobs for workers, both men and women, and the future of the area is happening now.

Accommodations and Food
To be honest, **Bill Bird Lodge,** tel. (6) 22092/ 22084, fax (6) 22253, is really *it* when it comes to Big Creek for the average traveler. Formerly called the Toucan Hotel, it houses a branch of the Belize Bank on the premises. Inside you'll find the **Admiralty Club** bar and restaurant. The lodge is generally used by businessfolk in the banana business. Parrots talk from their cages under the shady, screened veranda. All rooms come with a/c, h/c water, and private bath. The restaurant serves three meals daily. Rooms come with pool privileges at the banana industry compound nearby. Rates are US$44 s, US$58 d.

Another, more spartan lodging that may appeal to backpackers is the **Hello Hotel.** Try **Cardie's Restaurant** for simple meals.

Guide Service and Car Rental
The enterprising Gilbert Edwards is not only a guide with a Dodge Astro six-seater and a/c, he also has his own car rental agency, Toucan St., Big Creek, Belize, C.A., tel. (6) 22078, fax (6) 22386. His tours of the area cost anywhere from US$125-240 for a party of up to six people. He rents out a Ford Bronco for US$75/day, two-day minimum.

Getting There
Big Creek Airport is one of the busiest airports in Belize, thanks to the business atmosphere of the community. Check in Belize City for scheduled airlines that fly into Big Creek. Though there's little reason for most tourist types to do it, charter flights into Big Creek airfield are available through any of the Belizean airlines or charter services.

KATHY ESCOVIDO SANDERS

TOLEDO DISTRICT

INTRODUCTION

Toledo is the most southerly district in Belize and the third largest in the country. To the south and west it shares a border with Guatemala. The district has the highest population of Maya (Kekchi and Mopan) of any district in Belize.

The Land
The Toledo District presents the traveler numerous opportunities to experience the ocean, rivers, jungle, and mountains at their finest. Nearby, travelers find pristine cayes, wild rivers, Maya villages, and Garifuna communities. Stretches of pine and savanna, lowland broadleaf jungle, and the peaks of the Maya Mountains are just short distances from Punta Gorda, the major community in the district.

Things to Do
Bikers and hikers will find Maya villages where people still bathe in streams and cook over wood fires in their thatched huts. Or visitors might kayak down rivers that sparkle in the sun while the calls of birds and animals shatter the still-

ness. Others will dive on virgin reefs near small spits of sand or mangrove in the clear Caribbean or take swift boats acoss its surface to favored fishing spots or Guatemala ports. Some will thrill to catch a glimpse of an elusive animal. Still others will visit Maya ruins and view artifacts only recently unearthed from a sleep of a thousand years.

HISTORY

Maya Mysteries
The first Maya built several ceremonial centers in the Toledo area. Little is known about this group of people. However, as archaeologists continue to make discoveries, they learn more and more—some fact, and some fiction. One favorite mystery that lingers suspended between truth or fiction is the one surrounding the crystal skull found by the 17-year-old daughter of explorer Benson Hedges on her birthday. Experts have vacillated about the authenticity of the

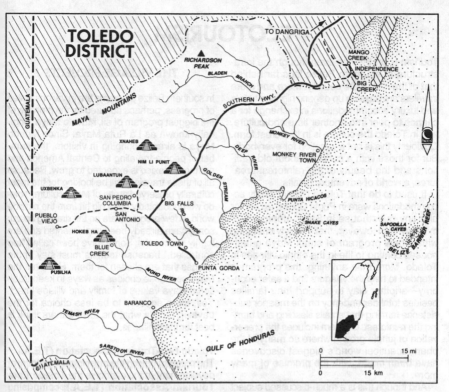

crystal skull for years. Was it made by the Maya? Does it have inexplicable powers? Is it a phony? Where did it *really* come from? Did Hedges plant it for the pleasure of his daughter? The questions persist over the decades. The skull still belongs to the Hedges family; you can see it in the British Museum in London.

Later Settlers

Just as in the Stann Creek District, the Garifuna followed the Maya into this remote area in the 1800s. Ironically, in 1866 they were followed by Americans—Southerners who'd been buying guns from the British during the American Civil War. When their side lost, they asked for and received refuge and land grants from the British, and then tried their hand at raising sugarcane. Most Americans eventually returned to the United States. Over the years laborers from distant parts of the world were brought into the country for logging and sugarcaning and made Toledo District their permanent home.

Today's Toledo

Today the district is a blend of many unrelated cultures—Caucasian, Kekchi and Mopan Maya, mestizo, Garifuna, Creole, Chinese, Palestinian, and East Indian.

ECOTOURISM

Tourism is on the rise even though the infrastructure of southern Belize lags far behind that of the rest of the country. More and more travelers are passing up generic highrise hotels and luxury accommodations in exchange for a chance to peer into another time and culture, and in Toledo the culture is in its purest form. Obviously this is not a vacation for everybody. But for those with a curiosity about old traditions and the beauty of the rainforest creatures, a world of adventure awaits.

It used to be that Toledo District's only accommodations were in Punta Gorda, except for one tiny guesthouse in San Antonio 15-20 miles away. However, that's slowly changing with a new program of small Maya guesthouses coming to life in the ethnic villages in Toledo. More than anything, this program is intended to help the villagers find a safer economy—another way to support their families besides total dependency on the meager subsistence farming that entails slashing and burning the rainforest. Concern includes the preservation of jungle growth where so many of the pharmaceutical world's biggest discoveries have been made, with the promise of many more.

And though this is a much-discussed subject worldwide, it's becoming a vital problem in southern Belize because of the growth of the various Maya communities. Not only will the guesthouse project protect natural resources, it is also designed to preserve an ancient culture that is in danger of becoming diluted by outside influences and lifestyles, especially with the increased interest from tourism.

THE VILLAGE PROJECTS

In southern Belize programs are in various states of progress, perhaps nurtured by the promise of the biggest program of all, **Mundo Maya**, originally known as La Ruta Maya. Since Mundo Maya is already bringing in visitors, the number of people traveling to Central America and southern Mexico is expected to grow. Because all of these travelers will be looking for the most culturally preserved areas of Maya culture, Toledo will undoubtedly get a big hit from the outside world. A few programs are on the drawing board; some have already been implemented and are highly successful. Some have been called "too controlled," because tourists must stay in the villages that are chosen for them. However, the Maya see these choices as ways to keep traditional Maya values of family and village intact. Yes, there appears to be less choice for the traveler, but it's what the town fathers think is best for their villages.

Toledo Eco-Tourism Association (T.E.A.)
The program having the most impact on tourism development in the district is the **Toledo Eco-Tourism Association (T.E.A.)**, comprising Mopan and Kekchi Maya, Creole, and Garifuna villages. Its purpose is to embrace ecotourism while allowing indigenous people to plan, control, and profit from it in their areas. An essential tenet promoted by the T.E.A., and different from other programs, is the belief that tourism should benefit the **entire community** instead of a few individuals. This is more in keeping with the

---

CONSERVATION ORGANIZATIONS IN BELIZE

Lighthawk; Box 8163, Santa Fe, New Mexico; tel. (505) 982-9656

Manomet Bird Observatory; Box 936, Manomet, Massachusetts; tel. (508) 224-6521

New York Botanical Garden; Dept. of Ethnobotany, Bronx, New York; tel. (212) 220-8763

Tropical Conservation Foundation; Box 31, CH-2074, Marin-Ne, Switzerland; tel. (038) 33-4344

Wildlife Conservation International; N.Y. Zoological Society, 185th St. & So. Blvd., Bronx, New York; tel. (212) 220-5155

U.S. World Wildlife Fund; 1250 24th St. Northwest, Washington, D.C.; tel. (202) 293-4800

Punta Gorda coast

communal values of these villages. Because of this fundamental difference, the T.E.A. will probably prove to be the dominant force of the several programs operating, because it better fits existing traditions and binds villagers together rather than divides them over profit. Granting organizations are beginning to focus attention on the program, and government support, which has been oddly lukewarm in the past, will ultimately be forthcoming.

By some standards, the **Village Guest House Program,** as organized by the T.E.A., would be small potatoes, since there are seldom more than four people per guide per village at one time. But for isolated communities that have stayed pretty much to themselves for hundreds of years, and whose citizens in modern times have had an annual income of about US$500, the sudden influx of people and money is a real boon. With education the people can see a reason to care for and nurture the environment that attracts the visitors. Maya guest villages include Santa Cruz, San Jose, San Miguel, San Pedro Columbia, and Laguna. Garifuna guest villages include Barranco and St. Vincent's Block.

Garifuna Village Project

Garifuna people make up one of the largest ethnic groups in Toledo. Life has never been easy for the Garifuna, and in recent years there's been a real danger of old traditions slipping

away entirely. Fortunately, a group of Garifuna volunteers have used 40 acres of a 1,000-acre plot (a legacy from their ancestors) to re-create an authentic Garifuna village at **St. Vincent's Block,** calling it **Habiabara Ginagu Cerro.** Farming is part of the project, and this re-created village is a small living museum. Something good usually is bubbling on the stove, and the workers in the field become docents, showing visitors around and serving them lunch Garifuna style. The project was originally an independent effort, but St. Vincent's Block volunteers have added themselves to the T.E.A. ranks.

Another Homestay Program

Sponsored by the **School for International Training,** Kipling Road, Box 676, Brattleboro, Vermont 05302-0676, tel. (800) 258-3500, fax (802) 258-3500, this program is part of a 15-week course for college-level students who want to earn credits in ecology while in a cross-cultural setting. Groups of students are sent around the country during their stay, two weeks of which are spent in a Maya or Garifuna village. Speaking with enthusiastic participants makes it obvious that they have benefitted from an experience they could never have had in a traditional classroom. The program is administered by Monkey Bay Wildlife Sanctuary. Contact the School for International Training for more information.

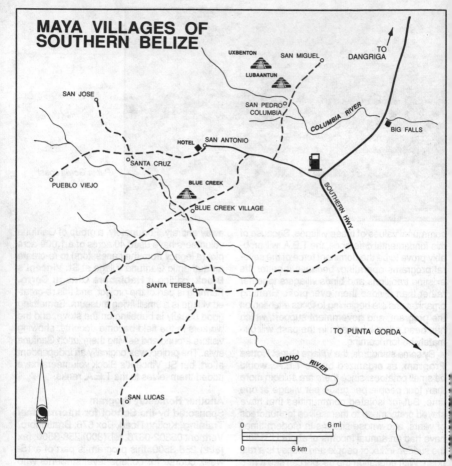

MAYA VILLAGES OF SOUTHERN BELIZE

VISITING THE VILLAGES

Visitors may choose to spend a 24-hour period in one or more villages, combining Maya and Garifuna stays and a range of activities if desired. You have the options of a couple of different village tours; a basic tour is a night's accommodations and a couple of guided activities (around US$38 per person). Villagers show visitors growing roots and herbs used for medicines, food still gathered and used in the villages, and local wildlife. A more ex-

tensive tour includes the above, plus traditional music, dancing, and storytelling (about US$83 per person).

Also available are individualized tours that combine a number of great adventures, such as exploring jungle trails and ancient ruins, horseback riding, river or sea kayaking, traditional dancing, camping, and fishing. Prices vary by budget and choices.

Benefits
The benefits go both ways. Travelers are certainly enriched by the cross-cultural exchange

and the exposure to nature. Observing and participating in making the day's tortillas, listening to the strains of Maya music by firelight in a thatched hut, trying to shape a pot out of ancient clay, swimming in the chilly waters of a clear forest stream, following a jaguar track down a jungle trail—these are the stuff of cherished memories that last a lifetime. The same can be said for fishing from dugout canoes, hacking open coconuts to slake a thirst, cruising twisting mangrove channels or flowing rivers, and dancing to the beat of Garifuna drums. On the communal level, everyone in the village benefits, even though he/she may not be directly employed as a guide, arts and crafts demonstrator, dancer, singer, or one of the other positions needed to provide service to the visitors. The money goes into a general village fund; salaries are paid first and the balance is used for education or health.

If This Is for You
Interested travelers in Toledo should check in at the **Toledo District Maya Guest House** office in Punta Gorda and ask for Chet Schmidt (for now the office is in **Nature's Way Guest House,** 65 Front St., tel. 7-22119). Here you will receive all information about a scheduled 24-hour stay, an orientation for your visit to a village, and a bag that contains the eating utensils you will use (cup, fork, spoon, bowl, plate) for your entire stay. Whichever village is next up on the list will

GUEST VILLAGES OF THE TOLEDO DISTRICT

Santa Cruz	San Pedro Columbia
San Miguel	Laguna
Barranco	San Jose

Some of these villages are within an hour's walk from each other. Most of them are surrounded by thick forest. Eventually the paths between villages will also revert to thick forest, if they haven't already; reforestation is a viable part of this program.

be the one you are assigned to visit. The orientation will give you some basic information about the Mopan and Kekchi Maya, how the program began, and what you can expect during your visit, and an explanation about the **Food Providers Workshop** that each village participant must attend; visitors can be assured of safely boiled water (I would still bring my own bottled water). Visitors will have each meal in a different home; this spreads the visitors around and keeps the event fresh and welcome to the villagers. In addition to paying the fee, the visitor has one other obligation: to write a report about his or her visit. The village elders want the truth: the good things, the bad things, anything that will help them improve this new project. Thanks to visitors' comments, the meals went from too

making tortillas at the T.E.A. guesthouse in San Pedro Columbia

T.E.A. guesthouse
in San Pedro

small to too big, and now the villagers are trying to hit a happy medium.

Visitors, please note: It's best to be very flexible when visiting Toledo District. Although accommodations can be as described one day, they can change overnight—especially those in the outback. In many cases these are new, small guesthouses, still ironing out the kinks in a whole new industry for most of these people. So to really enjoy the experience, be ready for *anything*.

Guesthouses are designed after the local style: thatched roof, wooden walls, and built on a cement platform. So far each village has one guesthouse that will accommodate eight people. Each room has beds with clean linens, mosquito netting, and male and female showers and outhouses.

Meals

Breakfast in Maya villages is generally eggs, homemade tortillas, and coffee or cacao drink. All meals are ethnic and lunch is the largest meal of the day; it is often chicken *caldo* (like a stew cooked with Maya herbs) and fresh tortillas. Supper is the lightest meal of the day, and

generally includes "ground" food (a root food such as potatoes) that the guide and visitors might "harvest" along the jungle trail. The *comal* (tortilla grill) is always hot and if you're invited to try your hand at making tortillas, go ahead—this is a wonderful way to break the ice with the usually shy Maya women. In a Garifuna village be prepared for simple but traditional cooking. It's some of the best in the country, especially the "serre" or fish in coconut milk.

What to Bring

Bring comfortable walking shoes, bug repellent (with 30% DEET or more), poncho, swimsuit, flashlight with extra batteries, and lightweight slacks and long-sleeve shirt. It never hurts to bring a tiny gift for the children—a pencil, a plastic barrette, or something similar really breaks the ice.

No matter how careful your hosts are, it's still possible to get a touch of traveler's diarrhea—you aren't accustomed to local strains of bacteria. All it takes is a touch of a less than aseptic hand and you will soon be on your way to the latrine. Bring your favorite remedy. (See the special topic "Simple First-Aid Guide.")

PUNTA GORDA

At about Mile 100 on the Southern Highway, Punta Gorda (or P.G. as it is frequently called) is the last sizable town you'll come to before reaching the Guatemala border and the biggest town in Toledo District. To the northwest lies a cluster of Maya villages; to the east, the Gulf of Honduras; to the southwest, Guatemala. Most folks in town speak English; the majority of inhabitants are Garifuna and East Indian. Fishing was the main support of the local people for centuries; today the industry has added high-tech shrimp farming. Farmers grow rice, mangoes, bananas, sugarcane, and beans—all important food crops.

A Base for Ecotourism
Few tourists who come to Belize ever make it as far as Punta Gorda. A great deal of the traffic comes from Guatemala, so much so that hotels and restaurants count on the tourist trade from the ferry and other small boats that cross the border. When they're out of commission, the local economy really suffers. That scenario is beginning to change.

In the areas surrounding P.G., Maya and, to a point, Garifuna carry on life much as their ancestors did. The visitors who seek out P.G. are intrigued adventurers looking behind the facade of tourism. And you had better be an adventurer, because this is not by any stretch an upscale resort area. But tourists' interest is starting to become a source of income for the area.

Most of the small outer villages are either Mopan or Kekchi Maya. Do your best to respect their ways; if you're backpacking, bring your own food and water or be prepared to pay your way in these small compounds. Punta Gorda is the best place around to stock up for a trek into the jungle.

ORIENTATION

This is a casual village! Many people in town know only a few street names. Coming into Punta Gorda across Joe Taylor Creek from the

north, you skirt the Caribbean on the left, and it's quite a view. The coastline describes a gentle arc south and around the Gulf of Honduras. On clear mornings the coast and mountains of Guatemala are in sight—and just barely visible on the horizon are the tall peaks of Honduras.

A hundred or so yards down the way, the road splits at a Texaco station, forming **North Park Street** (a diagonal street a block long) on the right and **Front Street** on the left. Following Front will take you through town past the ferry pier, the **Mira Mar Hotel,** several eating establishments, all the way to **Nature's Way Guest House** at the bottom of Church Street, and to **Curl's Gift Shop** just a little farther and on the left along Front Street. Behind Front, going away from the coast, only a few parallel avenues are of great interest to most travelers.

Main Street splits at the park to become **Main** and **Main Middle. Back Street** becomes **Jose Maria Nunez Street** as you head south of **Church.** The only cross streets besides Church to remember are **Prince Street,** which runs out to the airport, and two that straddle the pier: **Queen Street** to the south and **King Steet** to the north.

SIGHTS

The Waterfront
You won't find too many little port communities with a more simple, inviting waterfront than Punta Gorda. It has a balance, a symmetry of sorts. The sea laps over the reef, and closer, fishing boats bob at anchor. Kids jump over the low wall into the green Caribbean and splash in the shallows after school, and there's one regular who swims laps daily in front of town along with his dog. Activity accompanies the arrival of the ferry boat from Guatemala, and you can find vendors quietly selling "something" most every day.

Central Park
The town park, on a small triangle of soil roughly in the center of town, has an appropriately

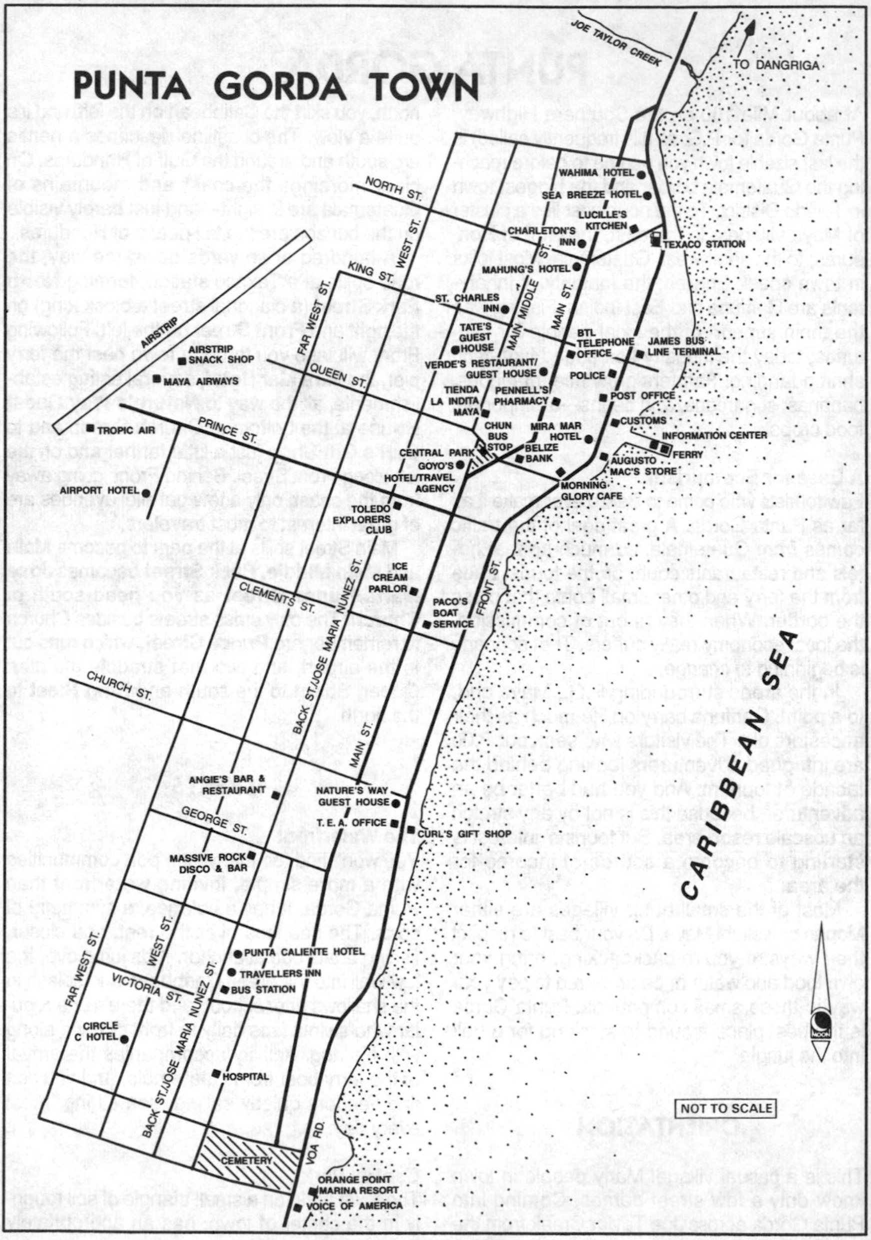

PUNTA GORDA TOWN

TO DANGRIGA

JOE TAYLOR CREEK

NORTH ST.

WEST ST.

KING ST.

FAR WEST ST.

QUEEN ST.

AIRSTRIP

AIRSTRIP
SNACK SHOP

MAYA AIRWAYS

TROPIC AIR

PRINCE ST.

AIRPORT HOTEL

CLEMENTS ST.

CHURCH ST.

BACK ST./JOSE MARIA NUNEZ ST.

ANGIE'S BAR &
RESTAURANT

GEORGE ST.

MASSIVE ROCK
DISCO & BAR

MAIN ST.

WEST ST.

FAR WEST ST.

VICTORIA ST.

BACK ST./JOSE MARIA NUNEZ ST.

CIRCLE
C HOTEL

HOSPITAL

CEMETERY

VCA RD.

ORANGE POINT
MARINA RESORT
VOICE OF AMERICA

WAHIMA HOTEL

SEA BREEZE HOTEL

CHARLESTON'S

LUCILLE'S
KITCHEN

TEXACO STATION

MAIN MIDDLE ST.

MAIN ST.

MAHUNG'S HOTEL

ST. CHARLES
INN

TATE'S
GUEST
HOUSE

VERDE'S RESTAURANT/
GUEST HOUSE

TIENDA
LA INDITA
MAYA

CHUN
BUS
STOP

CENTRAL PARK

GOYO'S
HOTEL/TRAVEL
AGENCY

TOLEDO
EXPLORERS
CLUB

ICE
CREAM
PARLOR

PACO'S
BOAT
SERVICE

NATURE'S WAY
GUEST HOUSE

T. E. A. OFFICE

CURL'S GIFT SHOP

PUNTA CALIENTE HOTEL

TRAVELLERS INN

BUS STATION

BTL
TELEPHONE
OFFICE

JAMES BUS
LINE TERMINAL

POLICE

POST OFFICE

CUSTOMS

INFORMATION CENTER

MIRA MAR
HOTEL

BELIZE
BANK

AUGUSTO
MAC'S STORE

FERRY

MORNING
GLORY CAFE

PENNELL'S
PHARMACY

FRONT ST.

CARIBBEAN SEA

N

NOT TO SCALE

sleepy air to it. At the north end is a raised stage dedicated to the "Pioneers of Belizean Independence." In the center of the park is a dry fountain and here and there, some green cement benches and a sliding board. A clock tower on the south end has hands everlastingly stuck as if holding time at bay. This is a pleasant spot to take a break, enjoy the blue sky, and watch the world go by.

Saturday Market
Don't miss the colorful Saturday market; many Guatemalans offer rich weavings from across the border—though basically it's a produce market. Here, you'll see people selling wild coriander, yellow or white corn, chiles of various hues, tamales wrapped in banana leaves, star fruit, mangoes, and much more. Laughing children help their parents. If you're inclined to snap a photo, it doesn't hurt to buy something, smile, ask permission, "¿Una foto, por favor?" in your best Spanish and say "gracias" when you are through. If refused, smile and put your lens cap in place.

The VOA Towers
Here the Voice of America beams programs to many places in the Caribbean. You can't miss the towers; they blink "redly" south of town. A quick phone call, (7) 22091/22147, is all it takes to arrange a visit (9 a.m.-5 p.m., Monday-Friday) and see close-up U.S. tax dollars at work .

RECREATION

The **Toledo Explorer's Club,** on the corner of Jose Maria Nunez and Prince streets, is a friendly, easygoing group of young entrepreneurs. They appeal to the young and hardy and combine adventure with education. They offer several jungle, barrier reef, river, and village tours of varying lengths for prices ranging from US$75-175. One seven-day adventure (cost about US$700) takes travelers to the deserted beaches of **Punta Negra, Monkey River, Bladen Nature Preserve,** and overnights in **Monkey River Village** and various southern cayes.

Boating Activities
Owned by Ernesto Requena, 12 Front St., Punta Gorda, Belize, C.A., **Rasham Charter Service** is a guide and taxi service specializing in Maya ruins and river tours.

Julio and Placida Requena run **Requena's Charter Service,** 12 Front St., Punta Gorda, Belize, C.A., tel. (7) 22070. They arrange boat trips both inland and ocean, especially to **Snake, Hunting,** and **Moho cayes.** They also transport you to caves, ruins, **Deep, Moho, Monkey, Sarstoon,** and **Temash rivers** and their associated villages. They offer scheduled trips to Puerto Barrios, Guatemala, on Monday, Wednesday, and Saturday, and charters on other days. Prices range US$150-250.

Saturday market in Punta Gorda

Southern Reef Charters, 4 Front St., Punta Gorda, Belize, C.A., tel./fax (7) 22682, is a charter boat service owned by Larry Smith. He takes travelers on a variety of boating, camping, fishing, and snorkeling trips.

The **Sundance,** Box 20, Punta Gorda, Belize, C.A., specializes in touring customers through the southern cayes and to Honduras and Guatemala. River tours are also available.

ACCOMMODATIONS

Accommodations are simple but relatively plentiful in Punta Gorda. Most accommodations have only cold water, are clean, offer shared bathrooms (a few are not much more than outhouses), and most don't take credit cards. The majority of accommodations in P.G. are family run, and that alone can be a great experience. However, do check out your room, sit on the bed, and take a peek into the bathroom before you sign your name.

Basic Rooms
Sixteen clean rooms with fans are available at the **Airport Hotel,** Ogaldes St., Punta Gorda, Belize, C.A., tel. (7) 22495, a block away from the airport. No meals are available but you can eat at the modest **Airstrip Snack Shop** just a block away or wander into town.

A block west of the bus station, the fine, but basic **Circle C Hotel,** 117 West St., Punta Gorda, Belize, C.A., tel. (7) 22726, is run by a local family. It's a quieter location, away from the action in town but convenient to the bus. Rooms are clean with ceiling fans and shared or private bath. With shared bath rates are about US$12.50 s, US$25 d; private bath US$17.50. You can arrange laundry services. A produce shop in the side yard sells cocoa, oranges, cassavas, bananas, yams, and other fruits and veggies.

Formerly called G & G's Inn, **Goyo's,** 49 Main Middle St., Punta Gorda, Belize, C.A., tel. (7) 22680, fax (7) 22469, is across the street from Central Park. Rooms come with ceiling fans, TVs, cold water, and private baths. Ask for one of the rooms with a family room in it or Room 2, a double corner room facing the ocean and clock tower. Rates are about US$16 s, US$17 d, with a family room US$20 d. Goyo's is also a travel agency.

If you're really tight in the pocketbook, check out **Verde's Guest House,** 22 Main St., Punta Gorda, Belize, C.A., tel. (7) 22069, behind the restaurant with the same name. Verde's has four simple rooms with louvered windows, screens, fans, cement floors, and shared outdoor outhouse-style toilets; rates are US$5 s, US$10 d.

Max Lewis runs **Wahima Hotel,** 11 Front St., Box 100, Punta Gorda, Belize, C.A., tel. (7) 22542, a four-room hotel at the far north end of

Punta Caliente Hotel

town. The ocean is literally steps from the front gate, probably the closest in town. Rooms have ceiling fans, cement floors, sinks, and toilets. Rates are about US$17.50 s, US$23 d. Two rooms with more amenities and higher price tags might be finished by this printing. The restaurant next door serves vegetarian fare and local foods. With screened windows on three sides it has an open, airy feeling.

The small **Mahung's Hotel**, Box 92, Punta Gorda, Belize, C.A., tel. (7) 22044, is just across from the Texaco station and at the corner of North and Main streets. Rooms have shared or private baths, h/c water, fans, and TVs. With shared bath rates are US$7.50 s, US$12.50 d; with private bath US$12.50 s, US$17.50 d. Car rentals and tours are available.

Moderate

On the main street of P.G. you'll find **Mira Mar Hotel**, 95 Front St., Punta Gorda, Belize, C.A., tel. (7) 22033. This old standard is easy to find (yellow and white, on the right) and convenient for those driving into town. It's half a block south from the community phone or the ferry pier and a half block north of the Saturday market. Once a favorite of the British military, it has a pool room and a bar/restaurant downstairs with funky Chinese decorations, photos of places such as Hong Kong and Hang Chow, and a beaded curtain. Locals and wayfarers hang out here on hot afternoons. The name means "sea view"— don't count on it. The hotel has about a dozen rooms, with three simple economy rooms mostly populated by hard-core budget travelers; they have ceiling fans and private bath for about US$14. In addition, eight doubles with h/c water, private baths, ceiling fans, and TVs with remotes run about US$24. One deluxe room has a/c, h/c water, full bath, stocked refrigerator, and a lamp that comes on with with a touch of the night table. And now for the ocean view (walk out on the balcony and look out over the rooftops). Rates are US$40 s, US$53 d. The restaurant serves a variety of Chinese dishes, among them a very tasty curried snapper in a brown gravy with potatoes for US$7; the full bar serves beer, fresh orange juice, and soft drinks.

The **St. Charles Inn**, 21 King St., Punta Gorda, Belize, C.A., tel. (7) 22149, is a two-story building with comfortable rooms and a shady veranda that allows you to observe village life below. Rates are US$12.50-18, depending on shared or private bath; laundry service is available. Downstairs you'll find a general store that sells juices, purified water, canned goods, slides, toiletries, fishing tackle, and bicycle parts—it's a good place for passing cyclists to stop.

The **Sea Breeze Hotel**, 6 Front St., Punta Gorda, Belize, C.A., tel. (7) 22243, is a newer building just north of the Texaco station. It houses a restaurant and bar as well as four rooms, with more in the planning stages. Rates are US$10 s, US$15 d. Eating around here should be no problem; a good restaurant downstairs is renowned for shrimp in tomato sauce. Wahima is next door to the north, there's a bakery with great cinnamon rolls just south, and check out the newish Bavarian spot farther down.

Those traveling by bus will find **Charleton's Inn**, 9 Main St., Punta Gorda, Belize, C.A., tel. (7) 22197, fax (7) 22471, at the north end of town convenient to everything. The Z-Line and James buses stop across the street. Rooms have h/c water, private baths, TVs, and have either a/c or fans (those with a/c have color TVs instead of b/w). Rates with fans are US$12.50 s, US$17.50 d; with a/c, US$22.50 s, US$30 d, US$35 t.

You're apt to run into all sorts of interesting travelers from around the world who have somehow heard of **Nature's Way Guest House**, 65 Front St., Box 75, Punta Gorda, Belize, C.A., tel. (7) 22119. Rooms and furnishings are simple but comfortable, clean with pleasant surroundings, fan cooled with friendly staff, and good breakfast (served on a regular basis; great meals are available for individuals and groups by reservation), and access to a string of intriguing activities. Room rates with shared bath are US$16 s, US$26 d, US$36 t; with private bath, US$25 s, US$36 d. The place is run by Chet Schmidt, an expat American, who after serving in the Vietnam War decided to move south . . . way south. He is also one of the guiding spirits of T.E.A. (Toledo Eco-Tourism Association), whose office is next to the hotel. Ask about kayak trips to nearby Joe Taylor Creek (US$20), jungle treks, camping, exploring uninhabited cayes, visits to archaeology sites, and Maya and Garifuna guesthouse stays. Write or call for information.

For those traveling by bus, **Punta Caliente Hotel,** 108 Jose Maria Nunez St., Punta Gorda, Belize, C.A., tel. (7) 22561, delivers great location, value, and food. Next door to the bus station, it's impossible to miss with its strings of tiny Christmas tree lights lending a festive air. It offers eight rooms, on-site laundry service (air dried, about US$5 per bag of laundry), a second-story common balcony, and a rooftop sundeck. The bright, airy rooms have cold water, private baths, cross ventilation, and ceiling fans; rates are US$20-25. The restaurant prepares delicious versions of local food, especially seafood. **Note:** It's one of very few places in town to serve meals on Sunday.

Tate's Guest House, 34 Jose Maria Nunez St., Punta Gorda, Belize, C.A., tel. (7) 22196, is a comfortable, classy lodging with five double rooms in a neighborhood setting. Rates range US$13-23 without a/c, with a/c US$60. Ask for rooms 4 or 5; they are spacious rooms with ceiling fans, color TVs/remotes, sunrooms, louvered windows, tile floors, and each has an additional entrance through the back yard.

If You Want Plush in Punta Gorda

"If you build it they will come"—that seems to be the guiding light behind the luxurious **Travellers Inn,** Jose Maria Nunez St., Punta Gorda, Belize, C.A., by the bus terminal. Compared to most hotels in P.G., this is a treat; large rooms, h/c water, the best bathrooms in town, a/c, expensive furnishings, thick carpets, rich woods, armoires, and all the things you'd least expect in such an isolated village. Rates are US$67 and up. For information call in P.G. (7) 22568, in the U.S., (800) 552-3419, (218) 847-4441, fax (218) 847-4442.

A Jungle Adventure

Near **Chano Creek,** the **Jose and Amelia Oh** family has opened a small jungle hostel with a few rooms with bathrooms and showers (solar-heated water), 12-volt lanterns, and an upstairs open-air porch for meals. For the backpacker they've built a hammock hut, all pretty basic. The hostel is a family affair; the Ohs' son Rolando is the head guide (after his father!). Mom does the cooking and prepares good Kekchi specialties such as *caldo* (chicken cooked with Maya spices and vegetables) and always lots of handmade tortillas.

By day Rolando will take you upriver about three or four miles to the **Rio Grande Cave.** You'll go in one side and all the way through to the other side, about two miles from Lubaantun. For a day-trek through tall primary forest, bring your hiking boots and Rolando will give you a close look at the jungle (never on the same trail twice), lunch, and a swim by the riverside. You'll see orchids, mahogany trees, and yellow-head parrots.

A trip downriver from the Ohs' takes you through lower, secondary forest, where you'll find fig trees, ceiba, howler monkeys, spiny-tailed wishwilly iguanas, six- to seven-foot-long iguanas that turn bright orange during the mating season. At the **Rio Grande waterfall** you'll swim and have lunch. You can also take a day-long canoe trip along the Rio Grande; about 12 miles downriver you'll be met by vehicle to take you back home.

Rolando is full of down-to-earth facts that come only from someone who has lived around the jungle. As he points out, you will not be burdened with mosquitoes in the primary jungle, but in the secondary jungle you'll definitely need bug repellent. His eyes are trained to see every little camouflaged creature. He explains that the traditional thatched roofs built by the Kekchi are of bay palm, and by the Mopan, cohune palm.

This type of adventure is not for everyone, but if you're looking for a *natural* expedition, ask around Punta Gorda for Rolando or Jose Oh. Remember, this is pretty basic, but an experience of a lifetime. Ask for prices in Punta Gorda.

FOOD

Don't expect gourmet in P.G.; most of the restaurants serve simple good food. Take the opportunity to taste local specialties, and there are lots. The town has several good bakeries, and fruit and veggies are cheap and abundant on market day (Saturday).

If you arrive on Saturday night, ask which cafes are open on the morrow. Many close on Sunday.

Restaurants

Angie's Bar & Restaurant, just south of the corner of Church and Back streets and just north of **Massive Rock Disco,** is a noisy little clap-board place but it's clean and the chicken, fish, or steak is well prepared for dining in or taking out.

Lucille's Kitchen, 3 North St., tel. (7) 22256, is the only garden restaurant in town, and dining alfresco amid the tropical plantings in Lucille's small outdoor garden area is a pleasant way to end a day. You'll see marigolds, roses, hibiscus, banana, breadfruit, and palm trees. Or you can escape the midday sun inside where fans chase away the heat. Lucille aims to please with vegetarian dishes cooked to order as well as standards such as stewed chicken, pork chops smothered in gravy, or fish grilled, fried, or sautéed. Prices are very reasonable. Most lunches and dinners are about US$6-7.

When you enter **Punta Caliente,** 108 Jose Maria Nunez St., tel. (7) 22561, and see the locals really tucking into plates of seafood, stewed pork (US$4), fried chicken (US$7), with sautéed vegetables and cole slaw, you know you've come to the right place. The conch soup (US$5) and the burgers (US$2) are particularly good. The restaurant is open seven days a week. You can arrange early breakfasts (6-7 a.m.) for groups.

Value is king at **Verde's Restaurant and Guest House,** 25 Main Middle Street. For US$2.50 you get fried fish or stewed chicken or beef, along with cole slaw, rice and beans, or white rice. Conch soup is US$3.50 and Verde's serves equally economical and tasty breakfasts, too.

Among other options, the **Morning Glory Cafe,** 59 Front St., has dependable breakfast fare, delicious fresh juice and great coffee. **Kowloon Restaurant,** 35 Main Middle, does a pretty good job on Chinese dishes. **Shaiba's Restaurant,** third building south of the Texaco on Front St., has decent food, if poor taste in wall hangings. **The Airstrip Snack Shop** serves basic local fare and fast food as soon as you step off the plane. **Sea Breeze Hotel,** 6 Front St., north of the Texaco Station, makes, among other dishes, a great shrimp in tomato sauce that draws regulars. **Travellers Inn,** by the bus terminal, is sometimes referred to as the fanciest place in town, with real table linens and a reputation for equally good food.

ENTERTAINMENT

Stop by **Angie's Bar,** Jose Maria Nunez St., for a reasonably priced beer and a lively environment in which to sit and drink it. Sometimes the music gets loud and the clientele a little rowdy. This can be a drag, especially if you're trying to eat.

Just down the road from Angie's is **Massive Rock Disco,** 153 Jose Maria Nunez St., another place for music. The massive part of the name must refer to the speakers because you can hear this place rocking a block or two away. And it does play some good tunes.

Honeycomb Bar, Front St. between Prince and Church streets, has a reputation for being wild. Others report having a good time and hanging out with the locals. You "takes your choice!"

SHOPPING

Gift Shops

You'll find **Curl's Gift Shop,** 72 Front St., tel. (7) 22159, just past the intersection with Church Street. This little shop makes the most of its limited space with a showcase of Belizean and other Central American jewelry as well as shelves of lacquered animal carvings, carved wooden kitchen spoons and forks, mahogany ashtrays, bowls and boxes with Maya motifs, and carved wooden plates. The quality is good and prices reasonable.

Tienda la Indita Maya, 24 Main Middle St., tel. (7) 22065, lies just north of Central Park (the end opposite the clock tower) and across the street from Kowloon Restaurant. This store specializes in arts and crafts by Maya Indians from Belize, Guatemala, and El Salvador. It also carries footwear and clothing.

A Little of This and a Little of That

In **Johnson's Store,** on Main Street over near Central Park, you'll find film of all types, shirts, cassettes of local musicians, pots and pans, mosquito netting, and more.

On Front Street "downtown" is where you'll find **Augusto Mac's Store,** a purveyor of mosquito netting (very important out in the boonies), canned foods, film, postcards, and more.

Wallace Supaul Store, at the north end of Main St., has great yogurt, cheese, juice, fruit, canned meat, and reasonable prices.

If you are going off into the jungle, check out the rubber boots, flashlights, and film at **Witz Wholesale//Retail** on Main Middle Street.

The small **K&K bookstore,** 47 Front St., is worth a quick look if you need reading material.

INFORMATION AND SERVICES

Toledo Visitors' Information Center
Look for this office at the Toledo Dock. Here you'll find a friendly group willing to answer questions about Punta Gorda and the entire Toledo District, and especially happy to talk about the "host family network," the Maya homestays. Also, contact the Toledo branch of the Belize Tourism Industry Association, Punta Gorda, Toledo District, Belize, C.A., tel. (7) 22119.

Post Office and Immigration
Near the ferry dock, you'll find the immigration office. Opposite that are a couple of government buildings, where you'll find the post office. There should be a new customs office soon.

Marina
The **Orange Point Marina Resort** eventually will have slips for boats, overnight accommodations, customs house, and other facilities. Take a left on VOA Road at the south end of town.

Money
Some businesses readily accept credit cards, but many don't, so it's best to have Belize currency along. The **Belize Bank,** 43 Front St., is open Mon.-Thurs. 8 a.m.-1 p.m., Fri. 8 a.m.-1 p.m. and 3-6 p.m. It's across from the Civic Center on the town square.

If you're headed toward Guatemala, go to the dock and look around for someone arriving from Guatemala who might want to exchange Belize dollars for Guatemala quetzals; often a freelance money changer hangs around the dock at boat time.

Medicine
Medical service is available at **Toledo Primary Health Care,** Main St., tel. (7) 22145.

Barona Mechanics
For years Ignacio Barona has built a reputation in P.G. for dependable car repair. Now, he offers rental vehicles: Dodge van, Chevy wagon and Cavalier, and Ford pickup. Rates are about US$65/day. You'll find him on Far West St. south of the water tank—called the *water supply area,* tel. (7) 22092.

Texaco Station
Fill your gas tank here and rent a car as well. The station is at the north end of Front Street, tel. (7) 22126/22926, fax (7) 22104.

marina under construction

PHIL LANIER

GETTING THERE

By Air
Some southbound flights from Belize City to Dangriga continue to Placencia and then to Punta Gorda. This is the quickest and most comfortable way to get to Punta Gorda and you have a choice of scheduled flights on **Maya Airways** or **Tropic Air.** In Punta Gorda you can buy your Maya Airways tickets at the airstrip. For a current schedule and fares, call Maya Airways at the airstrip, tel. (7) 22856. Or in Belize City, call its airport office, tel. (2) 44032/45968, fax (2) 30585. Call Tropic Air in Punta Gorda on Prince St., tel. (7) 22008, or in Belize City (2) 45671, fax (2) 32794. You can also arrange charter flights.

By Bus
Buses between Belize City and Punta Gorda make several trips daily. Check with **Venus** and **Batty** buses for current schedules and expect a long ride from Belize City—eight to nine hours. The trip is much shorter from Placencia and Dangriga. **Z-Line,** 53 Main St., buses run a daily service that departs Belize City at 8 a.m. and 3 p.m. except Sunday, when it departs at 10 a.m. and 3 p.m. The return trips are at 5 a.m. and 11 a.m. At least one bus, **James Bus,** meets the ferry from Guatemala and leaves for Belize City at 6 a.m. Thursday, Saturday, and Sunday; 1 p.m. Tuesday and Friday. You can board this bus across from the ferry dock on Front Street. Buses go off to the Maya villages from Punta Gorda next to the Civic Center. From here it's possible to get to Golden Stream, Silver Creek, San Pedro, and San Miguel. To get to Aguacate, Blue Creek, and San Antonio, check with **Chun's** and **Prim's** buses. Check at the **Toledo Visitors' Information Center** for more bus information and most recent schedules.

By Car
No matter who does the driving, this is one long trip! In wet weather certain of the small bridges can be slick; others are so narrow only one vehicle at a time can pass, so be ready to back off. On sunny days the going is long and hot. On rainy days the drive is interminable. If you choose to drive, the best plan is to break the trip up into small chunks, stopping several times along the way.

INTO GUATEMALA FROM PUNTA GORDA

Across the bay from Punta Gorda are Livingston and Puerto Barrios, Guatemala, mostly inhabited by Caribs. For those interested in doing a little exploring across the border, you have the option of flying or taking a boat.

By Air
Now that Punta Gorda has an international airport, **Maya Airways** flies into Puerto Barrios. Flights depart Punta Gorda Monday and Friday at 9:30 a.m., arriving in Puerto Barrios about 20 minutes later. Flights depart Puerto Barrios to Punta Gorda at 10:20 a.m., arriving 10:40 a.m. Fares are US$35 one-way, US$63 roundtrip (call the office at the airstrip, tel. 7-22856).

By Boat
The ferry, a large motorized dory, takes passengers two to three times a week to Puerto Barrios. From P.B. you can catch a bus to Livingston.

To make reservations and buy ferry tickets to Puerto Barrios, go to 24 Main Middle St., tel. (7) 22065. The fare is about US$6.50. You must buy your tickets on the day of departure, and you may be asked for your passport. The ferry leaves P.G. Tuesday and Friday at noon, arriving in P.B. at 2 p.m. However, like much in Central America, the schedule is not cast in stone. Once in a while the ferry doesn't run at all. But a lot of the hotels rely heavily on the business of Guatemalans who come to Belize to sell goods. Faster, small boats still make the trip to Livingston. Ask around the dock and you'll find one, but expect the cost to be higher. For instance, *La Paco* is a fast skiff that makes the trip to Barrios and Livingston nearly every day. The boat leaves from the pier downtown between 8:30 a.m. and 9 a.m., arriving 45 minutes to an hour later depending on the destination. The cost is US$12.50 one-way to Puerto Barrios, US$15 to Livingston, and a bit more on Sunday. In any event, check with the local police to have your passport stamped before you leave.

MAYA COUNTRY WEST OF PUNTA GORDA

San Pedro Columbia and San Antonio are just two of the Maya villages taking part in the **Toledo District Maya Village Guest House and Ecotrail Program** and the two easiest to reach. But for those interested in wandering the countryside on their own, Punta Gorda is a good starting point from which to wander off in many different directions.

ARCHAEOLOGICAL SITES

Nim Li Punit

At about Mile 75 on the Southern Highway near the village of Indian Creek, 25 miles north of Punta Gorda, you'll find Nim Li Punit (expect a 15-minute walk from the highway). The site was briefly surveyed in 1970, and about the only thing known for sure is that it held a close relationship with nearby Lubaantun. One of the memorable finds was a 29.5-foot-tall carved stela, the tallest ever found in Belize—and in most of the rest of the Maya world. It's possible to make arrangements to see these ruins and the villages before your arrival in Punta Gorda if you don't have your own car and would like a guide. In any case, if you plan on visiting these ruins, check with the Department of Archaeology in Belmopan before you go, tel. (8) 22106.

Lubaantun

North of the Columbia River and one mile beyond San Pedro is the Maya ruin of Lubaantun ("Place of the Fallen Stones"). It was built and occupied during the late Classic period (A.D. 730-890). Eleven major structures are grouped around five main plazas—in total the site has 18 plazas and three ball courts. The tallest structure rises 50 feet above the plaza, from which you can see the Caribbean Sea, 20 miles distant. Lubaantun's disparate architecture is completely foreign to Maya construction in other parts of Latin America. Maya buffs will want to examine this site. For more detailed information see "Maya Archaeological Sites."

SAN PEDRO COLUMBIA

To get there, take the main road in Punta Gorda that goes inland about 10 miles toward San Antonio. Just before you get to San Antonio, a dirt track to the right breaks off to the village of San Pedro. If you're without a vehicle, take the bus, which makes this trip about three times a week.

BUTTERFLIES IN SOUTHERN BELIZE

Most people know about the butterflies at Shipstern, and in the jungles of Belize you'll find the fluttering little beauties everywhere. However, as more civilization moves in, the butterflies move out. The folks at **Fallen Stones Butterfly Ranch and Jungle Lodge** have established a "breeding ranch," both for exporting into countries where there's nothing but concrete *and* for the protection and encouragement of the beautiful little critters right here in Belize.

Fallen Stones is in *real* rainforest country. The average yearly rainfall of 160 inches encourages the rich flora that attracts butterflies. Wandering through the trails, you'll see the intense blue Morpho as well as the white Morpho, which is pure white but shot with iridescent blue. Three species of the owl butterfly (Caligo) love to come and lunch on the overripe fruit the keepers of the ranch make sure to leave hanging on the trees—just for them. You'll also see tiny Heliconids and large yellow and white Pierids, among many, many more.

If you're interested in how the butterfly ranch is operated, just ask and you'll be taken on a tour of the structures and cages used to grow special plants that produce the favorite nectars of the adult butterflies. You'll also tour a room filled with plants that provide the larval food and another area where the pupae are hatched—up to 600 a week.

Or you can hire a cab by day—a bit pricey, but the most convenient way to come and go according to your personal schedule.

San Pedro is small and friendly. On the outskirts of town the dwellings are rather primitive; they often have open doorways covered by a hanging cloth, and hammocks and dirt floors. Chickens and sometimes dogs wander through the houses in search of scraps. People use the most primitive of latrines or just take a walk into the jungle. They bathe in the nearest creek or river, a routine that becomes more a source of fun than a cleaning procedure.

People work hard here to survive and support their families. In one household where we stayed, a T.E.A. guesthouse, the husband's daily routine begins at 5:30 a.m. when he leaves for work at a banana plantation. It takes him two and a half hours by foot and bus to reach his work site. At the end of his workday he reverses his trek, and is home for supper by 7:30 p.m. His wife takes care of the livestock, the children, and works with other villagers making craft items. Like parents all over the world, they harbor great hopes for the future of their children.

As you walk into town past the thatched homes on each side of the road, it becomes apparent that the effects of modern conveniences are only beginning to arrive. When a family can finally afford electricity, the first things that appear are a couple of lights and a refrigerator—the latter allows the family to earn a few dollars by selling chilled soft drinks and such. After that, it's a television set; you can see folks sitting in open doorways, their faces lit by the light inside.

A small Catholic church in town has an equally small cemetery. It sits on a hilltop surrounded by a few thatched dwellings. Not far away is a prefab-looking school that was erected, we were told, with the assistance of National Guardsmen from the U.S. who were getting jungle training.

Local guides take visitors out of town past a towering ceiba tree and into what appears to be secondary forest. If there's been rain, the going is muddy. We slogged up and down hilly trails, through little streamlets, and through glens. It's worth it. Everywhere is a stunning parade of life. Hummingbirds, toucans, parrots, and other birds flit about the canopy. Our guide pointed out a jaguar's track, plainly imprinted in the mud of the trail. We were able to follow it for a spell before it led off into the bush. We were impressed by the coolness of the jungle interior and with the guide's knowledge. He could point out and name every variety of flora and fauna along the path. He plucked wild coriander for us to savor and led us to a farmer's *milpa* (field), where corn was drying under a *palapa*. What a difference between the oppressive heat in the open corn fields and the cooling relief in the dark shadows of the jungle.

A Few Places to Stay

Formerly of Hawaii, the Villoria family runs a small farm, **Dem Dats Doin,** Box 73, Punta Gorda, Belize, C.A., tel. (7) 22470, that is self-described as being "an integrated, energy self-sufficient, mini biosphere." What that means is they raise pigs and use energy derived from the droppings to do about everything but go to the moon. A handy bio-gas digester is key to much of this, transforming the oinkers' "output" into methane that powers lights and appliances. What's left is put into the garden to raise food for pigs and people. It's a continuing cycle. Maybe this is an integrated, energy self-sufficient, mini biosphere after all. You be the judge. There's more to see, including a solar oven and home-made herbal potions. With an operation this offbeat and ecologically sensitive at the same time, the Villorias are definitely worth a chat.

Besides the T.E.A. program, **Fallen Stones Butterfly Ranch and Jungle Lodge,** Box 23, Punta Gorda, Belize, C.A., is the other most notable option for accommodations in the San Pedro area. Actually, the name is a bit misleading; the ranch is for the butterflies. For the people you'll find a very handsome lodge with a covered wooden outdoor deck/dining area and thatched-roof cabañas sprinkled about 42 acres of jungle hillside. Butterflies flutter about the grounds but the real work with the winged creatures takes place in buildings down the hill, where they are fed and bred.

The Butterfly Ranch is only one and a half miles from San Pedro, yet it could be a hundred; as far as the eye can see are rolling jungle hills and valleys stretching off into the Maya Mountains. The various trails about the property lead through Heliconia groves, forest trees,

solar energy at Fallen Stones

PHIL LANIER

and many native plants that appeal to the appetites of butterflies.

The cabañas are built along the lines of traditional Kekchi Maya homes, using rustic wood with high pitched ceilings and deep shady verandas. Screened louvered windows provide bug protection. Rates with half board are US$95 s, US$135 d.; full board, US$103 s, US$150 d. Meals are special, especially dinner, which might include pork chops in orange sauce with roasted potatoes and carrots. And for dessert, the house specialty—chocolate cake filled with sweet oranges and ginger that has been soaked in rum, sprinkled with shaved chocolate and served with cream. You can arrange various tours with local guides at reasonable rates. Contact Alistair King in Punta Gorda, owner of the Texaco Station, tel. (7) 22126, fax (7) 22104, and he'll put through a call to the ranch on the radio.

Another option is **San Pedro Village Guest House,** which you can reach by writing Box 75, Punta Gorda Town, Belize, C.A., tel. (7) 22119.

SAN ANTONIO VILLAGE

After leaving San Pedro and returning to the main road, make a right turn and you'll soon be in **San Antonio** just down the road. Inhabitants of these thatch-hut villages, Kekchi and Mopan Maya, are people who fled to Belize to escape from oppression and forced labor in their native Guatemala. The older folks continue to maintain longtime traditional farming methods, culture, and dress. No modern machinery here—they use a simple hoe to till the soil, and water is hand-carried to the fields during dry spells. The village of San Antonio is famous for its exquisite traditional Kekchi embroidery. However, the younger generation is being whisked right along into 20th-century Belizean society.

A local tourism representative lives in San Antonio. He is friendly and happy to give helpful advice about the area, and can direct you to local guides in town willing to take you to archaeological zones (including a trip to the caves) called **Hokeb Ha** and **Blue Creek** (bring your swimsuit). This is great birdwatching country. From here the road is passable as far as **Aguacate** ("Avocado"), another Kekchi village. But if you intend to visit the ruins at **Pusilha,** near the Guatemala border, you must travel either on foot or horseback. Another ruin, **Uxbenka,** is west of San Antonio near the village of Santa Cruz, easy to get to by trucks that haul supplies a couple of times a week. Not known by anyone but locals until 1984, Uxbenka is where seven carved stelae were found, one dating from the early Classic period.

Check out a tiny guesthouse, **Bol's Hilltop Hotel.** Rates are US$9.50 per person; no electricity.

MORE OPTIONS IN MAYA COUNTRY

A few more villages have guesthouses available for overnighters. You can contact **San Miguel Village Guest House, San Jose Village Guest House,** and **Santa Cruz Village Guest House** by calling (7) 22119 or writing to Box 75, Punta Gorda Town, Belize, C.A. Another contact for village guesthouses is the **Maya Host Families Network,** Box 73, Punta Gorda Town, Belize, C.A., tel. (7) 22470.

One Reader's Experience

I received a letter from a reader who gave us a little insight into one Maya family in the village of Santa Cruz. The traveler spent the night in a hammock in the family cottage. This was a great cultural exchange and the American traveler was impressed with the family, their English, and the discussions on subjects from slash-and-burn agriculture to how the Maya construct their huts. From Santa Cruz he went on to spend a night in the jungle. He described the overnight trip as very simple: he spent the night on the ground and saw small wildlife and a jaguar's footprints. Again, he was most influenced by the ideas the Maya have for tourism in their area. He said:

I have traveled in Guatemala and Honduras and even spent time in the refugee camps in the latter country. It was really satisfying for me to have a chance to interact with Mayans who do not live in fear, and who have a chance to take control of their own destinies. For that reason alone, my visit with these people was well worth it!

GETTING THERE

To get to Maya country from Punta Gorda, you have several choices. If you plan on an overnight with the homestay programs, T.E.A. will assist you.

Bikers will find a fairly easy ride of about 20 miles. Get directions from Chet Schmidt at Nature's Way Guest House.

Another alternative is **by bus** from Punta Gorda. Take the Chun Bus that makes the run to San Antonio Monday-Wednesday-Friday, returning Tuesday-Thursday-Saturday to Punta Gorda. Rates are US$1.75 one-way, US$3.50 roundtrip. The bus doesn't stop in San Pedro; instead you will have to trek in several miles. You can also catch a bus as far as Pueblo Viejo, "the edge of the known world." Catch the Chun Bus at Central Square. For times and additional information, call Antonio Chun, tel. (7) 22666.

If traveling **by car,** you have the option of exploring every little road you see. Yes, of course it's more sensible to drive a 4WD. From the turnoff for Punta Gorda at Mile 86 on the Southern Highway, take the road north. At about Mile 1.5 there will be a turnoff on the right that heads for San Pedro and other villages.

KATHY ESCOVEDO SANDERS

ACROSS BELIZE'S BORDERS
GUATEMALA (TIKAL)

The Tikal ruins, in the Petén (jungle) district of Guatemala, are among the more outstanding in the Maya world. They have been excavated and restored extensively, mostly by archaeologists and students from the University of Pennsylvania. What you'll see is only a small part of what is still buried and unexplored in the rainforest. It's been a national park for more than 30 years, so the forest has been protected from loggers—and parts of it are considered virgin. This is a *don't-miss* site.

As is the case with most Maya ceremonial centers, archaeologists are learning more and more about life in Tikal and its 3,000 structures (with 10,000 more foundations). They have mapped 250 stelae that the Maya left behind. In recent years, they have learned to decipher the Maya hieroglyphs, and about 80 percent of the Maya's written record has been translated.

Tikal is not only a treasure trove for the archaeology buff but also for nature lovers. You'll hear and, with luck (if you're up very early in the morning), see the howler monkeys that live in the treetops on the site. You'll see and hear hundreds of parrots squawking at you as you wander through **Twin Complex Q and R**—this is their domain. And while wandering the **Great Plaza** and the **Lost City,** you'll see colorful toucans fly between ancient stone structures and tall vine-covered trees.

Throughout the site, you'll see several twin complexes with identical pyramids facing each other across a central plaza. No one knows why they were built this way. At Twin Complex Q and R, one pyramid has been excavated and restored while its opposite is just as it was when found—covered with vines and jungle growth. You'll see this sort of juxtaposition frequently throughout Tikal. And if you saw the film *Star Wars,* you may recognize the five great pyramids of Tikal as the rebel base.

HISTORY

The Maya

The first Tikal Maya were farmers who, as far back as 750 B.C., chose the high ground that rose above the vast, steamy swamps of Petén for their settlement. The earliest evidence of their presence is some of the trash they left behind. Living on a major route between the lowlands and the cooler highlands, the Tikal villagers began a healthy trade in flint. The stone was plentiful here, and was prized for tools and weapons.

By 600 B.C., the Maya had begun their construction of Tikal ("the Place of Voices"). Over the next 1,500 years, they built their platformed city in layers, razing structures to gather material to build more.

By about 200 B.C., the Maya were building ceremonial structures. By 100 B.C., the great Acropolis was in place, and the Great Plaza was already as large as it would be hundreds of years later, when the population of Tikal reached its peak of about 55,000 people. From 50 B.C. to A.D. 250, the Maya created even more elaborate architecture on these early foundations. They also carved monuments, though they did not yet have hieroglyphics.

With the beginning of the early Classic period in about A.D. 250, the Maya's monuments grew larger, became more formal and less ornate, but the plans for their temples changed little. They built the causeways to connect the parts of their city, and carried on a thriving trade. Carvings on monuments and burial practices show a close relationship with Teotihuacán in Mexico. The monuments also describe Great-Jaguar-Paw and Smoking-Frog's conquest of nearby Uaxactún in A.D. 378. In 562, Lord Water of Caracol defeated Tikal in a great "ax war," and Tikal produced no monuments for 135 years. But in 682, Ah-Cacau took the throne and began to restore Tikal to its former glory. The great king was buried in the Temple of the Giant Jaguar.

Most of the construction at Tikal was in the late Classic period, which began in A.D. 550. (shortly before Tikal's defeat by Caracol) and ended in A.D. 900 (when the entire society collapsed). In and around the ceremonial parts of the city lie 200 stone monuments in the form of stelae and altars. Archaeologists have pieced together Tikal's history from the carvings. The burials at Tikal also hold a clue to the structure of the society.

In the six square miles of Tikal that have been excavated, archaeologists have found hundreds of little buildings that they believe were domestic. Usually they're found in small clusters on elevated sites suitable for housing an extended family. Most people were buried beneath the floors of their houses. Their bones were smaller and weaker than the bones of the folks buried in the great tombs. The range of the housing construction, in size and quality, also suggests great variety in people's status and wealth.

But in A.D. 900, the entire society fell apart, not only at Tikal but throughout the Maya world. Post-Classic Maya continued to use the site for several centuries, and even moved several of the stelae around in an attempt to restore the city for their own purposes, but the jungle eventually reclaimed Tikal.

The Archaeologists

Hidden Tikal was mentioned in 18th-century Guatemala archives, but not until 1848 did the government mount an official expedition. The governor and commissioner of the Petén visited Tikal, and their report, along with an artist's drawings of the stelae and lintels, attracted attention in Europe, where the report was published. A Swiss doctor, Gustav Bernoulli, visited in 1877. He had some of the lintels removed (from Temples I and IV); they are exhibited in the Museum für Volkerkünde in Basel, Switzerland.

The first maps of Tikal were drawn by Alfred Percival Maudslay, who visited in 1881 and 1882 and whose workmen liberated the temples from the forest. He published his accounts, along with the first photographs of the site. Teobert Maler continued in this vein; he visited in 1895 and 1904, mapping and photographing as he worked for the Peabody Museum of Harvard University. He wouldn't relinquish his site map, though, and the museum hired Mayanist Alfred Marston Tozzer and R.E. Merwin to finish the job.

Sylvanus G. Morley, for whom the Tikal museum is named and who was head of the Carnegie Institution's archaeology department,

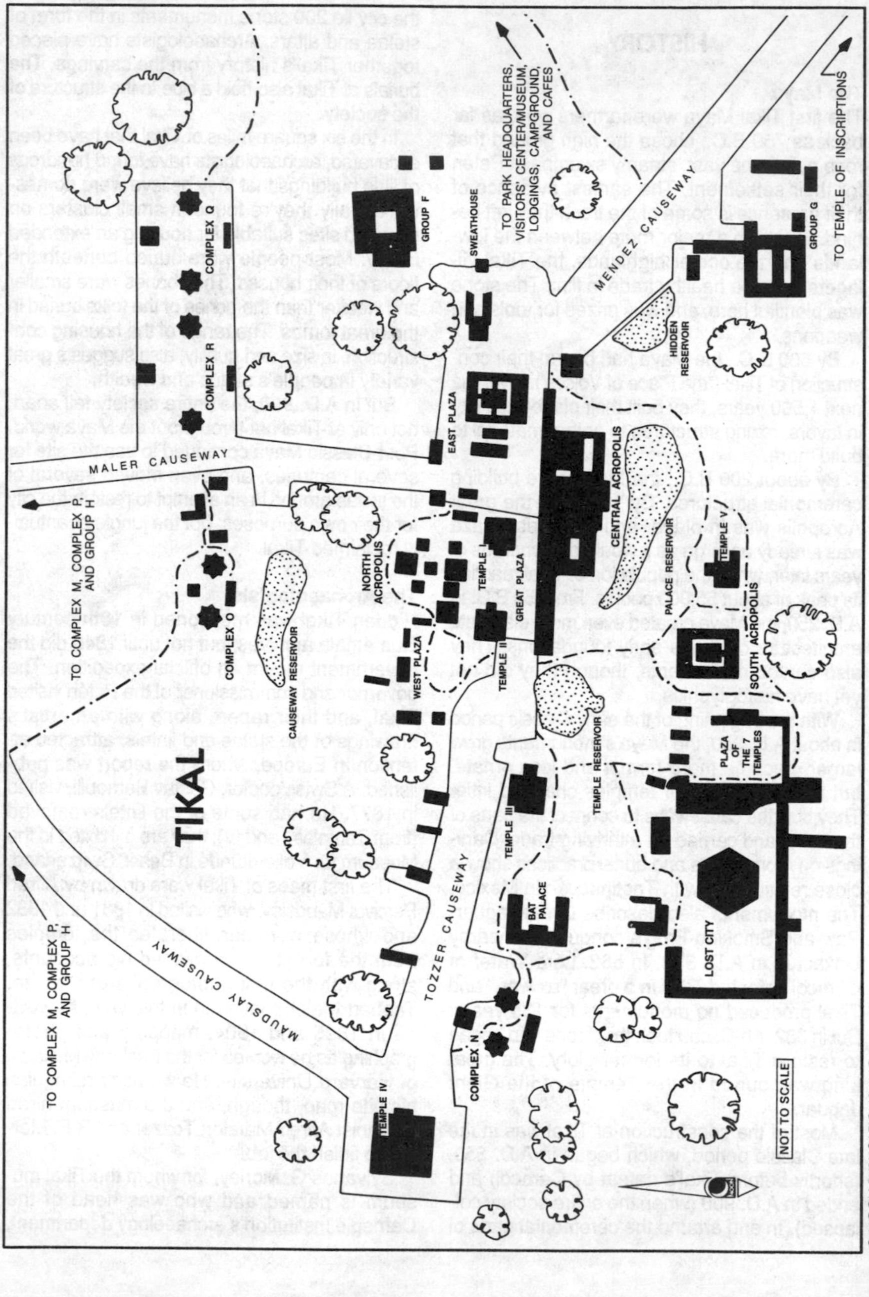

TIKAL

TO PARK HEADQUARTERS,
VISITORS' CENTER/MUSEUM,
LODGINGS, CAMPGROUND,
AND CAFES

MENDEZ CAUSEWAY

GROUP G

TO TEMPLE OF INSCRIPTIONS

GROUP F

SWEATHOUSE

HIDDEN
RESERVOIR

COMPLEX Q

COMPLEX R

EAST PLAZA

CENTRAL ACROPOLIS

PALACE RESERVOIR

TEMPLE V

MALER CAUSEWAY

NORTH
ACROPOLIS

TEMPLE I

GREAT PLAZA

TEMPLE II

SOUTH ACROPOLIS

TO COMPLEX M, COMPLEX P,
AND GROUP H

COMPLEX O

CAUSEWAY RESERVOIR

WEST PLAZA

PLAZA
OF THE
7 TEMPLES

TEMPLE RESERVOIR

TEMPLE III

TOZZER CAUSEWAY

BAT PALACE

LOST CITY

TO COMPLEX M, COMPLEX P,
AND GROUP H

MAUDSLAY CAUSEWAY

TEMPLE IV

COMPLEX N

NOT TO SCALE

© MOON PUBLICATIONS, INC.

used Maudsley and the Peabody Museum's reports as a base, and devoted himself to recording the writing of the Maya. In 1956 the University of Pennsylvania launched the project to excavate Tikal, and appointed Carnegie archaeologist Edwin Shook to lead the project. Since then, part of the immense site has been excavated and restored.

Exploring Tikal

It's so large and complex that unless you have a week to really explore Tikal, it pays to hire a guide. Official guides are available at the site and the fee is fairly standard (about US$30), varying according to the size of your group and the length of your tour. Try negotiating if the price is not to your liking. Wear good walking shoes to cover the six square miles of excavated sites. Photographers, bring lots of film because you'll become maniacal with your camera trying to capture it all—the white-gray stone buildings with the vibrant green of the grass and surrounding jungle.

THE RUINS

Site Entrance

At the gate to Tikal expect a fee (about US$10). Hang on to your ticket; you may be asked to show it. If you want to have the really memorable experience of watching the sunset from the top of Tikal pyramid, have the ticket man stamp yours for an after-hours stay; it's good till 8:30 p.m. Otherwise you must be out of the park by 5 p.m.

When you enter Tikal note the large visitors' enter/museum. Take a look at the scale model of the site and you'll get an idea of where everything is. The visitors' center has photos of the reconstruction, as well as some fine artifacts. The good little museum displays some excellent pieces of Maya history. Don't miss the fascinating tomb exhibit, including a skeleton and funerary offerings, just as they were found. Clustered around the visitors' center you'll find a few cafes, and nearby is a bazaar of Guatemala artisans selling mostly items made from their colorfully woven fabrics.

Tikal is huge, too vast to fully describe here. Listed below are a few highlights, but to get the most out of a visit, do some reading first. An indispensable book to read and then carry with you to read again at the site is prominent archaeologist William Coe's book, *Tikal, Handbook of the Ancient Maya Ruins*, available through the University Museum at the University of Pennsylvania (be sure to carry the map from the book with you—it's easy to get lost in this large complex). If you don't get it before you leave home, it's available at the site.

Note: Only VIPs of the park are allowed to drive on most of the roads; expect to walk a lot.

Tikal in all its glory

The Great Plaza

It's one mile from the museum to the Great Plaza. This plaza, considered the heart of ancient Tikal, is highly complex in design. The Great Plaza covers three acres; its plastered floor, now covered with grass, is made of four layers, the earliest laid in 150 B.C. and the latest in A.D. 700. Two great temples, I and II, face each other across the plaza, around which are scattered palaces, altars, a ball court, and 70 stelae—the memorial stones carved of limestone that tell of Maya life and conquest. Terraces and stairways lead up and down into a plethora of architecturally intense buildings. Most of these palaces were ceremonial centers, but a few are believed to have been apartments. If you climbed and poked around into every structure at the Great Plaza alone, it would take you at least an entire day.

Temple I

Because of its grace, form, and balance, this is probably the most photographed temple at Tikal. Also known as the **Temple of the Giant Jaguar** (named for a carving on one of its lintels), it rises 172 feet above the East Plaza behind it. Nine sloping terraces mark its sides, and its roof comb sits 145 feet above the Great Plaza floor. Atop the building platform is a three-room temple. Its central stair was used by workmen to haul building materials to the top of the temple. It's believed to have been built in about A.D. 700 for King Ah-Cacau, who brought Tikal out of its dark ages after its defeat by Caracol. His tomb was found inside during the restoration, and some of the grave goods, including 180 jade ornaments, pearls and bone carvings, are on display in the National Park Museum/Visitors' Center.

Temple II

Called the **Temple of the Masks,** for the carvings on its lintel, this smaller structure faces Temple I across the Great Plaza. One of the few Maya temples ever dedicated to a woman, it was built for Ah-Cacau's queen, and is smaller and less steep than his. It stands about 125 feet above the Great Plaza, though if its roof comb were intact, the temple would have stood close to 140 feet. Like its counterpart across

one of the temples of Tikal

the way, it also has three rooms at the crest. In front of Temple II lies a large block that archaeologists speculate served as a reviewing stand—priests standing on it could see the crowds in the plaza below and in turn they could be seen by all.

East Plaza

The immense East Plaza, east of the Great Plaza and backing up to the Temple of the Giant Jaguar, was once a formal plastered area covering 5.5 acres. Two of the city's causeways, **Mendez** and **Maler,** lead from here. This plaza is the site of the only known sweathouse at Tikal, and it's also the site of a ball court and what appears to be the marketplace. Trash and other evidence shows that the Maya continued to use the ball court after the collapse of Tikal in A.D. 900.

Temple IV

It's another long walk, but follow your map and visit challenging Temple IV, the **Temple of the**

Double-Headed Serpent. Facing east, it's a popular spot to watch the sunrise. The platform itself has not been excavated, and only those in good physical condition will want to climb the six ladders (sometimes all you can cling to are roots and branches) to the top. Yaxkin Caan Chac, the son and successor of Ah-Cacau, built Temple IV about 40 years after Temple I was built for his father. Today, Temple IV is the tallest surviving Maya structure from pre-Columbian history—212 feet from the base of its platform to the top. Not until the turn of the century, when elevators came along, were taller buildings constructed in this hemisphere. Temple IV also houses a three-room temple, with walls up to 40 feet thick. From the summit of Temple IV, the sight of the entire area is breathtaking. The jungle canopy itself rises 100 feet into the air, and the tops of the other white temples of Tikal rise above the tops of the trees.

Temple V

Though the climb to the top of Temple IV is strenuous, it pales in comparison with the ascent to the north-facing Temple V. Like Temple I, it was built about A.D. 700; it rises about 190 feet. After clambering through underbrush to reach the top of the former stairway, hardy climbers have the option of hoisting themselves up through a hole in the roof comb that appears to have been dug sometime before archaeologists discovered Tikal. Some travelers have reported that the dark, forbidding interior of the roof comb contains ropes and ladders to gain access to the very top of Temple V, from which there is a remarkably focused view of the other temples of Tikal.

Hieroglyphs and Stelae

The earliest stela at Tikal, number 29, was probably carved in A.D. 292. The latest is number 11, carved in 869. In between, the stelae record the births and deaths of kings, the cycle of festivals and seasons, and sagas of war. Even a long pause in the production of stelae, beginning in 557 and ending in 692, has a story to tell. Mayanists have deduced (now that they have discovered how to read as much as 80% of Maya writing here and at other Maya sites) that Tikal lost a great battle with Caracol, and the hiatus coincides

with Caracol's dominance of the region. The inscriptions of Tikal also show that a single dynasty ruled the kingdom from the early Classic period until the society collapsed in A.D. 900. Yax-Moch-Xoc founded the line and ruled from about 219 to 238. Though he was not the first leader to be be memorialized at Tikal, he apparently was so magnificent that he was recognized as the founder of a dynasty—the inscriptions are the first in which the Maya recorded the concept of a founding ancestor. His descendants made up the royalty of Tikal. Among them were kings with names such as King Great-Jaguar-Paw, the ninth successor of Yax-Moch-Xoc; Moon-Zero Bird, who took the throne in A.D. 320; and Curl-Snout (A.D. 379).

Other Sights

There's so much to see and experience in this lovely jungle—a lazy walk through one of many dirt pathways will bring you up close to striking or-

Temple IV is a challenge even for the hardy climber.

chids of all colors, bromeliads, exquisite ferns, delicate blossoms, and myriad trees of every variety. One of the Maya guides recalls hunting for a week at a time with his grandfather: they would wrap their game in a particular jungle leaf to keep it in "good health" and bury it in the ground at a convenient spot; then on the return trip home they dug it out, still fresh and ready for cooking.

TIKAL ACCOMMODATIONS AND FOOD

At the Ruins

Within the Tikal grounds you'll have the choice of staying overnight at three locales or camping. Accommodations are very simple; most do not have 24-hour electricity or hot water, and some have shared baths.

The **Jaguar Inn** offers rooms in the main building, as well as several bungalows around the pool. All beds have mosquito netting and you *do* need it. Rooms have private bathrooms and cold-water showers. Electricity (private generator) is on until about 10 p.m., candles for later. If you're a reader, bring a mini book light, and do bring a flashlight to light your way to the bathroom at night. Remember, you are in the middle of the jungle. Rates include three meals; US$55 s, doubles and triples available. The dining room is a low-key, screened-in porch with tile floors. Two additional on-site lodgings are the **Jungle Lodge** (budget rooms with shared bath US$15, or US$45 s) and **Tikal Inn** (US$55 d), which also serves meals. Camping costs about $6 per person.

Near the entrance to the Tikal ruins you'll find several cafes selling good food at reasonable prices. Vendors may also be selling breadnut tortillas near the temples. Try them; the taste is quite unusual. Usually a youngster at the foot of Temple IV will have an ice chest filled with beer and soda for sale, quite welcome after a hike up and down the tall pyramids.

Remate Petén—A Little Nicer

For those who want something a little nicer, go about 15 minutes south of Tikal to Remate Petén, just across from Lake Petén-Itza. Here you'll find the small, charming hotel called **Mansione del Pajaro Serpiente,** a group of cottages stepped up the side of a hill, giving wonderful views of the lake and the *petén*. The 10 rooms are really diminutive suites with sitting rooms, tile bathrooms, double beds, h/c water, electricity, and an open-air

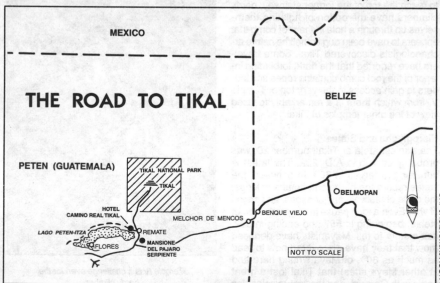

THE ROAD TO TIKAL

MEXICO

BELIZE

PETEN (GUATEMALA)

TIKAL NATIONAL PARK

TIKAL

HOTEL CAMINO REAL TIKAL

LAGO PETEN-ITZA

FLORES

REMATE

MANSIONE DEL PAJARO SERPIENTE

MELCHOR DE MENCOS

BENQUE VIEJO

BELMOPAN

NOT TO SCALE

© MOON PUBLICATIONS, INC.

dining room close by. The buildings are built of stone with *palapa* roofs and furnished with a flair. Across the road, a small group of shops sell wood carvings, jade jewelry, and more. Pickup at the Flores airport (no charge), and transportation to and from the park is available along with guided tours. Room rate is US$75 d; ask about two tiny rooms on the property without all the amenities, no sitting room, US$15 s, US$20 d. Add 17% tax to all prices. For more information, write Mansione del Pajaro, Remate, 17702, Guatemala.

Here also you can arrange to participate in the yearly **Maya Man Triathlon.** Usually held in the first week of March, the triathlon begins at Remate. It consists of a one-km swim, 34-km bike ride (to Tikal Park), and a seven-km run (through the park). For more information, contact the Mansione del Pajaro.

Another upscale hotel, the **Camino Real Tikal,** is about 40 minutes away from the Tikal site, but also in the village of Remate. The hotel sits on 220 acres that overlook Lake Petén-Itza and the *petén.* The hotel offers a wide selection of sporting options, including hiking, swimming, fishing, scuba diving, canoeing, bicycling, sailboarding, and sailing. In keeping with the area's environmental standards, no motor vehicles are permitted on Lake Petén-Itza. In 12 tri-level, thatched-roof bungalows, 72 attractive rooms provide luxurious bathrooms, a/c, minibars, international telephone service, cable TV, and individual balconies overlooking the lake. In the main building guests will find a full-service restaurant, swimming pool, snack bar, lounge, and lake-view bar open till midnight. Rates are US$90 s, US$100 d. Transportation to and from the Tikal archaeological site is US$15 roundtrip. A tour from the hotel, transportation, lunch, and guide costs US$55 per person. For more information and reservations, call (800) 327-373, (800) 228-3000, (9) 500-204, or write the hotel in San José Peté, Lote 77, 17702, Guatemala.

Flores

Flores, about an hour by road from Tikal, serves as a popular base for tourist excursions to the ruins. Many visitors opt to come by plane, and flights are available from Belize, Guatemala, and Mexico cities. The airport in Flores is newish and modern, much more so than the town it services. You'll find several hotels and numerous restaurants scattered around the area; most are very simple and very cheap.

GETTING THERE

On Belize's Western Highway from the Xunantunich turnoff, the road passes through Benque Viejo, an old town with aged wooden houses. It's a good place to stop and have a cold drink before the long ride into Guatemala, where the culture changes immediately. For Americans (with passports) crossing the border is usually no problem. First you must stop at the Belize side, show your passport, and fill out a departure form. At the Guatemala side you stop again, show your passport, and fill out some more papers for your visa. You'll be asked how long you expect to stay in the country; allow an extra couple of days just in case you are delayed. Expect to pay US$5 (unless you obtained the visa previously in Mérida, Belize, or the U.S.). You should not have to pay to have your passport stamped here, but as

An orphaned ocelot at Jaguar Inn in Tikal gets lots of TLC from Belizean archaeological guide Tessa Fairweather.

border guards often do, they may ask for more money. You can try and play dumb, act as if you don't hear or don't understand—it *sometimes* works—but be prepared to pay a few dollars! If you're driving your own car make sure you have all the necessary papers of ownership, which they *will* want to see. You are required to have your tires fumigated (by law), for which the cost is a few Belizean dollars.

Once across the border it's pretty easy sailing, but keep a couple of things in mind. When passing military camps (and you will pass several on the way to Tikal), do not take *any* photos (even of the large vicious sign of a soldier pointing his gun at you saying, "I dare you"). If you're aiming your lens at the lovely river and the water happens to flow in front of the guard station, you can get into difficulties no matter how innocent it seems to you. The Guatemala military is very touchy. Don't be surprised if you're stopped by the military and asked for your papers several times; keep your passport and visitor's permit handy, smile and answer all questions, and you'll soon be on your way.

The road in Guatemala is terrible, and it will take at least two hours to reach the entrance to Tikal National Park, after which the road is excellent for the final 30 miles to the site itself.

Note: If backpacking and taking public buses, be aware that no public transportation is available from the Belize border to Tikal. The only bus that runs from the Belize/Guatemala border is a Guatemala public bus that goes to Flores. You can spend the night here and take the morning bus to Tikal (board in front of the **San Juan**

Hotel.) The border/Flores bus is usually very crowded with chickens and the works. If you wish to bypass Flores and take your chances of hitching a ride straight to Tikal, ask the bus driver to drop you off at the park crossroad (about US$3) that leads to Tikal. You won't find any stores or restaurants here, and you may wait quite a while for a car or taxi headed for Tikal. Many hotels from the Cayo District and Belize City run minibuses to Tikal. If you see one, flag it down; the driver will pick you up if there's room. From the Belize border, fare is about US$40-50.

Note: The airstrip at Tikal is no longer used since the coming and going of planes was found to be damaging to the park's ecology. Now flights from Guatemala City and other points land in Flores. (See the chart "Airlines Serving Belize.")

Footnote about the Road Between Belize and Guatemala

Readers often write and ask why I don't mention driving between the Cayo District and Tikal more frequently. Well, it isn't that we haven't traveled it; we have, many times. It can be an interesting, though bumpy drive. In the rain, the road becomes a quagmire of very deep mud; we have seen it when the road was so scattered with abandoned cars that we just could not make it the entire way. But more to the point, often around Christmas, people traveling by car (and sometimes buses) on their way to or from Belize have been stopped by bandits and robbed of money and watches. I know of *no* case when the bandits have caused injuries, but some of them have been known to carry guns, making it a scary experience.

Many of the small cottage resorts offer escorted trips in vans, and they keep their ears open for any rumbles. At the first hint of a problem they will cancel the trip. In some cases drivers run their vans in tandem with other resort vans—safety in numbers! In spring of '92, after several robberies, we traveled in one van while another rode shotgun, both with Guatemala license plates and tinted glass. As many times as we have traveled that road, we have not been robbed, but we have spoken to those who have been.

TRAVEL IN GUATEMALA

As we go to press, several kidnappings of Americans held for ransom and bus holdups have been reported in Guatemala. For timely information as you depart for Guatemala, please call the **State Dept. Travel Advisory Office** in Washington, D.C., tel. (202) 647-5225. Or for more detailed information, contact the **Guatemalan Embassy** in Washington, D.C., tel. (202) 745-4952.

MEXICO

CHETUMAL

Chetumal, capital of the state of Quintana Roo, is a good base to visit the many archaeological sights in the southern section of Quintana Roo and the eastern section of Campeche. It's also a gateway to Mexico's well-known Caribbean resorts: Cancún, Cozumel, Playa Del Carmen, and Akumal. Chetumal is without the bikini-clad, touristy crowds of the north and presents the businesslike atmosphere of a growing metropolis. A 10-minute walk takes you to the waterfront from the marketplace and most of the hotels. Modern sculpted monuments stand along a breezy promenade that skirts the broad crescent of the bay. Also explore the back streets, where worn, wooden buildings still have a Central American/Caribbean look. The largest building in town—white, three stories, close to the waterfront—houses most of the government offices.

Wide, tree-lined avenues and clean sidewalks front dozens of small variety shops. The city was a free port for many years (but no longer) and as a result has attracted a plethora of tiny shops selling a strange conglomeration of plastic toys, small appliances, exotic perfumes (maybe authentic?), famous-label(?) clothes, and imported foodstuffs. This is a popular place for Belizeans and Mexicans to shop. The population is an eclectic mixture of cultures, including Carib, Spanish, Maya, and British. Schools are prominently scattered around the town.

Sights

On Avenida Heroes five miles north of the city is **Calderitas Bay,** a breezy area for picnicking, camping, and RVing. The trailer park is one of the few in the state that provides complete hookups for RVs, including a dump station and clean showers, toilets, and washing facilities. Right on the water's edge, the spotless camp is in a parklike setting, fringed with cooling palm trees. Even amateur divers will find exotic shells, and the fishing is great.

Nearby public beaches have *palapa* shelters that are normally tranquil, but on holidays they're crowded with sun- and fun-seekers.

Tiny **Isla Tamalcas,** 1.5 miles off the shore of Calderitas, is the home of the primitive capybara. This largest of all rodents can reach a length of over a meter and weigh up to 50 kilograms; it's found in only a few other places in the world (South America and Panama). The shaggy animal is covered with reddish, yellowish brown coarse hair, resembles a small pig or large guinea pig, has partially webbed toes, and loves to swim, even underwater. The locals call it a water hog, and it's a favorite food of the jaguar. Because it's been a favorite food, it's seldom seen anymore. Isla Tamalcas is easily accessible from Calderitas Beach.

Twenty-one miles north of Chetumal (on Highway 307) is **Cenote Azul,** a circular *cenote* 61.5 meters deep and 185 meters across filled with brilliant blue water. This is a spectacular place to stop for a swim, lunch at the outdoor restaurant, or just have a cold drink.

Accommodations

Chetumal has quite a few hotels in all price categories. We have just listed a few to check out.

Chetumal doesn't have a true luxury hotel. The **Hotel Los Cocos** (formerly the Del Prado), Avenida Heroes con Chapultepec, tel. (983) 2-0544, comes closest with clean pleasant rooms, a/c, pretty garden, and a large, clean swimming pool. You'll also find a bar with evening disco music and a quiet dining room with a friendly staff serving a varied menu. Rates are about US$80 d. The **Hotel Continental-Caribe,** Avenida Heroes #171, tel. (983) 2-1100, promotes itself as a luxury hotel (rumor has it that it will soon be a Holiday Inn?). It has a/c, restaurant, pool, bar with evening entertainment, and though the rooms are clean the overall appearance is not. Prices start at about US$48.

The moderately priced hotels for the most part are friendly (some clean, some not; look before you pay), usually fan-cooled, some with a/c, and they have h/c water. Prices range

US$24-35 d. **Hotel Marlon,** Avenida Juarez #87, tel. (983) 2-9522, fax (983) 2-1065, is a newish hotel with a very pleasant staff. Rooms are comfortable and clean, with a/c, hot water, telephones, and color TVs. It has a pool, a good restaurant, and the **Marquis** is a neat little piano bar. Rates start at about US$25 s, US$29 d. **Hotel Principe,** Avenida Niños Heroes #326, tel. (983) 2-4799, fax (983) 2-5191, offers ample rooms, a/c, h/c water, a pleasant courtyard, and the **El Arlequin** restaurant. Rates are US$25 s, US$29 d. Rooms at **El Marques Hotel,** Avenida Lazaro Cardenas #121, tel. (983) 2-2998, come with servibar, private bathrooms, and h/c water; rates US$28. **Restaurante El Marques** is on the premises. **Hotel Caribe Princess,** Avenida Alvaro Obregón #168, tel. (983) 2-0520, is very clean and has a/c, h/c water, and TV. A real budget spot is **Hotel Jacaranda,** Avenida Alvaro Obregón #201, tel. (983) 2-1455. Simple rooms come with fan or a/c; rates start at about US$11. Very reasonably priced food is available at its simple cafe.

Food

It's easy to find a cafe to fit every budget in Chetumal. Walk down the street to Avenida Alvaro Obregón for several fast-food cafes. On the same street, try **El Pez Vela** for seafood; for chicken go to **Pollos Sinaloa.** On the corner of Avenidas Efrain Aguilar and Revolución you'll find **Los Pozos,** a regional cafe serving typical Yucatecan dishes. Eat great tacos at **El Taco Loco** at Morelos #87, open 6 a.m.-3 p.m.; **Sergios Pizza** on Obregon and Cinco de Mayo is good. **Mandinga** serves good seafood on Belize St.; it's usually busy, with reasonable prices. **El Grill** at Hotel Los Cocos is great for a special night out. The **public market** has just about everything you could need.

Getting There

Buses between Belize and Chetumal travel throughout the day to the modern Chetumal bus station on the highway, 20 blocks south of town. **Taxis** are available from the station into town. With the expanding road system, bus travel is becoming more versatile and is the most inexpensive public transportation to the Quintana Roo coast. If you want to see more of Quintana Roo, buses from Chetumal make frequent trips to Playa del Carmen and Cancún. New express buses are appearing in many parts of Mexico. They are modern and clean, with bathrooms, a/c, and airline-type seats. Each bus has an attendant who will serve you coffee and cookies, and some buses have earphones for music—the 747s of the road. Chetumal is part of the loop between Campeche, Cancún, and Mérida. Check with a travel agent or **Belize Specialists,** tel. (800) 4-YUCATAN, for a pickup point in Chetumal or Cancún, usually at one of the hotels. Fares and schedules change regularly: to Cancún the fare is about US$30. Frequent bus service into Belize is provided by the **Batty Bus** or the **Venus Bus.** You will have to get off the bus when you go across the border into Belize. Have your passport handy; sometimes this takes a while.

If you're traveling **by car,** the drive is easy between Belize and Mexico on the Northern Highway. A good paved road connects Chetumal with Mérida, Campeche, Villahermosa, and Francisco Escarcega; Highway 307 links all of the Quintana Roo coastal cities. Expect little traffic, and gas stations are well spaced if you top off at each one. **Car rentals** are scarce in Chetumal; go to the Hotel Los Cocos for Avis. Chetumal is an economical place to rent your car (if one is available), since the tax is only six percent. If you're driving watch out for "No Left Turn" signs in Chetumal.

BACALAR

Twenty-four miles north of Chetumal (on Highway 307) lies a beautiful multihued lagoon called **Las Lagunas de Siete Colores** ("Lagoon of Seven Colors"). Bacalar, complete with 17th-century Fort San Felipe, is a small town founded by the Spanish to protect themselves from the bands of pirates and Maya that regularly raided the area. Today, part of the fort has a diminutive museum housing metal arms used in the 17th and 18th centuries. A token assortment of memorabilia recalls history of the area. The stone construction has been restored, and cannons are still posted along the balustrades overlooking the beautiful Bacalar lagoon. The museum is open daily except holidays, and charges a small entry fee.

Close by, built into the side of a hill overlooking the colorful lagoon, is **Hotel Laguna,** moderately priced, with clean rooms and private baths. Rooms each have a fan and a view of the sea. The dining room serves tasty Mexican food at moderate prices. Special touches make it an out-of-the-ordinary stopover: local shells decorate walls and ceilings, and ornate fences are neatly painted in white and green. A small pool (filled only during high season) and outdoor bar look out across the unusually hued Lagunas de Siete Colores. A diving board and ladder make swimming convenient in the lagoon's sometimes-blue, sometimes-purple, sometimes-red water; fishing is permitted and you can barbecue your catch on the grounds. Rates

are about US$36 d. Ask about a bungalow that includes a kitchen. Reserve in advance during the tourist season and holidays. To find the hotel, turn left off Bacalar's main street and follow the shore south. For reservations phone (983) 2-3517 in Chetumal, (99) 27-1304 in Mérida, or write to Avenida Bugambilias #316, Chetumal, Quintana Roo, Mexico. Allow plenty of time for the mail to reach its destination.

Close by is the **Laguna Milagros Trailer Park** with tent camping also permitted, about US$2-3 per person. Restrooms, showers, sun shelters, a narrow beach, small store, and open-air cafe combine to offer an exotic milieu on the edge of the lagoon.

MAYA SITES OF MEXICO

If you have several days and would like to take in more Maya history, drive north to **Tulúm** and then inland to **Cobá.** Both are outstanding Maya sites. Head west on Highway 186 to **Kohunlich,** and into the state of Campeche to the ruins of **Xpujil, Becán, Chicanná,** and **Calakmul Reserve.**

TULUM

In late 1994 many changes were made to Tulúm. A large new visitors' center, with restaurant, restrooms, museum, and arts and crafts shops were built a couple of kilometers beyond the old turnoff road. Maybe just in time, considering the hundreds of buses that blew their foul contaminated fumes on the already ancient structures. Services also include a shuttle for those who don't wish to take the 10-minute walk to the site (US$1.50 roundtrip). Guides are available for hire at the entrance as well (not included in the entrance fee).

Tulúm's archaeological zone is open daily 8 a.m.-5 p.m. At 8 a.m., few tour buses have arrived yet, making the cooler early hours a desirable time to explore and photograph the aged structures. You pay a US$5.50 per person fee (plus about US$10 to bring in your camcorder) at the new entrance to the ruins. Parking is available there as well, US$2.

In the past it was permissible to climb the ruins. Now, some have been chained off because of

concern for the stability of the structures, so please do not climb. Areas are clearly marked.

Tulúm is made up of mostly small, ornate structures with stuccoed gargoyle faces carved onto the corners of buildings. In the **Temple of Frescoes,** looking through a metal grate you'll see a fresco that still bears a trace of color from the ancient artist. Archaeologically, this is the most interesting building on the site. The original parts of the building were constructed around 1450 during the late Post-Classic period, and as is the case with so many Maya structures, it was added to over the years.

Diving God
Across the compound, a small *palapa* roof protects a carved descending god. This winged creature is pictured upside down and is thought by some historians to be the God of the Setting Sun. Others interpret the carving as representing the bee; honey is a commodity almost as revered on the Peninsula as maize. Visitors are no longer allowed to climb this ruin to view the carvings.

El Castillo
The most impressive site is the large pyramid that stands on the edge of a 40-foot limestone cliff overlooking the sea. The building, in the center of the wall on the east side, was built in three phases. A wide staircase leads to a two-chamber temple at the top; visitors are no longer allowed to climb this stairway, but the view from

the hill on which the Castillo stands encompasses the sea, the surrounding jungle with an occasional stone ruin poking through the tight brush, and scattered clearings where small farms are beginning to grow. Two serpent columns divide the entrance, and above the middle entrance is another carved figure of the Diving God. Until the 1920s, the followers of the "Talking Cross" kept three crosses in a shrine in this pyramid. It was only after curious visitors, as well as respectable archaeologists, showed an active interest in obtaining the crosses that the Maya priests moved the Tulúm crosses to Tixcacal Guardia, where they supposedly remain today, still under the watchful protection of the Maya priesthood.

Village of Tulúm

Tulúm pueblo is south on Highway 307 a short distance beyond the ruin's turnoff. It has always been the home of stalwart Maya people with the courage to preserve their ancient traditions; the descendants have vigorously chosen to enter the world of tourism (with tiny steps), and Tulúm pueblo is becoming a viable town.

COBA

This early Maya site covers an immense area (50 square km), and hundreds of mounds are yet to be uncovered. Archaeologists are convinced that in time Cobá will prove to be one of the largest Maya excavations on the Yucatán Peninsula. Only in recent years has the importance of Cobá come to light. Though Cobá was first explored in 1891 by Austrian archaeologist Teobert Maler, another 35 years passed before it was investigated by S. Morley, J. Eric Thompson, H. Pollock, and J. Charlot under the auspices of the Carnegie Institute. In 1972-75 the National Geographic Society in conjunction with the Mexican National Institute of Anthropology and History mapped and surveyed the entire area. A program funded by the Mexican government continues to explore and study Cobá, but the time-consuming, costly work will not be completed for many years.

Cobá was perhaps the favorite Maya ceremonial site of many independent travelers. The fact that the jungle hasn't been cleared away or all the mounds uncovered adds a feeling of discovery to the visit. For the visitor, it's important to know that the distances between groupings of structures are long (in some cases one to two km), and they're not located in a neatly kept park such as Chichén Itzá. Each group of ruins is buried in the middle of thick jungle, so come prepared with comfortable shoes, bug repellent, sunscreen, and a hat. A canteen of water never hurts.

Flora and Fauna

Cobá in Maya means "Water Stirred by the Wind." Close to a group of shallow lakes (Cobá, Macanxoc, Xkanha, and Zacalpuc), some very marshy areas attract a large variety of birds and butterflies. The jungle around Cobá is good for viewing herons, egrets, and motmots. Once in a while, even a stray toucan is spotted. Colorful butterflies are everywhere, including the large, deep-blue *morphidae* butterfly as well as the bright yellow-orange barred sulphur. If you look on the ground, you'll almost certainly see long lines of cutting ants. One double column carries freshly cut leaves to the burrow, and next to that another double column marches in the opposite direction, empty jawed, returning for more. The columns can be longer than a kilometer, and usually the work party will all carry the same species of leaf or blossom until the plant is completely stripped. It's amazing how far they travel for food! The vegetation decays in their nests, and the fungus that grows on the compost is an important staple of the ants' diet. The determined creatures grow to up to three centimeters long.

People

Thousands of people are believed to have lived here during the Classic period. Today, the numbers are drastically reduced. They plant their corn with ceremony and conduct their family affairs in the same manner as their ancestors; many villages still appoint a calendar-keeper to keep track of the auspicious days that direct them in their daily lives. This is most common in the Cobá area because of its (up till now) isolation from outsiders and low profile. The locals live in communities on both sides of the lake. Those by the ruins operate small artisans' shops and restaurants and typically speak a smattering of Spanish. The community on the far side of the lake has a small clinic and a basketball court that serves as the town plaza. The communities have electricity, but no telephone service; the only phone in the area is the cellular one at the Villa Arqueológica.

THE COBA RUINS

White Roads

The most important reason to visit Cobá is to view the archaeological remains of a city begun in A.D. 600. These structures built near the lakes were scattered along a refined system of *sacbe* (roads). The remains of more than 50 *sacbe* have been found crisscrossing the entire Peninsula, and there are more here than in any other location. They pass through what were once outlying villages and converge at Cobá, an indication that it was the largest city of its era. One such *sacbe* is 100 km long and travels in an almost straight line from the base of Nohoch Mul (the great pyramid) to the town of Yaxuna. Each *sacbe* was built to stringent specifications: a base of stones one to two meters high, about 4.5 meters wide, and covered with white mortar. However, in Cobá some ancient roads as wide as 10 meters have been uncovered.

Archaeologists have even found a massive stone cylinder that was used to flatten the masonry. They have also discovered the mines where the inhabitants excavated the sand used to construct the roads. Sacbe #1, the longest, was an apparent attempt to extend Cobá's realm and challenge Chichén Itzá's rising aggression. It did not work, because Cobá was defeated in a mid-9th-century war. Cobá had a minor resurgence during the late post-Classic when Tulúm-style temples were built on top of the site's pyramids and ceremonial platforms. In this last period its main function was apparently as a pilgrimage destination. (Many caches of offerings, including jade, pearls, and shells, have been found in La Iglesia and other temples.)

Most of the stelae have been found in the Macanxoc area of the site, also known as Group A. Until recently, Stela 1 here was one of the great enigmas of Maya translation. It is covered with incredibly long date glyphs that resemble no other Maya inscription. Now researchers believe that Stela 1 commemorates two very an-

cient dates. One of these is 13 August 3114 B.C., the day on which the current era—as reckoned by the Maya—began (it ends A.D. 23 December 2012). The other, more remarkable date is the longest one ever found in the Maya world; it marks the day that creation began: 41,943,040 followed by 21 zeros. Unfortunately, like most Cobá stelae, Stela 1 is badly weathered.

The Pyramids

While you wander through the grounds, it helps to use the map. When you enter, follow the dirt road a few meters until you come to the sign that reads Grupo Cobá directing you to the right. A short distance on the path brings you to the second-highest pyramid at the site (22.5 meters), called **La Iglesia.** After climbing many stone steps (the climb gets more dangerous each year as the steps disintegrate), you'll get a marvelous view of the surrounding jungle and Lake Macanxoc. Many offering caches, including jade, pearls, and shells, have been found in La Iglesia and other temples.

Back on the main path, a short trail leads to a stela with traces of carving, covered by a *palapa* to protect the stone from the elements.

From La Iglesia, farther on, the main path branches to the left, leading to **Nohoch Mul,** the tallest pyramid on the Peninsula (42 meters, a 12-story climb!). The view from atop Nohuch Mul is spectacular, and at the very top there's a small temple with a fairly well-preserved carving of the Descending God. After returning to the main path, turn left and continue to another fork. The path to the right leads to the **Grupo Macanxoc,** a collection of stelae covered with *palapas*.

From Grupo Macanxoc, the path to the left goes to **Conjunto Las Pinturas,** so named because of the stucco paintings that once lined the walls. Minute traces of the paintings, in layers of yellow, red, and blue, can still be seen on the uppermost cornice of the temple. This small building is well preserved, with groupings of pillars at the base and bright green moss growing up the sides of the gray limestone. It's nearly a half-hour walk from here back to the entrance to the ruins. Watch for signs and stay on the trails.

Scientists conjecture there may be a connection between the Petén Maya (hundreds of miles south in the Guatemala lowlands) and the Classic Maya who lived in Cobá. Both groups built lofty pyramids, much taller than those found in Chichén Itzá, Uxmal, or elsewhere in the northern part of the Peninsula.

Undiscovered

All along the paths are mounds overgrown with vines, trees, and flowers—many of these unexcavated ruins. More than 5,000 mounds wait for the money it takes to continue excavation. Thirty-two Classic-period stelae (including 23 that are sculptured) have been found scattered throughout the Cobá archaeological zone. Except for those at Macanxoc, most are displayed where they were discovered. One of the better preserved can be seen in front of the Nohoch Mul group. Still somewhat recognizable, it depicts a nobleman standing on the backs of two slaves and is dated 780 in Maya glyphs.

WEST OF CHETUMAL

Kohunlich

Forty-one miles west of Chetumal on Highway 186, turn right and drive five miles on a good side road to this Maya site. The construction continued from late pre-Classic (about A.D. 100-200) through Classic (A.D. 600-900). Though not totally restored nor nearly as grand as Chichén Itzá or Uxmal, Kohunlich is worth the trip if only to visit the exotic **Temple of the Masks,** dedicated to the Maya sun god. The stone pyramid is under an unlikely thatched roof (to prevent further deterioration from the weather), and gigantic stucco masks stand two to three meters tall. The temple, though not extremely tall as pyramids go, still presents a moderate climb. Wander through the jungle site and you can find 200 structures or uncovered mounds from the same era as the Palenque Maya archaeological site. Many carved stelae are scattered throughout the surrounding forest.

Walking through luxuriant foliage, you'll discover a green world. Note orchids in the tops of trees, plus small colorful wildflowers, lacy ferns, and lizards that share cracks and crevices in moldy stone walls covered with velvety moss. The relatively unknown site attracts few tourists.

mask of Kohunlich

The absence of trinket sellers and soft-drink stands leaves a visitor feeling that he or she is the first to stumble on the haunting masks with their star-incised eyes, mustaches (or are they serpents?), and nose plugs—features extremely different from carvings found at other Maya sites. Even the birds hoot and squawk at your intrusion as if you were the first. Like most archaeological zones, Kohunlich is fenced and opens 8 a.m.-5 p.m.; you'll pay an entrance fee. Camping is not allowed within the grounds, but you may see a tent or two outside the entrance.

STATE OF CAMPECHE

Several Maya sights in Campeche are close enough to the Belize border to be seen in a one-day (a long day) trip across the border, in conjunction with Kohunlich.

Xpujil, Becán, and Chicanná are the most accessible sites of south-central Yucatán's R'o Bec culture. They share the distinctive R'o Bec architectural style, whose hallmarks are "palaces" with flanking towers that appear on first glance to be Classic pyramids with temples on top. When you look closer, you realize that the "pyramid's" steps are actually reliefs and the temple is just a solid box with a phony door. It is as if they wanted the look of a Tikal-style temple without going through the trouble of building one. The towers are usually capped with roof combs, and sky serpent masks are frequent decorations on all ceremonial buildings.

The earliest occupation of the R'o Bec area occurred between 1000 and 300 B.C. The great earthworks at Becán, which were probably defensive, were built around A.D. 150. Shortly afterward, the distant city of Teotihuacán's influence appears at the site in the form of ceramics and other evidence. Researchers believe that during the early Classic, Becán was ruled by trader/warriors from that great culture. Most of the existing structures in the R'o Bec region were constructed between A.D. 550 and 830. Then the population gradually dwindled away; by the time of the Spanish conquest the area was completely abandoned. The R'o Bec sites were rediscovered early in this century by chicle tappers.

(The adventurous may also want to explore the sites of R'o Bec itself and El Hormiguero, which lie south of the road and are reachable only during the dry season along poor dirt roads.)

The sites of Xpujil, Becán, and Chicanná are easy to get to from Belize. Cross the border and take the main highway (186) that cuts across the peninsula from Chetumal (and on to Escarcega) in southern Quintana Roo. You will reach the sites once you're across the Campeche border. In order to further develop the Mundo Maya project (also called La Ruta Maya), the Mexican government has recently agreed to spend big bucks in this area of Campeche, where some of the most interesting archaeological sites have been fairly well ignored until now. Water has always been a stumbling block for tourist development, but rumors circulating say there will soon be plenty of water and electricity with which to begin upgrading the area. INAH (the archaeological arm of the Mexican government) has begun work on some of the main structures, and many more structures and

caves in the jungle continue to be "found." Because of the proximity to **Calakmul,** one of the largest Maya ceremonial centers found thus far, and the concentration of sites (though at present not fully developed), there will be many tourists coming through this part of Campeche.

By the time you visit, there may be an eco-tourism-style resort in the area called **Posada Chicanná.** Architect Jose Selem (who is also the general manager of the Ramada Inn in Campeche city) has designed the resort with 50 rooms in one- and two-story solar-powered buildings. From here, tours to the nearby ruins and Calakmul will be available.

Xpujil

About 110 km west of Chetumal, you'll pass the small village of Xpujil. Nearby stand three towers, a classic example of R'o Bec architecture: the remains of three false towers overlooking miles of jungle. On the back side of the central tower, check out what's left of two huge inlaid masks. Xpujil is one of the best-preserved R'o Bec-style structures, unique for having a taller central tower in addition to the flanking twin towers.

If you're in a vehicle that can handle a primitive jeep road, you can reach R'o Bec by taking the road south of the gas station near Xpujil.

Just past the small town of Xpujil, you'll see a large, circular *palapa* restaurant called **Maya Mirador.** This is a great lunch stop, serving good food and cold drinks (no wild game sold here!). The cafe is run by a transplanted Frenchman, Serge R'ou, and his Mexican partner/engineer Moises, both also heavily into archaeology and nature. Behind the cafe, Serge offers four tiny sleeping *palapas.* This is spartan simplicity in pole houses. There's no electricity, just a roof to protect you from the rain and the bigger critters, but for those willing to carry a sleeping bag or a hammock it's a convenient location to the ruins (there should be a few more cabins when you are there). Public restrooms are available. Serge speaks French, English, and Spanish and is a knowledgeable guide to the area. Recently he was involved in locating Maya caves that contained Indian drawings. At the newly discovered ruins, **Balam Ku,** robbers stripped the facing stones, but you can still see a portrait of kings. Sadly, guards are necessary at Maya sites to

*Xpujil in Mexico's
state of Campeche*

keep out robbers who sell the artifacts to private collectors not only in Mexico but around the world.

This is also an ideal place for birdwatching in thick jungle with little or no tourist traffic. Don't forget your binoculars and bug repellent! If you're traveling by bus from Belize to Chetumal, check with the tourist office or a travel agency for bus trips to these sites. Not fully restored, the ruins will give you an indication of what the archaeologists find when they first stumble upon an isolated site. You will have renewed wonder at how they manage to clear away hundreds of years of jungle growth, figure out a puzzle of thousands of stones, and end up with such impressive structures.

Although you should be careful of those few strangers who are always looking to rob and steal, the majority of the people in the Yucatán Peninsula are friendly, kind folks. On a recent trip, our car gave up without warning. There we were, stranded—it was almost dark, no phones, or much of anything else. We walked to the nearby Maya Mirador Restaurant, where we eventually flagged down a pickup truck, and a kind-hearted farmer agreed to drive us to the Mexico/Belize border (as long as we didn't mind riding in the back with various and sundry animals). We were grateful, animals and all, for the friendly helping hand.

Becán
Six km west of Xpujil along Highway 186 is the turnoff to Becán. Becán offers archaeology buffs some of the largest ancient buildings in the state. Excavation is proceeding according to schedule. Becán dates back to 500 B.C. Structure VIII, just off the southeast plaza, offers a labyrinth of underground rooms, passageways, and artifacts, indicating this to be an important religious ceremonial center. You'll see an unusual waterless moat, 15 meters wide, four meters deep, and 2.3 km in diameter, surrounding the entire site. It's believed this protective-style construction indicates that warring factions occupied this part of the Peninsula during the 2nd century. Historians claim that they were constantly at war with Mayapán, in what is now the state of Yucatán.

Chicanná
Another two km west is the turnoff to the Maya site of Chicanná, about a half km off Highway 186. The small city included five structures encircling a main center. An elaborate serpent mask frames the entry of the main palace, **House of the Serpent Mouth**—it's in comparatively good repair. Across the plaza lies Structure I, a typical R'o Bec-style building complex with twin false-temple towers. Several hundred meters south are two more temple groups, though not as well preserved. Throughout the area are small and large ruins. If you're curious to compare the subtle differences of design and architecture of the ancient Maya throughout the Peninsula, the group is worth a day's visit.

Calakmul Reserve

Located in the Petén region in the southern area of Campeche, 35 km from the border with Guatemala, Calakmul has given its name to one of the newest, largest biosphere reserves in Mexico. This site was once home to over 60,000 Maya. What may turn out to be the largest of all the structures built by the Maya, a massive pyramid, looms 175 feet over a base that covers five acres.

An archaeological team from the Universidad Autonoma del Sudeste in Campeche has mapped 6,750 structures; uncovered two tombs holding magnificent jade masks, beads, and two flowerlike earcaps; excavated parts of three ceremonial sites; and found more stelae than at any other Maya site. From the top of Pyramid 2, it's possible to see the Danta pyramid at Calakmul's sister site, El Mirador, and part of the Calakmul reserve on the Guatemala side of the border. Both of these sites predate Christ by 100 years.

Heading the archaeological team at Calakmul, William Folan has made startling discoveries, but even more important, he has been instrumental in pushing through the concept of the biosphere reserve. Today it has become a reality. Calakmul is not yet on the usual itinerary because of the difficulty reaching it; if you'd like more information contact the tourist office in Campeche city. See the October 1989 issue of *National Geographic Magazine* for color photos of the Calakmul archaeological site.

HONDURAS

Honduras is best known for its Bay Islands and Copan, ancient ceremonial city of the Maya.

San Pedro Sula

The gateway to Honduras, San Pedro Sula with its international airport is where many visitors land on their way to and from the **Bay Islands.** The ambience here is entirely different than in Belize; it has more the feeling of a Spanish colonial city, which of course it was hundreds of years ago. A day or two in the city, with its Spanish colonial buildings and lovely town square, will give you the flavor of another era. There's a good public market where arts and crafts from all over the country are sold—check out the great hardwood carvings. The **Gran Hotel Sula** across from the Plaza is a pleasant place to stay. Enjoy delicious (inexpensive) food at the hotel dining room. From San Pedro there are several other good side trips into the surrounding mountains.

Take a look at the cigar factory in **Santa Rosa de Copan** and then go on to the colonial town of **Gracias** at the base of **Celaque Mountain,** Honduras's highest peak, and the **Celaque National Park.** In the park take some time to roam the trails of this dense pine-clad cloud forest. Be sure to check out the hot springs for a soak before you leave the park. You can camp in this great park, but bring *everything* you need with you.

Starting from Tegucigalpa

Take a day or two to explore the city of Tegucigalpa, the capital of Honduras, with its colonial structures and left-over Spanish architecture. The graceful city offers a great **National Museum,** the **Presidential Palace,** and the beautiful **Basilica of Suyapa.** Don't miss the city market and wander through the streets to get acquainted. This is another good starting point into fascinating Honduran sites. The **Rio Platano Biosphere Reserve** is the forest habitat of the Pesch Indians. **La Tigra Cloud Forest** has myriad hiking trails and unique flora and fauna; birders would see more with a local guide. Mountain villages **Valle de Angeles** and **Santa Lucia** are typical with cobbled streets and red-tiled rooftops. Lush foliage makes everything green. Valle de Angeles is the home of the **National Artisans School** and a great place for shopping. The **Hotel la Ronda** and **Hotel Honduras Maya** in Tegucigalpa are good hotels. These are all places you can get to on your own with public transport. Or, for escorted tours and more information on prices and reservations and other destinations, contact Roatan Charters, Inc., tel. (800) 282-8932, or (904) 588-4131, fax (904) 588-4158.

COPAN

With an interest perhaps stronger than we had ever felt in wandering among the ruins of Egypt, we followed our guide . . . to 14 monuments of the same character and appearance, some with more elegant designs, and some in workmanship equal to the finest monuments of the Egyptians.

Although these are the words of John Lloyd Stephens describing his first view of Honduras, they could easily be mine—and probably yours as well. Those who have visited archaeological monuments of ancient societies around the world will more than likely come to the same conclusion as they explore Copan as did the erstwhile explorers Stephens and his fellow-traveler, artist Frederick Catherwood.

The Maya

For a thousand years Copan lay covered by trees, embraced by roots of the tall strangler ficus amid layers of dust, dead-plant material, and loose particles that floated on the Honduran breeze and gradually covered most of this archaic wonderland. Since Stephens and Catherwood's visit, much has happened. Astounding carvings of immense heads, stairways lined with rearing stone jaguars, and many plazas have been uncovered and revealed to the sunlight once again. Stephens describes a colossal stone figure:

The front was a figure of a man curiously and richly dressed, and the face, evidently a portrait, solemn, stern, and well fitted to excite terror. The back was of a different design, unlike anything we had ever seen before, and the sides were covered with hieroglyphics.

Maya Sites

Copan is on the Copan River in a valley about 2,000 feet high. Stonework continues to be revealed throughout the valley. In Copan's 1,500 years of existence, the Maya moved its centers from one place to the other, building impressive structures at each site, perhaps improving

Maya stelae at Copan site

each over the other until the middle of the 8th century, when it would seem that they reached the pinnacle of their accomplishments. Scientists believe Copan's beginnings were during the early Classic period, and these Maya continued in their advancements and structural designs until the late Classic period (A.D. 700).

While wandering through Copan with your guide (a guide is the way to go for good info), you will learn when the various structures were built and what archaeologists have learned about them over the years. The Acropolis, for example, is the largest complex at 130 feet high. This is where you'll find the well-known **Hieroglyphic Stairway,** covered with the longest "book" of hieroglyphics—2,500 glyphs on 63 steps. No, you cannot climb the steps; in fact, the public is not allowed to get too close. The Maya glyphs at Copan are considered the finest Maya art found to date. Look at the **Eastern** and **Western courts.** At the Eastern Court you'll find **Temple 22,** the most breathtaking structure in Copan. Though much of the intricate carving has been destroyed, enough is left that visitors can see what complicated, tedious work was devoted to this temple—believed to have been the most sacred of Copan. The **Great Plaza** is at the northern end of the **Main Structure,** and those who have visited Tikal will notice the similarities between this one and the Great Plaza at Tikal.

On 1 April 1995, a group of U.S. and Honduran archaeologists discovered what they believe to be the tomb of Kinich Ah Pop, the second king of the Copan dynasty. They found the well-preserved skeleton surrounded by jade offerings in the Margarita Tomb. The bones were stained red, signifying blood in a mark of respect. Hieroglyphics at the tomb read, "May you be venerated, Kinich, lord of the sun, lord of the lake, lord of Copan." Carved on the facade of the tomb are figures of a macaw and a quetzal, preserved so well that the archaeologists said they were among the most beautiful and most important of Maya finds. The remains of Yax Kuk Mo, Kinich's father and founder of the dynasty

Maya ruins at Copan

who ruled from 426-437, were discovered in 1993. Eventually Kinich's bones and the artwork will be displayed in the Copan museum.

Don't miss the museum on the main plaza in the small town of Ruinas Copan; you'll see a booth to buy your ticket to both the archaeology zone and the museum (about US$3). At the museum you'll find the usual collection of stelae, a tomb, and other artifacts from the site. From the museum expect about a half-hour walk to the site. By the time you have this book, the new museum on the grounds of Copan should be open. The entrance to this beautiful museum is a reproduction of the entrance to the marvelous **Rosalila Structure** discovered in 1991. It's best to plan at least one full day to take in the site; two days are even better.

Practicalities

Several very simple hostelries lie close by for an overnight stay. Probably the nicest (and the newest) is the **Hotel Marina,** and there are several budget-type hostels. Hotel Marina has excellent food and a friendly atmosphere. Try the new **Los Gauchos** restaurant—linen tablecloths in the middle of this jungle, and great food. Several simple eating places surround the small town square. If you're looking for a school to learn Spanish, what nicer place than **Ixbalanque,** Copan's Spanish language school? Room and board with families of the village are provided.

BAY ISLANDS

The Caribbean coast has many well-kept secrets. One that divers have kept to themselves for years is the Bay Islands of Honduras. Unspoiled and untouched by time, it's like living in your own private island world. Geologically the islands are an extension of the renowned barrier reef that runs from the tip of Mexico's Isla Mujeres south into the Honduras Bay, 35-70 miles off the Honduras coast. Reaching heights of 1,300 feet, the Bay Islands' spiny pine-covered hills drop to coconut-fringed, powder-fine sand beaches washed by the crystal water of the Caribbean. The reef is so close to many of the islands that often it means just a short swim from the beach to discover the flamboyant marine spectacle.

It's exhilarating to find a world without the interruptions of TV, fast-food hangouts, five-lane highways, glass-encased malls, or crowds of tourists. Geographically the island group includes **Utila, Morat, Barbarat, Roatan,** and **Guanaja,** along with some spectacular cayes. Whether you're a snorkeler or scuba diver, each is a diver's ecstasy. Add the pleasures of the '90s to the rich history of the island, which gives Honduras its "other" dimension, and you can't miss having a memorable vacation.

History

The first inhabitants of the islands were the pre-Columbian **Paya,** whose relationship to the mainland Maya is not completely understood. Some archaeologists say the Paya predated the Maya, but there's little left of these first inhabitants to really know—except for the *yapa ding dongs,* as the locals call the few artifacts remaining. A more recent (and exciting) history begins in the 1700s. The Bay Islands' past includes the British colonial government of 1741, pirate attacks, kidnappings, and a 300-year fight between the Spanish and the British for control of the islands.

The strong connection that links Belize, the Cayman Islands, Roatan, and the Mosquito Coast (the mainland across the bay from Roatan) began in the 1700s when settlers moved from one region to another, fleeing first Spanish and then British attacks. The musical chairs rotation of government takeovers in the strategically located islands was dominated by the British because of the islands' proximity to Belize and their British government. As a result, English family names particularly are common to all four areas, and despite the mixture of cultures, English has remained the commonly used language of the people on the islands, even though Spanish is the official language of Honduras. After traveling through the islands, you'll get the feeling that most islanders consider themselves separate from mainland Honduras.

Roatan

Shortly after Columbus's visit in 1502, during his last trip to the New World, the islands were either scenes of bustling activity or completely deserted. At the beginning of the 17th century buccaneers made the Bay Islands their hangout and Henry Morgan established his operations in the deep-water harbor of **Port Royal** on the southern coast of Roatan. Over the years, islanders harvested timber, small villages of diverse cultures maintained their purity, and eventually outsiders began to discover the tranquility and beauty of the islands. The largest island is 30-mile-long Roatan. **Western Caribbean Airlines,** and **Taca Airlines** make frequent trips to the international airstrip at the town of Coxen's Hole at the southwestern end of Roatan. Roundtrip from Belize City costs about US$180, and from Houston, New Orleans, or Miami, approximately US$380; the best deals are packages available from Roatan Charters, Box 877, San Antonio, Florida 33576-0877, tel. (800) 282-8932, fax (904) 588-4158.

The long slender island has a multitude of small bays, inlets, and cayes—and low-key rustic accommodations at each. The alluring water between sunrise and sunset displays multi-shades of blue, green, and purple. The marine-life is rich with lobster, conch, a variety of turtles, and colorful coral. The offshore reef, decorated with a constant ruffle of white foam, has boats of all sizes scattered about.

The people of Roatan seem happy with their lives. No one really wants to see a highrise, and most are already concerned that too much development will spoil the low-key lifestyle they enjoy. Talk circulates of condominiums, retirement villages, and more beach resorts. So far it is *just* talk.

Meanwhile, about 600 Americans are living on the island, many involved in the hotel business, some just enjoying the idyllic life of the tropics.

Coxen's Hole is a bustling community whose streets are filled with people all going somewhere in various modes of transport: cars, buses, bicycles, taxis, and, of course, lots of pedestrians. If you're a shopper you'll enjoy a stop at superstore **Casa Warren,** where you can buy everything from groceries to sunglasses to junior's underwear. At **Joanna's,** visitors will find the perfect gift to bring home to remember Roatan.

Not too far from Anthony's Key is the small village of **Sandy Bay.** This isn't much more than a group of stilted dwellings. From here visitors who can tear themselves away from the sea trek up the steep twisting path about a mile to the island's tree-covered spine, where the view takes in the southern and northern coasts of Roatan, with Anthony's just below. Divers will find excellent walls, pillar corals, fluffy yellow gorgonians, and reaching sponges.

At **Bailey's Key** you'll find a program involving diving with dolphins. Still in the experimental stage, the program allows only six divers at a time to dive with the dolphins and only in the holding pen; eventually this will expand to become an open-water experience—under supervision, of course.

Roatan Accommodations

Five miles from the airport the lovely **Anthony's Key Resort** climbs the steep hillsides of its island. This 50-room complex is on a private eight-acre island that caters mostly to divers year-round. Most of the guest bungalows are set in a grove of coconuts (this small island was formerly a coconut plantation). Anthony's has learned the secret of good service, and the resort lures visitors back year after year. Divers can explore the sea as often as they wish, day or night. Lectures and slide shows inform newcomers of what to expect. Tennis, horseback riding, and sailboarding give a variety of breaks from diving. At Anthony's you'll climb four flights of steps to get to the lobby, where the view is breathtaking.

Accommodations are available in a variety of styles and prices. Seven-day packages are available from US$500-650 per person plus seven percent tax. For more information contact Anthony's Key Resort, 1385 Coral Way, Ste. 401, Miami, Florida 33145, tel. (800) 227-348, (305) 858-3483.

A cozy secluded retreat with private beachfront bungalows and two guesthouses, the charming **Coco View Resort** offers unlimited diving on a beautiful reef right off the beach. After your arrival on Roatan Island, you'll be taken to Old French Harbor, where the hotel boat shuttle picks you up and takes you on a 10-minute ride up the coast. Winding through the cayes, you'll suddenly realize you've left civilization in the following wake. Forget about the world you left behind; give your return airline tickets to your hostess and you can forget everything until she taps you on the shoulder when it's time to go.

Along with Yaba Ding Ding, "super dive dog," you'll enjoy the cozy ambience, especially over a cold beer in the "sunset-enhancing station" (sometimes called the bar) when the sky is splashed with golden reds. This is the time when diving folk hash out the day's discoveries and nondivers enjoy once again the experience of doing "whatever feels good."

Divers come to Coco View to enjoy the wall just 100 yards off the beach, as well as **Mary's Place,** an immense volcanic crack where the delights of the underworld flourish. And there's more—the 140-foot tanker wreck of the *Prince Albert* awaits exploration in 25-65 feet of clear water. **Would-be divers:** Expect PADI and SSI American instructors, two dive boats with equipment lockers onboard, freshwater dunk tanks everywhere, and plenty of air. Complete gear rental and repair are available. Seven-night package trips start at US$625-775, depending on whether you are a diver or nondiver and time of the year. For more information and reservations, contact Coco View Resort, Box 877, San Antonio, Florida 33576, tel. (800) 282-8932. Accommodations include guesthouses and over-the-water luxury bungalows. You'll find them clean and comfortable with h/c water and private baths, overhead fans, 120-volt electricity, and each with its own porch to gather in the beautiful views of the sea.

For those who enjoy being pampered in luxurious surroundings or who think that living the life of the "rich and famous" is okay, check out **Fantasy Island,** the newest resort in the Bay Islands. Visitors will find 39 beautiful, a/c, beachfront rooms luxuriously appointed on a 15-acre private island just off Roatan. You name it, all water sports are available, from blue-water fishing to snorkeling and scuba diving to private yacht charters; don't forget the water toys, from wind-driven to mechanical. Excellent meals are served in a lovely tropical dining room. And for those who like to stay in touch, you'll find telephones and satellite TV. For more information, call (800) 676-2826; in Roatan call (504) 45-1222, fax (504) 45-1268.

Named for a couple of French families who moved to Roatan from the Mosquito Coast in 1823, **French Harbor** is the largest town on Roatan island and the most industrialized. The chief industry revolves around seafood (no surprise there) with a large fleet of boats that work the coastal areas as far south as Nicaragua. Conch, lobster, and shrimp are processed and frozen for world export.

While wandering around the city, check out the **Buccaneer Inn,** owned by Rita Silvestri, who is very much involved with the environmental protection of Roatan as well as a pro-development association that helps low-income citizens with a development bank. The Buccaneer Inn is a great beachfront hotel that some claim has the best chef on the island. Also at French Harbor, have a talk with transplanted American Eric Anderson, who first tried his hand at farming at Port Royal (until it was obvious the farm was not making it) and today owns and operates (with his wife Teri) **Hotel French Harbor Yacht Club.** Set on a hill overlooking French Harbor, 12 rooms offer an intimate resort with private baths, ceiling fans, cable TV, direct-dial telephones, some a/c (extra), porches with views, boat rentals, island tours, and car rentals. Dockage is available for boaters. For more information in Roatan call (504) 45-1478, fax (504) 45-1459; in the U.S. contact Tropical Travel, tel. (800) 451-8017.

Another Roatan harbor, **Oak Ridge,** is also totally engrossed in catching and processing seafood for export. The seagoing world recognized the key as the site of the original **Cooper Boatyard,** set up in 1870, where the 700-ton *Rubicon* was built in 1919—the largest ship ever built on the Caribbean side of Central America. This is a haven for historical tidbits of the French, Dutch, English, Spanish, and Americans.

One of the oldest Bay Island dive resorts, the **Reef House,** sits on a small caye at the entrance of the harbor and is still as popular as ever. A small unpretentious tropical hideaway designed for 30 divers, it has recently been remodeled and enlarged. When not diving you'll be pampered with excellent Creole, Caribbean, or American food served in your choice of candlelight dining room or at the terrace edge. Outdoors you'll find a poolside patio, bar, and a 120-foot blue lagoon with a sandy white bottom where protected swimming is only steps from your room.

Divers have access to a 37-foot diesel cruiser and a fully equipped dive shop. Five- to seven-day packages for nondivers, divers, and fishermen range from US$375-550 per person, plus seven percent tax. The resort's **Caribbean Institute** offers workshops and seminars, which explore a variety of areas of information, including marine biology, ecology, anthropology, and folklore of the islands. The programs provide a pleasant way to learn about the world around us: past, present, and future. For more information in the U.S. call (800) 451-8017.

Guanaja Island Accommodations

On the island of Guanaja, the discriminating traveler will find a relaxed elegance at the **Posada del Sol,** with gourmet food and perfect service. The luxurious Spanish hacienda is set in a beautiful mountainside location with more than 1,600 feet of waterfront. Besides the usual diving and deep-sea and light-tackle fishing, the visitor will enjoy tennis and horseback riding. Divers come to dive sites that include five shipwrecks, 10 miles of deep vertical coral walls (in 28-50 feet of water), and four miles of coral barrier reef. The resort has three dive boats and complete dive equipment. For a change of pace the Posada offers waterfall jungle trips, hiking, water-skiing, and charter sportfishing, plus lots more. Amenities include 24 Spanish-style rooms with a choice of poolside, hillside, or oceanfront accommodations. Package prices include three meals. Rates range US$730-1395 per person, depending on your activities. For more information contact Posada del Sol, 1201 U.S. Highway One, Ste. 220, North Palm Beach, Florida 33408, tel. (800) 624-DIVE, (407) 624-DIVE, fax (407) 624-3225.

Bayman Bay Club, a rustic resort of wooden bungalows built into a mountainside jungle, offers a tropical retreat for anyone who really wants to get away from it all—and the diving is great. Lodging is about as close to staying in a treehouse as it can get and still be termed a guesthouse, with the amenities that make traveling fun. Close to all diving activities on Guanaja Island, guests enjoy great food, offshore trade winds, and a feeling of being in another world. Seven-day packages start at US$650 nondiver, US$675 diver. For more information contact Tropical Travel, tel. (800) 451-8017 in the U.S.

Live-Aboard Boats

Roaming the waters of the Bay Islands and

making the dive experience convenient and luxurious is the live-aboard dive boat the *Isla Mia,* a 75-foot floating dive resort perfectly suited for exploring all the waters of the Bay Islands. The boat has five double cabins plus a cabin for six. Completely air-conditioned, the boat provides unlimited diving. A seven-day, six-night package costs US$1195 per person. For more information, in the U.S. call (800) 451-8017, (713) 298-2238, fax (713) 298-2335.

PRACTICALITIES

Safety

An important question on everyone's mind planning a trip to this part of the world is, "How safe is it to travel there?" I don't claim to be a political expert, but I feel comfortable enough to drop everything and go to the Bay Islands at any opportunity.

After looking into the safety issue, which means we have talked to ordinary residents of the islands (expats and locals), businesspeople, government officials, and returning visitors, including divers and nondivers who come back year after year, we have not encountered even one report of a problem. All of these people describe a very peaceful environment. Again, we have not been able to uncover a problem in the areas that we recommend: the Bay Islands, Copan, Tegucigalpa, or San Pedro Sula. So, my answer is, I believe traveling to the aforementioned places in Honduras is safe. Pitfalls await the unwary everywhere in life—travelers, like everyone, must take their steps carefully.

Getting to Honduras

Taca provides 727/737 service to the Honduras mainland and Bay Islands from U.S. gateways in Houston, Miami, or New Orleans. If you opt for an escorted two- or three-day tour from the Bay Islands, transportation, meals, and overnight hotel stay are arranged for you through several tour operators. Otherwise, to see Copan on your own, fly into either San Pedro Sula or Tegucigalpa and take a bus into the hilltop community of Ruinas Copan.

If you're traveling in Guatemala, it's a simple matter to cross the border into neighboring Honduras.

Miscellaneous Information

A valid passport is needed to enter Honduras; U.S. citizens do not need visas, but visas are required in advance for those traveling on Canadian passports. *Do* bring your passport. We read various reports to tourists saying that it's not necessary, especially if you're traveling into Copan for a day from Guatemala. However, we have also heard from travelers who found themselves stranded in Honduras for whatever reason, and without passports they had problems. So, be on the safe side, and bring your passport!

The official currency in Honduras is the **lempira,** referred to locally as the "lemp." Currently the exchange rate is US$1 to two lemps. Not all resorts accept **credit cards,** but **traveler's checks** are accepted almost every place (except the very smallest), and most resorts on the islands and the mainland are happy to take U.S. dollars. You must pay a **departure tax** of US$20 per person at the airport when leaving. Only a few hotels offer **car rentals;** as the roads improve, more are becoming available. **Hotel tax** is seven percent.

A San Pedro Sula businessman—the oranges look green on the outside but are orange, sweet, and juicy on the inside.

Divers, remember to bring your certification card; PADI or SSI certification courses are available. Spearfishing is not permitted, and removing coral, shells, or fish is prohibited without express permission from the Honduran government. Bring whatever film you think you might use, as it is much more expensive on the islands and all types are not sold.

AIRLINES SERVING HONDURAS		
American	US (800) 433-7300	from Miami
Continental	US (800) 231-0856	from Houston
TACA	US (800) 535-8780	from New Orleans

Medical Concerns

Emergency **medical treatment** is available at a clinic in French Harbor and good hospitals are 35 miles away (about 20 minutes away by plane) on the Honduras mainland. Although malaria is rarely encountered in the islands, you may wish to ask your doctor or contact the Centers for Disease Control and Prevention in Atlanta, Georgia, tel. (404) 639-2888, before leaving the United States. A recompression chamber with trained staff is located on Roatan. Prescription drugs are unavailable in the tiny villages so bring any necessary medicines in your carry-on luggage. Bring a bug repellent; though mosquitoes are a rarity, "no see-ums" and occasional sandflies can be a nuisance—Avon's Skin-So-Soft works great for *some* people (if you can stand the strong smell!).

BOOKLIST

ARCHAEOLOGY

Carrasco, David. *Religions of Mesoamerica: Cosmovision and Ceremonial Centers*. San Francisco: Harper & Row, 1990.

Coe, Michael D. *The Maya*. New York: Thames and Hudson, 1984.

Coe, William R. *Tikal, A Handbook of the Ancient Maya Ruins, with a Guide Map*. Philadelphia: University Museum at the University of Pennsylvania, 1967.

Freidel, Davis. *Archaeology at Cerros, Belize, Central America*. Dallas: Southern Methodist University Press, 1986-1989.

Garvin, Richard. *The Crystal Skull: The Story of the Mystery, Myth, and Magic of the Mitchell-Hedges Crystal Skull Discovered in a Lost Mayan City During a Search for Atlantis*. Garden City, NY: Doubleday, 1973.

Gifford, James. *Prehistoric Pottery Analysis and the Ceramics of Barton Ramie in the Belize Valley*. Cambridge: Peabody Museum of Archaeology and Ethnology, Harvard University, 1976.

Kelly, Joyce. *The Complete Visitor's Guide to Mesoamerican Ruins*. Norman: University of Oklahoma Press, 1982.

Mercer, Henry Chapman. *The Hill-Caves of Yucatán: A Search for Evidence of Man's Antiquity in the Caverns of Central America*. Norman: University of Oklahoma Press, 1975.

Schele, Linda, and David Freidel. *A Forest of Kings: The Untold Story of the Ancient Maya*. New York: William Morrow and Company, Inc., 1990.

CULTURES OF BELIZE

Kerns, Virginia. *Women and the Ancestors: Black Carib Kinship and Ritual*. Urbana: University of Illinois Press, 1983.

CONTEMPORARY READING

Belize First. Lan Sluder, Publisher. Quarterly magazine dealing with living and visiting Belize. Equator Travel Publications, Inc., 280 Beaverdam Rd., Candler, NC 28715 USA. Fax (704) 667-1717.

DIVING AND THE SEA

Burgess, Robert. *Secret Languages of the Sea*. Dodd, Mead, and Company.

Cousteau, Jacques-Yves. *Three Adventures: Galapagos, Titicaca, the Blue Holes*. Garden City, NY: Doubleday, 1973.

Kuhlmann, Dietrick. *Living Coral Reefs of the World*. New York: Arco Publishing, 1985.

Meyer, Franz. *Diving & Snorkeling Guide to Belize: Lighthouse Reef, Glover Reef, and Turneffe Island*. Houston: Gulf Publishing, 1990.

FICTION

Edgell, Zee. *Beka Lamb*. London: Heinemann Educational Books, Ltd., 1982.

Highwater, Jamake. *Journey to the Sky: A Novel About the True Adventures of Two Men in Search of the Lost Maya Kingdom*. New York: Thomas Y. Crowell, 1978.

King, Emory. *Belize 1798, the Road To Glory.* Belize: Tropical Books, 1991.

Westlake, Donald. *High Adventure.* New York: Mysterious Press, 1985.

HEALTH

Schroeder, Dirk. *Staying Healthy in Asia, Africa, and Latin America, 4th edition.* Chico, CA: Moon Publications, Inc., 1995.

Werner, David. *Where There is No Doctor.* Order from Hesperian Foundation, PO Box 1692, Palo Alto CA 94302.

HISTORY AND POLITICS

Barry, Tom. *Belize: A Country Guide.* Albuquerque: Inter-Hemispheric Education Resource Center, 1989.

Bernal, Ignacia. *The Olmec World.* Berkeley: University of California Press, 1969.

Bolland, O. Nigel. *Belize: A New Nation in Central America.* Boulder: Westview, 1986.

Grant, C.H. *The Making of Modern Belize.* Cambridge: Cambridge University Press, 1976.

Sawatzky, Harry. *They Sought A Country: Mennonite Colonization in Mexico. With an Appendix on Mennonite Colonization in British Honduras.* Berkeley: University of California, 1971.

Setzekom, William David. *A Profile of the New Nation of Belize formerly British Honduras.* Ohio: Ohio University Press, 1981.

NATURE

Lewis, Scott. *The Rainforest Book: How You Can Save the World's Rainforests.* Living Planet Press, 1990.

MacKinnon, Barbara. *Common Birds of the Yucatán Peninsula.* Cancún, Quintana Roo: Amigos de Sian Ka'an (Apto. Postal 770, Cancún, Quintana Roo, 77500, Mexico), 1989.

Poisonous Snakes of the World. Superintendent of Documents, U.S. Government Printing Office, Washington, D.C.

Rabinowitz, Alan. *Jaguar: A Struggle and Triumph in the Jungles of Belize.* New York: Arbor House, 1986.

Snakes Of Belize. Audubon Society, drawings by Ellen MacRae, 29 Regent Street, Box 100, Belize City.

Stephens, Katie. *Jungle Walk, Birds and Beasts of Belize.* Order through International Expeditions, (800) 633-4734.

Wood, Leberman, and Weyer. *Checklist of the Birds of Belize.* Pittsburgh: Carnegie Museum of Natural History, 1986.

RESTAURANT INDEX

See the Accommodations Index for the many hotels and resorts that also serve food.

ACCOMMODATIONS INDEX

INDEX

Page numbers in **bold** indicate the main reference; page numbers in *italics* indicate information in captions, charts, maps, or special topics.

Chicki Mallan

Tourism for an article she wrote about the Mexican Caribbean that was published in the *Los Angeles Times*. Chicki is a member of the SATW, Society of American Travel Writers.

ABOUT THE PHOTOGRAPHER

Oz Mallan has been a professional photographer since 1950. Much of that time was spent as chief cameraman for the *Chico Enterprise-Record*. Oz graduated from the Brooks Institute of Photography, Santa Barbara, in 1950. His work has often appeared in newspapers across the country via UPI and AP. He travels the world with his wife, Chicki, handling the photo end of their literary projects, which include travel books, newspaper and magazine articles, as well as lectures and slide presentations. The photos in *Belize Handbook* were taken during many visits and years of travel on the Yucatán Peninsula. Other Moon books that feature Oz's photos are *Yucatán Peninsula Handbook, Catalina Island Handbook, Cancún Handbook, Central Mexico Handbook,* and the soon-to-be-released *Mexico Handbook*.

ABOUT THE AUTHOR

As a child Chicki Mallan discovered the joy of traveling with her parents. She and her family would leave their Catalina Island home yearly, hit the road, and explore the small towns and big cities of the United States. Traveling was still an important part of Chicki's life after she had a bunch of kids of her own to tote around. At various times Chicki and kids have lived in the Orient and Europe. When not traveling, lecturing, or giving slide presentations, Chicki and photographer husband Oz live in Paradise, CA, a small community in the foothills of the Sierra Nevada. She does what she enjoys most, writing newspaper and magazine articles in between travel books. She has been associated with Moon Publications since 1983, and is the author of *Yucatán Peninsula Handbook, Catalina Island Handbook, Central Mexico Handbook, Cancún Handbook,* and with co-author Joe Cummings, the soon-to-be-released *Mexico Handbook*. In 1987, Chicki was presented the Pluma de Plata writing award from the Mexican Government Ministry of

ABOUT THE ILLUSTRATORS

The banner art at the start of the chapters was done by Kathy Escovedo Sanders. She is an expert both in watercolor and this stipple style, which lends itself to excellent black-and-white reproduction. Kathy is a 1982 California State University, Long Beach, graduate with a BA in Art History. She exhibits drawings, etched intaglio prints, and woodcut prints, as well as her outstanding watercolor paintings. In the April 1982 issue of *Orange Coast* magazine, a complete photo essay illustrates Kathy's unique craft of dyeing, designing, and etching eggs. Her stipple art can also be seen in Chicki Mallan's *Yucatán Peninsula Handbook, Cancún Handbook, Central Mexico Handbook,* and *Catalina Island Handbook*.

Bob Race, illustrator and cartographer, has always been interested in maps, especially the techniques and materials used to draw them. After receiving a BA in Art in 1974, he earned an MA in Painting and Drawing one year later. For the next 14 years he taught fine art at the college level, and in 1989 he began working at Moon Publications. Evolved from his teaching and personal work is an interest in the primitive and fine arts of other cultures.

COSTA RICA HANDBOOK
by Christopher P. Baker, 574 pages, $18.95
"There are numerous Costa Rica books on the market; but if only one comprehensive guide were to be chosen, this compact and thick paperback should be the item." —*Reviewer's Bookwatch*

JAMAICA HANDBOOK by Karl Luntta, 228 pages, $14.95
"Positively—without a doubt—the best guide book on Jamaica for the independent traveler. No other guide even comes close." —*The Shoestring Traveler*

STAYING HEALTHY IN ASIA, AFRICA, AND LATIN AMERICA
by Dirk G. Schroeder, ScD, MPH, 200 pages, $11.95
"Your family doctor will not be able to supply you with this valuable information because he doesn't have it." —*Whole Earth Catalog*

"Read this book if you want to stay healthy on any journeys or stays in Asia, Africa, and Latin America" —*American Journal of Health Promotion*

MOONBELT

A new concept in moneybelts. Made of heavy-duty Cordura nylon, the Moonbelt offers maximum protection for your money and important papers. This pouch, designed for all-weather comfort, slips under your shirt or waistband, rendering it virtually undetectable and inaccessible to pickpockets. It features a one-inch high-test quick-release buckle so there's no more fumbling around for the strap or repeated adjustments. This handy plastic buckle opens and closes with a touch, but won't come undone until you want it to. Moonbelts accommodate traveler's checks, passports, cash, photos, etc. Size 5 x 9 inches. Available in black only. **$8.95**

MOON TRAVEL HANDBOOKS

CENTRAL AMERICA AND THE CARIBBEAN
Belize Handbook (0370). $15.95
Caribbean Handbook (0277) $16.95
Costa Rica Handbook (0358). $18.95
Jamaica Handbook (0129) $14.95

ASIA AND THE PACIFIC
Bali Handbook (3379) $12.95
Bangkok Handbook (0595). $13.95
Fiji Islands Handbook (0382). $13.95
Hong Kong Handbook (0560) $15.95
Indonesia Handbook (0625) $25.00
Japan Handbook (3700). $22.50
Micronesia Handbook (3808) $11.95
Nepal Handbook (3646) $12.95
New Zealand Handbook (3883) $18.95
Outback Australia Handbook (3794) $15.95
Philippines Handbook (0048) $17.95
Southeast Asia Handbook (0021) $21.95
South Pacific Handbook (3999) $19.95
Tahiti-Polynesia Handbook (0374) $13.95
Thailand Handbook (3824) $16.95
Tibet Handbook (3905) $30.00
*Vietnam, Cambodia & Laos Handbook (0293) $18.95

NORTH AMERICA AND HAWAII
Alaska-Yukon Handbook (0161). $14.95
Alberta and the Northwest Territories Handbook (0676) . . . $17.95
Arizona Traveler's Handbook (0536) $16.95
Atlantic Canada Handbook (0072) $17.95
Big Island of Hawaii Handbook (0064) $13.95
British Columbia Handbook (0145) $15.95
Catalina Island Handbook (3751) $10.95
Colorado Handbook (0137). $17.95
Georgia Handbook (0609) $16.95
Hawaii Handbook (0005) $19.95
Honolulu-Waikiki Handbook (0587). $14.95
Idaho Handbook (0617) $14.95

Kauai Handbook (0013). $13.95
Maui Handbook (0579) $14.95
Montana Handbook (0544). $15.95
Nevada Handbook (0641). $16.95
New Mexico Handbook (0153). $14.95
Northern California Handbook (3840) $19.95
Oregon Handbook (0102). $16.95
Texas Handbook (0633). $17.95
Utah Handbook (0684) $16.95
Washington Handbook (0552). $15.95
Wyoming Handbook (3980) $14.95

MEXICO

Baja Handbook (0528). $15.95
Cabo Handbook (0285) $14.95
Cancún Handbook (0501). $13.95
Central Mexico Handbook (0234) $15.95
*Mexico Handbook (0315) $21.95
Northern Mexico Handbook (0226) $16.95
Pacific Mexico Handbook (0323) $16.95
Puerto Vallarta Handbook (0250) $14.95
Yucatán Peninsula Handbook (0242). $15.95

INTERNATIONAL

Egypt Handbook (3891). $18.95
Moon Handbook (0668). $10.00
Moscow-St. Petersburg Handbook (3913). $13.95
Staying Healthy in Asia, Africa, and Latin America (0269) . . $11.95

* New title, please call for availability

PERIPLUS TRAVEL MAPS

All maps $7.95 each

Bali	Hong Kong	Singapore
Bandung/W. Java	Java	Vietnam
Bangkok/C. Thailand	Ko Samui/S. Thailand	Yogyakarta/C. Java
Batam/Bintan	Penang	
Cambodia	Phuket/S. Thailand	

WHERE TO BUY MOON TRAVEL HANDBOOKS

BOOKSTORES AND LIBRARIES: Moon Travel Handbooks are sold worldwide. Please write to our sales manager for a list of wholesalers and distributors in your area.

TRAVELERS: We would like to have Moon Travel Handbooks available throughout the world. Please ask your bookstore to write or call us for ordering information. If your bookstore will not order our guides for you, please contact us for a free title listing.

Moon Publications, Inc.
P.O. Box 3040
Chico, CA 95927-3040 U.S.A.
Tel.: (800) 345-5473
Fax: (916) 345-6751
e-mail: travel@moon.com

IMPORTANT ORDERING INFORMATION

PRICES: All prices are subject to change. We always ship the most current edition. We will let you know if there is a price increase on the book you order.

SHIPPING AND HANDLING OPTIONS: Domestic UPS or USPS first class (allow 10 working days for delivery): $3.50 for the first item, 50 cents for each additional item.

EXCEPTIONS:

Tibet Handbook and *Indonesia Handbook* shipping $4.50; $1.00 for each additional *Tibet Handbook* or *Indonesia Handbook*.

Moonbelt shipping is $1.50 for one, 50 cents for each additional belt.

Add $2.00 for same-day handling.

UPS 2nd Day Air or Printed Airmail requires a special quote.

International Surface Bookrate 8-12 weeks delivery: $3.00 for the first item, $1.00 for each additional item. Note: Moon Publications cannot guarantee international surface bookrate shipping. Moon recommends sending international orders via air mail, which requires a special quote.

FOREIGN ORDERS: Orders that originate outside the U.S.A. must be paid for with either an international money order or a check in U.S. currency drawn on a major U.S. bank based in the U.S.A.

TELEPHONE ORDERS: We accept Visa or MasterCard payments. Minimum order is US$15.00. Call in your order: (800) 345-5473, 8 a.m.-5 p.m. Pacific Standard Time.

ORDER FORM

Be sure to call (800) 345-5473 for current prices and editions or for the name of the bookstore
nearest you that carries Moon Travel Handbooks • 8 a.m.-5 p.m. PST.
(See important ordering information on preceding page.)

Name: _____ Date: _____

Street: _____

City: _____ Daytime Phone: _____

State or Country: _____ Zip Code: _____

QUANTITY	TITLE	PRICE

Taxable Total_____

Sales Tax (7.25%) for California Residents_____

Shipping & Handling_____

TOTAL_____

Ship: ☐ UPS (no P.O. Boxes) ☐ 1st class ☐ International surface mail

Ship to: ☐ address above ☐ other _____

_____

Make checks payable to: **MOON PUBLICATIONS, INC.** P.O. Box 3040, Chico, CA 95927-3040
U.S.A. We accept Visa and MasterCard. **To Order:** Call in your Visa or MasterCard number, or send
a written order with your Visa or MasterCard number and expiration date clearly written.

Card Number: ☐ **Visa** ☐ **MasterCard**

☐ ☐ ☐ ☐ ☐ ☐ ☐ ☐ ☐ ☐ ☐ ☐ ☐ ☐ ☐ ☐

Exact Name on Card: _____

Expiration date:_____

Signature:_____

F-95 CA

International Expeditions'
Recipe for a
Rare Belizean Adventure

INGREDIENT LIST

Take: Time For A Vacation
Add: 200 miles of unspoiled barrier reef and an equal
measure of sugar white tropical beaches
1 bouquet of Maya, Carib, British and Chinese
cultures
1 generous helping of virgin rainforest
2 splashes of inland jungle rivers
A selection of the finest quality hotels and lodges
1 superb naturalist guide
Spice it up with exotic birds and animals
Season generously with adventure and fun

Combine all ingredients and stir with 10 years of expertise
in Belize travel for a rare and well done Belize adventure
EVERY TIME!

Group Departures

Custom Itineraries

Individual Travel

INTERNATIONAL
EXPEDITIONS INC

One Environs Park
Helena, Alabama 35080 • 205/428-1700

TOLL FREE **1-800-633-4734**

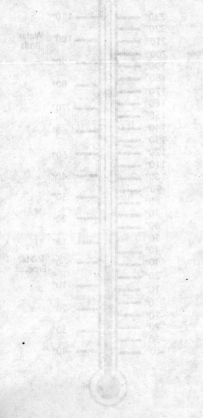

THE METRIC SYSTEM

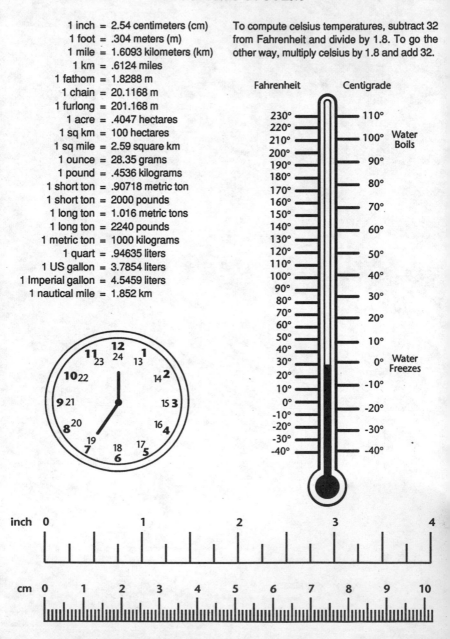

1 inch	=	2.54 centimeters (cm)
1 foot	=	.304 meters (m)
1 mile	=	1.6093 kilometers (km)
1 km	=	.6124 miles
1 fathom	=	1.8288 m
1 chain	=	20.1168 m
1 furlong	=	201.168 m
1 acre	=	.4047 hectares
1 sq km	=	100 hectares
1 sq mile	=	2.59 square km
1 ounce	=	28.35 grams
1 pound	=	.4536 kilograms
1 short ton	=	.90718 metric ton
1 short ton	=	2000 pounds
1 long ton	=	1.016 metric tons
1 long ton	=	2240 pounds
1 metric ton	=	1000 kilograms
1 quart	=	.94635 liters
1 US gallon	=	3.7854 liters
1 Imperial gallon	=	4.5459 liters
1 nautical mile	=	1.852 km

To compute celsius temperatures, subtract 32 from Fahrenheit and divide by 1.8. To go the other way, multiply celsius by 1.8 and add 32.

Fahrenheit   Centigrade

230° — 110°
220°
210° — 100°   Water Boils
200°
190° — 90°
180°
170° — 80°
160°
150° — 70°
140° — 60°
130°
120° — 50°
110°
100° — 40°
90°
80° — 30°
70°
60° — 20°
50°
40° — 10°
30°
20° — 0°   Water Freezes
10°
0° — -10°
-10°
-20° — -20°
-30° — -30°
-40° — -40°

inch   0   1   2   3   4

cm   0   1   2   3   4   5   6   7   8   9   10